SPECIAL EDITION

USING®

Macromedia®

Dreamweaver® MX

Molly E. Holzschlag

Jennifer Ackerman Kettell

que®

201 W. 103rd Street
Indianapolis, Indiana 46290

SPECIAL EDITION USING MACROMEDIA® DREAMWEAVER® MX

International Standard Book Number: 0-7897-2707-2

Library of Congress Catalog Card Number: 2001099708

Printed in the United States of America

First Printing: December 2002

05   04   03   02   4   3   2   1

Trademarks

All terms mentioned in this book that are known to be trademarks or service marks have been appropriately capitalized. Que cannot attest to the accuracy of this information. Use of a term in this book should not be regarded as affecting the validity of any trademark or service mark.

Macromedia is a registered trademark of Macromedia, Inc.

Dreamweaver is a trademark of Macromedia, Inc.

Warning and Disclaimer

Every effort has been made to make this book as complete and as accurate as possible, but no warranty or fitness is implied. The information provided is on an "as is" basis. The author(s) and the publisher shall have neither liability nor responsibility to any person or entity with respect to any loss or damages arising from the information contained in this book or from the use of the CD or programs accompanying it.

Associate Publisher
David Culverwell

Executive Editor
Candace Hall

Acquisitions Editor
Jeff Schultz

Development Editors
Sean Dixon
Laura Norman

Managing Editor
Thomas F. Hayes

Project Editor
Tricia Liebig

Production Editors
Megan Wade
Jennifer Lewis

Indexer
Chris Barrick

Proofreader
Kevin Ober

Technical Editor
Doug Scamahorn

Team Coordinator
Cindy Teeters

Multimedia Developer
Jay Payne

Interior Designer
Anne Jones

Cover Designer
Anne Jones

Page Layout
Michelle Mitchell

Graphics
Tammy Graham
Oliver Jackson

Contents at a Glance

CONTENTS

ABOUT THE AUTHORS

The following authors wrote and contributed material to *Special Edition Using Macromedia Dreamweaver MX*.

Molly E. Holzschlag, lead author, is a writer, an instructor, and a designer who brings attitude and enthusiasm to books, magazines, classrooms, and Web sites. Honored by Webgrrls as one of the Top 25 Most Influential Women on the Web, Molly has spent more than a decade working in the online world. She has written 20 books on HTML and Web design and development topics, including the bestselling *Special Edition Using HTML 4.0* and internationally acclaimed *Web by Design*.

Her popular column of 2 1/2 years, "Integrated Design," appeared monthly in the internationally popular *WebTechniques Magazine* until the magazine's closing in early 2002. Molly served for a year as the executive editor of *Web Review* and has contributed features and columns to *Adobe Studios*, *Adobe.com*, *Builder.com*, *Digital Chicago*, *Digital New York*, *IBM developerWorks*, *MacWorld*, *MSDN*, *PC Magazine*, and other developer publications.

When offline, Molly plays guitar and sings in the original acoustic duo Courage Sisters. For books, giveaways, training, speaking events, and other items of fun and interest, drop by her Web site at, where else, `http://www.molly.com/`.

Jennifer Ackerman Kettell, coauthor, is a seasoned author and freelance writer on computer and Internet subjects. She is a Web developer and designer with more than 11 years of experience building sites and communities in the online services industry and as a freelancer. Read more about Jenn at her site, `http://www.pendragn.com/`.

Jason Cranford Teague, contributing author, is a senior information architect for Lante and was previously with iXL, where he designed Web sites. He is the author of several bestselling books. Jason contributed material for the JavaScript, DHTML, and dynamic design topics in this book. He also served as technical editor for several chapters. Visit Jason's Web site at `http://www.webbedenvironments.com/` for more up-to-date information on his activities.

Dedication

For my stepfather, Ole Kenen.

Acknowledgments

From Que: Jeff Schultz for the opportunity, Sean Dixon for jumping into the fray for a bit, and Tricia Liebig for keeping everything on track. Laura Norman is, as always, an editor whose honesty is as helpful as her kindness. Also, a note of special thanks to Candace Hall for her incredible understanding and support.

From Waterside Productions: David Fugate, agent extraordinaire. Deep appreciation to the entire Waterside team for helping to make the business of being an author so much easier.

To my coauthor Jenn Kettell for her years of friendship and support and to contributing author Jason Cranford Teague for all his ongoing help. To my friends and family, you are what keeps me keeping on.

WE WANT TO HEAR FROM YOU!

As the reader of this book, *you* are our most important critic and commentator. We value your opinion and want to know what we're doing right, what we could do better, what areas you'd like to see us publish in, and any other words of wisdom you're willing to pass our way.

As an executive editor for Que, I welcome your comments. You can email or write me directly to let me know what you did or didn't like about this book--as well as what we can do to make our books better.

Please note that I cannot help you with technical problems related to the *topic* of this book. We do have a User Services group, however, where I will forward specific technical questions related to the book.

When you write, please be sure to include this book's title and author as well as your name, email address, and phone number. I will carefully review your comments and share them with the author and editors who worked on the book.

Email: feedback@quepublishing.com

Mail: Candace Hall
Que Publishing
201 West 103rd Street
Indianapolis, IN 46290 USA

For more information about this book or another Que title, visit our Web site at www.quepublishing.com. Type the ISBN (excluding hyphens) or the title of a book in the Search field to find the page you're looking for.

INTRODUCTION
THE BEST WEB DESIGN
SOFTWARE OF OUR TIME

IN THIS INTRODUCTION

DREAMWEAVER MX

Is Macromedia Dreamweaver MX perfect? No, it's not. And in all good humor, no one paid me to say that I like the software. I'm really just here to present it to you as well as possible via this book.

Macromedia is making tremendous strides to get in step with the realistic needs of anyone creating Web sites today. The company is paying real attention to the feedback of its clients, the Web design and development community, and grassroots organizations such as The Web Standards Project (WaSP) who advocate the implementation of standards and accessibility features within commercial Web design software.

Of the main competitors for a visual Web design and development tool, Macromedia has done the best job, bar none, at ensuring that it responds to the needs of the people who use its software. It's a rare and bold step for a software company to take, and the results are worth it. I have no doubts that you will be extremely pleased with the rich features to be found in this software.

Here are some of the features I am especially impressed with:

- **Extreme interface**—I've always admired Macromedia's savvy development practices. But I was forever frustrated with the interface designs of most of its products, which I've felt were not very intuitive. This is one of the coolest things about DW today: a brand-new design for the default interface. But if you preferred the DW 4 look, you can switch to that interface. And get this—Windows users can even make the Dreamweaver interface look like Homesite!

- **Standards support**—Dreamweaver MX is paying attention to the growing concerns of standards-related bodies, such as the World Wide Web Consortium (W3C). This translates into better tools to help address updates, variations in language (HTML, XHTML, and XML, for example), and other critical concerns such as accessibility.

- **Refined integration and extensibility**—The MX family of products brings the concept of integration to reality. Although Dreamweaver has long been well integrated with Fireworks and Flash, the entire Studio MX product line is focused on the broader concerns of interface, standards, and accessibility as well. So, no matter what problem you're trying to solve, the answer exists either within one of the associated tools *or* with extensible utilities that can be found via Macromedia Exchange and its related communities.

The time has come for Web design software products to get with the program. I am convinced Macromedia Dreamweaver MX is best-of-breed.

WHO SHOULD BUY THIS BOOK

The typical reader of this book is seeking intuitive, extremely customizable, and well-supported solutions to almost every challenge facing the creation of Web pages today. You might be a Web designer or developer seeking a visual interface and collaborative tools to speed up the development process. You might be a professional working in another field—medicine or law, perhaps—and are required to update an intranet or a public Web site. Either way, you want real solutions and up-to-date information that is presented in a direct and friendly fashion.

Many readers are looking for a bridge solution to the combined need of a visual editor and a hands-on approach to markup and code. Dreamweaver provides that combo platter. You can work in Design view, switch to Code view, or work in a combined Design and Code view. No matter where you do your work, Dreamweaver won't overwrite your decisions—you have ultimate control.

However, there are people for whom this book will not be ideal. Absolute newcomers to computers and the Web will find this book aimed at a more experienced audience. Any developer interested in working with server-side scripting will not find that information here, despite Dreamweaver MX's support for PHP, ASP, JSP, and other application and server-side mechanisms. This book focuses on the client-side uses of the software, with only very limited information on server-side features.

HOW THIS BOOK IS ORGANIZED

Special Edition Using Dreamweaver MX has eight parts divided into 33 chapters. Although you can read the book start to finish, you might prefer to use it as a reference. Or, read Chapters 1–9 for a short course on using Dreamweaver and return to the book later when you want to dig into certain areas more deeply.

Summary of Parts

Here's a guide highlighting the main topics within each of the book's parts:

- **Part I, "Designing Sites with Dreamweaver"**—Learn to define your site; add and present content using everything from text to Flash; and publish your site. This is a short course to using as many DW features as possible in the shortest possible time. Then, dig deeper in subsequent parts for those topics of greatest interest to you.

- **Part II, "Working More Efficiently in Dreamweaver"**—This section takes everything you learned in Part I and organizes it using DW tools and techniques. You'll learn how to use every window, toolbar, and panel; manage assets; work with templates; and build DW libraries.

- **Part III, "Writing and Editing HTML, XHTML, and CSS"**—DW offers a lot of help when it comes to professional-level authoring techniques. This section discusses the differences between HTML and XHTML, shows how CSS is growing to become the true language of Web design, and demonstrates how DW can help you achieve best practices.

- **Part IV, "Professional Page Design"**—Learn contemporary design concepts and applications for a wide range of sites; learn the art of layout from tables to frames to the more contemporary CSS techniques; learn to use DW libraries and templates to improve productivity.

- **Part V, "Designing for Interactivity"**—Add dynamic features such as rollovers and interactive navigation bars to your Web page using DW behaviors, JavaScript, and DHTML.

- **Part VI, "Adding Multimedia"**—Audio, video, applets, and Flash—many contemporary Web sites demand some kind of multimedia. Here's how to make the process easy, quick, and correct.

- **Part VII, "Managing Your Site"**—Two of DW's strongest features are its collaborative and management tools. This section focuses on how you can tap into the power of these tools for both professional and personal use.

- **Part VIII, "Extending Dreamweaver and Using Third-Party Software"**—Learn to find additional extensions, behaviors, and plug-ins through Macromedia Exchange and other locations. Use Dreamweaver along with other programs, such as Macromedia Fireworks and Adobe Photoshop for graphics and HTML Editors such as Macromedia Homesite and BBEdit.

Three appendixes also follow the book:

- Appendix A, "The Dreamweaver Interface"

- Appendix B, "Setting Preferences"

- Appendix C, "What's on the CD-ROM?"

CONVENTIONS USED IN THIS BOOK

Special conventions are used to help you get the most from this book and from Web markup.

Text Conventions

Various typefaces in this book identify terms and other special objects. These special typefaces include the following:

Type	Meaning
Italic	New terms or phrases when initially defined.
`Monospace`	Web addresses, names of files or folders, and onscreen messages.
`Bold monospace`	Information that you type.
Initial Caps	Menus, dialog box names, dialog box elements, and commands are capitalized.

Key combinations are represented for both Macintosh and Windows in the following format (Macintosh) [Windows]. For example, if the text calls for you to press Command-S for the Mac and Ctrl+S for Windows, you will see the following in the text: (Command-S) [Ctrl+S].

Helping You Dig Deeper

Because Dreamweaver is not without need for growth, a few challenging areas remain. I and co-author Jenn Kettell, as well as contributing author Jason Cranford Teague, address these challenges via sidebars and notes in our various chapters. Troubleshooting notes also point you to even deeper insight into using the program successfully.

I've also added a special feature to the end of each chapter called "Peer to Peer." I based the title of this section on Peer to Peer (P2P) technologies, which require a direct connection to work. In *Special Edition Using Macromedia Dreamweaver MX*, the Peer to Peer sections offer direct communication about the most up-to-date standards, accessibility, and global communications concerns. Many readers will need this information immediately; others will benefit in the future by reading the Peer to Peer section's contemporary viewpoints on using the software in a time of great change within the industry.

Special Elements

Throughout this book, you'll find Margin Notes, Cautions, Sidebars, and Cross References. These elements provide a variety of information, ranging from warnings you shouldn't miss to ancillary information that will enrich your Dreamweaver experience.

Cross References

Notes provide extra information related and relevant to the current topic but not specific to the given task at hand.

Caution
Watch your step! Avoid pitfalls by keeping an eye on the cautions available in many of this book's lessons.

Cross references are designed to point you to other locations in this book (or other books in the Que family) that will provide supplemental or supporting information. Cross references appear as follows:

⇨ *To learn more about adding a video file to your page, see "Inserting Video," p. 494.*

Troubleshooting Notes

Troubleshooting notes will be found in the text and will point you to an issue in the "Troubleshooting" section of the chapter that is relevant to the material being covered where the note is located. Troubleshooting notes will look like this:

⇨ *Does Dreamweaver contain these document interpretations? The answer is "sort of." Find out what Dreamweaver does have, how to access it, and where to learn how to add your own templates to Dreamweaver in "Available Standards-Based Templates" in the "Troubleshooting" section at the end of this chapter.*

Sidebars

Want to Know More?

Sidebars are designed to provide information that is ancillary to the topic being discussed. Read these if you want to learn more about an application or a task.

I

DESIGNING SITES WITH DREAMWEAVER

IN THIS PART

DEFINING YOUR SITE

IN THIS CHAPTER

BEFORE YOU START

Before you start using Macromedia Dreamweaver MX to design your Web site, you must *define* your site. Defining your site refers to setting up a directory structure locally and, in most cases, on a remote server where the site will appear. Then, you can begin working on your new pages and sites in an organized fashion.

Most readers will already have an idea of how best to create directory structures, and many of you might be running Web servers of your own. This experience will be helpful to you as you proceed to set up both your computer and the remote server for Macromedia Dreamweaver MX. In fact, if you already have a Web server set up, you can jump right into the following tasks.

To learn more about the types of hosting available and to find a hosting provider, please see the following article in The Web Host Industry Review, http://thewhir.com/find/web-hosts/articles/.

If you don't have service and would like to establish Web site service provision, please look into Web hosting options and find the best situation for your needs.

ESTABLISHING A WEB SITE

Before you can begin working with Dreamweaver to build your site or a page, your site must be defined. The following sections show you how to get started managing both local and remote settings in the software.

Defining and Saving the Site Locally

The first thing you'll need to do before being able to do any editing or design work using Dreamweaver is to define a local folder.

Follow these steps:

1. Make a new folder on your computer to store pages and Web site components. I called mine Sample Site I. In that folder, create an images folder, where you can store any images you'll use with the site.

2. Open Dreamweaver, and from the main menu, select Site, New Site. The Site Definition dialog box will appear (see Figure 1.1). You'll see two tab options, Basic and Advanced.

3. Click the Advanced tab. To the left, you'll see a list of category definitions for the site you're creating. For now, you're concerned only with Local Info. You'll have the opportunity to add other definitions later in this chapter.

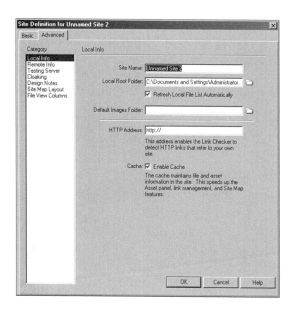

Figure 1.1
For any site you work with, you'll use the Site definition dialog box to name the site and set options for how you want to use it. The Basic tab is a wizard to help easily guide you through; more advanced users can click the Advanced tab and enter their own parameters.

4. Be sure that Local Info is highlighted. In the Site Name text box, add a name to identify this specific site from others you may have already created, or will create in the future.

5. In the Local Root Folder text box, type in the path to the site folder that you created. If you can't remember the complete path to the folder or are unsure of it, click the folder icon to browse your computer for the folder. After you've found the new folder, highlight it and click (Choose) [Select]. You'll now see that the path has been added to the Local Root Folder.

6. If the Refresh Local File List Automatically check box is unchecked, check it.

➪ *Files not updating properly? See "Refreshing Files" in the "Troubleshooting" section at the end of the chapter.*

7. Now add the path to the images folder by typing in the path to that folder in the Default Images Folder text box. You can also browse to the folder and add it. If you don't already have a folder defined, select Browse and then select a new folder through the dialog box. After you've created the new folder, you can select it and continue.

8. Leave the remainder of the dialog box as is, and click OK to apply your changes. You'll add the remote server information in the next section.

To see the new site added, select Window, Site from the main menu.

1

Creating the Best File Structure

With simple sites comprising just a few pages and images, file structure isn't an area of extreme concern. However, when sites grow to contain hundreds, thousands, or even greater numbers of files, it becomes imperative to architect a good file structure system to accommodate them.

The use of a local root folder is a good beginning. In this area should be any top-level files, such as the index page, and the main pages for the site. But, if your site contains a great deal of articles and resources, you might have to break this down into much greater detail. Let's say you are an e-zine and regularly publish articles, columns, comics, and classifieds. It is in your best interest to create subfolders for each of these, keeping things organized by topic.

Similarly, if you are using media other than images on your site, you might want to create subfolders for various media, such as images, audio, video, and so on.

The one potential problem that can arise out of creating too many subdirectories is that the resulting URLs can be very long, which makes them difficult to remember and bookmark and, depending on the way they are fashioned, even likely to cause problems with page validation (see the Peer to Peer section at the end of this chapter for more information).

A good exercise is to sketch out the file structure ahead of time. This will provide you a blueprint from which to work as you proceed in the building of your site. Although it's not always easy to anticipate the future, keep in mind that the site, if successful, will grow in size and that growth will need to be accommodated.

Setting the Remote Information

Gather all the information you have about your remote server. In most cases you'll be using FTP, but there are other connection options, as described in Table 1.1.

Table 1.1 Remote Information Options

Option	What It Does
None	Select this if you simply want to build your site on your local computer. You can always consider transfer options later.
Local/Network	If you are working on a network or running Web server software locally, select this option.
FTP	This is the File Transfer Protocol. This method is in widespread use for transferring files from a local machine to a remote machine.
RDS	This is Remote Development Services. It is used by people working with dynamic content in ColdFusion.
SourceSafe Database	A special Microsoft database that enables powerful management features for teams working on sites, SourceSafe must be installed and in use to use this option.
WebDAV	Certain servers use the Web-based Distributed Authoring and Versioning tools. If you are using a WebDAV system, select this option.

In most instances, you'll be using FTP, which is the process discussed here. If you are certain that you'll be using a different method, simply select the necessary option from the drop-down menu. Select FTP if you plan on moving your files to a live Web server, or select None if you plan on creating your site locally and figuring out what to do with it later.

To set up FTP, you'll need to obtain the following information:

> You can always change the Remote Information options at a later date by selecting Site, Edit Sites and then selecting the site you want to modify from the Edit Sites dialog box.

- FTP host name (such as `ftp.molly.com`)

- Login name (this is your user ID information)

- Password (this is a password selected by or provided to you by your service provider)

- Any additional information provided by your service provider regarding required settings

Typically, your service provider will have configured your login to default to the remote root folder. This folder corresponds to the local root folder as it will be the folder where the top-level documents and the subdirectories can be found.

With your FTP information in hand, you're ready to add the remote server information to the site you just defined. Follow these steps:

> In some instances, you'll want to create an area other than your default root on your Web server as a staging area for testing your site prior to publishing. Some individuals and companies actually use a different server for staging.

1. From the main menu, select Site, Edit Sites. The Edit Sites dialog box appears (see Figure 1.2).

Figure 1.2
Highlight the appropriate site in the Edit Sites menu to select it.

2. Highlight the site you want to modify by clicking it.

3. Click Edit. The Site Definition dialog box appears.

4. Select the Advanced tab, and under Category, highlight the Remote Info entry. A drop-down menu appears with a number of options. Select FTP. The dialog box updates with the necessary fields.

5. Enter your FTP host, host directory, login, and password. I recommend checking the Save check box. Unless your provider requires you to use passive FTP, leave the Use Passive FTP check box blank. Passive FTP is used for additional security but is usually not required in most cases (see Figure 1.3).

Figure 1.3
When you've finished filling out the Site Definition dialog box, your site will have most of the features necessary to manage the various files.

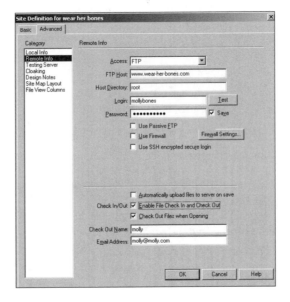

In most cases, this will be enough information to get you started. Click the Test button to see if, in fact, you get a connection. If you do, terrific! If not, carefully look over the information you entered and see whether everything is up to par. If it is and you are working from within a network and still having trouble, you might be behind a security firewall. If you are, you'll need to get those settings from your system administrator and enter them into the appropriate areas.

Unsure about how to get additional encryption security when using FTP to transfer files? See "Using Secure Shell" in the "Troubleshooting" section later in this chapter.

The two other options on the dialog box are as follows:

- **Automatically Upload Files to Server on Save**—If you check this option, Dreamweaver automatically transfers the site to the remote server when you save the site. Because this can actually upload files that are in the process of being edited, I don't recommend choosing this option unless you are using an external versioning system such as SourceSafe.

- **Check In/Out**—If you want to enable this feature, click once in the check box. The advantage of enabling this feature is that if multiple people are working on the site, Dreamweaver helps you manage team files, preventing overwriting and the need for additional edits.

To connect to and view your remote site, do the following:

1. Make sure the Site panel is open (select Site, Site files).

2. Select your site from the Site panel list by clicking it once to highlight it.

3. From the Site drop-down menu, select Connect.

4. Dreamweaver will connect with the site. Select Remote View from the drop-down box found to the far right.

You'll now see the current structure of the remote site. This changes as you publish files to the server (see Figure 1.4).

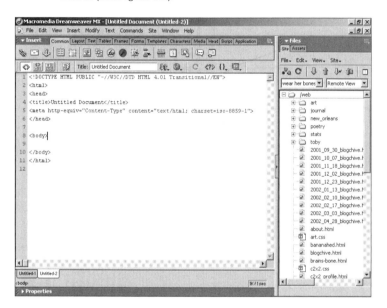

Figure 1.4
Using the Site panel to set features on your remote site allows quick access and updates to the files within your project.

After you've tested your connection, found it working, and made any modifications to the setup, click OK in the Site Definition dialog box; then click Done in the Edit Sites dialog box.

Importing an Existing Web Site

If you have existing Web sites on your local computer or a Web server you want to maintain using Dreamweaver, you'll need to first import them.

Importing a Local Site

If you want to bring a site that resides on your local computer into Dreamweaver, follow these steps:

1. Select Site, Edit Sites. The Edit Sites dialog box appears.

2. Click the New button. The Site Definition dialog box appears.

3. Define the Site Name just as you did in the previous section.

4. Type in the path to the Local Root Folder for the site, or find the Root Folder for the site using the browse feature. Highlight the site and click the Select button. Dreamweaver begins importing all the site files and directories. This might take a minute or two, depending on the size of the site you're importing.

5. After the import is complete, click OK. The Site Definition dialog box closes, leaving the Edit Sites dialog box open. You'll now see the name of the site you just defined in step 3.

6. Click Done.

Your site is now available from the Site panel, where you can see it in its entirety (see Figure 1.5).

Figure 1.5
The Site panel on the right shows the entire imported site. I've opened a page from the site, which is displayed in Design view.

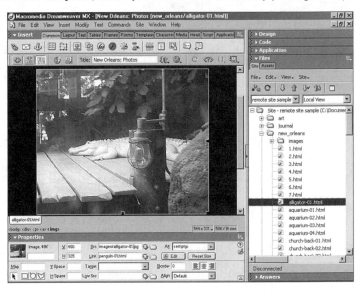

⇨ *To learn more about using the Site Window to manage files, please see Chapter 10, "The Workspace: Windows, Toolbars, and Panels in Detail," p. 169, and Chapter 16, "Using Cascading Style Sheets in Dreamweaver," p. 285.*

Importing a Remote Site

If you have a site on a server and would like to add it to Dreamweaver for management and editing, here's how:

1. Begin by creating a local folder just as you did for a new site.

2. Add the remote site options into the text boxes. This time, use the information matching the Web server and location within that server where your remote Web site resides. Click OK.

3. In the Site panel find the newly added remote site, highlight it, and then connect to it using the Connect icon (see Figure 1.6).

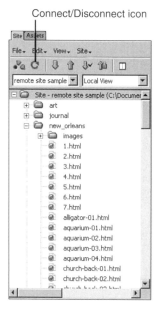

Connect/Disconnect icon

Figure 1.6
Clicking this icon connects you to a remote site. Once connected, clicking it disconnects you.

4. To import the entire site, click the root folder on the remote site.

5. Click the Site drop-down menu, and then select Get. Dreamweaver asks whether you're sure you want to get the entire site. Because you do, click Yes; the site will now be transferred to the local folder you created in step 1. This might take a few minutes, depending on how large the remote site is.

After the site is resident on your local machine, you can edit it as you see fit and then later transfer the edited files back to the remote server (see Figure 1.7).

If you are working on only one section of the site, you might want to transfer only the directories and files you'll be working on. Generally speaking, having all a site's assets on hand helps you get the most out of Dreamweaver MX tools, such as site mapping.

Figure 1.7
The remote site is now available on your local drive.

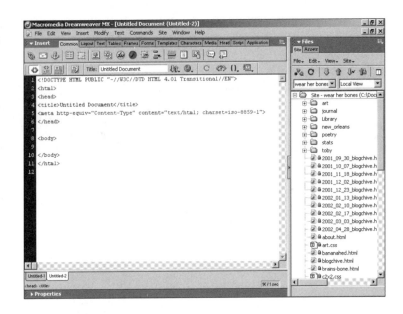

WORKING WITH DOCUMENTS

After you've defined your site, you'll want to start working with the documents—opening them, adding new documents, and even deleting or renaming them.

Opening an Existing Document

To open an existing document located on your hard drive, begin by selecting File, Open. The Open dialog box appears; browse for your file. Highlight the file you want to open, and then click the Open button.

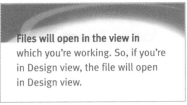

Files will open in the view in which you're working. So, if you're in Design view, the file will open in Design view.

The file will now open and be available for your modifications.

You can also open documents from the Site panel by simply double-clicking the document you want to open.

Adding a New Document

With the site defined, opened, or imported into Macromedia Dreamweaver MX, you're ready to add pages to your site. The software is very powerful and offers a wide range of page types that have been preauthored and categorized for your needs. These page types include HTML, XHTML, CSS, XML, and even a WML (Wireless Markup Language) option. Dreamweaver also offers several page designs that can be extremely useful. What's more, all these documents are customizable and can be used to generate new templates that conform to your own designs.

Whenever you open Dreamweaver, a blank, default page is automatically created. Close the page by selecting File, Close from the main menu. This clears the way for you to determine your own settings for the new page.

After the default page is closed, follow these steps to create and save a new page:

1. Select File, New from the main menu. The New Document dialog box opens (see Figure 1.8).

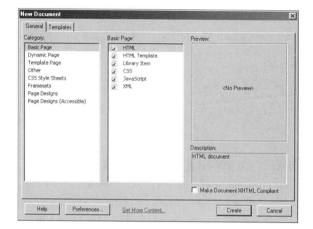

Figure 1.8
A variety of file type options are available in the New Document dialog box, including HTML and CSS.

2. In the General tab, you'll see the list of page types. For a standard HTML page, highlight the Basic Page category and then select HTML. If you want to author your document in XHTML, check the Make Document XHTML Compliant check box. For another kind of page, move to that category and then highlight the file type you want.

3. Click Create to create the page.

▭⇨ *For more information on HTML and XHTML, please see Chapter 14, "Working with HTML and XHTML," p. 237.*

You can now add text, images—whatever you want—to the page. After you've modified the page, you'll want to save the file. Here's how to do so:

1. Select File, Save As. The Save As dialog box appears.

2. Find the location where you want to save your file.

3. Name the file.

4. Click the Save button to save your changes.

Figure 1.9 shows a newly created document in Code view.

Figure 1.9
Here's a newly created XHTML document in Code view.

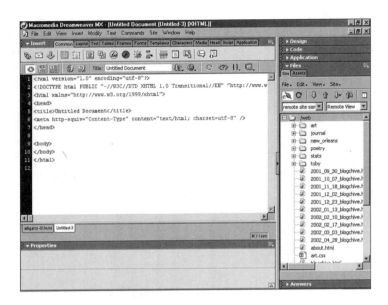

Deleting, Duplicating, and Renaming Documents

As you are developingyour site or reworking an existing site, there will be times that you'll find it necessary to duplicate a document to create a new document with similar items, rename an existing document, or delete documents that are no longer necessary. To do this, you simply (Control-click) [right-click] the document in the Site window and select the option to fit your needs (see Figure 1.10).

Figure 1.10
With the Site window open and a file selected, you can access a context menu with a variety of options, including Delete, Duplicate, and Rename.

To delete a file, select the Delete option from the context menu. A pop-up window will ask whether you really want to delete the selected file. Click OK. The file is now deleted.

Duplicating files is particularly handy when you want to use most of the information in a given page but modify some content. You can duplicate the page you want, make the modifications to the copy, and then rename the copy.

To duplicate a file, highlight the file to be duplicated in the Site panel. Then, bring up the context menu and select Duplicate.

A copy of the file will immediately appear with the words copy of in front of the original filename.

To rename a file, bring up the context menu, select Rename, and type in the new name for the file.

You can delete multiple files simply by selecting all the files you want to delete and then following steps 2 and 3 of the deletion process.

Caution

When renaming files, be sure to provide the proper file extension. If you rename a file with a different extension (or without one altogether), the file will open improperly or not at all.

USING DESIGN NOTES FOR A PAGE

As you work, you'll find there is information about the pages with which you're working that you'll want to jot down to remember later or to tell a co-worker about. Macromedia Dreamweaver MX provides a very handy tool called Design Notes that allows you to make notes for a page and save them to a separate file. You can also attach Design Notes to objects such as Flash files or applets, and you can use Design Notes in other programs such as Macromedia Fireworks MX. Here, the focus is on attaching a Design Note to a new or an existing document.

⇨ *For more information regarding Design Notes and objects, see "Working with Plug-Ins and Java Applets," p. 475; "Inserting Audio and Video," p. 485; "Understanding Flash and Shockwave," p. 498; and "Macromedia and Web Graphics," p. 570.*

When adding Design Notes to a page, you can mark a file's status as follows:

- Draft
- Revision 1
- Revision 2
- Revision 3
- Alpha
- Beta
- Final
- Needs Attention

1

You can also create a basic Design Note with your page, follow these steps:

1. Be sure the page is saved because you will not be allowed to write a Design Note if it isn't. Select File, Design Notes. The Design Notes dialog box opens with the Basic tab activated.

2. Select a status option from the Status drop-down menu. I selected Needs Attention.

3. Type your notes into the Notes text box (see Figure 1.11).

Date icon

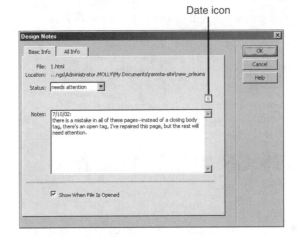

Figure 1.11
Add status and comments to a Design Note. You can modify Design notes to show author, date, and customized comments.

4. If you want the date to appear with your Design Note, click the Date icon above the Notes text box.

5. If you want the note to automatically show when the file opens, select the Show When File Is Opened check box.

6. Click OK.

Your Design Note is now saved with the page, and if you checked the Show When File Is Opened check box, the note will open every time the page is opened with Dreamweaver MX. If you leave that option unchecked, you can always see a Design Note by selecting File, Design Notes, and if a Design Note is attached to the file, it will appear. Design notes can also be seen by expanding the Site panel, which has a column indicating whether a given file has a note attached to it.

You can also use the All Info tab within the Design Notes dialog box to add name and value pairs to the notes. So, if you want to show that the author of the document is Harry, you can do so by adding the name of author and the value of Harry. Here's how:

1. With your page saved, select File, Design Notes.

2. When the Design Notes dialog box appears, fill in any basic information in the Basic tab; then click the All Info tab.

3. Click the plus (+) symbol (see Figure 1.12). Your cursor will move to the Name text box. Enter in a name that defines what you're trying to express—for example, **author**, **company**, or **project**.

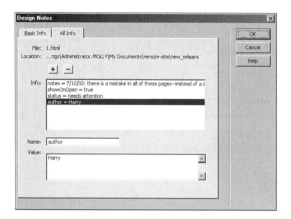

Figure 1.12
Using the All Info feature with Design Notes enables you to quickly and easily provide helpful information regarding a page or object.

4. Move to the Value text box and type in the value, which would in this example be an author, a company, or a project name or description.

5. Click OK to save the Design Note.

You can edit your Design Note at any time by selecting File, Design Notes. When the Design Note appears, make modifications using the Basic and All Info tabs. For example, if you want to remove a name value pair entry, simply highlight it in the All Info tab and click the minus symbol.

TROUBLESHOOTING

Refreshing Files

How can I make sure my site files are always up-to-date?

To ensure that all files are automatically refreshed, be certain to select the auto refresh feature. This is a helpful feature because it updates new files as you add them to the site.

Using Secure Shell

How can I make sure my site login is secure?

If you want to encrypt your login to the FTP server, you can do so using SSH, a popular security encryption for the Web. But you must first install PuTTY SSH Software from the Macromedia Web site, `http://www.macromedia.com/go/fp_dw_putty/`.

This is easily done by checking the Use SSH encrypted secure login check box, found in the Site Definition dialog box under the Advanced tab. Highlight Remote Info, select FTP for your access method—the check box, along with other information, appears. Check the check box, and a dialog box appears that enables you to download the program directly.

1

PEER TO PEER: PROBLEM URLS AND MODIFYING DREAMWEAVER FILES FOR STANDARDS COMPLIANCE

Two significant compliance issues come into play when defining sites and creating new pages using Dreamweaver MX. The first is dealing with long or problematic URLs, and the second is the unfortunate fact that some of the preconfigured files available via the New Document dialog box do not have the correct structuring required for validation and best practices.

Managing Problem URLs

The avoidance of very long URLs is a good practice from a usability standpoint. This means that, as you are defining your site and setting up directory structures, you need to keep things orderly and name files logically. A good rule of thumb is to try to not have more than two levels deep for information on your site and to keep directory and filenames as short as possible but still retain the logic. Also, wherever possible, avoid characters other than letters, numbers, and perhaps the occasional dash or underscore.

A reasonable structure would appear as such:

```
http://www.molly.com/seudw/index.html
```

A less reasonable example would be

```
http://www.molly.com/special_edition_using_dreamweaver/index.html
```

It's really a matter of common sense, and if you stick to it, you won't run into major problems. However, sometimes applications generate very long URLs with special characters in them. If you're working in XHTML, your pages will not pass a validation test to see whether all your syntax is correct if certain characters aren't escaped with character entities.

⇨ *To learn more about validation, see "Validating Documents," p. 520.*

Consider this URL:

```
http://www.stltoday.com/stltoday/entertainment/reviews.nsf/bydocid/
8B0C8EC6FD9760CF86256BDC005AEAFA?OpenDocument
&highlight=2%2Cstring%2Ccheese?opendocument
&headline=String+Cheese+Incident+stretches+out+for+good+and+ill
```

Not only is it terribly long, but it contains two instances of an ampersand, which must be escaped to validate within XHTML:

```
http://www.stltoday.com/stltoday/entertainment/reviews.nsf/bydocid/
8B0C8EC6FD9760CF86256BDC005AEAFA?OpenDocument
&amp;highlight=2%2Cstring%2Ccheese?opendocument
&amp;headline=String+Cheese+Incident+stretches+out+for+good+and+ill
```

Modifying Dreamweaver Files for Standards Compliance

Macromedia deserves a lot of kudos for taking a progressive stand and adding standards-related tools to its products. Naturally, major changes take time, so although some of these tools are working great, some are not yet available or up to par.

One such problem is the fact that an error exists in the default HTML document code. This file contains a portion of the DOCTYPE declaration, but it doesn't contain the associated URL. In the past, this didn't really matter because it was a fairly passive bit of code. But now, because of a new feature in browsers known as DOCTYPE switching, you can potentially cause problems with rendering if you don't include properly formed DOCTYPE declarations.

Whether you're interested in markup or not, there's a fairly easy solution to this problem, and after you've stepped through it, you'll not need to go back and fix it again.

To modify the default HTML document to contain the proper DOCTYPE declaration, follow these steps:

1. Select File, Open.

2. Locate the `Macromedia Dreamweaver` folder on your hard drive. You should see a subfolder titled `Configuration`.

3. Open the `Configuration` folder, and look for another subfolder titled `DocumentTypes`. Open this folder.

4. Look for another subfolder called `NewDocuments`. Open this folder, and then look for the file `default.html`.

5. Open `default.html`. In Code view, highlight this line:

```
<!DOCTYPE HTML PUBLIC "-//W3C//DTD HTML 4.01 Transitional//EN">
```

6. Replace it with this code:

```
<!DOCTYPE HTML PUBLIC "-//W3C//DTD HTML 4.01 Transitional//EN"
        "http://www.w3.org/TR/html4/loose.dtd">
```

7. Select File, Save.

The default HTML page is now properly marked up, and you won't need to make this change again.

➡ *Eventually, you'll want to create different Document Type Definitions (DTDs) pages and modify XHTML pages to contain the XML prolog or not. To learn more about what these things are and how to accomplish them with Dreamweaver, see "Transitioning from HTML to XHTML," p. 240.*

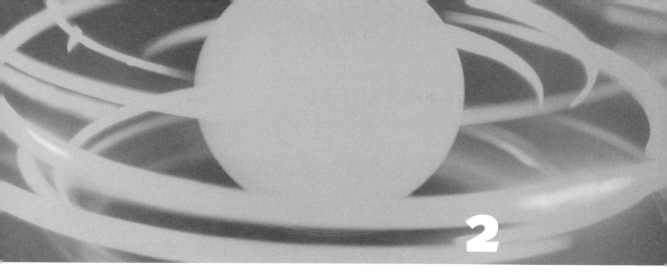

2

SETTING PAGE PROPERTIES WITH HTML

IN THIS CHAPTER

2

ADDING PAGE PROPERTIES

Web markup uses various attributes to format the colors and styles of text, links, and backgrounds. It is helpful to set other page features such as margins and title, and set the character encoding information of your documents.

Macromedia Dreamweaver collects all the attributes for the current document in a single window: the Page Properties window (see Figure 2.1). Using this window, you can set up the attributes for the page. In markup, most of these attributes can be set in the body element, although a few, such as the title and the character encoding, work with other elements such as head and meta.

Figure 2.1
Set the HTML attributes for the current page in the Page Properties window.

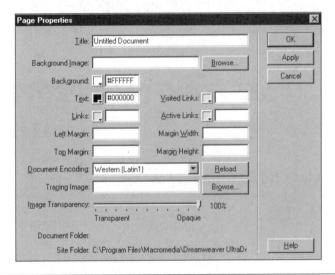

Setting Properties with HTML or XHTML Versus CSS

Although this chapter primarily deals with how to set page attributes using HTML, Web design is undergoing a steady migration away from HTML attributes and toward Cascading Style Sheet (CSS) properties to control layout and presentation. Unlike HTML attributes, which have to be set for each and every page, CSS allows attributes to be set either for a single page or for multiple pages simultaneously.

Currently, most professional Web sites use transitional HTML 4.01 or XHTML 1.0 in conjuction with CSS to ensure that browsers that do not support CSS, or only partially support CSS, are still sent the correct presentational information to display the page. Learning the techniques necessary to use HTML-based attributes, as well as learning how to use CSS, gives you the power to choose your method of setting page attributes.

➡️ *To find out how to set page attributes using CSS, see Chapter 16, "Using Cascading Style Sheets in Dreamweaver," p. 285.*

EXPLORING THE PROPERTIES WINDOW

To begin setting up your page properties, open the Page Properties window: select Modify, Page Properties.

Examine the Page Properties window. Table 2.1 describes each of the available fields and what purpose they serve. For most Web authors, these elements and attributes will be familiar, although some markup, such as those for document encoding, may be less familiar to the intermediate user.

Table 2.1   HTML Web Page Attributes

Name	Value	Element	Purpose
Title	Text	title	Sets a title for the page used in the browser window's title bar
Background Image	URL	body	Tiles a GIF or JPEG image behind all elements on the page
Background	Color	body	The color behind all elements on the page
Text	Color	body	The color of all text on the page
Links (Links, Visited, Active)	Color	body	The color of various link states: standard (no action), visited (already followed), and active (when the mouse clicks on the link)
Margin (Left, Width, Height)	Number (Pixels)	body	The space between the Top, edge of the page and elements on the page
Document Encoding	Text	meta	Sets the proper document encoding being used by the page

At this point, go ahead and set properties. The following sections will explain in greater detail how to do this and describe any special concerns you need to be aware of to create a valid page.

Adding the Page Title

Titling your page is essential for numerous reasons. The page title is displayed in the browser window's title bar and is used to:

- Denote bookmarks when a visitor bookmarks that page.

- Provide a marker for a browser's history feature.

- Promote better accessibility by assisting site visitors with orientation—your page title helps visitors know where on the Web they are, and specifically, where on your site they might be.

- Label the page should it be printed out.

The title is ASCII text that resides in the title container in the head of a Web page and can contain letters, numbers, and character entities as well as spaces.

> **Caution**
>
> Margin attributes used in the body of a document are proprietary attributes made available to certain browsers. These attributes can't be used if you wish to author pages that validate in accordance with W3C standards. When authoring valid pages, instead of setting these attributes in the body, you'll use CSS.

Whenever you create a new Web page in Macromedia Dreamweaver, it will have the default title `Untitled Document`.

To set your title, follow these steps:

1. With the Page Properties window open, highlight the default, `Untitled Document`.

2. Type in the new title.

3. Click OK. Your title will be updated.

Go ahead and save your page now.

Of course, Macromedia Dreamweaver MX provides alternative means of changing your title. You can change or modify the title:

- **In the Document window**—You can change its name by simply highlighting the name in the title field of the Document window and typing in a new title. This is the most frequently used method to change a Web page's title (see Figure 2.2) and is especially good when you'd like to modify your document's title as you are working in the Document window.

- **In Design view**—With the Document window open in Design view mode, select View, Head Content and then the title icon. In the Properties palette, you will see a title field. Highlight the current title and type a new one.

While you can use character enti-ties (such as   and so on) in the title, you *cannot* use any HTML or XHTML itself. So, if you want to add quotation marks or a copyright symbol to your title, you can do so by using an entity. However, you can't use any formatting, such as bold or italic.

Macromedia Dreamweaver places both the title and file name in parenthesis in the title bar of the document window.

Figure 2.2
For quick modifications to your title name, the Document window is a convenient alternative to reopening the Properties palette.

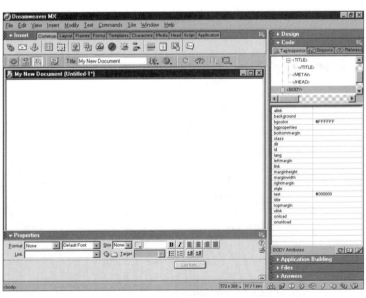

- **In Code view**—With the Document window open in Code view, scroll to the top of the markup until you see the `title` tag. Highlight the title between the open and close tags and type a new title.

Title Tips

As titles not only describe the page title but serve to help visitors orient themselves to your site, your title should be very clear. In fact, common practice is to place the name of the site first, followed by a colon or dash, and then the actual title of the document. So, if your site showcases and sells custom acoustic guitars, and you are working on a page about caring for your guitar, a good way to write your title would be:

 `Custom Acoustic Guitars: Caring for Your Guitar`

This way, the site name and specific topic are clear to a site visitor, as well as to one who bookmarks this specific page for later use. One caution with long titles: Certain browsers, such as the one for WebTV, truncate titles. So, if you can keep your titles short, doing so will be helpful to certain members of your audience. What's more, the longer a title, the longer and less clear it will appear when you bookmark the page. However, it's more important to be clear to the majority of your audience. A good rule of thumb is to use around five words, give or take a few for clarity's sake.

What happens when you don't add a title to your page? Find out in "Trouble with No Title Information" in the "Troubleshooting" section, later in this chapter.

Working with Backgrounds

Selecting the right background is important to the design process. You want to select a color that contrasts with the text (foreground) color so that reading is easier. If you decide to use a background image, use one that promotes readability, unless you are going for a completely visual effect. Selecting a background that is too distracting can cause eye strain, especially if the site has a lot of text to read.

Setting a Background Color

New documents are set to white by default. You can see this by opening the Page Properties window. Right below the Background Image textbox you'll see the Background option.

If you know the hexadecimal color value for the background of your page, type it into the Background textbox and click Apply. To set a color value for your background using the color chip, follow these steps:

1. Click the Background color chip to open a color palette from which to choose your color (see Figure 2.3).

Figure 2.3

Type the color value in directly or select a color from the drop-down menu.

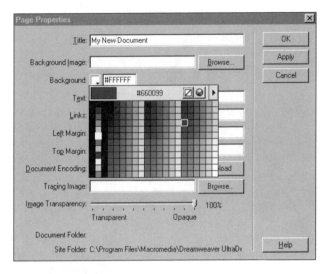

2. Move your pointer over the colors until you find one you like for your page. You'll see the hexadecimal value of the color appear in the top bar of the palette.

3. Click the desired color. The palette will load the hexadecimal value into the Background color text box, and the color chip will be updated to reflect your color.

4. Click Apply in the Page Properties window to see the background color in action.

Another option for changing your background color is to open your document in Code view and replace the color value for the bgcolor attribute with either a hexadecimal value or color name. If the background color has not already been set, you will type:

`bgcolor="#000000"`

directly into the body tag. Here, you see #000000, for black; you'll use the proper hex code for whatever color is appropriate to your design.

As you change the background color or image, the View mode will automatically update to show the new background image or color.

Look up hexadecimal and color codes on the book's companion page, which you can find by visiting http://www.molly.com/ books.php.

Setting Background Images

Using a background image can enhance the page both aesthetically and functionally, such as when using a background with a colored section for navigation.

Image Formats for Page Backgrounds

Background images can be any type of image that browsers can display.

Generally, the image format you choose should be the one that compresses your image the most with the least loss of visual quality (for graphics with large areas of solid color, the GIF format, and for more complex images and photographs, the JPEG format).

You can use a PNG graphic in the background. However, there are enough browsers that simply do not support PNG or poorly support PNG graphics. This makes the format a generally bad choice unless you know without a doubt that your audience is using browsers that have correct PNG support for your needs.

You can also use GIF animations as background graphics, but use background animations with extreme care and in special cases in which the visual or motion design of the page is more important than its readability.

⮕ *For more information on how to create background graphics, see "Creating Background Images," p. 573.*

All background graphics tile by default (see Figure 2.4). This means that your background graphic, no matter how large or small in dimension, will repeat horizontally and vertically across the page. So, when you create it, consider how it will look when placed end-on-end in two dimensions.

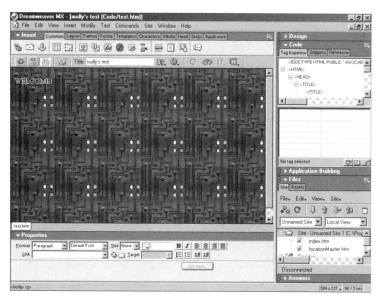

Figure 2.4

The Background image is automatically tiled behind all other content on the Web page.

Once you have created or chosen the background graphic you'd like to use, place it in your images folder. To add the background to your page using the Page Properties, follow these steps:

1. In the Page Properties window, click Choose (Mac) or Browse (Windows). This will open a browsing window.

2. Locate the file you just saved to your images directory and select it (see Figure 2.5).

3. Click Apply to apply your background image to the current page.

Alternatively, you can use Code view to add your background graphic. To do so, open Code view, scroll to the top of the document, and find the body tag. Replace the URL for `background` with the file path to the image you want to use. If you have not already set a background image, add the background attribute:

```
background="images/background.gif"
```

⇨ *For more details about how to manage backgrounds with CSS, see Chapter 16, "Using Cascading Style Sheets in Dreamweaver," p. 285.*

If the image dictated in the URL does not exist, no image is displayed—not even a broken image icon—and the background color will be used instead.

Adding Text Color

Text color is traditionally black for any text running longer than a few sentences. Black text on a white background provides the highest contrast possible and, arguably, is the easiest to read on screen and paper alike.

Of course, to create compelling designs, you might want to use other colors from your palette for the general text color. But remember that the higher the contrast, the better readability will result. What's more, many people are color blind and cannot see certain colors or combinations of colors. Your knowledge of audience and the intent of the site will help dictate your color choices.

Set a background color even if you set a background image. Choose a color close to the main color in your background graphic. The background color will display first, and even if your background graphic pops quickly into place, the subtle suggestion of the color will ease people into the visual presentation of the site. In addition, if for some reason your background graphic doesn't load, the color will take the image's place.

Caution

If the image file you selected is not within the current Web site's local root folder, you will be prompted by Macromedia Dreamweaver as to whether you want to move a copy of the image file into the Web site. This is usually a good idea, as it avoids the risk of losing the image when you upload the site.

CSS provides a lot more control over setting background images. In addition to tiling the image, you can choose to have it repeat horizontally only, repeat vertically only, or not repeat at all.

In new documents, Macromedia Dreamweaver sets the text color to black (#000000) by default.

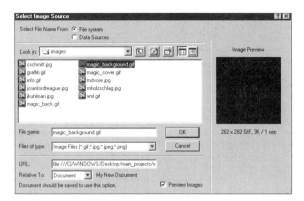

Figure 2.5

Type the URL for the background image (either absolute or relative) in directly or select the desired file from a local or networked hard drive.

Changing the Text Color

To change the text color using the Page Properties window, follow these steps:

1. Click the Text color chip to bring up the color palette.

2. Find the color you'd like and click on it. The hex code for the color will be entered into the Text color textbox, and the chip will change color from default black to the text color of your choice.

3. Click Apply to apply your text color changes to the document.

As with other page properties, you can set text colors manually in Code view. With the document open in Code view, scroll to the top of the page and find the body tag. Replace the color value for the text attribute with either a hex value or color name. If the text color has not already been set, you will need to type:

```
text="color value"
```

into the body tag (see Figure 2.6).

Managing Link Colors

By using HTML attributes in the body tag, you can set colors for three different link states:

- **Link**—This is the color of the link in its normal state and is expressed with the attribute name link.

- **Active link**—This is the link color that displays as the visitor clicks on the link. Its attribute name is alink.

- **Visited link**—When a link had been visited by a site visitor, setting the vlink attribute will change that link color to denote that it has already been followed.

When a new document is opened in Macromedia Dreamweaver, no default link colors are set. If left unset, the browser sets the link colors to its own defaults or to user specifications. Generally, the browser's default link colors will be blue for unvisited links, red for active links, and purple for visited links.

Figure 2.6
Type the color value for the text directly into the body tag using Code View.

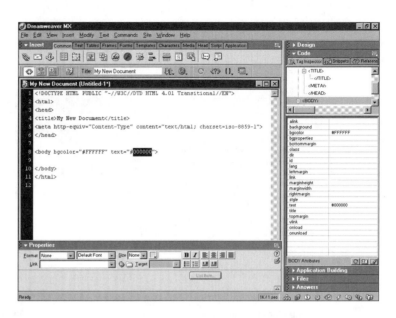

⇨ *Some concern exists over the coloring of links outside of the familiar browser defaults. Find out how this affects you in "Coloring Links" in the "Troubleshooting" section later in this chapter.*

Once again, you'll turn to CSS wherever possible because using it allows you to change not only the color of link text, but also any other text attribute (for example, you can make links bold), and it adds a fourth link state, hover, which is used when the visitor has his mouse over a link.

Setting Link Colors

As with other page properties, link colors can easily be set in the Page Properties window. To do so, follow these steps:

1. Open the Page Properties window. Click the color chip next to Links, and select your link color. If you already know your color, simply type the hex value into the Links color text box (see Figure 2.7).

2. Move to the Visited Links option and either use the color chip or enter the known hex color into the text box.

3. Continue on to the Active Links option, making your changes by following the same steps as with other link options.

4. After you have all the link colors added, click Apply to apply them to your page, or click OK to continue working.

If you'd like to make your changes using Code view, follow these steps:

1. With the document open in Code view, find the <body> tag.

2. Replace the color for any link style you'd like by typing it into the attribute value.

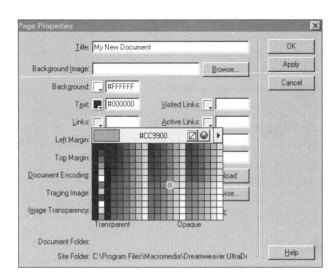

Figure 2.7
Select a color for the hypertext links on the page.

3. Save your page, and when you return to the document, your changes will have been applied.

Working with Page Margins

Page margins are considered to be between the edge of the viewable area of the browser window and the HTML content within it. Generally, Web pages will only have margins set for the top and left sides of the page (see Figure 2.8).

Top margin (height)

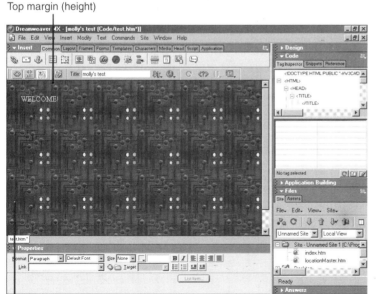

Figure 2.8
The top (height) and left (width) margins set the space between the content and the edge of the window. Note that the word Welcome now begins 30 pixels in and down.

Left margin (width)

Although margins can be set for the right and bottom sides of the page in most modern Web browsers, such attributes used in the body element are browser specific and therefore proprietary. They are *not* supported by the specifications, which of course recommend the use of CSS margins to control page concerns (see "Peer to Peer" later in this chapter).

Setting Page Margins

Macromedia Dreamweaver allows you to set the top and left margins for a page using the Page Properties window. To do so:

Hypertext links need to stand apart from other text on the screen so that users will recognize them. To that end, the colors you choose should sharply contrast the text color. Generally, it is best to select a more vibrant color for unvisited than for visited links.

1. Open the Page Properties window.

2. Type the margin number (in pixels) you'd like to use for the left margin into the Left Margin text box.

3. Repeat step 2 for your top margin.

4. Add margin width and height values in pixels into the Margin Width and Margin Height text boxes, respectively (see Figure 2.9).

5. Click OK and continue working.

Figure 2.9

Use the Page Properties dialog box to set margins.

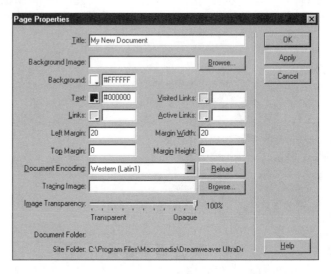

Should you desire to use Code view to add or modify margin properties, follow these steps:

1. With the document open in Code view, locate the <body> tag.

2. Replace the attribute values of each of the margin attributes with the pixel amount you want:

```
<body leftmargin="10" topmargin="0" marginwidth="10" marginheight="5">
```

3. Save the page to update your changes.

Changing Document Encoding

Document encoding defines the character set that your Web page will use. If creating a Web page in English or any other Western European language, keep this setting at its default, Western (Latin 1). This will insert the ISO standard code into a meta tag to define the character encoding for this page:

```
<meta http-equiv="Content-Type" content="text/html;
charset=iso-8859-1">
```

Macromedia Dreamweaver also offers built-in character sets for a variety of languages (see Figure 2.10), but if you do not see the language you need, that information is online at http://www.molly.com/books.php.

The Macromedia Dreamweaver Design view comes fully equipped with rulers to measure positions on the page in pixels (the default), centimeters, and inches. To turn the rulers on or off, select View, Rulers, Show.

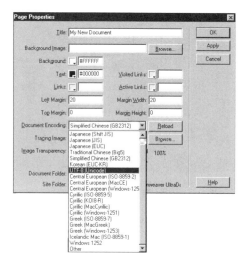

Figure 2.10

If you are not creating Web pages to be viewed in a Western European language, select one of the other options.

If you attempt to validate your markup with Dreamweaver or other tools and have not set a character encoding in your meta *element, you might end up with a warning. Find out why this happens and how to avoid it in "Validation Warnings and Character Encoding" in the "Troubleshooting" section at the end of this chapter.*

Using a Tracing Image

Now that your page properties are set, Macromedia Dreamweaver MX introduces a new and very helpful tool to the Page Properties window. This tool is referred to as *Tracing Image* and can be extremely useful as you build your page.

Caution

Character encoding is often set on the server side by your server administrator. This is considered the most effective and consistent way to provide documents in a given language. However, using the meta tag approach is important if you are unsure of what your ISP has set up or want to ensure that proper character sets are available for the page.

Designs often start as a series of static composition images (comps) created by a visual designer, art director, or creative director in a program such as Adobe Photoshop or Macromedia FireWorks (see Figure 2.11). A Web author then takes the comp and rebuilds it in HTML or XHTML. The challenge for the Web author is to realize the vision of the designer as accurately as possible within the confines of the Web.

Figure 2.11
This interface was created in Photoshop.

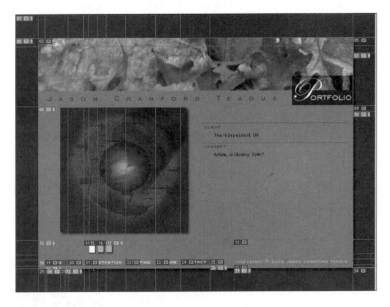

Tracing Image allows the Web developer to place the comp image as a background in the Macromedia Dreamweaver Design view. This, in turn, allows the Web author to build the page around the original composition, using it as a helpful blueprint.

The tracing image will not appear in the final Web page, only in Macromedia Dreamweaver. When the tracing image is visible, the page's background image or color will not be visible in the Design view. Fortunately, you can turn the feature on and off while working and see your actual progress.

Adding a Tracing Image to Your Page

To work effectively with a tracing image, follow these steps:

1. Open the Page Properties window and click the Browse button next to the Tracing Image text box.

2. The Select Image Source dialog box will open. Find the image you want to use as the tracing image. Select it, and click OK.

The image must be a format that Macromedia Dreamweaver can recognize. This does not, unfortunately, include Photoshop format, but does include PNG, GIF, and JPEG.

3. The Page Properties window will reappear, allowing you to set the transparency of the tracing image. When the tracing image opacity is subtle, it easily serves as a guide.

4 Click OK. The image will now appear in the Design view (see Figure 2.12).

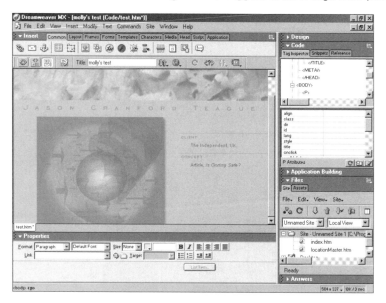

Figure 2.12

Use the tracing image as a guide while building your Web page.

Adjusting the Tracing Image's Position

The tracing image can be freely positioned or aligned with other objects in the Design view.

To set the tracing image's position:

1. Select View, Tracing Image, Adjust Position. The Adjust Tracing Image dialog appears.

2. Type in the X and Y coordinates where you'd like the top left corner of the image to appear. If starting at the top of your page, both the X and Y coordinates will be 0.

3. Click OK, and your tracing image will be positioned as to your needs.

To align the tracing image with another page component:

1. Highlight text or another page component in Design view to select it.

2. Now select View, Tracing Image, Align with Selection.

3. Macromedia Dreaweaver will automatically align the top left corner of the tracing image with the top left corner of the selected component.

To reset the position of the tracing image, simply select View, Tracing Image, Reset Position. Macromedia Dreamweaver MX will reset the position of the tracing image to the top left corner of the document.

You can quickly show and hide the tracing image by selecting View, Tracing Image, Show.

2

Using the Grid

Another useful layout tool is the grid (see Figure 2.13). Turning this on places a grid over top of the Design view that can help you while placing elements in the Web page. To show and hide the grid, select View, Grid, Show Grid.

You can also select View, Grid, Snap to Grid (Option-Shift-⌘) [Ctrl+G] to force elements that you move to align to the grid.

If you want to change the color of the grid, the spacing between grid lines, or whether the lines are solid or dotted, select View, Grid, Grid Settings.

Figure 2.13
The grid helps you accurately position elements on the screen.

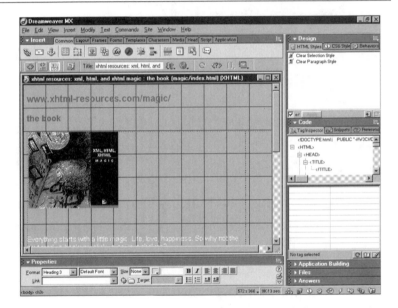

Your page properties are now set and can be easily modified using the tools described in this chapter. In Chapter 3, "Formatting Text with HTML," you'll learn how to use Macromedia Dreamweaver tools to work with a variety of text components.

TROUBLESHOOTING

Troubles with No Title Information

I'm not really sure what the title of my page should be. Is it really necessary?

If you leave title information out of your page, the title will publish to Dreamweaver's default `Untitled Document`. This gives your page visitors absolutely no help when trying to orient themselves to the page, figure out its purpose, and bookmark the page for further reference. Plus, the `title` element is required in HTML 4.0 and 4.01, and also in XHTML 1.0 and 1.1. Using a clear title is an important part of setting Page properties, so be careful not to overlook it!

Coloring Links

Are there any hard and fast rules for what color links should be? I'd like to make them match my site, but someone said that they have to be a certain color.

Many usability pundits—including Jakob Nielssen—have expressed that the use of colored links other than browser defaults cause usability problems with navigation. Although this might be true for people very new to using the Web (and nowadays, newcomers see so many different link colors, the point is almost moot), it's highly unlikely that any experienced user will fail to denote a link. Unless you are expressly asked by a client or superior to follow defaults, you should feel free to color links as you see fit.

Validation Warnings and Character Encoding

I'm getting a weird error when I validate my file. It says that no character encoding has been detected. What is causing this?

If you haven't added a `meta` tag and proper character encoding and then upload the file to the W3C validator to check your markup, you might get a warning saying that no character encoding has been detected. This can be fixed by ensuring you've set the encoding using the `meta` element, or better yet, by putting the page *without* any encoding *on* the Web server where it will reside and validating it from there. If you get no warnings and the page is properly interpreted, your server is configured accurately and the `meta` encoding is unnecessary (unless you're using foreign or unusual encodings and the server is using a more widespread encoding, such as UTF-8).

PEER TO PEER: PROPERTIES AND ATTRIBUTES; MARGINS AND TEXT

In this chapter, several issues come under scrutiny when compared to W3C specifications as follows:

- The use of margin attributes in the body element. The margin attributes `margintop`, `marginleft`, and `marginright` are all unavailable in any HTML or XHTL version.

- The term *properties* is used when describing that which modifies a CSS selector. The term *attribute* is used when describing that which modifies an HTML or XHTML element.

- Text and link attributes can be used in HTML 4.0, HTML 4.01, and XHTML 1.0 Transitional DTDs only. They cannot be used at all in XHTML 1.1.

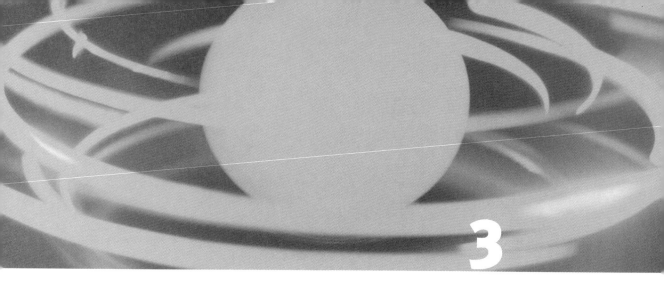

3

FORMATTING TEXT WITH HTML

IN THIS CHAPTER

TEXT AND THE WEB

Text on the Web is an intricate blend of focused content, word choice, writing style, and display. Although the former three require skills and techniques beyond the scope of this book, the display of your content can be entirely addressed by Dreamweaver.

Well-written, easily accessible content draws users to your site and keeps them there. It's not just the words themselves that grab visitors, but how easy it is to read them on the page. Several concerns when working with text content are

- **Use of typeface**—The font you choose plays a role in how your content looks visually, as well as how easy it is to read. Font colors are best when organized and consistent, and font sizing is an important issue when it comes to readability.

- **Chunking text**—How you break your content into separate paragraphs, use line breaks to format text, and add lists where appropriate can make or break a visitor's ability to scan and read without causing eye fatigue.

- **White space**—Also referred to as *negative* space, this is the space behind the words and objects. Use of margins, indents, and block quotes where appropriate will help you in arranging content effectively.

Garish fonts, blinking text, and poor contrast between the color of the text and the background are not a matter of style, but a matter of readability, or the lack thereof. Two different sites might cover the same topic—one with well-written but hard-to-read content, and the other with mediocre but well-displayed content. Chances are, most visitors will choose to return to the site that's most accessible, even if they can't get all the answers there.

Looking at this in real life, sites such as iVillage and most other e-commerce ventures generally write content that's at a fairly low reading level and only skims the surface of any topic. The display of that text is very easy to read, however, with good contrast in color, a standard font, small blocks of text on a page, and plenty of white space.

ADDING TEXT

Text is entered into Dreamweaver by either typing directly in the Document window or cutting and pasting text from another source. Text can be selected for editing or cutting and pasting within the document using many of the same keyboard shortcuts available in most word processors, as well as using the mouse (see Table 3.1).

Table 3.1   Common Editing Keyboard Shortcuts

Keyboard Shortcut (Win)	Keyboard Shortcut (Mac)	Result
Ctrl+X	Command-X (or Shift-Delete)	Cut
Ctrl+C	Command-C	Copy
Ctrl+V (or Shift+Insert)	Command-V (or Shift-Insert)	Paste
Ctrl+Z	Command-Z	Undo

Table 3.1 Continued

Keyboard Shortcut (Win)	Keyboard Shortcut (Mac)	Result
Ctrl+Y	Command-Y (or Command-Shift-Z)	Redo
Ctrl+A	Command-A	Select All
Shift+Page Down	Shift-Page Down	Selects rest of page from insertion point
Shift+Page Up	Shift-Page Up	Selects all text previous to insertion point
Shift+End	Shift-End	Selects rest of the line
Shift+Home	Shift-Home	Selects line previous to the insertion point
Shift+Left Arrow	Shift-Left Arrow	Selects character to the left of the insertion point
Shift+Right Arrow	Shift-Right Arrow	Selects character to the right of the insertion point
Ctrl-Backspace	Command-Backspace	Deletes the previous word
Ctrl+Delete	Command-Delete	Deletes the word to the right of the insertion point

After the text is entered into the document screen, you have many options for formatting it.

Paragraphs

A lot of the text in your documents is likely to be standard paragraphs. To create a paragraph break, simply press (Return) [Enter] and a blank line of white space is inserted below the paragraph.

Line Breaks

White space is important for control of design and readability. In most HTML editors, including Dreamweaver, when you press the (Return) [Enter] key, a new <p> tag is inserted.

From a markup standpoint, Dreamweaver assumes your text is in paragraph format by default until you apply formatting to the contrary. All text within the <p>...</p> tag pair is formatted as one paragraph.

Dreamweaver also automatically inserts a new HTML paragraph with a nonbreaking space   entity between the opening and end tags. If you then type on this new line, the nonbreaking space is replaced with your content. If you leave the paragraph blank, however, the paragraph remains with a nonbreaking space. Because the tag is not empty, browsers correctly interpret this paragraph as a blank line.

Conversely, you might want to start a new line of text without that blank line inserted by the paragraph tags. To do this, use a line break. A *line break* inserts a carriage return in the text without closing the paragraph tag and, thus, without inserting extra space between the two lines (see Figure 3.1).

Figure 3.1
The first paragraph of this text is formatted with a standard <p> tag pair. The second paragraph contains line breaks to place the food descriptions on separate lines within the same paragraph.

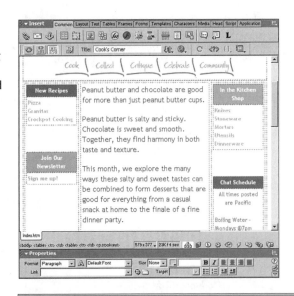

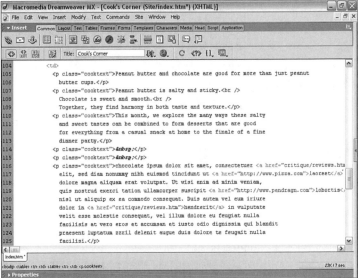

To add a line break, follow these steps:

1. Position your cursor where you want to force a line break.

2. Select Insert, Special Characters, Line Break from the menu, or press (Shift-Return) [Shift+Enter].

The text is forced to a new line without additional white space between lines. Line breaks can also be used to force more white space within a paragraph by adding multiple breaks consecutively.

⇨ *Find out why you'll get a validation error if text isn't properly formatted in strict HTML or XHTML documents in "Validation Errors Related to Text" in the "Troubleshooting" section at the end of this chapter.*

WORKING WITH FONTS

As you know, text is presented both online and offline using fonts. Fonts range from the plain to the elaborate, and from the highly readable to the highly illegible (see Figure 3.2). Fonts are grouped into categories, families, and faces. Font *categories* are the master families of type and describe the decoration or common features that denote families of fonts. Font *families* can be further broken down into font *faces*, which are specific font names. A font can also take on font *styles*, such as bold, italic, narrow, or regular/normal. The font categories and some of their faces are listed in Table 3.2.

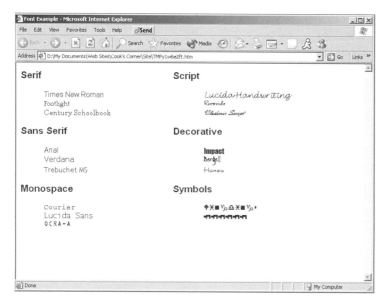

Figure 3.2
Fonts are grouped in categories with similar characteristics (as in serif fonts) or usage (decorative fonts).

3

Table 3.2   Common Fonts

Font Category	Common Windows Fonts	Common Mac Fonts	Additional Fonts
Serif— fonts with serifs, extra strokes at the points of the letters	Times New Roman, Garamond	Times, Palatino	Century Schoolbook, Goudy Old Style, Caslon, Footlight MT, Georgia
Sans Serif—fonts without serifs	Arial, Verdana	Helvetica, Geneva	Trebuchet MS, Franklin Gothic, Eras

Table 3.2 Continued

Font Category	Common Windows Fonts	Common Mac Fonts	Additional Fonts
Monospace (or Fixed Font)	Courier New	Monaco	Lucida Sans Typewriter, Ocra-A BT, TaxType Mono
Script	Lucida Handwriting Italic		Riverside, Lucia BT, Hancock, Vladimir Script
Decorative	Impact		Dragonwick, Bergell, Hansa
Symbol	Symbol, Wingdings	Symbol	Dingbats, Monotype Sorts, People, Puzzle

Of course, most of the fonts you see on the Web fall into either the serif or sans serif categories. That's because they're the most readable onscreen. As seen in Table 3.2, they're also the most common of all the preinstalled fonts on both major computer platforms. Monospaced fonts are generally used to signify a code listing or occasionally to integrate the text with a specific site design. Script and decorative fonts can be extremely difficult to read online and are generally not found on a broad range of users' computers, so they are usually used only in headings or the site logo. When used in this manner, they are created in a graphics package and inserted as images to bypass the font selection restraints and give the designer more control over appearance.

> Even the common fonts for each machine can vary. Each version of Windows ships with more fonts than the previous version. Mac OS X comes with many of the common Windows fonts as well as the Mac standards. Many fonts are also installed with such applications as Microsoft Office and Adobe Photoshop.

➪ *To read more about using images to replace text headings and similar elements, see "Adding the Image," p. 68.*

The font Element

Fonts are controlled in two ways. The font element is an inline method of setting fonts and attributes for a block of text. The font element's tags are automatically used by Dreamweaver when you use the Property inspector to modify text attributes such as font face, size, and color. Because it's so easy to use, many developers still use the font element.

Interestingly, however, the font element is deprecated by the W3C for HTML and is not to be used at all in any strict HTML or XHTML document. Instead, Cascading Style Sheets (CSS) should be used to define the form of your text, leaving the HTML document to contain only the content itself.

➪ *Cascading Style Sheets are covered in detail. See "Using Cascading Style Sheets in Dreamweaver," p. 285.*

⇨ *Want to use the font element and still follow best practices? Check out which HTML and XHTML document types allow you to use the* font *element in "Font Use" in the "Troubleshooting" section at the end of this chapter.*

The <font> tag allows for several attributes, the most common of which are accessible from the Property inspector (see Figure 3.3 and Table 3.2).

> Although the font element has been deprecated, font tags are still in such widespread use that they are covered in this chapter in detail. This shouldn't be interpreted as a recommendation of their use, however. CSS provides for much greater control over font presentation and is more easily modified on a page-wide or site-wide scale.

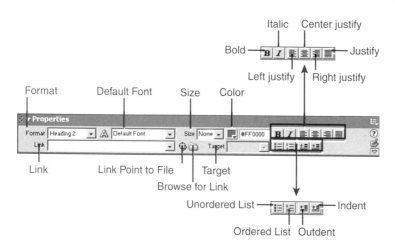

Figure 3.3
The Property inspector puts the most common <font> attributes within easy reach.

3

Table 3.3 font Attributes

Attribute	Purpose
size	Sets the relative size of the text
color	Sets the color of the text
face	Sets the font face or font group for the text
class	Sets the class ID for the text, enabling you to apply a style from a style sheet
dir	Controls the text direction, either left-to-right or right-to-left
title	Gives the block of text a title (similar to alt text for an image)
style	Defines in-line style rules

Setting the Font Face

The first roadblock in formatting your text is usually font choice. You can design a site that looks absolutely beautiful in Formal 436 BT font, but if users don't have that on their machines, the text reverts to the default font setting for their browsers. There's a big difference between Formal 436 BT and Times New Roman in both appearance and spacing. Thus, not only will the text look different than what you intended, but the layout of your page can also be set askew.

Fortunately, you can group fonts in attribute values and Cascading Style Sheet definitions. This is why it's important to understand which fonts belong to each category. Rather than choosing one nonstandard font and taking your chances on display, you can specify a range of fonts (usually in the same font category), such as `trebuchet ms, arial, helvetica, sans serif`. In this case, the browser first looks to display the text in Trebuchet MS. If that font is unavailable on the user's machine, it moves on to the next font in the list, and so on, until it finds a match. Usually, the final choice in a font group is a generic font category. Although you do lose some control over the specific presentation of your text when grouping fonts, you can be reasonably certain everyone has at least one sans serif font on their machine. Adding the font category to your font group ensures that text intended for sans serif Trebuchet MS isn't viewed in serif Times New Roman.

In Dreamweaver, fonts are chosen from one of the defined font groups. Select a range of text, and then select a font group from the Font Type drop-down menu in the Property inspector (see Figure 3.4).

Figure 3.4
The Font Type list contains preset font groups for the most commonly used Web fonts, along with any groups you add.

Adding Font Groups

You can add your own font combinations to the Font Type list. If you consistently use Trebuchet MS on your pages—either alone or in combination with other sans serif fonts—you can save time by adding it to the font list. To do this, perform the following steps:

1. Select Edit Font List from the bottom of the Font Type drop-down menu. This option is also available using the Text, Font, Edit Font List menu option.

2. In the Edit Font List dialog box, you can add or remove a font from an existing group by selecting that group from the Font List (see Figure 3.5). Otherwise, scroll to the bottom of the Font List to select Add Fonts in List Below.

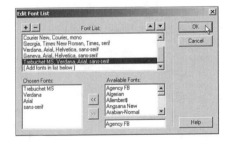

Figure 3.5
The Edit Font List dialog box lists all the fonts available on your computer to create and modify font groups.

3. To add a font, select it from the Available Fonts list. This list contains all the fonts installed on your computer, along with general font categories (found at the bottom of the list).

4. Click the arrows pointing to the Chosen Fonts list.

5. Continue steps 3 and 4 until the font group contains all the fonts or categories you require.

6. Click OK to add the new font group to the list and exit the dialog box.

Deleting Font Groups

You can also delete fonts and font groups. To delete a font from a group, do the following:

1. Select a font group from the Font List in the Edit Font List dialog box.

2. In the Chosen Fonts list, select the font you want to remove from the font group.

3. Use the arrows pointing away from the Chosen Fonts list to remove the selected font from the group.

4. Click OK.

> Even if you selected text before editing the font list, the new font group is not applied to that text until you select it in the Font Type drop-down list in the Property inspector.

To completely remove a font group, select the group in the Edit Font List dialog box and then click the minus (–) button at the top of the Font List.

Setting the Font Size

HTML font sizes are relative rather than a specific point size (unless you're using CSS, which gives you greater control over font size). When you select 3 or Default in the Property inspector, in theory, your site's visitors will see your text in the default size they've set for their browsers. Sizes 4–7 appear larger than the default, whereas sizes 1 and 2 are smaller.

When choosing a font size, keep in mind that browser differences exist between Windows and the Mac. The standard resolution for text on a Mac is 72dpi, whereas the standard is 96dpi for Windows. This means that text formatted to look good on a Mac might look too large on a Windows machine. If your site is also being read on the ever-increasing number of Web-enabled PDAs and cell phones, this issue is further compounded.

Another issue is browser settings. If a user has his browser set to display fonts in a large size and you pick a large size for your fonts, the output on the end user's screen can be enormous. The opposite is equally true; many Web surfers set their default text size to "smaller" to fit more text on the screen. When they visit a page coded to use small fonts, the text is too small to be legible. While savvy Web users know to increase their default text sizes in these instances, not all users will go to the trouble.

This problem is particularly of concern for those individuals who are visually impaired. Using relative font sizing (discussed in just a bit) can help. Even better, using style sheets, which have specific options to allow for resizing of fonts, is the best bet for providing site visitors with control over the size of text they're reading.

To set the font size, do the following:

1. Select the text to be sized. If no text is selected, the size change will be applied to subsequent text.

2. In the Property inspector, click the Size drop-down list (see Figure 3.6).

Figure 3.6
In the Size drop-down list, you can select from a specific size or an increased or decreased size relative to the default.

3. Select a size from the list.

As you can see from the list, you can pick a specific HTML size of 1–7, or you can choose to increase or decrease the size relatively from the default size by using the –7 through the +7 options. If a user's default size is 3, selecting +2 makes the font size a 5. If a different user's default size is 5, the same text would appear to that user as a size 7.

> **Choosing specific size settings** gives you more control as a designer, but it gives less control to the user. Choosing relative size settings reverses this control. It's up to you as the designer to apply size settings in a manner that balances your need to control design with the user's need to control readability.

Setting the Font Color

The default text color is set in the Page Properties dialog box. Unless you modified the page properties, the default color for text is black (#000000). To change the color of text from the default, select the text and then use the Color Picker in the Property inspector to select a new color (see Figure 3.7). The Text Color field uses the same Dreamweaver color picker as the Page Properties and other color tools. Alternatively, you can type the hexadecimal code in the text box to the right of the Color Picker.

> **To return text to the default text** color, click the Color Picker and then click the white square with the red strikethrough button.

Figure 3.7
Using the color picker to set the font color is a quick, visual way to colorize your fonts.

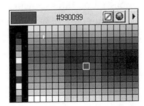

⇨ *For more on the process for changing the default text color using the Page Properties settings, see "Adding Text Color," p. 34.*

Setting Font Styles

A font style is formatting such as bold or italics applied to a font. The most typical font styles were seen in Figure 3.3 and can be applied from the Property inspector.

You can choose additional font styles by selecting Text, Style from the menu (see Table 3.4). You can also choose more than one style for the same text selection, such as when creating bold, italicized text.

Caution

Remember, if you underline text on your pages, it can be confused with a link.

Table 3.4   Font Faces and Their Uses

Font Style	HTML Element	Used For
Bold	b	Adding bold emphasis
Italic	i	Adding emphasis using italicization
Underline	u	Adding emphasis using underline
~~Strikethrough~~	s or strikethrough	Editorial purposes
Teletype	tt	Monospaced font
Emphasis	em	Usually displayed as italics
Strong	strong	Stronger emphasis than just using the emphasis style, usually displays as bold
Code	code	Text that represents a computer program listing
Variable	var	Text that represents a program variable
Sample	samp	Text that represents sample output from a program
Keyboard	kbd	Text that represents user input
Citation	cite	Source of a quote
Definition	dfn	Text that is a definition

If you select a style before typing, the style is applied to all subsequent text.

SETTING PARAGRAPH FORMATS

In addition to formatting the font, size, and color of text, the alignment and format of the block of text as a whole can be defined. A *paragraph format* displays the block of text according to the defaults of the formatting tag that is applied. Dreamweaver has three basic paragraph styles: paragraph, heading, and preformatted. They are applied using the Format drop-down list in the Property inspector (see Figure 3.8).

Figure 3.8

The paragraph format is used to signify text as being a paragraph, a heading, or preformatted.

Paragraphs

Most text on the page is formatted as the default Paragraph format. This format ignores white space, so sequential spaces within the paragraph appear as only one space when viewed in a browser.

Headings

Headings are used to identify different sections of content on a page. They range from largest and boldest (<h1>) to smallest (<h6>). Although designers have used them independently in HTML, ideally headers should be used hierarchically to divide the site into readable segments of information in much the same way as this book is laid out. Headings are applied to the entire paragraph, so you can't mix heading styles within the same line of text.

The proper use of headings is a serious part of document structure. For more details on why this is considered important, see the "Peer to Peer" section at the end of this chapter.

Preformatted

Preformatted text is the solution to instances in which the paragraph format is too restrictive. The preformatted format enables you to space text exactly as you want, including using white space and line breaks (see Figure 3.9). Text doesn't automatically word wrap, so you must press Enter to end a line. When put into practical use, your results with the preformatted format can vary depending on the fonts used and the default size settings on users' browsers.

Figure 3.9
The top heading, About Peanut Butter and Chocolate, is fashioned here using h1. The "This month . . ." subhead uses h2. Finally, the paragraph describing peanut butter has been reconfigured using the pre element. You can tell this by the fact that the font is monospaced.

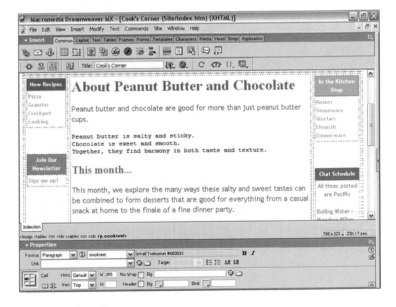

PARAGRAPH ALIGNMENT

Paragraph alignment is used to position text relative to its confining margins, whether those margins are the page margins, a table cell, or a layer. To change the alignment of text, follow these steps:

> **Alignment is considered presentational and therefore can be used only in HTML and XHTML transitional documents.**

1. Select the text you want to align, or insert the cursor at the beginning of the text.

2. Click Left Justify, Center, or Right Justify on the Property inspector.

You can also align text by selecting Alignment from the Text menu.

Increasing/Decreasing Indentation

Text can be indented or outdented in several ways. Select the desired text and use one of the following methods to indent or outdent the text:

- Use the Property inspector and click the Indent or Outdent button.

- From the menu bar, select Text, Indent or Text, Outdent.

- If the text you highlight is a list, you can right-click it and select List, Indent or List, Outdent from the context menu.

Indents and outdents can be applied multiple times until the text is positioned where you desire. Although this is easy to do, it's not the preferred method for positioning text. A better solution is to use a table or CSS.

⇨ *For more about using tables for positioning and layout, see "Adding a Table," p. 124.*

CREATING LISTS

Lists bring order and structure to text on the Web. Large blocks of text are difficult to read onscreen, so lists break things into manageable highlights.

Lists items are formatted in `<li>...</li>` tag pairs for each item. The list in its entirety also needs to be defined. The manner in which this is done depends on the type of list.

Unordered (Bulleted) Lists

An unordered list is used when the sequence of the items isn't important. Bulleted lists can be created from text you've already entered, or the list can be created as you type the text. Here's how to make an unordered list:

1. To configure the list and then type the list items, position the cursor where you want to start the list. If you're converting existing text into a list, select the text.

2. In the Property inspector, click the Unordered List button. You can also select Text, List, Unordered List.

3. Type in the text of your list.

4. To end the list after you enter all the items, press (Return) [Enter] twice or click the Unordered List button in the Property inspector.

List items are spaced more closely together than paragraphs (see Figure 3.10). If you look at the Code view, the unordered list is contained within a <ul>...</ul> tag pair.

Figure 3.10

An unordered list is used for items that don't need to appear in a specific order.

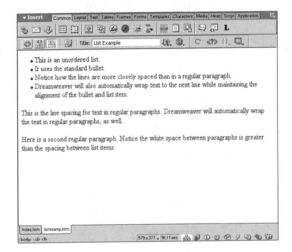

Font faces, colors, sizes, and styles can be applied to lists. Paragraph formatting, however, is likely to destroy the list layout, so it should be avoided. To remove list formatting, select the entire list and then click the Unordered List button in the Property inspector. The text itself remains, but the formatting of the list is deleted as is the markup that created the list.

Ordered (Numbered) Lists

Ordered lists are used when items should be followed sequentially. Create these lists in the same manner as unordered lists, but simply click the Ordered List button instead. Examining the code, you'll see that ordered lists are defined by the <ol>...</ol> tag pair.

One of the best features of an ordered list is its capability to renumber itself as items are added, deleted, or moved. To add an item to the list, position the insertion point at the end of the list item above where you want the addition to appear. Press (Return) [Enter] to add a new line; then type in the new item. To move an item in the list, either use the cut-and-paste method or highlight the list item and then drag it to its new location while holding down the left mouse button.

Changing List Properties

When you create lists, the bullet symbols or numbering sequence might need to be modified to meet your needs. To do this, select a list item and then click the List Item button on the expanded Property inspector (see Figure 3.11). Alternatively, you can select the entire list and use the Text, List, Properties menu option.

In the List Properties dialog box, select the style you want from the Style list (see Figure 3.12). The new style is applied to the entire list.

Figure 3.11
The expanded Property inspector has an additional option to format lists.

Click to expand or collapse Property inspector

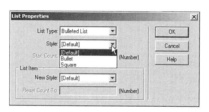

Figure 3.12
If you want to have a traditional disk-style bullet for your list, select Bullet. If you want a square, select Square.

3

To change the style of a single list item or an item and any subsequent items, change the New Style in the List Item section of the List Properties dialog box. Even if you later change the overall style for the entire list, items that have been individually formatted will retain their unique format.

Nested Lists

Lists aren't always one level deep. If you're outlining a project or giving step-by-step instructions, you might want to provide additional information relating to a specific list item. Nested lists enable you to insert sublists within lists.

To create a nested list, follow these steps:

1. Select the text you want to reformat from within an existing list, or insert a blank list item where you want the nested list to appear.

2. In the Property inspector, click the Indent button. Dreamweaver creates a separate list with the original list's properties.

3. Highlight the list, or place your cursor at one of the bullets in Design view. Click the List Item button in the Property inspector to open the List Properties dialog box.

4. Select a different list type from the menu if you want to use one.

5. Click OK.

Caution
If you don't indent the list item before you change the list type, Dreamweaver breaks the selected items into a separate list that's formatted in line with the original list. If more list items are below the selection, they are broken into yet a third separate list.

INSERTING SPECIAL CHARACTERS

Many special character entities, such as the copyright symbol or trademark symbol, are used frequently on Web sites. To add these symbols to your page, use the Characters tab on the Insert panel (see Figure 3.13).

Figure 3.13
The Characters tab on the Insert panel provides shortcuts to the most common special characters.

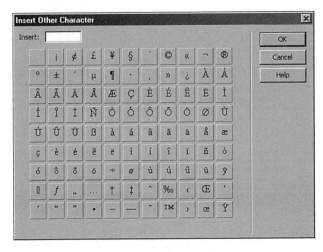

If you click the last button on the panel, you can insert additional special characters. The Insert Other Character dialog box displays 99 symbols (see Figure 3.14). Select the character you need, and then click OK.

Figure 3.14
Ninety-nine special characters are available on the Insert Other Character dialog box.

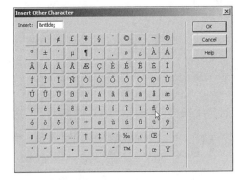

TROUBLESHOOTING

Validation Errors Related to Text

I'm getting validation errors related to text materials. Why?

This might be due to an issue with browser display.

Browsers rely on certain display models to interpret HTML and XHTML. Two such display models are referred to as *inline* and *block*. An element that is inline appears within the text itself, and therefore no carriage return is applied by the browser. Examples of inline elements include a, `span`, and any text
formatting such as b, i, and u. Block elements are complete sections after which browsers apply a carriage return automatically. Examples of block elements include all headers, p, div, and `table`.

Strict forms of markup expect that the author will place all inline elements within a properly described block. This means that text should appear within a header, paragraph, list, or any other block element but should not appear alone. So, in a strict document, the following is incorrect and causes a validation error:

```
Send <a href="mailto:molly@molly.com" title="email molly">me</a> an e-mail.
```

To avoid errors, make sure your text is properly placed within a block element, such as a paragraph:

```
<p>Send <a href="mailto:molly@molly.com" title="email molly">me</a> an e-mail.</p>
```

Interestingly, this problem doesn't occur with transitional DTDs, which do not require adherence to block and inline rules.

> **If you know the ASCII shortcuts** for the symbol you need, you can enter it directly on the Web page. For example, the copyright symbol is Alt+0169 in Windows and Option-G on the Mac. These are operating system shortcuts—not Dreamweaver shortcuts—and are fairly standard across applications on each platform.

Font Use

I want to use the font element and still have valid documents. Is that possible?

You can do so following these DTDs:

- HTML 4.0 transitional
- HTML 4.01 transitional
- XHTML 1.0

You can't use the font element in any strict HTML or XHTML document or with the XHTML 1.1 public DTD. As you are already aware, the use of the font element is highly discouraged in favor of CSS.

PEER TO PEER: THE ESSENCE OF STRUCTURE

Text structuring provides an excellent example of why the goal to separate document structure from presentation rules is so important.

If you add elements to text in a haphazard way, such as using paragraph tags to create white space; using headers out of numeric order; and using font elements, the document has no structure. An h1 header was labeled a level one with the precise goal in mind to label the content within the element as being a header of first-level priority, an h2 a second-level priority, and so on. This hierarchy is part of what creates structure. Add to that properly formatted paragraphs, line breaks, the reduction or elimination of font tags, and the use of lists to organize a document, and you get to the heart of what a structured document is all about.

When you structure documents using the hierarchical and logical methods described previously, that document becomes much more accessible not only to those with disabilities, but also for alternative devices such as PDAs, pagers, mobile phones, and so on. Follow these general guidelines, and your pages will be extremely flexible in how they can be used. What's more, you'll have returned to the original vision of the Web: a platform-dependent means of sharing documents.

3

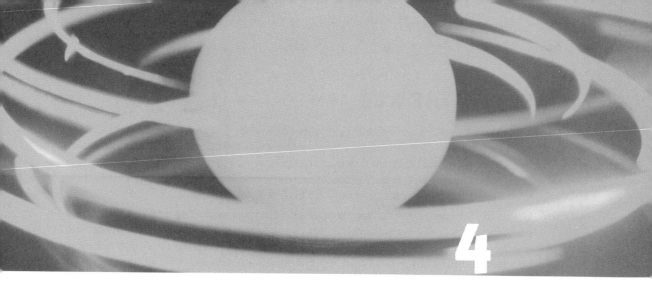

4

ADDING IMAGES

IMAGES ON THE WEB

The use of images on a site can enhance the user experience or make it a visual nightmare. Images can serve a purpose to visually make a point, or they can detract from even the best text content. To use images wisely, it's important to understand the differences between image types, how to use them appropriately, and how to optimize them to have the least impact on download time. When talking about creating a visual experience, it's important not to fly blind.

Images can take several forms. They serve as everything from navigation buttons to photo galleries. They can be used as decorative bullets in lists or as an animated eye-catcher to call attention to a new feature on the site. They can serve as backgrounds for an entire page or a table. When created with the effects available in the leading graphics applications, they can give visitors a new perspective on something old.

Images generally can be divided into three categories:

- **Page elements**—These are buttons, bullets, horizontal rules, and navigational icons that are essential to organizing and structuring a page.

- **Visual interest**—These are images that enhance the site's content. Visually interesting images can supplement the site's purpose or even be the sole purpose. Examples include a picture that complements the text and an online photo gallery. Animated GIFs often serve as visual interest when they're not serving a functional purpose as a page element or an advertisement.

- **Background elements**—These are images used as a backdrop in the body of a page, table, or layer. They are often subtle in design so as not to detract from the content that rests on them.

Web Image Formats

As you probably already know, several common file formats are available for Web images. GIF and JPEG formats have been used on the Web for years and are still the most popular. PNG is a more recent format but doesn't yet have widespread browser support, particularly for its most valuable features. The current cutting edge of Web imaging is vector graphics, particularly Flash and Scalable Vector Graphics (SVG).

To learn more about Scalable Vector Graphics, see the article *Scalable Vector Graphics* at `http://www.molly.com/articles/webdesign/2001-04-svg.php`.

GIF

Graphic Interchange Format (GIF) images are commonly used for line art and images with blocks of flat color. They're limited to only 256 colors, making them less suitable for photographs and detailed graduations in color. Their small size and transparency capabilities make them extremely popular on the Web. They can also be used for small animations.

JPEG

Joint Photographic Expert Group (JPEG or JPG) images are used for photos. They can take longer to load than GIFs and lose quality when they're very compressed, but they can display millions of colors with ease.

PNG

Portable Network Graphics (PNG) contains both bitmap and vector image data, giving it an edge over GIFs and JPGs (both of which are bitmap image formats). PNG also supports alpha channel and graduated transparency, but those features aren't yet supported by the current browsers. One advantage of the PNG format is that it has gamma correction, meaning it will appear the same on both PCs and Macs. Macromedia Fireworks MX uses PNG files to store source image files.

Bitmaps and Vectors

Vector images have been a part of the print world for years but are only recently finding wider support on the Web. To understand the attraction of vector images, you first need to understand the difference between bitmaps (such as GIF and JPG images) and vectors.

Think of bitmaps as a painting—each pixel on the screen is a drop of paint. The only way to change the painting is to add more paint to the canvas, thereby covering what previously appeared. If you stretch the painting, each drop of paint covers a larger area, making those individual drops expand. Shrinking a painting would reduce the size of the individual drops. Quality can, in either case, be compromised.

Vector graphics, on the other hand, are like a collage—each object is a shape, calculated mathematically. Shapes can be layered and stacked in different arrangements while keeping each shape intact. If you stretch or squish a vector graphic, each shape is mathematically recalculated to maintain its perspective and integrity.

The interest in vector graphics on the Web is largely due to the proliferation of Flash-based sites. Flash allows developers to create highly interactive, fully animated sites. One reason Flash is so attractive is the small file sizes of its images and animations. Unlike bitmaps, which need to store data about every pixel, vector images store the mathematical calculations only for drawing the shapes contained within it.

The popularity of Flash is leading to other forms of vector graphics on the Web. The World Wide Web Consortium (W3C) is currently working on specifications for SVG, mentioned earlier. These graphics are an XML construct in which the markup to draw the graphics is embedded into the Web page itself.

4

SVG currently requires a plug-in, but interest in it is avid due to Adobe and the W3C both focusing resources on it.

CREATING THE IMAGE

Images can come from many sources. Digital photography has enabled even novice developers to put a unique perspective on their sites. Even a low-end scanner can create image files of a high enough quality to use on the Web. Clip art and stock photography are other good sources for images.

Eyewire (http://www.eyewire. com) has a wide range of images grouped by theme and image type (illustrations and photos as well as fonts).

Using a Graphics Application

Whether you shoot the photo yourself or download a piece of clipart from the Web, you'll most likely want to edit some of those images in a graphics application. Graphics packages such as Macromedia Fireworks MX, Adobe Photoshop, Adobe Photoshop Elements, and JASC Paint Shop Pro enable you to create unique graphic images as well as edit and enhance existing images and photos.

Fireworks MX is often the graphics application of choice when developing in Dreamweaver. Fireworks is tightly integrated with Dreamweaver, streamlining the development cycle. You can use Fireworks to generate the code for rollovers and drop-down menus and then port the code directly into Dreamweaver. You can also edit images placed in Dreamweaver documents using Fireworks with just a couple clicks of the mouse.

⇨ *For more information about using Fireworks with Dreamweaver, as well as using other graphics programs with Dreamweaver, please see Chapter 32, "Working with Web Graphics," p. 569.*

Configuring Dreamweaver to Use an Image Editor

If you install Fireworks at the same time or prior to installing Dreamweaver, it is automatically configured as the default editor for images. If you install Fireworks later or choose a different graphics application as your image editor, you can set it up in the Preferences dialog box by doing the following:

1. Select Edit, Preferences from the menu.

2. In the Preferences dialog box, select the File Types/Editors category (see Figure 4.1).

3. Select a file extension from the Extensions list. If the extension you seek isn't in the list, you can add it by clicking the Add (+) button above the Extensions field and then typing in the **.xxx** extension.

4. Click the Add (+) button in the Editor field.

5. Navigate to the application you want to use when editing that file type.

6. Click OK.

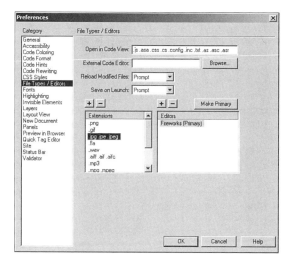

Figure 4.1

You can set one application as the image editor for GIFs and JPGs and another as the editor for PNG files.

Optimizing Images for the Web

The major graphics packages contain tools to optimize graphics to compress them into the smallest possible size with a minimal loss of graphic integrity. Adobe Photoshop ships with ImageReady to serve this purpose. Fireworks has integrated optimization tools. If you use Fireworks with Dreamweaver, automatic Design Notes will track an optimized image back to its original source PNG file to facilitate easy modification.

You can also use the Dreamweaver/Fireworks integration to launch a subset of the Fireworks tools and optimize a file from within Dreamweaver. To do this, follow these steps:

1. Select an image in a Dreamweaver document.

2. Select Commands, Optimize Image in Fireworks (or use the context menu to make the selection).

3. In the Fireworks Optimize window, change the options (see Figure 4.2).

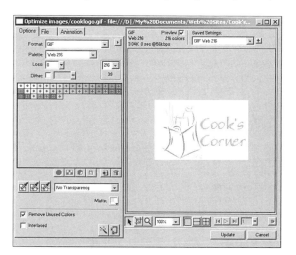

Figure 4.2

The Optimize features of Fireworks are available from within Dreamweaver.

4. Click Update to save the changes and return to Dreamweaver.

ADDING THE IMAGE

After the image is created and optimized, you can add it to your pages. To insert an image, do the following:

1. Position the insertion point where you want to add the image.

2. Select the Insert Image icon from the Insert Bar or select Insert, Image from the menu.

3. Select the image file from the File Selector.

4. Click OK.

> **If you didn't create the image in** Fireworks, you'll be prompted to locate a source file for the image. If such a source file exists, you should always work from that file instead of directly in the compressed GIF or JPG you inserted into the Dreamweaver document. If you attempt to optimize an existing JPG image, the quality will suffer tremendously.

Alternatively, you can use drag-and-drop to insert the image. Click and drag the Insert Image icon from the Insert Bar to the desired location on the page; then follow steps 3 and 4 from the previous procedure. You can streamline this process by selecting the image file in the Site panel or Assets panel and dragging it onto the Document window.

Although not necessarily recommended, you can insert images in file formats not used on the Web, such as TIF or BMP. In most cases these will not display in the Document window but will instead appear as a placeholder. This is useful when you're inserting images that have not yet been converted to an appropriate file format and is sometimes done as a reminder of what's intended for a specific location on the page.

You can add a Design Note or comment to the document to remind you to edit the image and convert it before going live. Remember that even though the image might not appear in the Document window, it can render correctly when testing in a browser. Don't let this fool you into thinking the image is Web-appropriate.

> **An image file won't be available** from the Library within the Assets panel until it has been placed elsewhere in the site at least once.

> ➡ *Design Notes are a way of commenting on a document without marking up the document itself. Learn more about them in Chapter 1, "Defining Your Site," p. 9.*

FORMATTING THE IMAGE

Images are generally sized and formatted in the graphic editor of choice because that provides the most control over the image's integrity. Several formatting attributes are still available for an `<img>` tag, however. Most of these are accessible from the Property inspector (see Figure 4.3). The attributes are listed in Table 4.1.

Table 4.1   Image Attributes

that specifies the location of the image file.

the image. This is used with JavaScript or CSS to identify an

value of this attribute identifies the image for a specific style
eet.

line style for the image.

ame or description, which might or might not be unique. The
n supported by a browser at all, usually appears as a ToolTip
the image.

text for users who cannot or choose not to view images. All
a descriptive alt attribute to make the site accessible.

y defined as the dimensions of the image itself, these attrib-
to scale the image within the browser.

nt of the image relative to surrounding content. This
eprecated in favor of using CSS for alignment.

ce or the width of a border around the image. If the border is
displayed. When an image is used as a link, this attribute
matic border that commonly identifies a link. This tag has
avor of CSS.

d vertical space around the image, typically used for adding
gin between the image and surrounding content. These
deprecated in favor of CSS.

Figure 4.3
The Image Property inspector contains the most common attributes of the <img> tag.

4

⇨ *Seeing a partial line around a linked image? The problem might be your markup's formatting. See "Managing Linked Images" in the "Troubleshooting" section of this chapter for more details.*

Naming Images

Of course, each image has a unique filename. But because images can be used multiple times in a site, or even a single document, the filename alone isn't very useful when pointing to a particular image. JavaScript and behaviors often refer to images by name to identify them as the target of an action, such as in a rollover.

> ### Caution
>
> Modifying the width and height of an image without physically changing its dimensions is not a recommended practice because the full image still must load. The only exception to this is when you are using spacer graphics, which are only 1×1 pixels to begin with. You can then modify width and height as required.

If you're planning to use JavaScript or behaviors on your images, give them unique names (which appear as the ID attributes in the code). Names should contain only alphanumeric characters, no punctuation. The more descriptive the name, the easier it will be to remember its purpose when putting together navigation bars and rollovers in the Behaviors panel.

⇨ *For more information about JavaScript and behaviors, see Chapter 22, "Working with JavaScript and Behaviors," p. 415. For more on rollovers and navigation bars, see Chapter 23, "Rollovers and Navigation Bars," p. 431.*

Setting the Image Size

As a rule, images should always be sized appropriately in the graphics application. There is only one real exception to this, and that's when you're creating a graphic to be purposefully stretched out of proportion with a spacer GIF.

⇨ *For more information on spacer GIFs, see Chapter 18, "Designing with Table-Based Layouts," p. 321.*

There are two ways to change the size of an image within Dreamweaver. The Property inspector shows the default width and height settings for a selected image. These settings are the dimensions of the actual image. To resize the image, type new values in the W and H fields.

You can also resize an image by selecting it in the Document window, positioning the cursor over the boundary box at one of the resizing points (the cursor will turn into a double arrow), and then dragging the boundary box to the desired size. As you can imagine, this method is far less precise.

If you've changed the width and height dimensions of an image but not the physical size of an image and then want to revert to the original settings, click the Reset Size button on the Property inspector or select Reset Size from the context menu for the image itself. As long as you've not edited the image physically, no data or detail will be lost.

Why Not Resize?

When you resize images within the HTML, expect the unexpected. Images may not scale quite the same across various browsers and platforms. Also, no matter whether you expand or shrink the size of the image, the file size remains the same because you're not editing the image itself. This means that even if you make the size of the image display smaller, the file can still take considerable time to load. If you need to change the dimensions of an image, it's worth the extra time it takes to resize it in the graphics editor instead of expecting the browser to do the job for you.

Setting the Image Alignment

Images don't always fall exactly where you want them within the context of surrounding content. The recommended method for aligning images is using Cascading Style Sheets (CSS).

If you're not using CSS for alignment, use the Property inspector to change the Align attribute.

You need to use the expander button at the bottom-right corner of the Property inspector to find the Align option.

The alignment options are as follows:

- **Browser Default**—Usually the Baseline (see Figure 4.4).

- **Baseline**—The text is aligned to the bottom of the image (see Figure 4.5).

- **Top**—The text is aligned to the top of the image (see Figure 4.6).

- **Middle**—The baseline of the text is aligned to the middle of the image (see Figure 4.7).

- **Bottom**—The text is aligned to the bottom of the image (see Figure 4.8).

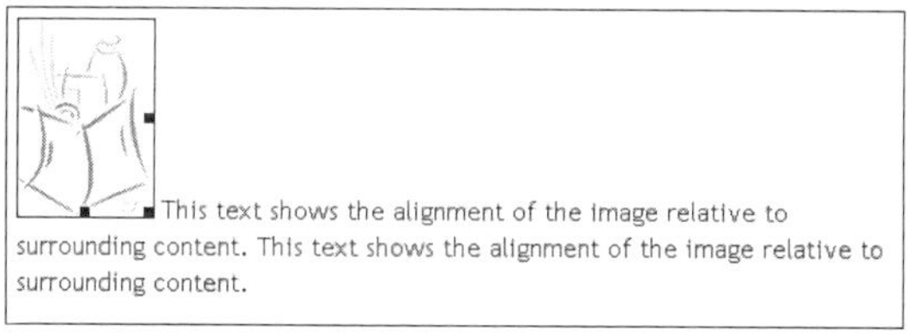

4

This text shows the alignment of the image relative to surrounding content. This text shows the alignment of the image relative to surrounding content.

Figure 4.4
This image is set for Browser Default alignment.

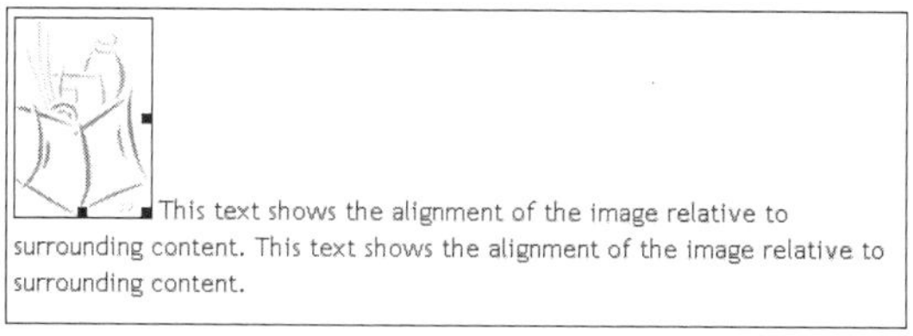

This text shows the alignment of the image relative to surrounding content. This text shows the alignment of the image relative to surrounding content.

Figure 4.5
This image is set for Baseline alignment.

Figure 4.6
This image is set for Top alignment.

This text shows the alignment of the image relative to surrounding content. This text shows the alignment of the image relative to surrounding content.

Figure 4.7
This image is set for Middle alignment.

This text shows the alignment of the image relative to surrounding content. This text shows the alignment of the image relative to surrounding content.

Figure 4.8
This image is set for Bottom alignment.

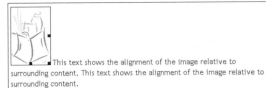

This text shows the alignment of the image relative to surrounding content. This text shows the alignment of the image relative to surrounding content.

- **Text Top**—The topmost point of the text is aligned to the top of the image (see Figure 4.9).

- **Absolute Middle**—The middle of the text is aligned to the middle of the image (see Figure 4.10).

- **Absolute Bottom**—The lowest point of the text is aligned to the bottom of the image (see Figure 4.11).

- **Left**—The image appears to the left of the text, and the text wraps along the right side of the image (see Figure 4.12).

- **Right**—The image appears to the right of the text, and the text wraps along the left side of the image (see Figure 4.13).

Although you might not notice much difference between default, baseline, and bottom at first, depending on how your individual image is cropped or treated with effects, you should try the different options to get the best balance between your text and image.

Figure 4.9
This image is set for Text Top alignment.

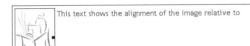

This text shows the alignment of the image relative to surrounding content. This text shows the alignment of the image relative to surrounding content.

Figure 4.10

This image is set for Absolute Middle alignment.

Figure 4.11

This image is set for Absolute Bottom alignment.

Figure 4.12

This image is set for Left alignment.

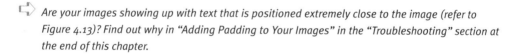

Figure 4.13

This image is set for Right alignment.

➪ *Are your images showing up with text that is positioned extremely close to the image (refer to Figure 4.13)? Find out why in "Adding Padding to Your Images" in the "Troubleshooting" section at the end of this chapter.*

➪ *For more about Cascading Style Sheets, see Chapter 15, "Designing with Style," p. 265, and Chapter 16, "Using Cascading Style Sheets in Dreamweaver," p. 285.*

Adding Alternative Text

Every visible image on your site—whether it's a photo of the Grand Canyon or a bullet icon—should have alternative text. Visually impaired Web surfers rely on this text to describe the images on a page, which can make the difference in them being able to use your site or moving on to one that's more accommodating. Even visitors with images turned on—most likely the vast majority of your site's visitors—will see the alternative text for an image before the image itself loads.

Spacer GIFs and the Visually Impaired User

Images that aren't used for visual purposes, such as a spacer GIF, should contain an `alt` attribute but no description, like so:

```
<img src="spacer.gif" width="25" height="1" alt="" />
```

This way, screen reading hardware and software won't read the image description. Because there is nothing to be seen, a description such as "spacer graphic" is just unnecessary information for the blind or visually impaired user.

Alternative text should be limited to a shorthand word or two. Provide a complete description where necessary to ensure your visitors can understand what's being displayed. Some designers even use alternative text to provide short quotes or haiku that make the site come alive for visually impaired users.

Alternative text is added in the Alt field of the Property inspector (see Figure 4.14). The length of the text can extend beyond what's viewed in that field.

Figure 4.14
Alternative text as seen within the Property inspector. Note that the Tag Inspector shows the Alt text as well.

TROUBLESHOOTING

Managing Linked Images

I linked an image and made some modifications to the image markup using code view. Now, my image has a strange line by it, even though my border value is set to 0.

This is an annoying artifact that results from breaking markup into separate lines. Keep the markup tight, and make sure the closing anchor tag, `</a>`, comes immediately *after* the img element, with no spaces whatsoever:

```
<a href="index.html"><img src="home.gif" /></a>
```

Adding Padding to Your Images

I have added images to my page as instructed here, but they are all too close to the text for my tastes. How can I position them more effectively?

There are two ways to add space around an image. If you are using HTML or XHTML transitional, you can use the hspace and vspace attributes right in the img markup. Set a pixel value for each, and then test it in a browser until you like the results.

CSS, however, is the preferred and most powerful means of adding these properties. You can add padding to any one or combination of an image's sides, and you can do so using a variety of measurements.

➡ *See Chapter 16, "Using Cascading Style Sheets in Dreamweaver," p. 285, to learn more.*

PEER TO PEER: BEYOND THE ALT ATTRIBUTE: CREATING ACCESSIBLE IMAGES

Although the alt attribute goes a long way in helping make a page more accessible, it's not the only means by which you can make your images more accessible. Here are some tips to help you make your images more useful to those who cannot see them or who see them poorly:

- Always provide in-text references to the image.

- If the image contains information critical to the comprehension of the page, you must also include a detailed description within the content as to what function the image provides.

- Try to use images of a good quality, with high contrast for low-vision site visitors.

- If you want to add detailed information about the image in addition to any contained in the content, consider using the longdesc attribute. This stands for *long description*. You can create a separate HTML page with the extended description in simple HTML markup. Then, you provide the location of this file as the value to this attribute:

```
<img src="growth-chart.gif" longdesc="growth-
chart.html"
alt="human growth chart, starting at age 1.">
```

Supporting browsers will provide an optional link called growth-chart.html.

Unfortunately, the longdesc attribute is very poorly supported in current user agents, but there should be progress in this area in upcoming releases of all major browser brands.

4

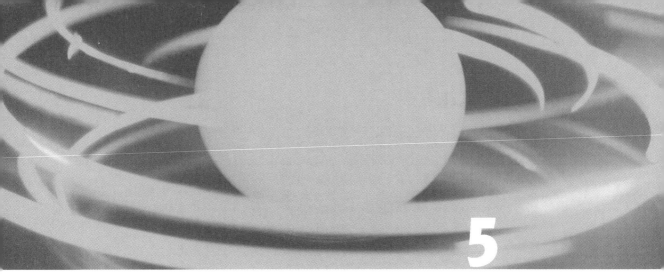

5

ADDING LINKS

ALL ABOUT LINKS

The foundation of navigation on the Web is the link. As you are probably well aware, the most common form of a link is from one page to another. A link can also take many other forms. You can link to an email address, creating a blank message with the recipient's email address (and even a subject) already inserted, which is useful for allowing visitors to send you questions. Links can navigate to a specific section of the same page or a selected point on another page, such as when creating a FAQ. Links can also open or save a file, as when creating a library. You can use a link to access a plug-in to display a movie or play music. Links can even be used to attach behaviors and JavaScript to text or images (called *null links*).

Links appear as part of a navigation bar, in an imagemap, or simply as plain text, but they still perform the same function—getting visitors from one place on the Web to another.

Hypertext links appear within the context of your site content. They are used to direct site visitors to sites or pages related to the topic at hand. This capability is the key strength and intrigue of the Web. The downside, unfortunately, is the very same—hypertext links can encourage visitors to move on to another site or subject, thus distracting them from reading the content on your site (see the "Encouraging Visitors to Stay on Your Site" sidebar later in this section).

Navigational links bring organization and usability to a site. Navigation bars are essentially a list of links represented graphically or textually in a menu format. Imagemaps are another method for displaying the navigational structure of a site. The key to navigation is consistency: The menu should appear on every page of the site with the options in the same order and displayed the same way. As with hypertext links, Cascading Style Sheets (CSS) can be used to modify the display of navigational links. Dreamweaver MX behaviors can also be used to create enhanced navigation bars with rollover states and other events (see Chapter 23, "Rollovers and Navigation Bars").

Encouraging Visitors to Stay on Your Site

Want to provide links but keep visitors on your site for a longer period of time? Try the following:

- Use CSS to create a link style that's less visually jarring to the visitor than the default underlines.
- Target links (particularly links to other sites) to open in a new browser window.
- Use frames, targeting links to open in a different frame than the source content.

PLACING A LINK

Constructing a link in Macromedia Dreamweaver MX is simple. A block of text or an image is designated as the source. A page, a site, an email address, or even a non-HTML file is designated as the destination.

To accomplish this in Dreamweaver, open the page in Design view and select the text or image for the source of the link. Assign the destination in the Link field of the Property inspector using one of the following methods:

- Typing the path

- Using the Link History pull-down

- Browsing

- Using the Point-to-File method

- Creating links in the Site panel

Typing the Path

The Link field of the Property inspector accepts direct input. If you know the full path of the link's destination, type it in the Link field (see Figure 5.1).

Figure 5.1
You can type a link directly into the Link field.

Although this might appear to be the easiest method for creating a link, it's also fraught with the most potential problems. If you make a typo in the name of the file or misdirect the path, the link will be broken.

Link History Pull-Down

When developing a site, it's common to use the same destination for multiple links. To save time, use the pull-down menu in the Link field to access the history of all links used on the page (see Figure 5.2).

External links must initially be typed manually. When creating an external link, type the full path, including the http:// designation. After the external link has been entered into the Link field for the first time, you can access it again using the Link history pull-down menu.

Browsing

To the right of the Link field is a folder icon. Clicking this icon opens the File Selection dialog box. This is a foolproof method for creating an internal link—the path is automatically generated by Dreamweaver when you select a file. You can also open the dialog box using the Modify, Make Link or the Insert, Hyperlink menu option. All these methods work the same; use the approach that best works for you.

If you're linking to a file located outside the local site on your drive, first copy it to the site folder to maintain the link's integrity and ensure it gets uploaded to the remote server.

5

Figure 5.2
The Link field can be used by typing directly into the field or accessing the pull-down history menu.

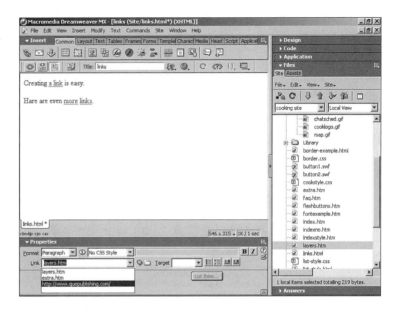

Using Point-to-File

Another way to create a link is to use the Point-to-File button in the Property inspector (see Figure 5.3). The Link text box is filled in when you drag your mouse to any file in the Site panel or to another open Document window. This method is usually faster than using the File Selector to browse through folders. It also automatically sets the filename, so if you're linking to an MP3 or HTML file, you don't have to remember the file extension—this method manages that for you.

Figure 5.3
As you drag the mouse to a destination file or anchor, a line extends from the Point-to-File button to the file.

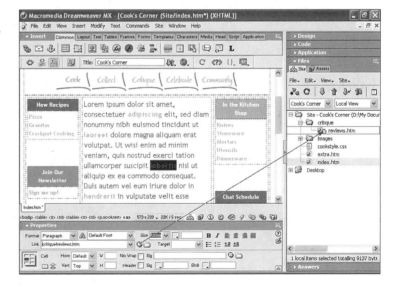

To use the Point-to-File method, follow these steps:

1. Select the source text, image, or file description for the link.

2. Access the Point-to-File feature by doing one of the following:

    • In the Property inspector, click the Point-to-File icon.

    • Drag the mouse from the selection to the destination file.

3. While still holding down the mouse button, drag the mouse until it's over another open Document window, an anchor (in either the current document or another open document), or a file in the Site panel.

4. Release the mouse button.

The correct link address is automatically entered into the Link text box.

Creating Links from the Site Panel

The site map, located in the Site panel, offers several methods to quickly establish links between pages that exist within your site.

Before using the site map, you must expand the Site panel into the full Site window. To do this, click the Expand/Collapse button on the Site panel toolbar. Macintosh users should select Window, Site to see the details.

The now-familiar Point-to-File icon is available in the site map (see Figure 5.4). Select a document, and the icon appears to the right of the page icon. Drag the mouse from the icon to the destination page. You can also drag the Point-to-File icon to an open document (or to an anchor within that document).

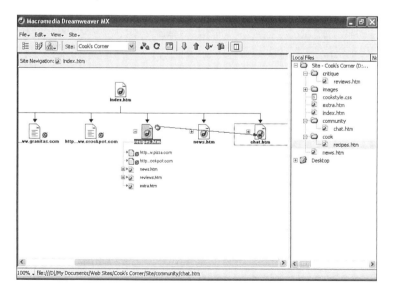

Figure 5.4
The Point-to-File icon is also available in the site map view in the Site window.

5

Using Windows Explorer and the Mac Finder

Another way to drag and drop a link is to select a file from Windows Explorer (or Finder on the Mac) and drag it to a page on the site map.

When you create links directly in the site map, you obviously cannot select source text or images in a page. Instead, Dreamweaver appends a text link to the bottom of the source document. This text can then be modified or even replaced with an image when you edit the document.

> You can also use the links generated in this manner to create a text menu at the bottom of your page to make it more accessible to visually impaired site visitors. This is especially helpful if your main menu is an imagemap.

Using the Site Map Menu

Just as the Document window has menu options to make links, the site map does too. Select a document, and then select Site, Link to Existing File.

You can also use the menu to link to a new file by selecting Site, Link to New File. This creates a new untitled document in the file list, as well as a link to it in the source document.

FORMATTING LINKS

Text links appear underlined by default to distinguish them from surrounding text (see Figure 5.5). Dreamweaver sets image borders to 0 by default, so you're unlikely to see borders around your image links. If you've modified the border setting, however, the border around an image link will be the same color as text links. Although these underlines and borders might be useful in some situations, they can detract from the design of the site. What's more, unless you're using a CSS method to add a border for a linked image, you can't use the border attribute in Strict versions of HTML and XHTML or XHTML 1.1.

Figure 5.5
Text links are underlined by default.

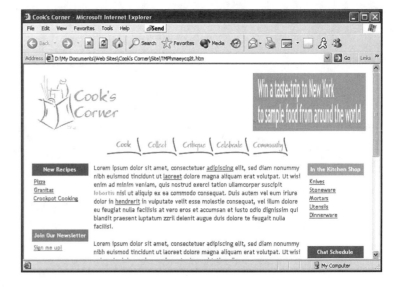

To remove the link border from an image, select it and then use the Property inspector to change the Border setting to 0.

Removing the underlining from text links requires the use of CSS (see Figure 5.6).

To change the format of a text link, do the following:

You might need to expand the Property inspector to access the Border setting.

1. Open the CSS Styles panel by either selecting Window, CSS Styles or clicking the CSS Styles tab in the Design panel group.

2. Click the New CSS Style icon on the CSS Styles panel.

3. In the New CSS Style dialog box, select Use CSS Selector; then select one of the link classes from the Selector drop-down menu (see Figure 5.7).

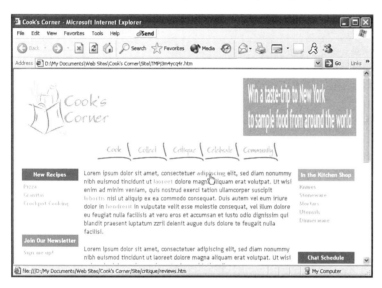

Figure 5.6
Links can be modified using Cascading Style Sheets to become more cohesive with the site's design.

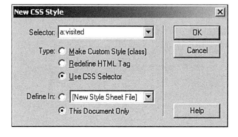

Figure 5.7
Using the New CSS Style dialog box, you can modify your link styles with CSS for greater efficiency and control.

4. In the Style Definition dialog box, change the Decoration field to None to remove the underlining from your links. You can also make other changes to the link style here.

5. Click OK to save your style changes.

⇨ *The available link classes in CSS are covered thoroughly later in this book. See Chapter 16, "Using Cascading Style Sheets in Dreamweaver," p. 285.*

Link Function and Form

Aside from the appearance of links, the function of links can also be changed. Adding attributes to the HTML tag does this.

Link Function

Each of these attributes has a different function, as described in Table 5.1.

Table 5.1 Link Attributes

Attribute	Purpose
Accesskey	Specifies a character that must be pressed by the site visitor to access the destination
Charset	Specifies the character encoding for the destination page
Cords	Used in imagemaps
Href	Specifies the URL as indicated in the Link field of the Property inspector
Name	Used to define an anchor position for an intra-page link
Shape	Specifies a shape in an imagemap
Tabindex	Determines the order in which links become active when visitors use the Tab key to navigate
Target	Determines where the destination page will open—in the current window, a new window, or replacing the current frameset in the current window

Link Form

Whether you're linking from page to page or to another site, the link must follow a specific format. URLs are made up of different segments in the format of *protocol://server/path/filename#anchor*.

In Dreamweaver MX, this breaks down into specific area components, as described in Table 5.2.

Remember, any presentational attribute is moved to CSS when working with HTML and XHTML Strict DTDs, and XHTML 1.1. The target attribute, for example, cannot be used with any of these DTDs. On the other hand, any attributes related to accessibility, such as accesskey and tabindex, are highly encouraged for use with all DTDs. See the "Peer to Peer" section at the end of this chapter for more details.

Table 5.2 URL Components

Component	Description
scheme	The protocol used to access the item, such as Hypertext Transport Protocol (HTTP), File Transfer Protocol (FTP), or email (mailto).
server	The domain name or IP address of the server hosting the site.
Path	The path that directs the link through the site hierarchy into the proper folder.
filename	The specific file sought by the link.
named anchor	A named anchor can be used to point to a specific (named) section of a page.

Absolute links enable users to move from site to site. They also require the scheme and server to be specified, as in `http://www.cookscorner.com/reviews.htm`. *Relative* links are used to link to pages within the same site. In relative links, the scheme and server are implied, so they don't need to appear in the link path. Instead, they simply point to the file in question, such as `reviews.htm`.

Document-Relative Versus Site-Relative Links

There are two types of relative links. *Document-relative* links provide the location of the linked file relative to the source document. Links are created based on the path required to navigate from the source document to the destination. To link to a page located in the same directory as the source page, use just the filename, such as `href="news.htm"`. If it's in a different directory, prepend the filename with the folder path, as in `href="info/news.htm"`. To navigate back toward the site root and into another directory, use two dots to move up a folder. For example, `href="../../shopping/sales.htm"` moves you up two directories from the source document, then into the `shopping` folder, and finally to the `sales.htm` file.

Site-relative links always use the site root as the starting point for the link path, even if the destination document is in the same folder as the source. This is signified in the link path with a leading forward slash (/). Using the last example, a site-relative link appears as `href="/collect/shopping/sales.htm"`. Site-relative links are difficult to use in a development environment because they can be fully tested only on the remote server. Unless you have a specific need to use them, you're better off sticking with document-relative links.

5

Targeting Links

As mentioned earlier, links can be distracting. One method for minimizing the impact of directing your visitors to other sites is to target your links. Targeting enables you to open a link in another window or frame. In doing so, the original content—your content—remains on the screen, encouraging visitors to return to it after reading the related information (see Figure 5.8).

The target options are

- _blank—Opens a new browser window containing the linked file.

- _parent—Used when designing with frames, this loads the linked file into the parent frameset of the source page. Frames are covered in Chapter 7, "Working with Tables and Frames," and Chapter 19, "Working with Frame-Based Layouts."

- _self—Loads the linked file into the same window or frame as the source page.

- _top—Also used with frames, this overrides the frameset to load the linked file into the full browser window.

Figure 5.8
Clicking the link on the Pendragn site opens a new window containing the Molly.com site.

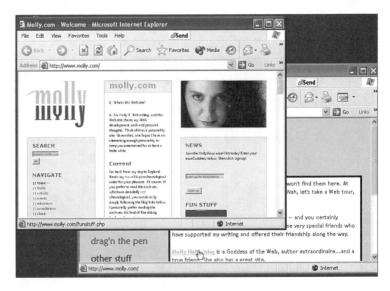

⇨ *Using magic target names and pages aren't loading properly? See the "Magic Target Names" topic in the "Troubleshooting" section later in this chapter.*

⇨ *For details on working with tables and frames, see Chapter 7, "Working with Tables and Frames," p. 121, and Chapter 19, "Working with Frame-Based Layouts," p. 351.*

To target a link, do the following:

1. Select the link source.

2. Create the link using one of the methods described earlier in this chapter.

> **Advanced markup authors can** add any attribute or element to a DTD using XHTML Modularization.

3. With the link source still highlighted, select a target by doing one of the following:

   - From the Property inspector, select it from the Target drop-down menu.

   - From the menu, select Modify, Link Target. In addition to the target options listed previously, this method allows you to target a frame in a frameset.

Targeting links, although a popular and useful method, can also be disruptive because they can drain the site visitor's resources with each new browser window that opens. What's more, as mentioned earlier in the chapter, the target attribute is not allowed in certain versions of HTML and XHTML. As such, you must be sure that you use target with care, and then only with a transitional DTD.

⇨ *For more information on working with markup, see Chapter 14, "Working with HTML and XHTML," p. 237.*

ANCHORING LINKS

Intra-page links have been mentioned throughout this chapter. An *intra-page* link navigates to a specific location on a page. The entire page loads, so visitors can scroll up and down from the anchor. Anchors are particularly useful for FAQs and other long documents (see Figure 5.9).

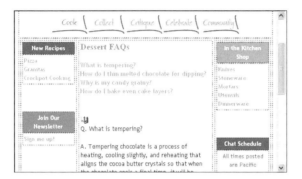

Figure 5.9
Anchors are useful in FAQs, where the questions are listed separately from the answers, with links between them.

Using a FAQ as an example, you'll see that all the questions can be listed at the top of the page, serving as link sources. The answer to each question is given a named anchor, which provides the destinations for the links.

Add a link under each question of a FAQ to return site visitors to the list of questions. This is also done using a named anchor.

Naming an Anchored Link

To create an anchor, you must first give the destination a name:

1. Place the cursor where you want to insert the anchor.

2. Click the Named Anchor icon on the Common tab of the Insert bar. You can also select Insert, Named Anchor from the menu.

3. The Insert Named Anchor dialog appears (see Figure 5.10). Type a name for the anchor in the Name text box.

4. Click OK.

Position the anchor one line above the content to which you're directing site visitors. This extra white space at the top of the browser window helps visitors' eyes locate the content.

5

If you set your preferences to display invisible tags, you'll see a yellow anchor icon in your document, representing the named anchor.

Figure 5.10
The Named Anchor icon opens the Insert Named Anchor dialog box.

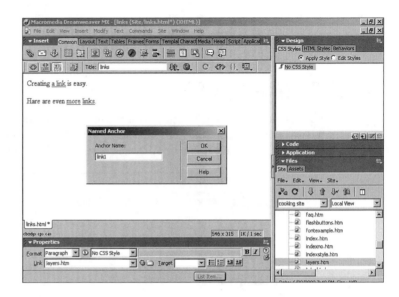

Linking to an Anchor

After you set the named anchor, you can link to it from any page or site. To create a link to the anchor, follow these steps:

1. Select the text or image source for the link.

2. Type the destination in the Link field of the Property inspector by using one of the following methods:

   - Type the anchor name preceded by the pound (#) symbol to link from the same page, such as **#shipping**.

   - To link to the anchor from another page, type the destination as **faq.htm#shipping** (preceded by the appropriate path to **faq.htm**, of course, including the scheme and server if linking from another site).

You can also use the Point-to-File method by dragging the cursor to the named anchor icon you want to use as the destination.

EMAIL LINKS

Rather than expecting users to cut and paste an email address from your site into their email applications, a mailto link automatically opens a pre-addressed message window. These links are somewhat unique and can be entered in two ways. To type an email link directly in the Link field of the Property inspector, the format is `mailto:email@domain.com`.

Another method for creating email links is to use the Email Link icon on the Common tab of the Insert bar. Follow these steps:

1. Place your cursor where you want the link to appear. Unlike other types of links, you don't have to preselect your source text—although you certainly can.

2. Click the Email Link icon. Alternatively, you can select Insert, Email Link from the menu bar.

3. The Insert Email Link dialog box appears (see Figure 5.11). If you preselected source text, it appears in the Text field. Otherwise, type the text you want to place as the source for the link.

Figure 5.11
The Email Link icon opens the Email Link dialog box.

4. Enter the email address in the Email text field.

5. Click OK.

Adding a Subject

Some email systems also allow you to specify a subject for emails sent from the mailto link. This is useful if you have mailto links to your address on multiple sites because you can give each link a different subject.

To add a subject to the mailto link, append a ? and the subject of the message immediately following the email address, without any spaces. Thus, a mailto link to webmaster@cookscorner.com with a subject of Recipes would be entered as `mailto:webmaster@cookscorner.com?Recipes`.

CREATING IMAGEMAPS

Imagemaps enable you to create multiple links from one image source. Unlike the rectangular constraints of standard image links, imagemaps can create irregularly shaped hotspots, allowing them to take on the exact dimensions of a piece of the image. Because each hotspot is defined with its own tags, you can apply alternative text and even behaviors to them.

It's important to set alt text for the entire image as well as each hotspot. The image alt text is displayed in areas of the image that don't have a hotspot.

To create an imagemap, follow these steps:

1. Insert an image into the document. Use the standard image properties to set the alignment and `alt` text for the image.

2. Select the image.

3. In the Property inspector, name the imagemap in the Map Name field. Names must be unique for the site.

4. Select a drawing tool from the Property inspector (see Figure 5.12).

Figure 5.12

The imagemap tools are located on the bottom half of the Property inspector.

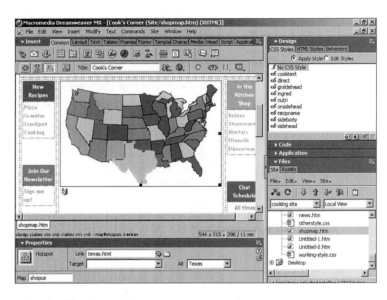

Then, create a hotspot using the following options:

- **Rectangle**—Position the cursor in one of the upper corners of the desired hotspot, and then drag the mouse to the opposite corner.

- **Oval**—Position the cursor at one of the upper corners of the hotspot location, and then drag to the diagonal corner to extend the circle. Although they're referred to as ovals, these hotspots are always perfect circles.

- **Polygon**—Position the cursor at a starting point, and then click at every point of the shape where it changes direction or angle. You must close the shape at the starting point to create the hotspot.

5. Click the hotspot you drew to display the Hotspot Property inspector (see Figure 5.13).

Figure 5.13

The Hotspot Property inspector is where you set the destination for the link.

6. Enter the link destination path and `alt` text for the hotspot. You can also set a target for the link.

7. Repeat steps 4–6 for each hotspot.

After creating your imagemap, you can test it using the Preview in Browser feature (see Figure 5.14).

Figure 5.14
This imagemap has hotspots for each of the contiguous 48 states.

Have you created an imagemap and are having trouble with precise linking? See the "Imagemap Overlap" section in the "Troubleshooting" section at the end of this chapter.

Adjusting and Moving Hotspots

Aligning hotspots perfectly when drawing them freehand is difficult. Rather than striving for the impossible, draw the hotspots as close as you can and then modify each by clicking the points of the hotspot and resizing or reshaping the element.

You can also modify the alignment of a group of hotspots using the Modify, Align menu. Follow these steps:

1. Select a hotspot.

2. Holding down the Shift key, select the other hotspots you want to align.

3. Select Modify, Align.

Alignment options include Left, Right, Top, and Bottom. You can also make all the selected hotspots the same width and height.

> **Caution**
>
> The imagemap techniques described here use *client-side* imagemapping, which simply means the mapping of the image is interpreted by the browser. Another much older method is called *server-side* imagemapping and uses the server to process the coordinate directives. For the purposes of accessibility, it is highly recommended that you use only the client-side method described here.

5

TROUBLESHOOTING

Magic Target Names

I'm trying to use a magic target name, but when I click the link, nothing happens. What's wrong?

You probably have either left out the underscore or failed to contain the magic target value in quotes. You must include the underscore, and many browsers expect quotes prior to the underscore symbol—otherwise, they might not correctly parse the markup.

Dealing with Imagemap Overlap

I've created an imagemap, but some of my hotspots overlap and it's causing people to miss their link destinations. What can I do?

Position your hotspots carefully. When they overlap, the one created first takes precedence. To change the pecking order, use the Modify, Arrange options to send some hotspots to the back and bring others to the front. But the best solution to this problem is to ensure the hotspots don't overlap in the first place.

PEER TO PEER: ADDING ACCESSIBILITY FEATURES TO LINKS

Because of their interactive nature, all links—whether standard, intra-page, email, or those around images (including those links within an imagemap)—come to the forefront of accessibility concerns. From a historical perspective, HTML 4.0 brought with it quite a few new accessibility features in the language. These features have followed into XHTML and are available for use in Macromedia Dreamweaver MX.

That's the good news. The not-so-good news is that many of these features—so necessary for those individuals accessing the Web via other means than the typical mouse, keyboard, and browser setup—are not yet implemented by many browsers. However, those browsers concerned with W3C compliance have at least partial support for these features or are working to include this support.

If an older Web browser, or one that does not support the features described in this section, is asked to interpret a page with language it doesn't understand, it simply ignores the markup. Using these techniques can't hurt, but they certainly can help, so using them is to the advantage of your site visitors.

The accessibility concerns with links that I will cover here are

- Ensuring that link text is specific and descriptive
- Adding a `title` attribute to every link
- Offering tabbing order of links
- Offering a keyboard access method to a link

Using a clear description within any link text and adding specific attributes for accessibility help your documents become more usable for all people, not just those with disabilities.

Descriptive Links

The W3C's Web Accessibility Initiative (WAI) suggests that all link text should be as sensible as possible. Remember, many site visitors don't use a mouse or even a keyboard in some cases. Terms such as "click here" don't really make any sense to these users as a result. So, you'll want the text of your link to be truly descriptive.

A bad example would be the following:

There's a great bread recipe available today. **Click here** for more information.

(where `click here` is hyperlinked).

A good example would be the following:

There's a **great bread recipe** available today.

(where "`great bread recipe`" is hyperlinked).

The emphasis is now placed on the topic at the heart of the link—a great bread recipe—instead of the much more vague `click here`.

The `title` Attribute

The `title` attribute is a helpful attribute that enables you to title links in much the same way as you would use `alt` text in an image.

In Macromedia Dreamweaver MX, you can add the `title` attribute and descriptive text using the following techniques.

Using the Hyperlink Dialog Box

When creating your link, you can use add a title by following these steps:

1. Select Insert, Hyperlink. The Hyperlink dialog box appears.

2. Fill in the descriptive text for your link, the hyperlink address, and descriptive text for your title.

3. Click OK.

Your markup now has the `title` attribute and a descriptive text value, making your page more accessible.

Adding the `title` Attribute by Hand

To add the `title` attribute to an existing link by hand, follow these steps:

1. In Code view, locate the link you'd like to modify.

2. Place your cursor after the link's URL.

3. Type one space; then type in the `title` attribute plus any descriptive text:

```
<a href="mailto:molly@molly.com" title="send molly an email">send
molly an email</a>.
```

Save the file. Alternatively, if you're in Design view, you can highlight the link, right-click it to get the context menu, and select Edit Tag Code from the menu. This will provide you with a pop-up, where you can quickly add the `title` attribute and descriptive value.

Defining Tab Order

Another helpful technique that appears in HTML 4.0 is the ability to set the tab order in a document. This means that link and form elements can be accessed in a specific order using the Tab key. This is helpful for people who don't use a mouse, as well as for experienced users who rely on keyboard actions to work with Web pages.

Defining tab order can be accomplished using the Hyperlink dialog box or by hand. When you create a link using the Hyperlink dialog box, place the value you want in the Tab Index box. So, if this is the first link on the page, the Tab Index can be 1.

To manually add a tab order to a link, use the described methods with Code view or Edit Tag Code to access the link markup. Then, add the `tabindex` attribute and the appropriate value:

Tab order does not have to be consecutive. In other words, you can set a link at the top of the page to be tenth in the tab order and a link at the bottom of the page to be first in the tab order. But think about the logical structure of the information in your document before using an order that is out of synch. In almost all cases, you'll find that setting the tabbing order consecutively makes the most sense.

```
<a href="mailto:molly@molly.com" title="send molly an email" tabindex="1">
send molly an email</a>.
```

Using the `accesskey` Attribute

The `accesskey` attribute allows those users not using a mouse to use the keyboard to access links and form elements.

Adding the `accesskey` attribute is as easy as adding the `title` or `tabindex` attribute. You can do so using the Hyperlink dialog box, which offers a text box where you can type in the key that you want a site visitor to press to access the link.

For more information on WAI, see `http://www.w3.org/wai/` at the W3C.

To add the `accesskey` by hand, follow the previous steps to get to Code View or Edit Tag Code. Once there, type in the attribute and desired value:

```
<a href="mailto:molly@molly.com" title="send molly an email" tabindex="1"
accesskey="s"> send molly an email</a>.
```

5

DESIGNING FORMS

IN THIS CHAPTER

FORM COMPONENTS

Interactivity on the Web is a big subject. There are a wide variety of choices for everyone who wants an interactive site to provide a means for their customers to communicate back to them, whether the feedback consists of message boards, guest books, or even just a survey.

Forms are often used to provide content for all of these and more. They have been around for a long time (since HTML 1.0) and are supported by just about every browser. They provide a standard way of returning information to the server that doesn't require client-side scripting, and they are flexible enough to be used in many situations where it isn't immediately obvious that a form is at work.

Most forms consist of two components, a client-side (browser) and server-side portion.

The client portion of a form consists of a collection of HTML form element tags that define the information that the form will collect, surrounded by a `form` tag that specifies where the form data will go and the method that should be used. In addition to the elements that make up the actual form, other HTML content is used inside the form tag to provide layout for the form elements.

The other form component is the server-side processing. Although forms can be handled completely on the client side using JavaScript, most end up being submitted back to the Web server. On the server, the form information is processed by a Common Gateway Interface (CGI) script, Java Server Pages (JSP) page, Active Server Pages (ASP) page, or some other server-side technology. At this point, the information can be used for just about anything—it can be used to generate a guest book entry, fire off an email to a customer support representative, or perform a search. The possibilities are endless.

ADDING A FORM

The first step in adding a form to a Web site is to place the `form` tag pair in the document and specify the attributes that it requires to function.

Inserting a `form` tag with Dreamweaver is done in much the same way as it is done with other objects. You can use either the Insert bar or the menu to insert the form.

The Forms category of the Insert bar provides ready access to all form-related tags, including the `form` tag itself (see Figure 6.1). Insert a form onto a page using one of the following methods:

- Place the cursor where you want to insert the form on your page, and double-click the Form icon in the Forms category of the Insert bar.

- Drag the Form icon on the Insert bar to the location on the page where you want the form.

- Place the cursor where you want to insert the form, and select Insert, Form from the menu.

Figure 6.1
The Forms category of the Insert bar provides a way to add all form tags and elements.

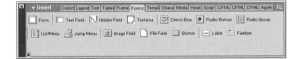

After a form has been inserted into a page, it can be seen in Design view as a dashed red box (see Figure 6.2). This box, the *form delimiter*, shows the portion of the page that is contained in the form—any form elements added inside this box automatically belong to the form.

⇨ *How are pages with more than one form managed? Find out in "Managing Multiple Forms" in the "Troubleshooting" section at the end of the chapter.*

The form delimiter box should be visible using the default settings. If it isn't visible, make sure that View, Visual Aids, Invisible Elements is checked and that Form Delimiter is selected in the Invisible Elements section of the Preferences dialog box.

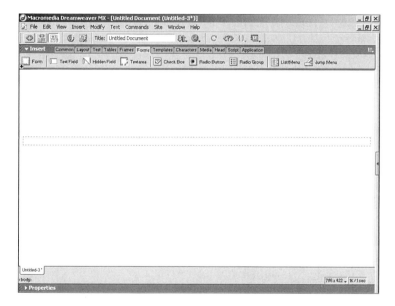

Figure 6.2
A red dashed border on the page shows the boundaries of the portion of the page included in a form.

Nesting Forms

When you add a form element to a page, it belongs to the container form—no matter how many levels of the tag hierarchy separate the two or how many other tags the form contains. A submitted form ignores all nonform tags between the `<form>...</form>` tag pair and automatically contains the value of all contained form elements. One tag that can't be contained in a form is another `form` tag. This leads to ambiguous ownership for all form elements contained by both `form` tags and can result in unexpected behavior in some browsers. Dreamweaver's form tools sometimes prevent you from adding nested forms, but not always. For example, if you already have a page with nested forms, it will allow you to add more.

6

Form Properties

The next step in creating a form is to set the form properties. These properties tell the browser how and where the form should be submitted.

To activate the Form Property inspector, click anywhere on the border of the form delimiter (see Figure 6.3). The Property inspector shows five properties that can be set for the form.

Figure 6.3
The Form Property inspector is used to set the details of how and where a form is submitted.

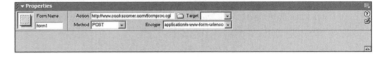

Naming the Form

You can enter a name for the form in the Form Name field of the Form Property inspector. Even though Dreamweaver automatically gives all forms a unique name, you might want to name the form a little more descriptively. The form name isn't submitted to the server with the form, but it can be used to refer to the form within the browser using JavaScript.

Defining the Action

The *action* is perhaps the most important form property. It contains the URL of the page that will process the form submission. Unless your form submits information to another Web site, the action usually points to the URL of a server-side program on your Web server that will process the form:

```
action="http://www.mysite.com/cgi-bin/formproc.cgi"
```

Alternatively, you can specify a JavaScript function to execute on the client instead of a server URL. A JavaScript action looks similar to the following:

```
action="Javascript: myfunction()"
```

Finally, you can also use a `mailto` link in the form action:

```
action="mailto: myemail@myserver.com"
```

A `mailto` link activates the email client on the browsing machine, allowing mail to be sent without any server-side processing.

The `mailto` action is the simplest method of form submission because it doesn't require any server-side application to work, but its use is not recommended. A `mailto` link requires the site visitor to have an email client and an email account accessible from that computer, which might not be the case if they are accessing the Web from a computer in a library or other public Internet access point. It is recommended that you use a server-side script to generate an email message instead.

Specifying a Method

The Method pop-up menu is used to select a method to submit the form data. The three choices are

- **POST**—Embeds the form information in the HTTP request sent to the server. The information in the form is hidden from the user's view with this method.

- **GET**—Appends the form information to the end of the URL.

- **Default**—Uses whichever method, GET or POST, the browser uses for a default.

Although your ultimate choice for a method is dictated by the Web server, you should try to use POST if possible. Information is hidden from the user, so it adds an element of confidentiality to the form. The GET method shows all the form information in the address line of the browser and allows only 8,192 characters to be sent, which might be inadequate for some forms.

Specifying a Target

The `target` attribute allows you to select a target window to display the results of the form submission. This works exactly like the target for an href. You can either specify a name for a window or frame or select one of the following options:

- `_blank`—Opens a new unnamed window.

- `_parent`—Displays the result in the current window's parent window.

- `_self`—Returns the result to the same window that contains the form.

- `_top`—Displays the result page in the topmost window containing the current window. This target is used most often to ensure that the result occupies the entire window even if the form is contained in a frame.

Specifying an Encoding Type

Finally, you can set the encoding type property for a form. This specifies the MIME encoding type to use for the form data. For most forms, this can be left blank or be set to `application/x-www-form-urlencoded`. *URL encoding* is the default encoding type. It's used to send plain text that has certain special characters encoded so they can be submitted as part of an HTTP request.

ADDING FORM ELEMENTS

Adding a form to a page is a good start, but to begin to make it truly useful you need to add form elements. Form elements are the individual controls on the page into which the user enters or selects values. These elements consist of single and multiline text fields, radio buttons, check boxes, lists, pop-up menus, drop-down list controls, and Submit and Reset buttons. Each of these form elements is discussed here in more detail.

Text Fields

A text field enables the user of the form to enter some text. To add a text field, do one of the following:

- Place the cursor where you want to insert the text field inside the form delimiter. Click the Text Field icon in the Forms category of the Insert bar.

6

- Drag the Text Field icon on the Insert bar to the location inside the form delimiter where you want the field.

- Place the cursor where you want to insert the text field, and select Insert, Form Objects, Text Field from the menu.

The properties of the text field are set using the Property inspector (see Figure 6.4).

Figure 6.4
The three types of text field are Single Line, Multi Line, and Password.

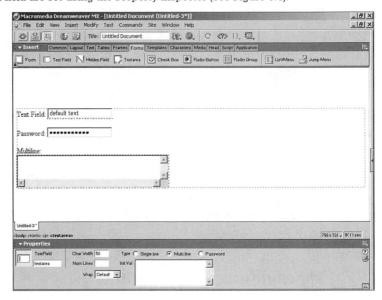

TextField Name

A unique name is automatically assigned to the text field, but you should enter a more descriptive name for the text field here. This name is used to refer to the value of the field on the server.

Char Width

The Char Width property is used to set the number of characters the text field can display at once. The default value for this property is 20, but the actual number of characters displayed is dependent on the font and browser. Any characters typed in the field in excess of the Char Width field will cause the text to scroll.

Max Chars

The Max Chars property is visible only for single-line and password text fields. It specifies the maximum number of characters to allow in the single line and password fields. If this field is not set, there is no limit to the amount of text allowed.

Num Lines

The Num Lines property is visible only for multiline text fields. It is used to set the number of rows to display in the field.

Type

The three types of text fields are as follows:

- **Single Line**—These fields show one line and are used to collect information entered by the user.

- **Multi Line**—These fields are typically used to collect larger amounts of text. Multiline fields are often used for requesting comments or submitting text to a guest book or message board. When Multi Line is selected as the type, you can also use the Wrap property to set how the text in this field should wrap: Physical specifies that the text wraps to the next line automatically, and Off specifies that text scrolls horizontally in the field until Enter is pressed. The other option, Virtual, specifies that text should wrap in the browser, but not in the text, when it is submitted to the server.

- **Password**—These are special, single-line text fields used to collect passwords and other confidential information. As characters are typed into a password field, they are not displayed. Asterisks or large dots are typically displayed instead.

Init Val

The Init Val property is used to specify the initial value for the text field. This can be used to specify default information for a form or instructions such as "Enter Comments Here" in a multiline field.

Hidden Fields

As the name implies, hidden fields are not visible to the user filling out the form. Hidden fields are used to hold information that doesn't need to change from form to form. For example, an email feedback form might have hidden fields to hold the target email address and a URL to navigate to after the form is processed. You can also modify hidden field values using a client-side scripting language such as JavaScript. To add a hidden field, do one of the following:

- Place the cursor where you want to insert the hidden field inside the form delimiter. Click the Hidden Field icon in the Forms category of the Insert bar.

- Drag the Hidden Field icon on the Insert bar to the location inside the form delimiter where you want the field.

- Place the cursor where you want to insert the hidden field, and select Insert, Form Objects, Hidden Field from the menu.

6

Although the hidden field isn't visible to a user of the form, it is represented in Dreamweaver by an invisible element marker. If the marker isn't displayed for your hidden fields, you might need to enable it in the Preferences. Select Edit, Preferences from the menu to activate the Preferences dialog box and make sure Hidden Form Fields is selected in the Invisible Elements section.

Clicking the marker activates the Hidden Field Property inspector (see Figure 6.5).

Figure 6.5
Hidden fields are represented in the editor by a marker.

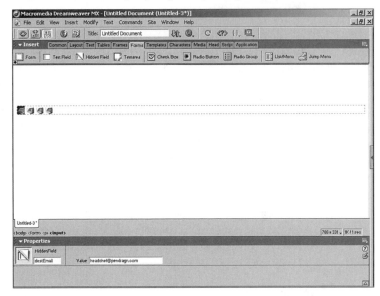

HiddenField Name

Dreamweaver automatically assigns a unique name for each hidden field that you add, but you should give it a descriptive name.

Value

The only other option that can be set for hidden fields is, of course, the value. The value is simply a descriptive value you want sent when the form is submitted so you can identify the hidden field's purpose.

Radio Buttons

Radio buttons enable users to select one option from a list of choices. An individual radio button can either be on or off, but they are typically used in a radio button group, which allows only one radio button at a time to be selected.

To add a radio button, do one of the following:

- Place the cursor where you want to insert the radio button inside the form delimiter. Click the Radio Button icon in the Forms category of the Insert bar.

- Drag the Radio Button icon on the Insert bar to the location inside the form delimiter where you want the button.

- Place the cursor where you want to insert the radio button, and select Insert, Form Objects, Radio Button from the menu.

Click the radio button to set its properties in the Property inspector (see Figure 6.6).

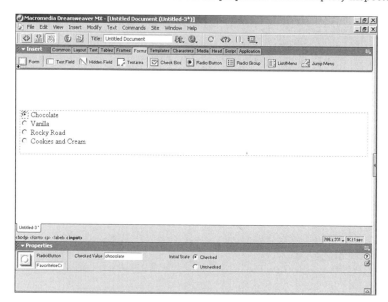

Figure 6.6
Radio buttons are used in groups to allow only one item to be selected from a list.

RadioButton Name

The name property has extra importance with radio buttons. Whereas other form elements should have a unique name to make them identifiable on the form, radio buttons that belong to a radio group all share the same name. The browser then allows only one of the controls to be the checked at a time.

Checked Value

The Checked Value property is the value that is submitted with the form if this radio button is checked. Make sure that this value is different from all the other radio buttons in the group.

Initial State

The Initial State option allows you to set whether the radio button is selected when the page first loads. The default selection for a radio button group should have a checked initial state, whereas all other buttons in the group should remain unchecked.

6

Radio Group

Although it is perfectly acceptable to add radio buttons one at a time, Dreamweaver has a Radio Group object that makes this task a little easier. You can insert a radio group in the same way that you do an individual radio button: Drag the Radio Group icon from the Insert bar, or position the cursor where you want the radio group to be placed and either double-click the Radio Group icon or select Radio Group from the Insert, Form Objects, Radio Group menu.

When you insert a Radio Group object, the Radio Group dialog box opens (see Figure 6.7). Configure the Radio Group by following these steps:

1. Enter a name for the radio button group in the Name field. This name will automatically be assigned to all radio buttons added using this dialog box.

2. Use the Plus button (+) to add new radio buttons to the group. Use the Minus button (-) to remove any buttons you don't want. By default, there are two in the list.

3. Click the individual button in the list to set a value and a label for it. Labels are automatically added as text after the radio button.

4. If you want to change the order of the buttons, select one and use the up and down arrow buttons to move it to a new position in the list.

5. Select a layout method. Your choices are for Dreamweaver to use line breaks (
 tags) after each button or use a table layout, which constructs a single-column table with each radio button on a new row.

6. Click OK to add the group.

> After a radio group is placed in a form using the Radio Group dialog box, the radio buttons are treated the same as radio buttons added individually. To modify any radio button's properties, you must click the button and use the Property inspector. Any additions to the radio group must be done by adding individual radio buttons one at a time.

Figure 6.7
The Radio Group object and dialog box is the fastest way to add a radio button group to a form.

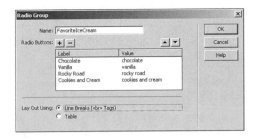

Check Boxes

Like radio buttons, check boxes are buttons that can be toggled on or off to make a selection. Unlike radio buttons, however, they are controlled individually and not in groups. Use check boxes when more than one selection is possible or if you just need a yes/no type of answer.

To add a check box, do one of the following:

- Place the cursor where you want to insert the check box inside the form delimiter. Click the Check Box icon in the Forms category of the Insert bar.

- Drag the Check Box icon on the Insert bar to the location inside the form delimiter where you want the button.

- Place the cursor where you want to insert the check box, and select Insert, Form Objects, Check Box from the menu.

Click the check box to set its properties in the Property inspector (see Figure 6.8).

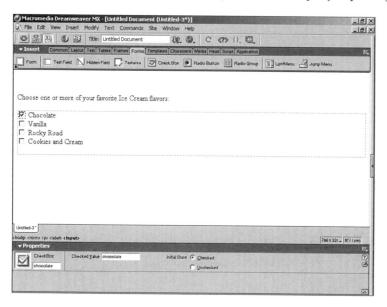

Figure 6.8
Check boxes are typically used to allow lists in which multiple selections are allowed.

CheckBox Name

A unique name for each check box should be entered here. This is the name that is used to identify the field when the form is submitted.

Checked Value

The Checked Value property is the value that is submitted with the form if this check box is selected.

Initial State

The Initial State option allows you to set whether the check box is checked or unchecked when the page first loads.

Submit and Reset Buttons

There are two more controls that are commonly used with forms: Submit and Reset buttons.

Most forms need a Submit button. It is used to send the form information to the URL specified in the form's action property, as discussed in the "Form Properties" section earlier in this chapter.

Reset buttons are used to set all the fields in the form to their default values.

To add a Submit or Reset button to your form, do one of the following:

- Place the cursor where you want to insert the button inside the form delimiter. Click the Button icon in the Forms category of the Insert bar.

- Drag the Button icon on the Insert bar to the location inside the form delimiter where you want the button to appear.

- Place the cursor where you want to insert the button, and select Insert, Form Objects, Button from the menu.

The button is automatically added as a Submit button. Use the Property inspector to change it to a Reset button (see Figure 6.9).

Figure 6.9
Buttons are used to submit the form to the server and to reset the content of the form to the default values.

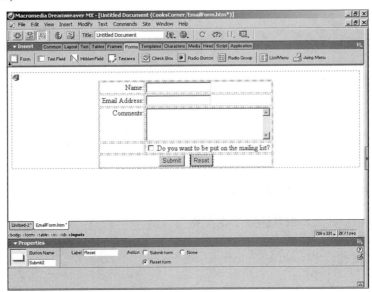

Button Name

By naming a button, you provide a way in which it can be identified. Typically, the button name and its label are the same just for the sake of consistency. If your button is a Submit button, you will likely name your button submit also.

Naming buttons is particularly helpful when adding JavaScript or using server-side scripts for more form functionality.

Label

The Label field is where you specify the text that is displayed on the button itself.

Action

Use the Action field to set the type of button. The options are Submit Form, Reset Form, and None. The None option is used to create a generic button. Although Submit and Reset buttons have a defined purpose, a button with a type of None is useful only when used to call a JavaScript function such as checking the submitted file to see that all required fields are filled in.

Lists and Menus

Lists and menus are used to provide a chance for the user to select an option. They are similar from a functional point of view and, in fact, use the same HTML/XHTML element—the `select` tag. The difference is in how they are rendered by the browser. A list shows more than one (and often all) of its options at once, whereas a menu shows only the currently selected option, with the other options accessible using a drop-down box.

Menus serve as the basis for Dreamweaver's Jump Menu object as well. This object enables you to use a menu for navigating your site by selecting a page from the list.

⇨ *For an explanation of Jump menus, see "Using Behaviors," p. 426.*

To add a list or menu to your form, do one of the following:

- Place the cursor where you want to insert the list or menu inside the form delimiter. Click the List/Menu icon in the Forms category of the Insert bar.

- Drag the List/Menu icon on the Insert bar to the location inside the form delimiter where you want the list or menu to go.

- Place the cursor where you want to insert the list or menu, and select Insert, Form Objects, List/Menu from the menu.

Use the Property inspector to set the type of list you want (see Figure 6.10).

Figure 6.10
Lists and menus both use the List/Menu Property inspector and the List Values dialog box to set their properties.

6

List/Menu Name

You can add a unique name to a list or menu. This name is used to identify the value when the form is submitted.

Type

You can select either Menu or List. If you select List, the fields for Height and Selections are enabled.

Height

Lists use the Height property to specify how many rows to show in the browser. If the list contains more items than rows, a vertical scrollbar is displayed to access the hidden items.

Selections

Lists allow multiple selections to be made at once. Selecting this means the resulting menu lets your site visitors choose one or more options from the list.

List Values

Click this button to activate the List Values dialog box (refer to Figure 6.10). In this dialog box, you can add, remove, and reorder list items.

Items added to the list are those items that actually appear in the menu. You have an optional value that can be specified. This allows the Item Label to show a meaningful option to the user and the value to be the actual information sent with the form. If no value is entered for a list item, the item label is used as its value. Consider this markup:

```
<option value="098765T">Chocolate Brown Sweater</option>
```

The site visitor sees chocolate brown sweater. However, when you receive the form, you will see not only the item, but also its product number, which has been used as the item's value.

Initially Selected

After you have items added to the list, you can select one of them to be the default selection by clicking it in this list.

File Field

A file field is a special type of text field with a Browse button that enables the user to select a file to upload to the server.

File fields are not commonly used, partly due to security issues. They leave your system vulnerable to allowing any type of file to be uploaded to your server. Contact your server administrator to confirm that file uploads are approved before using this element.

➪ *Having trouble with file fields? The problem might be your method or encoding. See "File Fields" in the "Troubleshooting" section at the end of this chapter.*

Image Fields

An image field is a special button that enables you to use an image instead of the text labels Reset and Submit buttons have. Image fields are used the same way as Submit buttons—to send the information to the server for processing.

To add an image field button to your form, do one of the following:

▪ Place the cursor where you want to insert the button inside the form delimiter. Click the Image Field icon in the Forms category of the Insert bar.

▪ Drag the Image Field icon on the Insert bar to the location inside the form delimiter where you want the button to be placed.

▪ Place the cursor where you want to insert the button, and select Insert, Form Objects, Image Field from the menu.

The Select Image Source dialog box opens to allow you to select an image.

⇨ *Images and the Select Image Source dialog box were explained in detail earlier in this book. See "Formatting the Image," p. 68.*

After you have chosen an image, click OK to create the button. Use the Property inspector to change the image field's properties (see Figure 6.11).

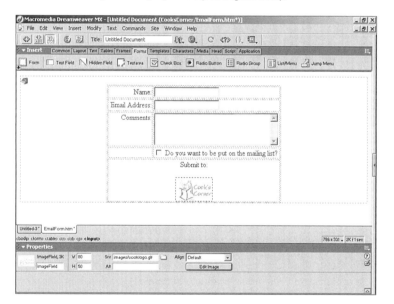

Figure 6.11
An image field is used to add a Submit button to your form that uses an image instead of a text label.

ImageField Name

You can add a unique name to a button to allow it to be accessible by JavaScript.

Width and Height

The W and H fields enable you to change the displayed dimensions of the image. As with the img tag, the actual image is not changed. Instead, it is either stretched or scaled down to fit within the specified dimensions.

Image Source

The Src field contains the path to the image file to use. To change the image, use the folder button to the right of this field to browse for a new image.

Alt

The Alt field enables you to specify alternative text to be displayed if the browser can't show images. This text is also usually visible in browsers with image capabilities by hovering the mouse pointer over the button.

Align

The Align menu enables you to set the alignment for the image on the page.

> **Clicking the Edit Image button** launches an image editor (Fireworks is default) so you can modify the image directly.

FORMS AND THE WEB SERVER

Now that you have the basics for creating forms with Dreamweaver, a discussion on how to write a server-side script to process form information is in order. A detailed explanation about server-side programming is beyond the scope of this book, but you should be able to get an idea of what form processing on the server might entail. Please note that this form would need a little more done with it to make it truly usable. If nothing else, adding validation will ensure that the data is good no matter which form processing technology you use.

➡️ *For a discussion of Dreamweaver's Form Validation behavior, see "Using Behaviors," p. 426.*

If you are averse to programming your own server-side form processing application, many sources of existing scripts are available on the Web. Your Web host might even have server-side form-processing applications already available for you to use.

> **If you do decide to write your own** server-side form processing script, contact your Web server administrator to discover which technologies are available to you on your server.

6

A Sample Form

The examples in this section of the various server-side technologies will all be used to process the same form, so you can compare and contrast what the code for each looks like. This form is a simple feedback form that provides fields for the user to enter an email address and comments and a check box indicating whether she wants to be put on a mailing list. In addition it has two hidden fields, one of which contains the destination email address. This form uses a table to provide layout for the visible form elements (see Listing 6.1).

Listing 6.1   Exploring a Sample Form

```
<form name="feedbackform" method="post" action="formproc.cgi">
<input name="destEmail" type="hidden" value="headchef@pendragn.com">
<table width="50%" border="0" cellspacing="2" cellpadding="2">
  <tr>
    <td align="right">Name: </td>
    <td><input name="name" type="text" id="name"></td>
  </tr>
  <tr>
    <td align="right">Email Address: </td>
    <td><input name="email" type="text" id="email"></td>
  </tr>
  <tr>
    <td align="right" valign="top">Comments:</td>
        <td><textarea name="comments" cols="40" wrap="VIRTUAL"
        id="comments"></textarea></td>
</tr>
  <tr>
    <td> </td>
    <td><input name="addtolist" type="checkbox" id="addtolist" value="checkbox">
        Do you want to be put on the mailing list?</td>
  </tr>
  <tr align="center">
    <td colspan=2>
      <input type="submit" name="Submit" value="Submit">
    </td>
  </tr>
</table>
</form>
```

Figure 6.12 shows the sample form.

Creating a Server-Side Script Page

A new feature in Dreamweaver MX is the ability to create server-side script pages. To create a dynamic page, do the following:

1. Select File, New.

2. Select Dynamic Page from the Category list of the New Document dialog box (see Figure 6.13).

3. In the Dynamic Page list, select the server-side technology in which you're developing your script.

4. Click Create.

6

Figure 6.12
The sample form to use for the server-side form handling.

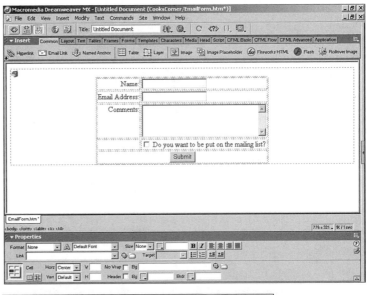

Figure 6.13
The New Document dialog box contains options for creating PHP, JSP, and ASP pages, all of which are well-suited for form processing scripts.

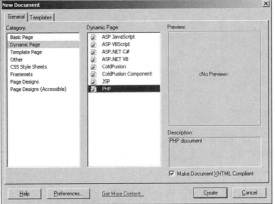

The Insert panel adds a tab for the technology you selected. The contents of the tab varies by technology, but it generally contains the most common tags for that technology and an option to access additional tags.

Exploring Server-Side Form Technologies

As mentioned at the beginning of the chapter, a discussion on using Dreamweaver MX with server-side technologies is very detailed and beyond the scope of this book.

The proper working of forms does require that the designer know at least a bit about which technologies can be used to process forms. With this information, you can at least discuss the issue with your ISP or systems administrator and make the best selection based on your personal and client needs.

Using PHP

One of the most popular languages for server-side development today is *Hypertext Preprocessor* (PHP). This is due to a number of factors, including the ease of integration with HTML pages and broad support for many platforms. It is also free. More information about PHP can be found at `http://www.php.net/`.

PHP is often compared to Perl, with good reason. Both languages are frequently used for server-side Web programming, and both are freely available on most platforms. PHP really shines because it was designed solely for Web scripting, whereas Perl is intended to be a general-purpose scripting language.

Because of its Web-specific nature, PHP is an excellent choice for writing a form processor. In fact, it includes built-in support for form processing and also for sending mail.

Here is a listing of a PHP form processor to handle the sample form:

```
<?
mail( $destEmail, "Comments Form",
    "$comments  Add to list: $addtolist , "From: $email ($name)" );
header( "Location: http://www.cookscorner.com/thankyou.html" );
?>
```

This form processing script couldn't be simpler. PHP automatically assigns form field values to PHP variables with the same name as on the form, and the built-in PHP function `mail()` makes sending mail a breeze.

Finally, the header function is used to redirect the browser to a thank-you page.

Using JSP

Another popular server-side technology is Java Server Pages, which uses the Java programming language (not JavaScript) to create Web applications.

JSP uses XML-like tags and Java scriptlets to provide logic for generating dynamic page content.

Like PHP, JSP has built-in support for form processing and sending email. Here's a look at some JSP code for forms:

```
<%@ page import="java.util.*, javax.mail.*, javax.mail.internet.*" %>
<%
  Properties props = new Properties();
  props.put("mail.smtp.host", "smtp.mail.example.com");
  Session s = Session.getInstance(props,null);

  MimeMessage message = new MimeMessage(s);

  InternetAddress from = new InternetAddress(request.getParameter("email"););
  message.setFrom(from);
  InternetAddress to = new InternetAddress(request.getParameter("destEmail"););
  message.addRecipient(Message.RecipientType.TO, to);
```

6

```
message.setSubject("Comments Form");
message.setText(request.getParameter("comments") + "Add to list:" +
                                request.getParameter("addtolist"));
Transport.send(message);
response.sendRedirect("http://www.cookscorner.com/thankyou.html");
%>
```

Using ASP

Microsoft's Active Server Pages is an established technology on Windows NT and 2000 Web servers.

ASP works by embedding server-side script (written in most cases in VBScript or JavaScript language) in a Web page with special tags marking it as server code. The server-side script is executed by the Web server, and the combination of the script output and the HTML on the page is sent to the browser.

The ASP script to process the sample form looks like this:

```
<%
  Dim oCDONTS
  set oCDONTS = Server.CreateObject("CDONTS.NewMail")

  oCDONTS.From = Request.Form("email")
  oCDONTS.To = Request.Form("destEmail")
  oCDONTS.Subject = "Comment Form"
  oCDONTS.Body = Request.Form("comments") & " Add To List: "
➥& Request.Form("addtolist")

  oCDONTS.BodyFormat = 1
  oCDONTS.MailFormat = 1
  oCDONTS.Send

  Response.Redirect "http://www.cookscorner.com/thankyou.html"
%>
```

The ASP example is reasonably concise and readable. The basis for sending email with ASP is through the collaboration data objects for NTS (CDONTS) objects, which is provided with Internet Information Server (IIS), Microsoft's Web server platform.

Form variables are accessed using ASP's `Request` object, and all form fields are automatically assigned to a collection called `Request.Form`.

Using Perl

The most common way to process form information on the server is by using a Common Gateway Interface program, and Perl has traditionally been the language of choice for CGI applications in the past. Although it has been supplanted in many cases by PHP, it's still a popular language for writing server-side applications.

Unfortunately, Dreamweaver doesn't provide coding support or server behavior for Perl pages. Fortunately, however, you can create Perl pages in any text editor, including Dreamweaver. You'll simply have to handle all the coding tasks yourself.

Perl has a daunting syntax that only a programmer could love, but for completeness, here is a Perl script that processes this form and sends the information using the sendmail program:

```perl
#!/usr/bin/perl

print "Content-type:text/html\n\n";

# Read in the form data and split it into name/value pairs
read(STDIN, $buffer, $ENV{'CONTENT_LENGTH'});

@pairs = split(/&/, $buffer);
foreach $pair (@pairs) {
    ($name, $value) = split(/=/, $pair);
    $value =~ tr/+/ /;
    $value =~ s/%([a-fA-F0-9][a-fA-F0-9])/pack("C", hex($1))/eg;
    $FORM{$name} = $value;
}

#define a mail program to use
$mailprog = '/usr/bin/sendmail';

# this opens an output stream and pipes it directly to the sendmail
open (MAILSTREAM, "|$mailprog -t") or &showerror("Can't access $mailprog!\n");

# printing out the header info for the mail message.
print MAILSTREAM "To: $FORM('destEmail');\n";
print MAILSTREAM "Reply-to: $FORM{'email'} ($FORM{'name'})\n";

print MAILSTREAM "Subject: Comments Form\n\n";

print MAILSTREAM "$FORM('comments');

# close the mail input stream to send the mail
close(MAILSTREAM);

print "Location:http://www.cookscorner.com/thankyou.html\n\n";

sub showerror {
    ($errmsg) = @_;
    print "<h1>Error!</h1>\n";
    print "$errmsg<p>\n";
    print "</body></html>\n";
    exit;
}
```

6

This program starts by decoding the form items from the HTTP request and storing them in a hash object. After the form values are obtained, the mail program is called and a mail message is generated from the form data. Finally, a response message is written back to the browser. Notice how much more complex it is compared to the PHP example with built-in support for forms and sending mail.

TROUBLESHOOTING

Managing Multiple Forms

How do I manage multiple forms on my pages?

Many pages contain multiple forms. A common example is a page containing forms that submit to multiple search engines. Each search engine has its own destination URL and form elements that are required. It is certainly possible to do multiple forms on a page with Dreamweaver. Simply use one of the form insertion methods to put a new form in a location on the page not contained by the first form. Form elements are submitted only with the form that contains them.

File Fields

I'd like to include file fields in my form, but they aren't working correctly. What could I be doing wrong?

For file fields to work successfully, they require the form to be submitted using the post method and an encoding type of multipart/form-data. See the "Form Properties" section of this chapter for information on setting these properties.

PEER TO PEER: ACCESSIBLE FORMS

Several elements and attributes are available by which you can ensure that your forms are accessible. These elements are used with other features, too, such as links. Table 6.1 describes the element or attribute, its function, and an example of its use.

For more information on Section 508, please see http://www.section508.gov/. If you are outside the U.S., you can find out which accessibility laws or rules apply to you at the WAI's International Program Office, http://www.w3.org/WAI/IPO/Activity.html.

Table 6.1   Elements and Attributes for Accessibility

Element or Attribute	Purpose	Example
tabindex	This attribute allows the site visitor to tab through form fields in an order you specify.	`<input type="text" name="tab1" tabindex="1">`
fieldset and legend	These elements help you group form controls in logical categories.	`<fieldset>` `<legend>` `<b>Name</b>` `</legend>` `Name <input type="text" name="name">` `E-mail <input type="text" name="email">` `</fieldset>`
accesskey	This attribute allows you to define a keyboard shortcut for a given option.	`<input type="submit" name="submit" value="submit" tabindex="5" accesskey="s">`
label	The label element activates the text content within it so a site visitor can click the text as well as the input control, making the area surrounding a small radio button or check box active and therefore more easily accessed. Note that the for and id values are the same.	`<label for="labelexample">` `This text is clickable now.` `</label>` `<input type="checkbox" name="check1" id="labelexample">`

Adding any of these elements or attributes to your forms will help those using assistive technologies to access your form with ease. If your documents are required to be Section 508 compliant, these features will help you reach that goal.

6

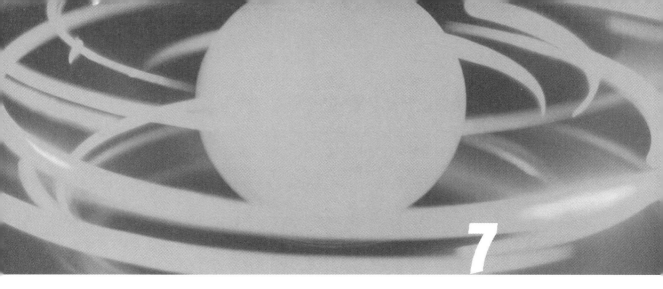

WORKING WITH TABLES AND FRAMES

ABOUT TABLES AND FRAMES

Tables and frames present unique challenges to designers, as well as tremendously powerful options in terms of layout and interface.

Tables were originally introduced to provide a way to organize data (see Figure 7.1). The resulting grid system created by tables could be used as a means of controlling the entire layout of pages (see Figure 7.2).

Figure 7.1
The intended use for HTML tables was to present tabular data via a Web page.

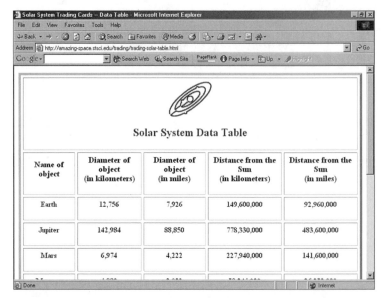

Figure 7.2
The most popular sites on the Web use tables for layout. Tables became the de facto means of laying out Web pages, but their use in this way is under scrutiny by supporters of standards.

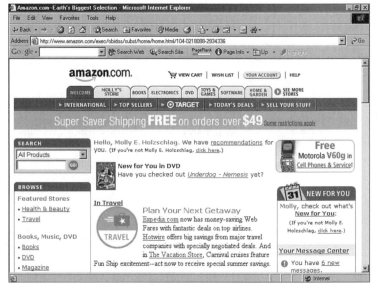

This realization grew beyond a means and into a convention—soon, the vast majority of sites on the Web came to embrace tables as their underlying structures. To this day, the infrastructures of most sites use tables for graphic placement, color arrangement, and text layout control.

But, as this book clearly points out, contemporary authoring practices are changing. The use of tables for structural layout of sites, while still dominant, is becoming less of a recommended practice in favor of style sheet layout. As browsers become more sophisticated, it becomes easier to imagine a time when the power of style can replace the limitations of tables as a layout tool (see Figure 7.3).

Figure 7.3

The columns and layout on Molly.com were created with Cascading Style Sheets and create a pleasing look without the complicated markup.

Similarly, frames have been a source of both frustration and empowerment for Web site designers and visitors alike. The frustration comes from a number of concerns. First, frames divide the available browser space, which is preciously restricted to begin with. Frames, particularly those using borders, literally take what is a small, contained space and break that space up into smaller, even more contained spaces (see Figure 7.4). This makes frames an unfortunate choice for certain audiences unless the author knows what she is doing.

Using frames requires an understanding of accessibility options for the site to be made useful to blind and disabled site visitors. Frames also make it more difficult to bookmark pages within a site in older browsers or to refer to specific pages within a framed structure via a URL. What's more, frames consume a lot more bandwidth. Finally, frames force the designer to do more work because they require more actual pages of markup per visible page.

Despite all the potential problems, frames can be very empowering from a design perspective. One aspect of this empowerment is that designers can keep sections of a page static whereas other parts of the page can be used to display other pages. Particularly handy for fixed navigation, this is a common approach to the development of menu bars and other specialty areas that are to remain in place.

7

Figure 7.4
Bordered frames take up valuable visual real estate as well as break up the visual continuity of a design.

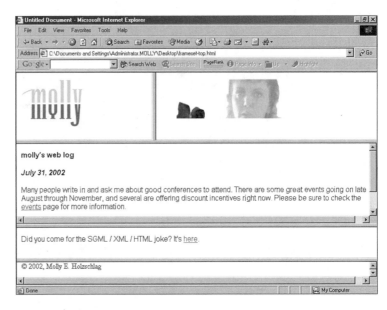

This chapter provides you with the basics of creating tables and framed pages. The goal here is to get you familiar with using tables and frames. Then, in later chapters, greater detail on how to approach various design problems is addressed.

☞ To delve more deeply into table-based design, see "Designing with Table-Based Layouts," p. 321.

☞ Frames are covered in-depth in "Working with Frame-Based Layouts," p. 351.

ADDING A TABLE

As mentioned, tables were originally designed to table data. This means that there are means to control the table's structure as well as presentational features. Here, you'll learn the basic components of a table, how to add one to your page, how to add content to the table, and how to make minor modifications to that table.

Table Components

Numerous elements and attributes define aspects of tables. Tables require three building blocks: the table element, at least one table row, and at least one table cell. Other elements and attributes are available to modify these elements.

When you create a table in Macromedia Dreamweaver MX, the following options to modify and customize your table are immediately available:

- **Rows**—Table rows determine how many vertical segments the table will have. They are represented by the `tr` element.

- **Columns**—Table columns are represented by `td` (for *table data*) and determine how many columns the table has.

- **Cell Padding**—The `cellpadding` attribute determines how much space will be placed between the content of a cell and the border of the cell.

- **Cell Spacing**—The `cellspacing` attribute determines the spacing between each cell.

- **Width**—The `width` attribute defines the width of the table. You can choose from pixels or a percentage to define the width. Width is a critical component of layout with tables, as you'll learn in Chapter 18, "Designing with Table-Based Layouts." Pixel-based tables used for layouts are refered to as *fixed-width* tables, and percentage-based tables for layout are referred to as *fluid* or *dynamic* tables.

- **Border**—Defining the `border` attribute with a numeric value determines the appearance and width of a border around your table's main components.

- **Bg Color**—This defines the background color of your table.

- **Brdr Color**—If you want to add a border color, you can do so using this feature.

- **Bg Image**—If you want to add an image to the background of the table, you can do so with this setting.

- **Table Id**—Here, you can provide a name to identify your table. This is helpful if you're going to be using JavaScript or DHTML to make dynamic modifications to the table.

> **Caution**
>
> The `bgcolor` attribute is only available in HTML and XHTML Transitional. The `bordercolor` and `background` attributes are considered browser specific and are therefore not to be used in any document conforming to W3C standards.

Options are also available to clear column width and height and convert widths from pixels to percentages. The importance of these issues is discussed in detail throughout the chapter.

Inserting a Table

Begin by ensuring that you are in standard, not layout, view. To do this, go to the Insert bar, click the Layout tab, and then click the Standard button.

To add a table to your page, follow these steps:

1. In Design view, place your cursor at the location where you want to insert the table.

2. Click the Common tab in the Insert bar. Click the Insert Table icon (see Figure 7.5). Alternatively, you can select Insert, Table.

7

Figure 7.5
To add a table, you can click the Insert Table icon, found in the Insert bar.

3. The Insert Table dialog box appears (see Figure 7.6). Here, you'll add the values you want to begin your table. For now, leave everything at default.

Figure 7.6
The Insert Table dialog box enables you to set up most of the preliminary attributes of the table.

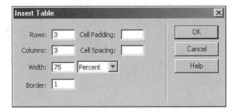

4. Click OK.

Dreamweaver MX will insert a table with 3 rows and 3 columns at a width of 75%, with a border value of 1. No cell padding or spacing is added by the program at this time. Figure 7.7 shows the results of inserting the basic table into Design view.

Modifying General Table Properties

After a basic table is created, you can modify the table's properties using the Property inspector.

Setting Rows and Columns

If you want to change the number of columns or rows in your table, follow these steps:

1. In Design or Code view, select the table you want to modify. The Property inspector will now display the table attributes available for modification (see Figure 7.8).

If you look at the markup generated for this table, you'll see that the nonbreaking space character entity   is used as a placeholder within each table cell. This enables you to view your table more effectively because, without content, table cells often collapse upon browser rendering. The character is removed automatically upon addition of content to the cell.

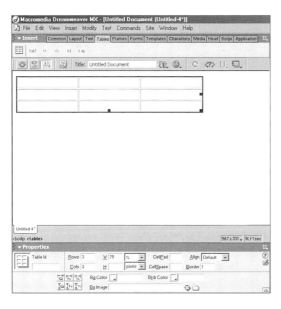

Figure 7.7
The table you've created using Dreamweaver MX default values is ready for modification.

Figure 7.8
The Property inspector for the `table` element enables you to make changes to your table, such as adding more rows.

2. To change the number of rows, simply type in the correct number in the Row text box. To change the number of columns, type the desired number of columns.

3. Press Enter.

The table will automatically update to display the rows and columns you've determined.

Rows and columns can be modified with a range of attributes that can influence the way your table works and looks, see "Designing with Table-Based Layouts," p. 321.

Adding a Border, Padding, and Spacing

If you want to add cell padding and/or cell spacing to your table, follow these steps:

1. In Design or Code view, select the table so the Property inspector displays the table attributes available.

2. In the Border text box, enter the width of border that you want to have. For table-based layouts, the value will most likely be 0. For tables that display data, you might want to have a thin border. Heavy table borders are not recommended because they can visually weigh down a page and distract the site visitor's eye from the content.

7

3. In the CellPad text box, enter the amount of cell padding you want to have. Any value other than 0 is usually used in data tables rather than layout tables because using cell padding can interfere with the control necessary in fixed-table layouts.

4. In the CellSpace text box, enter the amount of cell spacing for your table. As with padding, spacing is almost always set to 0 in fixed-table layout design.

5. Press Enter to update your changes.

> When you're creating tables for layout and don't want to have borders, padding, or spacing, it's recommended that you still include these attributes, each with a value of 0. This ensures that your layouts are better controlled. Note that all these attributes can also be controlled using Cascading Style Sheets (CSS).

Modifying the Table's Width

As referred to earlier, a table's width is a critical component of table-based layout. This is discussed in depth in Chapter 18. However, even if you're using tables for data, the difference between using pixels (fixed) or percentages (fluid or dynamic) is significant. A fixed table always stays the same size, no matter the resolution or size of the browser window. A dynamic table dynamically fills the available space. This means that all the content within the table is fluid—it moves to fit the resolution or browser window size.

To set or change your table's width, follow these steps:

1. Select the table in Design or Code view.

2. In the Property inspector, enter the numeric value (in pixels or percentages) for the table width in the W text box.

3. From the drop-down menu, select pixels or percentage.

Your table will update. Save your changes before continuing.

Setting the Table Height

You can set a table's height using Dreamweaver, too. To do so, follow these steps:

1. Select the table in Design or Code view.

2. In the Property inspector, enter the numeric value (in pixels or percentages) for the height in the H text box.

3. From the drop-down menu, select pixels or percentage.

The table height is now set.

> **Caution**
>
> The height attribute is not available in *any* HTML or XHTML recommendation. This results in browser support for it being quite limited. What's more, browsers that do render height do so inconsistently. As a result of these concerns, using height in tables should be avoided.

Adding Color and Images

Dreamweaver MX allows you to add several presentational features to the table element, including background color, border color, and background image.

Here's how to add a background color:

1. In Design or Code view, select the table to which you want to add color.

2. In the Property inspector, locate the Bg Color option. You can use the color palette to choose your color, or if you know your color's hexadecimal code, simply type it into the available text box.

3. The table automatically updates to reflect the color changes. Select File, Save to keep your modifications.

To add a border color, do the following:

1. Make sure the table is selected and the Property inspector is at the ready.

2. Locate the Brdr Color option. As with the background color, you can use the palette or type your hex code into the text box.

3. The table updates. Select File, Save to save your changes.

To add a background image, follow these steps:

1. Select the table.

2. In the Property inspector, find the Bg Image option. Select the folder icon and browse for the file on your computer.

3. Click OK to add the background image to your table (see Figure 7.9).

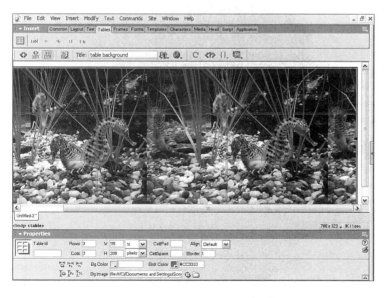

Figure 7.9
Adding a table background graphic can enhance the visual interest of a page. However, it can also be distracting, so choose the type of background you need with care.

7

Importing a Table

A very attractivefeature of Dreamweaver MX is Import Tabular Data. This tool enables you to take a table that has been created in another application (such as Excel), save it in a delimited format, and import it as a table.

Here's how to import tabular data into Dreamweaver MX:

1. Select File, Import, Tabular Data. If you prefer, select Insert, Table Objects, Import Tabular Data (they both work the same way). The Import Tabular Data dialog box appears (see Figure 7.10).

2. Use the Browse button to locate your file.

3. In the drop-down menu, select the delimeter type used in your file from these choices: Tab, Comma, Semicolon, Colon, or Other.

4. Set the table width as you see fit. Typically, the default Fit to Data is a good choice with imported files. You can always change this later if it doesn't suit your needs.

5. Set any padding or spacing that you want by typing the numeric value into the corresponding text boxes.

6. You can modify the appearance of the top row by selecting one of the following choices from the Format Top Row drop-down menu: No Formatting, Bold, Italic, or Bold Italic.

7. Enter a border value.

8. Click OK.

Caution

Background images and border colors are not supported by any version of HTML or XHTML and therefore are not available in a broad range of browsers, nor can they be used if you're interested in creating valid documents. Background color is allowed in transitional documents, so if you want some color without the problems associated with background images and borders, it's best to use a background color. Or, consider using CSS, which allows for more options with border styles.

Any type of delimited format, including tabs, commas, semicolons and so forth, can be transformed into a table using this feature.

Figure 7.10
Use the Import Tabular Data dialog box to customize the way an imported table will look and behave.

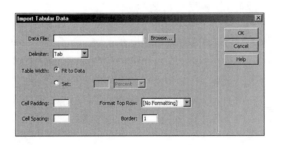

After the table is successfully imported into Dreamweaver MX, you can modify it as you see fit. Figure 7.11 shows the results.

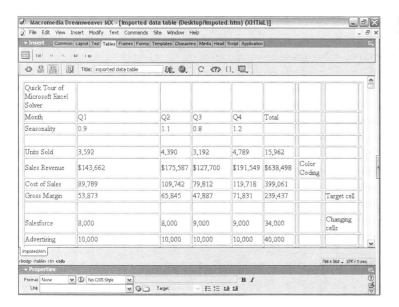

Figure 7.11
This alcohol moderation table was originally created in Microsoft Excel, saved as a tab delimited file, and imported into Dreamweaver MX as tabular data.

Adding Content

Now that you've got a table, you'll naturally want to add content to it. You can add any kind of content in a table cell, including text, images, applets, audio, video, Flash, Shockwave, and animation—if it can go on a Web page to begin with, it can be placed into a table cell!

To add content to a cell, follow these steps:

1. In Design or Code view, place your cursor into the cell where you want to add content.

2. If you want to add text, simply type in the text and then format it as you would any text outside a table. If you want to add an image or object, select Insert from the main menu. You can also add any library content. Select what type of file you want to insert and follow the remaining steps required to insert the file.

3. When you're finished adding content to the cell, you can move to the next cell and add content to it, continuing on through each cell within your table until the table is complete.

Figure 7.12 shows a table to which content has been added.

Figure 7.12
A simple table layout (border set to 0) complete with text and images.

7

⇨ *To add and format text, see "Adding Page Properties," p. 28.*

⇨ *To add Flash, see Chapter 8, "Adding Some Flash," p. 141.*

⇨ *To insert an image, see Chapter 4, "Adding Images," p. 63.*

⇨ *To create and add multimedia, see Part VI of this book, "Adding Multimedia," p. 473.*

BUILDING A FRAMESET

Whereas tables are document-based, frame technology actually modifies the interface through which a site is viewed. By creating a master document called a *frameset*, designers can break the browser viewing area into individual frames.

Frames-based pages are actually multiple pages delivered to the frameset. So, let's say you create a frameset to split the browser into two regions—a menu to the left and a main viewing area to the right.

Three documents are necessary to build this layout:

- The frameset document
- A complete document that contains the menu content
- A complete document that contains the main content

Of course, additional pages will also be needed to flesh out a site.

The frameset can be seen as a master control file because it only controls the layout and is never actually displayed by the browser. It determines how many rows and columns the frameset will be divided into, and it also can include presentational information about the frame layout, including whether borders are visible and if so, how those borders look and behave.

⇨ *To learn more about presentational modifications and advanced techniques using framed pages, see Chapter 19, "Working with Frame-Based Layouts," p. 351.*

The frameset markup also defines the location and name of each individual frame file. This is a critical aspect of frame construction because these settings determine how the site is navigated.

Dreamweaver MX enables you to create framesets in a variety of ways. In this section, you'll tap into Dreamweaver's predefined frames, which provide you with all the pages necessary to begin a frame-based layout, and you'll learn to create a basic frameset and framed pages.

Dreamweaver conveniently displays framed-based layouts so that as you're working you see the combined sum of the frameset and frame page parts. This helps you work more efficiently.

7

Using a Predefined Frameset

If you want to rely on Dreamweaver MX to set up the frameset and frame documents for you, you can use a predefined frameset. These are found in the New Document window and along the Insert bar.

To add a predefined frameset using the New Document approach, follow these steps:

1. Select File, New. The New Document window opens.

2. In the General tab, highlight framesets. The New Document window expands to show you the available frameset names as well as visually represent their layout (see Figure 7.13).

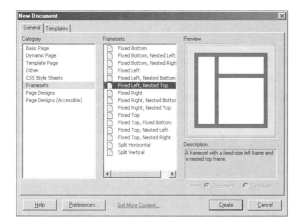

Figure 7.13
When you select framesets from the General options, you can choose individual frameset designs and see their layout in the corresponding window.

3. Find the frameset you want from the Framesets list. Click Create.

To add a predefined frameset using the Frames tab on the Insert bar, do the following:

1. Place the cursor within a document.

2. Click the Frames tab on the Insert bar (see Figure 7.14).

3. Select one of the icons available for framesets.

Dreamweaver MX will now generate the files necessary to create the frameset and its initial, associated pages. You will need to save and name each file accordingly—please see "Saving Framesets and Frame Pages" later this chapter.

Building a Custom Frameset

Two primary techniques are used individually or in combination to customize a frameset. The first involves using what Macromedia refers to as a *splitting item*. A splitting item is a directive to have the software split the selected frame. The second method is drag and drop: You drag the frame guide and drop it where you want the split to go.

7

Figure 7.14
Select a frame design from the options found on the Frame tab in Dreamweaver's Insert bar.

Frameset icons

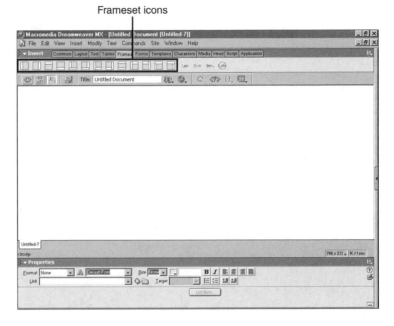

⇨ *Can't see your frame borders? Find out why in the "Viewing Frame Borders" in the "Troubleshooting" section at the end of this chapter.*

Using a Splitting Item

To use a splitting item, follow these steps:

1. Create a basic page by selecting File, New and using the New Document dialog box options for the basic page template. Be sure to set your work area to Design view.

2. Turn on the Frame Borders option by selecting View, Visual Aids, Frame Borders. This will provide a visual guide for you as you make your changes.

3. Choose a splitting item by selecting Modify, Frameset. Then select either Split Frame Left or Split Frame Right to split along the vertical, or select Split Frame Up or Split Frame Down to split along the horizontal. As soon as you make your selection, the frame splits according to that selection (see Figure 7.15).

You can continue splitting frames in this fashion as you see fit. Or, you can decide to employ the drag-and-drop method.

⇨ *Are the Modify Frameset options grayed out in the menu? If so, fix the problem with the information in "Frame Border Options" in the "Troubleshooting" section at the end of the chapter.*

Using Drag-and-Drop

Dragging and dropping frame sections is quite easy. Here's how:

1. With a frameset document at the ready, click and hold the mouse button down along one of the sides of the document window. If you want a vertical frame border, drag from the left or right. If you want a horizontal frame border, drag from the top or bottom.

2. Drop the section wherever you want it to go.

3. Continue adding sections until you're satisfied. If you want to split a section, use the splitting frames technique described earlier this section.

> You can duplicate a given frame design by pressing your mouse button down and dragging from the corner of the document window.

Figure 7.16 shows a complicated frameset. Although it would be very unusual to want to use such a complicated frameset in an actual Web site design, it's good to practice using splitting frames and drag-and-drop. Also, look at the resulting markup to learn more about the way frames are managed in HTML and XHTML.

Deleting Frames and Framesets

You can delete a frame at any time from the frameset by dragging the frame border off the page. However, if the file for the frame has already been saved, you should delete that file and modify any markup that is affected by the frame's deletion.

To delete a frameset, close the frameset file in Dreamweaver and delete the file itself from your hard drive.

Figure 7.16
A complex frameset created by
combining both the splitting
frames and drag-and-drop
method.

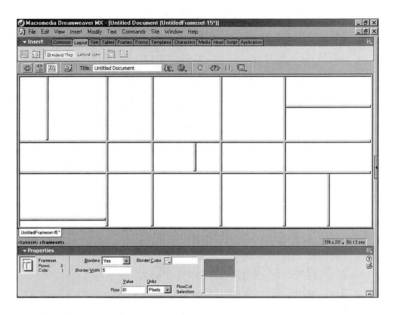

SAVING FRAMESETS AND FRAME PAGES

Frame pages are the individual documents that fill the frameset. They are generated in several different ways in Dreamweaver MX.

Frame pages are complete documents; they stand alone as well as within the context of the frameset. This means they can contain text, images, tables—anything you want to have delivered to the page's appearance in its determined portion of the frameset.

The main consideration when dealing with frame pages is ensuring that they are properly named and targeted. This means that your frameset document information defining the individual frame page name, ID, and filename must match with the frame page name, ID, and filename. Dreamweaver MX does this all for you after you step through the process of modifying and saving individual frame pages.

To begin working with frame pages, you should get your tools at the ready. You can work using the Frames panel, which can be opened and used as a means to navigate the frame pages within the frameset (see Figure 7.17). Open the Frames panel by selecting Window, Others, Frames.

To select the frameset within the Frames panel, click the outside border. To select an individual frame, simply click the frame within the panel.

You can also use the Document window in Design view to navigate your frameset and frame pages. The selection method is the same—click the outside border of the Document window or an individual frame to make your selection.

7

Figure 7.17
The Frames panel is helpful for managing frame pages.

Saving the Frameset

The first thing to do is save and name the frameset. To do so, follow these steps:

1. Select the frameset by using the Document window or Frames panel.

2. Select File, Save Frameset As. The Save As dialog box appears.

3. Type in a filename for your frameset. In frame-based layouts, the frameset is the file you'll want to point to in order to display the layout. So, you'll likely need to name your frameset as the index page.

4. Click Save to save the file to the appropriate folder.

If you look at the Property inspector with the frameset selected, you'll notice a variety of frameset attributes. You learn more about these attributes and how they influence the look and behavior of your frame-based site in Chapter 19, "Working with Frame-Based Layouts."

Saving and Naming an Individual Frame Page

To save and name an individual frame page, follow these steps:

1. Select the frame you want to save using the Frame panel or Document window.

2. In the Property inspector, provide a name for the frame. This is a very important step because the frame page name determines how linking and navigation will occur between pages. Use a name that makes logical sense. If the frame is being used as a menu, for example, you can simply name that frame menu (see Figure 7.18).

7

Figure 7.18
Name a frame using the Property inspector. Naming frames is a critical part of the frame process.

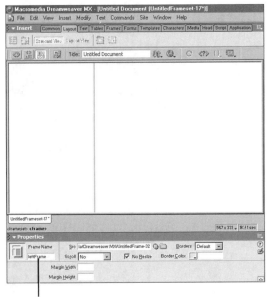

Type the Frame Name here

3. Select File, Save Frame As. The Save As dialog box opens. Name the frame file.

4. Click Save to save the file.

Continue this process for every frame page that appears within the frameset.

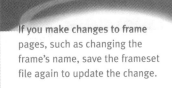

If you make changes to frame pages, such as changing the frame's name, save the frameset file again to update the change.

Importing an Existing Document into a Frameset

If you have an existing HTML or XHTML document that you want to import into a frameset, you can do so by following these steps:

1. In the frameset, select the frame into which you want to import the document.

2. Select File, Open in Frame. The Select HTML File dialog box appears.

3. Locate the file you want to import, highlight it, and click OK.

The file imports into the frame. Save the frame to update any changes (see Figure 7.19).

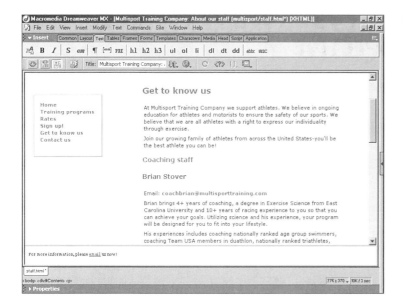

Figure 7.19
This page was imported into the frameset using Dreamweaver's Open in Frame feature.

TROUBLESHOOTING

Viewing Frame Borders

Why can't I view my frame's borders?

Save all pages related to the frameset before viewing them using the View Frame Borders feature. Save your files using the techniques described in this chapter. To view the borders, make sure you are in Design view. Then, select View, Visual Aids, Frame Borders.

Frame Border Options

I'm trying to add a frame border, but those options are grayed out. How do I access them?

If the frame border options are grayed out, it is most likely due to the fact that you're in the incorrect view. You must use Design view to set frame borders.

7

PEER TO PEER: TABLES AND FRAMES FROM A STANDARDS PERSPECTIVE

From a standards and best-practices perspective, both tables and frames pose some complicated challenges.

The primary issue with tables is already well-documented in this book, but it bears repeating because it is so incredibly important to the future growth of the Web. The use of tables for layout has been the mainstay of Web design for years now. However, using tables for layout is a method that is becoming less desirable as support for CSS layout becomes more available.

Tables used for layout goes against the W3C's ideal vision of HTML and XHTML, which calls for a separation of presentation from structure. This means that a table is ideally used only for tabular data and never used for presentation. What's more, tables used for layout prohibit easy access for those with disabilities.

Tables in presentations create a problem for people with disabilities, especially the blind. Many screen readers—a combination of software and hardware used by the blind to access computer documents and applications—can't read columns. Visual people know how to read columnar structures because we see them every day in the newspaper. The first column is read, then the second, then the third, and so on.

Tables that are marked up without special accessibility features can be used to create columns across a Web page that look visually fine. But, a screen reader might read the first line of the first column, followed by the first line of the second column and the first line of the third, making the page completely unintelligible to the user. The screen reader hardware and software doesn't understand the concept of visual columns; it just interprets the document as a single page.

With CSS layouts, the content is separated into divisions. You can create visual columns but stack the divisions in a specific order so the screen reader reads them without the barriers that table cells create.

So, should you use tables for layout or not? The decision has to be based on a very systematic evaluation of your audience. If you have demographic information about an existing site including the most frequently used browser versions, you can make your decision based on the ratio of support for CSS. Then, if you decide to use tables for layout, follow the guidelines in Chapter 18, "Designing with Table-Based Layouts," to ensure that those documents are as valid and as accessible as possible and that they use the special table features in HTML and XHTML.

Frames pose similar challenges. Frames are not considered presentational in and of themselves, despite the fact that they create a visual interface. Frames are a part of standards, and even though their use is controversial, they can be developed in such a way as to be accessible, attractive, and valid. This involves using such techniques as `noframes`, and ensuring that your frameset documents use only standard elements and attributes—there are numerous frame and frameset attributes that are presentational or browser specific that you should avoid in valid documents. The issues of accessibility, design sensibility, and validation of frame-based designs is covered in depth in Chapter 19.

ADDING SOME FLASH

IN THIS CHAPTER

8

USING DREAMWEAVER MX'S FLASH FEATURES

Macromedia Flash is a vector-based animation tool that has taken the Web by storm in the last several years. The passion for Flash is so intense that it has inspired many books; Web sites; and conferences where individuals can learn, create, and experience Flash's power.

But learning Flash is a commitment! And, although many readers will be Flash enthusiasts already or interested in learning more about Flash, the good news about Macromedia Dreamweaver MX is that it lets you use Flash text and buttons in your pages without ever having to open Flash itself or even know much about it.

In this chapter, you'll learn about vector graphics in general and then explore quick ways to add some Flash text and button features to your Dreamweaver MX compositions without actually needing to use Flash.

⇨ *If you'd like to learn about more advanced features in Flash MX itself, see Chapter 27, "Working with Flash and Shockwave," p. 497.*

> **If you'd like to learn Flash in** detail, check out *Special Edition Using Flash MX*, from Que.

ABOUT VECTOR GRAPHICS

Vector graphics are mathematically calculated images that consist of a series of lines and curves used to form different shapes. Each line and curve is generated using a mathematical instruction that provides the beginning, ending, and path of the line or curve.

Vector graphics are especially good for

- Creating illustrations with curves, hard-edged shapes, and smooth lines. Graphic designers typically use these programs to design logos and draw complex digital drawings.

- Technical drawings that can benefit from the sizing flexibility that vector formats offer.

- Animations and interactive presentations in the form of Flash (and other media, too).

> **Vector art does not appear on the** Web in its original format without a plug-in or special browser features. All images that appear inline in a Web page are pixel-based raster images. For a vector image to be positioned as a Web graphic, it must either be delivered to the plug-in or first be converted by saving or exporting it to JPEG or GIF.

Vector graphics are easy to scale because a simple process of altering the mathematical equations involved in the image is all that's required. If you save a vector graphic in its native file format using a vector graphic program, such as Macromedia Freehand (also part of the MX studio package) or the very popular Adobe Illustrator, you can later modify that file to make the graphic larger or smaller without losing quality or increasing file size.

Vector art is composed of Bèzier curves (see Figure 8.1). Bèzier curves define shapes or objects through the positioning of two anchor points, a segment, two direction lines, and two direction handles. Direction lines define the direction of a curve. It makes sense, therefore, that straight paths or sharp corners do not have direction lines.

The first drawing programs for computers were *pixel-based*. Pixel-based programs produce results with stair-stepped pixelated lines and shapes, which can result in jagged edges (this is known by a very serious technical term: *jaggies*).

Adobe Illustrator, released in 1988, was the first vector-based computer program to be made available to the general public. Illustrator allowed artists to draw hard-edged graphics on a computer and print out an image composed of clean, sharp lines and edges.

This advance was valuable not only for illustrators, but also for typographers. Type fonts could be rendered using the same technology, enabling typographers to design hundreds of new fonts with ease. This is one of the most exciting features of Macromedia Flash in general because the quality and control over typographic elements are extremely rich.

FILE TYPES AND OBJECT PROPERTIES

Two primary types of Flash objects are available for your use in Dreamweaver MX: text and buttons. In addition, several file types are used in the creation of Flash objects that will be helpful to know about as you work through the exercises in this chapter.

For an interesting article on Flash and Flash file types, see http://www.techtv.com/callforhelp/howto/jump/0,24331,3376912,00.html.

Understanding Flash File Types

Three Flash file types are important to know about. Table 8.1 shows these file types and explains their purposes.

Table 8.1   Flash File Types

File Type	File Extension	Purpose
Flash file	.fla	The source file for any Flash project. This file type requires Flash MX to open so you can export it as a .swf or .swt file for delivery to Web browsers.
Flash Movie file	.swf	This is a Web-ready compressed version of the .fla file. You can view this in a browser with the proper support, but you can't edit the file in Flash. The .swf file type is used when you create Flash buttons and text in Dreamweaver MX.
Flash Template files	.swt	These templates provide a means for you to make modifications to a .swf file. In Dreamweaver MX, this file type is used to create and modify buttons, which are then saved as .swf files for use on a Web page.

Flash Object Properties

Certain properties are available for you when working with Flash text and Flash buttons, as well. When you insert a Flash object into your document using the methods described in this chapter, you will be able to select the object and set specific properties for that object.

The following properties are common to both text and buttons:

- **Name**—The name identifies the button or text object so it can be used with scripts and behaviors. Simply type the name you want the object to have into the Name field in the Property inspector.

- **Width**—This specifies the width of the object in pixels, picas, points, inches, millimeters, centimeters, or percentages.

- **Height**—Use this to specify the object's height. You have the same measurement options available for height as you do for width.

- **File**—The file is the location of the Flash object file in question. You can browse for the file or, if you know the path, simply type it into the available field.

- **Edit**—When you click this button, the Flash object dialog box opens so you can modify your Flash button or text with ease.

- **Reset Size**—Use this features to reset the object to its actual size.

- **Vertical Spacing**—Allows you to specify, in pixels, the amount of whitespace above and below the object.

- **Horizontal Spacing**—Allows you to specify, in pixels, the amount of whitespace to the left and right of the object.

- **Quality**—The higher the quality of an object, the better it will look. However, high-quality Flash objects—especially complex ones—take longer to load and require more computer processing power to work well. The available settings are Low, which is good for speed with a lower-quality appearance, and High, which opts for appearance over speed. Auto Low emphasizes speed but delivers higher quality wherever possible. Conversely, Auto High emphasizes quality *and* speed but opts for speed over quality if achieving both is not possible.

- **Scale**—The scale paremeter for objects specifies how the movie will display. One option is Default, which makes the full object appear within the area defined by the width and height attributes. In this instance, the aspect ratio remains intact, preventing distortion. If you choose No Border, borders will be cropped. Exact Fit means that the object will fit into the exact width and height you determine, even if that's not its original size.

- **Align**—This attribute specifies the object's alignment.

- **Background Color**—This allows you to specify a background color for the object.

- **Play/Stop**—The Play button allows you to preview your work. If you're in the preview, you can click the button, which will now be labeled Stop, to stop the preview.

- **Parameters**—If you'd like to add or modify object parameters, you can do so directly by clicking this option. The Parameters dialog box opens.

Figure 8.1 shows the Property inspector with a Flash object selected so you can see the properties.

Figure 8.1
You can format your Flash text and buttons using these Flash object attributes in the Property inspector.

8

Finding that your Flash text or button objects aren't displaying properly? The problem might have to do with the scale type you've set. See "Problems with the Exact Fit Feature" in the "Troubleshooting" section later in this chapter.

INSERTING FLASH TEXT

Flash text is a Flash movie with only text in it that can be inserted into your Web pages in Dreamweaver. The advantage of Flash text is that you have a lot more control over the typographic choice and quality because of the inherent nature of vector graphics. Vector type tends to be smoother and crisper, which improves readability.

Inserting Flash text into your design is very straightforward. Just be sure the document with which you are working is saved before trying to add the object.

To Insert a Flash text object, do the following:

1. Open a previously saved document, or save any new document or a document in progress. Make sure the file is updated and saved; otherwise, Dreamweaver won't let you add the object.

2. In the document, place your cursor where you'd like the text object to appear.

3. Select the Media tab on the Insert bar. You can click the Flash text icon, shown in Figure 8.2, or drag and drop it onto the page where you'd like the text object to appear. Alternatively, you can select Insert, Interactive Images, Flash Text. The Insert Flash text dialog box appears (see Figure 8.3).

Flash
Flash text

Flash button

Figure 8.2
The Media tab on the Insert bar contains three important icons relative to Flash objects.

4. Add the text you require into the text box labeled Text.

5. Modify the text as per your needs (see Table 8.2).

Figure 8.3
The Insert Flash Text dialog box contains numerous options for styling your Flash text.

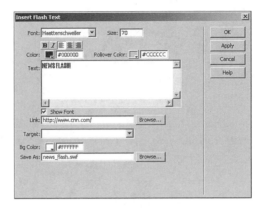

6. Customize a name for the Flash object file in the Save As field.

7. Click Apply or OK.

The Flash text will now be inserted into your document.

Table 8.2 Flash Text Features in Dreamweaver MX

Text Option	Application
Font	Select from any TrueType font on your machine. Dreamweaver MX automatically loads your available font choices into the drop-down menu.
Size	Choose the size of your font. Size in this case is represented by points, not pixels.
Font Styles	Style your text by applying bold or italics and justifying the text to the left, center, or right.
Color	Apply color to your font choice.
Rollover Color	You can choose a second color for use when the mouse passes over the text. This is especially useful if the text is a link.
Show Font	Check this if you'd like to see the text displayed in the text box with styles applied.
Link	You can make your Flash text object a link by providing a URL in the Link field.
Target	Here you can specify a target frame or window for the link.
Background Color	Allows you to define a background color for the text.

➪ *Having trouble with links in your Flash text? The problem might have to do with the way browsers interpret links in a Flash file. See "Link Problems" in the "Troubleshooting" section later in this chapter for more information.*

Figures 8.4 and 8.5 show a linked Flash text object that changes color when the mouse passes over the link.

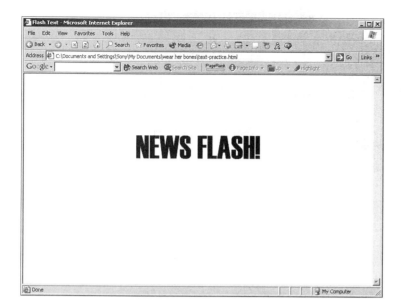

Figure 8.4
Here you see a Flash text object styled black using the Color swatch in the Insert Flash Text dialog box.

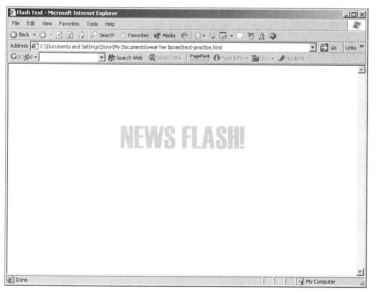

Figure 8.5
Because a rollover color was defined in the Insert Flash Text dialog box, when the mouse passes over the text—which is a link—the color changes from black to light gray.

ADDING FLASH BUTTONS

If you'd like to get a little more adventuresome and add Flash buttons to your page, Dreamweaver MX makes it remarkably easy to do so—as easy as adding and modifying Flash text. Some of the advantages of Flash buttons include smoother text, built-in mouseovers, and other effects.

Do the following to Insert a Flash button object:

1. Just as with Flash text, you must make sure the file with which you are working is updated and saved; otherwise, Dreamweaver won't let you add the object.

2. Place your cursor where you'd like the button object to appear in the document.

3. Select the Media tab on the Insert bar. You can click the Flash button icon or drag and drop it onto the page where you want the button object to appear. Alternatively, you can select Insert, Interactive Images, Flash Button. The Insert Flash Button dialog box appears (see Figure 8.6).

Figure 8.6
The Insert Flash Button dialog box provides everything you need to create a Flash button in Dreamweaver MX.

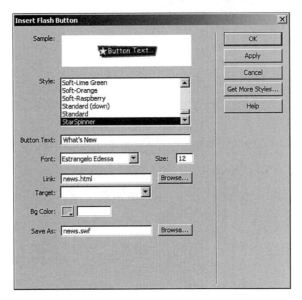

4. In the dialog box, browse the button style you'd like. Several styles are available, and you can get more from the Macromedia Exchange site by clicking the Get More Styles button found on the right side of the dialog box.

5. In the Button Text area, type in the text you want to appear on the button.

6. Customize the text style using the Font and Size options. As with Flash Text objects, you can make a Flash button object a link.

7. You can select a background color for your button. Once you are happy with your choices, name your file and click Apply or OK to insert the button.

If you're working in Design view, you can click the Apply button in the Insert Flash Button as you work with the dialog box to make your style choices. The Apply button applies your current choices and leaves the dialog box open, allowing you to continue to modify your button's features.

Dreamweaver MX will now create the button and insert the Flash button object into the document (see Figure 8.7).

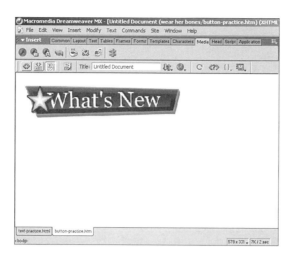

Figure 8.7
Here's a close-up of the customized button within the document window. You can create an entire set of buttons in this way, providing an attractive navigation feature for your page.

8

PREVIEWING, EDITING, AND RESIZING FLASH BUTTONS AND TEXT

As you are working with Flash buttons and text objects, being able to preview their features is helpful. You can do this easily in Dreamweaver MX. You can also easily make additional edits and sizing changes to your objects, perfecting them as you work on your page.

Previewing Flash Buttons and Text

To preview your Flash button or text object, follow these steps:

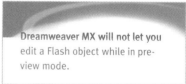

Dreamweaver MX will not let you edit a Flash object while in preview mode.

1. If you're not already there, switch over to Design view.

2. Select the Flash object by clicking it once.

3. In the Property inspector, locate the Play button and click it.

The Flash button or text object is now active, and you can test it out. Click Stop at any time to end the preview.

Editing Flash Buttons and Text

Here are several ways to open a Flash button or text object for editing:

- Double-click the object.

- Click the Edit button in the Property inspector.

- (Control-click) [Right-click] and select Edit from the contextual menu.

8

In the case of a Flash text object, the Insert Flash Text dialog box will appear. If you are working with a button, the Insert Flash Button dialog box will appear. You can now make any required modifications to the object.

Resizing Flash Objects

Resizing Flash objects is easy and can be accomplished in Design view. First, select the object; then use the visual resize handles as follows:

- Adjust the width of the object by dragging the selection handle to the right.

- Adjust the height of the element by dragging the selection handle at the bottom of the object.

- To adjust both width and height, drag the selection handle found in the corner.

In many cases, preserving the object's aspect ratio (its width and height relationship) is required. To do this, be sure to hold down the Shift key while resizing.

If, at any point, you want to return the object to its original size, simply click the Reset Size button in the Property inspector.

> **Caution**
>
> Not preserving an object's aspect ratio can result in a distorted or blurry display of that object.

TROUBLESHOOTING

Link Problems

Clicking a linked Flash object isn't bringing me to the link. What's the problem?

You probably used a site-relative URL, such as

`../articles/cooking.html`

Browsers have trouble with site-relative URLs in Flash objects. Although you can refer to a file in the same directory as the Flash object using a relative URL, like so:

`cooking.html`

you shouldn't try to use relative URLs in your Flash objects. Instead, use the absolute form in all other cases:

`http://www.molly.com/articles/cooking.html`

Problems with the Exact Fit Feature

While previewing Flash button and text objects, the objects appear to be distorted. What's going on?

You probably have the scale feature set to Exact Fit. The problem with Exact Fit is that the movie can distort because the aspect ratio of the object is not preserved. Typically, it's recommended that you avoid this problem.

PEER TO PEER: ACCESSIBLE TEXT AND NAVIGATION ALTERNATIVES

In our ongoing peer-to-peer discussions regarding standards, accessibility, and best practices, it's important to point out that Flash objects, as with many objects, have specific problems in the context of accessibility.

The Web Accessibility Initiative (WAI) has 14 primary guidelines for accessibility, and Flash objects are affected by several of them. Here you'll find three key problem areas with recommendations for alternatives:

- **Provide equivalent alternatives to auditory and visual content**—In the context of text and buttons, be sure to provide a text equivalent for Flash text in your HTML, or on another page, and be sure to provide text link alternatives to Flash-based navigation buttons.

- **Don't rely on color alone**—Be sure your colors are contrasting enough so as to be readable, and don't rely on color to express any important navigation or text instructions. If your Flash text or buttons do not conform to this, provide some alternative so site visitors with color blindness or other forms of visual and cognitive impairments can access your information.

For details on Web Content Accessibility Guidelines, see http://www.w3.org/TR/WCAG10/.

- **Ensure that pages featuring new technologies transform gracefully**—Flash is not exactly new, but it does require a plug-in and in many cases, an end user might not have one. So, again, be sure that there are alternatives to the Flash content you provide on your Web pages.

PUBLISHING YOUR SITE

IN THIS CHAPTER

TESTING ON YOUR MACHINE

Some developers view Web design as a race to get a site from the drawing board through the development process to the finish line—the live server. In actuality, there are many steps between developing the site's pages and putting out the virtual "Open" sign. The difference between a mediocre site and a great site is often the attention paid to these interim details.

By the time you've designed a table layout, added navigation, inserted images and text, and linked everything to the Web at large, you might be rather sick of looking at your site. It's worth resigning yourself to a last look or two to ensure that everything's in place.

Cleaning Up Your HTML

As you well know, even the best Web developers sometimes have errors in their markup. Dreamweaver writes fairly tight markup, but it can sometimes leave behind extraneous or redundant nested tags. Or, it's possible that you inadvertently used the Property inspector to change the font face or size when you intended to develop a CSS-based site. If you made any additions or changes in Code view, you might have introduced extra tags or attributes.

One method of fixing these mistakes is using the Find and Replace commands in a well-planned pattern to hunt down common problems. Dreamweaver offers a better solution, however. The Clean Up HTML command systematically has the following options:

- **Empty Container Tags**—Removes tags that don't have content between the opening and end tags (for example, `<blockquote></blockquote>`).

- **Redundant Nested Tags**—Removes tags that are nested redundantly within the exact same tag, (for example, `<font color="FFFFFF">Most chefs <font color="FFFFFF">use </font>three basic knives.</font>`).

- **Non-Dreamweaver HTML Comments**—Removes comments inserted by developers. This command does not remove comment tags inserted by Dreamweaver to mark templates or library items, (for example, `<!--insert image of kitchen knives here when graphics are complete-->`).

⇨ *Do you prefer comments to Design notes? See "HTML Comments and Design Notes" in the "Troubleshooting" section at the end of this chapter to determine which is best for you.*

- **Dreamweaver Special Markup**—Removes comments inserted by Dreamweaver to identify templates and library items. For example, `<!-- TemplateBeginRepeat name="..." -->` is markup inserted by Dreamweaver to define a repeatable region in a template.

If the tag and its attributes are not identical to those in which they're nested, Dreamweaver will not change them. For example, if the font tags also contained an attribute for font size that is different in each of the two tags, Dreamweaver will not alter the nested tag, not even to remove the redundant attribute.

- **Specific Tag(s)**—Allows you to specify a tag or tags to remove. Any content that appears within that tag is preserved. Multiple tags can be separated with commas in the tag field. So, if you type **font, i** into the tag field, all instances of the `<font>` and `<i>` tags will be removed from the document.

As in the Redundant Nested Tags option, this command does not combine redundant attributes from `<font>` tags that only control a subset of the text block.

- **Combine Nested `<font>` Tags when Possible**—Combines multiple `<font>` tags if they surround the same block of text. For example, `<font color="FFFFFF"><font size="3">basic knives</font></font>` would be combined into `<font color="FFFFFF" size="3">basic knives</font>`.

- **Show Log on Completion**—Displays a report showing how many changes were made.

To use the Clean Up HTML command, do the following:

1. Open the document you want to clean up.

2. Select Commands, Clean Up HTML. If you're developing in XHTML, the Commands menu automatically changes this option to Clean Up XHTML.

3. Select the options for Dreamweaver to find and repair (see Figure 9.1).

4. Click OK.

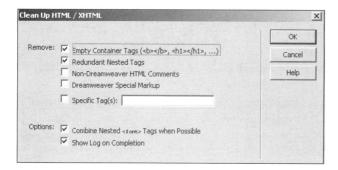

Figure 9.1
The Clean Up HTML/XHTML dialog box lists the many options of this command.

If you select the Show Log on Completion option, Dreamweaver displays a report listing how many items were fixed or removed after the command is executed (see Figure 9.2). If you ran the Clean Up XHTML command, this report also states the number of img tags that don't have alt text attributes.

Estimating Download Speed

Even with the advent of broadband, download speed is still an issue for many Web surfers. If anything, faster Internet access has made visitors even more impatient for sites to load. You can estimate the speed at which a page will download by looking at the Download indicator at the bottom of the Document window (see Figure 9.3).

If the Clean Up XHTML command reports missing alt tags, it's a simple matter to use the Find command to search for img tags to find those without alt attributes.

9

Figure 9.2
This alert box details the number of changes made to the document after executing the Clean Up XHTML command.

Figure 9.3
The Download indicator displays the file size of the page and all its components and approximates the download time at a preselected connection speed.

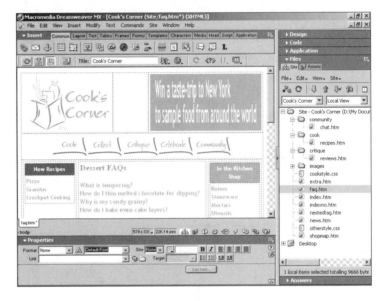

The Download indicator settings are controlled by the Status Bar category of the Preferences dialog box (accessed by selecting Edit, Preferences and then clicking the Status Bar category). As you work, set this option to match that of the expected average visitor of your site. When your page is complete, you should set this preference at various connection speeds to get an estimate of the download times on both extremely fast and very slow connections.

If the download time appears significant, use the Clean Up HTML/XHTML command to remove any extraneous tags and comments. Be sure you've optimized all your images to their fullest without sacrificing too much quality. Audio files are also quite large and can greatly increase download time.

Spell Checking

There are very few truly great spellers on the planet, and even the best spellers make mistakes. Dreamweaver's spell-check feature helps the best and the worst spellers hide their flaws from public view. To run the spell-checker, do the following:

> Remember, the Download indicator only provides an approximation of download speed. Dreamweaver can't assess factors such as traffic and server speed.

1. Select Text, Check Spelling from the Document window menu.

2. The spell-checker stops at the first word in the document that isn't in its dictionary. The word is highlighted in the document and is also displayed in the Check Spelling dialog box (see Figure 9.4).

3. If you know the word is spelled correctly, click the Add to Personal button to add the word to your dictionary.

➡ *Work for a specific industry or profession that uses many words not in a standard dictionary? No problem! See "Adding Dictionary Terms" in the "Troubleshooting" section at the end of this chapter.*

4. If the word is spelled correctly, but you don't want to add it to your personal dictionary—such as when you're using an intentional misspelling to make a point within the context of your site—click the Ignore button. To ignore all instances of this spelling, click the Ignore All button.

5. If the word is indeed misspelled, either manually type the correct spelling in the Change To field or select one of the words in the Suggestions list. Click Change to replace the misspelled word with the new spelling. Or, click Change All to replace all instances of the same misspelled word.

6. When the Spelling Check Completed alert appears, click OK to end the spell-check.

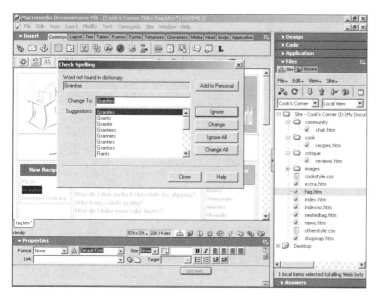

Figure 9.4
The spell-check highlights the misspelled word so you can see it in context. The dialog box makes suggestions as to the proper spelling or allows you to manually type the correct word.

A Final Manual Review

The Dreamweaver tools mentioned previously in this chapter all help you prepare your site for its final journey to the remote server. Nothing, however, beats a good eye. After you've cleaned up your HTML, spell-checked the site, and ensured that everything is optimized, it's worth taking one last look at each and every page of the site. Be especially on the alert for

- Table layouts that have gone awry as you inserted images and text

- Missing page titles, descriptions, and keywords

- Commonly misused words that wouldn't be picked up by the spell-checker

- Images that don't suit the final content

- Placeholder images that weren't replaced with final graphics

- Cross-browser compatibility and design integrity

As with all spell-checkers, Dreamweaver won't catch misuse of homonyms (by, bye) or commonly misused words (affect, effect).

⇨ *For more information on browser testing, see "Cross-Browser Compatibility," p. 525.*

Creating Backups

The final pre-upload step is critical, yet it's often one of the most overlooked. Always back up your entire site and all source files. Many developers rely on the remote server as failsafe storage for their completed sites. Particularly in the volatile world of the Internet, this is extremely risky. Web hosting services come and go, sometimes without any advance notice to their customers. Servers also crash, and modems or broadband connections go down. As I'm sure you've encountered, these things usually happen just when you're counting on them most to access your pages for updates.

Of course, retaining the local folders is one method of backing up the site. Consider keeping an additional copy on CD, though. This backup stands as a record of the previous state of your site. If you somehow decimate one of your local pages during an edit—and certainly if the error is compounded by replacing the remote page before the error is noticed—the additional backup is a tremendous relief.

UPLOADING PAGES WITH THE SITE PANEL

When it's time to make the leap to the remote server, you'll once again turn to the Site panel. If you defined your remote server information when you defined the initial site, you're ready to go online. If you left the remote information blank, you'll need to edit your site definition to add this information. Follow these steps:

1. Select Site, Edit Sites from either the Document window or the Site panel.

2. Select the name of the site from the Edit Sites dialog box (see Figure 9.5).

3. Click the Edit button to open the Site Definition dialog box.

4. Edit the Remote Info category, as described in Chapter 1, "Defining Your Site."

5. Click OK to close the Site Definition dialog box.

6. Click Done to close the Edit Sites dialog box.

Figure 9.5
The Edit Sites dialog box lists all the sites you've created, enabling you to modify the site definitions.

9

Going Online

At this point, most of your work will involve the Site panel. If you're still editing and tweaking pages, keep the panel docked to quickly move between views. Otherwise, use the Expand/Collapse button on the Site panel to open the Site window (see Figure 9.6). The larger site view will enable you to quickly move between the local and remote file lists and use drag-and-drop to upload and download files.

The Site window is divided into two panes, the local folder list and the remote server. The Remote Site pane remains empty until you connect to the remote server to update the file view. To connect to the remote server, simply click the Connect to Remote Host button on the Site panel toolbar (see Figure 9.7). When you connect to the remote server, the Remote Site pane is automatically updated with a current file list. The same button is used to disconnect from the server.

If you're already comfortable using file transfer applications such as WS_FTP or CuteFTP, you might prefer to continue using what's familiar. These applications provide better control over files and directories on the remote server and enable you to transfer files outside the defined remote directory. You should still enter remote server information, however, for occasional file uploads from Dreamweaver.

Toggling the Local/Remote Views

One key advantage of the Site window is its display of both the local and remote file lists in the same window. After your site is live and you're doing more maintenance and updating than initial development, however, the Site panel might be more convenient. The upside of the Site panel is that it shares the screen real estate with the Document window, making it easy to edit files on-the-fly and then immediately upload them without changing views. The downside is that the Site panel can display only one file list at a time. To switch views, use the Site panel view drop-down menu.

Figure 9.6
Unless you're still editing pages as you go, the expanded Site window makes transferring files between the local and remote servers easier.

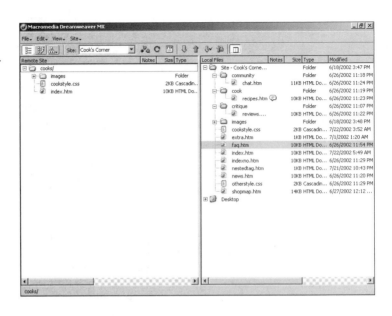

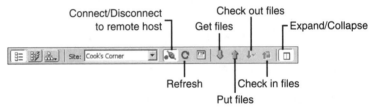

Connect/Disconnect to remote host
Get files
Check out files
Expand/Collapse
Refresh
Check in files
Put files

Figure 9.7
The Site toolbar contains the most important options of the upload/download process.

Putting Files (Uploading)

Until you upload files to the remote server, the Remote Site pane will be remarkably empty. Unless you're working in a development group, the commands you use to transfer files are Get (download from the remote server) and Put (upload to the remote server).

▭▷ *To learn more about using Dreamweaver in a collaborative team environment, see Chapter 29, "Working with Others," p. 535.*

Initially, you'll most likely want to upload the entire site to the remote server. To do this, simply click the Put button on the Site window/panel toolbar (refer to Figure 9.7). Because this can be a lengthy process, Dreamweaver asks whether you want to proceed.

To put individual files onto the remote server, follow these steps:

1. Highlight the file or files you want to transfer in the Local Folder.

2. Click the Put button on the toolbar. The Dependent File dialog box appears and asks whether you want to include any dependent files or images.

> **Caution**
>
> You *must* select the site's root folder in the local pane to upload all the files and directories within the site. If you choose only one file or directory, just that element will transfer.

3. Click either Yes or No. You can also choose to not have this option appear in the future by selecting the Don't Show Me This Message Again check box (see Figure 9.8). The transfer then begins.

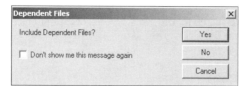

Figure 9.8
Dreamweaver's automatic detection of dependent files can be a time-saver.

If you select a file that has not been saved, you'll be prompted to save the file before putting it on the server. In the Site category of the Preferences dialog box, you can set Dreamweaver to automatically save all files before transferring, although advanced developers might opt to retain control over this process.

More About Dependent Files

Because Web pages are rarely self-contained in one file, it's important to upload the images, multimedia, and CSS style sheet files to the remote server as well. Dreamweaver helps in this area by asking whether you want to upload dependent files when putting a document on the remote server. This feature is extremely useful when you upload pages initially. Later, however, you should use this option only if you've changed several of these dependent files. If only the document itself has changed—or if you've changed only one or two dependent files—it's much less time-consuming to upload only those files that have changed.

Set your preferences for how Dreamweaver handles dependent files in the Site category of the Preferences dialog box. The settings for getting and putting files can be customized to your tastes. A common setting for this option is to get/download dependent files only when prompted, but to automatically put/upload dependent files. The rational for this setting is that the most current version of an image or other dependent file usually resides in the local folder, thus you don't want it automatically overwritten by an older version on the remote server when you get a file. However, you do want to upload the most current version of a dependent file when you put the page on the server. Again, however, you might want to manually get and put dependent files if only a few of them have changed.

Use the (Shift) [Ctrl] key to select multiple files in the list.

Getting Files (Downloading)

The opposite process to uploading pages is getting them from the remote server to work with them locally. To download, select a file or files in the Remote Site pane and click the Get button on the Site toolbar or drag and drop the files into the local folder (refer to Figure 9.7).

If you're using the Site window as suggested, you can also select the files in the Local Folder and drag them to the Remote Site pane, which automatically initiates the Put command.

TESTING YOUR SITE ONLINE

After the site has been transferred to the remote server, the testing process starts all over again. Although you've checked the site for approximate download speeds, accessibility, cross-browser compatibility, and code validation using Dreamweaver's tools, nothing can replace real-life experience.

Testing Download Speed

As mentioned earlier, the download speed provided by Dreamweaver in the status bar is only an approximation based purely on the size of the document and its components and the speed of the user's connection. After the site is on the server, you can test the accuracy of Dreamweaver's prediction. If you're using a broadband connection, it's very important to visit the site using a standard modem, especially if your intended audience will include a significant number of dial-up users.

Note, however, that even if you're testing the site at various speeds, the true test comes when the site is live. If you're lucky enough to have a high volume of visitors, you might be unfortunate enough to have slow-downs in access speed as the server struggles to keep up.

Fixing Problems

Putting the site onto the remote server also enables you to check for real-life cross-browser compatibility. Again, Dreamweaver can alert you if your code is not compatible with certain browsers or platforms, but even valid code can appear very different on various configurations. Even if you don't have the necessary platforms and browsers to personally test your pages, having the site on the remote server enables you to get the opinion of others with different configurations.

Taking a fresh look at the site can also draw your attention to other minor problems, such as typos or slow-loading images that you didn't catch in earlier testing.

Editing on the Server

When you find mistakes, you can edit pages directly on the server. To do this, connect to the server using the Connect to Remote Host button on the Site toolbar. If you're using the Site window, select a file from the Remote Site pane and open the file. If you're using the Site panel, the view automatically changes to the Remote view upon connecting to the server. Select a file from this view, and open it. You can then edit the file as normal. When you save the file, it is automatically saved to both the remote server and the local folder, ensuring that your local folder remains an accurate replica of the live site.

GOING LIVE

Releasing a site to the public is often just the beginning. After the site is in action, it needs to be promoted, maintained, tracked, and updated.

⇨ *For more on the methods for tracking usage of your site, see Chapter 30, "Learning About Your Site," p. 543.*

Getting the Word Out

The final step in the process of publishing a site is promoting it to the masses. Site promotion is a fine art, and many firms charge hundreds or even thousands of dollars to increase a site's visibility. There are several steps you can take to promote your own site without resorting to these services.

Search Engine Listings

If site promotion is a science, search engines are a specialty. There are several types of search engines on the Web. The most popular are services such as Google (www.google.com) and Yahoo! (www.yahoo.com), although there are many others. Each service varies slightly in how it finds and ranks sites. Services such as Yahoo! require you to submit the site for entry onto their list, a process which can take several weeks. Others run *spiders*, automatic programs that seek out new sites on the Web by following links. Of course, some programs and services will help you get your site listed in as many search engines as possible. You can help this process by ensuring that your site is coded to maximize these opportunities.

> **Don't try to fool the search** engines with false keywords. If caught, your site will be de-listed. For more is a science, search engines are a specialty. There on standards items related to search, see the "Peer to Peer" section at the end of this chapter.

> **9**

Meta tags can be used to provide keywords and a description of your site. Although the keywords are important, the description is often the most important criteria used by these engines to determine relevance for ranking purposes. Be sure your description contains the most important keywords for your site, but don't go overboard and try to include every keyword in the description. Be succinct, but also think about marketing.

Getting Linked

Another method of promotion is getting your site linked from other related sites. This is where networking comes into play. Be an active Web surfer and get to know the competition and complementary sites. If a site has a guest book or email link, try to negotiate a co-linking arrangement. The advantages of linking are twofold. First, the other site's visitors will be exposed to your site. But possibly even more important, some search engines rank their site listings based on how many other sites link to yours.

Becoming an Expert

Direct word-of-mouth is another effective technique. If your visitors like what you have to offer, they'll tell others. In many cases, they'll do this on a Web-based forum specific to that area of interest. One way to encourage this is to become active in these forums yourself. Answering questions and demonstrating your vast knowledge of the subject will entice people to see what else you have to offer.

TROUBLESHOOTING

HTML Comments and Design Notes

Which is better, HTML comments or Design Notes?

Which do you prefer? Either HTML comments or Design Notes can provide useful information about a site and its various assets. Either way is a perfectly legitimate course. However, if you determine that you need to communicate information mostly with co-workers—*all* of whom are using Dreamweaver—then the Design Note method might be the better option because it reduces your overhead.

However, if you do use comments, you can use the Non-Dreamweaver HTML Comments command when cleaning up your HTML or XHTML. If you've used comments instead of Design Notes to communicate with other members of the development team or as reminders to yourself, this command removes all said comments. However, Design Notes are left intact. Comments might no longer be useful after the page is complete and might unnecessarily pad a page, thus increasing its download time. Design Notes do not affect a page's download time.

Adding Dictionary Terms

This spell-checker is driving me nuts! None of the words that come up as wrong are really misspelled. How can I get around this?

If you develop sites that are specific to a particular field, such as psychology or engineering, you can seed the dictionary by creating a document with a list of correctly spelled terms. Run the spell-checker and as it highlights each term, use the Add to Personal button to add them to the dictionary.

One very cool fact: The dictionary isn't site specific, so words you enter into the dictionary in one site are applied to other sites.

PEER TO PEER: STANDARDS AND SEARCH

Sometimes, aspects of following best practices and standards can have unexpected but positive effects in other areas of the work.

A properly structured document complete with accessibility features such as `alt` text and `noframes` content for framed pages can enhance your search engine ranking. The reason is because a well-structured document contains a natural hierarchy of topical logic that you can tap into, placing keywords in helpful places.

Images should always contain `alt` text for accessibility reasons, but this can also be used to increase search engine rankings by judicious use of keywords in the text. Similarly, if headings using structured, hierarchical h1, h2,... tags contain keywords, this can increase the site's ranking with some engines. Other methods for increasing search engine rankings include ensuring that imagemaps have alternative text menus, putting essential text as close to the top of the page as possible by designing your table and frame layouts well, and putting `noframes` content on frameset pages.

Of course, nothing can beat a site where the content itself is well written, fits the description of the site, and makes good use of the site keywords in its text. Aside from increasing search engine rankings, good content increases word-of-mouth promotion by your site's visitors.

9

WORKING MORE EFFICIENTLY IN DREAMWEAVER

IN THIS PART

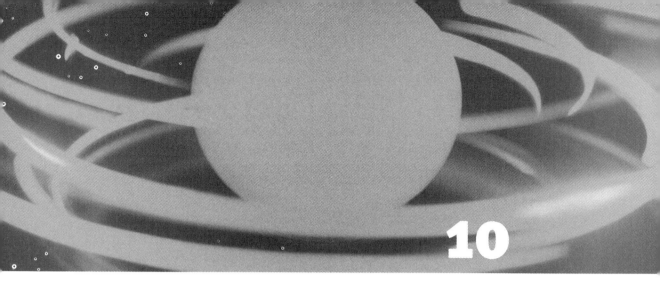

10

THE WORKSPACE: WINDOWS, TOOLBARS, AND PANELS

THE DREAMWEAVER MX INTERFACE, IN-DEPTH

Dreamweaver has so many tools and features it's unlikely that you'll use all of them for every site. Some you might not ever need at all, particularly if you're an advanced Web developer. However, knowing all about what's available in Dreamweaver will help you maximize your workspace to put oft-used tools within easy reach while removing extraneous toolbars and panels from view. Most importantly, to feel truly comfortable with the Dreamweaver environment, you'll want to know how to move things around to suit your needs and work style.

WORKSPACE LAYOUTS

If you're using Windows, your first decision is choosing a workspace layout. When you installed Dreamweaver, you were prompted to select an initial Workspace Setup (see Figure 10.1). If you've used previous versions of Dreamweaver, you possibly chose the Dreamweaver 4 workspace, opting for familiarity. New Dreamweaver users most likely opted for the Dreamweaver MX Workspace. Now that you're familiar with Dreamweaver itself, you have the opportunity to change your workspace, if you desire.

Figure 10.1
The Workspace Setup dialog box appears when first installing Dreamweaver on a Windows system. You can also access Workspace Setup from the Preferences dialog box.

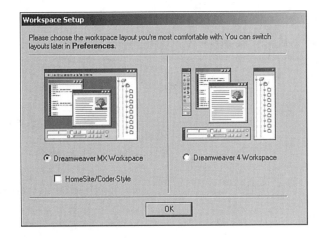

To change the workspace, do the following:

1. Select Edit, Preferences.

2. In the General category, click the Change Workspace button.

3. Select a workspace from the Workspace Setup dialog box (see Figure 10.2).

4. Click OK to return to the Preferences dialog box.

5. Click OK to close out of the Preferences dialog box.

The changes you made to the workspace won't take effect until you exit and restart Dreamweaver.

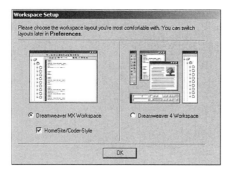

Figure 10.2
Selecting a workspace from the Workspace Setup dialog box.

The workspace layouts are

- **Dreamweaver MX Workspace**—All windows, panels, and inspectors are contained within one application window, in the same manner as Fireworks and other Macromedia applications (see Figure 10.3). All panels are docked on the right side of the application window. Documents are opened in Design view by default, and multiple documents are tabbed at the bottom of the Document window.

- **HomeSite/Coder-Style**—Similar to the Dreamweaver MX Workspace, but with panels docked on the left in the same manner as HomeSite and ColdFusion Studio (see Figure 10.4). This workspace opens all documents in Code view by default.

Dreamweaver refers to a Document *window* in the Dreamweaver MX workspace, although it's actually a pane contained within the application window. This is intended to provide consistency in terminology between workspaces.

10

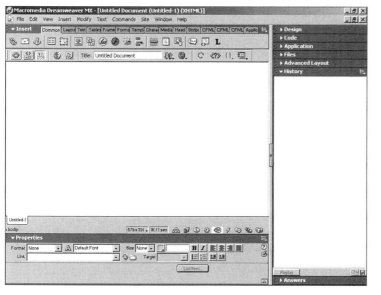

Figure 10.3
The Dreamweaver MX workspace contains all documents, panels, and inspectors in one application window.

Figure 10.4
The HomeSite/Coder-Style work-space is similar to that of the Dreamweaver MX workspace, but the panel groups are positioned on the left side of the window.

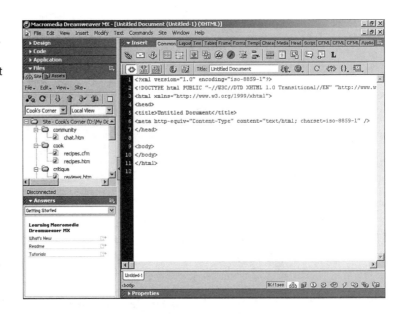

- **Dreamweaver 4 Workspace**—Good for users of previous versions of Dreamweaver. Documents and panels are contained in separate windows (although panels are docked together by default), and documents open in Design view by default. Other open applications remain visible behind these multiple windows, which can be distracting unless you're familiar with this workspace (see Figure 10.5).

Figure 10.5
The Dreamweaver 4 workspace is a carry-over from previous versions. The panels and documents appear in separate windows.

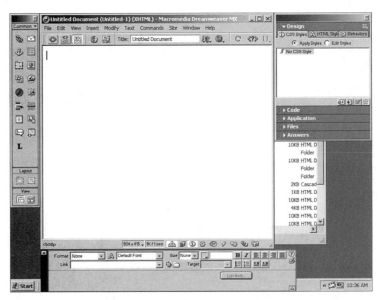

No matter which workspace you choose, it can be customized as you wish. You can select the Dreamweaver MX workspace but manually move the panel groups to the left side of the screen. Panels that are regrouped or undocked from the panel group remain in that new state even in future

Mac users only have the floating layout available.

Dreamweaver sessions. The Property inspector is initially collapsed, showing only the most common options. If you expand the Property inspector, it remains expanded in future sessions unless you manually collapse it.

EXPLORING THE DOCUMENT WINDOW

The Document window is where all the action takes place. The Document window contains a title bar, menus, toolbars, and a status bar. All the other panels, inspectors, and toolbars exist to add to or modify the contents of the Document window. The Document window displays a visual representation of the site in Design view (see Figure 10.6), the HTML code for the site in Code view (see Figure 10.7), or a split window containing both the design and the code (see Figure 10.8).

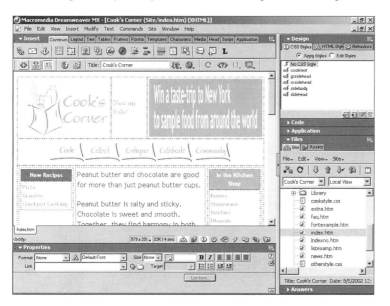

Figure 10.6
Design view enables you to work in a what-you-see-is-what-you-get (WYSIWYG) atmosphere.

Most likely, you'll use all three views at some point or other. Even with the advancements of WYSIWYG development environments, it's still good to know how to get your hands dirty, so to speak, in the markup.

In Code and Design view, changes you make to the code aren't reflected in the Design pane unless you refresh the view. You can do this by clicking the Refresh button on either the Property inspector or the Document toolbar, or simply by pressing F5.

Figure 10.7
Code view enables you to develop or edit the markup directly.

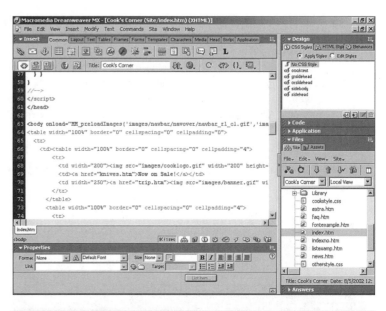

Figure 10.8
Code and Design view enables you to make changes to either pane and see how changes in one affect the other.

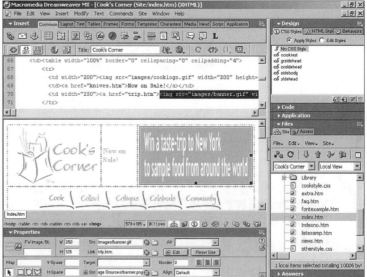

Title Bar

The title bar displays the title and filename of the open document. Aside from being a reminder of the name of the page on which you're currently working, it can also serve as a reminder that you haven't yet given the page a title. As you work, an asterisk is appended to the filename, signifying that you've made unsaved changes to the document. Use the Save keyboard shortcut (Command-S) [Ctrl+S] or select File, Save to save your file.

Menu Bar

The menu bar contains nearly all the commands and features of Dreamweaver. Most of these comands are also accessible from panels and the Property inspector, as well as context menus that pop up when you (Control-click) [right-click] your mouse.

➡️ *Still don't have quite the layout or menu options you'd like? Read more in "Extending the Dreamweaver Interface" in the "Troubleshooting" section at the end of this chapter.*

Toolbars

Two toolbars are available in the Document window. To toggle these toolbars from view, select View, Toolbars and select from the two options. Both toolbars can be visible at the same time, but they'll cut down on your workspace.

The Standard toolbar contains the usual File, Save, Copy/Cut, and Paste commands (see Figure 10.9). If you already know the keyboard shortcuts for these common commands—they're the same as those for most Windows or Mac applications—this toolbar simply takes up screen real estate.

Figure 10.9
The Standard toolbar is useful for novices, but it takes up valuable screen real estate.

The Document toolbar, shown in Figure 10.10, also contains options available elsewhere in Dreamweaver, but it's convenient to have them at your fingertips (see Table 10.1).

Figure 10.10
The Document toolbar makes it easy to switch views, title the page, and preview the document in a browser.

Table 10.1   Document Toolbar Options

Option	Function
Show Code View	Changes the Document window to Code view.
Show Code and Design Views	Changes the Document window to the split Code and Design view.
Show Design View	Changes the Document window to Design view.
Live Data View	When designing dynamic database-driven sites, this displays the document in Design view with live data pulled from the connected database.
Document Title	Has a text field to enter a title for the page; if you've already added a title, it will appear in this field.

Table 10.1   Continued

Option	Function
File Management	Activates a drop-down menu containing the Get/Check In and Put/Check Out commands, Design Notes, and the Locate in Site command. Using the Put command uploads the open Document to the remote server, whereas the Get command downloads the file of the same name from the server and prompts you to overwrite the existing local file.
Preview/Debug in Browser	Activates a drop-down menu giving you access to the Preview in Browser and Debug in Browser commands and enables you to configure the Browser List (also found in the Preferences dialog box).
Refresh Design View	Available only in Code and Design view, this refreshes the Design pane when you make code changes in the code pane.
Reference	Opens the Reference panel in the Code panels group to access information on HTML, CSS, and other scripting and server technologies.
Code Navigation	Available only in Code view, this enables you to set breakpoints and navigate through JavaScripts in the document.
View Options	Activates a drop-down menu enabling you to change the visibility of head content, rulers and grids, and borders around certain elements in Design view. Also lets you change the order of the panes in the Code and Design view to position the Design pane on top.

Status Bar

The Status bar is located at the bottom of the Document window (see Figure 10.11). It provides information about the weight and download time for the document. Dreamweaver calculates an approximate download time based on the Connection Speed setting in the Status bar category of the Preferences dialog box (Edit, Preferences). You can change these settings to calculate download time for faster or slower means of connection.

Figure 10.11
The Status bar displays the Tag selector, Window Size selector, Download size/speed indicator, and possibly the Launcher bar.

Window Size Selector

You can change the dimensions of your default screen size to match those of your typical site visitor. This enables you to design for a wide range of browser dimensions or to test the general appearance of the document in a specific configuration. You can create custom window size dimensions in the Preferences dialog box, available by selecting Edit Sizes from the Window Size Selector pop-up menu.

If the Document window is maximized, you cannot change the Window Size Selector settings. The window size is automatically set to the maximum available screen real estate.

Choosing the Right Viewing Size

More and more Web visitors are using upgraded monitors, enabling them to view pages in a broader array of colors and at a higher resolution. As a result, many designers are now developing based on an 800×600 screen size or even higher. For the most part, this is acceptable, but keep in mind that there are always those who are still satisfied with 640×480 displays. WebTV owners have a display size of only 560×384 (and an equally limited range of colors and other limitations).

When choosing a window size in Dreamweaver, also keep in mind the chrome of most browsers. Chrome is the space taken up by the browser's status bar, toolbars, and menus. Many of the default Window Size Selector settings take this into account.

Tag Selector

The Tag Selector combines the best of working in Design view with the need to occasionally—and sometimes frequently—make changes to the underlying code by hand. The Tag Selector shows the HTML tags (see Figure 10.12) relative to the position of the cursor in Design view.

Tag Selector

Figure 10.12
The Tag Selector allows you quick access to tags used in your document.

This feature is often overlooked because there are so many methods for accessing and editing code. But when you're working on nested tables or have multiple layers on the page, the Tag Selector can help you find your place in the code. Just click a tag in the Tag Selector to highlight it in Design view. You can then make modifications to that element in the Property inspector or by using the menus and panels. You can also select a tag from the Tag Selector and then switch to Code view. The element and its contents will be highlighted.

The Tag Selector also makes deleting blocks of content easy. You can delete tables or blocks of text easily by choosing their container tag in the Tag Selector and then pressing the (Backspace) [Delete] key to erase it.

➪ *All your document content disappears upon deleting a tag? Find out why, and how to avoid this problem, in "Deleting Content" in the "Troubleshooting" section later in this chapter.*

Finally, the Tag Selector can be used to edit tags. Select a tag, and then bring up the context menu (Ctrl-click) [right-click]. The context menu provides one of many methods for setting the class of a tag, used extensively with Cascading Style Sheets. You can also use the context menu to access the Quick Tag Editor.

The Tag Selector isn't visible in Code view because other code tools are more useful in this environment. Thus, if you're using the HomeSite/Coder-Style workspace, the Tag Selector doesn't appear at the bottom of the Document window.

⇨ *For more information on the Quick Tag Editor, see "Editing Markup Using Macromedia Dreamweaver MX," p. 250.*

Launcher Bar

The last element of the Status bar is the Launcher bar. The Launcher is displayed only if you've selected Show Icons in Panels and Launcher in the Panels category of the Preferences dialog box. These buttons make opening and closing various panels and inspectors easier without having to scroll through the Document window menus or poke around the panel groups. The only downside to making the Launcher bar visible is that it can limit the tags listed in the Tag Selector because of crowding in the Status bar. If you're using the Tag Selector extensively, you might decide not to keep the Launcher bar visible.

The following panels are included in the Launcher bar by default:

- Site
- Assets
- CSS Styles
- Behaviors
- History
- Bindings
- Server Behaviors
- Components
- Databases

If screen space is an issue, add the Insert panel button to the Launcher bar. You can then toggle the visibility of the Insert panel with the press of one button, eliminating it from view when you work but still having it readily accessible.

Figure 10.13 shows the Launcher bar and its related options.

Figure 10.13
The Launcher bar provides quick access to panels from the status bar.

Panels and inspectors can be added to or removed from the Launcher bar in the Preferences dialog box (see Figure 10.14). If you're not doing any development with databases and advanced server technologies, you can eliminate related panels from the Launcher bar. You might want to replace them with options for the Layers and Timeline panels if you're using those elements in your sites. If you're doing a lot of hand-coding, the Snippets panel is another good choice.

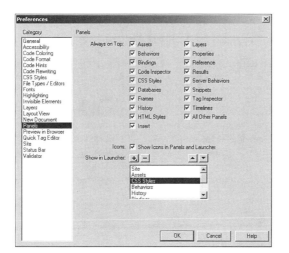

Figure 10.14
Modify the Launcher bar in the Preferences dialog box.

To modify the buttons on the Launcher bar, follow these steps:

1. Select Edit, Preferences from the menu.

2. Select the Panels category.

3. Check the Show Icons in Panels and Launcher option.

4. In the Show in Launcher option, do the following:

   • Select an item from the list and press the minus (-) button to remove it from the Launcher.

   • Press the plus (+) button and select a panel from the pop-up menu to add an item to the Launcher.

   • Use the up and down arrows to rearrange the list of panels.

5. Click OK to exit the Preferences dialog box.

WORKING WITH THE INSERT BAR

One of the most useful panels in the workspace is the Insert bar—also called the Insert panel group (see Figure 10.15). The Insert bar is similar to other panel groups except that it can be docked only at the top or bottom of the screen. If you attempt to dock the Insert bar with the other panel groups, it instead becomes a floating panel group. In the classic Dreamweaver 4 view (which includes Macs), the Insert bar appears in a vertical orientation—yet still separated from the other panel groups—with a pull-out menu containing the list of categories (see Figure 10.16).

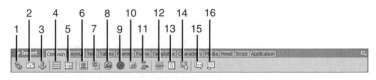

Figure 10.15
The Insert bar contains numerous tabs and buttons that assist you in quickly adding features to your pages.

1. Hyperlink
2. Email
3. Named Anchor
4. Insert Table
5. Draw Layer
6. Image
7. Image Placeholder
8. Fireworks HTML

9. Flash
10. Rollover Image
11. Navigation bar
12. Horizontal rule
13. Date
14. Tabular data
15. Comment
16. Tag Chooser

Figure 10.16
The floating Insert bar, found in Dreamweaver MX for Mac and Dreamweaver 4 view for Windows.

The Insert bar contains 12 tabs (a 13th appears if you're designing a dynamic page using a server technology), each containing icons for the most frequently used options in that category (see Table 10.2).

Table 10.2   Insert Bar Tabs

Tab	Function
Common	Contains image, table, link, layer, third-party code (Fireworks), comment, and other commonly used objects.
Layout	Enables toggling of standard and layout views for creating tables and provides the tools to use Layout view to draw tables and cells.
Text	Adds text formatting such as bold and italic and paragraph formatting such as headings and lists. It can also be used to access the Font Tag Editor to set multiple attributes at once.
Tables	Used to insert tables and related table elements.

Table 10.2   Continued

Tab	Function
Frames	Creates a frame-based layout from the many object options and adds noframes content.
Forms	Inserts form containers and elements.
Templates	Used to create templates and add editable, optional, and repeating regions and tables.
Characters	Inserts special characters such as copyright and monetary symbols and opens a dialog box containing additional characters.
Media	Used to insert Flash, Shockwave, Java applets, plug-ins, and ActiveX controls.
Head	Inserts head content such as keywords, descriptions, and links to external style sheets.
Script	Adds scripts and server-side includes to the document. Also contains a noscript object to include for browsers that have scripting disabled or unavailable.
Contextual Server Technology	Appears only when creating dynamic pages using ASP, JSP, PHP, or other server technologies and contains objects that can be inserted in Code view.
Applications	Adds server behaviors.

The Insert Bar Buttons

To insert an element from one of the Insert bar categories, position the cursor at the insertion point and then click the object button in the Insert bar (or drag the object button to the insertion point). In the case of inserting images or creating links, among others, a dialog box appears in order to complete the insertion, such as selecting an image file or defining in the link parameters. To insert placeholders for these elements, when available (such as for images), press the (Option) [Ctrl] key while clicking the Object button. You can then select a final image or fill in other required attributes later in the development process.

Insert Bar Controls

The Insert bar can be set to display buttons as text only, icons only, or both text and icons. To do this, follow these steps:

1. Select Edit, Preferences, and the Preferences dialog box appears.

2. Highlight the General option in the Category list. The Preferences dialog box displays general options.

3. Find the Insert Panel drop-down menu, and select your preference for the Insert bar style.

4. Click OK.

10

The Insert bar now reflects your changes.

When you use the text and text and icons settings, the number of objects in a tab can exceed the available space on the bar. In that case, a small arrow appears in the lower-left corner of the Insert bar. Click the arrow to view additional objects.

USING THE PROPERTY INSPECTOR

The Property inspector is arguably the most important tool in Dreamweaver (see Figure 10.17). Whereas other panels place objects on the page, the Property inspector modifies the attributes of those objects. The context of the Property inspector changes depending on the selected element or view. As with all panels, the Property inspector can be moved. It can be docked either above or below the Document window or undocked to become a floating panel.

Figure 10.17
The Property inspector changes with the context of the selection.

The Property inspector is initially in a minimal state, containing only the most popular attributes for an element. In many cases, however, additional attributes are available in the expanded Property inspector. To expand the panel, click the arrow in the bottom-right corner.

In addition to the standard text fields and buttons, the Property inspector contains several other features. The color picker is used to select a color for text, table borders, and other objects. The Point-to-File and Folder icons are used to locate files to insert images or links; the Quick Tag Editor, signified by a pencil-and-paper icon on the right side of the Property inspector, enables you to add element attributes not found on the inspector. Selecting the question mark icon launches the Using Dreamweaver help system.

WORKING WITH PANELS

Unless you've changed the default workspace to remove all the panels and inspectors from view, you'll see that the Document window is surrounded by groupings of additional options and site information. Some of these panels are critical to the ease-of-use of Dreamweaver, whereas others can be removed without fanfare.

Most of the panels appear to the right of the Document window in both the Dreamweaver MX and Dreamweaver 4 workspace settings. In the HomeSite/Coder workspace, most of the panels appear to the left of the Document window. The Insert bar and Property inspector, however, can appear only at the top or bottom of the workspace.

Panels are grouped by default in logical panel groups. Of course, this logic might or might not apply to your workflow. The arrangement of panels into groups and even the panel group names can be modified to meet your needs.

To open a panel group, click the arrow to the left of the panel group name. This button is a toggle, so panel groups can be minimized when not in use (see Figure 10.18).

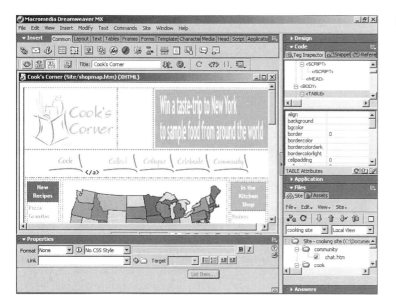

Figure 10.18
Click the arrow next to panel groups to open and close panels. Here, you see Design, Code, Application, Files, and Answers, with the Code and Files panel groups open.

Arranging Panel Groups

Each panel group has several controls (see Figure 10.19). The icon to the right of the panel group name activates a drop-down options menu containing several commands within the context of the panels contained in the group. At the bottom of each menu is also a series of panel group commands.

Figure 10.19
The panel group controls include a gripper and a drop-down menu with group commands.

To the left of the group name is a tool called the *gripper*. Clicking and dragging the gripper for a group enables you to undock that panel group. These floating panels can then be moved around the workspace. To dock a floating panel group, drag it by its gripper until the insert indicator is positioned where you want in the panel dock. Thus, you can use the gripper to rearrange the order of the panel groups in the panel dock.

Panels can be moved into other existing or new panel groups. To do this, follow these steps:

1. Select the tab for the panel you want to relocate.

2. Open the options menu for the panel group in which the panel is currently located.

3. Select the Group [*panel name*] With command.

4. Select an existing group, or select New Panel Group to create a new panel group.

The Dreamweaver help files claim that you can drag a panel tab out of the panel group to undock it from that group. This is incorrect. If you attempt this, an alert box appears warning you to use the options menu commands to regroup panels.

The moved panel immediately appears in its new group. Or, if you created a new panel group, open the options menu in the new group and select Rename Panel Group to give it an appropriate name. You can then add other panels to the new group.

Panel groups can be sized to take up more or less space in the panel dock. When you position the mouse between panel groups, the cursor changes into a double-headed arrow, which can be clicked and dragged up or down to modify the size of expanded panel groups. To maximize a panel group to take up as much space in the panel dock as possible, select Maximize Panel Group from the panel menu. This minimizes other open panel groups to give the select group full use of the vertical space.

If you're making extensive use of the Reference panel, move it into its own panel group and then undock that group. You can then expand the size of the panel without resizing the Document window. As an added benefit, the floating panel remains on top of the Document window even as you work on a page, eliminating the need to switch between viewing the panel and your document.

Some panels—particularly the Reference panel, located in the Code panel group—benefit from additional horizontal space as well as vertical. Position the mouse cursor between the panel dock and the Document window until it becomes a double-headed arrow; then click and drag horizontally to give additional space to the panel dock. Keep in mind, however, that this decreases the size of the Document window.

If you're not using a panel group at all, you can close it by selecting Close Panel Group from the options menu for that group. To reopen a closed panel group, select it from the Window menu in the Document window.

Exploring the Panels

Individuals use Dreamweaver MX differently, combining aspects of menu commands, context menus, and panel-based commands along with other options to work quickly and efficiently. In this section, you'll get an idea of what the various panels do and learn to make some modifications to them should you need to do so.

Design Panels

The Design panel group contains panels that control the styles and behaviors of the elements on the page. The three panels in the group are HTML Styles (see Figure 10.20), CSS Styles (see Figure 10.21), and Behaviors (see Figure 10.22).

Figure 10.20
The HTML Styles panel modifies element attributes to set styles.

Figure 10.21
The CSS Styles panel is used to define and modify Cascading Style Sheets, which is the preferred method for establishing the presentation of elements.

Figure 10.22
The Behaviors panel is used to add JavaScript behaviors to create navigation bars, preload images, make jump menus and pop-up menus, and design disjoint rollovers.

➪ *For more information about HTML Styles, see Chapter 15, "Designing with Style," p. 265. For information on behaviors, see Chapter 23, "Rollovers and Navigation Bars," p. 431.*

In addition to the three panels grouped here, some developers choose to add the Frames and Layers panels, making more of the design elements available in one panel and eliminating the need for the Advanced Layout panel group.

Files Panels

The Files panel group contains the necessary tools to control the files and assets for the entire site.

Site Panel

The Site panel can be expanded into a full-size Site window (see Figure 10.23). In the integrated Dreamweaver MX workspace, the expanded window replaces the Document window until it's collapsed or a file is opened. In the Dreamweaver 4 (and Mac) workspace, the Site window becomes a distinct window, so both the Site window and Document window can remain on the screen.

Figure 10.23
The Site panel is used to maintain all the files for the site and communicate with the remote server.

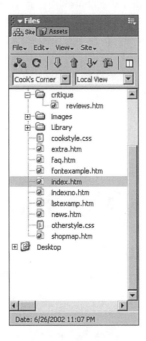

Assets Panel

The Assets panel, shown in Figure 10.24, contains all the assets of the site—links, colors, images, multimedia, scripts, templates, and library items.

⇨ *For more detailed information about the Site panel, see "Establishing a Web Site," p. 10, and "Uploading Pages with the Site Panel," p.158. For more about the Assets panel, see "Working with the Assets Panel," p. 198.*

Code Panels

The Code panels can be used in either Code or Design view.

Tag Inspector Panel

The Tag Inspector lists each of the tags in the site; clicking a tag in the Inspector lists the attributes of the tag and highlights that element in the Document window (see Figure 10.25). The tag's attributes can be edited directly in the Tag Inspector or in the Document window.

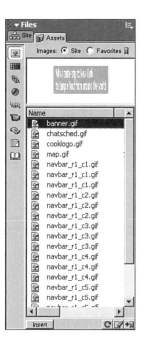

Figure 10.24
The Assets panel stores the intangibles for the site, such as color choices and external links.

10

Figure 10.25
The Tag Inspector puts all the selected tag's attributes in one editable list.

Snippets Panel

The Snippets panel contains predefined code snippets, grouped in related folders (see Figure 10.26). You can also add your own snippets and folders in this panel.

10

Figure 10.26
The Snippets panel contains small, reusable portions of code, which can be inserted into a page.

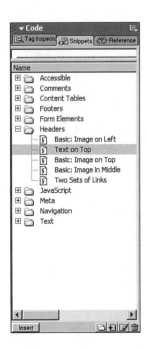

Reference Panel

The Reference panel provides reference material for HTML, CSS, JavaScript, dynamic server technologies, and accessibility issues (see Figure 10.27).

Figure 10.27
The Reference panel is a tremendous resource of Web development information.

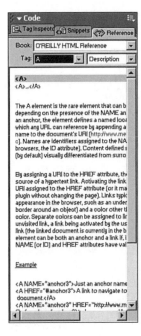

⇨ *For more information on the Tag Inspector and Snippets features, see "Editing Markup Using Macromedia Dreamweaver MX," p. 250.*

Application Panels

When you're creating dynamic pages using databases and advanced server technologies, you'll want to open the Application panel. Initially, each of the panels in this group prompts you to configure the test server and other requirements (if you haven't already done so in the Site Definition).

If you don't design dynamic pages, you can close this panel group entirely to save space.

Advanced Layout Panels

The Advanced Layoutpanel group contains tools for controlling non-table-based layouts.

Layers Panel

The Layers panel lists all the layers in the document and controls their visibility and z-index (see Figure 10.28). You can prevent layers from overlapping by clicking the check box at the top of the panel.

Figure 10.28
The Layers panel controls the visibility of layers.

Frames Panel

The Frames panel represents the frames and frameset for the page (see Figure 10.29). The frameset and each frame displays its name, making it useful when targeting frames during development.

Figure 10.29
The Frames panel displays a visual representation of the frameset for the document, along with the name of each frame.

For more information about layers, see Chapter 20, p. 369, and Chapter 24, p. 445. For more on frames, see Chapter 7, p. 121, and Chapter 19, p. 351.

Timelines Panel

The Timelines panel is used to animate layers (see Figure 10.30). Like the Property inspector, the width of the Timelines panel means it can be docked only above or below the Document window.

Figure 10.30
Layer animation is controlled by the Timelines panel.

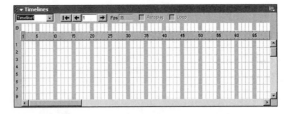

For more detailed information on layer animation and timelines, see Chapter 24, p. 445.

Results Panel

The Results panel automatically appears to display the results of searches, validation checks, and various reports.

Search Panel

The Search panel is displayed at the bottom of the workspace whenever you issue a Find command (see Figure 10.31). This panel displays the results of a search; you can click the results to edit them in the Document window. Buttons on the left side of the panel enable you to initiate or cancel Find commands.

Figure 10.31
The Search panel lists the results of searches in a document or site.

Validation Panel

The Validation panel, shown in Figure 10.32, lists any coding errors in the site or document when you validate the site (by selecting File, Check Page, Validate Markup/Validate As XML). This validation can also be initiated directly from the panel, and corrections can be located from it.

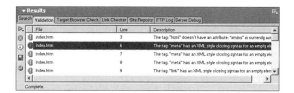

Figure 10.32
The Validation panel lists coding errors.

Target Browser Check Panel

The Target Browser Check panel, shown in Figure 10.33, lists browser compatibility issues as a result of running the Check Target Browsers report (File, Check Page, Check Target Browsers or directly from the Target Browser Check panel). The panel provides options to save the report for future reference. By highlighting an item in the report and clicking the More Info button, you can view a dialog box explaining exactly why an item is marked. If you double-click an entry, it opens in the Document window in Code and Design view with the offending code highlighted.

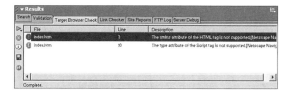

Figure 10.33
The Target Browser Check panel lists elements that can't be viewed properly in the target browser.

Link Checker Panel

The Link Checker panel, shown in Figure 10.34, lists the results of the Check Links report (File, Check Page, Check Links or run from within the Link Checker panel). This report lists broken links, orphaned files within the site, and all external links.

Figure 10.34
The Link Checker panel enables you to fix broken links, eliminate orphaned files, and manually validate external links.

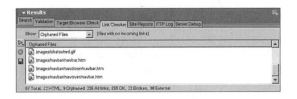

Site Reports Panel

The Site Reports panel, shown in Figure 10.35, displays the results of the Site Report (Site, Reports from either the Document window or Site panel menus). The Site Report can be quite extensive, depending on the options you choose when initiating the report. As with the other Results panels, you can use this report to get more information on the items listed and use the items to locate the specific code in question to make modifications.

Figure 10.35
The Site Reports panel lists problems found with accessibility, incomplete tags, or missing alt attributes.

FTP Log Panel

The FTP Log tracks communication with the remote server (see Figure 10.36). You can also enter commands directly to the server from this panel, which is useful to experienced developers.

Figure 10.36
The FTP Log tracks the communication between the local and remote servers for each session.

Server Debug Panel

The Server Debug panel is used with dynamic pages to locate errors in the code (see Figure 10.37). To use this feature, select View, Server Debug from the menu. The Server Debug panel displays the results of this command, including the server variables and values, execution time, and SQL queries on the page. If you didn't configure your testing server correctly, this panel prompts you through the required steps.

Figure 10.37
The Server Debug panel displays the results of the server debugging feature when developing dynamic database-driven sites.

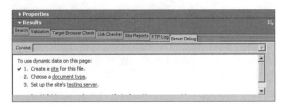

⇨ *For more about validation and browser checking, see Chapter 28, p. 517. For more information on site testing and reports, see Chapter 30, p. 543. Dynamic pages are covered in minimal detail in Chapter 6, p. 97, although the full potential of them is beyond the scope of this book.*

Answers Panel

The Answers panel provides application help and resources for Dreamweaver itself (see Figure 10.38). You can use this panel to access the Help files and tutorials. You can also use it to connect to Macromedia tech support to get information about updates to Dreamweaver and to download extensions.

This panel is useful when you're first starting to use Dreamweaver, but its value diminishes over time as you become familiar with the application. This is an easy panel to discard to save space in the panel dock.

If you find yourself using this panel as a resource, you can increase its usefulness by regrouping the Reference panel here. That will put all your application and development support in one panel group.

10

Figure 10.38
The Answers panel provides access to the Macromedia Support Center as well as local help files.

History Panel

The History panel maintains a list of all your actions in the current document (see Figure 10.39). You can use this list to create new commands for repetitive, time-consuming actions. You can also use the History panel to undo multiple steps at once or to replay steps.

The last item on the list is the most recent, and the panel scrolls upward. To undo the last several actions, drag the slider that's to the left of the steps upward to select the steps you want to undo. After you've made your selection, continue editing. The selected steps are not undone until you take another action that overwrites those steps in the history.

To repeat steps, use the slider to select them and then click the Copy Steps button.

After you've undone multiple items and overwritten them with other steps, you cannot redo the original steps.

The History panel tracks only a limited number of steps per session. You can increase or decrease this number in the Maximum Number of History Steps field of the General Preferences settings.

Figure 10.39
The History panel tracks every action you've performed on the current document, enabling you to retrace your steps and even create commands based on repetitive actions.

To create a command, select a series of steps with the slider and then click the Save As Command button. You'll be prompted to give the command a name, and the new command will appear on the Commands menu.

CODE INSPECTOR

The Code Inspector contains all the same features as the Code view but is located on a floating panel (see Figure 10.40). The Code view was new in Dreamweaver 4, and the Code Inspector remains primarily for long-term Dreamweaver developers who were used to accessing their code in this manner.

Figure 10.40
The Code Inspector duplicates the functionality of the Code view in the Document window. The only advantage of the Code Inspector is its capability to be positioned elsewhere on the screen because it's a floating panel.

TROUBLESHOOTING

Extending the Dreamweaver Interface

I'd still like further interface features to meet my preferences. Do I have additional options?

You can modify menus yourself or download extensions from the Macromedia Exchange. To learn more about customizing menus and other aspects of the MX interface, see the Macromedia Dreamweaver Support Center at `http://www.macromedia.com/support/dreamweaver/custom/customizing_dwmx/`.

Deleting Content

I selected a tag and deleted it, only to find all my content had disappeared. What happened?

You likely selected the body tag and pressed Delete while attempting to delete another tag or some portion of your content. When you use the Tag Selector for deletion, select the body tag, and then press Delete, the head content remains but the body tag returns to a completely empty state. Of course, this also means you should use this feature with care when selecting the body or other large containers on a page.

PEER TO PEER: DREAMWEAVER AND PERSONAL INTERFACE STYLE

Is there a way to approach the Dreamweaver MX interface from a perspective of standards and best practices? Is it better to use one method provided in the program over another? The answer is *it depends on you.*

Interface design is a tricky thing. You know this because you design or are learning to design Web sites, which require that you develop some kind of interface for your site visitors. You already know that audience will help drive this.

Prior to the interface advances that have now been made available in Dreamweaver MX, the default interface was difficult for many to deal with. This became truer over time because Dreamweaver expanded from a Web design tool to one that also accommodates developers. So, you're dealing with a range of people, which means you're dealing with a range of learning types and spatial skills.

It has taken a bit of time for Macromedia to extend the interface in such a way that it can suit a variety of needs, but as you can see, the options now available to you are quite powerful and extensive.

One of the greatest challenges to Web builders today is creating a desktop working environment that offers all the tools to manage tasks at hand, collaborate with others assigned to the task, and do these things with efficiency and speed.

When you study the Dreamweaver MX interface, it's easy to see that it is a program destined to supply you with as many options as possible. In some ways, this can get very confusing because figuring out which option will help you best perform a task becomes difficult. On the other hand, having so many options means you can set up a situation in which you work effectively with the tool. Your office mate might have a completely different interface configuration, but you are still able to collaborate effectively because you are each relating to the interface in the way that works best for you.

Try different configurations of the interface, and determine which one you feel most comfortable with. Ultimately, your relationship to the Dreamweaver interface will be a uniquely personal one. And, the more extensibility that Macromedia offers, the more variations on the theme will be found.

10

MANAGING ASSETS

IN THIS CHAPTER

KEEPING TRACK OF SITE COMPONENTS

Designing and developing a working, growing Web site often means keeping track of an ever-increasing assortment of HTML pages, images, links, color schemes, templates, Flash, and multi-media. As your site grows, it's harder and harder to keep everything in one place. Even if you organize your site well with folders for images, multimedia, and style sheets, you'll soon find the need to add a separate folder for navigational images or perhaps another for movies or articles relating to a particular section of your site. Navigating to these separate folders time after time during the development process can become tedious and fraught with opportunities for mistakes.

Links and color schemes present different challenges, of course. These items aren't stored in files, so you can't just navigate the folders of your site to find the link you used on one page or that very color of blue you used on another. If the same color scheme isn't used from page to page, site consistency is lost. Templates can solve the color consistency issue to some extent, as can Cascading Style Sheets (CSS), but they certainly don't completely solve the problem.

Enter Dreamweaver's Assets panel (see Figure 11.1). Dreamweaver stores every major element of a site in a cache. The Assets panel is a complement to the Site panel, and indeed, they're both docked in the same Files panel group. The Site panel lists the tangible files for the site. The Assets panel lists the intangibles—the colors, URLs, templates, images, and multimedia used on the site's pages.

Figure 11.1
The Assets panel breaks the site cache into nine categories, each of which can be viewed as a site-wide list or a user-generated favorites list of oft-used assets.

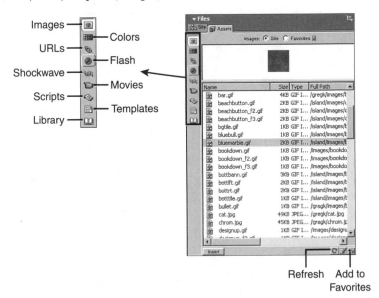

WORKING WITH THE ASSETS PANEL

The Assets panel doesn't recognize every asset type, but it does recognize many of the most common ones. The left side of the Assets panel has a column of buttons that let you choose the category of assets to display—Images, Colors, URLs, Flash, Shockwave, Movies, Scripts, Templates, and Library. The right side of the panel lists the assets within the selected category. A preview version of a selected asset is displayed above the list.

Unfortunately, Dreamweaver doesn't track assets such as audio files, Adobe Acrobat PDFs, or Java applets. Also, don't be misled by the generic Movies category because it doesn't list unsupported media formats such as Windows Media or RealVideo.

> **Expand the preview area by dragging** the splitter bar between the preview and list areas.

⇨ *For more on the Library category of the Assets panel, see Chapter 13, "Building a Library," p. 225.*

CREATING A FAVORITES LIST AND FAVORITES FOLDER

The Assets panel has two different views. The Site list provides a complete list of all the assets in every folder and page of the site. The Favorites list displays only the assets you choose to put there (see Figure 11.2). If you create a well-planned Favorites list for your site, you'll have all the colors, URLs, and other elements within easy reach while still having convenient access to the less-used assets from the Site list. To change between the two views, click the Site or Favorites radio button at the top of the panel.

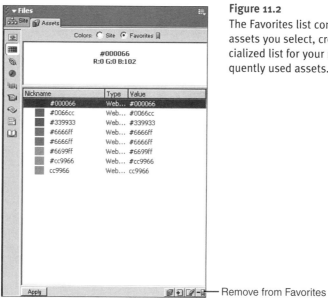

Figure 11.2
The Favorites list contains only assets you select, creating a specialized list for your most frequently used assets.

Remove from Favorites

Adding an Asset to the Favorites List

To add an asset to the Favorites list, follow these steps:

1. Select an item in the Site list.

2. Click the Add to Favorites button on the bottom-right of the panel, or (Command-click) [right-click] and select Add to Favorites from the context menu.

3. A confirmation alert will appear (see Figure 11.3). Click OK.

Figure 11.3
This alert box confirms the addition of an asset to the Favorites list. You can opt to remove this confirmation from future additions.

You can also add images and media files to the Favorites list directly from the Site panel. Select an appropriate file and select Add to Favorites from the context menu. The exact name of this menu option changes depending on the type of asset—in the case of an image, the option is labeled Add to Image Favorites.

Assets added to the Favorites list remain on the list unless you manually remove them. Even if you refresh or re-create the site cache to update the Assets panel, the Favorites list remains the same. To remove an asset from this list, select it and then click the Remove from Favorites button.

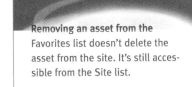

Removing an asset from the Favorites list doesn't delete the asset from the site. It's still accessible from the Site list.

➪ *Have you ever designed a site and lost track of exactly which site belongs to which obscure URL or which shade of blue you're using for a particular item? This can happen even when using the Assets panel because URLs are often not descriptive even in a list, and all the hex values and slight color variations begin to blur in your mind. Find out how to avoid losing track of your site's stuff in the "Nicknaming Assets" topic of the "Troubleshooting" section, found at the end of this chapter.*

Creating a New Favorites Folder

Even using the Favorites list, it's easy to become overwhelmed with assets, particularly on a large site. An advantage the Favorites list has over the Site list is that it enables you to organize assets into groups called Favorites folders.

Favorites folders can be useful for organizing and quickly locating images you want to use together on your pages. For example, on a cooking site, you might have movies with demonstrations of cooking techniques, gadgets, and recipes. By grouping these into Favorites folders, you'll know exactly where to look to find the movie you seek. For organizational overkill, you can even nest Favorites folders.

To create a Favorites folder, do the following:

1. Click the New Favorites Folder at the bottom of the Assets panel.

2. Type in a name for the folder.

3. Drag assets from the Favorites list into the new folder.

Of course, this feature is purely for convenience. The actual location of the files within your local site remains the same.

ASSET TYPES

Along with their general usage as assets, each type of asset also has some specific purpose or limitations.

Images

The Images category lists any image files that you've placed within your local site, even if you've not yet used them on a page yet. Dreamweaver recognizes GIFs, JPEGs, and PNG formats.

⮕ *Forget to give sliced image portions a unique name? You can use the Assets panel to solve the problem. Please see "Sliced Images and the Assets Panel" in the "Troubleshooting" section at the end of this chapter.*

Colors

The Colors category lists any colors that have been used for text, backgrounds, or links on any page within the site. Dreamweaver will not include colors from images or media files.

You can add a new color to the Favorites list directly in the Assets panel by doing the following:

1. In the Favorites view, select the Colors category.

2. Click the New Color button.

3. Use the color picker to choose a new color.

The Dreamweaver documentation states that the Assets panel will list colors used in style sheets as well as directly on pages. In practice, however, this is not the case. To view colors from a style sheet in the Assets panel, they need to be added manually to the Favorites list.

11

CSS Colors and Assets

If you're using CSS, the Colors asset won't be of much use because it inserts colors using `font` tags. You can, however, use this category as a guide to the colors in your style sheet.

To do this, add each of the color references in your style sheet to the Favorites list. Then, change the nickname of each color to the name of the style class. Although you won't want to use this list to insert the color or style, you can use it in conjunction with the CSS Styles panel as a reminder of the color of each of your text styles.

URLs

A URL asset is a reference to an external URL to which a page in your site has a link. When the Assets list is created, every page in the site is scanned for HTTP, FTP, Gopher, HTTPS, JavaScript, email (`mailto`), and local file (`file://`).

As with colors, you can create new URLs directly in the Favorites list. Follow these steps:

1. In the Favorites list, select the URLs category.

2. Click the New URL button (this is the same button used to add new colors, it's just renamed within the context of the category).

3. Enter a URL and a nickname in the Add URL dialog box (see Figure 11.4).

Figure 11.4
Enter a URL and nickname for the new asset. The nickname can be used as the source text for the link when inserted into a document.

4. Click OK.

If a URL has a nickname, the name is used as the source text if the asset is inserted into a document, unless a selection of the link source has already been made.

The New URL button won't work unless one of the assets in the URLs list is selected. This won't overwrite an existing Favorite— it's just a quirk of the application.

Flash

If your site contains Macromedia Flash (SWF) files, they'll be listed in the Flash category. This list also includes Flash buttons or text objects that you create in Dreamweaver. The Assets panel lets you preview your Flash content. When one of these assets is selected, a small Play button appears in the upper-right corner of the preview area. Most likely, you'll need to resize the Assets panel to view the Flash movie. Another way to preview the movie is to double-click the file in the Assets list.

The Assets panel doesn't list Flash source (FLA) files.

▷ *Want more information on Flash? Please see "Adding Flash Buttons," p. 147.*

Shockwave

This category shows any movies in Macromedia Shockwave format. As with Flash movies, Shockwave files can be previewed in the preview area or the standalone QuickTime player.

Movies

If your site has any movies in the MPEG or QuickTime format, they'll be displayed in the Movies category. As with Flash and Shockwave movies, you can preview them in the Assets panel or the standalone QuickTime player.

Scripts

JavaScript and VBScript files are listed in the Scripts category. The list only contains scripts in files with JS or VBS extensions—scripts contained in your HTML files aren't listed. The text of the script file is displayed in the preview pane when you select the asset.

Inserting a script asset into a document creates a `<script src="file://...>` tag, with the `src` attribute containing a link to the script file.

⇨ *For more information on using JavaScript with Dreamweaver, see "Adding JavaScript to a Web Page," p. 420.*

Templates

This category lists Dreamweaver template (DWT) files. A *template* is a document you can use to provide a standardized layout for your pages. Templates are one of the few assets you can create from the Site list.

⇨ *For more information on templates, see Chapter 12, "Working with Templates," p. 207.*

Library

Library assets are elements you want to use in multiple pages. They are easily updated on all pages containing them when you edit the library item.

⇨ *For more information on Library assets, see Chapter 13, "Building a Library," p. 225.*

ADDING AN ASSET TO A WEB PAGE

Of course, the real power of the Assets panel is in its capability to streamline your development time. You can insert most types of assets directly into a document by dragging them to the Design view of the Document window or by using the Insert button at the bottom of the panel. On the Colors and Templates categories, the Insert button changes to the Apply button.

The asset is added to the page at the insertion point. In the case of colors, text typed after the insertion point appears in the selected color. If you've inserted a URL asset, the destination path of the URL appears as the source for the link; the source text can, of course, be modified.

For assets such as URLs and colors, you can also apply them to selected text in Design view. To do this, follow these steps:

1. Select the text to which the color or link should be applied.

> **Caution**
>
> When you use the Assets panel to control color, the color is applied to text using the `font` tag. If you're using CSS, the `font` tag overrides any style previously applied to that text (because the `font` tag takes precedence being closest to the content). This also causes your page to be out of compliance with strict HTML/XHTML because the `font` tag is deprecated.

2. Select the asset from the Assets panel.

3. Click Apply, or select Apply from the context menu.

To apply scripts to the head of the page, select View, Head Content; then drag the script from the Assets panel into the Head Content area of the Document window.

MAINTAINING THE ASSETS PANEL

The Assets panel requires regular maintenance to retain its value. As the site evolves, so do the assets, but the Assets panel lacks the capability to automatically keep up with its listings. Assets themselves might need to be updated. And, finally, sites might need to share assets already listed on another site.

Refreshing and Rebuilding the Site Assets List

The first time you open the Assets panel for a site, it scans for assets to build a site assets list. After the initial list is created, however, assets are not added to the list unless you refresh the Site list. To do this, follow these steps:

1. Make sure the site list is showing by clicking the Site button at the top of the Assets panel.

2. Click the Refresh Site List button at the bottom of the panel. You can also (Command-click) [right-click] the Assets panel and select Refresh Site List from the context menu.

Refreshing the site list updates the Assets panel with any assets that have been added or deleted within Dreamweaver. If you've made changes to the site outside Dreamweaver, however, these assets are not updated even when you use the Refresh Site List feature. Instead, the list must be re-created. To do this, hold down the Ctrl key when clicking the Refresh Site List button or select Recreate Site List from the context menu.

> **Proper updating within** Dreamweaver suggests that, ideally, you will perform all maintenance on your site within the Dreamweaver application.

Editing Assets in Other Programs

To edit an asset, either double-click it in the Assets panel or select it and click the Edit button. Some assets, such as images, must be edited by an external application. The application to use is determined by the settings in the Dreamweaver Preferences tool. If you want to use a different application than the default, select Edit, Preferences and select the File Types/Editors category. Then, add the application you want to use to edit that file type.

Assets that don't reside in physical files but are, instead, scanned from your documents—such as URLs and colors—can be edited only in the Favorites list.

HTML-based assets, templates, and library items are edited in Dreamweaver. Double-clicking assets of this type opens a new Document window containing the asset.

11

Using the Assets Panel Between Sites

Assets are often useful on multiple sites. For an asset to be available to a site, the asset must first be copied to the Favorites list of the new site. To do so, follow these steps:

1. Select the asset or Favorites folder from the Assets panel.

2. (Command-click) [Right-click] and select Copy to Site from the context menu.

3. Select a site from the list of defined sites.

The assets are copied to the other site into corresponding folders as those on the source site.

TROUBLESHOOTING

Nicknaming Assets

I'm getting so much stuff in my Assets panel that I can no longer remember what's what. Is there an easy way to keep things straight?

One of the more useful features of the Favorites list is the ability to nickname your assets. Instead of assets appearing in the list as "http://www.pendragn.com," you can nickname the asset as "Jenn's Site," which will hopefully jog your memory more easily.

To change the nickname of an asset, be certain you're in the Favorites view, select the asset, and then select Edit Nickname from the context menu. You can also edit the Nickname by single-clicking the current nickname twice. After entering the nickname, press (Return) [Enter] or click elsewhere in the Assets panel. The actual filename, color, or URL will still appear in the Value column of the Favorites list, and the preview display will remain unchanged.

Sliced Images and the Assets Panel

How can I have more control over individual images I'm working with while constructing a table?

The display on the Assets panel is helpful when piecing a sliced image back into a table, particularly if you forgot to give each slice a unique name in your graphics application. Unlike selecting image files from the Insert Image dialog box or dragging from the Site panel at random, the Assets panel displays each image, so you can drag and drop the pieces into the table like a puzzle.

PEER TO PEER: ASSETS AND BEST PRACTICES

One of the primary goals a full-throttle development application such as Dreamweaver MX aims to achieve is providing management tools. In fact, one of the most alluring aspects of Dreamweaver MX

11

is the very fact that it can be successfully used to manage almost every aspect of a Web site. This fact is made even more attractive because the product is so highly integrated with other Macromedia products and also because of the quality of Dreamweaver's collaborative tools.

Using Assets addresses the concern of how the many components of a Web site are organized and maintained. Without the tool, you'd have to find another external management tool, keep running lists of assets by hand, or just plain "wing" the management of your site. Although these bootstrap methods might suffice for a small site, try it on one that has hundreds or even thousands of documents, and you'll be running for the aspirin in no time.

Management tools such as the Assets panel aren't just there as a value-added service. Get used to using it to manage your site, and you'll find you save time and significant frustration if you do so.

11

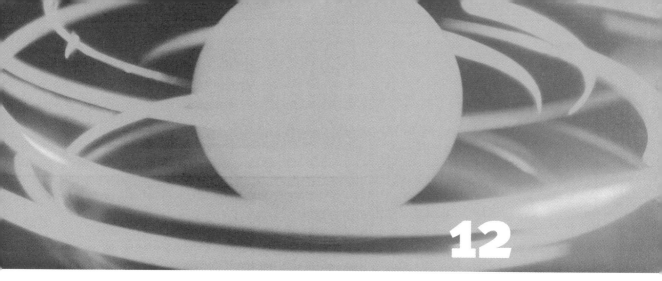

WORKING WITH TEMPLATES

IN THIS CHAPTER

WORKING WITH TEMPLATES

Web sites tend to reuse many of the same elements and layout from page to page. This provides a consistent look and feel across the entire site. It also speeds up development time when you can reuse your images and code. You can, of course, cut and paste your images and layout elements from page to page. This approach, however, is not without its own problems. For example, changing the layout on one page means that you have to make the same changes by hand on all your pages, which can be tedious and prone to mistakes.

Dreamweaver's solution to this error-prone process of reusing page layouts is templates. Dreamweaver *templates* are special documents you can build that contain the layout for your site's pages. The template contains the structure and elements used for page layout, along with regions you designate as editable that will be used later for adding content.

When you create a page using a template, it remains attached to that template even after the unique content of the page is added (unless you detach it yourself). This lets you make changes to the template document and have those changes applied to all pages that are attached to it, a very powerful ability that saves you time and helps prevent errors.

CREATING A TEMPLATE

There are essentially two ways to create templates in Dreamweaver. You can create a template document from scratch or use an existing document as a template. Perhaps the easiest method is to convert an existing document into a template. This is especially useful when you're experimenting with different layouts or when you decide to reuse a page layout you weren't originally planning to use again.

Starting a New Template

There are two ways to create a new template document in Dreamweaver. The first and most obvious method is to use the File menu, like so:

1. Select File, New.

2. In the New Document dialog box, select Template Page under the General tab.

3. Select the type of template page to create from the Template Page list. Unless you're using a server-side technology such as ASP or ColdFusion, select HTML Template.

The second way to create new templates is in the Assets panel. This is convenient because the Assets panel is also the place where you keep track of and use your templates. To use the Assets panel, do the following:

No matter which method you use to create a template—making it from scratch or saving an existing document as a template—Dreamweaver places the template in a folder named `Templates` in your site's root folder. If this folder does not exist, it is automatically created when you save your first template.

1. Select Window, Assets to open the Assets panel.

2. Select the Templates category (see Figure 12.1).

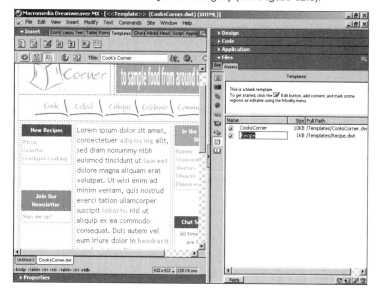

Figure 12.1
The Templates category of the
Assets panel is the place to create
and use templates for your site.

3. Click the New Template button at the bottom of the Assets panel, or select New Template from the context menu. An untitled template document is added to the list.

4. Enter a name for the template.

5. Click Edit to open the document.

Saving a Document As a Template

You can also choose to save an existing document as a template, by following these steps:

1. Open the document in the Document window.

2. Select File, Save As Template.

3. In the Save As Template dialog box, enter a name for the template.

Either method you use to create templates places them in the Templates folder in the site's root folder.

Creating Editable Regions

After you've created a template and designed your layout, you need to indicate which sections can be edited in documents that use the template. By making you choose which

> If you add a template region to a document that is not already a template (using the Insert, Template Objects command, for example), Dreamweaver automatically converts the document into a template. Unless you disable it, a warning dialog box pops up informing you of this when you add a template region.

12

parts of the document are editable, the rest of the document is locked from accidental changes. All templates need to have at least one editable region to be useful. If you try to save a template with no editable region, Dreamweaver will give you a warning message.

An editable region must contain an entire block in your document. If you are using a table for layout, you can make the entire table editable or just an individual cell. You can make multiple cells of the table part of the same editable region if you don't make the entire table editable.

To create an editable region on a template, do the following:

1. Select the region you want to make editable.

2. Select Insert, Template Objects, Editable Region. You can also (Ctrl-click) [right-click] and select Templates, New Editable Region from the context menu or select the Editable Region button on the Templates category of the Insert bar.

3. In the New Editable Region dialog box, enter a unique descriptive name for the region (see Figure 12.2). You can use spaces, but not any characters that are used to define HTML or JavaScript elements such as question marks, quotation marks, curly brackets, or angle brackets.

Figure 12.2
A descriptive name for your editable region helps you easily identify the purpose for the section.

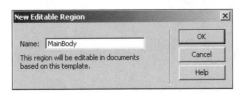

4. Click OK to finish adding the region. The editable region is displayed in the designer as a box with a tab showing the region's name (see Figure 12.3).

Figure 12.3
Editable regions are shown in the template as a box with a tab indicating the region's name.

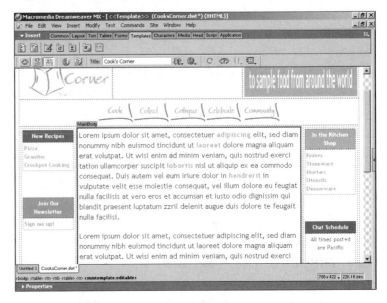

Creating Optional Regions

Dreamweaver allows you to mark regions as optional. Optional regions can be used to specify content that may or may not be shown in the final document. Thus, if certain pages need to show repetitive content—such as a disclaimer or copyright notice—and others don't, you can turn the optional regions on and off as each page requires. In Design view, the tab of the optional region is preceded by the word "if." Based on the condition set in the template, a template user can define whether the region is viewable in pages she creates.

> **You might decide later that a** region you previously marked as editable should be locked. You can remove editable regions by selecting the region you want to detach and selecting Modify, Templates, Remove Template Markup.

Here's how to insert an optional region:

1. Select the element or section you want to make optional.

2. Select Insert, Template Objects, Optional Region from the menu. You can also select Templates, New Optional Region from the context menu or click the Optional Region button on the Templates category of the Insert bar.

3. Specify the options for the region in the Optional Region dialog box. These options are described in the next section.

4. Click OK to create the optional region.

Setting Optional Region Options

Optional region options are set in the New Optional Region dialog box (see Figure 12.4). This dialog box is used to set template parameters and define the conditional statements that determine whether the optional region should be shown.

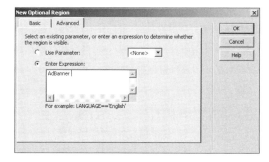

Figure 12.4
The New Optional Region dialog box is used to specify parameters and conditional statements used to control an optional region's display.

On the Basic tab of the New Optional Region Dialog box, you can define a new template parameter for the region. Template parameter values can be set for each page that uses the template and are used to determine whether the region is displayed. If you have multiple optional regions, simply use the same parameter name for each one. To define a template parameter, do this:

1. Open the New Optional Region dialog box for an optional region.

2. In the Basics tab, enter the name of the parameter.

3. Make sure Show By Default is checked if you want pages created with this template to have this parameter set to TRUE by default. Uncheck it if you want the region to be hidden by default.

4. Click OK.

You can also choose existing template parameters from a pop-up menu by clicking the Advanced tab and selecting the parameter you want to use. Note that only existing parameters are displayed in this menu.

Editable Optional Regions

Editable optional regions can be added as well. To add an editable optional region, follow these steps:

1. Position the pointer where you want the region positioned in the document. A selection can't be changed into an editable optional region, so do not select any elements or text.

2. Select Insert, Template Objects, Editable Optional Region, or click the Editable Optional Region button on the Templates category of the Insert bar.

3. Specify the options for the region in the Optional Region dialog box as described previously.

4. Click OK to create the editable optional region. It is shown in the editor with tabs for both the editable and optional content.

Creating Repeating Regions

Templates can also contain regions that repeat. Repeating regions are used to allow the user of the template to expand sections of the document in a controlled manner. For example, a template might have a table to which the template author can add new rows. Making a row of the table repeatable enables the table to expand without giving up control of the layout.

Repeating Tables

A repeating table can be used to provide a structured way to expand a document. The table row can contain one or more editable cells that the template user can fill with content.

To insert a repeating table to a document, do the following:

1. Put the insertion point in the document where you want the table.

2. Select Insert, Template Objects, Repeating Table from the menu. The Insert Repeating Table dialog box appears (see Figure 12.5).

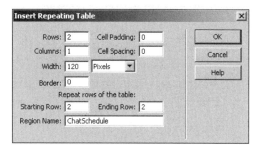

Figure 12.5
You can also click the Repeating Table button on the Templates category of the Insert bar to open the Insert Repeating Table dialog box.

3. Enter the values for the table in the dialog box. Rows, Columns, Cell Padding, Cell Spacing, Width, and Border are standard table attributes that you can set accordingly. The following parameters are unique to repeating tables:

- **Starting Row**—Specifies the first row to use in the repeating region. By default this is row 1, but it can be changed if the first row contains information, such as a column headings, that shouldn't be repeated.

- **Ending Row**—Specifies the ending row of the table to use as the repeating region. This can be the same as the starting row for simple tables, or it can be one or more rows later to repeat more complex table layouts.

- **Region Name**—Lets you specify a unique name for the region.

4. Click OK to insert the table.

Repeating Regions

A more freeform repeating option is the repeating region. Repeating regions typically contain tables, but they can also contain other elements and attributes.

Repeating regions are not editable by themselves, but they can contain one or more editable regions inside them to allow the region to be customized. To create a repeatable region, do the following:

1. Either select the existing content you want to make into a repeating region or place the insertion point where you want it to go.

2. Select Insert, Template Objects, Repeating Region from the document menu, or (Control-click) [right-click] the document and select Templates, New Repeating Region from the context menu. The New Repeating Region dialog box appears (see Figure 12.6).

3. Enter a unique name for the region in the New Repeating Region dialog box.

4. Click OK.

5. Insert one or more editable regions in the repeating region to allow it to be customized by the template user.

Figure 12.6
The New Repeating Region dialog box is used to give a unique name to a repeating section of a template. You can also open the dialog box by clicking the Repeating Region button on the Templates category of the Insert bar.

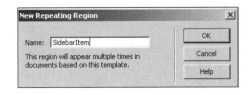

Making Attributes Editable

To allow the template user to set certain attributes of an element, but not control anything else about it, you need to make certain attributes editable. For instance, you might want to allow a different iconic image in the heading of the page and allow the template user to specify a new value for the src attribute. You could make only this attribute editable while leaving other attributes such as the height and width locked.

To create an editable attribute for an element, follow these steps:

1. Select the element in the Document window.

2. Select Modify, Templates, Make Attribute Editable from the main menu. The Editable Tag Attributes dialog box appears (see Figure 12.7).

Figure 12.7
Templates can have elements that are locked but contain editable attributes.

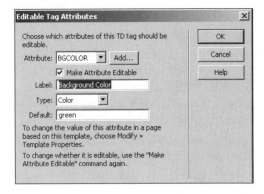

3. Select the attribute you want to make editable from the list. Only attributes that are currently defined for the element are shown—if the one you want isn't shown, click Add and enter the attribute name.

4. Check the Make Attribute Editable box.

5. Enter a descriptive label for the attribute in the Label field. This is necessary to make it easier to identify what the attribute is for when a template-based page is created.

6. Select the type of attribute. This tells Dreamweaver what type of data the attribute contains and how to prompt the template user for a value. Select one of the following:

   • **Text**—Specifies a text element. For example, use this for alignment attributes so the user can enter left, center, or right.

- **URL**—Specifies a link or an image source attribute. Using this type enables Dreamweaver to automatically keep track of and update the link path.

- **Color**—Specifies a color value. A color picker is used to prompt the template user to enter a color.

- **True/False**—Specifies a Boolean value. Use this to set attributes that have only true or false values.

- **Number**—Specifies a numeric value. For example, this could be used to specify an image height and width.

7. Enter a default value for the attribute. This should be a value consistent with the type you chose.

8. If you want to make other attributes of the element editable, you can repeat steps 3–7 without leaving the dialog box.

9. Click OK to apply the changes.

Macromedia Markup in a Template

Template documents are standard HTML documents, but Dreamweaver adds special comments to identify the various regions and parameters of the template. If you view the template in Code view, you will see that editable regions are specified using a `<!-- TemplateBeginEditable name -->` `<!-- TemplateEndEditable -->` block. Repeating regions similarly use a `TemplateBeginRepeat`/ `TemplateEndRepeat` comment block. Template parameters for editable attributes and optional region parameters are contained in `<!-- TemplateParam -->` comments. You can edit values for these template values directly in Code view, but take care not to change the comment identifier; otherwise, the template can break.

12

USING TEMPLATES

After your template layout is defined, you're ready to use it to create your site. You can use a template in one of two ways:

- Create a new document from a template.

- Apply template changes to an existing document.

Creating a New Page from a Template

The most common way to use a template is to create a new document in a site. A new document is created just like any other, but the content of the document contains the template code along with any regions that are editable (see Figure 12.8). If an editable region had text or other content in it in the template, that content is also included in the document.

Figure 12.8
New documents created using a template automatically get the template content, including the default content in any editable regions.

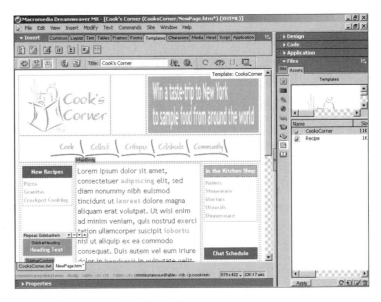

To create a new page from the template, do one of the following:

- Select File, New from the document menu, and click the Templates tab in the dialog box. Select the site and a template (see Figure 12.9).

- Select a template from the Templates category of the Assets panel. (Control-click) [Right-click] the selected template to bring up the context menu. Select the New from Template option.

Figure 12.9
The New from Template dialog box lets you browse your sites for templates. It shows a thumbnail preview of the template to make finding the one you are looking for easier.

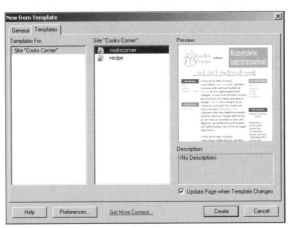

Controlling highlighting for templates is something you might want to do. See "Highlighting Template Code" in the "Troubleshooting" section at the end of this chapter.

Changing Template Code Colors

If you don't like the colors Dreamweaver uses to show template region borders and tabs in the document view, you can change these settings in the preferences. This can be useful if the default colors are hard to see over your site's color scheme. Follow these steps:

1. Select Edit, Preferences from the document menu.

2. Select the Highlighting category in the Preferences dialog box (see Figure 12.10).

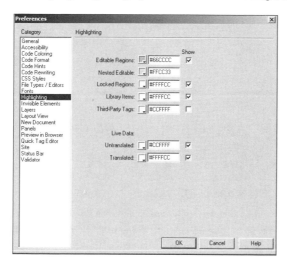

Figure 12.10
The Highlighting category of the Preferences dialog box lets you change the colors Dreamweaver uses for highlighting template regions.

3. Enter new values for the highlighting colors you want to change. You can also click the color swatch to bring up the color picker, and then select the colors.

Keep in mind that these settings are saved globally and used no matter what site you are editing. It is best to try to keep the colors neutral, especially if you work with multiple sites.

Making Changes to the Page

After you have a document created using the template, editing it is a lot like editing any other document. The only difference is that you can modify only the content of the editable portions of the page.

To change content in an editable region, simply click the region and enter the new content. You can use any of the Dreamweaver editing features in this content region.

Repeatable regions have additional options. On the right side of the Region tab, you have the option to add, remove, or select a new repeating section.

Changing Page Properties with the Template

To set any values for optional region parameters or editable attributes, select Modify, Template Properties from the Document menu to activate the Template Properties dialog box (see Figure 12.11). All optional region and editable attribute parameters are displayed, along with their current or default values. This gives you one convenient place to change all the template properties for a page and reduces the possibility of missing one.

Figure 12.11
The Template Properties dialog box is where you set values for optional region parameters and the page's editable attributes.

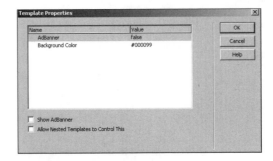

Applying a Template to an Existing Page

Although creating new pages that automatically use a template layout is what templates are primarily about, it is also nice to be able to take an existing document and apply a template layout to it. Dreamweaver enables you to do this, and it does so by attempting to match the page content with the regions of the template.

Pages originally created with a previous version of the template are likely to have some regions that match the new template. These pages are matched by Dreamweaver automatically.

If you apply the template to a document that doesn't have matching editable regions, Dreamweaver allows you to select a template region to apply mismatched content to or to delete content that doesn't match. To apply a template to an existing document, do this:

1. Open the document to which you want to apply the template using the Site panel or by selecting File, Open from the Document menu.

2. Select Modify, Templates, Apply Template to Page from the Document menu. You can also select a template in the Templates category of the Assets panel and click Apply, or you can drag a template from the Assets panel to the document.

3. If there is content that can't be matched to a template region, the Inconsistent Region Names dialog box is displayed (see Figure 12.12).

4. Select an editable region from the list. Then, using the Move Content to New Region drop-down menu, select a template region into which Dreamweaver should move the content.

5. Repeat step 4 for other editable regions of the document.

6. Click OK.

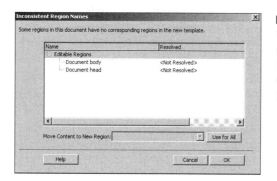

Figure 12.12
When you apply a template to an existing page, the Inconsistent Region Names dialog box lets you choose which region of the template to use for existing content.

Detaching a template is possible, too. See "Detaching a Template" in the "Troubleshooting" section at the end of this chapter.

Editing a Template

Editing a template is similar to editing any other document. Double-click the template in the Assets panel to open it in the editor, or select it in the list and click the Edit button.

After you've made changes to a template, you need to apply the changes to any document that uses the template. If you specified the option to automatically update a page, the Update Template Files dialog box appears when you save the template and gives you the option of updating or not updating pages in your site. If you don't have a page marked to automatically update, apply the template to it using the Apply button in the Assets panel. Any editable regions that can't be matched to regions in the new template cause the Inconsistent Region Names dialog box to be displayed.

You can use the Update Pages dialog box to quickly apply a template to all pages that use it in your site. To use this dialog box, do the following:

1. Select Modify, Templates, Update Pages. The Update Pages dialog box appears (see Figure 12.13).

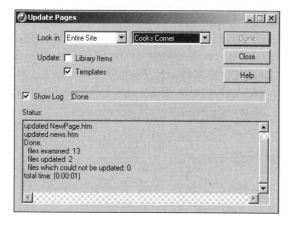

Figure 12.13
The Update Pages dialog box enables you to quickly apply a template to any template pages on your site.

12

2. Select one of the following options:

- **Entire Site**—Select this option in the Look In list to update an entire site; then select the site in the drop-down list.

- **Files That Use**—Select this option in the Look In field to update only those pages that use a particular template file; then select the appropriate template from the drop-down list.

3. Leave the Show Log check box checked to see the changes that are made to your pages.

4. Click Start to update the pages.

The log window shows the pages that were updated. If any errors occurred in the update, they are shown in the log's status window as well.

EXPORTING A TEMPLATE SITE

Templates have one other capability beyond providing a consistent look and feel. You can also export template data as name/value pairs for each editable region of a document as XML. This enables you to easily work with it outside Dreamweaver using an XML or text editor. XML data can also be used by other applications or stored in a database for later retrieval.

Exporting Template Data to XML

To export a document's editable regions as XML, do the following:

1. Select File, Export, Template Data As XML from the Document menu. The Export Template Data As XML dialog box opens (see Figure 12.14).

Figure 12.14
You can export data from a template document's editable regions as XML for use in other applications or databases.

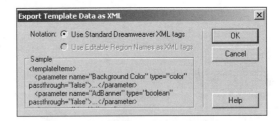

2. Select the notation you want to use for the export. You can choose the standard Dreamweaver notation or use editable region names for the tag names. If your document contains repeating regions, you can select only the standard Dreamweaver notation.

3. Click OK.

4. Select a name for the XML file and click Save.

Conversely, you can import XML data into a document or use it to create a new document. To import XML data into a document, select File, Import, XML into Template.

Exporting Without Template Markup

Although using templates is a great idea, what happens when you merge your site into another site that does not use templates or provide files to others for whom the template markup is unnecessary because they are working outside a Dreamweaver environment? You can export your site in a way that enables Dreamweaver to strip out the template-related markup. To export the site without template markup, follow these steps:

Want to learn more about XML? Check out *Special Edition Using XML* by David Gulbransen (ISBN 0-7897-2748-X).

1. Select Modify, Templates, Export Without Markup from the Document menu. The Export Site Without Template Markup dialog box appears (see Figure 12.15).

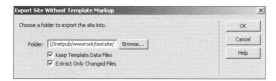

Figure 12.15
A site can be exported without template markup to allow it to be used in a new site that might not have the same template.

2. Enter a path to the folder in which you want to save the site in the Folder field. You can also click Browse to find the folder. The folder must be outside the current site.

3. Select Keep Template Data Files to keep any exported XML data files for your documents.

4. Select Extract Only Changed Files if you are exporting over previously exported files and you want to update only those files that have changed.

TROUBLESHOOTING

Detaching a Template

I've changed my mind, and now I no longer want the template attached to a certain document. How do I get rid of it?

Although templates are nice for maintaining a consistent look across your pages, sometimes it is necessary to have a little more control over a page. Dreamweaver enables you to detach a template from a document so you can edit all the regions of the page without the constraint of the template. Select Modify, Templates, Detach from Template to remove the template. Keep in mind that any later changes to the template will not be applied to this page.

12

Highlighting Template Code

I want to see my editable regions. How can I ensure that I do?

Template editable regions are shown in your document as a colored border with a tab in the upper-left corner with the region name. For repeating regions, controls are also shown that enable you to add and remove repeating sections. These tabs are only shown while in the designer—they won't be on the live version of the page. You can control whether this highlighting is seen by selecting or deselecting View, Visual Aids, Invisible Elements.

PEER TO PEER: ADDING STANDARDS-BASED TEMPLATES

Way back in Chapter 1, "Defining Your Site," some of the missing pieces in Dreamweaver HTML templates were covered.

To assist you in working with standards-based templates, a series of seven standards-complaint documents have been provided on the CD. You can make these into templates. The files include

- **HTML 4.01 Transitional (h4t.html)**—Use this template any time you want to use HTML 4.01 Transitional. Transitional HTML 4.01 allows font tags and other presentational elements and attributes, but no proprietary (browser-specific) elements or attributes can be used.

- **HTML 4.01 Strict (h4s.html)**—Use this template any time you're developing an HTML page using CSS for all presentational elements and attributes.

- **HTML 4.01 Frameset (h4f.html)**—This template is for any HTML frameset.

- **XHTML 1.0 Transitional (xht.html)**—This template is an excellent choice for developers who want to have the flexibility of HTML 4.01 Transitional with the advantage of using XHTML markup.

- **XHTML 1.0 Strict (xhs.html)**—If you are writing CSS-based layouts, are relying on CSS for all presentational attributes, and are interested in using XHTML, this is the template for you.

- **XHTML 1.0 Frameset (xhf.html)**—This template is for an XHTML frameset.

- **XHTML 1.1 (xh1.1.html)**—There is only one public Document Type Definition for XHTML 1.1. Essentially, XHTML 1.1 is the XHTML 1.0 Strict DTD. Use this for the same reasons you would use XHTML 1.0 Strict. The difference is that, at the time of this writing, XHTML 1.1 is the recommended version. It allows no presentation, so you must use CSS for all layouts and design concerns.

12

Here's how to create a template out of any (or all!) of these files:

1. Open the document in the Document window.

2. Select File, Save As Template.

3. In the Save As Template dialog box, enter a name for the template. Click OK. If a warning message pops up saying that the template has no editable regions, bypass this and save the file anyway.

Your templates will now be available any time you want to use them. Simply select File, New. When the New Document dialog box opens, click the Template tab, find the document, highlight it, and click OK.

12

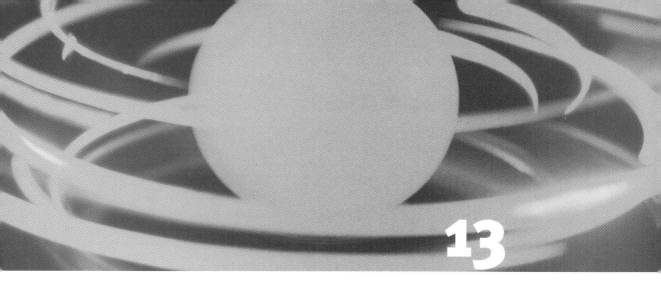

13

BUILDING A LIBRARY

CREATING LIBRARY ITEMS

As any experienced Web designer knows, site development often consists of placing the same elements on multiple pages to create a cohesive whole. Assets and templates help in these situations—as do snippets if you're code-inclined—but they aren't always the right tools for the job. Assets are very specific and apply only to one type of element or file. Templates are used to create entire pages. But what about reusing specific portions of a page?

Library items complete the triumvirate of design tools for accessing reusable elements. Despite being one of the Assets panel categories, Library items are used to re-create elements (or a group of elements) defined by the designer.

These can include anything from portions of text to an entire table structure. Library items can be used to add a copyright notice to the bottom of each page; this notice can then be updated each year by changing only the Library item instead of every page on the site. Library items can also be used to create a sidebar table structure that can then be inserted as needed on pages throughout the site.

When you create your first Library item, Dreamweaver generates a Library folder in your local site. This folder contains all the Library items for the site, each of which is identifiable to a Windows user by its `.lbi` extension.

Although you can edit library files directly in this folder, the best place to work with Library items is in the Library category of the Assets panel (see Figure 13.1). In this panel, you can create and edit Library items, insert them into pages, and even copy them to another site's library.

Figure 13.1
The Library category of the Assets panel displays a preview of the Library item and tools to create and edit items.

Library Items and Server-Side Includes

If Dreamweaver Library items sound a lot like Server-Side Includes (SSIs), you're right—they essentially work the same way.

SSIs are small files that are inserted by the server upon delivery of a page to a requesting browser. These small files contain the same information that a Dreamweaver Library item can—although SSIs are more flexible in that they allow you to include *any* portion of a document, including head elements (which Library items do not allow).

Any document that will receive the SSI must contain the include statement. This statement will look something like this (servers vary, as do the syntax for SSIs):

```
<!--#include virtual="/includes/footer.ssi" -->
```

Dreamweaver does allow you to create SSIs via the specific application you might be using: PHP, ASP, and so forth. To use SSIs, you'll need to check with your server administrator to ascertain proper syntax and usage.

> A comprehensive Webmonkey article on extending Dreamweaver also contains good information on using SSIs, including converting Library items to SSIs, `http://hotwired.lycos.com/webmonkey/99/11/index2a.html`.

Library Items Versus Dreamweaver Templates

The biggest advantage Library items have is how easy they are to edit. Just as with templates, when the Library item is edited, every instance of the item on your site's pages is updated automatically. Also just like templates, Library items are coded into the document with comment tags. These tags surround the code for the Library item and contain a link back to the library source code.

The comment text for a Library item is distinguishable from that of template comments. The comments will appear as

```
<!-- #BeginLibraryItem "/Library/Sidebar.lbi" -->
```

and

```
<!-- #EndLibraryItem -->
```

The path included in the #BeginLibraryItem comment will reflect the name of the Library item.

⇨ *Learn more about templates, see "Working with Templates," p. 208.*

Library items can be comprised of any element or combination of elements on a page, with the exception of head content (such as script, style, and meta tags).

To create a Library item, do the following:

1. Select the elements you want to create as a Library item. In my sample site, I've selected the description section of my gallery page so I can reuse it on other pages.

2. Drag the selection to the Library category of the Assets panel. Alternatively, click the New Library Item button at the bottom of the panel or select Modify, Library, Add Object to Library from the menu (see Figure 13.2).

3. Enter the Library item's name. The more descriptive, the better because this becomes the filename for the Library item.

When you create the Library item, the original selection becomes the first instance of your new object, linked to the new item you created from it. The Property inspector changes context to provide tools for editing the Library item, detaching the selected instance of the item from its source, or re-creating the item from the selected instance (see Figure 13.3).

13

Figure 13.2
The New Library Item button can be used to create a Library item. You can also insert a Library item, refresh the site list, edit a Library item, or delete one using the Assets panel Library options.

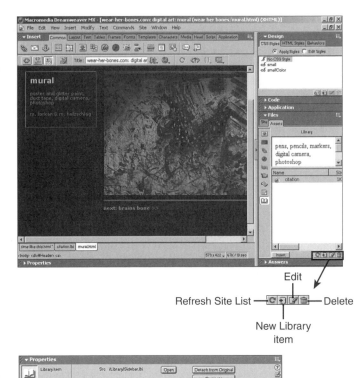

Edit

Refresh Site List ——— Delete

New Library item

Figure 13.3
The Library Item Property inspector enables you to modify the Library item and the selected instance of it on the page.

USING LIBRARY ITEMS

When you create your first Library item, you can immediately see how it appears in Design view when inserted into a page because the selected elements become a library instance (see Figure 13.4).

To insert the Library item elsewhere in the site, follow these steps:

1. Position the insertion point in the Document window where you want the Library item to be placed.

2. Open the Library category of the Assets panel.

3. Select the Library item you want to insert.

4. Click the Insert button at the bottom of the Assets panel, or drag the Library item to the Document window.

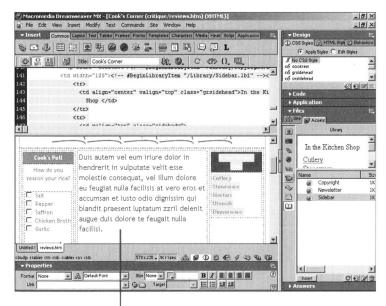

Inserted Library item

Figure 13.4
When you insert a Library item, the markup for the elements is inserted, surrounded by comment tags. The item appears high-lighted in Design view to distin-guish it from regular, editable content.

You can insert the Library item content and immediately detach it from the library by pressing the Ctrl key as you drag or click the Insert button. If you do this, the content will be copied into the doc-ument at the insertion point, but the inserted content assumes the same status as any other element on the page and must be manually changed in Design or Code view.

The status of the Library item itself remains unchanged. You can still insert the Library item else-where in the site, either retaining its attachment to the item or detaching it, as necessary.

Editing Library Items

As mentioned earlier, the advantage of the library is that modifications made to an item are updated site-wide.

Here's how to edit a Library item:

1. Select the item.

2. Click the Edit button in the Assets panel. You can also open the Library item for editing from the Property inspector when an instance of the item is selected in the Document window.

3. Edit the syntax and content as you require.

When you edit a Library item, the content of the item appears in a new document window. After making your changes, save the document. An alert box will prompt you to update any pages con-taining the Library item (see Figure 13.5).

13

Figure 13.5
When you save changes to a Library item, you're prompted to update all instances of the item throughout the site.

If you don't update pages at this point, you can use Modify, Library, Update Current Page or Update Pages later. If you choose to update, the Update Pages dialog box appears and lists the number of updates made (see Figure 13.6). You can also use this opportunity to update the remainder of the site's library and template instances.

Figure 13.6
The Update Pages dialog box is used to update both Library items and templates used in the site.

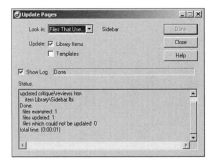

If the Library item is updated, all markup between the comment tags is modified to reflect the changes. In templates, certain regions can be locked so you don't inadvertently modify pieces of the template.

Library items, however, have no such constraints. Changing the content of the inserted Library item doesn't break the link to the library. However, if you manually modify the content of the Library item within the document—adding content to a table inserted using a Library item, for example—those changes will be lost when and if the Library item is updated. If you don't want your changes to be overridden, you need to detach the inserted Library item from the source.

> **Caution**
>
> When editing Library items, you can't use Cascading Style Sheets (CSS) or timelines. This is because these features insert code into the head section of the page. Library items can only insert a consecutive block of code into the body of the document.

Detaching from the Original

To detach an instance of a Library item from the library and thereby prevent it from being edited and updated when the Library item itself is modified, you need to break the link between the document and the item.

To detach a Library item from the original, do the following:

1. Select the instance you want to detach in the Document window. The Property inspector modifies to manage your item.

2. Click Detach from Original (see Figure 13.7). The highlighting around the item will disappear, signifying that the content is now simply a part of the document.

3. Save any changes.

Figure 13.7 shows the detach button in the Property inspector.

Figure 13.7
Detaching a Library item from the original merges the content and code from that item with the document at hand.

Deleting Library Items

To delete a Library item, follow these steps:

1. Make sure the Assets panel is open and the Library is selected. Then, select the item to be deleted.

2. Click the Delete button at the bottom of the Assets panel.

The item is deleted from the Assets panel, but any instances of it remain in their respective documents.

⇨ *Did you accidentally delete a Library item? See "Re-creating Library Items" in the "Troubleshooting" section of this chapter.*

Although you can't include style rules in a Library item, you can include class attributes. When the Library item is inserted, it assumes the styles set for that class in the attached internal or external style sheet, thus assuming the appearance of the rest of the site. To learn more about class attributes, see Chapter 15, "Designing with Style."

Behaviors in the Library

When you create a Library item out of content containing Dreamweaver behaviors, the elements and event handlers are copied, but the associated JavaScript is not. This is because, as noted earlier, the Library item can't update head content.

Caution
The delete process is irreversible. After a Library item is deleted, it is removed from the hard drive.

Fortunately, though, when you insert the Library item into a document, Dreamweaver is smart enough to know to add the appropriate JavaScript functions. If those functions are already in the head, Dreamweaver knows not to duplicate it.

You can't edit behaviors using the Open option in the Property inspector. This only opens the Library item itself, which won't contain the necessary JavaScript and access to the Behaviors panel.

Editing behaviors in a Library item, therefore, requires a workaround. Follow these steps:

13

1. Open a document that contains an instance of the Library item.

2. Select the Library item in the document.

3. Click Detach from Original in the Property inspector to make the item editable.

4. Use the Behaviors panel to change events and actions as necessary.

5. In the Library category of the Assets panel, delete the original Library item by clicking Delete at the bottom of the Assets panel.

6. In the Document window, select all the elements contained in the Library item.

7. In the Assets panel, click the New Library button, giving the Library item the same name as the original.

> **Caution**
> Be sure to note the exact name of the original Library item before you delete it. If you give the new Library item a different name, the link to all other instances of the Library item will be broken.

After the Library item has been re-created in this manner, you'll need to update the site to bring all the other instances of the Library item up-to-date. To do this, select Modify, Library, Update Pages from the menu.

▷ *To learn more about working with behaviors, see Chapter 22, "Working with JavaScript and Behaviors," p. 415.*

COPYING TO ANOTHER SITE

Library items can be copied to another site in the same manner as any other asset on the Assets panel. Select the Library item and (Command-click) [right-click] and select Copy to Site from the context menu. A pop-out menu will list all the defined sites to which you can copy the Library item. If this is the first Library item being added to the other site, Dreamweaver will create a Library folder in the local site.

▷ *Have you copied a Library item to another site just to find all your links and images are broken? Find out how to troubleshoot this problem in "Moving Library Items" in the "Troubleshooting" section of this chapter.*

13

TROUBLESHOOTING

Moving Library Items

I copied a library item to another site, and now many links and images are unavailable. What happened?

When you copy a Library item to another site, images and internal links contained in the item will be broken. The image files to which a Library item may refer aren't copied to the new site. Links aren't automatically updated to reflect the new path to the destination file. Nor would you want them to be because any links between the two sites would need to be reformatted as external links (or the link would need to be edited to point to a file on the new site).

Re-creating Library Items

I deleted a Library item and then realized I need it again. What can I do?

If you accidentally delete a Library item, your only recourse is to re-create it from one of the instances of it in a document. To do this, select an instance of the Library item and click the Recreate button in the Property inspector.

If there aren't any instances of the Library item in your site—which could occur if you made the original instance editable and either didn't create any other instances or made all of those editable, as well—you'll need to create a new Library item from scratch.

PEER TO PEER: LIBRARY ITEMS AND VALID DOCUMENTS

Library items are yet another means by which Dreamweaver assists designers in achieving best practices. By creating Library items, you can save significant time when updating or modifying your site. Simply update the item, and that update is then applied to all the documents within the defined site.

Because Library items are simply saved selections of markup that belong to a larger document, it's very important to ensure that the markup within the item and any document to which the Library item is added correspond to one another. Any missing or additional piece of markup, be it a bracket, a quotation mark, an element, an attribute, or a value can cause problems with rendering and also create invalid documents.

A surefire way to avoid this issue is to validate your documents *after* a Library item has been added.

➭ *To find out about validation, see " Cross-Browser Compatibility," p. 525.*

WRITING AND EDITING HTML, XHTML, AND CSS

IN THIS PART

WORKING WITH HTML AND XHTML

IN THIS CHAPTER

MARKUP TRENDS

Those readers who have been following along with Web design and development trends over the past several years are most certainly aware that many changes are occurring with both the languages used for the Web and the way we use those languages. And, as you've seen throughout this book, there is a strong emphasis right now on following standards.

Despite the renegade spirit of the Web, there are rules that, when followed, make the job of creating documents and sites more accessible, more available to international audiences, and more available to a wide range of Web browsers and other user agents such as those for PDAs and wireless devices. Macromedia is working hard to ensure that its products in general—and Dreamweaver specifically—contain tools to help you follow these standards. In this chapter, you'll learn about HTML and XHTML, how these languages came about, and how Macromedia Dreamweaver MX allows you to work with them.

Macromedia and Markup

Macromedia Dreamweaver was one of the first Web design tools to ensure that its users could customize the way the program manages markup. The term *Roundtrip HTML* emerged to describe the ability to move HTML documents between editors, within Dreamweaver, and within Dreamweaver views with limited or no changes being made to your markup.

The following are a few issues in Macromedia Dreamweaver MX that you need to be aware of and which you'll want to modify to maintain as much control as possible over the resulting document markup:

- **Overwriting of tags**—Dreamweaver MX attempts to repair mistakes such as poorly formed tags, adding a closing tag where appropriate and removing unnecessary tags. This feature generally is disabled by those experienced Web authors who will be working directly with a document's markup at least some of the time and validating documents against existing World Wide Web Consortium (W3C) recommendations.

- **Error marking of appropriate tags**—If Dreamweaver MX sees a tag it doesn't recognize, in most instances it marks it as an error. This can be problematic if you're using XML or a tag that for some reason is unknown to the program. Fortunately, Dreamweaver MX does *not* modify a tag it doesn't recognize, but be aware that it will likely mark it as an error when it in fact might not be an error at all.

- **Error correction**—You can set up the software so that it performs checks on given markup. If that markup is browser specific or unsupported in some way, Dreamweaver highlights the markup. Click the highlight, and you'll get assistance from the program to help you fix the problem.

As you work through this chapter, you'll first learn the details necessary to determine which, if any, changes you want to make to these options. Then, you'll learn how to customize these options and use the various views and editors within Dreamweaver to generate markup that conforms to your needs.

The Value of Understanding Markup

There is no doubt that the challenge of working with Web-based documents and sites today requires a broad range of skills. Many readers are likely to be frustrated by the sheer volume of information about and changes to the languages and trends being used and followed. You've spent some good money on Dreamweaver, and you might be wondering why the program just doesn't manage all this code stuff for you.

The good news is that Dreamweaver makes every attempt to do just that. By providing you with multiple views and as up-to-date information as possible, you can conceivably use Dreamweaver without ever once looking at the markup.

But there are problems and concerns with that approach, especially for those readers who are concerned with balancing browser needs with future growth as well as balancing design value with concerns such as accessibility. To manage these issues, learning about the languages—at least enough to be fluent in their primary concepts—can be a huge help to you.

Following W3C recommended markup approaches creates consistency between documents, saving time and frustration when trying to find errors within a document. What's more, multiple people are working on a site, so adhering to standard practices creates a much more efficient work environment.

If you're frustrated by browser and platform inconsistencies, you'll find that following recommendations (along with some common sense) will eliminate many of your struggles. Documents become more interoperable, reducing testing time and increasing portability of documents from one place to another. Documents conforming to W3C recommendations pay attention to the needs of the disabled, ensuring that the information within them can be easily accessed and clearly understood.

Formal markup also provides a means by which documents can be prepared to display in a variety of languages using different character sets.

As the world moves from Web to wireless and alternative means of accessing Web-based data, clean markup becomes an imperative. Markup adhering to current recommendations and approaches can easily be interpreted by a much wider range of user agents beyond the browser—making your information very widely accessible.

ORIGIN OF THE SPECIES: SGML, HTML, XML, XHTML

To understand HTML, you need to step back to its parent markup language, the Standard Generalized Markup Language (SGML). SGML has been around for many years and became a standard for document markup specialists in government and especially industries such as medicine, law, and finance.

SGML is what's referred to as a *meta-language*. It exists to create other markup languages. SGML is essentially a collection of language rules that authors use to create their own document languages. HTML is one of the resulting languages—a child, if you will, of its meta-parent SGML.

From SGML, HTML took its structure, syntax, and basic rules. However, HTML—even in its current seemingly complex state—is much less complex and detailed than SGML. Especially in its early life, HTML was very simple. It existed to allow for some very basic markup of pages for the Web: paragraphs, line breaks, and headers. Remember, the Web was first a text-only environment. HTML

14

was not developed with detailed presentation concerns in mind; rather, its goal was the simple structuring of data.

Enter the visual browser, which changed the Web environment from one constructed of text documents to one that promised growing opportunities for visual design. HTML—and Web browsers themselves—were stretched out of proportion to accommodate the rapid-fire pace of the Web's visual and interactive growth. Designers were naturally more concerned with creating designs that were visually rich and esthetically pleasing.

Trying to manipulate HTML to get it to do what you want is pretty frustrating. There are no consistent methods for creating layout. For example, to lay out a page in columns, you probably rely on tables, instead of style sheet positioning, because you must achieve total cross-browser compatibility for your clients. You also have little control over white space—relying on workarounds such as single pixel spacer GIFs—and there's essentially no stable way to manage type within HTML itself. HTML is in many ways a designer's nightmare—born of the very fact that the Web was never intended to be a visual environment. But it became one, and how to manage that reality has been a challenge ever since.

Another child of SGML is XML, the Extensible Markup Language. Interestingly, XML is also a meta-language. It, too, exists as a means of creating other languages. Although SGML is a very complex and extremely detailed meta-language, XML has emerged as a streamlined meta-language suitable for creating Web markup languages that are customizable and flexible for the needs of specific applications. Examples of XML markup applications include Scalable Vector Graphics (SVG), Synchronized Multimedia Integration Language (SMIL), and Wireless Markup Language (WML).

People working on the evolution of markup languages via the W3C began to look at HTML and the problems it was facing due to this stretching and manipulating to accommodate design. Donning the glasses of XML, it becomes very clear that HTML had become in many ways a linguistic mess. So, work was done to take the very best of HTML and apply the strength and logic of XML. From this work came a new, refined markup language, the Extensible Hypertext Markup Language (XHTML).

XHTML is the reformulation of HTML as an XML application. In other words, the rules and methodologies of XML are applied to HTML, bringing syntactical strength back into HTML, which lost that strength during its rapid evolution from text document markup language to the de facto language of visual design. By strengthening markup in this way, markup is brought a lot closer to the interoperable, accessible, international, and growth-oriented goals mentioned at the beginning of this chapter.

TRANSITIONING FROM HTML TO XHTML

Because XHTML is the current recommended markup language of the W3C, many people are beginning to transition their practices to XHTML. However, XHTML is not always the best choice because it is often stricter than HTML 4. So, it takes experience and understanding to be able to choose which markup methodology to use.

To balance shifting trends in convention and approach the demand for better standardization across browsers, HTML 4 emerged with some potent rules. Your challenge is that these rules, in their strictest incarnation, don't always work in cross-browser/cross-platform design, and they often are not backward compatible.

To address these issues, HTML 4 has built-in accommodations for them. Interestingly, it is this flexibility within HTML 4 that is the least understood—and yet it's a seminal aspect of the HTML 4 specification.

These accommodations are found in the document type definitions (DTDs) found within the HTML 4 specification. DTDs are essentially a laundry list of all the elements, attributes, and syntax conformance rules that must be adhered to for a document to conform to the real language in question. In formal markup, the DTDs are declared within the document, which you'll see later.

The following DTDs exist in HTML 4:

- **Strict HTML 4**—This is the purest of HTML 4 interpretations. Anything deprecated (made obsolete) in this version of the language is not used, ever. Most presentational elements and attributes are left out of the interpretation—you can't use a font tag, for example, when writing a document that conforms to a strict interpretation. As such, the strict interpretation is also the most optimistic version of HTML 4 because if you want any presentation at all, you'll use CSS—something that is difficult to achieve in specific environments.

- **Transitional, or "loose" HTML 4**—By combining aspects of the prior version of HTML (HTML 3.2) with elements from the strict HTML 4 standard, a more realistic, usable version of the language emerges. This is where you will find the most backward-compatibility for many public and contemporary Web site designs. In transitional HTML, you can use font tags, attributes for presentation, and tables for layout, and the concern with document structure is slightly less demanding than in strict interpretations. Most readers will likely use transitional HTML (or XHTML 1.0) to accommodate their goals.

- **Frameset HTML 4**—This includes all the information within the transitional version combined with the newly adopted frame-based elements such as frame, frameset, noframes, and iframe. The frameset interpretation exists as an interpretation to confirm the standardization of frames within HTML and offer a regulated method of using them.

The standard expects that you will insert the appropriate document version and the document type definition (see the section "Features of XHTML," later in this chapter) information identifying the specification to which the document conforms. So, if you're creating a strict HTML document, the shell of the document will appear with the document version, as shown in Listing 14.1.

Listing 14.1 Sample HTML Strict Document

```
<!DOCTYPE HTML PUBLIC "-//W3C//DTD HTML 4.0//EN"
"http://www.w3.org/TR/REC-html40/strict.dtd">
<html>
<head>
<title>Strict HTML Sample Shell</title>
</head>
<body>

</body>
</html>
```

14

Transitional documents will appear with the document type and structure demonstrated in Listing 14.2.

Listing 14.2   Sample HTML Transitional Document

```
<!DOCTYPE HTML PUBLIC "-//W3C//DTD HTML 4.0 Transitional//EN"
"http://www.w3.org/TR/REC-html40/loose.dtd">
<html>
<head>
<title>Transitional HTML Sample Shell</title>
</head>
<body>

</body>
</html>
```

Finally, any page you build with frames in HTML 4 should be denoted as being within the frameset interpretation. Frameset documents contain the frameset version information, as follows:

```
<!DOCTYPE HTML PUBLIC "-//W3C//DTD HTML 4.0 Frameset//EN"
"http://www.w3.org/TR/REC-html40/frameset.dtd">
```

⇨ *Does Dreamweaver contain these document interpretations? The answer is "sort of." Find out what Dreamweaver does have, how to access it, and where to learn how to add your own templates to Dreamweaver in "Available Standards-Based Templates" in the "Troubleshooting" section at the end of this chapter.*

Along with these interpretations are three primary concepts HTML 4 encourages authors to adopt. These concepts exist to ameliorate problems and concerns with the language's past (and often current) use:

- **Separate document structure from presentation and style**—Much of HTML 4 is focused on taking any element from prior language versions used for presentation or style of information and setting it aside. Instead, style sheets for presentation and design are typically recommended.

- **Think carefully about accessibility and internationalization**—Because HTML was originally built for all people to access documents, including those on a variety of platforms, those using different languages, those using different user agents, and those with a special concern for people having physical impairments, the standard asks that we keep these issues in mind when authoring code. A good example of this is adding `alt` attribute descriptions to `img` tags, helping visually impaired users to better understand Web documents.

- **Make documents load more quickly via careful table design**—HTML 4 has several element additions that help tables render incrementally. In fact, HTML 4 highly encourages developers to move away from using tables for an underlying grid system, implementing the use of style sheet positioning in its place. Of course, choosing to use style positioning over table grid systems is difficult to achieve. Style sheet positioning is highly unstable and unreliable, and no backward-compatibility is built in.

14

XHTML builds heavily on these foundations. Whether you choose to employ XHTML or HTML, the bottom line is that you should use recommended markup rather than arbitrary markup. This is especially important when you move from HTML into the realm of XML and beyond because without the foundational concepts and techniques, you run the risk of making mistakes such as introducing proprietary or even nonexistent markup into a document. If that happens, and you try to share it with another colleague, company, or application, significant and time-consuming problems can ensue.

FEATURES OF XHTML

As you delve more deeply into XHTML, you can begin to see how it uses aspects of both familiar HTML concepts and strict ideas influenced by XML. In XHTML, document conformance and DTDs are essentials. This is true, too, of HTML 4.

Document Conformance and Document Type Definitions

For a document to conform to XHTML 1.0, it must adhere to the following:

- The document must validate against one of the three DTDs: strict, transitional, or frameset.

- The root element of an XHTML 1.0 document must be `<html>`.

- The root element must designate an XHTML namespace using the `xmlns` attribute.

- A `DOCTYPE` (document type) definition must appear in the document prior to the root element.

As mentioned earlier, the vocabulary rule sets used in Web markup are called document type definitions. In XHTML 1.0, as with HTML 4.0, there are only three preset DTDs. How you write your XHTML documents—and how they're validated by various tools—relies on the DTD you choose.

In XML, and for future versions of XHTML, DTDs can be customized. This adds a great deal of power to your toolkit because you can define the rules and the actual tags a document must use to conform to that common language. So, if a company makes a special product, it can create its own vocabulary to manage that product. Or entire industries, such as medical or financial, can share DTDs specific to their unique needs.

The three DTDs currently available for your use in XHTML 1.0 are

- Strict

- Transitional

- Frameset

You should immediately recognize these DTDs because they are the same as in HTML 4.01. The actual vocabularies are somewhat different, however, reflecting the rigor and syntactical shifts that have occurred in XHTML since HTML became an XML application.

XHTML 1.0 that follows the strict document type definition is the most rigorous—and the purest—of XHTML syntax. When writing a strict XHTML 1.0 document, you'll use the strict `DOCTYPE` declaration, as follows:

14

```
<!DOCTYPE html PUBLIC "-//W3C//DTD XHTML 1.0 Strict//EN" "DTD/xhtml1-strict.dtd">
```

Listing 14.3 shows a strict and conforming XHTML 1.0 document with the XML prolog in place.

Recommended, Not Required: The XML Prolog

A recommended, but not absolutely necessary, component to XHTML 1.0 documents is the XML declaration, `<?xml`. The XML declaration is used to define the document as an XML document and describe the XML version. Many XHTML authors leave the XML declaration out because it is not understood by many browsers and causes the code to render improperly or not render at all if used.

There is a problem with leaving the XML declaration out, however. Because the XML declaration allows you to specify the character encoding within a document (this is important for documents that use non-ASCII encoding), omitting it leaves your pages vulnerable to improper rendering of special characters. As a workaround, you can include a META tag in the head portion of your document that defines the character encoding you're using (this usually is UTF-8 or UTF-16):

```
<meta http-equiv="Content-Type" content="text/html;charset=UTF-8" />
```

This META workaround for character encoding works only for UTF-8 or UTF-16 (standard ASCII characters). If you are using any other encoding method, you must include the XML declaration for the encoding to work.

If you're working on documents in English, you won't need to worry too much. However, if you are creating documents using other character sets, such as those in Japanese for example, you'll need to research and employ the appropriate character set. You can do this with a visit to http://www.unicode.org/.

Listing 14.3   A Strict and Conforming XHTML 1.0 Shell

```
<?xml version="1.0"?>
<!DOCTYPE html PUBLIC "-//W3C//DTD XHTML 1.0 Strict//EN"
"http://www.w3.org/TR/xhtml1/DTD/xhtml1-strict.dtd">
<html xmlns="http://www.w3.org/1999/xhtml">
<head>
<title>Strict Document Sample with XML Prolog</title>

</head>
<body>


</body>
</html>
```

Transitional XHTML 1.0 is the more forgiving vocabulary within the standard. This forgiveness appears in general concepts rather than syntactical adherence. In other words, you must follow syntax rules and the rules for well-formed documents. But, you do have leeway with certain elements, attributes, and code approaches. For example, in transitional XHTML 1.0, you can use deprecated tags, such as font or center. These are considered presentational and are therefore unavailable in the strict DTD.

Transitional XHTML 1.0 documents use the transitional DOCTYPE declaration:

```
<!DOCTYPE html PUBLIC "-//W3C//DTD XHTML 1.0 Transitional//EN"
"DTD/xhtml1-transitional.dtd">
```

Listing 14.4 provides a look at a Transitional XHTML 1.0 document.

Listing 14.4   A Transitional XHTML 1.0 Shell

```
<?xml version="1.0"?>
<!DOCTYPE html PUBLIC "-//W3C//DTD XHTML 1.0 Transitional//EN"
"DTD/xhtml1-transitional.dtd">
<html xmlns="http://www.w3.org/1999/xhtml">
<head>
<title>Transitional Document Sample</title>

</head>
<body>


</body>
</html>
```

The Frameset DTD denotes a document as a frameset. Any frameset you create in XHTML 1.0 must be declared as such; otherwise, it will not validate. The Frameset DTD in XHTML 1.0 requires the following DOCTYPE declaration:

```
<!DOCTYPE html PUBLIC "-//W3C//DTD XHTML 1.0
Frameset//EN" "DTD/xhtml1-frameset.dtd">
```

Listing 14.5 is a conforming frameset in XHTML 1.0.

Listing 14.5   Frameset in XHTML 1.0

```
<?xml version="1.0"?>
<!DOCTYPE html PUBLIC "-//W3C//DTD XHTML 1.0 Frameset//EN"
"DTD/xhtml1-frameset.dtd">
<html xmlns="http://www.w3.org/1999/xhtml">
<head>
<title>Frameset Document Sample</title>

</head>
<frameset>


</frameset>
</html>
```

14

Well-Formedness and Syntactical Rules in XHTML 1.0

What about the ways in which XML has influenced HTML's familiar syntax? Several key concepts are inherent to XHTML as a result of XML's influence, but they are perhaps significantly different from the way you've been authoring HTML.

First, the concept of *well-formedness* is key. This means that any document you write must follow the correct order of elements and the correct method of writing those elements. As you probably realize, browsers forgive. So, if I were to write the following in HTML:

```
<b><i>Welcome to my Web site!</b></i>
```

A browser is likely to display my text as both bold and italic. However, look at the markup. It opens with the opening bold tag and then the italics tag. But instead of nesting the tags properly, the bold tag is closed first. This is improper nesting, and as a result, the code is considered poorly formed. To be well-formed, the code must be properly ordered:

```
<b><i>Welcome to my Web site!</i></b>
```

This is a well-formed bit of markup. Well-formedness is a critical concept in XHTML 1.0, and you must get used to following logical order within your documents.

Some other issues related to markup are necessary in XHTML 1.0. They include

- **All elements and attribute names must appear in lowercase**—HTML is not case sensitive. You can write HTML elements and attribute names in lowercase (`<p align="right">`), uppercase (`<P ALIGN="RIGHT">`), or mixed case (`<P aLiGn="right">`). All those mean the same thing— in HTML. But in XHTML, every element and attribute name *must* be in lowercase: `<p align="right">`. Note that attribute values (such as `"right"` in this case, but especially true for case-sensitive filenames in URLs) can be in mixed case.

- **All attribute values must be quoted**—In HTML, you can get away without quoting values. So, you can have the following:

  ```
  <img src="my.gif" height=55 width=65 alt="picture of me">
  ```

  Some attributes are quoted, some aren't. But when writing XHTML, you *must quote all attribute values*. There are no exceptions to this:

  ```
  <img src="my.gif" height="55" width="65" alt="picture of me">
  ```

- **All non-empty elements require end tags, and empty elements must be properly terminated**—A non-empty element is an element that might contain content or other elements. A paragraph is non-empty because within the tags exists text, images, or other media. In HTML, you could open a paragraph but not close it. In XHTML 1.0, you must close any non-empty element. Use this:

  ```
  <p>This text is content within my non-empty paragraph element.</p>
  ```

  not this:

  ```
  <p>This text is content within my non-empty paragraph element.
  ```

Another good example of this is the list item element, `<li>`. In HTML, you can simply open the list item and never close it—it's optional. But in XHTML, you must close it. Use this:

```
<li>This is the first item in my list.</li>
```

not this:

```
<li>This is the first item in my list.
```

Empty elements are those elements that do not contain content. Good examples are breaks, horizontal rules, and images. In the case of empty elements, a termination is required. In XML, and thus in XHTML, this is done by using a slash after the element name, so `<br>` becomes `<br/>`. But because some browser bugs cause pages to render improperly, in XHTML 1.0, you must add a space before the final slash to ensure the page is readable:

```
<br />.
```

Remember that image element just a few paragraphs ago? Even with all the attributes quoted, it's not proper XHTML 1.0. Because it's an empty element, it must be terminated accordingly:

```
<img src="my.gif" height="55" width="65" alt="picture of me" />
```

As you can see, the rules here are not so daunting. It just takes a bit of knowledge and precision, and you can easily author documents that are readable by current user agents *and* adhere to the XHTML recommendation.

➩ *This is a lot of information! Fortunately, Dreamweaver provides helpful tips and information about HTML and XHTML. See "Dreamweaver Help for XHTML" in the "Troubleshooting" section later in this chapter.*

➩ *To learn more about how to incorporate proper DOCTYPEs and DTDs into your Dreamweaver documents, see "Peer to Peer: Problem URLs and Modifying Dreamweaver Files for Standards Compliance," p. 24, and "Peer to Peer: Adding Standards-Based Templates," p. 222.*

SYNTAX

Many Dreamweaver MX users might be familiar with but not have a clear understanding of the building blocks of HTML and XHTML: elements, attributes, and values. The following sections will help clarify those building blocks.

Elements

There are specific as well as general rules and conventions regarding elements. The first is that all standard element identifiers are contained within a less-than and greater-than symbol, as follows:

```
<link>
```

14

Note that there are no spaces between the symbols and the tag and no spaces between the letters that denote the tag.

Elements that appear in the body of a document are defined by the concept of *block* or *inline*.

Block

Block-level elements refer to structural elements. These elements can contain other block-level elements (as in a division containing paragraphs) and inline elements. Usually, block-level elements are rendered by browsers as beginning on a new line.

Inline

Inline elements, also referred to as *text-level* elements, are those elements that contain content. They can also contain other inline elements, but they should not contain block-level elements. Inline elements typically work within the content of a document without causing any line breaks.

In transitional HTML and XHTML, inline elements can appear alone. However, in strict HTML and XHTML, all inline elements must be contained within a reasonable block-level element. So, let's say you are using the img element and you do not place it within a division, paragraph, or other block-level element. In a transitional document, this will cause no problems with validation. However, in strict documents, you will get an error while attempting to validate the document because the inline element must be properly contained by a block-level element.

Attributes

Many elements can act perfectly fine alone, but one variety of tags *must* have attributes to function properly.

An *attribute* actually consists of two properties: the attribute name and the attribute value.

Many attributes in HTML have historically had to do with modifying the way something on a page looks. In the strict DTDs of HTML 4.0, HTML 4.01, and XHTML 1.0, and the XHTML 1.1 DTD, any attribute that defines a style is not allowed; instead, you must use style sheets. However, you can use these attributes and their companion values in transitional HTML 4.01 and XHTML 1.0.

Other attributes are fundamental to the proper interpretation of an element and have nothing to do with presentation at all. Examples would be src, alt, href, and so on.

Attribute names can be whole words, partial words, abbreviations, or even acronyms. Some whole word attributes include align, color, link, and face. Partial word examples include src for "source" and vlink for "visited link."

Attributes follow the tag and are separated by at least one space:

```
<body bgcolor...
```

These are then set by the attribute value before the tag is closed.

A tag can have more than one attribute, and, in fact, some tags take on many attributes at the same time. In this case, the syntax follows the same concept: first the tag, then a space, and then an

14

attribute. The attribute receives a value, and then a space is again introduced *before* the next attribute:

```
<body bgcolor="#ffffff" text="#000000">
```

and so forth, until all the attributes and their values are included.

Values

Values, like attributes, can be made up of a whole word. If you're using the div, or division, element and want to align all the information in that division in a transitional HTML or XHTML document, you can select from several values that modify the align attribute. Such values include left, right, center, and justify.

A resulting statement would be

```
<div align="right">
</div>
```

Some attribute values are numeric, referring to pixels, percentages, browser-defined sizes, or hexadecimal numbers to define color. A pixel value example is well described by the width attribute:

```
<table width="768">
```

Similarly, you can use a percentage value in the same instance. The markup would then be

```
<table width="100%">
```

In this case, the table would flex to 100% of the available space.

Browser-defined sizes are those sizes that the browser selects. In other words, you can't predetermine the exact size, such as with pixels, but you can approximate the size. The best example of this is with the deprecated font tag attribute size. The size attribute can opt to take a value ranging from 1 to 7, with 1 being the smallest and 7 the largest:

```
<font size="5">
```

Any text between this and the closing font tag takes on the browser's interpretation of a size 5.

An example of a numeric type of value would be hexadecimal color codes:

```
<body bgcolor="#FFFFFF">
```

There are other kinds of values you should be aware of. One such value is a relative or absolute link to another document, meaning that a directory, series of directories, and specific filename can be included in certain attributes to fulfill a value:

```
<a href="http://www.molly.com/">Go to My Home Page</a>
```

This markup creates a link that, when activated, goes to my home page. The a, or anchor element, creates a link; the attribute is href, or hypertext reference; and the value is the URL, http://www.molly.com/.

Similarly, I can point to a directory and an image:

```
<img src="images/molly.gif" />
```

In this case, the tag is `img`, or image (which, again, is an empty element and must be terminated in XHTML); the attribute is `src` ("source"); and the value is a combination of the path to the images directory and the specific file, `molly.gif`.

Another interesting example is the `alt` attribute. This attribute appears in image or object tags and offers a description of the image or object for those individuals who can't or don't want to see the image or object:

```
<img src="molly.gif" alt="picture of Molly" />
```

In this situation, the value assigned to the `alt` attribute is actually a series of words used to describe the picture. You can also see in this example how a tag can have multiple attributes with corresponding values.

By now you probably have noticed that all values are preceded by an = symbol (the equal sign), and the value is within quotation marks.

EDITING MARKUP USING MACROMEDIA DREAMWEAVER MX

Dreamweaver offers numerous ways to customize and edit HTML and XHTML. If you're primarily a designer, you'll likely be working in Design view and modifying elements, attributes, and attribute values using the Properties toolbar. If you're primarily a document specialist or programmer, you might find yourself more comfortable working in Code view, switching back and forth to Design view to see your results. Dreamweaver MX also offers a combination Design and Code view, which is a great way to use both views simultaneously.

Regardless of how you work with Dreamweaver, it's important to customize your code settings to adhere to best practices and accommodate, or at the very least work toward, standards-based design.

The use of the word "code" to describe markup languages such as HTML and XHTML is controversial in certain sectors. The reason for this is that many professionals feel that "code" refers to higher levels of programming, whereas markup is just that: marks on a document, not a *code* per se. Even though Dreamweaver uses the word "code" to include HTML and XHTML, use caution when referring to markup as "code" in professional circles.

Customizing Preferences for Best Practices

Different designers and developers have developed preferences for the way their markup is displayed during editing and viewing. Also, your company might have preferences in terms of the way the resulting markup should look. This helps with consistency, especially when a team of people is working on a given project.

What's more, overriding default settings can give you more control over how Dreamweaver treats your markup and over the outcome of your documents.

Setting Formatting Preferences

The following formatting preferences can be modified in Macromedia Dreamweaver MX:

- **Use (Space or Tabs)**—This option enables you to set spaces or tabs for indentation.

- **Indent Size**—With this option, you can set the indent size by number of tabs or spaces.

- **Automatic Wrapping**—This feature adds a hard return at the end of a column.

- **Line Break Type**—Different types of operating systems manage line breaks differently. To ensure your line breaks properly on your server, you might want to modify this type.

- **Default Tag Case**—This controls the capitalization of your elements. This feature is especially important when working with case-sensitive languages such as XHTML or XML.

- **Default Attribute Case**—Controls the case of attributes.

- **Override Case of: Tags and Attributes**—This lets you override the case of elements and attributes from external files or type it in yourself. This is very handy for people who are used to authoring HTML but are transitioning to XHTML, where tags and attributes should be lowercase.

- **No Break After TD**—This option ensures that no line break appears after a table cell tag. This feature is important when designing fixed-width tables with sliced graphics because it prevents gapping.

- **Centering**—Here, you can choose whether to center using `center` or `div align="center"` when centering elements on a page.

To modify any of these settings, follow these steps:

1. From the main menu, select Edit, Preferences, Code Format. The Code Format dialog box appears (see Figure 14.1).

2. Find the check box, drop-down menu, or radio button of the option (or options) you want to modify.

3. Click OK.

Default tag and attribute case settings will not affect anything you type yourself into Code view, nor will they influence any previously authored document imported into Dreamweaver. These settings influence only the markup that is generated using Design view *unless* you select the Override case option.

Using `div align="center"` and the `center` element are both appropriate in transitional HTML and XHTML documents. However, these methods are considered presentational and are therefore not available if you are using strict interpretations of HTML and XHTML.

To apply your preferences to a document that was created in another editor, or in Dreamweaver prior to changes in your preferred format, simply open the document and select Commands, Apply Source Formatting. Your document will update to the current preferences.

14

Your preferences are set! You can change these preferences at any time should you need to do so.

Figure 14.1
The Preferencesfor Code Formatting screen controls the appearance of your documents.

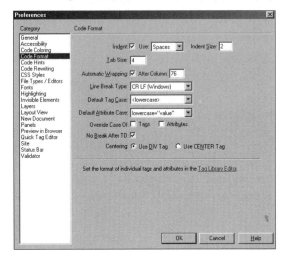

Setting Rewrite Preferences

Macromedia's Roundtrip HTML, discussed earlier in the chapter, is an important feature because you can use it to ensure that the work you do in Code view or that you import into Dreamweaver retains (or does not retain) a variety of markup concerns.

Here are the rewrite features you can control in Macromedia Dreamweaver MX:

- **Fix Invalidly Nested and Unclosed Tags**—Fixes tags that are poorly formed (see the section "Well-Formedness and Syntactical Rules in XHTML 1.0," earlier this chapter).

- **Rename Form Items when Pasting**—Ensures you don't duplicate the name value for form objects.

- **Remove Extra Closing Tags**—Deletes any closing tag that has no opening tag.

- **Warn when Fixing or Removing Tags**—Generates a summary of those invalid tags that Dreamweaver can't correct, providing you with line numbers so you can go in and troubleshoot the situation on your own.

- **Never Rewrite Code: In Files with Extensions**—Prevents Dreamweaver from rewriting any of the code if there's a specified filename extension.

- **Encode Special Characters in URLs Using %**—Checks your URLs to make sure they contain only legal characters.

- **Encode <,>, &, and " in Attribute Values Using &**—Encodes brackets, ampersands, and quotations in attribute values. Doing so is important in XHTML, which requires that certain characters are escaped to be properly valid.

To set any of these rewrite preferences, do the following:

1. Select Edit, Preferences, Code Rewriting (in Mac OS X, select Dreamweaver, Preferences, Code Rewriting).

2. When the Code Rewriting dialog box appears, make any adjustments to the preferences you want (see Figure 14.2).

3. Click OK.

Your rewrite features are now customized to your needs.

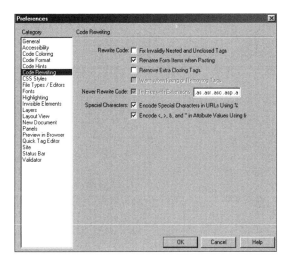

Figure 14.2
Setting preferences for rewriting gives you more control over the way Dreamweaver handles Roundtrip HTML.

Setting Viewing Preferences

Along with formatting and rewrite preferences, you can also set viewing preferences. These preferences will be helpful to you as you work in Code view and use the Code Inspector.

The viewing preference settings available are

- **Word Wrap**—Visually wraps the markup and content so you can view it within the screen. No line breaks are actually added, so setting this feature to your own screen size and preference doesn't affect the final document itself, just the way you see it.

- **Line Numbers**—Turns on or off the appearance of line numbers for each line of markup or code in the screen. This is very helpful when trying to locate problems or when you want to let others know where a problem exists.

- **Highlight Invalid HTML**—Highlights invalid HTML that Dreamweaver finds. You can then use the Property inspector to make corrections.

- **Syntax Coloring**—Coloring syntax helps authors find element and attribute types quickly, making troubleshooting much easier and faster. You can turn the syntax coloring feature in Dreamweaver on or off by using this option (see the sidebar "Syntax Coloring," later in this section, for more detail).

14

■ **Auto Indent**—Ensures that any time you press the Enter key, your markup automatically indents.

To set viewing preferences, follow these steps:

1. Open a page in Code view.

2. Select View, Code View Options. The Code View Options submenu appears (see Figure 14.3).

3. If you want to turn off something, highlight the option to remove the check. If something has a check by it, the option is enabled.

Figure 14.3
Viewing features with a check mark beside them are turned on, and those without check marks are inactive.

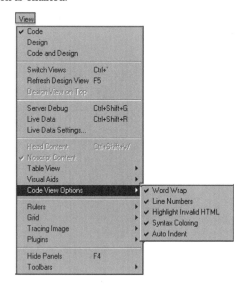

Syntax Coloring

Whenever you're working with documents—especially large ones—it becomes important to have as many tools available to make that work fast and easy. Color-coding syntax has long been a favorite means of assisting with the identification of various components of syntax within code and markup.

Many programming editors offer syntax coloring, including the very popular HTML editors Homesite and BBEdit. Dreamweaver also offers this option if you want to use it.

To use syntax coloring in Dreamweaver, first make sure it's available by selecting View, Code View Options. If there's a check next to Syntax Coloring, it is available and Dreamweaver will use a default color scheme. Otherwise, highlight it to turn it on.

If you want to customize the scheme, select Edit (Dreamweaver in Mac OSX), Preferences, Code Coloring. The Preferences dialog box appears. From the Document Type list, select HTML. Then, click the Edit Coloring Scheme. You can now modify the color and appearance of your code, enabling you to work more quickly and efficiently in the environment of your choice.

Editing HTML and XHTML in Code View

If you do a lot of hand-coding, you're likely to be spending most of your time in Code view. After you've set up your preferences for this view as you like them, you're ready to get to work.

To begin authoring or editing documents in Code view, simply open a new or an existing document. Switch to Code view using the menu icons or by selecting View, Code. You'll see the document or document template ready for you to begin typing.

A number of helpful tools are available to assist you as you work in Code view. You'll want to try them and see what you find helpful.

Working with Code Hints

Code hints are Dreamweaver's means of providing you with a list of helpful elements and attributes that you can insert or simply examine as you are entering your markup.

To add a tag using Code Hints, follow these steps:

1. Type the starting bracket of your element, <. The Code Hints list appears (see Figure 14.4).

Figure 14.4
The Code Hints list is a handy way to quickly add or make changes to your markup.

2. Scroll down the list until you find the tag you want. Double-click the tag to insert it.

3. To see the attributes available with the tag, press the space bar. Select the attribute you want and press Enter.

4. You can type in a value or select one from the attribute value menu.

5. Type the end bracket, >, after the last attribute you require to close the tag.

To add attributes to an existing tag, do the following:

1. Place your cursor immediately to the left of the closing bracket (>) of the opening tag.

2. Press the spacebar to bring up the Code Hints list.

3. Select the attribute and appropriate value.

When you're done, save the file to update the changes. Working with Code Hints takes a little bit of dexterity, but after you have the hang of it, you'll likely use Code Hints often.

Using Code Snippets

Code snippets have been a saving grace for people who are working on sites that reuse certain markup and content. Essentially, you store a section of code for reuse. Dreamweaver also has a few preset snippets you can use as needed.

14

To make your own snippet, follow these steps:

1. Open the Code panel and click the Snippets tab.

2. Click the New Snippet icon (see Figure 14.5). The Snippet dialog box appears (see Figure 14.6).

Figure 14.5
Code snippet options enable you to easily insert regularly used portions of code and content.

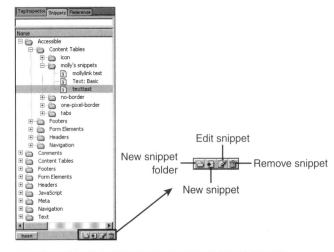

Edit snippet

New snippet folder

Remove snippet

New snippet

Figure 14.6
The Snippet dialog box enables you to customize the way in which your snippets will be inserted into a document.

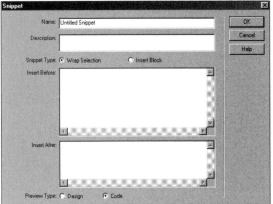

3. Add a name for your snippet in the Name text box. You should create a name for the snippet that is descriptive, such as "Molly.Com alpha menu." Add a description of the snippet to the Description text area.

4. If you want to have the snippet appear before or after selected code within your document, select the Wrap Selection radio button and then type (or copy and paste from another document) the code you want to insert in either the Insert Before or Insert After text area.

5. If you want to have the snippet appear at the insertion point, select the Insert Block radio button and then type or copy and paste the snippet into the main window.

6. If you want to have the code render and be able to preview it in the Preview pane of the Snippets panel, select the Design radio button. If you want to see only the code, select the Code radio button.

7. Click OK.

Your new snippet is now available in the Snippets panel. To insert a snippet—one you've created *or* a preset Dreamweaver snippet—either highlight the section of code in Code view that you want the snippet to appear before or after or place your cursor where you want the block snippet to go. Simply double-click the snippet in the Snippet panel, and the snippet will be added to your code. Or, you can click the Insert button along the bottom of the Snippets panel.

You can edit or delete a snippet by highlighting it and then clicking the appropriate icon (refer to Figure 14.5). Or, (Ctrl-click) [right-click] over a snippet to access the context menu, from which you can choose from a number of snippet management options.

You can also organize your snippets into custom folders. To do so, follow these steps:

1. Click the New Snippet Folder icon in the Snippets panel (refer to Figure 14.5).

2. A new snippets folder appears in the panel with the cursor in the Folder Name field. Name the folder.

3. Drag the snippets directly to the folder.

> **If you want to create a new snippet in that folder, open the folder before clicking the New Snippet icon.**

Using the Tag Chooser

Another helpful tool in Dreamweaver is the Tag Chooser. You can use the Tag Chooser to insert HTML or XHTML tags into your documents.

To add a tag using the Tag Chooser, follow these steps:

1. In Code view, place your cursor at the point in the document where you want to add the tag.

2. From the main menu, select Insert, Tag or (Ctrl-click) [right-click] and select Insert Tag. The Tag Chooser dialog box appears (see Figure 14.7).

3. The left window of the Tag Chooser contains a list of different tag types. Highlight the tag type you want in that window. The available tags will now appear in the right window.

4. To insert a tag, highlight the tag of your choice and click the Insert button. Or, simply double-click the tag name.

> **A great advantage of using the** Tag Chooser is the helpful Tag Info window along the bottom. When you highlight a tag, the tag's proper use and description appear in this window.

14

Left window   Right window

Figure 14.7
The Tag Chooser provides an interface for you to select the proper tag for your needs. Its Tag Info window is especially helpful, providing a tag description and proper usage.

Tag Info window

Working with the Tag Inspector and Tag Editor

If you're unsatisfied with the editing choices thus far, there are still more options for you! You can use the Tag Inspector and Tag Editor to manage tag editing in Dreamweaver Code view.

To use the Tag Inspector to edit a tag, do the following:

1. Open the Tag Inspector by selecting Window, Tag Inspector.

2. With your document open in Code view, click inside the tag you want to edit. Dreamweaver displays any available attributes that exist within its libraries.

3. Use the Tag Inspector property sheet to add your attributes. Predefined values appear within the list (see Figure 14.8).

4. Click Enter to update your tag.

Alternatively, you can edit tags using the Tag Editor. You can do this from within the Tag Inspector or from a context menu.

Here's how to edit a tag using the Tag Editor from within the Tag Inspector:

1. Open the Tag Inspector, and highlight the tag you want to edit.

2. Highlight the opening tag within the Tag Inspector. Available attributes appear in the property sheet. Click an attribute.

3. Click the Edit Tag icon in the Tag Inspector. The Tag Editor appears (see Figure 14.9).

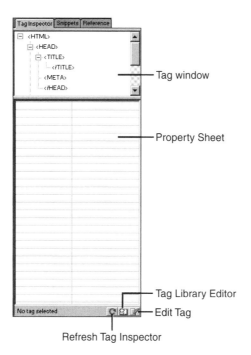

Figure 14.8
The Tag Inspector can be used to edit tags.

Tag window

Property Sheet

Tag Library Editor

Edit Tag

Refresh Tag Inspector

Figure 14.9
Using the Tag Editor, you can modify attributes and attribute values. Helpful information about the tags with which you're working is available, too.

4. Use the Tag Editor to make your modifications. If you have questions about what you're doing, click the Tag Info button to get information about the tag you're modifying.

5. Click OK.

At any time that you want to use the Tag Editor, you can do so by placing your cursor in the tag you want to edit. Then, (Ctrl-click) [right-click] and select Edit Tag. The Tag Editor appears, ready for your modifications.

14

Editing HTML and XHTML in Design Mode

Even if you're working in Design mode, you can make easy changes to the underlying markup. You can make edits using the Property inspector, a Tag Editor, the Quick Tag Editor, and a tag selector. This section shows those of you who prefer working in Design view how to accomplish these tasks.

> The Tag Editor options change according to the type of tag with which you're working and the amount of options available for that tag.

Editing Tags with the Property Inspector

While you're working in Design view, you might want to edit a feature such as a link color. To edit any element or attribute within Design view using the Property inspector, follow these steps:

> Want to add comments to your code? Comments are helpful to denote code sections and identify important areas or issues within the document. To add a comment to your document in Code view, simply click the Comment icon on the Insert bar. This inserts the comment code. Then, simply type your comment between the open and close comment tags.

1. Select the text or object you want to modify. The Property inspector will change to offer you appropriate options for what you've selected.

2. Make changes using the options within the Property inspector.

3. Save your file to update your changes.

You will now see the rendered results of your modifications. Continue to modify as you see fit. You can always switch to Code view if you want to see how working with the Property inspector affects the underlying code.

Using the Tag Editor

The Tag Editor is available in Design view as well as Code view. If you're working in Design view and want to harness the power of the Tag Editor, here's how:

1. Highlight the text or object you want to modify.

2. (Ctrl-click) [Right-click] and select Edit Tag. The Tag Editor for that element appears.

3. Make modifications to the tag, and when you're finished, click OK.

Changes affecting appearance will be available onscreen. If you want to look at the changes to the code, switch to Code view. Or, if you like to work using both, switch to Show Code and Design view.

Using the Quick Tag Editor

The Quick Tag Editor is available to you in Design view and offers three modes as follows:

- **Insert HTML**—Use this mode to insert new HTML markup.

- **Edit Tag**—Use this mode to edit an existing tag.

- **Wrap Tag**—Use this mode to wrap a tag around a selected section of text, objects, and other markup.

To insert an HTML tag using the Quick Tag Editor, follow these steps:

1. With your document open in Design view, place the cursor where you want to insert the new tag.

2. Press (Command-T) [Ctrl+T]. Or, click the Quick Tag Editor icon in the Property inspector (see Figure 14.10). Insert HTML mode is activated.

Quick Tag
Editor icon   Quick Tag Editor

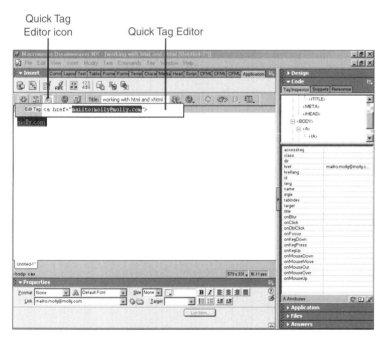

Figure 14.10
Insert HTML using the Quick Tag Editor in Design view.

3. Type in the tag, or select it from the tag list that appears and press Enter.

Your tag is now added to the document.

If you want to edit a tag using the Quick Tag Editor, select the link, object, text—whatever you want to modify—and press (Command-T) [Ctrl+T]. Then, type or select the attributes you want to use to modify the tag.

If you want to have the tag wrap around an object, select that object and then bring up the Quick Tag Editor. The tag you enter will wrap around the selected page component.

14

Using the Tag Selector

Still another handy tag management tool is the Tag Selector, which runs along the bottom of the Document window in all views (see Figure 14.11).

Figure 14.11
The Tag Selector keeps track of your document. You can click any tag to make modifications to it.

You can use the Tag Selector to edit and remove tags. Here's how to do so:

1. Click in the document to propagate the Tag Selector with the tags you want to manage.

2. (Ctrl-click) [Right-click] and select Edit Tag Code to bring up the Quick Tag Editor. Make your modifications.

3. If you want to remove the tag, select Remove Tag from the contextual menu.

Save your file to update any changes.

⇨ *Still not enough control over code? There are other options; check them out in "Using External Editors" in the "Troubleshooting" section of this chapter.*

TROUBLESHOOTING

Available Standards-Based Templates

I want to ensure that my default templates contain all the necessary basics to adhere to standards. How can I do this?

14

As mentioned, not all the templates available in Dreamweaver MX are standards compliant. Homesite offers a range of templates similar to those described in this chapter, but they, too, have some problems associated with them.

In the "Peer-to-Peer" section of Chapter 1, "Defining Your Site," you can learn how to take the templates provided in this chapter (and the expanded set, available on the CD) and bring them into Dreamweaver.

Dreamweaver Help for XHTML

I just don't understand all this XHTML stuff. I need help!

There are several interesting ways that Dreamweaver MX shows its support for XHTML in terms of documentation. Open the Help section of Dreamweaver by selecting Help, Using Dreamweaver. Once in the Help interface, click the Search tab and type the term **XHTML** into the search keyword field. Dreamweaver documents concerned with explaining and assisting you with XHTML will be listed. Of special interest is the "About the XHTML Code Generated by Dreamweaver" and the "Web Resources for XHTML" articles, which point you to the W3C and its validators for additional help.

Using External Editors

I know Dreamweaver MX has a lot of options for working with markup, but I'm used to using a specific editor. Can I use an external editor with Dreamweaver?

The integration of external HTML editors for use with Dreamweaver is a very easy process. In fact, Homesite is distributed along with Dreamweaver for precisely this purpose. To learn more about using external editors with Dreamweaver, please see Chapter 33, "Working with Other HTML Editors."

PEER TO PEER: MACROMEDIA AND THE WEB STANDARDS PROJECT

The Web Standards Project (WaSP) Dreamweaver Task Force was created in 2001 to accomplish two tasks of vital importance:

- To work with Macromedia's engineers to improve the standards compliance and accessibility of Web pages produced with Macromedia Dreamweaver, the market-leading professional visual Web editor and development tool. This part of the group's mission was largely fulfilled with the May 2002 release of Dreamweaver MX, although the Task Force will continue to work with Macromedia as the company fine-tunes subsequent versions of its product.

14

- To communicate effectively within the online Dreamweaver community, raising awareness of Web standards and helping others discover how their tools can be used to create standards-compliant, accessible sites. This work will continue indefinitely and is a key component of WaSP's developer education outreach program.

Since that time, advances have been made. Several books by WaSP members and standards evangelists specifically written for designers and developers (including this one) contain ample information on using Dreamweaver tools to achieve standards. Tools continue to be developed by third parties to address accessibility and other compliance concerns, and conferences such as Web Builder are including Dreamweaver MX training focused on these new features.

There is a special report of interest to readers by the WaSP Dreamweaver Task Force about Macromedia Dreamweaver MX that can be found at `http://www.webstandards.org/act/campaign/dwtf/mxassessed.html`. The mission, history, and participants of the Task Force are described at `http://www.webstandards.org/act/campaign/dwtf/`.

14

15

DESIGNING WITH STYLE

15

THE EVOLUTION OF STYLE

Ever since the Web took off as a popular medium in the early 1990s, designers have been scrambling to find new and more effective ways of adding style to their pages. In the early days of HTML, tags were merely intended to provide structure for content, specifying that selected content should be contained in a table, for example, or a line of text should be rendered as a heading. The actual display of this structure was left to the browser. Each browser had its own variations on the font size of a heading or whether it should appear in bold or italics. This worked for a while, back when the Web was more about information than entertainment. But it wasn't long before designers wanted to present their material but also wanted it to be visually appealing. In response, new tags and attributes were developed and Web design became much more complex. Black monospaced text on a gray background just didn't cut it anymore.

The Web is certainly a bigger and brighter place now, with eye-popping designs and interactive pages. Somehow, though, the form and function of HTML pages have become confusingly intertwined, and the adherence to HTML standards is getting lost. Novice developers, in particular, don't concern themselves with the difference between using a heading tag to denote a section head and simply formatting a block of text with a font tag and appropriate attributes. Even though the two might appear the same in a browser, a paragraph doesn't perform the same function as a heading.

Although this might appear to some as quibbling, the reality is that a document's proper structure affects many things, including whether it is portable or accessible. And, in the case of headers, it's important to note that some search engines use heading content as one of their criteria to determine site ranking. Also consider how much easier it is to perform a Find on a heading tag than to manually cull through dozens of paragraph tags.

WHAT ARE STYLES?

The current movement in standards-based Web design is to separate document structure from presentation. HTML documents without HTML-based presentational elements are smaller, are easier to modify, and can be readily adapted to numerous design themes. Web designers aren't about to give up their hard-won control over the visual presentation of their material, however, so leaving display totally up to the browser is unacceptable. In fact, designers want even more control over their designs, not less. Therefore, a component was needed to provide designers with presentation control. Enter the Cascading Style Sheet (CSS).

Designing Beyond HTML

CSS meets the requirement of separating form and function while also expanding the design possibilities beyond anything HTML could hope for. Font control, color management, margin control, and page layout are only a few of the design elements that are improved with CSS.

Perhaps the greatest advantage of style sheets is their updatability. When presentation is intermingled with the content and structure of the page, each change to font color or size must be made individually. Using CSS, a change to the style sheet updates any and all iterations of that style. If you're using an external style sheet, changes can be reflected across every page in the site that's linked to that style sheet. In some cases, you can give a site an entirely new appearance without touching a single page of HTML.

CSS is also one of the critical components of Dynamic HTML (DHTML), along with HTML and JavaScript. DHTML can make pages come alive using layers and timelines. It's also a means of providing interactivity for site visitors.

CSS Versus HTML Styles

Dreamweaver offers both CSS and HTML Styles. Although they both control the style and appearance of a document, their actual functionality is quite different. CSS can be applied to a wide range of HTML tags, either by redefining the tag itself or by adding a class attribute. CSS can be defined within the HTML document or in an external file, which in turn can be linked to multiple files. CSS can also be modified by changing the CSS declaration itself, with those modifications automatically applied to each occurrence when it's rendered in the browser.

HTML Styles is the way Dreamweaver describes any presentational attribute from within HTML—not CSS—to stylize a page. These are much more limited. Rather than serving to separate structure from presentation, these styles are intended to let you more easily apply inline formatting. They can be applied only to paragraphs or blocks of selected text, so they can't be used to format the appearance of a table or layer. The styles are applied using font tags, which cannot be used in Strict HTML and XHTML. HTML Styles are saved so you can use them in multiple documents. However, if you modify a style, those changes are applied only to future uses of the HTML Styles; they won't change existing formatting in any document.

HTML Styles are useful if you're designing for older browsers that most likely can't interpret CSS. Under most other circumstances, however, CSS is far preferable as a means to apply style.

HTML STYLES

Although HTML Styles aren't as powerful or standards-compliant as CSS, they still serve a purpose in some situations. If your site is targeted to those with older browsers, won't be modified often, and doesn't require adherence to the latest strict standards, HTML Styles are a quick method of formatting your text.

HTML Styles are created and applied using the HTML Styles panel (see Figure 15.1). The panel can be found in the Design panel group by default. You can also access it by selecting Window, HTML Styles from the menu.

Users of previous versions of Dreamweaver will notice that HTML Styles aren't quite what they used to be. This is most likely due to the increasing popularity of CSS. The HTML Styles panel is no longer included on the Launcher Bar by default (although it can be added in the Panels category of the Preferences dialog box). The HTML Styles panel also no longer comes with preset styles.

15

Selection style
Paragraph style

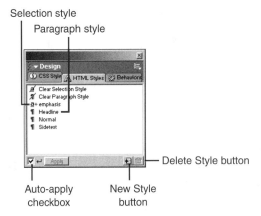

Figure 15.1
The HTML Styles panel controls the creation and application of HTML Styles.

Delete Style button

Auto-apply
checkbox

New Style
button

HTML Styles are divided into two types, designated with ¶ for paragraph styles and an underlined lowercase *a* (a) for selection styles. A paragraph style is applied to an entire paragraph, whereas selection styles are applied only to the selected text within a paragraph. Styles can be set to over-write any other formatting or to add the new formatting in addition to those previously applied. Styles that add formatting appear with a plus sign (+) next to their style type designation.

Creating HTML Styles

Before you can apply HTML Styles, you need to create them. After they're created, the styles can be applied to any text in the document or even multiple documents.

To create a new custom style from scratch, follow these steps:

1. Click the New Style button in the HTML Styles panel (or select Text, HTML Styles, New Style from the menu).

2. In the Define HTML Style dialog box, enter a name for the style (see Figure 15.2).

Figure 15.2
The Define HTML Style dialog box contains the most common text formatting options.

3. Choose whether this style will apply to paragraphs or selections of text in the Apply To field.

4. In the When Applying field, select whether this style adds to the existing style of the text or whether it clears any existing formatting and only applies the formatting specified in the new style.

5. Select font settings from the Font, Size, Color, and Style options:

   • The Font field contains a list of all the existing font groups. Select Edit Font List to add a new font group.

   • Font Size lists all the same size settings as the Property inspector. Remember, sizes preceded by a plus or minus are relative.

   • Font Color enables you to access the color picker or enter a hexadecimal color value.

   • The Bold and Italics buttons are self-evident. The Other button provides a list of all the same font style options that are listed in the Text, Style menu.

6. If you're creating a paragraph style, select the format and alignment of the paragraph:

   • Format enables you to designate the paragraph as a Heading or Preformatted text.

   • The Alignment options are Left, Center, and Right.

7. Click OK to save the HTML Style.

⇨ *For more information about font groups, see Chapter 3, "Formatting Text with HTML," p. 45.*

You can create an HTML Style from existing text. Select text that has been formatted. Then click the New Style icon in the HTML Styles panel. The Define HTML Style dialog box will open with all the formatting options of the selected text. Follow steps 2–7 of the previous procedure to finalize the new style.

You can modify any style in the HTML Styles list with the exception of the preset Clear styles. To modify a style, (Control-click) [right-click] it and then select Edit from the context menu.

The new HTML Style isn't automatically applied, even if a paragraph or selection has been made. The new style must be applied by selecting the new style from the HTML Styles panel and using either the auto-apply feature or the Apply button.

Caution

You can double-click a style to edit it, but this has the added result of applying the style to any selected text (or a paragraph, in the case of paragraph styles), which might not be your intention.

Applying HTML Styles

To apply a style, as shown in Figure 15.3, position the insertion point within a paragraph (for paragraph styles) or select a block of text (for selection styles). Select a style from the HTML Styles panel by clicking it.

Figure 15.3
The body text of this page is formatted with the Normal style. The bold text has an Emphasis style applied, and the sidebar is formatted with a Sidebar style. All were created in the HTML Styles panel.

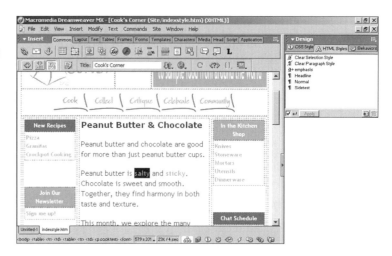

The HTML Styles panel has a check box in the lower-left corner. Check this box to have styles automatically applied when they're selected from the list. If this box isn't checked, you must click the Apply button to apply a style.

HTML Styles can also be applied from the menu. There are two default style options when you first begin using Dreamweaver, but as you create more HTML styles, those styles will appear on the menu. To choose a style from the menu, select Test, HTML Styles and make your choice from the available options. Selecting a style from this menu automatically applies it.

⇨ *Applied a style inadvertently to the wrong page element? Find out how to avoid, and fix, problems of this nature in "Editing HTML Styles" in the "Troubleshooting" section at the end of this chapter.*

The auto-apply feature in the HTML Styles panel is useful when you're applying a style to multiple selections in the document because it's fast. The Apply button ensures you don't unintentionally apply a style as you click in the HTML Styles list, particularly if you're editing styles and don't necessarily want them applied to a paragraph or selection. Choose the method that works best for you.

Default Styles

There are two entries on the HTML Styles panel by default. Clear Selection Style removes all text formatting tags for the selected text, and only for the selected text. If necessary, it places appropriate tags before and after the selected text, so surrounding text remains formatted with whatever style you select for it. This is useful when formatting a paragraph with one style and then removing the style from a block within that paragraph.

Clear Paragraph Style removes all formatting tags from the paragraph. If you don't like the effect of something you try, you can remove it easily.

CASCADING STYLE SHEETS

Cascading Style Sheets are far more powerful than HTML Styles and are the preferred method for applying styles to a site, except in certain situations. One of these considerations is browser compatibility. To date, no browser completely supports all of CSS, although the most recent versions of each major browser come close. Table 15.1 lists each of the major CSS properties and the earliest version of each major browser that supports it (if any).

15

Using one of the Clear styles removes formatting even if it wasn't applied using an HTML Style. Thus, if you've used the Property inspector to change the font size of a selection and then later use the Clear Selection Style on the selected text, it removes the font size attribute. If you use the Clear Paragraph Style, it removes formatting from the paragraph as a whole as well as from any formatted text blocks within the paragraph.

Table 15.1 CSS Compatibility in Major Browsers

CSS Background Properties	Browser Support
background	IE3, NN4, Opera 3
background-attachment	IE4, NN6, Opera 4
background-color	IE3, NN4, Opera 3
background-image	IE4, NN4, Opera 3
background-position	IE4, NN6, Opera 3
background-repeat	IE4, NN4, Opera3
CSS Block Properties	**Browser Support**
letter-spacing	IE4, NN6, Opera 3
text-align	IE3, NN4, Opera 3
text-indent	IE3, NN4, Opera 3
vertical-align	IE4, NN4, Opera 3
white-space	IE5.5, NN4, Opera 4
word-spacing	NN6, Opera 4
Box Properties	**Browser Support**
clear	IE4, NN4, Opera 3
float	IE4, NN4, Opera 3
height	IE4, NN6, Opera 3
margin	IE4, NN4, Opera 3
margin-bottom	IE4, NN4, Opera 3

15

Table 15.1 Continued

Box Properties	Browser Support
margin-left	IE3, NN4, Opera 3
margin-right	IE3, NN4, Opera 3
margin-top	IE3, NN4, Opera 3
max-height	None
max-width	None
min-height	None
min-width	
width	IE4, NN4, Opera 3

Border Properties	Browser Support
border	IE4, NN4, Opera 4
border-bottom	IE4, NN6, Opera 4
border-bottom-color	IE4, NN6, Opera 4
border-bottom-style	IE4, NN6, Opera 4
border-bottom-width	IE4, NN4, Opera 3
border-color	IE4, NN4, Opera 3
border-left	IE4, NN6, Opera 4
border-left-color	IE4, NN6, Opera 4
border-left-style	IE4, NN6, Opera 4
border-left-width	IE4, NN4, Opera 3
border-right	IE4, NN6, Opera 4
border-right-color	IE4, NN6, Opera 4
border-right-style	IE4, NN6, Opera 4
border-right-width	IE4, NN4, Opera 3
border-style	IE4, NN4, Opera 3
border-top	IE4, NN6, Opera 4
border-top-color	IE4, NN6, Opera 4
border-top-style	IE4, NN6, Opera 4
border-top-width	IE4, NN4, Opera 3
border-width	IE4, NN4, Opera 3
padding	IE4, NN4, Opera 3
padding-bottom	IE4, NN4, Opera 3
padding-left	IE4, NN4, Opera 3
padding-right	IE4, NN4, Opera 3
padding-top	IE4, NN4, Opera 3

Table 15.1 Continued

Extensions Properties	Browser Support
text-shadow	None
cursor	IE4, NN6, Opera 3

List Properties	Browser Support
list-style	IE4, NN6, Opera 3
list-style-image	IE4, NN6, Opera 3
list-style-position	IE4, NN6, Opera 3
list-style-type	IE4, NN4, Opera 3

Positioning Properties	Browser Support
bottom	IE5, Opera 3
clip	IE4, NN6, Opera 4
display	IE4, NN4, Opera 3
left	IE4, NN4, Opera 3
overflow	IE4, NN6, Opera 4
position	IE4, NN4, Opera 3
right	IE5, Opera 3
top	IE4, NN4, Opera 3
visibility	IE4, NN6, Opera 3
z-index	IE4, NN6, Opera 4

Text Properties	Browser Support
color	IE3, NN4, Opera 3
direction	IE5
font	IE4, NN4, Opera 3
font-family	IE3, NN4, Opera 3
font-size	IE3, NN4, Opera 3
font-style	IE4, NN4, Opera 3
font-variant	IE4, NN5, Opera 3
font-weight	IE3, NN4, Opera 3
line-height	IE3, NN4, Opera 3
text-decoration	IE3, NN4, Opera 3
text-transform	IE4, NN4, Opera 4

Unlike HTML Styles, CSS truly separates presentation from structure. Deprecated tags are avoided, making CSS the perfect choice to use with Strict DTDs. Styles can be applied to any tag or even to a specific class of that tag. A complete discussion of CSS could fill its own book, and indeed, there are several excellent books on the subject. This section merely serves as an overview of the structure and versatility of CSS.

15

INSIDE CSS MARKUP

As you saw in Table 15.1, CSS properties can be applied to a wide range of elements. To use these properties, you first create a rule for the display of a particular tag. A rule is made up of the following components:

■ **Selector**—The element to which you're applying the style. If you want to format the paragraph tag to display text in burgundy, for example, the selector is the <p> tag.

■ **Declaration**—The properties and values that describe how to display the selector, including

● **Property**—The property of the selector being modified, such as the color, size, font, margin, or position. For example, to display the burgundy paragraph text, you must modify the color property.

● **Value**—The setting for the property. For burgundy paragraph text, for example, the value of the color property is #660033.

When you put these parts together, the result is a rule that looks like this:

```
p {color: #660033;}
```

Notice the declaration is enclosed in curly brackets. A rule can contain multiple declarations within the brackets, each separated with a semicolon. Thus, a rule with many declarations can be grouped like this:

```
p {
color: #660033;
font-family: Trebuchet, san-serif;
font-size: 14pt;
text-align: center;
}
```

This results in centered, burgundy text in either the Trebuchet MS font or a similar san-serif font in a 14-point size.

Grouping

Declarations can also be used for multiple selectors at the same time, which is called *grouping*:

```
p, h1, h2 {color: #660033; font-family: Trebuchet MS;}
```

This rule defines a style for the paragraph, heading 1, and heading 2 tags.

> **Caution**
>
> Keep in mind that even if a CSS property has widespread support among current browsers, many Web surfers don't update their browsers. This is particularly true of the latest releases of each browser because many users choose to wait for the bugs to be worked out before upgrading.

> To learn more about working with CSS in the context of HTML and XHTML, try *Special Edition Using HTML and XHTML* from Que.

Grouping can also be used in style declarations. You can group font properties, for example. A typical body style might look like this:

```
body {
font-family: Trebuchet MS, san-serif;
font-size: 13pt;
line-height: 14pt;
font-weight: bold;
font-style: normal;
}
```

By grouping the arguments, the same style can be shortened to the following:

```
body {
font: bold normal 13pt/14pt Trebuchet, san-serif;
}
```

When grouping arguments, the order of the properties is very important. Notice that although font-style is the last declaration in the expanded rule, it is the second value listed in the shorthand declaration. Also notice that no commas appear between the values, other than the one separating the font family values.

The semicolon is important for separating declarations, but it's optional after the last declaration in a rule. If you forget to include a semicolon between declarations, the entire rule might be ignored by a browser. It's best to just get into the habit of always adding a semicolon to the end of declarations, including those at the end of a rule.

Nesting Style

Styles can even be nested. Let's say you want to define all paragraph text to be burgundy except when it's contained in a table—you want that text to be dark blue (#333366). The style sheet for these rules would appear like this:

```
p {color: #660033;}
td p {color: #333366;}
```

The ungrouped example also shows how an extensive style rule can be declared over multiple lines. The selector and opening curly bracket are placed on the first line, and each property/value group is displayed on another line, ending with the closing curly bracket on the last line.

Notice that, unlike the structure of a rule being applied to multiple tags, the second rule in this style sheet doesn't separate the selectors with a comma. This lack of a comma is what tells the browser to render the style only when the tag is nested as such.

Selectors: HTML, Classes, and IDs

There are several types of selectors of which to be aware:

- **Element selectors**—Refer directly to an HTML element, such as p, h1, a, and so on.

- **Class selectors**—Class selectors can be considered "custom" selectors. They are defined with a name preceded by a period, such as .bodytext, followed by the style declaration. They are applied within the HTML document using the class attribute:

```
<p class="bodytext">This paragraph will take on the style you've defined
for the class selector "bodytext".</p>
```

■ **ID selectors**—Similar to class selectors, ID selectors have several differences. First, they begin with a hash mark (#) instead of a period. They are called on in the document with the `id` attribute. IDs also differ from class selectors in that a specific ID is used only once within a document.

▷ *Unclear or confused about the use of* `id`? *It might be the browsers you're using. See "Browsers and the* `id` *Attribute" in the "Troubleshooting" section at the end of this chapter.*

Posting a recipe is an example of the use of class selectors. You might want the ingredients list to appear in a large font size in burgundy. The directions can appear in a smaller size in dark blue, and the nutritional information could appear in an even smaller size in black. You could try to be clever and use a different format tag for each section. This changes the structure of your document, however, which can have functional implications, particularly as browsers change their support for various tags. Instead, each of these styles can be declared as a different class.

Class tags can be defined in two ways. If the style is to be applied only to paragraphs of a particular class, you can define the class within the paragraph selector. On the other hand, if you want the style to be available to a wide range of elements, such as to headings and list items as well as paragraphs, you can define the class as a selector itself. Thus, the style rules for the previous example could appear as follows:

```
.ingred {color: #660033; font-size: 13pt;}
p.direct {color: #333366; font-size: 11pt;}
p.nutri {color: #000000; font-size: 9pt;}
```

Notice in the example that the directions and nutrition information classes are defined as being a subset of the paragraph element, whereas the ingredients are defined as a standalone class. This is because ingredients can appear either in paragraph format or in lists. Defining the classes this way gives you the flexibility to apply the styles where they're best served.

In the HTML document, you place the class name wherever the style should apply:

```
<p class="direct">Directions</p>
```

To apply a class style to a selection instead of an entire paragraph, use the `<div>` and `<span>` tags with the class attribute. When giving recipe directions, the name of each ingredient can appear in the `.ingred` class style—yet another reason to define that class independently of a tag element. The directions would appear as such:

```
<p class="direct"> Heat oven to 300 degrees F. Place aluminum foil
on cookie sheet; generously brush with 1 tablespoon of the
<span class="ingred">oil</span>.
Arrange <span class="ingred">tomato halves</span>, cut sides up,
in single layer on foil; brush with 2 teaspoons of the oil. Sprinkle
with <span class="ingred">sugar</span>, <span class="ingred">salt</span>
and <span class="ingred">pepper</span>. </p>
```

Figure 15.4 shows how a recipe appears in the browser when using this style sheet.

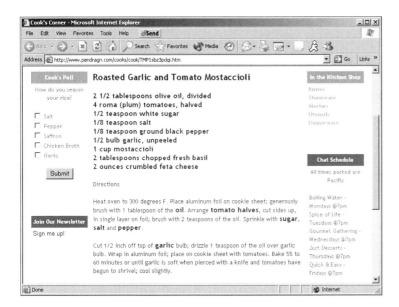

Figure 15.4
This recipe applies the three classes declared in the style sheet.

As you can see, defining classes takes advance planning, both in structuring your style sheet and in coding your document.

Link Classes

One of the most common uses of style is to format links to suit the design of a site. The a tag can be styled to remove the underlining on links. Links have four states—active, hover, link, and visited—and each of these states can be defined separately in a style sheet. The active state of the link is when it's clicked by a user. The hover state displays when the mouse is over the link, whereas the link state applies to links that have not been visited. The visited state is how links are displayed after they've been recently visited.

Because of their popularity, Dreamweaver makes these pseudo-classes readily available when creating a new style.

⇨ *For a complete explanation of the CSS Styles panel, see Chapter 16, "Using Cascading Style Sheets in Dreamweaver," p. 285.*

Style Integration

Style sheets can be used by HTML documents in three primary ways. The relating of a style sheet to a document is referred to as *integration*. The location of your style rules is just as important as the declarations within them.

External CSS

An external style sheet is also called a *linked* style sheet because it's a separate document that is linked to one or more HTML documents. This type of style sheet offers the greatest amount of flexibility because changes to the style sheet update the display of every page from which it's linked.

External style sheets simply contain the rules you defined for your page or site, and they're saved with a .css extension. To apply the style sheet to an HTML document, you add a <link> tag to the head of the HTML document, such as

```
<link rel="stylesheet" href="cooksite.css" type="text/css">
```

This link must be added to the head of every HTML document that uses the style sheet. To modify the appearance of a site, simply edit the style sheet. Whenever a page is viewed in a browser, the current CSS rules are adopted.

Dreamweaver can display many styles in the Document window, whether they're applied internally or from an external style sheet. Some styles, however, can be displayed only in a browser. When testing your style sheets, use the Preview in Browser feature of Dreamweaver.

Internal CSS

Internal style sheets, also known as *embedded* style sheets, are used to control a single HTML document. The style rules are placed in the <head> of the document in a <style> tag pair, such as the following:

```
<head>
<title>Cook's Corner</title>
<style>
<!--
p {color: #660033;}
p.ingred {font: 12pt Trebuchet MS;}
-->
</style>
</head>
```

Notice the actual style rules are contained in a comment tag. This is to prevent them from being displayed in a browser that doesn't support the <style> element. The element itself would be ignored by older browsers—just as older browsers ignore other tags they don't recognize—but the contents of the tag would be rendered as regular text if they weren't enclosed in a comment tag.

Applying Styles in a Tag

The third type of style, the inline style, is an attribute applied directly to a tag within the body of the HTML document, such as

```
<p style="color: #660033;">There are three new recipes.</p>
```

Inline styles can also be used in <div> and <span> tags to apply a style to a selection.

This method gives you complete control over that particular instance of that specific element, but it doesn't apply the style anywhere else within either the document or the site. Thus, the inline style

15

is most useful for exceptions to either the default display or an internal or external style sheet. It's far less easy to update inline styles, so they generally shouldn't be used as a matter of course.

Other Styles

There are other style sheet types besides external, embedded, and inline. Two other forms of style sheets, *imported* and *user-defined*, are in use as well. You can create these sheets just as you would an external sheet. An imported sheet is integrated with an HTML or XHTML document using the @import rule, which is beyond the scope of this book. A user-defined style sheet is simply one that a user writes and places as a default within her browsers to override all styles on any site. This technique would be useful in a situation in which an individual requires a certain font style, size, and contrast to read onscreen effectively.

Understanding the Cascade Order

The three main types of style sheets aren't mutually exclusive. Quite to the contrary, if you look at the level of control each method has over certain portions of your site, you can begin to see how you can use various style sheets together to gain an incredible amount of control over the presentation of your site.

Using the cooking site as an example, the overall design of the site would use an external style sheet containing rules for the sidebar text, the body content, and other site-wide elements. The recipes appear on only one page, however, so the recipe styles can be embedded internally onto that page. If a particular recipe has special instructions you want to emphasize, you can apply an inline style to that selection of text.

This emphasizes the cascading nature of CSS. This cascade also applies to the precedence of contrary style rules. The closer a style declaration is to the content it's defining, the more precedence it has over that content. In other words, if an inline style contradicts an external style sheet, the inline style takes precedence because it's closest to the actual content.

Caution

Site visitors can set their browsers to ignore style sheets and apply their own browser settings or user-defined style sheets to all pages. The CSS standard provides methods to get around this—most of which aren't yet implemented in the popular browsers—but think carefully about whether it's worth risking the loss of a user by wresting control away from him. When users override CSS rules, they usually have their reasons (usually involving accessibility), and that should be respected.

CHOOSING A STYLE SHEET EDITOR

Now that you have a better understanding of CSS, you need to choose an environment for developing and maintaining your style sheets.

15

Inheriting Properties

Certain HTML tags exist only within other tags. The `<body>` element contains all the content of the page and its markup. The `<body>` tag is the parent, and all the tags within it are considered children of this element. Table rows and cells appear only within `<table>` tags, for example, and form elements appear within `<form>` tags. Children inherit the style applied to their parent tag unless the child tag itself is defined.

Browsers are becoming better about their capability to keep the containment hierarchy intact when it comes to inheritance of style sheet rules. There are still inconsistencies, however, especially when applying style to a table.

Dreamweaver's Internal Editor

Dreamweaver enables you to create and edit style sheets in several ways. The Dreamweaver Document window can also serve as a text editor (see Figure 15.5). Thus, you can create an external style sheet by opening a new document, manually adding style rules, and saving the document with a `.css` extension.

Figure 15.5
This external style sheet can be modified in the Document window, as shown here, or in the CSS Styles panel.

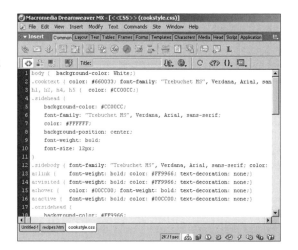

To manually add internal styles to an HTML page, open the page in Code view and type the styles into the `<head>` of the document, being sure to use the `<style>` and comment elements appropriately (see Figure 15.6).

> Inline styles must always be added in Code view using the `style` attribute.

The most common method for managing both internal and external style sheets in Dreamweaver is to use the CSS Styles panel in the Design panel group. The CSS Styles panel automates the style sheet process and offers an extensive array of style declaration options.

⇨ *For a complete explanation of the CSS Styles panel, see Chapter 16, "Using Cascading Style Sheets in Dreamweaver," p. 285.*

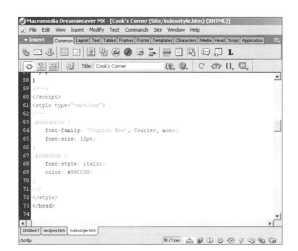

Figure 15.6
Internal style sheets can be edited either in Code view, as seen here, or through the CSS Styles panel.

Setting an External Style Sheet Editor

Although Dreamweaver offers powerful CSS tools, many experienced developers prefer to use a third-party style sheet application. The most popular of these applications is TopStyle by Bradbury Software (http://www.bradsoft.com), shown in Figure 15.7. TopStyle Lite ships with Dreamweaver MX. The full, Pro version of the application is available from the Bradbury site.

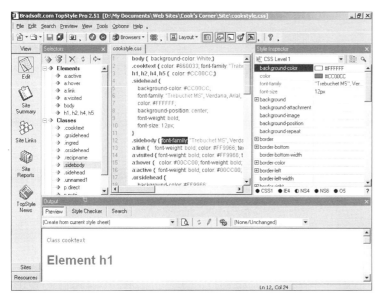

Figure 15.7
TopStyle is a third-party CSS application that can be fully integrated with Dreamweaver.

Because TopStyle is a dedicated CSS application, it includes features beyond the scope of Dreamweaver. TopStyle provides CSS validation to alert you to styles that aren't implemented in target browsers. It also points out styles that are defined in style sheets but aren't used in the site and style sheets that aren't linked from any pages in the site. Another useful feature is the capability to group styles according to the elements to which they're applied or the context of the style.

TopStyle Pro, if installed, is integrated with the Dreamweaver interface. When you double-click a style in the CSS Styles panel to edit it, TopStyle automatically opens. You can also edit an external style sheet by right-clicking it in the Site panel and then selecting Open With, TopStyle in the context menu.

Changing the Default CSS Application

If TopStyle is already installed when you install Dreamweaver, it automatically is set as the default CSS editor. If you install TopStyle or another third-party editor later, you can set it as an external editor:

1. Select Edit, Preferences from the menu.

2. Select the File Types/Editors category from the Preferences dialog box.

3. Select the .css extension from the Extensions field. If it's not present in the list, click the Add (+) button and type .css in the new field.

4. Click the Add (+) button above the Editors field.

5. From the Select Editor dialog box, navigate to the third-party CSS application you want to use, and then click Open.

6. Click OK to exit the Preferences dialog box.

> If TopStyle is your third-party application of choice, you can open TopStyle and select Enable Dreamweaver Integration from the Third Party page. This automates the external editor process in Dreamweaver as well as TopStyle.

TROUBLESHOOTING

Editing HTML Styles

I was working with editing HTML styles and inadvertently applied a style where I did not want it. How can I avoid this?

If you want to edit an HTML Style, be sure not to have any text selected in the document and turn off the auto-apply feature to prevent a paragraph style from being applied to the paragraph containing the insertion point. If auto-apply is engaged, an HTML Style will be applied any time you select a style from the list, even if you double-click to edit the style.

Browsers and the `id` Attribute

I inadvertently used `id` instead of `class`. It kept working, so I didn't realize I was doing something wrong. How'd this happen?

Despite the fact that IDs are supposed to be used only once in a document, browsers tend to forgive this. Therefore, you might see multiple IDs relating to the same rule in documents that render just as if the ID selector were a class selector. This is, however, not valid, and you will get errors when you go to validate such a document—to say nothing of causing problems with scripts that expect valid markup.

PEER TO PEER: CSS RESOURCES

Attention to CSS is really ramping up. Here are a few must-read CSS books, articles, and references to get you started learning more about CSS.

Articles

The following articles will provide insight into CSS:

- "CSS: The True Language of Web Design. Part I: The separation of presentation from structure." `http://www.molly.com/articles/markupandcss/2002-02-truelanguage1.php`.

- "CSS: The True Language of Web Design. Part 2: primary concepts and methods found in CSS." `http://www.molly.com/articles/markupandcss/2002-03-truelanguage2.php`.

- Eric A. Meyer has written exhaustively on CSS. Check out his writing page for direct links, `http://www.meyerweb.com/eric/writing.html`.

Web Resources

The following Web resources will be very helpful to you:

- The W3C style pages and CSS specifications can be found at `http://www.w3.org/Style/`.

- Eric A. Meyer has created exhaustive comparison charts for browser support, at `http://style.webreview.com/`.

Books

Several recently published books are helpful to those interested in CSS. Recommended readings include

- All four books from Eric A. Meyer are excellent to read and keep as references: *Cascading Style Sheets: The Definitive Guide* (O'Reilly & Associates, May 2000); *Cascading Style Sheets 2.0 Programmer's Reference* (Osborne/McGraw-Hill, March 2001); *CSS Pocket Reference* (O'Reilly & Associates, May 2001); *Eric Meyer On CSS* (New Riders, June 2002).

- *Cascading Style Sheets: Separating Content from Presentation* is a good book for those folks just starting out. It's written by some top leaders in the field of markup and CSS, including Owen Briggs, Steven Champeon, Eric Costello, and Matt Patterson (Glasshaus, 2002).

- *Designing CSS Web Pages* by Christopher Schmitt (New Riders, 2002) is an especially good choice for designers seeking a better understanding of what CSS can actually do for them.

- *Sams Teach Yourself CSS in 24 Hours* by Kynn Bartlett is an easy-to-read, tutorial-style book. It's perfect for beginners.

USING CASCADING STYLE SHEETS IN DREAMWEAVER

IN THIS CHAPTER

16

DREAMWEAVER MX AND CSS

If you're a novice reading this book in sequence, you should now have most of the CSS basics out of the way and be ready to put them to work in Dreamweaver. If you're an experienced developer new to Dreamweaver, you want to get down to the details of how to use CSS in Dreamweaver.

The first rule of using CSS in Dreamweaver is to ignore all the text formatting options available in the default Property inspector. Formatting applied in that manner adds `<font>` tags and other HTML-related attributes to the page, which is exactly what you're trying to avoid. Instead, click the Toggle CSS/HTML Mode button, located between the Format and Font fields on the Property inspector (see Figure 16.1). Switching to the CSS view prevents you from making inadvertent format changes to the HTML rather than applying a CSS style.

CSS/HTML Mode button

Figure 16.1
The Property inspector has a toggle between HTML and CSS views.

THE CSS STYLES PANEL

Inline styles are made by hand because they're infrequently used and are defined and applied as needed, rather than predefined at the page head or external style sheet level. *External* and *embedded style sheets*, however, use the CSS Styles panel (see Figure 16.2). This panel facilitates both the creation and application of style rules.

Figure 16.2
The CSS Styles panel lists all the internal and external styles available for the current document.

The CSS Styles panel has two views. The default is the Apply Styles view, which lists all the styles available to use in the current document. To apply a style, select a tag or block of text and then click the style in the CSS Styles panel.

The Edit Styles view displays the declarations for each style rule (see Figure 16.3). When you're in Edit Styles view, the only way to apply a style is to use the context menu (right-click) or double-click to edit the style and then select Apply from the dialog box.

Figure 16.3
The Edit Styles view of the CSS Styles panel lists the properties and values of each style, making it easier to select and edit the styles.

MANAGING STYLE SHEETS

Styles can be created internally or externally. If you haven't attached an external style sheet to the page, new styles will be added internally to the HTML document by default. Before you can add styles to an external style sheet, you need to create a link to one.

Creating an External Style Sheet

Whether you're creating a new external style sheet or linking to an existing external style sheet, the process is similar:

1. In the CSS Styles panel, select Attach Style Sheet.

2. In the Link External Style Sheet dialog box, provide the name of the style sheet (see Figure 16.4).

Figure 16.4
The Link External Style Sheet dialog box can be used to attach existing style sheets or create new style sheets.

You can name the style sheet using the following options:

- Type the name directly if you already know the complete path.

- Use the File Selector to navigate to the .css file.

- If you're creating a new style sheet, use either method to name a new .css file. Filenames must be in lowercase, contain no punctuation, and end in a .css extension.

3. Select either Link or Import as the method to attach to the external style sheet.

Link is the most common method for attaching external style sheets. Import is not supported by some browsers, so it should be used only in limited situations.

16

4. Click OK to create a link to the external style sheet.

5. If you're creating a new `.css` file, an alert box will state that the file doesn't exist and ask whether it should be created. Click OK to create the new file.

After an external style sheet has been attached, you'll be able to choose to add new styles either internally in the HTML document or to the external sheet.

Another method for creating a new external style sheet is to click the New Style button on the CSS Styles panel and select New Style Sheet File from the Define In field. This opens the File Selector dialog box, in which you can navigate to the folder where the new `.css` file should be stored and give the file a name.

Exporting Styles

You can also create an external style sheet by exporting the styles from an internal style sheet. Do the following:

1. Open the HTML document that contains the internal styles.

2. Select File, Export, Export CSS Styles.

3. In the Export Styles As CSS dialog box, navigate to the folder in which the style sheet should be saved.

4. Give the new style sheet a name. The name should end with a `.css` extension.

5. Click Save.

CREATING A NEW STYLE DEFINITION

Whether you're using internal or external style sheets, the next step is to define the styles you need for your page or site. To create a new style, follow these steps:

1. From the CSS Styles panel, click the New Style button.

2. The New CSS Style dialog box appears (see Figure 16.5). In the Define In field, choose to add the new style to an external style sheet or in This Document Only (an internal style sheet).

Figure 16.5
The New Style dialog box determines the location of the new style as well as the type.

3. Select a style type:

- **Make Custom Style (Class)**—Creates a class style. If you select this option, you need to name the class in the Name field above the style type selector. If you don't precede the class name with a period (.), as is required by the style sheet, Dreamweaver adds it for you.

> To create a nested style or tag-specific class, use the Use CSS Selector option and then type in the selector(s). Type the tag names without angle brackets.

- **Redefine HTML Tag**—Applies a style to an HTML tag. When you select this option, you also must select a tag from the Tag field above the style type selector. These styles are automatically applied to the appropriate tags after they're defined. You won't see a difference in the code itself. Rather, the style to be applied to the tag is interpreted from the style sheet—whether external or embedded—and applied to all instances of the tag.

- **Use CSS Selector**—Applies a style to one of the link types listed in the Selector field above the style type selector. These styles enable you to remove the underlining from links and otherwise change the appearance of the various link states. They're automatically applied after they're defined.

4. Click OK.

5. The Style Definition dialog box opens. Set the style rules by choosing from the various style categories and options (explained later in this chapter).

6. Click OK to complete the style definition and return to the Document window.

After you create a style, it's easy to apply. Styles defined for an HTML tag are automatically applied when viewed in a browser. Class styles are applied by doing the following:

1. In the Document window, select the content to which you want to apply the class style.

2. In the CSS Styles panel, select a style from the list.

If the selection is only a small portion of content within a tag, the `<span>` tag is used with the `class` attribute. If the selection extends across multiple paragraphs or tag pairs, the style is applied using the `<div>` tag.

DEFINING STYLES

The Style Definition dialog box contains almost every available option for CSS. Some of these options can't be rendered in any browsers, as yet, but Dreamweaver makes them available to plan for future support. Most style options can be displayed in the Document window, but you should preview your documents in a browser to be certain they're rendering correctly.

To access the Style Definition dialog box, click the New CSS Style button in the CSS Styles panel. The New CSS Style dialog box appears. Name your style and fill in the dialog box as per your needs; then, click OK. The CSS Style Definition dialog box now appears (see Figure 16.6).

Figure 16.6
Using the Style Definition dialog
box to manage a style sheet.

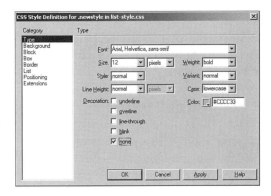

The Style Definition dialog box is divided into logical categories to group the style properties. You can choose freely among the categories and properties even within one style rule.

Setting the Type

The Type category contains properties pertaining to the appearance of text (see Figure 16.7). If you're removing the underlining from links—one of the most common applications of CSS—select None in the Decoration properties. Table 16.1 lists the other type options available in Dreamweaver.

Figure 16.7
The Type category of CSS styles
pertains to text appearance,
which replaces the deprecated
<font> tag.

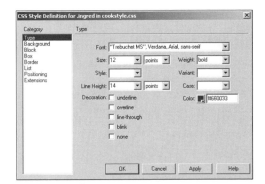

Table 16.1 CSS Type Options in Dreamweaver MX

Option	Purpose
Font	Sets the font family, using font groups established in the Font List settings.
Size	Sets the font size. If you specify a numerical value (small, larger, and so forth), you can also set the unit of measure. Choosing a percentage unit of measure increases or decreases the size of the font relative to the default. The most common unit is points.
Weight	Sets the heaviness of the text boldness. Normal text has a weight of approximately 400; bold text has a weight of 700. A weight below 400 results in lighter text.
Style	Sets the font as normal, italic, or oblique.

Table 16.1 Continued

Option	Purpose
Variant	Sets the text to display in small caps. Small caps have the same appearance as capital letters but are the size of lowercase letters.
Line Height	Sets the leading before a line of text. Leading is the space above a letter to separate it from the text above within a paragraph.
Case	Sets the text to display in uppercase or lowercase, or with initial caps.
Decoration	Sets additional properties for the display of the text, whether it should be underlined, overlined (a line appearing over the text), line-through (strikethrough), or blinking.
Color	Sets the color for the text using the standard color picker.

⇨ *Fonts not showing up properly? To find out at least one reason this might be happening, see "Font Concerns" in the "Troubleshooting" section at the end of this chapter.*

If you come from a word processing background, you're used to setting bold type using text styles, but this isn't the case here. Boldness is set by weight, not style.

Setting the Background

The Background category offers control over background images and colors (see Figure 16.8). Not only do these styles ensure consistency throughout the site, but they also offer greater control over the repeating and scrolling of background images. Most background styles aren't supported in Netscape 4 but are fully supported in Netscape 6. The properties in this category are listed in Table 16.2.

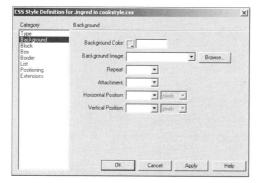

Figure 16.8
The Background styles set background images and colors.

Table 16.2 CSS Background Options

Dreamweaver Option	Purpose
Background Color	Sets the background color for an element. This style can be applied to the `<body>` tag to set a color for the entire page. It can also be applied to `<p>` and other tags to set a background color only for that particular selection. Using this style with link tags makes them stand out on the page.
Background Image	Sets a background image for the page or element. This is most commonly used with the `<body>` tag or table cells (`<td>`).

Table 16.2 Continued

Dreamweaver Option	Purpose
Repeat	Sets the repeat tiling for a background image. No Repeat sets the image to display from the upper-left corner of the element to which it's applied and not repeat at all. Repeat tiles the image horizontally and vertically as needed to fill the entire area used by the element. Repeat-x tiles the image horizontally, but not vertically. Repeat-y does the opposite.
Attachment	Sets the scrolling for the background image. A fixed image remains anchored to its original position, even as the text is scrolled. This creates the effect of the text moving over the background image and also enables you to set a background image to specific dimensions to avoid tiling. A scrolling image scrolls with the text, which is the default.
Horizontal Position	Sets the initial horizontal position of the background image. The position can be set with numerical coordinates or relative to the positioning of the element to which the style is applied.
Vertical Position	Sets the initial vertical position of the background image.

Setting the Block Properties

Block styles are used to control the alignment and spacing of text blocks (see Figure 16.9). Support for these styles is, at best, spotty and buggy in Netscape 4 but is fully implemented in Netscape 6. Support in Internet Explorer is still rather limited. The block style properties are listed in Table 16.3.

Figure 16.9
Block styles are used to control the alignment and spacing of blocks of text.

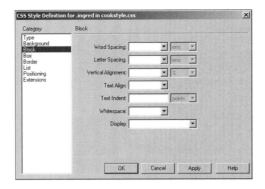

Table 16.3 Block Style Options

Dreamweaver Option	Purpose
Word Spacing	Sets the space between words. The default unit of measure for word spacing is an em, which is the space taken up by the *m* character, although the unit of measure can be changed. Positive values increase the spacing between words, whereas negative values set words closer together.
Letter Spacing	Sets the space between letters.
Vertical Alignment	Sets the alignment of the element relative to the elements near it.
Text Align	Aligns text relative to the elements surrounding it. Text can have left, right, center, or justified alignment.

Table 16.3 Continued

Dreamweaver Option	Purpose
Text Indent	Sets the indentation of the first line of the text block by the specified value. To outdent text, use a negative value.
Whitespace	Sets the control of spaces and tabs within an element. Normal causes the text block to be formatted in the same way as a default paragraph tag, where extra whitespace is ignored. The Pre value preserves whitespace. The Nowrap value causes text to extend horizontally until a ` ` tag is encountered, rather than wrapping to conform to the browser window.

Setting the Box Properties

Box styles are used to control the positioning and spacing of elements, much in the same way as tables (see Figure 16.10). With appropriate browser support, which is still somewhat spotty even in the current browsers, you could design your entire site using box and positioning styles rather than tables. The Box style properties are listed in Table 16.4.

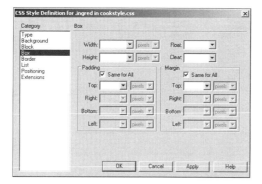

Figure 16.10
Box styles set the positioning and spacing of elements, similar to the layout of tables.

Table 16.4 Box Options in Dreamweaver

Option	Purpose
Width	Sets the width of the element.
Height	Sets the height of the element.
Float	Sets the positioning of the element. Floating elements are positioned against the margin for which they are set, with the other elements of the page flowing around them.
Clear	Clears the area around the box and doesn't let other elements flow around it.
Padding	Sets the amount of space between the element and its border or margin.
Margin	Sets the spacing between the element and other page elements.

Setting the Border

Border styles are used to set borders to surround an element (see Figure 16.11). Each side of the rectangular border can have a unique line thickness and color. Borders can also be applied only to select sides of the element, creating text surrounded on top and bottom while the sides remain open or similar combinations. Eight border styles exist, giving the border an inset, grooved, or dotted-line appearance—unlike the line thickness and color, these styles are applied to all sides of the border (see Figure 16.12). Many of the border properties are buggy in earlier browsers, so they should be applied cautiously and thoroughly tested. The properties of the Borders styles are listed in Table 16.5.

Figure 16.11
Border styles are used to create borders around an element. Each side of the element can have a unique border style.

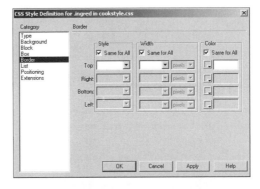

Figure 16.12
Border style examples: dashed, dotted, solid, double, groove, ridge, inset, and outset.

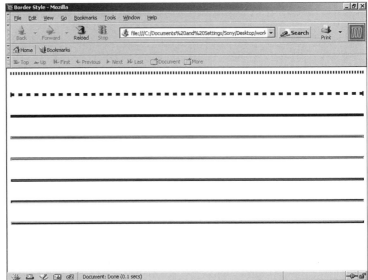

Table 16.5   Border Style Options

Option	Purpose
Style	Sets the style of the border. The options are Dotted, Dashed, Solid, Double, Groove, Ridge, Inset, and Outset.
Width	Sets the thickness of the border for each of the sides.
Color	Sets the color for the border.

Setting the List Properties

List styles offer control over the appearance of lists (see Figure 16.13 and 14). The List style properties are shown in Table 16.6.

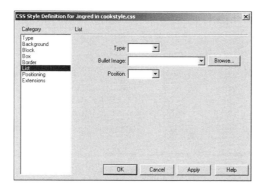

Figure 16.13
List properties are controlled in the CSS Style Definition dialog box and enable you to control the appearance of bullets and the wrapping of the list contents.

16

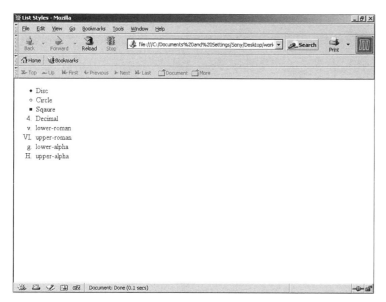

Figure 16.14
List styles include a variety of means of labeling list items. Here, you see, from top to bottom: disc, circle, square, decimal, lower-roman, upper-roman, lower-alpha, and upper-alpha.

Table 16.6 List Properties

Property	Purpose
Type	Sets the appearance of bullets in unordered lists from the following options: Disc, Circle, Square, Decimal, Lowercase Roman, Uppercase Roman, Lowercase Alpha, and Uppercase Alpha.
Bullet Image	Sets a custom image for unordered list bullets. This image can be any of the common formats, including animated GIF. Bullet images aren't supported by Netscape 4 browsers but have been implemented in Netscape 6.
Position	Sets the wrapping of the list item. An outside position wraps the text to the indent of the list, whereas an inside indent wraps the text to the page margin.

Setting the Position

Positioning styles control the exact placement of elements on the page (see Figure 16.15). These properties form the basis of working with layers. The Position properties are listed in Table 16.7.

⇨ *Learn about using layers and CSS in Chapter 20, "Advanced Layout with CSS Layers," p. 369.*

Figure 16.15
Positioning styles control the placement of an element.

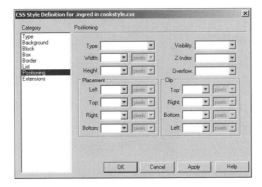

Table 16.7   Positioning-Related Options

Option	Purpose
Type	Sets the positioning format. The types are Relative, Absolute, and Static (at its exact placement within the document, rather than independently of the rest of the content).
Visibility	Sets the visibility of the layer. Layers can inherit the visibility of their parent tags or be set independently of the parent to be either visible or hidden.
Z-Index	Sets the stacking order of the layers. A higher z-index means a layer is closer to the top of the page in depth. A lower value means a layer could be hidden under others.
Overflow	Sets the flow of the layer's content when it overflows the dimensions of the layer. The overflowing content can be hidden; scrolled using scrollbars that are added to the element; or auto, which automatically applies the appropriate formatting.
Placement	Sets the actual positioning of the layer on the page.
Clip	Sets the size of the element, which then determines where the element is clipped.

Setting Extensions

Extensions are specialty properties, shown in Figure 16.16, used to manage page breaks, cursor design, and add filters (which really are DHTML, rather than CSS). They're listed in Table 16.8.

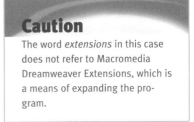

Caution

The word *extensions* in this case does not refer to Macromedia Dreamweaver Extensions, which is a means of expanding the program.

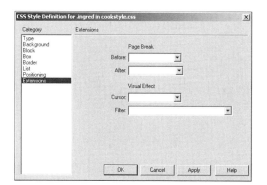

16

Figure 16.16
Setting extensions, which are CSS properties and filters used for paged media and screen.

Table 16.8 Extensions to CSS

Property	Purpose
Page Break	Used to facilitate printing a Web page, this style forces a page break in a long document.
Cursor	Sets the style of cursor that appears to the user while on your page.
Filter	Sets effects independently of Fireworks or other graphics packages. These effects control the opacity, glow, and masking features of the element.

EDITING STYLE SHEETS

The biggest benefit of using style sheets is being able to update the format of a site or page quickly. To edit your style sheets, follow these steps:

1. Click the Edit Style Sheet button in the CSS Style panel.

2. Select the name of the style sheet in the Edit Style Sheet dialog box, and then click Edit (see Figure 16.17).

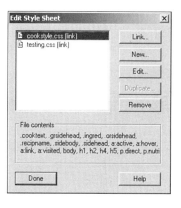

Figure 16.17
The Edit Style Sheet dialog box lists all the style sheets attached to the current document.

3. In the style sheet dialog box, select a style and then click Edit (see Figure 16.18).

Figure 16.18
All the styles within the selected style sheet are listed. Choose which style to edit.

4. This opens the Style Definition dialog box, from which you can change the style.

⇨ *Having trouble with inline styles and the Edit Style Sheet feature? See what the problem is in "Problems with External Style Sheets" in the "Troubleshooting" section at the end of this chapter.*

Using Design Time Style Sheets

Design Time style sheets are new in Dreamweaver MX. This feature enables you to temporarily display or hide the effects of various style sheets within the site. This feature works only in the Document window; what the user actually sees in the browser is determined by the style sheets attached to the final HTML document. For development purposes, however, this tool can be quite convenient.

To use Design Time style sheets, do the following:

1. (Control-click) [Right-click] in the CSS Styles panel to open the context menu.

2. Select Design Time Style Sheet.

3. In the Design Time Style Sheets dialog box, use the plus and minus buttons to open the File Selector and select which style sheets should be visible or invisible while you develop the site (see Figure 16.19).

Figure 16.19
Setting up Design Time Style sheets, allowing you to see how certain styles will or will not influence a document.

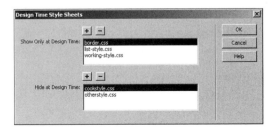

4. Click OK.

To see at a glance which style sheets are visible or hidden, look at the CSS Styles panel. You'll notice the word "design" or "hidden" next to the style sheet's name if you've set that style sheet using the Design Time feature.

TROUBLESHOOTING

Font Concerns

I set up a style sheet to control my fonts, yet the faces I chose are not appearing. Why is this? I thought CSS offered more flexibility when it came to fonts!

Although fonts can be easily controlled by style sheets, CSS falls under the same limitations as HTML in font delivery. The specific typeface must be available on the computer viewing your page. As with the font element, style sheets allow you to stack font groups to maximize the possibility that a visitor's browser will be capable of seeing your text as you designed.

More information about font families can be found in Chapter 3, "Formatting Text with HTML."

Problems with External Style Sheets

I'm trying to edit styles for an external style sheet, but the CSS Style Definition dialog box keeps opening and expecting me to edit my inline styles. What's going on?

If your document contains internal styles, the Edit Style Sheet button automatically opens the CSS Style Definition dialog box to edit the style surrounding the insertion point or selection. To get around this bug, (Control-click) [right-click] in the CSS Style panel and select Edit Style Sheet from the context menu. The rest of this process will proceed normally.

PEER TO PEER: PROPERTIES AND ATTRIBUTES

Dreamweaver often uses terminology that doesn't synch up with the terminology used by the W3C. This gets confusing. So, to clarify a few concerns that arise when studying HTML versus CSS, consider these terms and their definitions:

- **Attribute**—An *attribute* is a portion of markup that extends or modifies the element to which it is being applied. In Dreamweaver, *attributes* are often referred to as *properties*, which is technically not correct. Examples of attributes include `align`, `bgcolor`, `width`, `height`, `border`, and so on.

- **Property**—A *property* is the portion of a style rule that defines what type of style is being applied to the selector or class for that rule. A property has a value that further defines the style. Examples of properties in CSS include background-color, font-family, line-height, margin, and so on.

In Dreamweaver, *property* is used a bit more loosely to describe interface components (the Property inspector and the options therein), HTML attributes, *and* CSS properties.

16

PROFESSIONAL PAGE DESIGN

17

DESIGN ESSENTIALS, SITE ARCHITECTURE, AND USABILITY

IN THIS CHAPTER

WEB DESIGN ESSENTIALS

Whether you are an experienced Web designer or just starting out, this chapter will provide you with the essentials of creating intelligent, well-designed, and well-architected Web sites. You'll learn about tools and techniques for page layout; you'll read about site architecture; and you'll explore primary concepts of user interface (UI) design. Finally, you'll enjoy a contemporary discussion of Web usability, a current topic that will have a long shelf life when it comes to providing your site visitors with the best possible experience.

Several important concepts with which to begin include

- **Understand your audience**—Who are you designing the Web site for? Learn as much about the overall personality, culture, limitations, strengths, and technical capabilities of your site visitors. With existing sites that you are redesigning, this might be easier if you can access server statistics, which provide a lot of this information in detail, particularly the technical concerns. If you're just starting out, use any information you might have from prior advertising or surveys of audiences. If you have no information whatsoever, write a list of the features you imagine your "typical" site visitor to have and design to that outline.

- **Clarify the intent of the site**—Before you even begin to design your site, you must have a clear understanding of what your intentions are. Do you want to sell something? Inspire? Educate? Know exactly what your intent is because this will help guide you through the design process as well as clearly communicate to your site visitors what the site is for and how it can best be used.

- **Understand browser concerns and work with them effectively**—Because so many Web browsers are in use, designing for total compatibility as well as adhering to Web standards can be a nightmarish undertaking. This means you must be prepared for a testing cycle in your production timeline, but you should also begin with the intent to deliver to as many browsers as possible.

➪ *To learn more about cross-browser design, see "Cross-Browser Compatibility," p. 525. [chapter 28]*

DOCUMENT MANAGEMENT AND FILE STRUCTURE

Although this subject might seem quite basic to some readers, the reality is that significant problems arise when directories are poorly structured and files are named improperly. One reason this is such a common occurrence is that many computer professionals are accustomed to working on one primary platform and files are managed differently on each platform. Another reason is that tools such as Dreamweaver MX must be combined with your awareness of various issues in order to be most effective.

Consider the following points:

- For files to be correctly rendered in a browser or located properly on a Web server, those files—and the directories in which they reside—must adhere to specific rules to be readable across all platforms.

- Case causes countless hours of frustration, especially for entry-level Web designers. By mixing case in file and directory names, case sensitivity on certain platforms can cause inconsistently written directories and files to be inaccessible.

- As sites grow and change, smart file management will flex and grow with the sites as well. Poorly managed documents and directory structures can really inhibit growth by placing additional responsibilities on the Webmasters responsible for dealing with the growth of a given site.

The bottom line? One of the best-known rules in Web design and development is that faulty document management causes even more challenges down the line. Learning good document management can help prevent these problems.

Directory Structure

It is best to work with Dreamweaver MX locally while considering the structure of your site as it will appear on the server. If possible, set up a system that you can use consistently, whether you are managing your documents locally or on a server.

If you have a very small site, just a few pages say, you can place all the files for a site into one directory. But when you start working with larger sites containing numerous documents, countless graphics, and other media, managing one directory of files becomes nearly impossible.

> The topmost directory in any given structure is referred to as the *root directory*, and any directory within the root is referred to as a *subdirectory*. A *parent* directory is the directory immediately above any given subdirectory.

Fortunately, Dreamweaver MX allows you to set up directories and reflect them accurately on the remote server (see Figure 17.1).

To set up a logical directory structure, follow these guidelines:

- **Categorize areas of your site**—Examples would include Articles, Recipes, Photos.

- **Use subdirectories carefully**—Be careful to create subdirectories only when necessary, and when you do so, to name them clearly and use them for their predetermined purpose.

- **Follow conventional practices**—For the sake of professional consistency, it helps to name directories conventionally. For example, images are typically kept in either an "images" or "graphics" subdirectory.

Figure 17.1
Using the Site tab in the Files panel at full view can help you compare files and directories both locally and remotely. Here you see the structure of both the local and remote site is consistent.

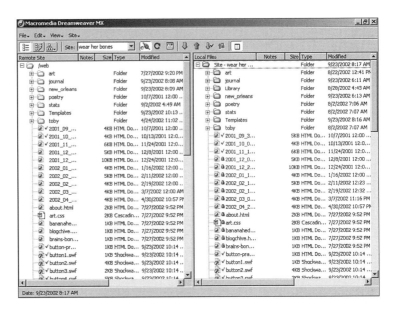

17

Filenaming Concerns

The primary problems with naming are

- **Improperly formed filenames**—To allow for platform-independent access, filenames must adhere to specific naming formats.

- **Unclear filenames**—Filenames get confusing if you don't create a system that clearly identifies, at least to you, what each file contains.

- **Names that are too long**—There's already enough length to many URLs—don't add to the problem by naming your file with an unreasonably long filename.

- **Names with no or improper prefixes and suffixes**—If you don't use the proper prefix and suffix locally, you will have trouble when they are on the Web itself. It's great to get familiar with and use the proper suffixes for your files.

➡ *Unable to bring your site up after you've posted it to the Web? You might have incorrectly named your default file. See "Setting the Default Page" in the "Troubleshooting" section at the end of this chapter.*

To ensure you don't encounter any problems with filenaming, follow these simple rules:

- **Don't use spaces**—Even if you're used to doing this on your local computer, you'll have trouble testing your file locally and running it on the Internet if you have a space in the name. In place of spaces, you can use underscores or dashes.

- **Don't use any extraneous characters**—Stick to letters, numbers, underscores, and dashes. Especially troublesome characters include apostrophes (as in `molly'swebsite`), dollar signs, percent signs, pound signs, parenthesis, and so on, which might have special meanings for operating systems or Web software.

- **Name your files in all lowercase**—Even though at this point you're working locally and this won't trouble your individual computer, it's a good practice to get into early. Many servers still perceive filenames by case, meaning that `index.html`, `INDEX.html`, and `IndEX.html` are three different files! You'll avoid many a future headache by following this simple guideline.

One of the best ways to stay organized is to give your files understandable names. This becomes especially important when you begin managing many documents in a single project.

You can always assign a project a two- or three-letter code and then give the filename a logical identifier. This is something you can consider for larger sites. For smaller sites, it's best to stick to simple names such as `news.html`, `resume.html`, `about.html`, and so forth.

The important issue is to be consistent. Pick a style that works for you and stick with it.

Many Web professionals write information regarding naming conventions into a style guide. For an excellent example of a style guide that covers both markup and document management concerns, see the New York City Public Library's style guide, `http://www.nypl.org/styleguide/`.

Filename Length

Have you ever come across a URL so long that you couldn't copy it to send along to someone who might find it useful, even though the information at that location was really something to write about?

You can avoid adding to the often-lengthy naming process on the Web by working with shorter filenames locally. This sets you up for a longer-term consistency rate with filenaming conventions.

A good rule of thumb with filename length is to make the name sensible and logical without exceeding many more than eight characters in the prefix. Ten characters would be perfectly acceptable; twenty characters would not. Good examples are `about.html`, `contact.html`, and `history.html`; problematic names would be `aboutourcompany.html`, `contactustoday.html`, and `company history.html`.

Correct Prefix and Suffix Names

The only time a prefix name matters is when a file goes live on the Web. Locally, you can start with any name. However, plan ahead and find out which prefix your server will allow you to use for the default page. Name that file accordingly, and you'll be prepared when the time comes to upload your pages.

Think about the following prefix and suffix naming possibilities:

- A few possible prefixes are `index`, `default`, and `welcome`.

- For standard HTML files, two primary options exist for the suffix: `.html` and `.htm`. In most cases, you can use either one. As always, follow the consistency rule and choose one when the option is available, but do check with your systems administrator to be sure. And, never mix too many file types within a site—that spells trouble.

- If you're serving dynamic content with an application such as ASP, .NET, PHP, Perl, and others, you might have a different suffix. You'll have to check with your network systems administrator or ISP for the information specific to your server.

- Graphic files must be named properly at all times. For GIFs, always use the `.gif` extension, and for JPEGs, use the `.jpg` (not `.jpeg`) extension.

A variety of other file types can be incorporated into your structure. Their suffixes vary depending on the file type. When in doubt, consult the documentation for the suffix information, or check with the system administrator who manages the server on which your local documents will eventually be placed.

Looking for extension information? Try the amazing File Extension Source, an enormous catalog of filename extensions at `http://filext.com/`.

17

SAVING FILES

File management is easy, but it can also be risky. You can overwrite files, lose data, and save files to the wrong area of your computer. You also can run the risk of saving files improperly. Dreamweaver's management tools help you a great deal with this, but there are still some good guidelines to follow.

Here are some tips for general saving and file management:

- **Save your work regularly**—Whenever you begin a new file, immediately name it properly and save it to the correct location in your directory structure.

- **Back up your work**—Whether you make a copy of the file to floppy disk, Zip disk, or CD is no matter—just make sure you keep a copy! There's no more awful a feeling than losing your hard work.

- **Create your directory structure first, and save files to that area**—Use Dreamweaver's Site Definitions dialog box to ensure you set up your directory structure before trying to manage a project (see Figure 17.2). This way you'll know where your files are, setting up a logical structure upon which to form the linking of pages and page assets within a given document.

Another problem with file management has to do with saving files to the wrong format. Let's say you're in Fireworks MX and want to save a file as a JPEG, but you mistakenly select another format. If you give the file the wrong suffix name, the program will save the file improperly.

This problem holds true when saving HTML, XHTML, and Cascading Style Sheets (CSS) files and related documents. It's important to remember that HTML, XHTML, and CSS are saved in ASCII, or *text* format. If you save a file as a binary file or transfer it as a binary file, the file will be corrupt. The same is true with binary formats—you can't try to save or transfer a GIF or JPEG file in ASCII, for example, because you will destroy the file's integrity.

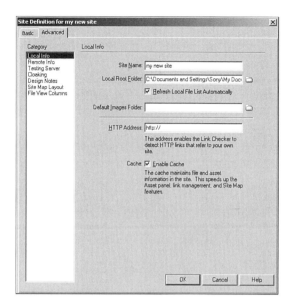

Figure 17.2
When you first define a site in Dreamweaver MX, be sure to set up your local information and then your remote information. This will help you keep your local and remote sites organized from the beginning.

PAGE LAYOUT TECHNIQUES AND TOOLS

Before you get too deeply into page layout with tables, frames, and CSS, it's important to learn some of the methods and features Dreamweaver MX provides so you can enjoy a streamlined and successful process of page design and production.

Storyboarding and Wireframing

Generally speaking, it's helpful to know what your design is going to look like before ever jumping into laying out your pages in Dreamweaver MX. A great way to get your creative juices flowing is to begin with a sketch board and pencils. Simply draw a rectangle representing each screen for the individual pages you require. Then sketch your ideas. This is akin to storyboarding, which is used in TV, animation, and film. In recent years, Web designers have taken to calling this process *wireframing*.

Some designers don't bother with wireframing, but most contemporary thinking suggests that it is a great way to begin designing your site because you have a very detailed map that can help you architect the site more efficiently. You will also reduce errors and avoid many potential problems with usability. You get to imagine the site before ever actually designing it.

Wireframing gives you a preliminary starting point, and from there, you can progress to laying out your ideas in detail in an imaging program such as Macromedia Fireworks or Adobe Photoshop.

To learn more about working with imaging tools, see Chapter 32, "Working with Web Graphics," p. 569.

Page Compositing

After you're to this stage, the first step is to create a page mock-up. This is known as *compositing*, and it is an important step in ensuring that your overall look is what you like. When you composite, you use an imaging program—preferably one with layers—and lay out the various elements. Doing this in an imaging program prior to working in Dreamweaver enables you to plan your layout approach, make decisions on how to approach laying out the design in Dreamweaver, and actually create the graphics you'll be using in your design.

In your imaging program (Fireworks is being used for this example, but you can follow along with the general steps in most available imaging programs), lay out your page by following these steps:

1. Open Fireworks MX and select File, New.

2. In the New dialog box, enter your width and height in pixels (see Figure 17.3). For this example, the page is set to a width of 768 and a height of 500. This more or less emulates average screen space at a common resolution of 800×600.

Figure 17.3
Setting up your composite's main features in Fireworks MX.

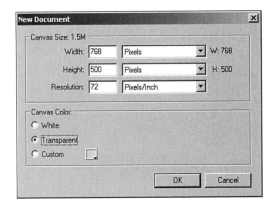

3. Select a canvas color or fill that will match your background color or background design. You can choose from white, transparent (use this if you're undecided), or a custom color.

4. Click OK.

Fireworks MX generates the canvas (see Figure 17.4). Now you're ready to add content to the composite.

Adding Content Using Layers

Perhaps one of the most powerful aspects of today's imaging tools is that they contain a feature called *layers*. Layers enable you to place content on separate layers of a single document, allowing you to modify just that content without influencing anything else in the design.

You'll want to tap into the power of layers to manage your composite files because layers give you much greater control and flexibility while modifying and perfecting your composite design.

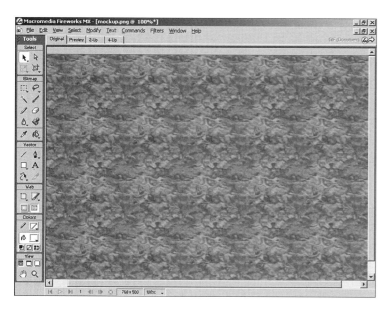

Figure 17.4
With the background design in place, the canvas is now ready for content.

To create a new layer and add content to it, follow these steps:

1. In the Layers panel, click the New Layer icon (see Figure 17.5). A new layer appears.

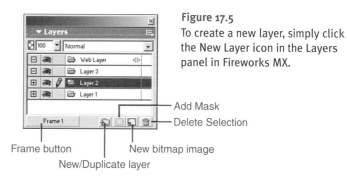

Figure 17.5
To create a new layer, simply click the New Layer icon in the Layers panel in Fireworks MX.

2. Double click the new layer and give it a name describing the contents it will contain, such as **header text**.

3. Add your content to the layer.

4. Continue adding layers and content until you are satisfied with your initial page mock-up design.

5. Save the file to the native Fireworks format, PNG.

When you open this file again in Fireworks MX, the layers will be intact and editable.

If you're using a different imaging program that has layers, save to that program's native format (such as Adobe

> **Caution**
>
> Make sure you save the file with the layers intact. Never rasterize a file that you want to use as a composite, unless you're making a copy of it for another purpose. If you do, you'll lose the ability to manipulate the position, size, color, or other attributes of the element on that layer.

Photoshop's .psd format). This way, you can later make any necessary adjustments to the fonts, colors, and positions of your page elements.

Of course, you can later use the composite not only to make adjustments to the design, but also to actually generate your graphics.

SITE ARCHITECTURE OVERVIEW

Designing a Web page to be effective means understanding a bit about the structure of hypermedia documents—taking the time to plan your page and how it will interact with other pages on the site.

> Visually designing via compositing and developing a site's architecture are often done by different members of professional development teams.

The structure of a site directly relates to the effectiveness of your page because by understanding the underlying, interactive technology available to you, you can make choices for your site and your audience—eliminating potential problems on either end. Similarly, planning plays a big role in making sure you know what you want and need before you start to work. You spend less time and, in a professional situation, less money by ensuring that your work is well thought out in advance.

A compelling aspect of the Web that stems from the hypertext environment is that the Web's format can be interpreted as being *nonlinear* rather than linear. Books are read page-by-page, which is a linear activity. Another familiar, linear act is how most Westerners perceive time. We see it as a logical order of days, one following another in a line. It's interesting to note that in some cultures, time is perceived as a spiral. Linear activities dominate Western civilization, however, and that the Web is such a curiosity—and challenge to its developers—often relates to the fact that it is essentially unlike most of our familiar constructs.

⇨ *Are linear sites good for audiences? Find out in "Linearity" in the "Troubleshooting" section later in this chapter.*

Web sites, unlike books, can be constructed to take you from the middle of a sentence or a thought to another, ancillary thought. Or, that link can take you to some data whose relationship to the originating data is not immediately clear.

What happens when a person is interacting with information in this way is that he can, and often does, depart from this linear structure into one that allows for a more free-flowing, nonlinear event. That by-now tired term, *surfing the Web*, sums up this freedom well—suggesting that moving from Web site to Web site is a fluid journey, rather than a strict, regimented one.

It becomes imperative that the individual designing Web pages understand how this environment offers organizational structures that are both like and unlike those with which we are most familiar—books and flow charts are linear and are perfectly acceptable for certain designs on the Web. But to tap into the nonlinear world and make it a relevant experience for the Web site visitor is to enhance his experience and challenge your own capabilities.

Because most readers are accustomed to linear structure and are most familiar with organizing information into such structures, it's very important to give most functional sites enough linearity to be comfortable and navigable.

A linear Web site is similar to a book. Each page is placed to the conceptual "right" of the next, and there's an opportunity to page forward or backward (see Figure 17.6).

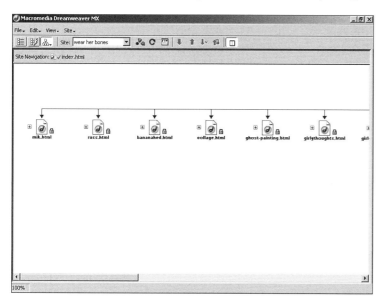

Figure 17.6
This portion of the site is linear in that site visitors move from one page to the next in a timeline fashion.

Another familiar structure in our linear world is the *hierarchical*, or flow-chart, method of mapping a Web site. In a case of this nature, you can offer links that move from level to level as well as from side to side. In Figure 17.7, a hierarchical site is shown. As you begin to add links that take visitors to multiple areas inside and outside the site, the linearity becomes less evident.

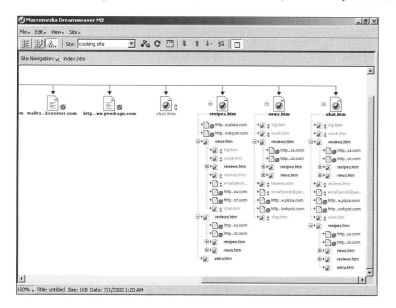

Figure 17.7
Using Dreamweaver MX to map a site provides a perfect example of a hierarchical construct of this site section.

So, what of a nonlinear site? Well, a true nonlinear site would have completely random links. What this means is that no matter where a visitor clicked, he wouldn't know where in the Web world he was going to end up! This isn't an optimal choice for most people, but many sites do choose to put a random link generator somewhere, so site visitors can try a random site.

Is there a middle ground? You bet, and it's one that is encouraged because, in most cases, we want to give site visitors enough linearity so they are comfortable within the environment. How do we add some nonlinear options to a site?

- Begin with a linear or hierarchical structure.

- Add links from any place within that site to another section of that same site.

- Add links to external sites.

The nonlinear experience in the result comes from the allowance for and encouragement of user choice. Every person coming to this site can conceivably surf it differently. This, in turn, creates an individual, flowing experience, rather than a highly structured one. However, we've been cautious by beginning with a linear structure to make the site sensible and help people maintain a sense of place.

> For more information on site architecture, see the excellent tutorial at http://www.evolt.org/article/Web_Site_Architecture_101/4090/635/.

USER INTERFACE DESIGN ESSENTIALS

Interfaces serve to welcome, guide, and provide the functional elements required to assist your visitor in getting to the information or experience she is seeking. Considered a critical aspect of multimedia design, a well-built interface is particularly important for the Web. If an individual isn't finding the information required or isn't having a meaningful adventure on your pages, she can simply choose to take a sharp turn off the road and visit another site—one, perhaps, that will be more interesting and informative for the visitor and profitable to your competitor.

One step to avoid creating sites that act as pit-stops or U-turns on the Web's highways and byways is to ensure that the sites you build make the visitor feel comfortable and provide that visitor with the goods she is after. This is done via a number of methods, including intelligent design as well as an attractive and useful site interface.

Several time-honored principles of user interface design should be applied to your Web site plans. These concepts are drawn from other media, such as interactive CD-ROMs, kiosks, and even television. The hypermedia environment of the Web—with its links to here, there, and everywhere in the vast and complex Internet world—is often bereft of these foundational principles. The results are ill-designed interfaces that confuse and frustrate rather than inform and assist the people who visit those Web sites.

> User interfaces might have complex underlying technologies making use of behaviors, DHTML menus, and server-side features, but ideally the visual results are easy for anyone to understand.

The reason for the abundance of problems with user interfaces on the Internet has a lot to do with the fact that very frequently Web sites are built by computer engineers, high school students, and even fine artists—all of whom have much to contribute content-wise to the Web environment but little or no experience in what it takes to communicate in the unusual, nonlinear structure of the Web.

The following principles can assist you in avoiding the potholes that inexperienced Web designers can find themselves driving into. Apply these ideas to the sites you build, and you stand a much better chance of a smooth ride toward your Web success.

Metaphor

In design, *metaphor* refers to the symbolic representation of the structure you're attempting to build. A metaphor acts as a familiar visual aid around which you build the entryway, interiors, windows, doors, and exits of your environment.

In fact, metaphor was used to construct the previous paragraph. The Web site is defined as though it were a building—with a selection of the elements you expect to find in a building. Metaphor helps people feel comfortable because they are familiar with the rules of the setting. A simple example of this can be found on Yahoo!, which uses a series of visual metaphors for its navigation, as you can see in Figure 17.8. Users relate the airplane image, which represents "travel," to the link that has travel information, and so forth.

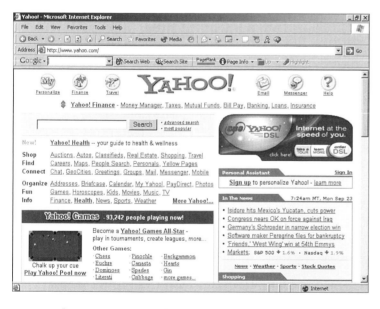

Figure 17.8
Visitors relate easily to metaphor and are able to interact with the interface without having to think too much about how to do so.

One common pitfall of metaphor is the use of overly vague—or overly specific—references. People everywhere can identify with an airplane metaphor. But the less specific you make your metaphor, the greater the chance that at least some of your visitors will become confused.

Achieve metaphor, and you're one step closer to helping that person make herself comfortable and visit with you awhile.

⇨ *Is metaphor necessary for your design? See "Metaphor" in the "Troubleshooting" section at the end of this chapter.*

Metaphor should use common, everyday concepts that people from any part of the globe who come upon your site will be able to understand immediately.

Clarity

To increase a visitor's desire to stay, be sure that he understands the elements in your pages. There should be no critical pieces that are abstract or difficult to decipher. This is not to say that abstraction as an art form isn't allowed—a good designer can use abstract art in a very clear Web site. What a good designer cannot do is use abstractions when it comes to those elements necessary to navigate the site, locate information, or return to critical areas in the site.

Elements that fall into this category include any buttons, imagemaps, or links that are necessary for site navigation. A button that leads the visitor to the left shouldn't have an arrow that faces up, and a link that offers a mail option shouldn't pull up your newsreader. It's that simple, and that clear. Clarity is a must for precise communication.

Consistency

Consistency is not only one of utmost importance in interface design, but also one of the skeletal necessities of a Web site. Haven't you ever found yourself landing on a Web page and thinking, "Wow, this looks great!" Then, as you move to the next page, you find yourself wondering what happened to the inviting design and promise that first page offered!

Consistency can be gained by developing a site palette and sticking to the color theme in some regular fashion. Location and order of navigation also are significant aspects of consistent UID design.

If you stay long enough to move through the site, backgrounds change, font styles are inconsistent, headers and navigation are completely irregular—in short, you can't tell from one page to the next where the heck you are. Being consistent with design elements allows for a cohesive presentation. This keeps your visitors calm instead of tense, confused, and ready to take a hard right—right off your site, that is.

Orientation

Following closely along with each of the prior concepts is the idea that a site visitor must know where she is at any given time. This is *orientation*. If you're deep into a site that has hundreds of pages, it helps to know where in that site you are. It's also really good if you have quick access to other areas of the site and can go back where you came from if you find out you're somewhere you really don't want, or need, to be.

Orientation is achieved by ensuring that each site has either a header that defines that page's purpose or another, familiar element that instantly defines the location. You have probably seen a variety of methods to ensure orientation, including

- **Use of breadcrumbs**—Breadcrumb navigation ensures that a page within a Web site contains some clear means of where within the site structure a visitor is (see Figure 17.9).

- **Use of titles**—Be certain that when your site is ready to publish, you've titled all your pages accordingly (see Figure 17.10).

- **Use of design features to help denote location**—You can help the site visitor identify where she is by changing the navigation design for the current page. You might also consider disabling any link that will cause the same page to reload.

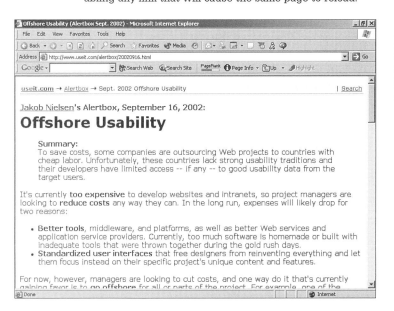

Figure 17.9

In this example, the site visitor knows that she is at the site useit.com, in the `alertbox` section, reading the September 2002 column called Offshore Usability.

17

Navigation

Just as you want your visitors to remain oriented as they look around your site, you also want them to be able to figure out how to successfully navigate from page to page—and back again. Navigation and orientation are closely linked because your navigational tools—the icons, buttons, and menus on each page—can provide some much-needed consistency for your site.

Navigation goes beyond creating a uniform set of buttons, however. Give careful thought to where those buttons are going to lead your visitors. A menu with too many choices will overwhelm people and detract from the flow of your site.

A menu with too few choices will force people to guess at which option will take them to the information they seek.

Caution

If you make your visitor click more than three times to get to the information he is after, you run the risk of disorienting him. Ideally, no piece of data on your site is more than three clicks away from a related piece of data.

Figure 17.10
Titling pages is a critical point
that is often missed by designers.

Title

Suffice it to say that navigation is an integral part of interface design and a critical element of any Web site. It's all about getting from way over there to right where you want to be, logically, quickly, and with ease.

Learning More about Design Principles, Site Architecture, and User Experience

To learn more about information architecture, simplicity, and user experience, check out the following columns in *Digital Web Magazine*:

- **Keep it Simple**—This series, written by Peter-Paul Koch, offers perspectives on keeping your site designs simple and therefore easily manageable (`http://www.digital-web.com/columns/keepitsimple/`).

- **Wide Open**—David Wertheimer talks about information architecture from a very practical, easy-to-swallow perspective (`http://www.digital-web.com/columns/wideopen/`).

- **IAnything Goes**—This is Jeff Lash's thoughtful column on information architecture (`http://www.digital-web.com/columns/ianythinggoes/`).

TROUBLESHOOTING

Linearity

I want to create a site that moves from page to page without many links within the pages. I understand that this is a linear site. Is it going to upset visitors if I use strict linearity on the Web?

The answer lies in the intent of the site. If you're creating a portal site, a page-to-page design without many links is simply not going to work. However, if you're creating a guided tour where you want to bring your visitor from one piece in an art exhibit to the next in a precise fashion, the linear site will be absolutely appropriate.

Metaphor

Is metaphor necessary to create good sites?

Many sites choose not to use metaphorical images to represent navigation elements. Instead, choosing words for the navigable content, such as New, About Us, and Contact, works perfectly well.

Setting the Default Page

I created a Web page, but it doesn't appear when I type the domain name. What could be the problem?

You might have created your file with a name that is not recognized as a default by your Web server. A default Web page name is the filename used by your server to deliver a file when the URL or directory, but not a filename, is given. So, if I type in `http://www.molly.com/`, my server will know to send the default page for that location and directory, which is `"index"` no matter the suffix (I use PHP so my suffix is `.php` on most documents on my site). If you named the file `index.html`, for example, try renaming it as `default.htm`. Alternatively, contact your Web service provider and ask for the default naming convention required by its servers.

PEER TO PEER: WEB USABILITY TRENDS

As you've read through the general ideas presented in this chapter, it becomes clear that the proper approach to design, management of file structure when architecting the site, and use of UI conventions helps make a site easier for visitors to enjoy.

The last several years have seen a dramatic increase in the concern for usability (also referred to as *user experience* or *user experience design*). Usability refers to a site visitor's ability to fully use your site and its features. There are currently extreme perspectives in the usability field, from the well-known conservatism of usability pundit Jakob Neilsen to the more free-flowing ideas embraced by other communities of designers and developers, such as those from Flash and Peer-to-Peer (P2P) technologies.

Despite the fact that usability is currently a hot topic, there are some common usability concerns that most people creating Web sites share:

- **Web sites should be accessible**—As you are already aware, the ideal is to have sites that are accessible to anyone, anywhere, using any platform, browser, or device.

- **Web sites should be appealing**—This is a little vague because what appeals to me might not appeal to you. The real point is will it appeal to your site visitors? That's why the very first point made in this chapter—understand your audience—remains the first and most important step when creating a media project of any kind.

> You can read Jakob Neilsen's regular Web site for his take on usability at http://www.useit.com/alertbox/. An excellent article by Clay Shirky, "An Open Letter to Jakob Neilsen," provides a high-level perspective on why Neilsen's ideas are thought to be too rigid (http://www.shirky.com/writings/nielsen.html).

- **Sites should be consistent**—As mentioned earlier, a significant part of user interface is ensuring consistency. The location of navigation systems is very important in this regard, as is ensuring that other presentational features—color, type, and layout—should all be managed sensibly.

- **Sites should forgive**—If a user makes a mistake and ends up somewhere he doesn't want to be, can he find the way home? A site should always let a visitor make a mistake but be able to undo that mistake with ease.

17

DESIGNING WITH TABLE-BASED LAYOUTS

IN THIS CHAPTER

Table Elements	**322**
Creating Advanced Tables	**322**
Using Layout View	**336**
Advanced Table Techniques	**344**
Troubleshooting	**348**
Peer to Peer: Dreamweaver Features for Accessible Tables	**349**

TABLE ELEMENTS

If you've been reading this book sequentially, you've already learned a bit about tables and how to create a basic data table. In this chapter, you'll get an in-depth look at the elements used for tables, how table rows and cells are modified, and how to use tables for layout.

➩ *If you missed the foundational information on tables, see Chapter 7, "Working with Tables and Frames," p. 121.*

The first step in becoming aware of how best to use tables as a fundamental tool in Web design is to understand the HTML and XHTML elements used to create them (see Table 18.1).

Table 18.1   Table Elements in HTML and XHTML

Element	Purpose
table	The main table tag, it denotes the beginning and subsequent end of a table.
tr	The table row tag and its companion closing tag, <tr> ... </tr>.
td	The table data or table cell. This tag is used to define individual table cells.
th	Defines a cell with header information. Typically, this renders in bold.
caption	A caption describes the nature of a table. You are allowed only one caption per table. Captions are especially helpful for accessibility and are rarely used in table layout, but rather are reserved for table data.
thead	Table head, used for table header information.
tfoot	Table foot, used for footer information.
tbody	Table body, defines the table body.
colgroup	Defines a group of columns. There are two ways to specify the group. One is to use the span attribute to specify the number of columns to be grouped. The other way is to use the col element.
col	Used to define columns within a group.

The trick now is knowing when and how to use and modify these elements. Fortunately, Dreamweaver provides a lot of help.

CREATING ADVANCED TABLES

Tables are quite flexible for both data and layout purposes. There are a lot of detailed issues that need to be addressed, especially if you're using tables for layout. In this section, you learn Dreamweaver methods to set table properties, work with table cells and table rows, nest tables, and stack tables.

Setting Table Properties

If you have experience designing with tables or have created a few working through Chapter 7, you know that there are three primary foundations of a table—the table element itself, the table row (tr), and the table cell (td). You can't have a table if you don't have at least these three elements in place.

The attributes that modify these elements are numerous. And, how these attributes work with one another is important because there is a hierarchical order to the application of attributes with the cell taking precedence over the row and the row taking precedence over the table.

The dominance of table cell attributes over other attributes within a table demonstrates how critical the table cell element is. In fact, many Web authors choose to not apply formatting to rows at all. Rather, they focus only on the table cells and the table element itself because more control over layouts can be achieved.

To view a table's general properties, open a document that contains a table, select the table, and select Window, Properties. The Property inspector appears.

Within the Property inspector, you can examine the table's properties (see Figure 18.1). These properties relate to the table element itself and can be modified to fit your needs.

> **Caution**
>
> The height and bordercolor attributes do not exist in any version of HTML or XHTML. They are therefore considered browser-specific and should be used only with careful consideration. The align, valign, and width attributes do exist for tables in HTML and XHTML. Interestingly, you can even use these attributes in XHTML strict and XHTML 1.1, despite the fact that they are unavailable for other elements, such as p, in those language versions.

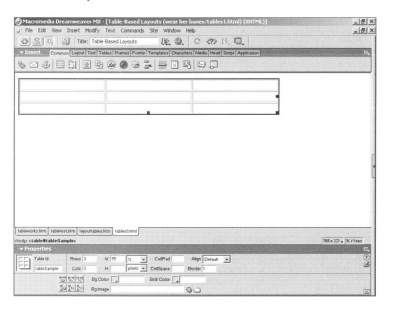

Figure 18.1
The Property inspector enables you to view a table's general properties.

18

A variety of attributes can be used to modify table cells and rows. The attributes available within Dreamweaver are described in Table 18.2.

Table 18.2   Table Formatting Options

Dreamweaver Option	Associated Markup Attribute	Action
Horz	align	The horizontal alignment of the cell or row
Vert	valign	The vertical alignment of the cell or row
W	width	The width of the cell or row
H	height	The height of the cell or row
NoWrap	nowrap	Prevents line wrapping so the table will expand to display all the content within that cell or row
BG	background	Enables a link to a background graphic for the cell or row
BG	bgcolor	Enables the use of a background color for the cell or row
Header	th	Transforms a table cell to a table header (th), which as noted in Table 18.1, usually renders in bold
Brdr	bordercolor	Defines a border color for your cell or row

Figure 18.2 shows the Property inspector's options for working with table cells and rows. When you select a row, the Property inspector will read "row." When you select a column of cells, the menu will read "column." Otherwise, the options within the inspector are the same for each.

Figure 18.2
You can modify tables and rows using the options found within the Property inspector when a table is highlighted.

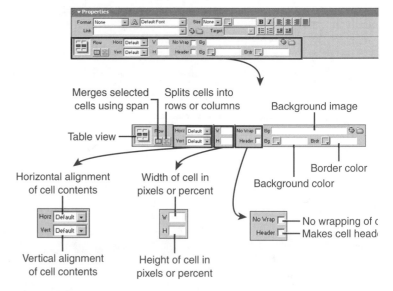

Managing Table Rows and Cells

Using the Property inspector, you can manage all aspects of your table and its rows and cells. Managing a table includes knowing how to insert, delete, split, and merge cells and rows.

Inserting and Deleting Table Rows and Cells

To insert a table row, follow these steps:

1. Open a document with a table, or create a new table.

2. In Design view, click in a table cell.

3. Select Modify, Table, Insert Row (see Figure 18.3).

A complete row is now inserted.

Inserting a table cell follows the exact same process, although you select Modify, Table, Insert Cell to insert a cell rather than a row.

When you don't add attributes to a tag, browsers seek the default. Table borders default to 0, whereas cell padding and cell spacing default to 1. Alignment defaults to the left, and width becomes dynamic. This means that the width of a table and the cells within adapt to the combination of browser space and the data you've placed within the cells.

Figure 18.3
Insert a table row using the main menu. You can also use Code view and the Table tab on the Insert bar to add a table row to your table.

18

To insert multiple table rows or cells, follow these steps:

1. In Design view, click in a table cell.

2. Select Modify, Table, Insert Rows or Columns. The Insert Rows or Columns dialog box appears (see Figure 18.4).

3. If you want to insert rows into your table, select the Rows radio button. If you want to insert cells into a row, select the Columns radio button.

4. Type the number of rows you want to insert into the Number of Rows text box.

5. If you want the row or cell to be above your insertion point, select the Above the Selection radio button. If you want for your row or cell to appear below, select the Below the Selection radio button.

6. Click OK.

Figure 18.4
The Insert Rows or Columns dialog box allows you to add rows or columns in multiples. Because table cells become a table's viewable columns, the term *column* is used to describe a stack of cells.

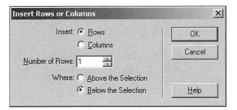

Dreamweaver now adds the rows or columns as per your specifications.

Aligning Rows and Cells

You can align rows and cells horizontally and vertically. Horizontal alignment uses the `align` attribute and a value of `left` (default), `center`, or `right` (see Figure 18.5). This causes content to align along the horizon to the left, center, or right, respectively. Vertical alignment is achieved using the `valign` attribute with a value of `top`, `middle`, `bottom`, or `baseline` (see Figure 18.6). Content shifts accordingly to the top, middle, bottom, or baseline position within the cell.

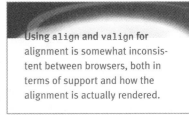

Using `align` and `valign` for alignment is somewhat inconsistent between browsers, both in terms of support and how the alignment is actually rendered.

Figure 18.5
Examine the horizontal alignment of these table cells. The image in the top cell is left aligned, the image in the middle cell is center aligned, and the bottom cell is right aligned.

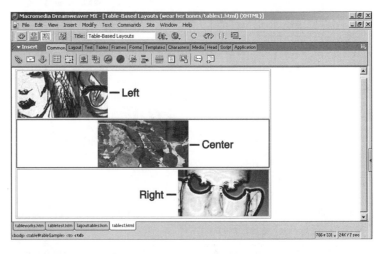

To align a row or cell horizontally or vertically, in Design view, click in a cell or select the row you want to align. Using the Property inspector, select your alignment preference from the Horz (horizontal) or Vert (vertical) drop-down menu.

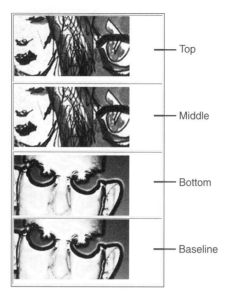

— Top

— Middle

— Bottom

— Baseline

Figure 18.6
Vertical alignment in table cells from top to bottom: top, middle, bottom, and baseline. Note that the `baseline` attribute, when supported by a browser, will try to arrange all objects, in this case image and text, to the baseline point.

The row or cell is now aligned horizontally. How Dreamweaver achieves this in the markup it generates is interesting. When you align a row of three cells, the alignment attribute is placed in the `tr` element. The individual cells will *not* get the alignment attribute or value. If you select a column, the individual cells get the attribute.

Adding Backgrounds and Color to Rows and Cells

To add a background color to a single table cell, follow these steps:

1. In Design view, click in the cell for which you want to have a background color.

2. Find the bottommost BG option on the Property inspector. You'll see a color chip and a text field at the ready.

3. Either click the chip and select a color from the color picker or enter the color name or hexadecimal equivalent into the text box.

The color is automatically applied (see Figure 18.7).

To add a background color to an entire row, begin by selecting the row you want to colorize. Then, follow steps 2 and 3 of the previous procedure to get the results shown in Figure 18.8.

If you want to have one type of alignment across a group of rows or cells, you can align more than one row or column at a time by first selecting the multiple rows and columns you want. Once selected, choose your alignment preference for the group.

18

Figure 18.7
The background color is now visible. In this case, the bgcolor attribute is applied to that individual table cell only.

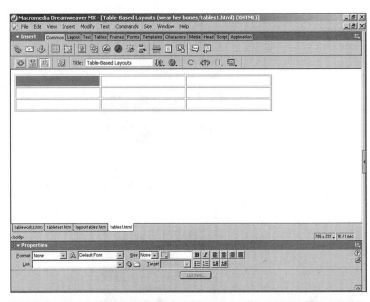

Figure 18.8
Here, the top and bottom rows have had a background color added. In this case, the bgcolor attribute is added to the tr element only, and not the table cells within it.

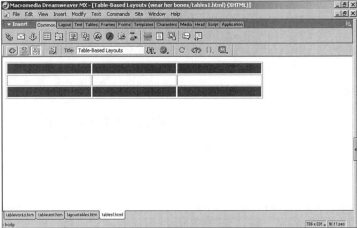

You can also add a background graphic to your table rows or cells. To add a background to a row (or several rows), make sure you're in Design view. Select the rows or cells to which you want to add the background graphic. Then, in the Property inspector, type the path to the graphic, or use the file browser to find the file and select it for use. The background then tiles into the rows or cells that make up the selected row (see Figure 18.9).

You can always add color to an entire row and then click in a specific cell and change the color of that cell to vary your design.

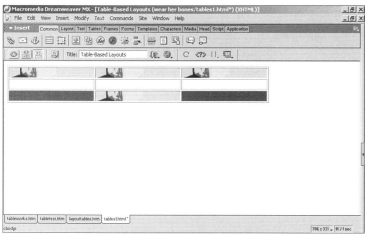

Figure 18.9
Adding a background to table cells and rows. Just as with background graphics, these graphics tile into the available space.

If you selected rows, the background attribute appears in the tr elements corresponding to those rows. If you selected a cell, or several cells, the background attribute appears in the td elements corresponding to those cells.

The background attribute is a bit problematic because, as you'll see if you study Table 18.3, while you have good rendering support with current browsers for backgrounds in table cells, IE and Opera do not support the attribute for table rows (see Figure 18.10). So step lightly when using this approach. Eventually, support might disappear in any standards-compliant browser because it is simply not a part of the languages they are being built to accommodate.

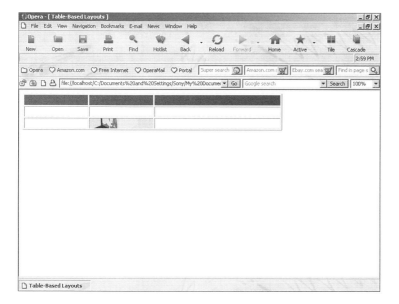

Figure 18.10
Opera 6 successfully interprets the background of the table cell but not that of the row, even though the markup is the same as what generated the table in Figure 18.9.

18

Table 18.3 Browser Support for the `background` Attribute

Browser	background in `tr`	background in `td`
Netscape Navigator 4.0	Yes	Yes
Netscape Navigator 6.0	Yes	Yes
Netscape Navigator 7.0	Yes	Yes
Mozilla 1.0	Yes	Yes
Internet Explorer 6.0	No	Yes
Opera 6.0	No	Yes

Because the `background` attribute is not supported in any standard language version, those readers attempting to follow standards should use Cascading Style Sheets (CSS) layouts. Interestingly, CSS layouts offer a lot more flexibility in terms of backgrounds—you can not only attach a background graphic to a table or division, but also control whether it tiles, how it is positioned, which parts of it are seen, and so forth.

So, despite the unfortunate situation regarding the `background` attribute in table design, the CSS options do offer much more control. Designers will be limited, however, by the CSS support within the target audience's browsers.

Content Wrapping

The `nowrap` attribute ensures that your content will have no line feeds. This means the table cell must flex to accommodate the content. As such, you have to be cautious so as not to override any widths within the table cell you want to keep intact (see Figure 18.11).

Figure 18.11
The `nowrap` attribute ensures that the table cell contents do not wrap. This overrides any width values you might have used in a cell, so use this attribute with caution.

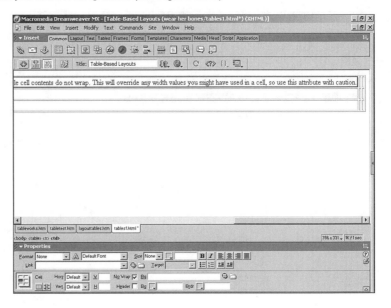

To set the nowrap attribute in a table cell, simply click in the cell in Design view and then check the No Wrap check box in the Property inspector.

The nowrap **Attribute in XHTML**

Although you are allowed to use the nowrap attribute in XHTML transitional, you must accommodate its status as a *minimized attribute.*

You'll recognize minimized attributes by the fact that in HTML they stand alone as a single word:

```
<td nowrap>
```

The practice of attribute minimization is not allowed in XHTML. As a result, you must use the attribute name as its value for the syntax to be valid:

```
<td nowrap="nowrap">
```

Splitting Cells into Rows or Columns

This is a quick method to add more rows or columns of cells to existing cells. You'll find that this is helpful from time to time as you're creating your table layout or moving page elements around.

To split a cell, follow these steps:

1. In Design view, click in the cell.

2. Select Modify, Table, Split Cell. Alternatively, you can click the Split Cell button within the Property inspector.

3. The Split Cell dialog box appears (see Figure 18.12). Set whether you want rows or columns by selecting the corresponding radio button.

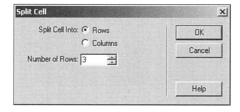

Figure 18.12
The Split Cell dialog box enables you to modify your table rows and columns.

4. Determine the number of rows or columns you want, and type that number into the Number of Rows text box.

5. Click OK.

The table row or cell is now modified as per your specifications (see Figure 18.13).

Figure 18.13
Dreamweaver splits the cells of
the table, adding the appropriate
markup elements and attributes.

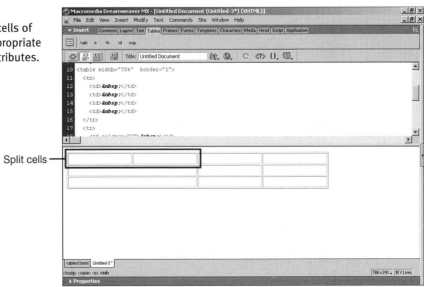

Split cells

Merging Cells with Span

To modify your table for layout or data purposes so a column of cells can span several rows or columns without any internal boundaries, you can merge cells.

Merging cells taps into the power of two attributes: rowspan and colspan. Row spanning enables you to have a cell span several rows, giving you more options regarding how your table is designed. Column spanning enables you to have a cell span several columns (see Figure 18.14).

Figure 18.14
The merged cells result in a
columnar structure using the
rowspan attribute.

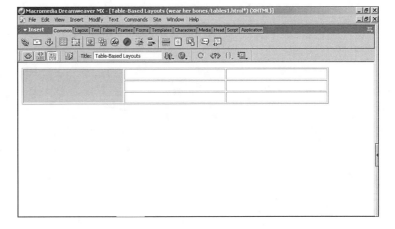

To merge cells, follow these steps:

1. In Design view, select the cells you want to merge.

2. Select Modify, Table, Merge Cells. Alternatively, you can use the Merge button in the Property inspector.

3. The cells are now merged (see Figure 18.15). Save your file so the attributes are updated.

> **You can merge only those cells** that appear next to each other on the horizontal or vertical. You cannot merge cells that are separated from one another or diagonal to one another.

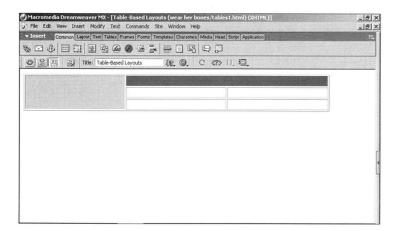

Figure 18.15
Merging cells creates new options for your table's layout. This is helpful for creating both compelling data tables and layout tables.

Nesting and Stacking Tables

Nesting and stacking are table techniques that are used to achieve more complex table designs. *Nesting* tables is exactly what it sounds like: One table is placed inside another. *Stacking* is just as self-explanatory: It is simply the placement of one table on top of another.

Nesting Tables

To nest a table, follow these steps:

1. In Design view, click in the cell of a table into which you want to insert another table.

2. Select Insert, Table (see Figure 18.16). The Insert Table dialog box appears.

3. Determine the features your nested table should have. Enter your choices into the dialog box.

4. Click OK.

Figure 18.17 shows the outlines of a nested table.

Figure 18.16
Inserting a table into a page using the Insert Table dialog box.

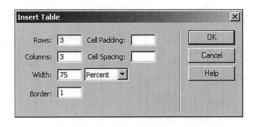

Figure 18.17
You can nest as many tables as you like, but typically any more than two or three nests deep creates overly complicated markup.

Nested table

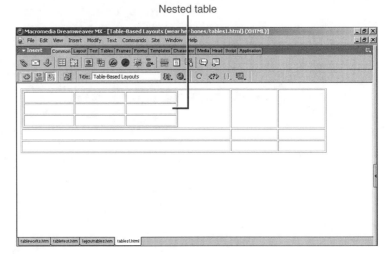

Stacking Tables

Stacking tables can be effective in table-based layout if you want to have two or more areas of a page that can be arranged independently. For example, you might choose to have a fixed table above a dynamic one or combine tables of different sizes.

To stack a table this way, follow these steps:

1. In Design view, place your cursor after your table. Press (Return) [Enter] to get to the next insertion point within the document.

2. Select Insert, Table.

3. The Insert Table dialog box appears. Determine your table's parameters and enter them into the dialog box.

4. Click OK and save your changes.

You can now add any content, presentation, and style to the table you want. Figure 18.18 shows a series of stacked, empty tables.

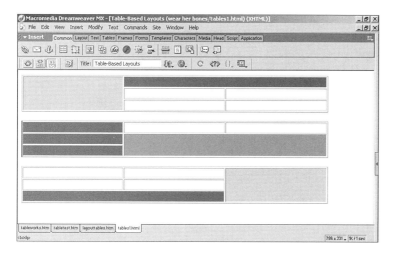

Figure 18.18
Each of these stacked tables has different layout and presentation attributes. You can stack as many tables into a document as seems logical to meet your needs.

Using a Design Scheme

One of Dreamweaver's many attractions is that it has built-in tools to make your life easier. If you're looking to build an attractive data table quickly, you can do so using Dreamweaver's preset table designs. Although they're somewhat limited (preset tables in Dreamweaver do not allow for some advanced features such as spanning), preset table design schemes are a great choice in many instances.

To use a design scheme for a table, follow these steps:

1. Create a table with the amount of rows and columns you require.

2. Select Commands, Format Table from the main menu. The Format Table dialog box appears (see Figure 18.19).

3. Select from any of the 17 preset tables listed at the upper-left of the dialog box. Customize the table colors as you desire.

4. Click Apply to see the formatting and presentation changes.

5. Click OK to accept the changes.

You can change the preset design at any time by simply following steps 2–5 and applying a new theme. The new theme simply overwrites the old one.

Figure 18.19
The power of Dreamweaver table design schemes is that they are highly customizable. You can create great looking data tables that match your designs precisely.

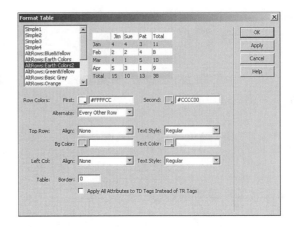

USING LAYOUT VIEW

Layout view is a special view Dreamweaver MX supplies you with as you work to achieve table-based layouts. This way, you can move portions of your design around the page with a freedom you would not have working in traditional Design or Code view. The underlying markup is still tables, but you get more visual interface options along the way.

To see how a table you created looks in Layout view, follow these steps:

1. Open a table and switch to Design view (you must first be in Design view to get to Layout view).

2. Click the Layout tab along the Insert bar. Alternatively, you can select View, Table View, Layout View from the main menu or press (Command-F6) [Ctrl+F6].

3. Examine your table. You'll notice that in Layout view, your table now appears as a layout table rather than an HTML table (see Figure 18.20).

> To return to working on your tables outside of Layout view, select View, Table View, Standard View. Dreamweaver switches back to Design view, where you can continue working or switch to Code view, depending on your preference.

You are now ready to modify your table using Layout view's tools and options.

Drawing Layout Tables and Cells in Layout View

A layout cell is very similar to a table cell in that it contains your content. However, the purpose of layout tables and cells is to help you organize and move tables around in such a way that would be prohibitive if you were just inserting table cells and rows. So, this method is especially helpful if you're using the table to create a layout.

> You also can nest layout tables, enabling you to create more complex layouts.

As with table cells, layout cells cannot exist outside a layout table. If you create a layout cell, Dreamweaver automatically contains it within a layout table. Create an additional layout table anywhere on the page where you want more control over that portion of the page.

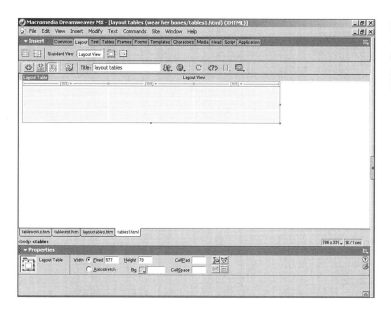

Figure 18.20
In Layout view, layout tables appear as measured, outlined grids, whereas the underlying HTML tables appear in gray.

Drawing a Layout Table

To create a Layout table, follow these steps:

1. In Layout view, click the Draw Layout Table button to create a single layout table.

2. Position your cursor in the Document window.

3. Drag to create the layout table. The layout table now appears on your page.

4. You'll notice a green tab in the upper-left corner of the layout table (see Figure 18.21). If you (Shift-click) [right-click], you'll see a drop-down menu from which you can perform a variety of layout actions.

Drawing a Layout Cell

To draw a layout cell, follow these steps:

1. In Layout view, click the Draw Layout Cell button.

2. Position your pointer within the layout table where you want the layout cell to go.

3. Drag to create the cell.

4. Continue adding cells as needed, or begin adding content to the cells (see Figure 18.22).

Figure 18.21
Each layout table appears in green, with a tab denoting Layout Table at the upper-left. The width of the table is also available when the layout table is selected.

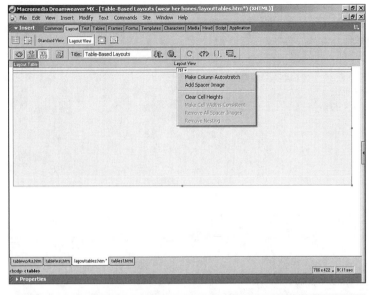

Figure 18.22
Here are several layout cells within a layout table. Layout cells appear outlined in blue. A grid of fine lines in the background provides you with an idea of what the HTML table structure beneath your layout table looks like.

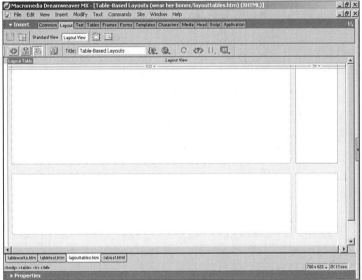

➪ *You can modify the default colors of your layout tables and cells. See Appendix A, "Setting Preferences," p. 617.*

Nesting a Layout Table

To nest a layout table within another layout table, follow these steps:

1. Select the layout table into which you want to insert a new layout table.

2. Click the Draw Layout Table button.

3. Move your cursor to the location within the Layout table where you want to draw the nested table. Remember, the layout table is gray.

4. Click and drag to create your new nested table.

> **Caution**
>
> In fixed design, you must never exceed a cell's parameters. In other words, if you have a cell that is 125 pixels wide, but you put a 200-pixel–wide graphic in it, you will cause the table to render improperly.

➪ *Feeling a little out of control regarding your layout tables and cells? Check out "Using the Grid" in the "Troubleshooting" section at the end of this chapter.*

Formatting in Layout View

A range of utilities is available to assist you in creating a great table design within Layout view. You can use the Property inspector to modify your layout table and cell attributes; you can add content to a layout cell and modify that cell to more effectively manage that content; and you can let Dreamweaver help you make decisions about using spacer graphics for table integrity.

Setting Layout Table and Cell Attributes

A range of options exists for modifying layout tables and cells. When you're working in Layout view, these settings apply to the layout tables and cells, as well as to the way the markup will be generated to create the underlying table-based design.

Most of these settings are familiar by now and include width, height, background, no wrap, cell padding, and cell spacing.

However, several options for layout tables and cells you might not have seen before include

- **Fixed**—Selecting fixed allows you to specify a pixel value width for your table or table cell.

- **Autostretch**—Selecting this feature results in the table or table cell having a percentage value. The resulting table or cell is therefore dynamic and will automatically flow to fill the available space.

- **Clear Row Heights**—Selecting this removes the row heights.

- **Make Widths Consistent**—In fixed designs, selecting this feature matches the width of the cell to its contents. So, if you have created a layout cell that is 300 pixels wide and the content is only 250 pixels wide, this feature resets the width to 250, resulting in a visual match between the layout table and cell, and the underlying HTML table and content.

■ **Remove All Spacers**—This feature removes any spacer GIFs used in your layout.

■ **Remove Nesting**—This setting removes any nested layout tables.

To select options for a layout table, follow these steps:

1. Select the layout table. To do this, click the layout table's tab, or click the `<table>` tag in the tag selector above the Property inspector.

2. In the Property inspector, make modifications to the properties available as you see fit.

3. Press (Return) [Enter] at any time to apply a property.

4. Save your file to update the changes.

To select options for a layout cell, the process is the same. Simply select the layout cell by clicking the edge of the cell, or (Command-click) [Ctrl-click] anywhere in the cell. Make your selections using the Property inspector, and save your changes.

Adding Content

You can add any kind of content you would like to a layout cell, just as you would with a traditional HTML table cell. Follow these steps:

1. Select the cell to which you want to add content.

2. If you want to add text to the cell, click in the cell and begin typing. You can format your text normally by using the Property inspector.

3. If you want to add an image (not a background image) to your cell, place your cursor in the cell and then select Insert, Image. Alternatively, you can click the Insert Image button on the Insert bar. Insert the image and modify as you want.

You also can add other elements, such as objects and applets. Simply add them to the layout cell as you would to a normal document (see Figure 18.23).

Because Dreamweaver adds heights as you work on your design in Layout view, you will likely want to remove that markup. To do so, select the Clear Row Heights option, but only after you've added the content to the cells within that row. To remove heights from cells, you need to switch to Code view and manually remove them.

Caution

If you select the Remove Nesting option, any nested tables are removed from the design. The content remains, however, and Dreamweaver incorporates any content into the remaining table. You will likely have to adjust Dreamweaver's modifications to fit your goals.

After your content is completely entered into the table, you might want to clear cell heights. As mentioned several times in this book, heights are problematic and usually nonstandard. Using them is not recommended. Each layout cell column has a drop-down menu with options for modifying that area. Select Clear Cell Heights to remove all height attributes from that cell.

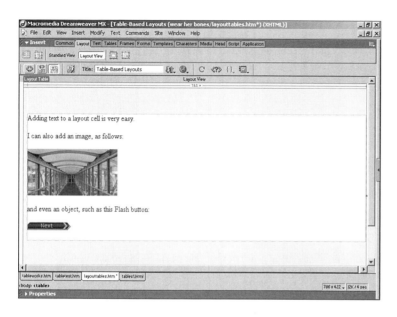

⇨ *Trying to add content to a layout table but having difficulties? See "Adding Content" in the "Troubleshooting" section of this chapter.*

Moving and Resizing Layout Cells and Tables

As you work with your page layout, you'll likely want to move and resize various components within it. You can move and resize table cells and nested tables, and you can resize the outer table, but you cannot move it.

⇨ *You can learn more about overlapping and clipping. See "Creating Draw Layers," p. 447.*

To move a layout cell, first select the cell. Selection handles appear around the cell, which you can grab, and then drag the cell to its new location. To resize the cell, select it and then use one of the selection handles to resize it according to your needs.

To move a nested layout table, select the table by clicking its tab. Selection handles will appear, and you can move the nested layout table. To resize it, simply select it and use the selection handles.

Layout cells, similar to table cells, cannot overlap, and a layout cell cannot be made smaller than its contents. Interestingly, overlapping and clipping can be done using Draw Layers.

Caution
You cannot move a main layout table—only a nested one.

Ensuring Column Integrity

The width and behavior of your table and its elements are critical to the way the resulting design will work in real-world applications. To ensure that table columns do not collapse or that they flow appropriately, or to fix to your specifications, review some of the concepts and techniques used to achieve column integrity.

Here are the primary concepts to remember:

- Individual columns, like tables, can have a fixed or dynamic width. When you create these columns as having fixed widths, those widths appear in the column header. When you create these columns as having dynamic (percentage) widths, the column header shows a wavy line to represent its dynamic features.

- Autostretching columns alerts Dreamweaver to add spacer images in any fixed-width columns to help retain the structure of the table.

Ideally, you will manage autostretching only after your content has been added to the layout because this avoids unexpected problems with markup. By keeping the process streamlined, you avoid errors and keep your resulting markup neat.

One way to achieve the best of both worlds is to combine fixed and dynamic approaches. The wisdom here, however, is to ensure that only one cell is fixed to a percentage width—and that width should be 100%. This approach helps you maintain the shape of the layout but allows for dynamic positioning of text.

This approach works well, for example, if you have a left and right margin you want to remain fixed and still have the center body area autostretch. You could achieve this effect by fixing the columns to the left and right using both a fixed width cell and spacer GIF set to the dimensions of the cell, but leaving the center cell dynamic.

Spacer Images

A helpful means of ensuring structure within a table, spacer images have been in use for a long time. But they are controversial for several reasons. First, they add some minor download time to your page. Secondly, they are at the heart of the presentation versus structure argument. A spacer image really has no logical place within HTML, although it does have a logical place in the layout method that has become de facto for HTML.

Spacer images are single pixel images that are made transparent. When inserted into a design, you can modify their widths or heights to fix that portion of a table so it won't collapse because, although the content in it is transparent, it is structurally maintaining the cell.

Making a Column Autostrech

To make a column autostretch, follow these steps:

1. Select the column you want to stretch.

2. In the Property inspector, select the Autostretch radio button. The Choose Spacer Image dialog box appears if you have never created a spacer before.

3. Select Create a Spacer Image file if you have no spacer image for this site. If you do have one, select Use an Existing Spacer Image file. Click OK and follow the prompts until your modifications have been made.

Inserting a Spacer into a Column

To add a spacer image into a column, follow these steps:

1. Select the layout table that contains the column to be modified.

2. Along the column header menu, click the arrow to bring up the drop-down menu.

3. Select Add Spacer Image. You will be prompted as to whether you want to have Dreamweaver create one for you or use an existing one. Make your selection, and follow the remaining options to insert the spacer.

The spacer image is now placed within the column. The image will not be visible (see Figure 18.24).

Caution

When working with tables in this fashion, it really is wiser to let Dreamweaver create the spacer images for you. Unless you're an advanced user, not using them can mean collapsed areas within your layout that you cannot see, making your work harder—the exact opposite intention of using these features in the first place!

Caution

When using spacer images in a table, be sure to include an alt attribute in the image, and leave the attribute value undeclared. The reason you should do this is so that screen readers for the visually disabled will ignore the spacer image. If you don't do this, the word "image" will be repeated to the user over and over again.

18

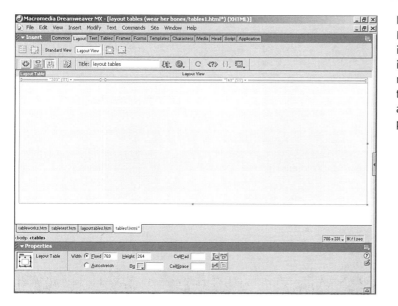

Figure 18.24
Despite the fact that the spacer image can't be seen, you know it's there because the column menu header now appears with two lines rather than one line across the top. This denotes the presence of a spacer image.

Removing Spacer Images

If you want to remove spacer images, you can do so one at a time or from the entire table at once.

To remove a spacer image in one instance, select the layout cell in which the spacer resides. From the column header's drop-down menu, select Remove Spacer Image. The image is removed, and the header returns to having only one line, indicating that there is no spacer image within it.

If you want to remove all spacer images from your layout table, follow these steps:

1. Open the document containing the layout table from which you want to remove all spacers.

2. Click the Remove All Spacers button, found within the Property inspector.

3. All the spacer images will be removed. Save your file to update these important changes.

One of the problems that might occur at this point is the collapse or disappearance of cells within the layout that didn't have content within them. At this point, you'll likely have to make some additional modifications so your layout can be achieved.

ADVANCED TABLE TECHNIQUES

HTML 4.0 introduced several additional means of organizing tables to enable better rendering of tables and to make those tables more inherently accessible.

Although Dreamweaver MX contains reference information on these elements, as well as provides some guidance as to how to enter them in Code view, these features are not yet available within most of the Dreamweaver tools with which you are familiar. So, to learn these features, you'll switch to Code view for a bit.

Column Grouping

Column grouping is the act of defining groups of cells within a table. The technique is useful for streamlining your markup by applying structure- or content-related information to grouped columns within your tables.

Column grouping involves the use of the following elements:

- colgroup—Defines a group of columns. There are two ways to specify the group. One is to use the span attribute to specify the number of columns to be grouped; the other way is to use the col element.

- col—Used to define columns within a group.

As mentioned previously, you can use the span attribute to define your groups. You also can use the col element. In the case of the span attribute, the number of columns to be grouped is determined by the numeric value of span. So, if you write

```
<colgroup span="5">
</colgroup>
```

the number of columns to be spanned is five.

In Listing 18.1, a table has been created with three rows of four cells each. The columns are grouped together with the colgroup element, and then an alignment is applied to each group using the align attribute in the colgroup tag.

Listing 18.1   Column Grouping

```
<!DOCTYPE HTML PUBLIC "-//W3C//DTD HTML 4.01 Transitional//EN"
        "http://www.w3.org/TR/html4/loose.dtd">

<html>
<head>
<title>Column Grouping</title>
</head>

<body>

<table border="2" width="100%">

   <caption>Column Grouping</caption>

   <colgroup align="right">
   <colgroup align="left">
   <colgroup align="center">
   <colgroup align="right">
   <tr>
   <td>content</td>
   <td>content</td>
   <td>content</td>
   <td>content</td>

   </tr>

   <tr>
   <td>content</td>
   <td>content</td>
   <td>content</td>
   <td>content</td>

   </tr>

   <tr>
   <td>content</td>
   <td>content</td>
   <td>content</td>
   <td>content</td>

   </tr>
```

18

Listing 18.1   Continued

```
</table>


</body>
</html>
```

So, instead of having to put the alignment in each of the individual table cell tags, I simply applied it using column grouping, and it subsequently applies to all the grouped columns.

Figure 18.25 shows how the grouping controls look when applied to a table. Many browsers do not support these features, but Internet Explorer 6.0 does, as you can see in this figure.

Figure 18.25
Here is an example of a table that uses the colgroup element. Note the varied alignments in each column are based on the grouping, not individual alignment within each cell.

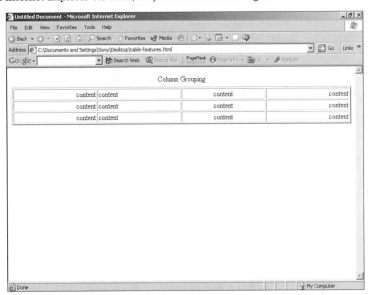

Table Head, Table Foot, and Table Body

Whereas colgroup and col work to group columns, the thead, tfoot, and tbody elements within HTML and XHTML can be seen as working to combine rows. Using these elements, rows can be grouped according to their functions, described in Table 18.1 in the first section of this chapter.

In HTML 4.0 and 4.01, colgroup has an optional closing tag and col is considered an empty element (closing tag forbidden). So, if you're writing XHTML documents, you'll need to accommodate this by always closing your colgroup element and terminating the col element:

```
<col width="100%" />
```

There are a few idiosyncrasies when working with these, as follows:

- Each of the thead, tfoot, and tbody elements must contain a row group of at least one row. The tbody element can be left out in HTML for backward compatibility with older table models.

- Interestingly, the tfoot appears *above* the tbody.

- In HTML, tbody end tags can be omitted. In XHTML, you must use the end tag.

- In HTML, when both the thead and tfoot elements are in place, you can use a start tag only. However, in XHTML, you must use both start and end tags.

Listing 18.2 shows the use of these elements.

Listing 18.2   thead, tfoot, and tbody in Action

```
<!DOCTYPE HTML PUBLIC "-//W3C//DTD HTML 4.01 Transitional//EN"
        "http://www.w3.org/TR/html4/loose.dtd">
<html>
<head>
<title>Working with Tables</title>
</head>

<body>

<table>
<thead>
    <tr><td>This is the table head</td></tr>
</thead>
<tfoot>
    <tr><td>This is the table foot</td></tr>
</tfoot>
<tbody>
    <tr><td>This is the table body</td></tr>
</tbody>
</table>

</body>
</html>
```

Figure 18.26 shows the results of the markup in Listing 18.2.

18

Figure 18.26
Despite the fact that the foot appears in the markup before the head, it visually renders in its appropriate position.

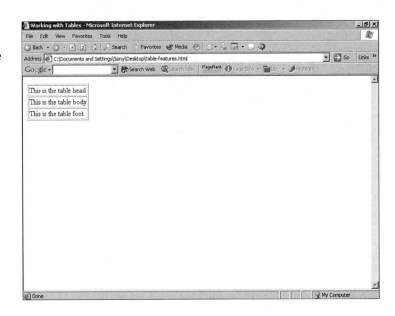

TROUBLESHOOTING

Using the Grid

I'm having trouble getting my layout to line up right. What tools in Dreamweaver will help?

Turning on the grid can provide a visual guide while working with layout tables. The grid also enables you to control snapping, which when turned on, allows the elements on your page to snap to the grid's parameters instead of floating randomly. To control the grid settings, select View, Grid, Grid Settings. When the Grid Settings dialog box appears, you can modify the display of the grid and the snap settings. If you want to turn on snapping, check the Snap to Grid check box. If you want to turn it off, make sure the check box is clear.

Adding Content

I'm having difficulties adding content to a layout table. What's the solution?

You can place content only in a layout cell, not a table. So, if you have no cells in the layout table, you need to create some for your content. Or, you might be clicking outside the layout cell. Be sure that, if you have an existing layout cell, you are working within that cell. Cells will be white rather than gray.

PEER TO PEER: DREAMWEAVER FEATURES FOR ACCESSIBLE TABLES

Creating accessible tables involves adding certain elements and attributes to them that have been created to enhance accessibility.

Macromedia's ongoing commitment to adding accessibility and standards-compliant tools has resulted in a great feature for creating accessible tables. By setting up accessibility attributes for tables, you can make it so all your tables are, by default, accessible.

To turn on accessibility features for tables, follow these steps:

1. Select (Dreamweaver, Preferences) [Edit, Preferences] and the dialog box appears.

2. Select Accessibility from the Category list. In the Accessibility menu, check Tables.

3. Click OK. Accessibility options for tables will now be available to you.

To insert accessible tables, follow these steps:

1. Select Insert, Table. The Insert Table dialog box appears. Set the parameters for your table.

2. Click OK. The Accessibility Options for Tables dialog box appears (see Figure 18.27).

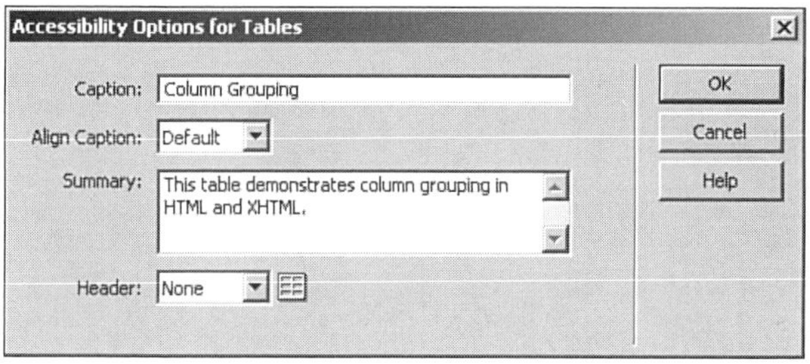

Figure 18.27
Adding information to the Accessibility Options for Tables dialog box.

3. In the Caption text box, enter a descriptive caption for your table. Align the caption using the Align Caption drop-down menu options.

4. In the Summary text window, add as detailed a summary that describes the table and its contents as is possible.

5. You can make headers out of either the first row or first column, or both. This means that the text content within a header will appear in bold, as well as using a different element th to denote that element as a header.

6. Click OK.

You now have a table that will be much easier for those using accessibility devices to interpret.

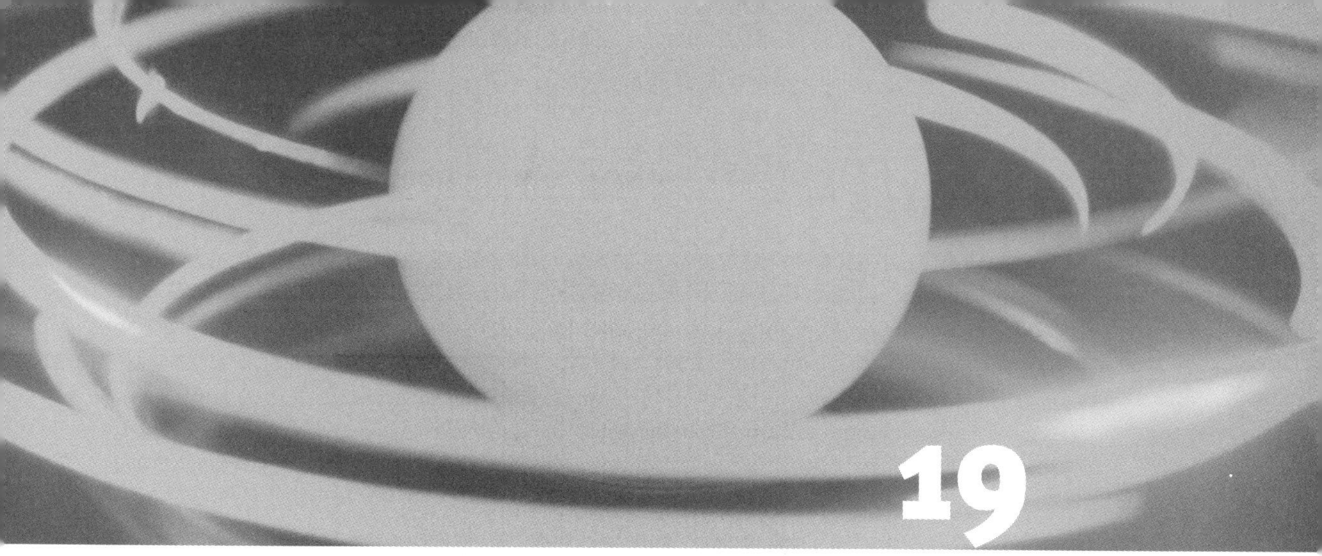

WORKING WITH FRAME-BASED LAYOUTS

IN THIS CHAPTER

ABOUT FRAMES

In Chapter 7, "Working with Tables and Frames," an early introduction to the creation of basic tables and frames was provided. In this chapter, you'll delve more deeply into the rationale for using frames; you'll learn how to modify frame and frameset features and how to make frames more accessible.

Frames can be very empowering from a design perspective. One aspect of this empowerment is that designers can keep sections of a page static while other parts of the page can be used to display other pages. Particularly handy for fixed navigation, this is a common approach to the development of menu areas and other items, such as a company logo, that are to remain in place (see Figure 19.1).

Figure 19.1
This frame-based site keeps the main, left navigation, and top logo areas static. New content is loaded into the main window.

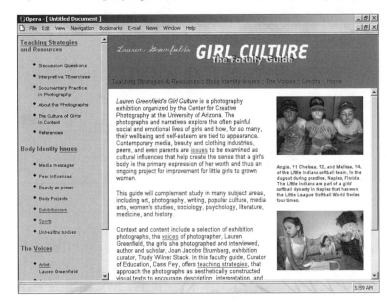

Despite their interesting applications, frames have their own unique set of problems. First, creating a frame-based site these days requires an understanding of accessibility options for the site to be made useful to blind and disabled site visitors. This makes frames an unfortunate choice for specific audiences unless the designer is clear as to how to manage frames for accessibility or is prepared to create an alternative, non-framed site. Frames also make bookmarking pages in a site or referring to specific pages in a framed structure via a URL more difficult. Finally, frames force the designer to write more markup and manage more documents because frames require more actual pages.

> Frames were formally adopted as standard in HTML 4.0, and they carry over into XHTML 1.0 with their own DTD. In XHTML 1.1, frames are in a unique module.

Because of these difficulties, only the most technologically adept, design-literate of authors should use frames—and even then at the risk of causing difficulty to certain users for the pages they build. Fortunately, the tools in Macromedia MX make it easier for you when you do decide to use frames by providing accessibility options and easy development tools to modify your frame choices.

Frames, particularly those without borders, give designers another method to create a grid system upon which to base a design. Borderless frames expand frames from their original role as an organizational tool to include page format and design control. With borderless frames, as with borderless tables, individual sections of a page can be defined and controlled (see Figure 19.2).

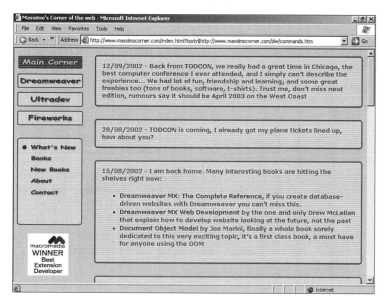

Figure 19.2
A borderless frame gives a clean method of creating a design while still tapping into the value of static page areas.

Whereas tables can be used only on a page-by-page basis, frame technology introduces the static concept, discussed previously, and the aspect of *targets* allowing a variety of powerful controls.

Webmasters and site designers can now make better choices about how to employ frames. Whether the choice is to use borders for an attractive interface or to create pages with frames as the silent and strong foundation beneath a complex and multifaceted design, the Web designer is ultimately empowered by having these choices.

🖙 *Concerned with issues related to linking to other Web sites from within your frames page? See "Using Frames to Contain Other Sites" in the "Troubleshooting" section at the end of this chapter.*

BUILDING FRAMED PAGES IN DREAMWEAVER MX

As with tables, only three components are absolutely necessary to build a framed page. Yes, frames can get a bit complicated, depending on the ways in which you want to employ them, but at the most basic level, all framed sites begin with the factors introduced here.

If you worked through the exercises in Chapter 7, "Working with Tables and Frames," some of the preliminary information regarding the creation of framesets and frames will be a review. If you feel as though you've learned these techniques well enough, feel free to skip to "Modifying Frameset and Frame Elements" later in this chapter.

19

Any framed page requires a controlling HTML/XHTML document that gives the instructions on how the framed page is to be set up. This control is called the *frameset*. Then, an HTML or XHTML page is required for each individual frame.

The frameset page is the control page of your framed site. In it, you'll argue primarily for the rows or columns you want to create and the HTML pages that will fill those rows or columns. This is done using two major elements:

> **Caution**
>
> It's important to remember that the frameset is a conceptual replacement for the body in the frameset HTML or XHTML document. Therefore, *no* body tags should appear. The one exception to this is the noframes element, which allows you to place a body element within it. This is covered in the "Peer to Peer" section at the end of the chapter.

- frameset—This element defines the way the framed page will look, and its basic attributes help to define rows and columns.

- frame—The frame element arranges individual frames in the frameset. This includes the location of the document required to fill a frame, using the src="x" (where x assigns the relative or absolute URL to the location of the page). A variety of other frame element attributes are covered later in the chapter.

In this section, you'll step through a series of exercises to get you working immediately with frame documents. The first exercise will be to create a frameset, and then you'll move on to build framed pages.

Creating Framesets

There are two means by which you can create a frameset in Dreamweaver MX. You can create your own, or you can use a predefined frameset style.

Building Your Own Frameset

Building your own frameset is similar to building tables in Dreamweaver MX. The first thing you'll want to do is turn on the viewing borders so you can visually work to create the frameset.

To build your own frameset, do the following:

1. Begin with a new HTML or XHTML document by selecting File, New. Or, open a document that you'd like to have converted into a frame.

2. Set the borders to view by selecting View, Visual Aids, Frame Borders.

3. To create the frameset, select Modify, Frameset and then choose the correct type of initial split you want from the selection (left, right, up, or down). Figure 19.3 shows a frame being split.

4. Click and drag the splitting item to where you'd like it.

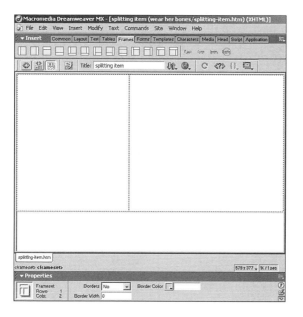

Figure 19.3
Using splitting items, you can break the frame up as you need it without ever worrying about how to generate the complex frameset markup.

If you are happy with the frameset you've created, save the file and continue working. If you'd like to have more splits, follow these steps:

1. Place your cursor into the frame you'd like to split.

2. Select Modify, Frameset, and again select a splitting option.

3. Continue to split frames, dragging the splitting items to the visual location where you require it.

To delete a frame in your frameset, drag that frame's border off the page. Delete any related content.

19

Using a Predefined Frameset

Using a predefined Dreamweaver MX frameset is helpful if you want to quickly create a frameset document with various features intact.

To create an empty, predefined frameset using the New Document Window, follow these steps:

1. Select File, New.

2. In the General tab of the dialog box, highlight Framesets. The Framesets options will appear. Highlight each option in turn to get a view and description of what the resulting frame layout will look like.

3. When you've found the frameset you want to use, click the Create button.

Dreamweaver MX generates the frameset (see Figure 19.4).

Figure 19.4
This frameset design would normally be complicated to mark up, but using predefined framesets allows you great design options.

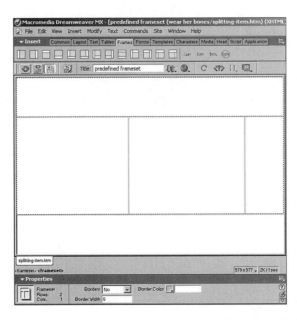

You can also create a predefined frameset using the Frame tab on the Insert bar. To do so, follow these steps:

1. Open a regular HTML or XHTML document. It can be a new document with no content or an existing document with content you want to have modified as a framed page.

2. Place your cursor in the document.

3. From the Insert bar, click the Frame tab. Select the frameset style you'd like.

Dreamweaver MX automatically applies the frameset (see Figure 19.5). This means that it has also generated the individual documents that are delivered to each individual frame. If you're starting from scratch, these should be saved because you will eventually be adding content to them.

↪ *To review how to save frame documents, see "Saving Framesets and Framed Pages," p. 136.*

You can now make modifications to the frameset using the Property inspector.

Using Frame Selection Tools

Dreamweaver MX provides you with two primary visual means to help you make selections when working with your framesets and frame elements. You can work in the Frames panel or the Document window.

To select frames in the Frames panel, follow these steps:

1. Be sure the panel is available. Select Window, Others, Frames. The panel appears, as shown in Figure 19.6.

2. To select a frame, simply click in the frame.

3. To select a frameset, click the border that surrounds the frameset.

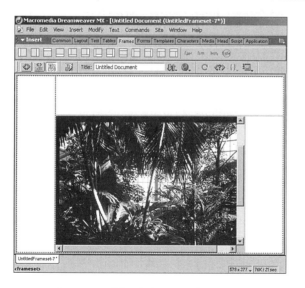

Figure 19.6
The frames panel is a helpful way of selecting your frames and frameset so as to make modifications to your frame options.

You can now make any modifications to the frame or frameset as you require.

To select frames in the Document window, use this method:

1. With your frameset document open, switch to Design view.

2. To select a frame, (Option-Shift-click) [Alt+click] inside a specific frame.

3. To select a frameset, be sure the frame's visual borders are on so you can see what you're doing. Select View, Visual Aids, Frame Borders. Then, click any of the frameset's internal borders (see Figure 19.7).

> **Caution**
>
> Simply clicking in a frame in the Document view does not select it. Instead, a single click in a frame allows you to begin editing the document content of that frame.

Figure 19.7
Select Dreamweaver MX visual frame border aids to make frame and frameset selections.

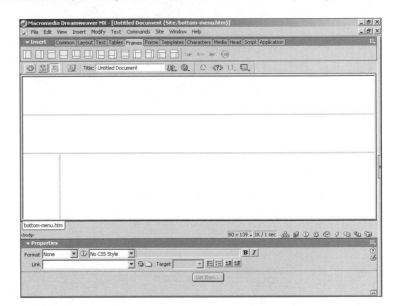

MODIFYING FRAMESET AND FRAME ELEMENTS

There are a variety of means by which you can modify framesets and frame elements in the frameset.

Modifying the Frameset Element

Table 19.1 shows the Property inspector's options, the various elements and attributes that result from selecting those options, and the purposes those options serve.

> **Caution**
>
> The `framespacing`, `frameborder`, `border`, and `bordercolor` attributes are not available for the `frameset` element in the W3C specifications. This means browser implementation for them is available but inconsistent, and you should use these features with care.

Table 19.1   Modifying Framesets

Dreamweaver MX Option	Corresponding Attribute Name in HTML/XHTML	Available Attribute Values	Purpose
Borders (yes, no, default)	frameborder	yes, no	A yes value provides a means for the frameborder to appear. A no value makes the frameset borderless. A default value leaves this attribute out.
Border Width	framespacing and border	Numeric value in pixels	To manage cross-browser differences, both the framespacing and border attributes are added by Dreamweaver MX with the numeric value of your choice.
Border Color	bordercolor	Name or hexadecimal value of color	Colorizes the frame border to your design.
Column	col	Pixels, percents, or relative (*)	Defines the width of a given column in the frameset.
Row	row	Pixels, percents, or relative (*)	Defines the width of a given row in the frameset.

To make any modifications to your frameset, open the frameset and select the frameset in the Document window or by using the Frames panel. Use the Property inspector options available to make the desired changes (see Figure 19.8).

Figure 19.8
When a frameset document is open and the frameset is selected, frameset-related options are available.

19

Modifying Frame Elements in the Frameset

How you set up your frames is very important because the information in the frame element relates to the way in which these elements will behave.

Table 19.2 shows the available features Dreamweaver MX offers for modifying frames.

Table 19.2   Frame Options in the Property Inspector

Dreamweaver MX Option	Corresponding Attribute Name in HTML/XHTML	Available Attribute Values	Purpose
FrameName	name, id	name (where the value is the name you assign the frame)	To identify the frame for proper targeting and scripting.
Src	src	Location of frame file	

Table 19.2 Continued

Dreamweaver MX Option	Corresponding Attribute Name in HTML/XHTML	Available Attribute Values	Purpose
Borders	`frameborder`	`yes, no, default`	A value of `yes` provides a frame border. A value of `no` disallows a frame border. A `default` value doesn't add the attribute to the markup at all.
Scroll	`scrolling`	`yes, no, auto, default`	A value of `yes` means a scroll will always be available when needed. A value of `no` means that a scroll will never be available. A value of `auto` provides a scroll only when needed, and a value of `default` doesn't apply this attribute.
NoResize	`noresize`	`noresize*`	Disables resizing of the frameset borders.
Border Color	`bordercolor`	Any color name or hexadecimal value	Adds a colored border to the frame.
Margin Width	`marginwidth`	Numeric value in pixels	Defines the margin width for the frame.
Margin Height	`marginheight`	Numeric value in pixels	Defines the margin height for the frame.

As with frameset attributes, some of the frame attributes available in Dreamweaver MX are considered proprietary, as follows:

- `bordercolor` is proprietary and does not appear anywhere in the HTML or XHTML specifications.

- A value of `yes` or `no` for the `frameborder` element in a frame is browser specific. Instead, you can use either `1` or `0` but no other value.

To modify any of your frame's features, select the frame you want to modify and then use the Property inspector options to make the desired changes (see Figure 19.9).

It's important to point out that in HTML, the `noresize` attribute is minimized. In other words, it takes no value and simply appears as a single word. Attribute minimization is disallowed in XHTML, so the value of `noresize` becomes `noresize`, as in `noresize="noresize"`. Fortunately, Dreamweaver MX has support for this, so if your pages are set to XHTML compliant mode (select File, New and check the check box labeled Make Document XHTML Compliant), the attribute will be written properly.

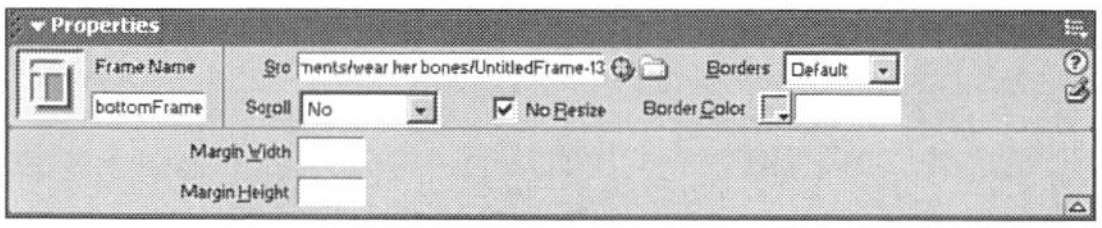

Figure 19.9
When you select a frame to modify, the Property inspector provides all the available options for the frame.

TARGETING WINDOWS

To effectively use frames, a designer must decide where link options will load. For example, you might have set up your frameset to contain a menu on the left and a larger frame field on the right. The goal is to ensure that the links in the menu always load in the content area, unless you want a different behavior.

The following are two basic ways to link, or *target*, documents to specific windows:

- Combine target and name attributes to specifically target windows.

- Use a magic target name.

> **Caution**
>
> Although you can use any combination of attributes in a frame that you require—even if they are proprietary—you *must* include two options for your framed site to work. First, you must include the source for the frame in question. Then, you must name the frame because this is imperative for linking and targeting.

The target and name attributes allow you to add pages to your framed site and target a specific window by naming that window and targeting the link.

⇨ *Trying to print out a frame in your framed page but having no success? See "Printing Frames" in the "Troubleshooting" section of this chapter.*

Linking a Frame Using the target and name Attributes

To target a frame to open properly using the target and name attributes, you need to ensure that all your individual frames have been properly named in the frameset. Then, follow these steps:

> A *magic target* name is a special name reserved by browsers to perform a distinct function.

1. Select a link or linked object in the frame where you'd like the link to reside. In our example, that would be the left menu, which is named leftFrame.

2. Provide the source file of the page you're going to have load in the main area by clicking the folder icon and finding the appropriate file.

3. In the Property inspector, you'll find the Target drop-down menu. If you properly named all your frame files and are working in the frameset, the name of your frame should appear in the list. Because you want this page to load in the mainFrame frame, select that frame as your target.

The target element has now properly been added to the link. When you click the link, the page you want to load in the main frame will do so (see Figure 19.10).

Figure 19.10
Using targeting, this page loads into the main window when any "Teaching Strategies" menu item in a frame is clicked.

Using Magic Target Names

As you look at the Target drop-down menu, you'll find several predefined target names that cause certain actions to occur when a target link is created:

- `target="_blank"`—The "_blank" argument causes the targeted document to open in a completely new browser window.

- `target="_self"`—The targeted document will load in the same window where the originating link exists.

- `target="_parent"`—This loads the targeted document into the link's parent frameset.

- `target="_top"`—Use this attribute to load the link into the full window, overriding any existing frames.

The following are issues to bear in mind when using magic target names:

- You should avoid naming standard targets with anything other than an accepted alphanumeric character. An underscore, or any other symbol, will be ignored.

- The magic target name "_blank" always forces a new browser window to open. Be careful to use this only when a new window is absolutely necessary; otherwise, you run the risk of angering Web site visitors, who, depending on their settings, might end up with numerous, resource-draining browser windows on the desktop.

- The `target="_top"` attribute and value is usually the right choice when a link takes the visitor out of your framed site into a new site. Some Web authors like the idea of keeping external sites inside their own sites by targeting the remote site into a local frame, allowing the native site's menu or advertisement to remain live while surfing elsewhere. This not only is considered an annoyance, but might get you into legal trouble. Avoid this at all costs unless you have express permission from the site you are incorporating within your own. See the "Troubleshooting" section for more information on this topic.

WORKING WITH BORDERLESS FRAMES

Choosing to use borderless frames is a critical issue because using, or not using, borders, is the point where the designer makes decisions about how to use frame technology as a format tool. Removing borders makes formatting a page seamless, and this is a powerful, as well as a currently popular, method of designing pages.

Designing Borderless Frames Across Browsers

The first rule in cross-browser design is to know which browsers you are attempting to reach. With borderless frames, that rule is clarified by the fact that only certain browsers and certain browser versions interpret borderless frame attributes in the correct manner. Although contemporary browsers have typically good compliance for `frame` and `frameset` attributes, if you have to cater to older browsers, you'll want to pay careful attention to the information found in this section.

Caution

Borderless frames are not supported in the Netscape and Microsoft browsers earlier than the 3.0 version.

The way borderless attributes evolved was mostly proprietary—in a given browser, and then later some of those attributes were brought into the HTML specifications. So, using some of these attributes will cause your documents not to validate. If you are having problems with your Dreamweaver MX-generated borderless frames, you might have to get into the markup via Code view to make some changes by hand and just have a nonconforming document.

The challenge of borderless frames doesn't lie in the markup per se, but in the differences in the ways popular browsers interpret the markup or require the markup to read.

Fortunately, a workaround is available: You can stack attributes in tags, and if a browser doesn't support that attribute or its value, it will ignore it and move on to the attribute and related value that it does interpret.

Managing Suitable Workarounds

In HTML 4.0 and XHTML 1.0, marking up a borderless frameset is easy. You simply add the attribute and value `frameborder="0"` in the `frame` element.

However, browsers without consistent support, which includes most popular browsers before their 4.0 and later versions, require a little jostling to get the borderless effect.

19

The Netscape browser (3.0+) allows for borderless frames when

- The `border` attribute is set, in pixels, to a numeric value of `"0"`.

- The `framespacing` attribute is assigned a `"no"` value.

Microsoft's Internet Explorer, browser version 3.0, produces borderless frames if

- The `frameborder` attribute is set, in pixels, to a numeric value of `"0"`.

- The `framespacing` attribute is assigned a width, in pixels, to a numeric value of `"0"`.

> **Frame design is most elegant** when borders are turned off and the use of graphics and layout in the framed pages is maximized. More important, however, frame design should never be frivolous. You should always use frames for a good reason, such as when you want static navigation, banner, or branding areas or are using borderless frames for fixed layout.

If it seems like there's a conflict, well, there really isn't because each browser either requires a different attribute to control width or a different value to control spacing. It looks confusing, but if you stack attributes, you can easily create borderless frames that will be read by both browsers without difficulty.

This technique results in two workable syntax options:

```
<frameset frameborder="0" framespacing="0" border="0">
```

or

```
<frameset frameborder="no" framespacing="0" border="0">
```

Either one will work, and it's just a matter of personal preference as to which you'll use. Remember to add your columns and rows to the string to create a full range of frameset arguments.

WORKING WITH INLINE FRAMES

Originally introduced by Internet Explorer 3.0, I-Frames—*inline*, or *floating*, frames—were officially adopted in HTML 4.0. This is good news because they're very effective when put to appropriate use. The bad news, however, is that they aren't supported by Netscape 4.0 and many other 4.0-level browsers. However, with IE support and support in current Netscape, Mozilla, and Opera browsers, inline frames have become very usable.

Understanding I-Frames

I-Frames work quite a bit differently from regular frames. First, you don't create a separate frameset for the frame. You place the I-Frame information directly inline in any HTML or XHTML page. Think of an inline frame as a window in your browser canvas through which you can look at another HTML or XHTML document. Inline frames are frequently used when delivering ads to a site because the ads can be dynamically updated on a distant server and picked up by any Web sites linking from their inline frame to that advertising service (see Figure 19.11).

Figure 19.11
The ads on webreview.com are generated by an advertising company and then linked to via inline frames in the document pages.

Correct Markup for I-Frames

Although Dreamweaver MX does supply an Inline Frames icon on the Frames Insert bar, it doesn't provide a lot of support to work with them. So, if you'd like to add inline frames to a page, you'll need to work in Code view and mark them up by hand.

Consider the following markup:

```
<iframe width="350" height="200" src="text.html">
</iframe>
```

In this scenario, an inline frame with a width of 350 and a height of 200 will be created. The page that will be served to this "window" of the independent frame will be `text.html` (see Figure 19.12).

You can add scrolling and border attributes as well:

```
<iframe width="350" height="200" src="text.html" scrolling="no" frameborder="0">
</iframe>
```

Figure 19.13 shows the inline frame with a border set to 0.

Inline frames support the name attribute, as well as magic target names.

Caution

As with regular frames, the only standard values for the `frameborder` attribute are 0 or 1.

19

Figure 19.12
In this inline frame, the 1-pixel border isn't defined, but it is the browser's default. In most browsers that support inline frames, the default value of the inline frame border is 1.

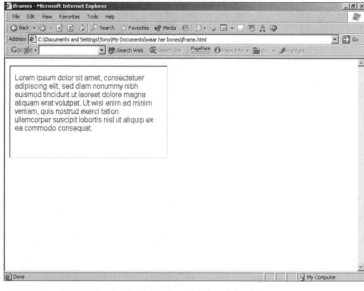

Figure 19.13
This inline frame has no scrolling and a frameborder value of 0. As a result, the inline frame appears seamless.

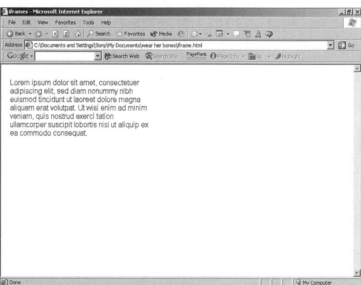

Because there is no content in the `iframe` element, when you mark up an inline frame in XHTML you can use the closing tag, as shown previously, or simply use the trailing slash:

```
<iframe width="350" height="200" src="text.html" scrolling="auto"
frameborder="0" />
```

In this instance, you'll not need the closing tag.

TROUBLESHOOTING

Using Frames to Contain Other Sites

What if I want to keep part of my site available at all times? Can I just link the external site into one of my own frames?

Can you? Technically speaking, yes. Legally speaking? Questionable. People have argued over this very issue, and the general sense is that if doing this isn't exactly illegal, it is a complete lack of etiquette. What's more, it doesn't make experienced Web visitors very happy—when I get to a site I want to experience *that* site, not a hybrid. Newcomers to the Web might be completely confused by this action as well. There have even been court cases in which framed content has been considered copyright infringement when incorporated into someone else's site. So, it is recommended that you never do this, at least without explicit permission.

Printing Frames

How can I make my framed pages easily printable?

Provide a link to a printable format, a downloadable text file, an HTML or XHTML document, or even a Portable Document Format (PDF) file so that individuals who want to print out portions of your site can do so with ease.

PEER TO PEER: BUILDING ACCESSIBLE FRAMES

19

One of the most important considerations when designing Web documents is to ensure that individuals who cannot use frames, such as the blind or mobility impaired, can still have access to important information on a Web site.

Keeping to the current trends *and* incorporating no-frame and text access addresses cross-browser issues by enabling not only those who *require* text access, but those who prefer it as well.

One of the ways to achieve this in a framed site is by employing the `noframes` element. This is placed into the frameset document automatically by Dreamweaver MX, but if you don't use it, it just sits there, ignored by the browser.

Critical information can be provided in the `noframes` element at the same URL as the frameset page, and an entirely accessible site can be formed by using the same pages as the framed site.

It's important to point out that tables also are problematic in terms of accessibility, but slightly less so. Tables can be read fairly well by line-based browsers assuming they are marked up properly. Graphical browsers used with screen readers often do not perceive table columns as separate entities and therefore will read right across columns. However, frames, without the `noframes` element in use, are inaccessible in either case.

Creating an accessible portion of a frameset is easy. Here's how:

1. Create a new frameset or open an existing one.

2. Add any HTML or XHTML syntax and content in the `noframes` element. An example could be as follows:

```
<p>Welcome! If you don't have a browser that supports frames, you can follow
<a href="index_noframes.html" title="go to frameless version of site">this
link</a> to enjoy our content. If you are interested in a browser that
supports frames, please upgrade your Web browser to a current version.</p>
```

3. Save the file. You've now made the page accessible to non-frame browsers.

Because you can format an entire document in the `noframes` element, consider using the index page as the Welcome page to your site. From there, link to internal pages that are external to the frame design.

20

ADVANCED LAYOUT WITH CSS LAYERS

LAYOUT WITH STYLE

Layers is the term used by Dreamweaver MX to refer to box containers on a Web page. Using Dreamweaver layers—a feature made possible through the use of Cascading Style Sheets (CSS)—designers can gain as much control over their sites as traditional print layout offers. Dreamweaver layers can be visible or hidden. When used with behaviors, they form the basis of pop-out menus on cutting edge sites. Layers can even be animated using timelines.

Layers, Draw Layers, and the Layer Element

Unfortunately, the use of the terms *layers* and *Draw Layers* can become confusing. So, for the purposes of this book, when referring to CSS-based layouts using divisions (as described in this chapter) without any kind of animation, the term *layers* will be used.

When discussing the use of behaviors with layers, the term *Draw Layer* will be used. This is in part because, after scripting is added to a CSS division, you are no longer working with just with scripting or CSS but are developing in the technology referred to as *Dynamic HTML (DHTML)*.

Another problem with Macromedia's naming convention is that there is a proprietary tag known as layer, whose relationship to the Draw Layer and the layer in Dreamweaver is clarified in the "Peer to Peer" section in Chapter 24, "Draw Layers and Animation."

⇨ *For a detailed discussion of the true meaning of layers in markup, see Chapter 24, "Draw Layers and Animation," p. 445. Layer animation and timelines are also detailed in Chapter 24.*

Although Dreamweaver treats layers as objects unto themselves, layers are actually CSS constructs. A <div> or <span> tag is given an ID (to identify the layer from amongst multiple layers) and styled with positioning declarations. A typical layer would look like this:

If you've worked with DHTML before, then you have probably heard of or used the layer element. This is a special element that Netscape added to its version 4 browsers that was in many ways similar to Macromedia Dreamweaver Draw Layers layers, but they are *not* the same thing.

```
<div id="Layer1" style="position: absolute; left: 400px;
➡top: 100px;
width: 100px; height: 75px; z-index: 3"></div>
```

The contents of the layer would appear within the <div> tag pair.

⇨ *For more information on positioning styles in CSS, see Chapter 16, "Using Cascading Style Sheets in Dreamweaver," p. 285.*

LAYER PREFERENCES

Before you create layers for layout purposes, you should indicate your preferences for the default settings new layers should use. This is done in the Layers category of the Preferences dialog box (see Figure 20.1).

The preferences are as follows:

- **Tag**—This sets the default HTML tag to use when creating layers. By default, Dreamweaver uses the `<div>` tag, and this is usually preferable.

- **Visibility**—Specifies the default visibility of a layer. Inherit should be used with nested layers to assume the visibility of the parent. Visible and Hidden are exactly what they describe. Default specifies that the browser default should be used, which gives control to the user but takes some control away from the developer.

- **Width and Height**—Sets the default width and height for inserted layers (those created by dragging from the Insert Bar or selecting Insert, Layer).

- **Background Color**—Sets the color to use for the background of layers. Use the color picker, or enter the hexadecimal value of the color.

- **Background Image**—Sets a default background image. Enter the image file to use in the text box, or click the Browse button to locate the file.

- **Nesting**—When you draw a layer within the boundaries of another layer, it becomes nested in that layer when this option is checked. Whatever you choose for this setting can be suppressed by holding (Option) [Alt] when drawing a layer.

- **Netscape 4 Compatibility**—Netscape 4 browsers have a known bug that causes layers to be positioned incorrectly when a user resizes his browser. This option inserts a JavaScript function into the document head that forces the page to reload whenever the browser window is resized. This option can also be toggled on and off using the commands Add/Remove Netscape Resize Fix.

Many of these preferences are also discussed in later chapters when you use Draw Layers to create DHTML animations. However, for the purposes of this chapter, the context is specifically related to CSS layout techniques, *not* animation.

You should generally reserve the `<span>` tag for inline selections, such as when applying a CSS style to a selection within a paragraph. This makes the `<span>` tag less appropriate for layers, even though it will work.

20

Figure 20.1
The Layers preferences control the default settings for layers.

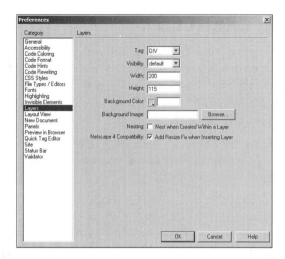

THE LAYER "BOX"

Dreamweaver provides several ways of creating layers that you'd like to use for layout on a page. You can insert a layer using the menu, drag it from the Insert Bar, or simply draw it on the page.

To create a layer, do one of the following:

- Insert a layer by selecting Insert, Layer from the menu. A layer is created at the insertion point with the default size settings.

> When Invisible Elements are active, the elements on your page can appear in a shifted position in Design view. Turn off this option to get a better idea of how your page will look in a browser.

- Drag the Draw Layer option from the Insert Bar into the Document window. The layer is created in the closest position possible to where you release the button.

- To draw a layer, click the Draw Layer button in the Insert Bar. Then click in your document where you want the layer to be positioned and drag from the upper-left corner to the lower-right corner of your intended layer (see Figure 20.2).

- To draw multiple layers, click the Draw Layer button in the Insert Bar. Then hold down the (Command) [Ctrl] key while you draw. This enables you to continue drawing layers without having to repeatedly click the Draw Layer button.

If you have Invisible Elements turned on (select View, Visual Aids, Invisible Elements), a layer marker is shown in the Document window for each layer. Even if you move the layer box, the layer marker remains where it was originally positioned.

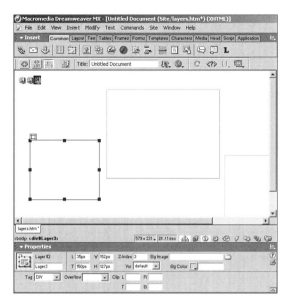

Figure 20.2
Draw a layer by clicking the Draw Layer icon in the Insert Bar; then click and drag in the Document window to define the size and position of the layer.

Adding Content to the Layer

You can insert HTML elements into a layer just as you can with your base document. Before placing elements in a layer, you must first activate the layer by clicking anywhere within the layer border (don't click the layer border itself, though, because that selects the layer for resizing or moving).

When you activate a layer, the insertion point is shown inside the layer box and any objects you insert or text you type is placed inside the layer (see Figure 20.3).

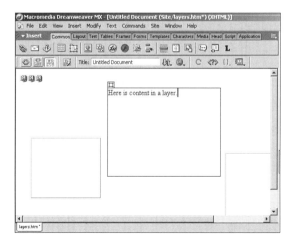

Figure 20.3
Activating a layer places the insertion point inside it. Any text or objects inserted here are placed within the layer and are then moved or hidden as you manipulate the layer itself.

20

Selecting, Moving, and Resizing a Layer in the Design View

When you insert layers, they are seldom exactly where you want them in your document. Fortunately, manipulating layers is easy. You can move, resize, or align layers in Design view. If you're well-versed in CSS, you can also use Code view to enter exact values for the layer properties. Use the following steps when working with layers:

1. Select a layer that you want to remove or resize in Design view by clicking its border. You can also select a layer in the Layers panel by clicking its ID. A resize border is created around the layer, and a drag box appears in the upper-left corner (see Figure 20.4).

Figure 20.4
You can resize a layer by clicking its border and dragging one of the resize points around the edge. Move the layer by dragging on the drag box in the upper-left corner.

Drag box

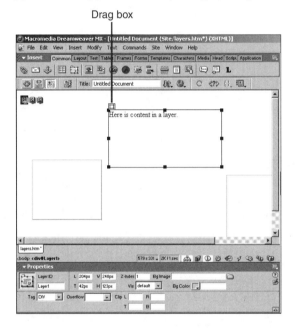

2. To move a layer, position the cursor over the drag box in the upper-left corner or anywhere over the border except where the resize points are located. A quad arrow cursor is shown, enabling you to drag the layer to a new position.

3. To resize a layer, position the cursor over one of the eight resize points on the sides and corners. A double-arrow cursor indicates the direction in which you can resize. Click and drag to resize the layer.

You can align multiple layers by selecting them (press (Shift) [Ctrl] as you select the layers) and selecting one of the alignment options in the Modify, Align menu. All alignment actions are relative to the last layer selected. The last layer selected is represented by solid resize points on the border; the other layers are represented by hollow resize points.

20

USING THE LAYERS PANEL

The Layers panel, located in the Advanced Layout panel group, provides a convenient way to view and modify the layout properties for the layers in a page (see Figure 20.5).

Figure 20.5
The Layers panel lists all the layers in the document, along with the visibility setting and z-index (stacking order).

Layers are shown in the list in the reverse order from which they were inserted, from the most recently inserted layers at the top to the previously inserted layers at the bottom. Nested layers (layers contained within other layers) are shown as a tree view descending from the parent layer. From the Layers panel, you can select layers, set their visibility, rename them, change their stacking order, nest them, and set the layer overlap setting.

Layer Visibility

The initial visibility of a layer can be changed from the default value using the Layers panel. The leftmost column of the panel (showing an eye at the top) indicates the current visibility state for each layer. If the eye is open, the layer is visible. If the eye is closed, the layer is hidden. If the eye icon does not appear, it indicates the layer is set for the default value for the browser. You can toggle the initial visibility for the layer by clicking its position in this column.

You can also set the visibility for all layers at once. Click the eye icon in the column header to toggle through the visibility states.

Renaming Layers

Although Dreamweaver inserts unique IDs for layers it creates, you'll frequently want to rename the layers to make them easier to remember and indicate their purpose. This way, you can easily tell which layer is being targeted by a JavaScript operation or behavior.

To rename a layer from the Layers panel, double-click its name. The name then becomes editable, and you can simply type in a new name (see Figure 20.6).

20

Figure 20.6
Give your layers IDs that are easy to remember, particularly when using multiple layers for pop-out menus and such.

Changing the Stacking Order

The stacking order for layers, otherwise known as the *z-order*, specifies which layer is seen on top when two layers overlap. Let's say you want to create content boxes that have a slight overlap. Layers with a higher z-index are shown on top of layers with a lower number. You can change the stacking order for layers in two ways:

- Select the layer you want to change and drag it up or down the layer list to the desired position (see Figure 20.7). A line is shown indicating the new layer position. Release the mouse button when the layer is in the correct position. The values in the z-index column are then renumbered to accommodate the new order.

Figure 20.7
The z-index for a layer can be changed by dragging the layer upward or downward in the Layers panel.

- In the Z column, click the number for the layer you're changing. An edit box appears, and you can type a new number. Enter a higher number to move the layer up in the stacking order, or click a lower number to move it lower. The numbers you enter needn't be in sequence, which is convenient when moving your layers out of order. Press (Return) [Enter], and the layer is then moved to the new position in the list.

Nesting Layers

Nested layers are layers contained within other layers. You can nest layers when creating them or by using the Layers panel. To nest a layer using the Layers panel, hold down the (Command) [Ctrl] key and drag a layer onto another layer.

Layer Overlap

When individuals size their browsers, content layers often overlap. To prevent this from happening, you should indicate whether you want to allow layers to overlap in two different ways:

- In the Layers panel, check the Prevent Overlaps box.

- Check the Modify, Arrange, Prevent Layer Overlaps menu item.

When the Prevent Layer Overlaps option is on, you cannot create a layer in front of another layer. If you try to move or resize a layer, you won't be able to make it overlap other layers.

Dreamweaver won't fix existing overlapping layers when you activate this option.

The Prevent Layer Overlaps option takes precedence over the Snap to Grid option. If both are enabled and you move a layer, it won't snap to the grid if doing so would cause it to overlap another layer.

SETTING THE LAYER'S ATTRIBUTES

The Property inspector can be used to set attributes for layers after they're created. To view the Property inspector for a particular layer, select it in the Layers panel or click the layer border in the Document window (see Figure 20.8). Click the Property inspector expander button if you don't see all the options. The attributes available within the Layer Property inspector are listed in Table 20.1.

Figure 20.8
The Layer Property inspector lets you set layer options.

Table 20.1   Layer Property Inspector Options

Option	Purpose
Layer ID	Specifies the name of the layer to use for scripting and as identification in CSS. Every layer must have a unique name, and the name cannot contain any special characters (spaces, hyphens, or periods).
L and T	Specify the left and top coordinates for the layer. You can change these by entering new values here. These control the placement of the layer on the page, not the dimensions of the layer box.
W and H	Specify the dimensions of the layer box. These are the minimum sizes to use for the layer. If the layer's content exceeds the dimensions of the layer, the layer can be automatically increased depending on the Overflow setting.
Z-Index	Specifies a value to use for stacking layers. Layers with higher values for this option are always shown on top of layers with lower values.
Vis	Specifies the initial visibility of the layer. This can be changed using behaviors, such as when creating a pop-out menu.
BG Image	Specifies an image to use for the layer background. You can enter a filename directly into the text box or use the Browse button to locate it.
BG Color	Uses the color picker to select a background color for the layer.
Tag	Specifies the HTML tag to use for the layer, either <div> or <span>.

Table 20.1 Continued

Option	Purpose
Overflow	Specifies what happens if the content of a layer exceeds its dimensions. If Visible, the layer is resized to show all the content. If Hidden, any content exceeding the layer size is clipped. If Scroll, scrollbars are visible at all times in the layer, enabling the user to scroll through the layer's content. If Auto, scrollbars appear only when the content exceeds the layer dimensions.
Clip	Defines the visible area of a layer. This can be used to cut content from the edge of a layer to focus on a specific area. The values represent the distance in pixels from the layer's boundaries, relative to the layer.

If you select more than one layer at once (press (Shift) [Ctrl] as you select the layers in the Layers panel or the Document window), the Property inspector changes to the Multiple Layers Inspector (see Figure 20.9). This Inspector offers only a subset of the layer attributes—L and T, W and H, Vis, Tag, BG Image, and BG Color.

> Remember the rules of inheritance, discussed in Chapter 15, "Designing with Style." If the layer has a background color, that color is also applied to any content within the layer unless contradicted by another CSS rule.

➾ *Finding font tags in your CSS-based layouts? See "Toggling CSS/HTML Modes" in the "Troubleshooting" section at the end of this chapter.*

Figure 20.9
You can set attributes for multiple layers simultaneously by using the Multiple Layers Inspector.

CONVERTING LAYERS

Layers are supported in current browsers, but those few Web surfers still using 3.0 version browsers are out of luck. If your target audience is among those using these outdated browsers, you're also out of luck. Dreamweaver provides a method for converting a document that contains layers or CSS, which is also not supported by most version 3 browsers, to one that uses a table and HTML font attributes instead. Use the File, Convert, 3.0 Browser Compatible command to open the Convert to 3.0 Browser Compatible dialog box (see Figure 20.10). This box gives you the option of converting CSS styles to the equivalent HTML attributes and also lets you convert layers to a table to maintain the position of the layer's contents. When you click OK, Dreamweaver creates a separate document, preserving the original formatting, and opens the converted file in the Document window. So, you'll end up with two separate documents—one that uses CSS for layout and another that reverts to conventional HTML layout.

➾ *Having difficulty converting layers properly? See "Conversion Concerns" in the "Troubleshooting" section at the end of this chapter.*

Figure 20.10
The Convert to 3.0 Browser Compatibility feature is useful to convert cutting-edge layer- and CSS-based designs into tables and HTML-based pages that can be viewed in older browsers.

Converting Layers to Tables

Using the 3.0 Browser Compatible option creates two documents that then need to be maintained separately.

Another method for converting layers to tables is to use the Layers to Tables option:

1. While in Design view, select Modify, Convert, Layers to Table to open the Convert Layers to Tables dialog box (see Figure 20.11).

Figure 20.11
The Convert Layers to Tables options are another method for making pages accessible from older browsers.

2. Select the following layout properties:

- **Most Accurate**—Creates a table cell (`<td>`) for every layer, plus placeholder cells necessary to fill the space between layers.

- **Smallest: Collapse Empty Cells**—Causes layer edges to be realigned if they're currently positioned within the specified number of pixels. This option is designed to create a simpler table at the expense of accurate positioning.

- **Use Transparent GIFs**—Causes the table's last row to be filled with transparent spacer GIFs to ensure the table will be displayed with the same column widths in all browsers.

- **Center on Page**—Causes the table to be centered on the page. Otherwise, it's aligned left.

- **Prevent Layer Overlaps**—Turns on the Prevent Layer Overlap feature. Any new layers you then create won't be able to overlap existing layers. Whether or not you check this box, if your layers overlap, you won't be able to convert them to table cells.

Whenever you convert layers to tables, or vice versa, something is always lost in the translation. The more times you convert a file, the further you'll get from the original specifications of your design. Always make a copy of the original document before converting in case you're not happy with the results.

20

- **Show Layers Panel**—Displays the Layers panel.

- **Show Grid**—Shows the grid to be displayed in the Document window.

- **Snap to Grid**—Activates the Snap to Grid option.

3. Click OK. Any layout changes you select will take effect.

You can also convert tables back to layers using the Modify, Convert, Tables to Layers option. This completes the same process, in reverse.

DESIGNING WITH LAYERS

Among the many advantages of layers is that you can use them to create dynamic content. By adding JavaScripts and behaviors to layers, they become incredibly powerful and enable interaction with your users.

⇨ *For an explanation of JavaScript and behaviors, see Chapter 22, "Working with JavaScript and Behaviors," p. 415.*

Behaviors that can target layers include Change Property, Set Text of Layer, Show-Hide Layers, and Timelines. Layers can also be used in conjunction with other elements and behaviors to create advanced navigation systems.

Change Property

The Change Property action can be used to change the value of a layer's attributes (see Figure 20.12). You can use it to set the size, position, z-index, and other properties in recent browser versions.

Figure 20.12
The Change Property behavior is used to change the value of a layer's attributes.

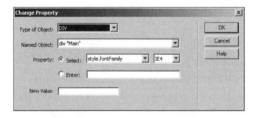

Other properties can be set as well:

- **Type of Object**—Select the kind of object you want to target. For layers, select one of the layer tags. This limits the name choices in the Named Object drop-down list.

- **Named Object**—This is a list of the objects in your document that match the type of object you choose.

- **Property**—You can select a target browser from the drop-down list on the right side, which provides a list of supported properties on the left. As an alternative, you can check Enter and enter the name of any property directly. This enables you to set properties you know about but that aren't listed as choices.

- **New Value**—Enter the value you want the property to have after the event is fired—for instance, a new color if you're changing a color property.

Set Text of Layer

The Set Text of Layer action enables you to completely replace the content of a layer with new text you supply. This text can be any valid HTML markup, letting you dynamically update an entire layer at once. The Set Text of Layer dialog box provides an input box where you can type or paste the JavaScript code you want to use (see Figure 20.13).

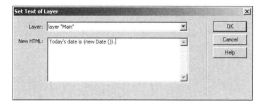

Figure 20.13
The Set Text of Layer dialog box lets you input JavaScript code to dynamically change the content of a layer.

You can embed JavaScript statements or function calls to generate the text for the layer by enclosing it in braces, like this:

```
Today's date is {new Date()}.
```

The result is shown in Figure 20.14.

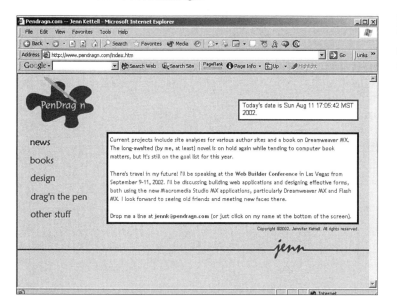

Figure 20.14
The Set Text of Layer behavior can be used to provide the current date in a layer.

20

Show-Hide Layers

One of the most useful features of layers is the capability to be shown or hidden on demand. A page might have layers to make up pop-up menus, which become visible when the mouse is moved over the navbar buttons. The Show-Hide Layers behavior makes tying this process to a variety of events easy.

The Show-Hide Layers action lets you show, hide, or return to a default state of any and all layers you choose with a single action. The following steps show you how to use the Show-Hide Layers action:

1. Select an object to trigger the action. This object can be anything except another layer.

2. Open the Actions menu of the Behaviors panel and select Show-Hide Layer. The Show-Hide Layer dialog box provides a list of all layers in your document (see Figure 20.15).

Figure 20.15
The Show-Hide Layer dialog box lists all the layers in the document that you can trigger with an action.

3. Select each layer you want to affect with this action individually, and then click a new state for it: Show, Hide, or Default.

4. When you finish, click OK.

TROUBLESHOOTING

Toggling CSS/HTML Modes

I am using layers to create my content. I don't want any HTML presentation, yet Dreamweaver is adding <font> tags. What's going on?

Unless you're in the CSS mode of the Property inspector (use the Toggle CSS/HTML Mode icon in the inspector), any changes you make to text properties using the upper section of the Multiple Layers Inspector will insert <font> tags, just as when using the text Property inspector.

Conversion Concerns

I'm attempting to use the conversion feature, but my design isn't being preserved. Any suggestions?

If your layers overlap, are on a timeline, or are hidden, as in pop-out menus, this conversion process can't preserve your design. You'll still need to make considerable modifications to the converted file to make it acceptable for view.

PEER TO PEER: CSS LAYOUT RESOURCES

CSS layout is perhaps the most difficult aspect of CSS to achieve consistently with browsers. A lot of "hacks" and "workarounds" are used to deal with these difficulties. There are also some terrific repositories for CSS-based layouts with some of these workarounds built in that you can use as a template of your own and modify from there.

Several great resources for layout and CSS exist. Some favorites include

- Eric Meyer's Tricking Browsers and Hiding Styles can be found at `http://www.ericmeyeroncss.com/bonus/trick-hide.html`.

- Eric Costello's resources at Glish.Com include layouts, explanations, and insights (`http://www.glish.com/`).

- Owen Briggs's Problem and Workaround set for a variety of CSS layout concerns can be found at `http://www.thenoodleincident.com/tutorials/box_lesson/index.html`.

- BlueRobot.Com is an excellent resource with a great layout reservoir (`http://www.bluerobot.com/`). A BlueRobot CSS Layout forms the basis for Molly's XHTML 1.1 and CSS site (`http://www.molly.com/`).

20

21

DESIGNING WITH ALTERNATIVE DEVICES

DREAMWEAVER MX: BEYOND WEB DESIGN

One of the primary motivations for adding standards and related technologies to tools such as Dreamweaver MX is to embrace the range of alternative devices to which Web content is being delivered.

Want to create a site that works well on a PDA? A cell phone? WebTV? No matter the markup language you choose to use—traditional HTML, XHTML, or Wireless Markup Language (WML)—Macromedia Dreamweaver MX enables you to use the design techniques and languages you require, right now. Even if you haven't ventured into the world of alternative device design, it's helpful to get a look now, so you'll be more prepared for the way you might want to work in the future.

TYPES OF ALTERNATIVE DEVICES

It's amazing to think that in just less than a decade, we've come to a world where not only has the Internet—and the Web—become pervasive at work, in our schools, and in our homes, but related technologies are advancing beyond the standard computer's scope.

Numerous devices are available that enable us to access and send email and browse the Web without the need to have a heavy desktop or even lightweight notebook computer around! In fact, many of these devices sit in the palms of our hands. Or, they are attached or built into other devices in our world—our televisions and even some automobiles. Eventually, it's thought that we'll be able to access online services using home appliances. Need a recipe? Simply look it up from a built-in browser on your refrigerator.

It might sound a little odd, and perhaps these technological advances don't suit everyone's tastes. But it's really happening, and developers who are aware of new and even experimental applications and methods will be better enabled to make choices about their career goals. Instead of working to create a traditional Web site, you might find yourself writing WML or other, proprietary languages for special devices. The opportunities are only as endless as the new ideas coming to light.

Operating Systems for Alternative Devices

Alternative devices require operating systems to, well, operate. As most readers are aware, an operating system (referred to as an OS for short) is the meta-management software found on your computer or related device. Its job is to manage memory, allocate system input and output, communicate with and between applications on your computer, and so forth.

Operating systems for alternative devices are essentially no different from the OSs with which we are already familiar: Windows, MacOS, Unix, Linux, and the like. However, their job is modified due to the hardware and software that exist in the alternative environment. In most cases, the alternative devices discussed in this chapter are pretty small—some

It's interesting to point out that where Java was once considered to be a contender for the delivery of Web-based content, the language has in fact found one unforeseen use: the development of mobile operating systems and applications. Many small devices use Java as the underlying language driving their systems. Another popular language for this is C++.

21

smaller than your hand. This means that processing speed and memory are relatively limited, at least as compared to desktops and notebook computers.

The primary OSs in use by mobile devices are

- **Windows CE**—Developed by Microsoft, Windows CE is a pared-down version of Windows. It draws from the same iconography and interface design as Windows, making the products that support it very user-friendly to individuals familiar with Windows.

- **EPOC**—Designed for wireless phones and related devices, EPOC has its origins in an operating system that Psion (see the following section, "PDAs") introduced. Originally an open source OS, EPOC has been further developed by Symbian and is now a license-based OS.

- **PalmOS**—Totally proprietary to the Palm computing platform, PalmOS was developed by 3Com and is used in Palm and some related products.

- **Linux**—This popular open-source computer OS is starting to be used in mobile devices, to the delight of Linux and open-source fans.

> For developer information about Windows CE, see http://www.microsoft.com/windows/embedded/. Information on EPOC can be found at http://www.symbian.com/developer/index.html, and PalmOS resources and developer sites are available from http://www.palmsource.com/. A great overview by Derrick Story, managing editor of O'Reilly Networks on the state of Linux on Palm devices is available at http://www.oreillynet.com/pub/a/network/2000/09/01/magazine/linux_pda.html.

PDAs

Do you have a PDA? PDAs are *personal digital assistants*. These devices are small, mobile computers that help you manage your schedules and keep your personal and business contacts organized. Some PDAs have built-in or add-on modems, enabling you to send and receive email and surf the Web wirelessly.

New developments in PDA technology are occurring at a rapid-fire pace. Color support and even sound and video are showing up in numerous new PDAs.

Developers interested in extending their Web site information to PDA environments need to be aware of the limitations of PDAs. They include

> Check out some PDA products: For information on the PocketPC, see www.pocketpc.com/. Palm PDAs are showcased at www.palm.com, Visor's at www.handspring.com, and Psion's at www.psion.com/. Information for developers wanting to develop for a given platform is available at each of these sites.

- **Very small screen size**—Most PDAs are the size of your hand. Screens tend to be limited in their capability to display complex visual or lengthy text-based data.

- **Limited color support**—Many PDAs don't offer color at all, and those that do, offer limited color. So, special care regarding how color is used for PDA device development must be taken.

■ **Limitations on technology**—Although some PDAs support multimedia such as audio, video, Flash animation, JavaScript, and Java applets, many do not. When developing for specific PDAs, I advise researching which technologies are supported by a given PDA, and when developing for broad-spectrum audiences, avoid the use of the technologies listed previously.

Mobile Computers

Mobile computers are typically the same size or bigger than a PDA, but smaller than an ultra-light notebook. These computers pack more power than a PDA but typically have fewer resources available than a desktop or notebook computer. Handheld computers run on scaled-down OSs such as Windows CE.

For developers, the often low processing power and limited screen resolution of mobile computers mean pared-down pages that use very straightforward markup or table-based layouts specifically designed to fit the available screen resolution. Avoidance of multimedia and processor-intensive technologies is advised.

You can check out some interesting mobile computers online. Casio's personal PCs are available at http://www.casio.com/personalpcs/. Clio can be found at http://www.pinaxgroup.com/store/, and IBM Blackberry can be found at http://www.pc.ibm.com/us/accessories/services/blackberry/.

Smart Pagers and Phones

A *smart* pager or phone has features beyond the basics of paging or voice communications. Many smart pagers and phones offer PDA-style software, including contact lists, calendars, email, and Web browsers. They use a variety of OSs, including proprietary technology.

Of course, the restrictions of screen space and color support on these very small displays also limit the developer. Information has to be tightly organized for display, and screen space is especially variegated in these devices.

Set-Top Boxes

The convergence of television and the Web has been discussed for some years. *Set-top boxes* are appliances that enable televisions to connect to the Internet. One current technology is WebTV, the most familiar application of the merging of television and the Web. WebTV has been bought by Microsoft, who is expanding on it and integrating it into a range of TV/Internet-related projects. PersonalJava from Sun Microsystems is a technology being used to enable Web connectivity devices, including set-top boxes.

Set-top boxes also are being used to enable analog TVs to decode digital broadcasts. For more information on WebTV, see http://resourcecenter.msn.com/access/MSNTV/default.asp. PersonalJava information can be found at http://wwws.sun.com/software/communitysource/personaljava/.

eBooks

These devices enable users to download digital books and other related material from the Web. Although the idea of getting cozy with a digital device and a hot cup of tea seems remote for most people who were raised with paper books, the eBook is a concept that bears consideration.

> See http://www.
> gemstar-ebook.com/
> ebcontent/devices/default.
> asp for more information on
> eBook devices.

This is especially true when we think about technical documentation, search features, and wireless Internet connectivity. Conceivably, an individual working in the field and requiring a remote update to a troubleshooting document could use an eBook to retrieve the necessary information immediately and then read it on a screen display that's more comfortable than a mobile computer.

Whether the eBook concept will take off is yet to be seen. Introduced in 1998, eBooks are of mild interest but do not seem to be as popular as other mobile technologies.

ALTERNATIVE DEVICE LANGUAGES

The following sections cover a few of the languages you'll need to be familiar with if you want to design sites that can be handled by tomorrow's handheld devices.

XHTML and XML

As a metalanguage, XML allows the development of applications for a wide range of data types and therefore is attractive to developers working with alternative languages and protocols, including the Wireless Application Protocol (WAP). WML and XHTML are both examples of this. Both are applications created from XML and used for wireless delivery. WML tends to be more specific to wireless, whereas XHTML is a little broader in its scope.

XHTML enables Web pages to be backward-compatible but positions them to integrate with XML and other related technologies. Part of the rationale for XHTML is to position Web content for easy modification and access by alternative devices. This is most clearly seen with XHTML Basic, a subset of XHTML Modularization that pares XHTML down to

> Read more about XHTML Basic at
> http://www.w3.org/TR/
> xhtml-basic/.

only what can be delivered to alternative devices. This includes such things as headers text, lists, links, and basic tables and forms but excludes such things as frames, which are resource intensive and not suitable for this type of design.

Of course, by now you are aware of the support Dreamweaver MX has for XHTML, and an XHTML Basic template is available for your use in the "Peer to Peer" section of this chapter.

XSL/XSLT

Extensible Style Language/Extensible Style Language Transformations embody a write-once, display anywhere concept. Developers using transformations create a style sheet that basically says, "If this device requests the page, deliver it using this style."

The advantage to transformations is that multiple options for display can be offered. Let's say you want a page to display using specific design parameters on a standard computer screen but to also be available to display on a PDA. Ideologically, XSLT enables you to do this.

Because XSL and XSLT can be marked up in text editors, you can use Dreamweaver MX in Code view to create XSL/T documents.

Exploring WML and WAP

The Wireless Markup Language (WML) works in tandem with the Wireless Application Protocol (WAP), helping to deliver content to wireless applications. Although WAP has, at least for its early years, been left in the domain of the wireless industry, WAP is becoming of greater interest to the standard Web developer. This is particularly true for those Web designers interested in developing for wireless devices. Inevitably, those individuals will come across WAP information and want to know what WAP is. This becomes even more important as the demand for get-it-anywhere Web and Internet access increases.

The protocols that manage Internet data, especially TCP/IP and HTTP, were built for land-based connections. They are not particularly well suited to managing wireless transmissions. Two of the major problems with current protocols are that

- They demand high processing power.

- The speed of current methods of sending wireless data via current Internet protocols is very slow, resulting in long transmission delays, referred to as *latency*.

So, a couple of things could have occurred here. A completely new network could have evolved, leaving the Internet to itself. Or, a network using the available intelligence and enormous content base of the Internet and Web could have emerged. As it happens, WAP grew out of the latter.

Instead of a completely new network structure, WAP uses the client/server concept of the Internet. The *client*, in the case of a wireless transmission, is the WAP-enabled phone, pager, or other wireless device. The *server* is usually a preexisting Web server that also is configured to serve WAP content.

However, for this relationship to work, there are two additional components. They are the wireless network, which is a network employing radio or satellite transmission, and a WAP gateway, which interprets Web content from the server and makes it suitable for transmission and interpretation on a WAP client.

WAP has its historical origins in Unwired Planet, an early wireless company that introduced HDML. In an effort to encourage a wireless future, those developers teamed up with Ericsson, Nokia, and Motorola (three top manufacturers of mobile devices).

Out of this meeting of businesses came the WAP Forum, which later coordinated with the Open Mobile Architecture Initiative to create the Open Mobile Alliance (OMA). OMA is an organization dedicated to the development and promotion of wireless devices, protocols, and languages. Visit OMA at `http://www.wapforum.org/`.

WML is an application of XML. In other words, XML is the metalanguage from which WML is derived. As a result, its syntax and structure will be familiar to those readers who've worked with XHTML, which also derives from XML. WML uses a "card" concept, organizing content for wireless pages to be delivered in a stacked rather than distributed fashion.

Interestingly, WML is supported by Dreamweaver MX, and in fact, you'll step through the creation of a short WML card stack later in this chapter.

HDML

The Handheld Device Markup Language (HDML) was submitted for discussion to the W3C in 1997 by Unwired Planet. HDML proposed the concept of cards and decks, as well as providing a DTD and syntactical structure for the management of wireless content.

You can find the HDML submission to the W3C at `http://www.w3.org/TR/NOTE-Submission-HDML-spec.html`.

HDML has been set aside for WML, but the early concepts of HDML have contributed significantly to the development of wireless markup.

Web Clippings

Web Clippings is a proprietary methodology of developing miniature Web applications for use with the Palm VII and later. Web Clippings draws from simple HTML, using a pared-down version of HTML and a restricted technologies menu to achieve delivery of specialized Web content to this wireless PDA.

ALTERNATIVE DEVICE DESIGN

Although currently only specialized developers are working to deliver content to alternative devices, alternative device design is a field that's getting more interesting over time. This is particularly true in Europe and parts of Asia, especially Japan, where the proliferation of cell phones and other devices has become much more widespread than in the U.S. Designers who want to break out beyond the Web and who find designing for wireless of interest are sure to find growing opportunities in years to come.

Demystifying Future Delivery Systems

The overview of these new technologies will help you get comfortable with the devices you need to know about. Some readers will be familiar with one or two of these systems, and a few of you might already be working with them. Take a moment to view or review some of the languages and protocols that you could be working with in the coming years.

21

You're probably asking, "Do I really need to know this stuff?" You might very well need to expand your language and protocol horizons beyond XHTML and HTTP, depending on your personal and professional goals.

However, many designers work in teams and can leave the weighty technology to others. Although those of you in this group might not need to know how to work with these technologies, you'll need to know how to design for them. Moreover, being aware of what the technologies are, what they do, and how they influence the way you design will put you in better control of your work and make you infinitely more attractive to recruiters in years to come.

Understanding Alternative Environments

So, how do designers actually plan and design for alternative applications? Simplest is best in the alternative world. This is because displays on most of these devices are very small and almost wholly text based. Were you getting excited over the growing room available to you on PCs? Using fixed table designs at 800×600 or larger? That's great for the Web as it's delivered to the desktop, but you're going to have to reorient yourself entirely if you also want to design for teeny, tiny alternative devices.

Those of you who designed for the Web back in the days of the line-based browser Lynx appreciate these limitations (see Figure 21.1). You might remember that a page had limited display features, basically allowing for a bit of text, some links, and some minimal text formatting. The text-based Web forced designers to plan intelligent content that displayed logically.

Figure 21.1
Browsing the Web with Lynx. A reminder of days past and alternative device days to come.

Designing for alternative devices means studying the device, looking at its limitations and features, and thinking about how your information will be structured. Set aside beautiful visual designs—at least for now. Think instead of content and structure. Later, as certain handheld interfaces become more advanced, you can return to more complex visual presentations. For now, simplicity reigns supreme.

First of all, let's examine why people are attracted to appliances for accessing Web content. Aside from the "toy" factor that drives many to purchase the latest and greatest technology just because it's cool, many people are looking to their Palms, pagers, and cell phones as methods of gathering personal and professional information. They want that information quickly. They also want it on the run—whether checking a stock quote while catching a plane or checking baseball scores at the opera, the alternative device user needs the requested information to be fast, accurate, and easy to access.

Data must be very streamlined for these devices. You won't be able to have three screens of options and information or multiple areas that users click through to get to the data they want and need.

If you examine your cell phone or pager, you'll immediately notice that not only is the display quite small, but there are few buttons to press. This means people will navigate your content and make choices in limited and awkward ways. Simplifying navigation for these devices is not just a guideline, it's an imperative.

If these limitations haven't injured your design-oriented soul, wait until you hear this: At least for now, wireless networks are very, very slow. Add to that the fact that alternative devices have very limited processing speed and memory, and those of you who had been pouring a cold one to celebrate the growing distribution of broadband access had better grab a quick breath and hold it. If you're planning to deliver alternative device content, everything you create will have to weigh less, be more precise, and somehow still be intelligent.

Alternative Device Design Tips

Speaking of intelligence, I'm sure you want more details about the concepts you'll need to design effective alternative device information. The following sections contain some basic guidelines.

Sensible Architecture

A good place to begin is by understanding the architecture of device design. When beginning a site map, most designers use some type of hierarchical structure to build pages. This structure might have a home page and branch from there into subgroups of pages. Designing for an alternative device doesn't allow you this much leverage. Instead, you have to bring as much information to the top as possible. Instead of the page metaphor, wireless development uses a card deck metaphor. In this methodology, information is stacked rather than distributed over pages. The first card in your stack might have the identity of the site and a few links to the information, such as stock quotes, sports scores, or weather. One click, and the users are at the data they seek.

Clean Markup

As you know by now, XHTML exists largely because of the need for syntactical rigor in HTML. Whether you're working with XML, XHTML, WML, or proprietary methods such as Palm's Web Clippings, you'll be at a significant disadvantage from both design and technological standpoints without good coding practices. Technologically speaking, keeping markup and code clean and accurate makes it readily portable. Good markup helps deliver content that's clean and fast. From a design perspective, the integrity of a document's structure is imperative to the way it appears onscreen. Using logical structure, including properly labeled headings, text formatting, and text emphasis, makes these limited playing cards of information more sensible both logically and visually.

21

Meaningful Navigation Cues

When developing for the visual Web, designers can choose from a variety of navigation metaphors. You can opt to use concrete visual cues or abstract cues or mix text and abstract visual design to make a composition that's compelling and unique. Every navigation element must be clearly denoted. If you want someone to scroll down, an arrow pointing down with the words "scroll down" might be your best bet to ensure people know how to navigate your information. Every navigation cue, whether symbolic, textual, or some combination thereof, should be very clear in its intent.

Images and Color

Not every alternative device is limited to text content. When you use images, keep in mind that they must be extremely light, weighing in at less than 1.5KB. Also, *never* use images to replace text. Rather, use images to enhance or extend the meaning of text. In addition, if the language with which you're developing enables an image to contain an alternative text `alt` attribute, use it. Because of the limited memory, processing, and access speeds of wireless devices, many people with image support turn it off.

It's interesting to point out that color is starting to appear on more Palm-style devices. Color support can be very limited or more mature, such as on devices using thin film transistor (TFT) active-matrix displays. This is good news for the designer interested in adding some visual interest to his alternative device design. However, if it doesn't degrade gracefully to traditional text displays, it's unwise to rely on color until the market offers more devices that support color numbers and values.

Back to the Future

Does this mean that the days of expanded design opportunities via traditional Web browsers are limited? Not in the least! Take comfort in the fact that some of you will never have to design for alternative devices. Others among you will jump at the opportunity, knowing that a limited design environment can encourage innovation. Still others will want the flexibility and options born of expanded knowledge and technique.

If XSLT and profiling through the proposed CC/PP framework take off—and many say they will—ideally you'll be designing information that will be written once and played anywhere. Although designers will certainly have to prepare their content for a wide array of devices, the desktop will still be a popular choice on the Web browsing menu.

The grand irony is that designers, especially those who once designed for a kinder, simpler Web, have little to fear. Aside from learning some new concepts that should not be as daunting as they might first appear, it looks as though our jobs will be very much like creating pages for the Web in 1993. But this time, we'll be using different languages and protocols to achieve our designs.

CREATING A WML PAGE IN DREAMWEAVER MX

Now that you have a sense of alternative devices, you can tap into the help Dreamweaver MX offers when it comes to designing for them. In this section, you'll create a WML page using Dreamweaver MX.

As with HTML and XHTML, WML expects that you have basic structural components in every WML document. Dreamweaver provides these structural components in a WML template. Then, you'll manually add the additional components in Code view.

To begin creating your WML page, follow these steps:

1. In Dreamweaver, select File, New. The New Document dialog box will open.

2. On the General tab, find the entry titled Other and highlight it. In the Other window, you'll see an option for WML. Highlight the option (see Figure 21.2).

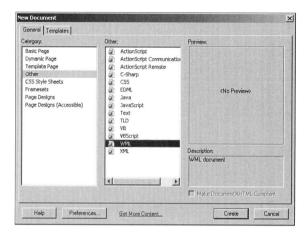

Figure 21.2
Using the New Document dialog box, you can choose the Other category and then select WML.

3. Click the Create button. Dreamweaver MX now creates a WML document that opens directly in Code view.

Listing 21.1 shows the Dreamweaver MX template for WML, consisting of the XML Prolog, the DOCTYPE declaration for WML, and the structural tags required to create the card sections in the document.

Listing 21.1   The Dreamweaver MX WML Template

```
<?xml version="1.0" encoding="iso-8859-1"?>
<!DOCTYPE wml PUBLIC "-//WAPFORUM//DTD WML 1.3//EN"
"http://www.wapforum.org/DTD/wml13.dtd" >
<wml>
<card>

</card>
</wml>
```

At this point, you should begin building the page in Code view. In the following exercise, you'll add paragraphs and content to your WML file. Note the use of id and title in the card element.

21

To add paragraph content to your cards, follow these steps:

1. With the document open in Code view, add the id with a value of `"top"` (it's the top card), and add a `title` with a value of `"welcome"`. Here's the code for it:

```
<?xml version="1.0" encoding="iso-8859-1"?>
<!DOCTYPE wml PUBLIC "-//WAPFORUM//DTD WML 1.3//EN"
"http://www.wapforum.org/DTD/wml13.dtd"
<card id="top" title="Welcome!">

</card>
</wml>
```

2. Add the opening and closing paragraph tags within the first card:

```
<?xml version="1.0" encoding="iso-8859-1"?>
<!DOCTYPE wml PUBLIC "-//WAPFORUM//DTD WML 1.3//EN"
"http://www.wapforum.org/DTD/wml13.dtd" >
<card id="top" title="Welcome!">

<p>

</p>

</card>
</wml>
```

3. Add your content:

```
<?xml version="1.0" encoding="iso-8859-1"?>
<!DOCTYPE wml PUBLIC "-//WAPFORUM//DTD WML 1.3//EN"
"http://www.wapforum.org/DTD/wml13.dtd" >
<wml>
<card id="top" title="Welcomme!">

<p>

Welcome to my WML document!

</p>


</card>
</wml>
```

4. Save the document.

5. View your document in a phone or an emulator. I used the Deck-It WML Previewer (see Figure 21.3).

Figure 21.3
Using the Deck-It WML emulator to view the WML document. Check out the Deck-It emulator at http://www.pyweb.com/tools/.

> ⇨ *Are your pages not fitting properly into the device window? Find out one of the reasons why in "Baby-Face Limitations" in the "Troubleshooting" section at the end of this chapter.*

Adding Paragraphs and Line Breaks

To break lines where you'd like them to break, you should use both the paragraph (necessary to display the text) *and* the line break. A good example of this is an address, in which line breaks are desirable.

To create a line break, follow these steps:

1. Begin a new WML document for this exercise. Identify your card and add a title:

```
<?xml version="1.0" encoding="iso-8859-1"?>
<!DOCTYPE wml PUBLIC "-//WAPFORUM//DTD WML 1.3//EN"
"http://www.wapforum.org/DTD/wml13.dtd" >
<wml>
<card id="contact" title="Get in Touch">

</card>
</wml>
```

2. Add the paragraph tags:

```
<?xml version="1.0" encoding="iso-8859-1"?>
<!DOCTYPE wml PUBLIC "-//WAPFORUM//DTD WML 1.3//EN"
"http://www.wapforum.org/DTD/wml13.dtd" >
<wml>
```

21

```
<card id="contact" title="Get in Touch">

<p>

</p>

</card>
</wml>
```

3. Add your content:

```
<?xml version="1.0" encoding="iso-8859-1"?>
<!DOCTYPE wml PUBLIC "-//WAPFORUM//DTD WML 1.3//EN"
"http://www.wapforum.org/DTD/wml13.dtd" >
<wml>
<card id="contact" title="Get in Touch">

<p>
Please get in touch with us!
We are located at:
2001 Sunrise Drive
Wilmotshire, USA
</p>

</card>
</wml>
```

4. Add the break tags where desired:

```
<?xml version="1.0" encoding="iso-8859-1"?>
<!DOCTYPE wml PUBLIC "-//WAPFORUM//DTD WML 1.3//EN"
"http://www.wapforum.org/DTD/wml13.dtd" >
<wml>
<card id="contact" title="Get in Touch">

<p>
Please get in touch with us! <br/>
We are located at: <br/>
2001 Sunrise Drive<br/>
Wilmotshire, USA
</p>

</card>
</wml>
```

5. Save the file as breaks.wml. You can now upload and test your files with your smart pager, phone, or wireless device, or with an emulator (see Figure 21.4).

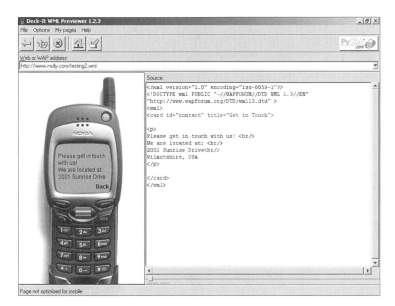

Figure 21.4
Paragraphs and breaks are in use, but you'll see that the content still wraps to fit the small screen. You can add text styles to your content wherever you see fit.

Adding Links

To add a link from one card to another, you can use the combination of the anchor and go tags, as shown in Listing 21.2.

Listing 21.2 Linking Between Cards

```
<?xml version="1.0" encoding="iso-8859-1"?>
<!DOCTYPE wml PUBLIC "-//WAPFORUM//DTD WML 1.3//EN"
"http://www.wapforum.org/DTD/wml13.dtd" >
<wml>

<card id="welcome" title="Welcome">

<p>
Welcome to Wilmotshire. We are pleased to have you here visiting.
<anchor>
<go href="#contact"/>Next
</anchor>
</p>

</card>

<card id="contact" title="Get in Touch">
```

21

Listing 21.2   Continued

```
<p>
Please get in touch with us!<br/>
We are located at:<br/>
2001 Sunrise Drive<br/>
Wilmotshire, USA<br/>
</p>

</card>
</wml>
```

Figure 21.5 shows the first card with the link item Next. Figure 21.6 shows the card that appears when a user follows the link.

Figure 21.5
The first card in the deck displayed in an emulator.

If you'd like to link to an external page, you can use the anchor and go method, as shown in Listing 21.3, or use a standard link, as shown in Listing 21.4.

Listing 21.3   Linking Externally with Anchor and Go

```
<?xml version="1.0" encoding="iso-8859-1"?>
<!DOCTYPE wml PUBLIC "-//WAPFORUM//DTD WML 1.3//EN"
"http://www.wapforum.org/DTD/wml13.dtd" >
<wml>

<card id="anchor_method" title="Welcome">

<p>
Welcome to the wireless web.
```

Listing 21.3   Continued

```
<anchor>
<go href="http://www.molly.com/ "/>Next
</anchor>
</p>


</card>
</wml>
```

Figure 21.6
Follow the link, and the second card loads.

Figure 21.7 shows the anchor external link example in the emulator.

Listing 21.4   Linking Externally with a Standard Link

```
<?xml version="1.0" encoding="iso-8859-1"?>
<!DOCTYPE wml PUBLIC "-//WAPFORUM//DTD WML 1.3//EN"
"http://www.wapforum.org/DTD/wml13.dtd" >
<wml>

<card id="standard_method" title="Get in Touch">

<p>
<a href="http://www.molly.com/">Next</a>

</p>

</card>
</wml>
```

21

Figure 21.7
An anchor example of external linking.

At this point, you should have a basic understanding of how to create WML documents. For additional resources, check out the Wireless Developer's Network, `http://www.wirelessdevnet.com/`.

➡️ *If you are unsure about the validity of your WML documents, see "WML and Validation" in the "Troubleshooting" section later in this chapter.*

DESIGNING FOR MSN TV (WEBTV)

Despite the fact that WebTV users are still a small part of the browsing population, knowing how to properly accommodate those users can only serve to broaden the scope of your Web sites. What's more, the Web and TV will become more closely entwined over time—and the savvy developer will do well to learn what's up and coming in our convergent future. This is especially true now that Microsoft has bought WebTV and its related technologies and has brought them into the fold of Microsoft Network (MSN) offerings.

Why MSN TV/WebTV?

The demographic of the Web is changing. What used to be the domain of skilled computer users and motivated curiosity seekers has become a public utility. Technically interested but less-adept audiences want—and deserve—an easy way to get online. We see this clearly in the senior audience, which happens to be one of the largest growing Web populations. WebTV makes the Web approachable by putting it in the context of a familiar medium.

From a more technical standpoint, convergence is something developers have foreseen for some time now. Convergence (a late-90s word describing the integration of the Web and other media, such as TV and handheld devices) is realistically a critical concern for developers. The familiar (albeit already frustrating) domain of the Web browser isn't the only focus of our futures. We need to become aware that we'll soon be dealing with user agents running on devices as small as pagers and at least as large as big-screen TVs. That means negotiating changes in the languages we use and the way we do design.

WebTV is a perfect place for developers to start because, although there are concerns unique to working with WebTV, these concerns aren't too far outside the ones we already deal with today. We stay in the realm of the familiar—a browser and conventional HTML methods—but make a move into the realm of a user agent that's not running on a standard computer.

Design Principles for WebTV

How is designing for WebTV different from designing for standard browsers? For starters, the WebTV browser is a proprietary technology that's significantly different from the more familiar browsers such as Microsoft Internet Explorer and Netscape Navigator. But some unusual concerns are common to both WebTV and conventional TV. Here are the major concerns for designers broken down into four groups: resolution, markup and code rendering, design, and technology. Within each category are specific considerations for Web developers when working with MSN TV/WebTV. Here's a closer look.

Resolution

The resolution of a television screen in the United States is akin to a 640×480 computer screen. European TVs use a PAL standard, equivalent to an 800×600 computer environment. Upcoming HDTV standards will be considerably different by virtue of the technology they encompass. I say "akin" and "equivalent" because certain factors, such as technical concepts including scan lines, blanking intervals, and interlacing, affect TV and make TV resolution different from that of a computer monitor.

However, knowing that you have some familiar equivalents is a good starting point. As mentioned earlier, just as most designers recognize a lowest common denominator of around 585 pixels for fixed-design Web sites, WebTV browsers are a bit smaller, due to the capabilities of North American and Japanese displays. The width for a WebTV screen is 544 pixels, and the height per screen is 372 pixels.

I can hear the screams of agony now. Please don't despair! If you're designing with tables, you have several options. You can design fixed-width tables to accommodate WebTV at 544 pixels. You can also use dynamic table layouts and use a browser detect and route for WebTV along with other resolutions.

Of course, you can ignore resolution issues altogether. But beware: WebTV restricts fixed tables by wrapping or compressing them to the size it can accommodate, squeezing your graphics to fit. In some cases, this can result in spliced graphics being rendered in bizarre ways, as shown in Figure 21.8.

21

Figure 21.8
Tables in WebTV are often compressed, potentially rendering your spliced designs in strange, ineffective ways.

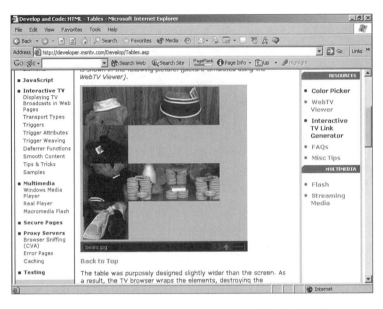

To ensure that fixed tables (and the images within them) that are wider than 544 pixels behave, use the guide shown in Table 21.1 to accomplish the results you'd like. If any of these options are not present, and your table is wider than 544 pixels, the WebTV browser will wrap any information that can't fit in this maximum width.

Table 21.1   WebTV Table Design Options and Results

Option	WebTV Result	Markup Sample

Store all images in separate table cells.	All images will be compressed in a given row to fit the screen.	`<tr>`
		`<td><img></td>`
		`<td><img></td>`
		`</tr>`

Keep images in the same cell, but use the `<nobr>` element around the images.	Images will first be compressed in an attempt to have all images fit on the same line. Any images that still don't fit will wrap to the next line.	`<td> <nobr>`
		`<img><img><img>`
		`</nobr> </td>`

Fix the width of the table cell containing the images.	Images will first be compressed and then wrapped if necessary.	`<td width="600">` `<img><img><img> </td>`

Markup Rendering

WebTV renders HTML differently in some cases from what you might expect. We've already seen this in the resolution example described previously, in which compression and wrapping of tables by the browser can occur.

Page titles, frames, forms, and imagemaps have specific issues to contend with, as follows:

- **Page titles**—Page titles for the title bar tend to be truncated to 35 total characters or less. Therefore, it's wise to keep titles concise. "Molly.Com: Home" will work just fine, but "Welcome to the Web Site of Molly E. Holzschlag" will truncate.

- **Frames**—In terms of frames, it's interesting to note that the WebTV browser converts frames into tables. This means that any static portion of a frame viewed in a browser will not remain static if there's a scrollbar. Figure 21.10 shows a framed page with the top static navigation in place. Figure 21.9 shows the same page in the context of WebTV.

- **Forms**—Forms will work just fine if they're kept simple, with very clean HTML. Complex forms and incorrectly coded attributes can cause the WebTV browser to choke. Interestingly, there are some fun attributes specific to WebTV browsers, enabling the addition of background color, cursor color, text color, and even having selections automatically activated. Forms using JavaScript might not work properly.

- **Imagemaps**—It's important to know that WebTV doesn't support server-side imagemapping. It does, however, support client-side imagemapping. The one caveat is that any shape other than a rectangle might prove problematic because WebTV users don't use a mouse to navigate. Rather, links are surrounded by a selection box (see Figure 21.10). If you're using imagemaps when designing for WebTV, be sure to include client-side mapping information and keep your map areas rectangular.

➡️ *To learn to create client-side imagemaps using Macromedia Fireworks MX, see "Designing Imagemaps," p. 584.*

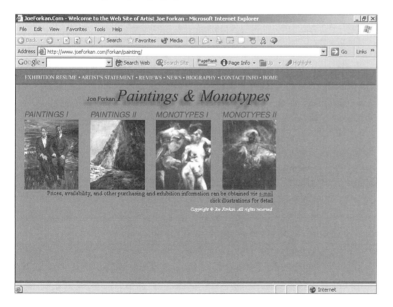

Figure 21.9
A standard framed page. When you get to this site, the top menu bar remains static.

21

Figure 21.10
WebTV turns the framed page into a table, so all the content moves with the page. Note the selection box around the Home button.

Design

There are several visual concerns of which to be aware. In general, because TV uses different technology from computer monitors to generate images, things will look somewhat different in the TV environment.

The good news is that TV supports many more colors than browsers—and, what's more, no colors will dither, ever. The bad news is that certain colors, especially red and white, can appear very bright and disconcerting when displayed on a TV. Television backgrounds are generally better dark, with light text. The Web is more flexible in this regard.

So, you'll need to think carefully about who you're designing for and why. Obviously, white backgrounds are simply too important in Web design to restrict them just to accommodate the smaller population of WebTV users. Furthermore, the use of colors that are not Web-safe when designing for diverse audiences is a consideration developers always need to think carefully about. However, if you're developing content specifically for WebTV, you should keep these issues in mind.

For more information on WebTV support and information, visit the WebTV site at http://developer.msntv.com/. You can also download the WebTV viewer (for Windows and Mac platforms) from http://developer.msntv.com/Tools/WebTVVwr.asp, which simulates the way your work will look on WebTV right from your computer. It's an excellent way to test your pages for MSN TV/WebTV compatibility.

Another critical difference in terms of visual design is the way fonts are rendered. WebTV ignores most HTML and CSS fonts unless you stick to the two fonts the WebTV browser uses—Helvetica for proportional text and Monaco for fixed-width text. WebTV also has its own sizing system for fonts. Users control the size by setting up their preferences to read fonts as small, medium, or large.

21

Therefore, designers will always be at the mercy of having their information displayed to user preference. This especially affects any floating images in text and wraps headers or display text that you've so carefully designed.

At this point, the only thing you can do about these concerns is to test your pages to see just how they render at different sizes.

Technology

WebTV browsers are limited in the technology they support. Because audio, video, and multimedia such as Flash are naturals for the TV environment, you won't encounter technological problems there, although file formats and Flash versions are still limited because of restrictions in the WebTV browser. Flash 1 is supported by both WebTV Classic and WebTV Plus (two WebTV browsers), whereas Flash 2 is available only in WebTV Plus, Flash versions 3 and 4 are available in more recent MSN TV browsers, but Flash 5 has not yet been implemented at this writing. In terms of scripting, a version of JavaScript known as JellyScript is in use with certain restrictions. In general, most technologies that rely on the browser or browser plug-ins to work, such as JavaScript and DHTML, Java applets, and style sheets, all have quirky support in WebTV or aren't supported whatsoever.

There's also significant contention as to how seamlessly server-side technologies work. There's not a lot of information out on this, but I found no problems with ColdFusion. Conceptually, nothing happening on the server side should affect the end results in a browser. However, if you take a peek into the Web Design for WebTV Forum, you'll see numerous problems encountered by designers using CCI, SSL, ASP, and other server-based technologies.

> **For the MSN TV Developer's** Forum, point your browser to `http://developer.msntv.com/`.

As with all Web development, testing plays a critical role in the way design decisions are made or revised. If you're seriously committed to developing for WebTV, owning a WebTV unit might be desirable. Alternatively, you can simulate WebTV by using the helpful WebTV Viewer.

As more and more media becomes intertwined, developers are finding that instead of technologies scaling down into some semblance of routine, the daily code demands are getting more complex. Fortunately, extensible markup languages such as XML and XHTML are gaining more attention and support because their native customization features allow for ways in which to better integrate the diverse platforms and agents available.

TROUBLESHOOTING

WML and Validation

I am new to working with WML. Is there a way I can validate my work?

Macromedia Dreamweaver MX provides validation for you. Select File, Check Page, Validate Markup to get a report.

21

⇨ *To learn more about validation, see "Validating Documents," p. 520.*

Baby-Face Limitations

I created a WML page, but I'm having problems seeing it all and have to scroll. What can I do?

Although you can create as many paragraphs in a card as you want, bear in mind that the displays of mobile devices are very small and the methods used to scroll down pages are often cumbersome. The simplest workaround is to keep your content very, very concise.

PEER TO PEER: A CLOSER LOOK AT XHTML BASIC

XHTML Basic was created as a standard by the W3C specifically for use in mobile and alternative devices such as smart phones, PDAs, pagers, automotive navigation systems, and computerized vending machines. These devices require streamlined markup because they don't have a lot of RAM or processing speed. Therefore, they don't have room for a complex browser to interpret detailed code. Because of these limitations, XHTML is just that—basic.

XHTML Basic is meant to include only those methods in HTML and XHTML that are appropriate for these types of appliances. Given these restrictions, many elements and methodologies used in standard Web design are left out of XHTML Basic to let it deliver consistent information to special appliances.

Only some HTML and XHTML features can be used safely among all such appliance types without causing rendering problems. These include the use of text and basic text formatting, such as standard headings, paragraphs, and lists.

A critical feature for all hypermedia is, of course, the link. Basic forms are important for managing input and basic tables—in this case not for design or layout, but for their original intent, which is tabular data formatting. Images can be used in many instances, although they should be kept very small. Meta information can also be included and is helpful for document identification, character set encoding, and search engine keywords.

What's in XHTML Basic

Many items can be included in XHTML Basic, but some can't. Sometimes a technology is included, but only in part. The following technologies and modules are allowed in XHTML Basic:

- **Text**—Standard text is supported in XHTML Basic. Formatting, including paragraphs, headers, breaks, and lists, is also supported. It supports emphasis, but not italics.

- **Forms**—Very basic forms are allowed. These forms must comply with the Basic Forms Module. This module supports form elements common to HTML 3.2: `form`, `input`, `select`, `option`, and `textarea`.

- **Tables**—Tables from the Basic Tables Module are supported, including the following elements: caption, table, td, th, and tr.

- **Style sheets**—External style sheets are supported via the link element. Elements including div, span, and class are also supported to enable the use of style. It's recommended that developers ensure graceful degradation for user interfaces that don't support style.

- **Images**—Images are supported using the img element, but use images very sparingly, and then only when they're extremely small in size.

So, with XHTML Basic, you can have body markup that's limited to paragraph markup:

```
<p>Welcome to Molly's Wireless Web</p>
```

Or, you can also include paragraphs, headers, and lists:

```
<h2>Welcome to Molly's Wireless Web</h2>
<p>Here you will find:</p>
<ul>
<li>Book Updates</li>
<li>Speaking Engagements</li>
<li>Contact Information</li>
</ul>
```

Or, you can create a more complex sample using a basic table:

```
<p>Select one:</p>
<table border="1" cellspacing="0" cellpadding="2">
<tr>
<td><a href="updates.html">Book Updates</a></td>
<td><a href="speaking.html">Speaking Engagements</a></td>
<td><a href="contact.html">Contact Information</a></td>
</tr>
</table>
```

For a forms page, you could have a complete (but simple) form, and you could also use an external style sheet to apply style as you see fit.

What's Not in the Specification

So, what's been left out of XHTML basic? Lots! The limitations of alternative appliances make authoring for them quite restricted. Here's what you can't use in XHTML Basic:

- **Scripting**—The script and noscript elements aren't supported. Scripts demand processing power, which many of the smaller, alternative devices simply don't have.

- **Frames**—Frames are based on the interfaces provided by a Web browser. Because the user agents in alternative devices are very limited and very small, frames don't make sense. As such, they're completely unsupported in XHTML Basic.

21

- **Objects**—The object element, used for things such as Java applets or Flash files, is prohibited. Once again, the simplicity of alternative devices doesn't allow for this kind of advanced functionality.

- **Imagemaps**—Because mapping requires input from a pointing device, and only a few alternative devices use pointers (for example, PDAs do, but pagers don't), imagemaps have been left out of XHTML Basic.

So, any inline script using the script element won't be allowed. Conceivably, the link attribute could be used to link to an external script. However, scripting for alternative devices currently has limited usage, if it's useful at all. You'll also never see framesets in XHTML Basic because the user agents don't have the power to support them.

The same is true of objects. Imagine trying to deliver a Flash file to a pager. Hardly! And, even though small images are supported, imagemapping features aren't. Recall that original mapping was a server-sided process, and later it was browser based. Most user agents for small devices need to be lean, so support just doesn't exist. What's more, the point-and-click options available on a computer aren't available on most alternative devices.

If all this feels limited, it is. But these limitations empower you to deliver content to alternative devices. XHTML Basic doesn't exist for standard browser design. Rather, it's pared down, especially because alternative devices are, as a group, limited.

The XHTML Basic Document

An XHTML Basic document follows rules familiar to XHTML (and XML) authors. Documents must conform, validate, and contain specific syntax to enable this conformity and validation.

An XHTML Basic document must comply with the following guidelines:

- The document validates to the XHTML Basic DTD.

- The document must contain a DOCTYPE definition denoting the proper DTD.

- The document's root element (as in XHTML itself) is html.

- The root element contains the default namespace for XHTML, further defining it as an XHTML-based document.

- Conformance is an absolute in XHTML, and therefore, in XHTML Basic. As a result, XHTML Basic documents must validate against the named Basic DTD.

To establish the document as an XHTML Basic document, and to allow for validation, the DOCTYPE definition must be included. The root element is html because HTML is the vocabulary in use in the XHTML Basic markup.

The uses of modularization will become much more diverse in the future, but XHTML Basic is a perfect example of how to make modularization for wireless and alternative devices work today. You can create documents that are accessible by Web browsers and existing mobile devices such as cell phones and Palm handhelds. The reason you can do this is that the vocabulary is defined by HTML. But the syntactical rules evolved from XML, which in turn has given us XHTML. And that, in turn, has inspired modularization, taking us to an entirely new level of extensibility.

An XHTML Basic Template for Use in Dreamweaver MX

If you'd like to add an XHTML Basic template for use in Dreamweaver MX, follow the directions in Chapter 12, "Working with Templates," and add the template found in Listing 21.5 and on the CD-ROM.

Listing 21.5   The XHTML Basic Template

```
<?xml version="1.0"?>
<!DOCTYPE html PUBLIC "-//W3C//DTD XHTML Basic
1.0//EN" "xhtml-basic10.dtd" >

<html xmlns="http://www.w3.org/1999/xhtml">

</html>
```

21

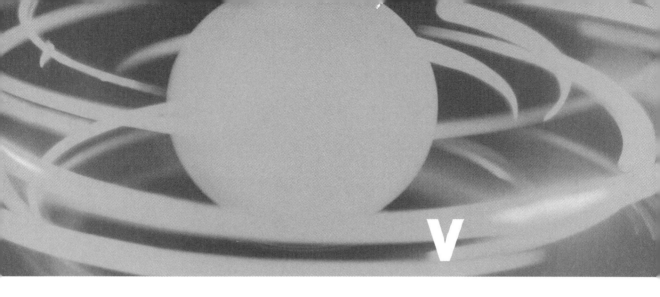

V

DESIGNING FOR INTERACTIVITY

IN THIS PART

WORKING WITH JAVASCRIPT AND BEHAVIORS

IN THIS CHAPTER

SCRIPTING CONCEPTS

The primary function of HTML and XHTML is to define how a Web page should be structured, provide references to other pages through links, and accept input using forms. After the Web page loads, the web markup in use has preformed its job.

But, if you'd like your pages to have interactive components, you should use scripting. Scripts can be combined with events that are interpreted by the browser (referred to as *intrinsic events* or simply, *events*) that react to the site visitor as he or she performs a given action.

Scripting allows you to add code telling the Web page what to do at the point of this action. What the Web page does in response to the viewer's action is referred to as an event. With scripts, you have the power to control events that happen on the screen, such as changing a graphic when the viewer's mouse pointer passes over it.

Scripts used with a document and interpreted by the browser are referred to as *client-side* scripts. These scripts are most often JavaScript (or some version thereof) but can be other types of scripts, such as Visual Basic Script (VBScript). Scripts can be used inline (embedded scripts) or linked to using the `src` attribute along with the `style` element.

It's also important that I mention the *Document Object Model* (DOM). The DOM is a means within browsers that allows authors to access parts of a document, and add programs and scripts to dynamically modify that document: its structure, its presentation, and its contents.

This DOM *should* be platform and language neutral. However, the implementation of the DOM in browsers has varied enormously over the past years, leading to a lot of confusion about how browsers interpret and deal with scripting. The DOM is especially important in scripting and the creation of dynamic pages in general, and specifically, to what has become known as *Dynamic HTML (DHTML)*.

Many readers will be familiar with DHTML, but others will want to better understand what DHTML is—and what it is *not*. DHTML is not a language in and of itself. What it *is* technically, and from the point of view of the W3C, is a combination of technologies, as follows:

- **HTML or XHTML**—An HTML or XHTML document and its elements provide the matrix.

- **CSS**—Using Cascading Style Sheets, numerous presentational effects can be accomplished.

- **Scripting**—Some form of scripting, primarily JavaScript, is used to carry out dynamic events.

The major frustration with DHTML has focused on two main concerns. The first is that the implementation of the DOM from one browser type and version to the next has been very rocky. The second is that browser-specific elements that did not make it into specifications have caused many DHTML authors frustration.

▭⟩ *How do designers manage the browser support difficulties and still create great DHTML sites? See "Managing Cross-Browser Design" in the "Troubleshooting" section at the end of this chapter for more information.*

Want more details about DOM related activities and resources? See http://www.w3.org/DOM/.

If you do not know how to use scripts or JavaScript, never fear! Macromedia Dreamweaver takes all drudgery out of creating JavaScript by providing dozens of useful pre-programmed scripts for you to customize (called *snippets* in Macromedia Dreamweaver) and by allowing you to quickly add common actions for a variety of common events (called *behaviors* in Macromedia Dreamweaver).

In this chapter, you will explore both how to add your own JavaScript and how to quickly add JavaScript using Macromedia Dreamweaver's built-in tools. First, I'll go over a few important JavaScript concepts to help you gain better control and decision making as you work with Macromedia Dreamweaver's scripting tools.

Understanding JavaScript

For the sake of clarity, it's important to recognize that JavaScript is *not* a part of HTML. Rather, JavaScript and HTML are different technologies that work closely together, and JavaScript can exist within a Web page built using HTML to tell the HTML what to do.

JavaScript has three main components: event handlers, functions, and code.

Event Handlers

Event handlers are JavaScript's front line. They can be associated with particular elements on the page—a link for example—to detect a particular action, such as when the mouse pointer passes over the link. When that occurs, the event handler tells the browser what to do about it, which in this case is to execute a JavaScript function (see Figure 22.1). JavaScript functions are described in greater detail in the next section.

Macromedia Dreamweaver has many configured scripts that allow you to create behaviors (see Table 22.1).

22

Sometimes the naming of things in software programs and in the actual languages they support is inconsistent. *Actions* and *events* are technology terms, but *behaviors* is a term often used in software to describe what results from the script—a modification in the behavior of the components being scripted.

Caution

Despite name similarities, JavaScript and Java are not the same thing. JavaScript is a scripting language developed by Netscape. Java is a programming language for application development developed by Sun. Both were being developed at the same time, and Sun and Netscape decided to market them together, creating a bit of confusion because of the similarity of their names.

Virtually all the browsers on the market today have JavaScript capability. However, that does not mean that they will all support JavaScript in the same way. For the most part, Macromedia Dreamweaver will assist you in creating JavaScript that works on the majority of browsers.

Figure 22.1

The onMouseOver event handler is located in a link.

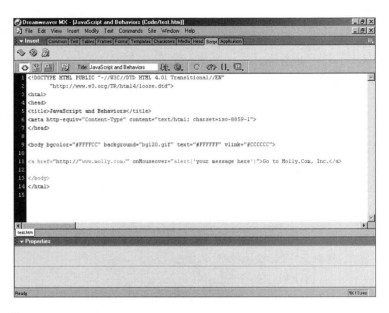

Table 22.1   Common Event Handlers

Event Handler	Event
onAbort	Element is not completely loaded.
onBlur	Element is deselected.
onChange	Form element is changed.
onClick	Element is clicked.
onDblClick	Element is double-clicked.
onError	Page or image generate an error while loading.
onFocus	Element is selected.
onKeyDown	Any keyboard key is down.
onKeyPress	Any keyboard key is clicked.
onKeyUp	Any keyboard key is released.
onLoad	After an element loads (including the Web page).
onMouseDown	Mouse button is pressed down.
onMouseMove	Mouse is moved.
onMouseOut	Mouse pointer passes out of an element.
onMouseOver	Mouse pointer passes over an element.
onMouseUp	Mouse button is released.
onResize	Browser window or frame is resized.
onUnload	After the element is no longer loaded (including the Web page).

JavaScript Functions

A JavaScript *function* is a collection of JavaScript code given a specific and unique name, with a unique corresponding result, to be called on by an event handler. Functions can be very simple or very complex depending on what they are intended to do (see Figure 22.2). Although the range of functions is fairly broad, a single function does only one thing.

If you aren't a JavaScript programmer yourself, Macromedia Dreamweaver includes dozens of preprogrammed scripts to use. Macromedia Dreamweaver MX provides you with two ways to add JavaScript functions to a Web page: *snippets*, which allow you to add chunks of JavaScript, and *behaviors*, which allow you to add events and simple JavaScript code to elements as stated earlier.

All of these events are supported by popular Web browsers, although onResize is not supported in IE 4.0. The W3C HTML and XHTML specifications express some, but not all, of these event handlers. For more information on the actual specifications, see the Peer to Peer section later this chapter.

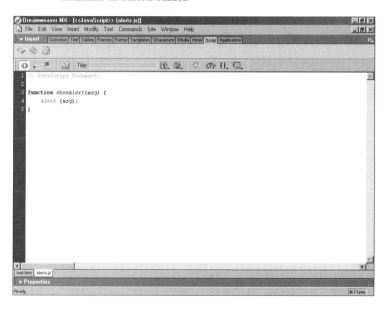

Figure 22.2
This simple JavaScript function causes a message to pop up.

JavaScript Code

JavaScript code is often associated with an event handler or a function, but JavaScript code can stand alone in a Web page. If left outside of an event handler or function, the code is executed as soon as the page is loaded—the equivalent of an onLoad event handler.

JavaScript uses variables to record values for different purposes while the page is loaded. These values can change throughout the course of the user interaction with the page, allowing the browser to keep track of what is happening. For the most part, you will not need to interact with JavaScript variables unless you want to create your own JavaScript code.

ADDING JAVASCRIPT TO A WEB PAGE

JavaScript can be added to all versions of HTML and XHTML documents via the `script` element. Although most browsers will immediately recognize whether you are using JavaScript or another scripting language such as VBScript, it is a good idea (and necessary in certain versions of HTML and XHTML) to define, in the opening `<script>` tag, the type of script you are using.

Another means of adding scripts to a page is placing them in an external file and referencing them. See "Using External JavaScript Files" later this chapter.

Adding the `script` Element

JavaScript can exist either in the head of a document or in the body, but it always has to be within a `script` element. Otherwise, the JavaScript code is displayed as text within the document. The only exception to this is when placing your JavaScript in an external file. In that case, you do not use any HTML markup; you just place the code into the file.

To add the script container, follow these steps:

1. With the document open in the Code view, place your cursor either in the head or body of the document at the point you want to insert the new JavaScript.

2. Open the Script Insert panel and click the Script icon (see Figure 22.3). The Script window will appear.

3. Select the Language type. This can be a generic JavaScript (covering all versions), a specific version of JavaScript (1.1 or 1.2), or VBscript. I recommend using JavaScript.

4. Type your JavaScript code into the Content field. You do not have to type all of the JavaScript at this time, but you must enter something in this field for the `script` element to be inserted.

In the Design view, a JavaScript container is represented by a script tag icon.

5. You can type content for browsers that are not JavaScript compatible or for those cases in which a user has turned off JavaScript. To do this, type your content into the No Script field. This is optional, but it is generally a good idea to add a link or other message.

6. Click OK. A `script` element with the JavaScript you entered will be inserted in your page at the cursor. If you added no script content, the JavaScript you entered will appear in a `script` container at the location of your cursor.

Caution

In XHTML, the `language` attribute has been deprecated in favor of the `type` attribute. In this case, you add the MIME type as the value for the attribute as follows:

```
<script type="text/
javascript">

</script>
```

A Web page can contain as many script containers as needed. Repeat these steps as many times as you want within a single document.

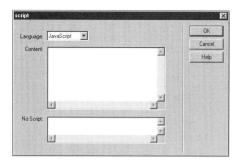

Figure 22.3
Using the Script dialog box.

Adding noscript Information

The noscript element allows you to include HTML content that will be displayed only by browsers that do *not* support scripting or that have JavaScript turned off by the visitor. You can place any HTML you want between these tags. You can add no script content while adding a script container to your page (as shown previously), or you can add a noscript element independently, as follows:

1. With the document open in the Code view, place your cursor either in the head or body of the document at the point you want to insert the content for browsers that can't understand JavaScript.

2. Open the Script Insert panel and click the No Script icon. The Tag Editor - No Script window will appear.

3. Click OK and the noscript element will appear at the cursor.

> Because you can add any markup you like to the noscript element, it's best used in the body of the document with additional markup. Many Web designers provide a link to a page with alternative content that does not rely on scripts. This helps address accessibility concerns and is especially useful on those sites wanting to comply with accessibility guidelines.

Using External JavaScript Files

As mentioned, JavaScript code can be included directly within the Web page or set up as a standalone file and imported into a Web page using the script element. The advantage of using an external JavaScript file is that the code can be reused in as many different Web pages as you need. Any changes made to the master JavaScript file will be reflected in all pages using the external file.

Using an external JavaScript file in a Web page is a two-step process. First, you must create the external JavaScript file, and then you must set up a script tag in the Web page to import the external file.

> The code in an external JavaScript file will not be viewable within the Web page's source itself.

Setting Up an External JavaScript File

Before you can add an external JavaScript file to a Web page, you must set up the file. The easiest way to set up an external JavaScript file using Macromedia Dreamweaver is to access the JavaScript template.

22

To set up an external script, do the following:

1. Select File, New to open the New Document window.

2. In the New Document window, select Basic Page in the General tab (see Figure 22.4). Then select Javascript from the Basic Page column. Finally, click Create.

3. A new, untitled document is opened with nothing but a JavaScript comment at the top. Enter your JavaScript into this page.

4. Save your external JavaScript file by selecting File, Save or File, Save As. The Save As dialog will appear.

5. Type a name for your file, select the location you want the file saved, and click Save.

> ## Caution
>
> External JavaScript files should *not* include any HTML tags unless they are within a `document.write()` or `document.writeln()`. In addition, you should not include a `script` element in an external JavaScript document. Including any HTML can cause the script to fail or act unpredictably.

You'll notice that Macromedia Dreamweaver automatically adds a `.js` extension to the end of the file name. JavaScript files don't have to use a `.js` extension, but this has become the convention and helps avoid confusion with other file types.

Figure 22.4
In the New Document window, there is an option for creating JavaScript documents.

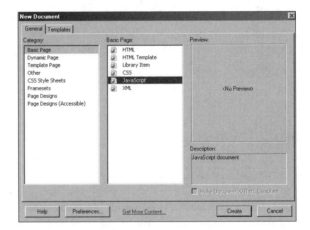

Be sure to save the external file in a location easily accessible by the Web page(s) you will be importing it into. If you are likely to be using several different external JavaScript files, you might want to set up a separate folder named `javascript` in your directory to save your scripts in.

➪ *What if you want to have more than one JavaScript effect on a page? See "Using Multiple Scripts" in the "Troubleshooting" section at the end of this chapter.*

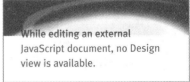

While editing an external JavaScript document, no Design view is available.

Adding the External JavaScript File to a Web Page

Now that the external JavaScript file has been set up, you can import the file into any number of Web pages using the `script` element as follows:

1. Add a `script` element as explained earlier in this chapter.

2. With the Document window open in the Design view, click the Script icon to see the script options in the Properties window. Here, you can change the scripting language and whether the code is client-side or server-side code. If you want to use an external JavaScript file, set the source here.

> You can attach as many pages as you like to the external script. It's one of the advantages of using such a script because it can be modified and all the pages linking to it will automatically accept the modification without you having to touch those files—only the originating `.js` file.

3. Click the Folder icon next to the Source field, and the Select Script File window will appear.

4. Select the external JavaScript file you want to import, and click (Choose) [OK].

Alternatively, you can simply type the source location for the external JavaScript file directly into the opening `<script>` tag in the Code view. The script's location will be displayed in the source file. The external file will be used at the location in the Web page, but the code itself will not appear in the main Web document.

Editing JavaScript

After you have set up the script container, you can add to, change, or edit your JavaScript code.

To modify JavaScript using the Script Properties Editor, follow these steps:

1. Open the document in Design view.

2. Click the Script icon where your script resides in the document.

3. In the Properties window, click Edit.

4. Modify or change the script as necessary. Click OK to update the changes to your script.

You can also modify your scripts manually in Code view. To do so, open the document that contains the script, or if the script is an external one, open that file directly. Make any changes you want and save the file to update the changes.

Figure 22.5
You can add your JavaScript in the Script Properties window.

USING JAVASCRIPT SNIPPETS

Macromedia Dreamweaver includes several dozen code snippets and functions to help quickly add JavaScript to your Web pages. These self-contained JavaScript code fragments and functions perform common tasks including everything from calculating the area of a circle to opening a new pop-up window.

Being self-contained, these snippets usually do not have to rely on any other code to work. However, some snippets do require other snippets. If additional snippets are required, these dependencies will be listed in the JavaScript comments at the beginning of the snippet.

Macromedia has carefully tested the snippets to ensure cross-browser compatibility, but in practice, this is difficult, if not impossible, to guarantee. If you find that a function does not seem to be working properly, and you have experience with scripting, you can try to troubleshoot and debug it on your own. Or you can remove it and try a different solution to the problem.

Inserting JavaScript Snippets

To add a snippet into a page, follow these steps:

1. With the document open in the Code view, add a script element to either the head or body of the HTML code as described previously in this chapter. Alternatively, add snippets into existing `script` elements.

2. Place the cursor at the point within the script where you want to add the JavaScript snippet. You can also select code in the document, and some snippets will insert code before and after the selected code.

3. Select Window, Snippets to open the snippets panel if it is not already open (see Figure 22.6).

4. In the panel, folders for a variety of code snippets include HTML and a special folder for JavaScript snippets. Click the JavaScript folder to open it. Inside the JavaScript folder are a variety of subfolders, each holding code snippets or additional subfolders. Select the snippet you want to add and click the Insert button at the bottom of the panel.

5. The snippet code will be inserted after your cursor.

Creating New JavaScript Snippets

Although Macromedia Dreamweaver includes several dozen JavaScript snippets in its library, if you are developing your own code, you will want to add your own customized snippets. Follow these steps to do so:

1. If you have already created the code you want to turn into a snippet, select the code from its original source and copy it.

2. If it is not already open, open the snippets panel by clicking the Snippets tab.

> **Caution**
>
> Remember, if adding the script to an external JavaScript file, you should *not* include a `script` element.

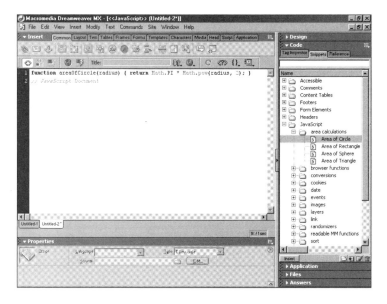

Figure 22.6
The code snippet panel. Each snippet has a brief description to the right of its name.

3. In the JavaScript Snippets folder, select the subfolder you want the new snippet placed in. You can also create a new subfolder by clicking the Folder icon. The new subfolder will be placed in the currently selected folder and can be immediately renamed.

4. Click the New Snippet button, which will open a blank Edit Snippet window.

5. In the Edit Snippet window, type a name and a description for the new snippet (see Figure 22.7). Then select whether you want to have the code wrap around other code (place code both before and after the selected code when inserted) or behave as a block (insert all code immediately after the cursor).

6. Click OK to add the snippet to the library. You can now insert this snippet into a Web page as described earlier in this chapter.

Editing JavaScript Snippets

You can edit JavaScript Snippets in much the same way as you add them:

1. In the snippets panel, select the code snippet you want to edit and click the Edit Snippet button, or just double-click the snippet.

2. The Edit Snippet window will open with all the fields filled in with existing information (see Figure 22.8). Make changes as desired (see "Creating New JavaScript Snippets" earlier in this chapter for details about each field), and then click OK.

This will not update any existing uses of the snippet, but from this point forward, the new code will be used when you insert the snippet.

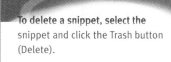

To delete a snippet, select the snippet and click the Trash button (Delete).

Figure 22.7
The Edit Snippet window with a browser redirect JavaScript snippet.

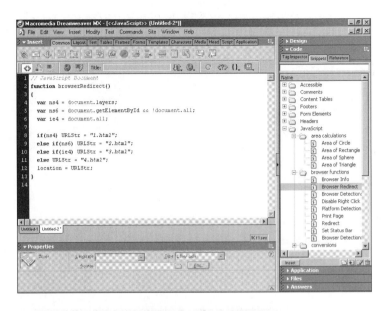

Figure 22.8
The information about the snippet you want to edit is already entered and ready for you to change.

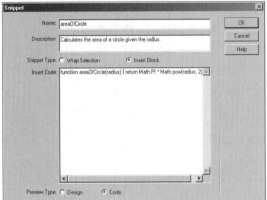

USING BEHAVIORS

A behavior is a combination of an event with an action. Adding behaviors to a Web page allows visitors to interact with your page and the page to perform important tasks without having to reload.

Behaviors are attached to particular elements on the page, or to be more accurate, to HTML tags on the page that define particular elements. Whenever the specified event happens to that element—whether it is the entire Web page, a graphic, or a text link—the associated action is performed.

Caution

Behaviors do not work with Internet Explorer 3 for the Mac, so these behaviors will be disabled. However, they should not cause other problems with rendering the nonscripted portions of the page or generate an error. It's always a good idea to test your work in a number of browsers to find out how your various visitors will see the site.

As with JavaScript snippets, behavior actions are prewritten JavaScript code. In fact, many of the behaviors available are also included as standalone snippets.

Macromedia Dreamweaver comes with several built-in actions to choose from, all of which have been tested to be as cross-browser and cross-platform compatible as possible (see Table 22.2). In addition, you can build your own behaviors or download additional behaviors from the Internet.

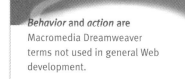

Behavior and *action* are Macromedia Dreamweaver terms not used in general Web development.

22

Table 22.2   Macromedia Dreamweaver Behaviors

Behavior Action	Results
Call JavaScript	Executes a specific JavaScript function.
Change Property	Changes a specific attribute (such as image source) for an element.
Check Browser	Redirects browser depending on the browser type and version.
Check Plugin	Redirects browser depending on whether a particular plugin is available.
Control Shockwave or Flash	Starts, stops, or rewinds Flash movies on the page.
Drag Layer	Allows layers to be moved in the Browser window.
Go To URL	Opens a Web page in a specified window or frame.
Hide Pop-up Menu	Hides a particular pop-up menu (see Show Pop-up Menu).
Jump Menu	Changes a currently placed form drop-down into a jump menu.
Jump Menu Go	Creates a Go button for a particular jump menu (jump menu must already exist).
Open Browser Window	Opens Web page in a new document.
Play Sound	Plays a sound file. Browser must be able to play the sound format.
Pop-up Message	Displays alert message.
Preload Images	Preloads specific graphics to increase display speed of the page.
Set Nav Bar Image	Changes the image used in a Navagation bar (see Chapter 23, "Rollovers and Navigation Bars").
Set Text	Changes the text in a frame, a layer, the browser status bar, or a text field.
Show Pop-up Menu	Creates a pop-up menu to be displayed.
Show-Hide Layers	Shows or hides a particular layer.
Swap Image	Changes the source of a particular image.
Swap Image Restore	Reverts the image to its previous source before it was swapped (see Swap Image).
Timeline	Allows Control over existing Timeline (see Chapter 24).
Validate Form	Checks the input of form elements.

22

The Behaviors Panel

Behaviors are added to elements on the page (or to the page itself) through the Behaviors panel (see Figure 22.9).

Figure 22.9
The Add Action button is the "+" in the upper-left corner of the Behaviors panel.

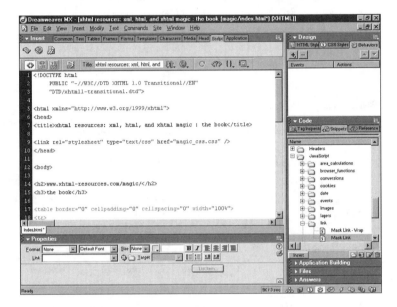

Not all behaviors and events will be available at all times since not all events will be relevant to all page elements. For example, you cannot have an onChange event with a link tag. Some behaviors require certain elements to exist before use. A case in point would be that an image must be on the page to use image swap.

Attaching Behaviors

To be used by an element, a behavior must be attached to it. This process involves selecting an element, selecting a behavior to attach, and following a series of screens tailored to the behavior. Do the following:

1. Select the element to which your want to attach a behavior. If you want to attach a behavior to text or to an image, type **javascript:;** into the link field in the Properties window to turn it into an empty link. To select the body, place the cursor in the opening <body> tag in the Code view.

2. Open the Behaviors panel by clicking the Behaviors tab. Click and hold the Add Behavior button (the "+") and select an action from the pop-up menu.

3. A dialog box will appear specific to the action you selected. This box will include fields, which allow you to customize the parameters of the action, and instructions. Make changes as needed and click OK.

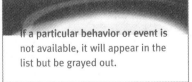

If a particular behavior or event is not available, it will appear in the list but be grayed out.

4. A behavior is added to the element with both the action and the default event to trigger it defined. To change the event, click on the triangle next to the event name and select a different event.

You can repeat steps 2 and 3 to add additional behaviors for this element, or start from step 1 to add behaviors for other elements.

Deleting a Behavior

Behaviors are most easily deleted using the Behaviors panel. Simply select the behavior you want to remove and click the delete button which is the "-" in the upper-left corner (Delete). If you mistakenly delete an event, simply select Edit, Undo.

If you feel particularly adventurous, you could try to remove the behavior from the code manually, but unless your scripting skills are very good, this is likely to lead to errors and is not recommended.

Editing Behaviors

After a behavior is in place, it can be changed in a variety of ways:

- To edit the action's parameters, double-click the behavior in the Behaviors panel to reopen the action's dialog box. Make changes as needed and click OK.

- To reorder actions with the same event handler (thus changing the order in which they will be run), select the behavior you want to move, and then click the up or down arrows.

- To update behaviors from older versions of Macromedia Dreamweaver, select the element with the behavior to be updated, double-click (select+Enter) the behavior in the Behavior panel, and click OK. This behavior will now be updated for all instances on the page. Do this for each individual behavior used on the page.

You can set Macromedia Dreamweaver to show only events that work in particular browsers by selecting the Show Events option at the bottom of the Actions and Events menus and selecting a particular browser and version. This will ensure that the events you choose will work on the intended browser.

In addition to the behaviors that come with Macromedia Dreamweaver, you can download and add behaviors made by Macromedia Dreamweaver and third parties. For more information on downloading behaviors from the Web and installing them in Macromedia Dreamweaver, see Chapter 31, "Downloading and Installing Extensions, Behaviors, and Plug-Ins."

TROUBLESHOOTING

Managing Cross-Browser Design

I'm getting really frustrated trying to create DHTML across browsers! How does one deal with this difficult issue?

- **Learn the latest cross-browser DHTML techniques**—One way to do so is to get involved in a community of developers who are interested in creating and distributing scripts that will work on multiple browsers. One such community can be found at `http://www.siteexperts.com/`.

- **Develop for just one browser type**—Although this is very controversial and not recommended for contemporary design, it is still a valid option if you are catering to a specific audience. If, for example, you know that everyone on the intranet for which you are creating an application is using a specific browser, you can use DHTML that is applicable to that browser only.

- **Use DHTML for specialty areas, not for primary navigation**—If you want to use some DHTML but don't want to compromise site visitors, don't rely on the DHTML for major components of the site, such as navigation. Instead, create a special area of the site to show off your DHTML work and express clearly which browsers support which DHTML features.

Some designers never touch DHTML, which is a reasonable choice if you decide that the needs of your audience would be compromised if you used it.

Using Multiple Scripts

Can you use multiple scripts in a page?

Of course, you can. Simply place the `<script>` element with the script you want to use. Some scripts will be in the head of the document; others will be in the body. Just be sure to test your pages to see whether all the scripts will properly execute.

PEER TO PEER: SCRIPTING AND SPECIFICATIONS

Several specification issues of which to be aware when marking up documents are as follows:

- Intrinsic events in HTML 4.0 and XHTML 1.0—The following intrinsic events are the only events allowed in conforming HTML and XHTML documents. All other events are specific to the browser that developed them and are considered to be proprietary: `onload`, `onunload`, `onclick`, `ondblclick`, `onmousedown`, `onmouseup`, `onmouseover`, `onmousemove`, `onmouseout`, `onfocus`, `onblur`, `onkeypress`, `onkeydown`, `onkeyup`, `onsubmit`, `onreset`, `onselect`, `onchange`.

- In XHTML, events should not be camel-case (for example, `onClick`). Rather, they should be written in all lowercase (`onclick`) to conform with XHTML rules.

- The European Computer Manufacturer's Association (ECMA) is working to standardize a form of JavaScript referred to as ECMAScript.

> For more information on the history of JavaScript, and how ECMAScript fits into the picture, visit The Digital Samarai, `http://www.thedigitalsamurai.net/javascript_history.asp`. The ECMAScript specification can be found at `http://www.ecma.ch/ecma1/stand/ecma-262.htm`.

ROLLOVERS AND NAVIGATION BARS

IN THIS CHAPTER

EFFECTIVE NAVIGATION

Letting your site visitors know where they are and where they are going are the key ingredients for good navigation, successful usability, and as a result, happy visitors.

Yet, a variety of challenges with the Web keep designers limited to certain locations for navigation—typically top, left, or right within the browser viewing space. A primary concern is the limited amount of space on the computer screen. Web designs must walk the narrow line between providing enough information to let the visitors know what is going on and not overwhelming them with so much information that they cannot find what they are looking for.

> **Although the term** *rollover* **implies** the onMouseOver and onMouseOut events, image swapping can be applied to a variety of events including onClick, onMouseDown, and onMouseUp. However, Macromedia Dreamweaver's built-in rollover tool defaults to onMouseOver and onMouseOut.

Fortunately, Macromedia Dreamweaver offers several solutions via JavaScript to help you design attractive and interactive navigation systems.

One of the most common and powerful ways to achieve interesting navigation schemes is to use JavaScript *rollovers*. JavaScript rollovers allow you to swap a linked image on-the-fly. With image swapping, you can add visual cues to indicate which link the user is about to click and even add additional information about the link.

A more advanced form of the rollover is termed the *navigation bar*. Macromedia Dreamweaver allows you to quickly assemble a collection of menu options with rollovers, which you can conveniently edit at any time.

Macromedia Dreamweaver of course did not invent the rollover or the navigation bar, but it does allow you set them up quickly and easily without knowing all the complexities of JavaScript. Even if you are seasoned at coding JavaScript, you will enjoy exploring Macromedia Dreamweaver's built-in rollover capabilities, which can save you hours of coding time.

CREATING A ROLLOVER

The concept behind creating a rollover is quite simple: When the visitor places her mouse over a linked image, that image is replaced with another image. Then, when the visitor moves her mouse out of the image, the new image is replaced by the first image. This easy technique is extremely popular when designing Web interfaces.

Hand scripting rollovers can be time-consuming and tedious, requiring you to set up code to load each image separately and to control the rollover states for each linked image. In addition, hand coding is often error-prone. One misplaced semicolon can take hours to track down in a really complex script.

> **You can place anything you want** within a rollover graphic, including drawn images, photographic images, and text.

Macromedia Dreamweaver's controls make setting up and editing rollovers easy.

Creating the Images

You will need two graphics to create a rollover using Macromedia Dreamweaver: An *off* state and an *on* state. The off state is how the image appears when the page first loads and how it should appear after a rollover (see Figure 23.1). The on state is how the image will look during the rollover (see Figure 23.2).

Figure 23.1
Before the image is rolled over, it is an outlined arrow with a deep drop shadow.

Figure 23.2
After the visitor rolls over the image, it changes to a solid arrow with a shallower drop shadow giving the illusion that it has been pressed.

You can use any program to create the images as long as it can save the two images in a Web-ready format. GIF or JPEG are recommended, although some browsers can display PNG or SVG.

> For information on working with images, see "Working with Images," p. 604.

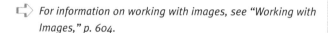

The on and off rollover images should be exactly the same size; otherwise, the second image will be distorted to fit the space of the first image.

The easiest way to create consistent rollover graphics is to use the Layers features available in Adobe Photoshop and most of the popular graphic programs. For example, in Adobe Photoshop, you can set up a layer for each rollover state but keep the same background image.

This is crucial because it allows you to keep a consistent background for all the states as well as ensures that all the images will be the same size when saved (see Figure 23.3).

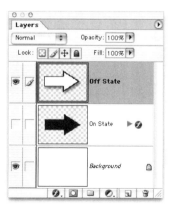

Figure 23.3
In Adobe Photoshop (Mac), the graphic for the on and off states each has its own separate layer with the third layer for the background.

No matter how you create these images, save them as separate graphic files with a filename that helps you remember what they are and which state is which (see Figure 23.4).

Figure 23.4
The on and off versions of the image have been saved in the Web sites images folder. Note the naming of these files makes it clear which purpose they serve.

Adding a Rollover to Your Page

Now that you have created your rollover graphics, add them to your Web page. To begin, open the Web page you want to add the rollover to and then follow these steps:

1. With Macromedia Dreamweaver open to Design view and the cursor in the location you'd like the image, click the Rollover Image button in the Insert palette. The Insert Rollover Image dialog box appears (see Figure 23.5).

Figure 23.5
With the cursor in place, click the Rollover Image button.

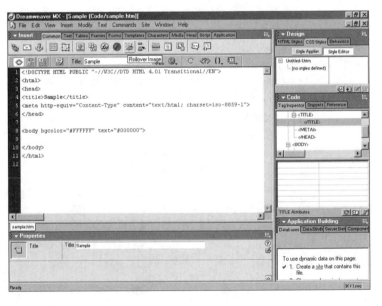

2. In the Insert Rollover Image dialog box, type a name for the image (see Figure 23.6).

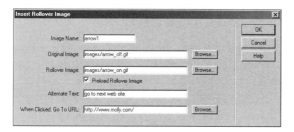

Figure 23.6
The Insert Rollover Image dialog box allows you to set the name and images for up (original) and over (rollover) states, as well as a URL for the image to be linked to.

23

3. Define the location of the original image (used during off state) and the rollover image (which appears during on state) by either typing the path from this page to the image or using the browse buttons to locate them.

4. You can have the rollover image preloaded (that is, loaded invisibly in the background). This is recommended because it prevents an unattractive pausing that can occur while the rollover image is being loaded after the onMouseOver event.

5. Add the URL for the link in the When Clicked, Go to URL field by typing in the URL directly or using the Browse button to locate the Web page to be linked to. If this is not a link, leave this field blank; Macromedia Dreamweaver will automatically fill in the link with a number sign (#) to indicate a null link.

6. Click OK for the new rollover image to appear on your Web page. If you need to make changes to the rollover—for example, if you want to change the link URL—select the image and make your changes in the Properties panel.

Using Animated GIFs with Rollovers

Any graphic format that the browser can display can be used as a rollover, including animated GIFs. So, rather than using a solid black arrow for the over state in this example, you could create an animated GIF with the black arrow slowly fading in and out (see Figure 23.7).

One caution when using animated GIFs with rollovers: Netscape 4 has a bug that causes image distortion if you try to use too many different animated GIFs with different rollovers on the same page.

Using one on a page should not cause a problem, but I do not recommend using more if your work is likely to be viewed in Netscape 4.

Figure 23.7
In this animation, the arrow fades down to almost nothing and then fades back up to full strength.

Although JavaScript rollovers are very common, Java applets are occasionally used for rollovers. Why is the JavaScript method so much more popular? See "Java Applets and Rollovers" in the "Troubleshooting" section at the end of this chapter.

DESIGNING REMOTE ROLLOVERS

Although rollovers are most often used to change the image being rolled over, you can use a rollover of one link (image or text) to change any remote graphic on the screen as long as the image being changed has a unique ID. This is referred to as a *remote rollover*. A common use of this technique is image toggling, where a remote image changes as the mouse passes over the referring links.

Adding a Rollover to Control a Remote Image

The Insert Rollover Image button is a convenient way to add rollovers to a Web page, but rollovers can also be added using the Behaviors panel discussed in Chapter 22, "Working with JavaScript and Behaviors." That method is useful here because it gives greater control over which image is being changed:

1. Place an image into the Web page that you want to swap and give it a unique name.

2. Add a link to the page. The link can be a text link, another linked graphic, or another page component (see Figure 23.8). The image being changed does *not* have to be a link itself.

Figure 23.8
The graphic arrow has been added next to a link for the home page.

3. With the link selected, select the Behaviors panel; then select Window, Behaviors. Click the Add Behaviors button (+) and select Swap Image from the drop-down menu. The Swap Image dialog box will appear (see Figure 23.9).

Figure 23.9
Swapping images using the Add Behavior drop-down menu.

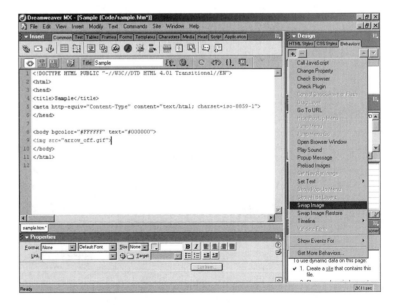

4. The Swap Image dialog box will have a list of all the images on the page (see Figure 23.10). Select the image you want to change and set the new source for the image by either typing the URL to the new image or browsing to find it. Then choose whether to have the new image pre-loaded (recommended). You can choose to have the image restored to its original state: onMouseOut.

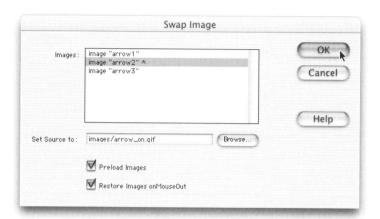

Figure 23.10
The Swap Image dialog box (Mac view) provides control over all images on the page from this link. Select an image and specify with which image you want to replace it when the visitor rolls over the link.

5. You can do this for any image in the list, allowing you to change multiple images from a single link. Just select another image name from the list and specify its replacement image.

6. After you have set all the images you want, click OK.

Image names with asterisks (*) next to them already have a swap image associated with them.

7. An onMouseOver event is added to the behaviors for this link with the Swap Image action. If you selected to have the image restored, there will also be an onMouseOut event with a Swap Image Restore action. The link will now cause the specified image(s) to change their sources when the visitor passes his mouse over it (see Figure 23.11).

Figure 23.11
The Swap Image and Swap Image Restore (Mac view) actions have been added to the behaviors for this link.

If you want to add the Restore Image functionality separately, simply select the link and then Swap Image Restore from the Add Behavior drop-down menu. A dialog box will appear to confirm; click OK, and the Restore action will be added to the link.

⊏⟩ *Preloading images is a recommended practice. Find out why in "Preloading Images" in the "Troubleshooting" section later in this chapter.*

CREATING NAVIGATION BARS

Most Web sites include a menu to help the visitor move around in the Web site, and these menus are likely to use rollovers to help communicate what is going on. Simple rollovers are helpful but limited for this task, so Macromedia Dreamweaver includes a navigation bar to collect menu options into one element and provide four rollover states: up, over, down, and over while down (see Table 23.1).

Table 23.1   Rollover States and Events in Navigation

State	Event
Up	Normal.
Over	Mouse Over.
Down	Mouse click. Also used to indicate that the menu option is the current selection.
Over While Down	Used for Mouse Over if the menu option is currently in the down state. Generally speaking, this is the same as the down state.

Creating the Navigation Bar Graphics

As with the rollovers already presented in this chapter, you first create the menu images in a graphics program such as Photoshop or Fireworks. The obvious difference between the rollovers already discussed and the navigation bar rollovers is that you will create four different states for each menu item in a navigation bar.

How you design these four states is up to you and the needs of your project, but here are a few helpful guidelines by state:

■ **Up**—This is the off state for the link. It should let the visitor know that it can be clicked but should not necessarily overwhelm other elements on the screen. For example, in Figure 23.12, light text indicates an up state for the link.

■ **Over**—This is the on state for the menu option and should let the visitor know the link is ready to be clicked. You can communicate this through color changes, shifting size, shifting position, or adding additional markers (such as a pointer). The idea is for an obvious change to occur between the up and over states. For example, in Figure 23.13 text is black with a drop shadow.

Figure 23.12
The up state is represented using light blue text for the menu options. In this grayscale figure it is the lighter text on the page.

Figure 23.13
The over state uses black text with a drop shadow to set it apart from other menu options.

- **Down**—This is the current state for the menu option and should be clearly contrasted from the up state. Generally, it is used to indicate that this is the currently selected menu option (in other words, the current page). For example, black text is used in Figure 23.14.

- **Over While Down**—This is the on state used for an element currently in the down state. Because the element is already down, indicating that it is selected, this is a special case. You need to either communicate to the visitor that this link is already active or simply leave it looking the same as the down mode. Red text is used to indicate this state in Figure 23.15.

Figure 23.14
The down state is simply black text, which is more distinct than the light blue.

Figure 23.15
The over while down state is red to let the user know he is already at this link.

Adding the Navigation Bar

The most difficult part of putting the menu together is creating all the images you need. Unlike a simple rollover, every menu option requires at least three different images (though technically you could still get away with two) and can use up to four. But adding the bar to Macromedia Dreamweaver is simple, accomplished by following these steps:

1. Open the Web page you want your navigation bar on, place your cursor where you want the bar, and click the Navigation Bar button to open the Modify Navigation Bar dialog box (see Figure 23.16).

2. When the Insert Navigation Bar dialog box opens, it automatically creates a blank default button, called unnamed1, for you to modify (see Figure 23.17). Type a new and unique element name for the first navigation element (button), replacing the default value.

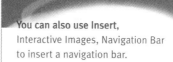

You can also use Insert, Interactive Images, Navigation Bar to insert a navigation bar.

Figure 23.16
The Navigation Bar button opens the Modify Navigation Bar dialog box.

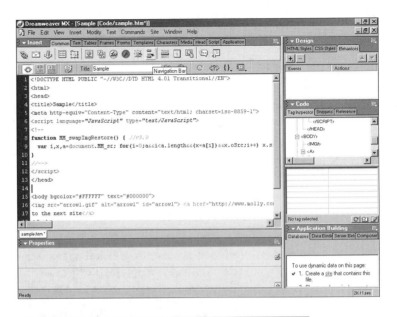

Figure 23.17
When the Insert Navigation Bar dialog box opens for the first time, Macromedia Dreamweaver sets up a blank button for you.

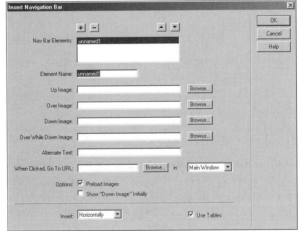

3. Specify the images to be used for the four states by typing the path to the image or by using the Browse button to locate it. You can reuse the same graphics for different states if you want. For example, you might want to use the same graphic for the down and over while down states.

4. Enter the URL for the button to link to and specify where the link should target. If you leave the URL field blank, Macromedia Dreamweaver automatically inserts a number sign. If you are working with a frames document, the frames appear in the targeting list.

5. Select whether you want the graphics for this element to be preloaded. This is generally recommended to prevent a potentially unattractive pause as the image loads for the first time during a rollover.

6. Select whether this element should initially be in the down state. Because the down state generally is used to indicate the current page, this allows you to set the initial page for the menu. Elements that have been set to show the down state initially have an asterisk by their names in the Nav Bar Elements list.

7. You can add as many navigation bar elements as desired by clicking the plus sign and following steps 2–6 for each.

> You can adjust elements up or down in the menu hierarchy or delete an element entirely by selecting it in the Nav Bar Elements list and using the up and down arrows or the minus (–) sign to delete them.

8. Select whether you want the navigation bar to run horizontally across the page or vertically down the page and if you want to use tables to create the layout.

After you have added all the navigation bar elements, click OK; the new navigation bar will appear on your Web page.

Editing the Navigation Bar

You can use only one navigation bar per Web page using Macromedia Dreamweaver, but you *can* change and add to the navigation bar as much as you want. You can edit the navigation bar in four ways:

- The Navigation Bar button
- The Properties panel
- Code view
- The Behaviors panel

Editing the Navigation Bar with the Navigation Bar Button

To edit the navigation bar using the Navigation Bar button, follow these steps:

1. Click the Navigation Bar button. You'll get an alert explaining that you can use only one navigation bar per Web page (see Figure 23.18).

Figure 23.18
Macromedia Dreamweaver will let you know you already have a navigation bar on this page and ask whether you want to edit the existing bar.

2. Click OK. The Modify Navigation Bar dialog box appears.

3. Make your changes, and click OK.

The only properties you can't change here are the navigation bar's orientation (horizontal or vertical) and whether it uses tables for layout.

Editing the Navigation Bar with the Properties Panel

If you want to edit the navigation bar via the Properties panel, follow these steps:

1. In Design view, select the image within the navigation bar you want to modify.

2. Move to the Properties panel and make any necessary modifications.

3. Save the file to update your changes.

The navigation bar will now function according to any changes you might have made.

Editing the Navigation Bar with Code View

Using Code view, you can edit the navigation bar directly into the JavaScript code. Readers uncomfortable with scripting might not want to use this method, but if you are skilled with scripting or want to experiment, you can open the code in Code view and type your changes directly into the document.

Editing the Navigation Bar with the Behaviors Panel

Each element in the navigation bar will have four events associated with it in the Behaviors panel: onMouseOver, onMouseOut, onClick, and onLoad. Each of these events has a Set Nav Bar action associated with it. You can edit the Set Nav Bar action for each of these separately by double-clicking the behavior to open the Set Nav Bar Image dialog box.

TROUBLESHOOTING

Java Applets and Rollovers

Why are Java applets for rollovers so problematic?

The answer is very simple: Applets tend to drain system resources to run, whereas JavaScript is quickly interpreted by the Web browser itself. So, if you have numerous images within the applet, the applet has to not only reload on each page, but execute as well.

Preloading Images

I've heard that preloading images is a recommended practice. Why is this so?

The answer is easy: speed. The preloading of images means that the browser caches these images, so when you move from page to page, they aren't downloaded again. This speeds up the entire navigation process yet provides your site visitors with a pleasant visual experience.

PEER TO PEER: ADVANCED CSS ROLLOVER TECHNIQUES

Although JavaScript and DHTML are perfectly acceptable for rollovers and navigation, with the improvement in browser rendering of CSS comes the opportunity to do some nice rollover techniques using CSS. As a result, you can use few or no images, which is very desirable for quick loading yet attractive Web sites.

CSS Edge is available at
http://www.meyerweb.com/
eric/css/edge/.

23

For an interesting look at CSS rollovers, visit Eric A. Meyer's CSS Edge, an experimental site for CSS on the edge.

There, you'll find two excellent examples of rollover techniques:

- **CSS pop-up using text**—This example, as shown in Figure 23.19, allows a remote rollover to occur using text.

- **CSS pop-up using images**—Instead of the remote rollover triggering text, in this case an image is triggered (see Figure 23.20).

⌐ Home link

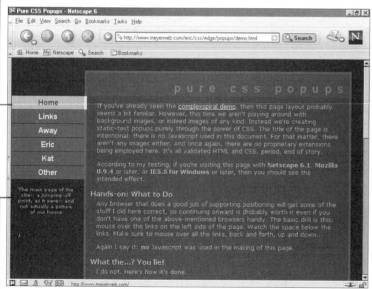

⌐ Rollover text

Figure 23.19
CSS rollovers using text.

Figure 23.20
CSS rollovers using images.

Home link

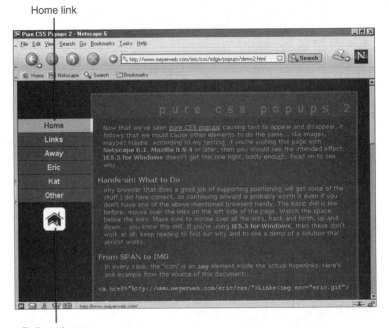

Rollover image

The method to create these techniques is clearly explained on Meyer's site. Open Code view and give it a try.

DRAW LAYERS AND ANIMATION

ABOUT DRAW LAYERS

As you discovered in Chapter 22, "Working with JavaScript and Behaviors," DHTML relies on Cascading Style Sheets (CSS) as much as it does on JavaScript. Using CSS, you have the power to position elements with much greater control.

CSS works on a foundation referred to as the *Box Model*, which is a model that controls how and where things within a browser window are displayed. By tapping into CSS, you can signify locations onscreen that can be absolutely positioned in relation to the page and other page components. This provides an alternative way to lay out Web pages and is the current recommended practice over using tables for layout.

With Draw Layers, you can set up a section containing graphics, text, forms, or any other markup elements and then position that box precisely within a page.

Dreamweaver Draw Layers provide special tools, not only to add and move these layers, but also to animate these layers, show and hide them, change their sizes, or even allow site visitors to move the Draw Layers around in their browser windows (see Figure 24.1).

> ## Caution
>
> It's very important not to confuse Macromedia Dreamweaver's use of the term *layers* with the Netscape `layer` and `ilayer` elements, which are proprietary, non-standard elements that have been dropped from Netscape 6.0 and higher. Please see the Peer to Peer section at the end of this chapter for more details.

Figure 24.1
A Draw Layer with content. This layer can be positioned anywhere you want in the browser window.

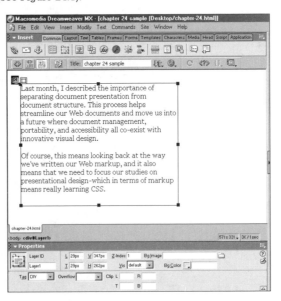

Draw Layers are created in markup using either a `div` or `span` element associated with an ID using CSS positioning. Within these divisions or spans, you can place any markup or JavaScript that would normally be placed within the body of a Web page (see Figure 24.2).

⇨ *To learn more about IDs, please see "Selectors: HTML, Classes, and IDs," p. 275.*

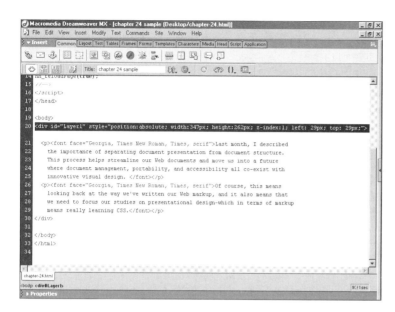

Figure 24.2
The markup used to create the Draw Layers includes the div element and id and style attributes.

CREATING DRAW LAYERS

You can have as many different Draw Layers as you want on a single Web page, each independently positioned. Macromedia Dreamweaver provides three ways to add Draw Layers to a Web page: Menu, Draw, and Drag and Drop.

To place a Draw Layer using the menu, follow these steps:

1. Open your document in Design or Code view.

2. Place your cursor at the point in the page where you want to add the Draw Layer.

3. Select Insert, Layer. A layer 115×200 pixels will be inserted there.

To create a Draw Layer using the Draw Layer tool, follow these steps:

1. Open your document in Design view.

2. Click the Draw Layer icon on the Common tab in the Insert bar.

3. Using the cross-hair, define the Draw Layer in Design view.

A Draw Layer of the dimensions created as you draw will be placed on the page (see Figure 24.3).

You can also drag and drop a Draw Layer. To do so, open your page in Design view and then drag the Draw Layer icon from the Insert panel to the design area. A Draw Layer 115×200 pixels will be placed on the page where you drop it.

In addition to the bounding box you just created, every other Draw Layer on the page is also represented by a small, square yellow icon in the upper-left corner of Design view. These icons appear in the order in which the layers appear in the HTML markup and are for use in Dreamweaver only—they do not show up when the Web page is presented in the Web browser—and are used to select layers in Macromedia Dreamweaver without having to directly click the layer itself. The more layers you add to a page, the more useful this is because layers can often be hard to distinguish when overlapping.

Figure 24.3
Use the Draw Layer tool to draw a layer in Design view. This gives you maximum control over the initial placement and size of the layer.

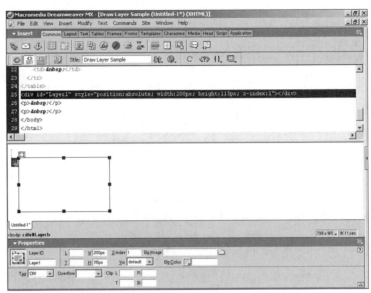

What's more, each layer has a selection handle in its upper-left corner and resizing handles (black squares) on all four sides and all four corners. You can move the layer around by dragging any of the edges of its bounding box (except on the resize handles) or the selection handle (see Figure 24.4).

Figure 24.4
A Draw Layer has been added to the page. Its bounding box (with selection handle and resizing handles) is shown along with the Draw Layer selector.

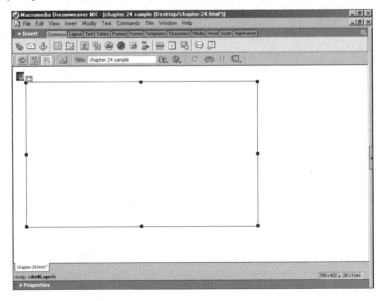

Macromedia Dreamweaver includes a panel to help you organize Draw Layers. With this panel, you can view and change a layer's features, including visibility state, name, and Z-Index.

To open the Layers panel, select Window, Others, Layers (see Figure 24.5).

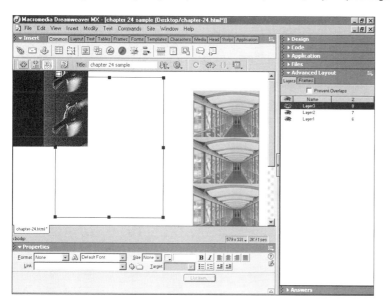

Figure 24.5
The Layers panel gives you easy access to a specific layer in your document.

Setting Up a Draw Layer

After the Draw Layer has been placed and selected, its attributes can be changed and manipulated in a variety of ways either directly in the code (using the Property inspector) or in the Layers panel. Draw Layer attributes are changed using the Property inspector or by hand using Code view (see Figure 24.6).

Naming a Layer

The Draw Layer name is a unique identifier given to each layer in a Web page and is assigned to the ID attribute. When a layer is first added, Dreamweaver automatically names it Layer 1, with each new layer given an increasing number.

> **Caution**
>
> Although you can give multiple Draw Layers (or other objects) the same name, the last one defined in the markup is the object that will actually use that name. To avoid confusion, Dreamweaver prevents you from using the Property inspector to change a Draw Layer's name to one that already exists.

Dreamweaver provides three ways to change a Draw Layer's name, including the Property inspector, the Layers panel, and Code view.

Figure 24.6
The Property inspector displays Draw Layer attributes.

To name a Draw Layer in the Layers panel, do the following:

1. Open the Layer panel under Advanced Layout or by selecting Window, Others, Layers (F2).

2. Double-click the name of the Draw Layer.

3. Type in the new name.

To properly name a Draw Layer using the Property inspector, follow these steps:

1. In Design View, click the Draw Layer icon you want to modify. The Property inspector will show the Draw Layer's properties.

2. Under Layer ID, you'll find a text box with the Draw Layer's name. Highlight the name.

3. Type in a new name.

4. Press the (Return) [Enter] key on your keyboard to update the name.

To name a Draw Layer using Code View, follow these steps:

1. Find the id attribute.

2. Highlight the attribute value within the quotation marks.

3. Type in the new name.

Although some designers might want to stick with Dreamweaver's default names during production for each Draw Layer, many designers prefer to customize the name at this stage of the game in such a way as to help identify its content or use during the production process.

Changing Element Type

Draw Layers can be created using either the span or div element, with the default being the div element. Because the div element is considered a block-level element, it places a hard return before and after the content. The span element is an inline element, so it can be used without the risk of a carriage return being entered. This means you can style elements in a paragraph without causing any line breaks.

To change the element type, you can use the Property inspector as follows:

1. In Code view, highlight the Draw Layer in question. The Property inspector is now available for modifying the Draw Layer.

2. Find the Tag drop-down menu, and click the drop-down arrow.

3. Select the element type you want to use.

Dreamweaver automatically rewrites the opening and closing tag to the element you've chosen.

Modifying Position (Left and Top)

The great advantage of using Draw Layers is that they can be absolutely positioned anywhere on the Web page—even off the currently visible area of the page. The position is set by defining how far from the top and left corners of the Web page the top and left corners of the Draw Layer should be placed. All content in the layer is displayed to the right and below that point (see Figure 24.7).

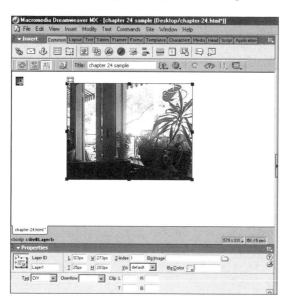

Figure 24.7
This layer has been positioned 25 pixels from the top and 123 pixels from the left.

You can define the position of the Draw Layer using Code view, Design view, and the Property inspector.

To define position in Code view, first locate the `style` attribute in the Draw Layer you want to modify. Depending on the document you're working with, you might already see the `left:` and `top:` properties, with related pixel values. If you do see these values, replace them with the ones you want. So, if you want your Draw Layer to be positioned 50 pixels from the left margin, you'd type in **left: 50px;**. To modify the top margin to be 10 pixels from the top, you'd type in **top: 10px;**. Save the file to update the changes.

To define a position using the Property inspector, do the following:

If you have more than one Draw Layer in your document (which, of course, is very likely), you can align those Draw Layers in a variety of common ways. To align two or more Draw Layers, select the Draw Layers and then select Modify, Align and the alignment option you want.

1. In Design view, select the Draw Layer by clicking its icon. The Property inspector for Draw Layers appears.

2. To modify the left value, find the L text box and input the pixel value you want, such as **50px**.

3. To modify the top value, find the T text box and input the appropriate pixel value, such as **10px**.

The Draw Layer bounding box will now move to the new location.

You can also modify the position by clicking and dragging in Design view. To do so, click but do not release any of the edges of the Draw Layer and move it to the desired position on the page. Alternatively, you can select the layer and then use the arrow keys to move it in 1 pixel increments or, if you hold the Shift key down while using the arrows, 10 pixel increments.

3D Positioning with Z-Index

In addition to the top and left positions, Draw Layers can be stacked on top of each other, just as a deck of cards is stacked together. The *Z-index* is a number (positive or negative) that defines the Draw Layer's stack position in ascending order in relation to other Draw Layers, with positive numbers being higher and negative numbers being lower.

Macromedia Dreamweaver automatically sets the first Draw Layer in the stack to a Z-index to 1 and the next layer to 2, and so on.

Modifying the stacking of Draw Layers is quite powerful because not only can you stack information directly on top of each other to use for hiding and unhiding page elements using scripting, which you'll put to practical use later in the chapter, but you can also offset Draw Layers so that portions of a given Draw Layer are visible in the stack.

As usual, there are several ways to change the Z-index. You can use Code view, the Property inspector, and the Layers panel. In Code view, find the element for the Draw Layer you want to modify and then simply replace the value in the Z-Index property. If no Z-index is available, you can type it in yourself. Either way, if you wanted a Draw Layer to have a Z-index of 10, the markup to use would look like this:

```
z-index:10;
```

To modify Z-index in the Property inspector, select the Draw Layer in question. When the Draw Layer properties appear, locate the Z-index textbox and type in a new value.

If two layers have the same Z-index, whichever one is defined last in the markup will be on top. You can also drag and drop layers in the Layers panel to change the Z-index much as you would layers in Photoshop.

If you want to change Z-index using the Layers panel, follow these steps:

1. Open the Layers panel by pressing F2.

2. Double-click the Draw Layer you want to modify. A live text box appears beneath the Z.

3. Type in the new value.

In Design view, you can move a Draw Layer's icon to change its stacking order in relation to other layers with the same Z-index. To do so, click the icon, move it to the left or right, and drop it. Moving it to the right moves it up in the stacking order, whereas moving the icon to the left moves it down (see Figure 24.8).

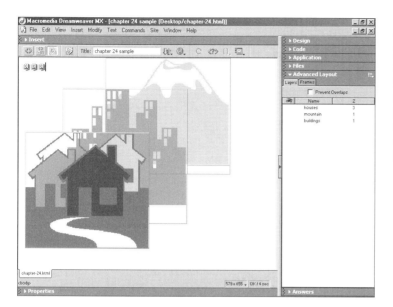

Figure 24.8
These three layers (houses, buildings, and mountains) have been stacked on top of each other. The houses have the highest stacking order, so they appear on top. The mountains and buildings have the same Z-index, but the buildings come last in the markup, so they appear on top.

24

Working with Width and Height

Draw Layers have a specific width and height that define how the content in the Draw Layer should be formatted for display. For example, if the width is set to 200 pixels, content is placed in a column 200 pixels wide. However, the height value is used only to demonstrate how the overflow should be treated, which is discussed later in this section.

> If you're using a graphic that is larger than the Draw Layer you create, the width and height will be ignored, and the graphic will take whatever space is needed in order to display.

You can set the width and height of a Draw Layer in the familiar three ways, using Code view, the Property inspector, or directly in Design view.

In Code view, locate the tag for the Draw Layer and replace the width and height style values with the pixel values defining the new dimensions. So, if you wanted your Draw Layer to be 200 pixels wide and 200 pixels high, your markup within the div or span for that Draw Layer would read as follows:

```
width:200px; height:200px;
```

Using the Property inspector, select the Draw Layer; then replace the width (W) and height (H) values with the pixel value defining the new dimensions for the Draw Layer. You will see the Draw Layer resize in Design view to correspond to the new dimensions.

When working in Design view, simply click and hold any of the resize handles on the edges of the Draw Layer and drag it up or down to the desired size; then release it (see Figure 24.9).

Figure 24.9
Grabbing a resize handle enables you to resize on that side or corner. Here, the selected houses area is being resized.

Resize handles

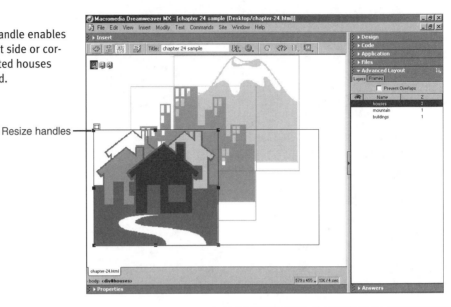

Making Draw Layers the Same Width or Height

You can set multiple Draw Layers to be the same height and width. Select the Draw Layers, using (Shift-click) [Ctrl+click] to select multiple layers, and then select Modify, Align, Make Same Width or Make Same Height. All the selected Draw Layers are set to the width or height of the last layer selected in that group.

Defining Visibility with Clipping

In addition to having a width and height, Draw Layers can also have their four sides clipped. Clipping enables you to define which area of the Draw Layer will be visible onscreen. Imagine cutting a rectangular hole in a piece of paper and placing it onto the Draw Layer. If the hole is smaller than the Draw Layer, the edges of the Draw Layer are not visible behind the paper.

Clipping is frequently used with scripting to hide or unhide portions of objects during dynamic operations within the browser. A clip is defined in pixels from the top, left, bottom, and right sides of the Draw Layer. As with dimensions, the clip is subject to what you do with the overflow (see Figure 24.10).

If you want to see a great example of clipping in action, check out the clipping demo at http://www.yasd.com/tutorials/xobjects/clip.htm.

Caution

Browser support for overflow is inconsistent. For example, Internet Explorer 4 does not have this feature, whereas II 6 does.

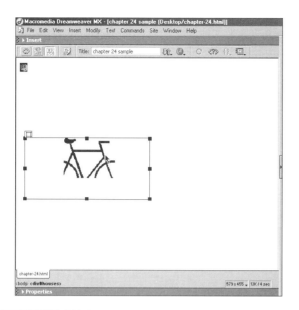

Figure 24.10
In this image, the bike's tires have been clipped off.

About Overflow

If the content of a Draw Layer does not fit within the width and height set or within the clipping area set, the parts not showing are referred to as *overflow*. You can set one of four ways to treat the overflow content for a particular Draw Layer:

- **Visible**—This setting basically ignores the dimension and clip settings and shows the overflow anyway.

- **Hidden**—The overflow is completely hidden and cannot be viewed without the use of scripting.

- **Scroll**—Places horizontal or vertical scrollbars around the Draw Layer to view the overflow content (see Figure 24.11).

- **Auto**—Places horizontal or vertical scrollbars around the Draw Layer as needed to view the overflow content.

Background Images and Background Color

You can add a lot of visual interest to your designs by adding images and colors to the background of Draw Layers. These backgrounds and colors can be completely different from full-page backgrounds.

To add a background color to a Draw Layer, do the following:

1. In Design view, select the Draw Layer to which you want to add a background color.

2. In the Property inspector, find the BgColor option. You'll see two options there: a pop-up palette and a text box.

3. Use the palette by clicking the arrow. When the palette appears, use the eyedropper to select your color. Or, you can simply type the hexadecimal value or color name you want to use directly into the color text box.

Figure 24.11
Although the layer has been clipped, the scrollbars enable you to view the rest of the bike.

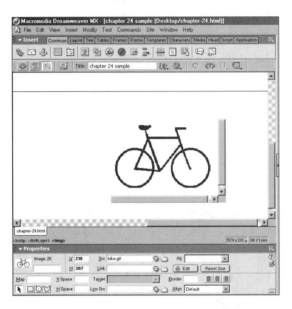

The background color of your Draw Layer will now update. If you'd prefer to add a background image, follow these steps:

1. Select the Draw Layer.

2. Locate the BgImage text box. You'll notice a text box and a folder icon.

3. If you know the path and filename of your background image, simply type it into the text box. If you don't know the location, click the folder, browse your hard drive, select the file, and click (Open) [OK].

Visibility

Draw Layers can be either visible or hidden when the Web page first loads. Then, JavaScript can be used to make the Draw Layer active.

There are four values for Draw Layers. Table 24.1 describes the values and their actions.

Caution

You can use any supported graphic type, including PNG, for a Draw Layer background, but there is a concern with PNG in that although Internet Explorer 5 Mac supports PNG alpha channels (transparency), it does not support alpha channels for PNGs in a Draw Layers background. No other browsers support PNG alpha channels for any use. So, if you want to try making a transparent image, you have to use GIF format.

Table 24.1   Draw Layer Values

Value	Action
Default	No visibility value, Draw Layer is visible when the page loads.
Hidden	The Draw Layer is not displayed when the page loads.
Visible	The Draw Layer is displayed when the page loads.
Inherit	The Draw Layer uses whatever visibility is set for the surrounding Draw Layer or the body of the Web. If no visibility is set in surrounding Draw Layers, the Draw Layer will be visible.

Dreamweaver provides three ways to add or modify the initial visibility of an element. You can use Code view, the Property inspector, or the Layers panel.

To change the visibility using Code view, follow these steps:

1. Locate the div or span element for the Draw Layer in question.

2. If there is no visibility property, add the property and value. So, if you wanted the visibility to be inherited, you'd write

   visibility: inherit;

3. If a visibility property already exists and you want to change it, simply highlight the property value and type in the value.

➪ *To learn more about inheritance, please see the sidebar "Inheriting Properties," p. 280.*

Hidden Draw Layers do not show up onscreen at all until a JavaScript action has been added to allow them to do so.

24

To change the attributes of multiple layers simultaneously in the Property inspector, select the Draw Layer either in Design view or in the Layers panel and then (Shift-click) [Ctrl+click] additional layers. Changes made in the Property inspector will affect all selected layers.

The visibility property is now updated. If you'd prefer to use the Property inspector, here's how:

1. Select the Draw Layer icon in Design view, or highlight the Draw Layer's div or span element in Code view.

2. In the Property inspector, click the Vis menu arrow and select the value from the drop-down menu.

The visibility property will update.

To use the Layers panel, open the panel, found under Advanced Layout (F2). Then, click the space found to the left of the Draw Layer name. Keep clicking, toggling through the three states: blank (default), eye (visible), and closed eye (hidden).

Setting Global Draw Layer Preferences

You can create your own default settings for Draw Layers using the Edit menu. Select Edit, Preferences, and then highlight the Layer option. Set preferences from the list to determine the default values for the element type, visibility, width, height, background color, and background image. In addition, check whether you want Draw Layers that are inserted into other Draw Layers to automatically be nested and whether you want to include a bug fix to make the layers more compatible with Netscape 4.

Adding Content to a Draw Layer

Content is added to Draw Layers the same way it is added to any other part of a Web page. This means you can type directly into Draw Layers, copy and paste, drag and drop, use the Insert panel, and so on.

Nesting Layers

Draw Layers can be placed inside other Draw Layers. As when you place a table within another table, or a list within a list, this technique is referred to as *nesting*. A Draw Layer nested inside another Draw Layer moves with the primary (also referred to as *parent*) Draw Layer and inherits the primary Draw Layer's visibility if set to do so. Nested layers position themselves to the upper-left corner of the parent Draw Layer, not to the upper-left corner of the Web page.

Nesting is especially useful for grouping like elements together, such as background or foreground elements. These elements can then be controlled independently or as a group using scripting, allowing for animation and dynamic events (see Figure 24.12).

Figure 24.12
The three background elements (houses, buildings, and mountains) have been nested inside a layer called Background.

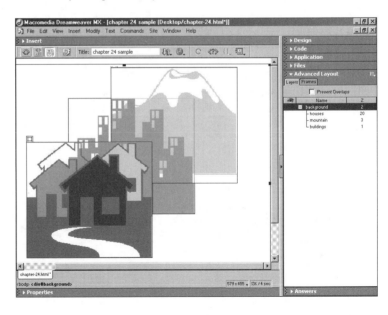

Dreamweaver provides three ways to add a nested Draw Layer into an existing Draw Layer. You can

- Place the cursor in a Draw Layer and select Insert, Layer. The new Draw Layer will appear inside the primary Draw Layer at the mouse cursor.

- Drag the Draw Layer icon from the Insert panel and drop it in an existing Draw Layer at the point you want the nested Draw Layer to appear.

- Select the Draw Layer tool from the Insert panel and draw a new Draw Layer inside an existing Draw Layer. If Nesting is turned off (see the sidebar titled "Setting Global Draw Layer Preferences," later in this chapter) then press and hold the (Option) [Alt] key to create a nested Draw Layer.

> **Caution**
>
> Netscape 4 has a severe bug when working with nested layers. To overcome the bug, Dreamweaver provides the Netscape Resize Fix, which can be turned on from the Layers Preferences or directly using Commands, Add/Remove Netscape Resize Fix.

In addition, you might have Draw Layers that have already been created that need to be nested in another Draw Layer. In the Layers panel (F2), select the Draw Layer you want to nest in another Draw Layer, press and hold the (Command) [Ctrl] key, and drag and drop it onto the Draw Layer in which you want it nested. The nested Draw Layer will now appear indented under its parent Draw Layer.

Preventing Layers from Overlapping

So, if Draw Layers can be independently positioned, they can overlap each other. This can be problematic because the overlapping content may become unreadable.

Dreamweaver allows you to prevent this from happening while you are creating your Web page by turning on the Prevent Overlaps feature. If you turn this on by checking the option on the Layer panel (F2) or by selecting Modify, Arrange, Prevent Layer Overlaps, Dreamweaver will not allow you to place one layer over another.

Layers will instead slip around each other in Design view while you are moving and sizing them, but this does not reflow layers that were overlapped before you turned on Prevent Overlapping.

Converting from 3.0 Draw Layers

If you are upgrading from Dreamweaver 3 to 5, the layers you added in your older pages might not work properly. However, conversion is a snap. Open the old Dreamweaver 3 file and select File, Convert, 3.0 Browser Compatible. In the dialog box, select your conversion options and click OK. Dreamweaver opens the converted file as a new, untitled document.

24

ADDING BEHAVIORS TO A DRAW LAYER

It's one thing to create a Draw Layer and add content to it, but a Draw Layer really comes to life when you add behaviors to it.

A few special behaviors are used exclusively with Draw Layers that you should consider: Showing, Hiding, and Dragging.

Showing and Hiding Draw Layers

Unlike images, Draw Layers cannot simply have their sources changed in order to change their appearance. Instead, Draw Layers must have their visibility changed to make them either hidden or visible, and you can turn on one layer while turning off another layer.

To add the Show-Hide behavior to control a layer's visibility, do the following:

1. Select an image or a link on the Web page (either in or out of a layer), and in the Behaviors panel, select the Show-Hide Layer behavior from the Add Behavior drop-down (see Figure 24.13).

Figure 24.13
Add the Show-Hide behavior to the Draw layer.

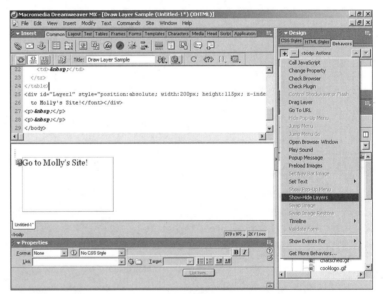

2. In the Show-Hide dialog box that appears, select the Draw Layer you want to influence (it does not have to be the one the image or link is in), and then choose whether you want to make that layer show, hide, or use the default display.

3. Click OK. The behavior is now associated with the image or link you selected in step 1.

Text links default to using the `onClick` event, whereas images default to using the `onLoad` event. When the event is triggered, the Draw Layer is either hidden or shown (see Figure 24.14).

Figure 24.14
When the mountain is clicked, it disappears. When the buildings are clicked, the mountain reappears.

Dragging a Draw Layer

Draw Layers can be set by you to be repositioned by your site visitors, giving them a great deal of customization power. You've no doubt seen similar applications on portal pages, where you can move information boxes around the page to suit your tastes.

A site visitor simply clicks the Draw Layer, and the Draw Layer can be freely repositioned on the Web page.

The Drag Layer behavior is either on or not, so it is best associated with the onLoad event handler for the Web page or an element in the Draw Layer being moved. To add repositioning capability for a Draw Layer, follow these steps:

1. Select an image or a link on the Web page either in or out of a layer. In the Behaviors panel, select the Drag Layer behavior from the Add Behavior drop-down, which opens the Drag Layer dialog box.

2. In the dialog box you'll find two tabs, Basic and Advanced. In the Basic tab, select the Draw Layer you want to have dragged (see Figure 24.15).

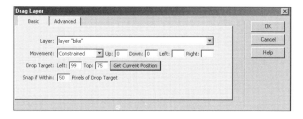

Figure 24.15
These are Basic options for a dragged layer. The motion has been constrained so that the object will only move left and right.

3. Choose whether the motion should be unconstrained (the site visitor will be able to move it anywhere on the screen) or constrained (if constrained, set the maximum amount the Draw Layer can move up, down, left, or right from its current position).

4. Enter the target zone for dropping the Draw Layer and whether the Draw Layer should snap into the target zone if it's within a certain number of pixels.

5. In the Advanced tab, select which part of the element can be clicked to be dragged (either the object generating the event or the entire Draw Layer).

6. Select whether the Draw Layer should be brought to the front as the user drags it and dropped to the back once she releases it. Then, any JavaScript will be executed to create these drag features.

7. Click OK.

The behavior is now associated with the image or link you selected in step 1 (see Figure 24.16).

Figure 24.16
The bike can be dragged back and forth. Its movement has been constrained so that it will not move up or down, only left to right. We don't want the bike flying off the page!

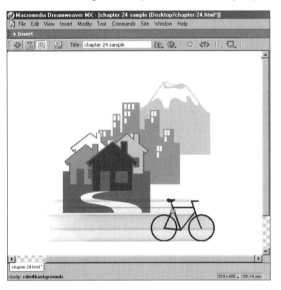

Text links default to using the onClick event, whereas images default to using the onLoad event. The layer can now be moved about the screen.

ANIMATING LAYERS WITH THE TIMELINE

Most people are familiar with traditional cell animation, which works by rapidly flipping a series of still image frames—replacing the previous image with a new slightly different image—to create the illusion of movement. This is, in fact, how GIF animation works as well. A GIF animation is simply a stack of images that rapidly appear and disappear. If this is done fast enough, the human eye does not notice that every few tenths of a second a new image is appearing and instead sees a fluid action.

Animation using Draw Layers and JavaScript (DHTML animation) does *not* work this way. Instead, DHTML animation moves an object (usually a Draw Layer) slightly (maybe only by a few pixels) and then moves it again and again and again. If done quickly enough, say every few tenths of a second or so, this creates the illusion that the Draw Layer is moving.

Although the results of the two methods are a moving image, both methods have their strengths and weaknesses. DHTML animation is more processor intensive, meaning that the audience member's computer controls how smooth the animation is. However, DHTML animations result in smaller file sizes and thus are faster to download than GIF animations because only one graphic or HTML text is used. In addition, DHTML animations are easier to make changes to, enable you to change the visible area, visibility, and Z-index of the objects, and can be controlled by the end user.

Understanding the Timeline Window

DHTML animations in Dreamweaver are controlled using a timeline, and, although it does not use frames to create the animation, Dreamweaver's timeline uses a frame metaphor to control the animation. This makes sense because, as mentioned, most people are familiar with frame-based animation. Just keep in mind that, although it looks like you're doing cell (also known as *frame*) animation, the technology is different.

One important difference between frame animation and DHTML animation using a timeline, however, is that you can have multiple objects animated in a single timeline using DHTML.

24

The timeline (Shift+F9) is set up as a grid with animation channels running horizontally and frames running vertically. Table 24.2 describes timeline features and their associated actions.

Table 24.2 Timeline Features

Timeline	Timeline Action
Animation Channel	An animation channel can contain only a single Draw Layer at a time (over a series of frames). You can add as many Draw Layers as you want to different animation channels over the same frames, and you can add multiple Draw Layers to the same animation channel, but not in the same frames.
Frame	This is an individual point in the animation. The more frames shown per second, the smoother the animation will be, but the more processor intensive it will be (see the Frames Per Second entry later in this table).
Timeline Name	A single Web page can have multiple timeline-based animations, each of which can be named. Move between different timelines on the page using the pop-up menu.
Playhead	Shows the current frame being displayed in Design view. Move this back and forth to scrub (play) through the animation. Changes made will be made to the frame currently under the playhead.

Table 24.2 Continued

Timeline	Timeline Action
Playhead controls	Allow you to move the playhead to the beginning of the animation or move frame by frame forward or backward in the animation. Hold down these controls to play the animation forward or backward. You can also type the frame number to which you want to move directly into the frame field.
Frames Per Second (fps)	Set how many frames will be played in a second. The higher this number, the smoother the animation. Obviously, the higher the fps, the faster the animation will play. At 15fps, 60 frames play in 4 seconds, but at 20fps the same animation plays in 3 seconds. In addition, a higher fps requires more processor time to display the frames more quickly. Whether this will be a problem depends on the user's computer. If she has a slower computer, the animation might actually end up looking jerky.
Autoplay	Check this, and Dreamweaver adds an `onLoad` event to have the animation play as soon as the page is loaded into the browser.
Loop	Check this, and the animation loops continuously until the page is unloaded.
Animation Bar	A light blue bar displayed in an animation channel to show the length of a particular animation for a particular Draw Layer.
Keyframe	Within an animation bar, frames where you want to set a new action to take place are indicated with a small white circle. These are referred to as keyframes.
Behavior Channel	In addition to the animation channels, each frame has a behavior channel where behaviors can be added at certain points while the timeline is running. (For more on behaviors, see Chapter 22.)

Figure 24.17 shows the timeline and its associated features.

Figure 24.17
The Dreamweaver timeline.

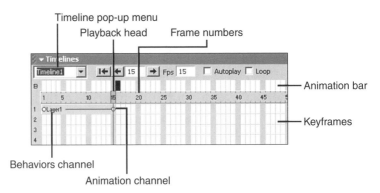

Adding and Changing Draw Layers Within the Timeline

A timeline starts as a blank slate. To create animations, one or more Draw Layers have to be added to it from the Web page.

To add a Draw Layer to the timeline, follow these steps:

1. With your Web page open in Design view, select Window, Timelines (Option-F9) [Alt+F9] to open the Timeline window.

2. Select a Draw Layer.

3. In the timeline, set the playhead to the frame at which you want to begin the animation for the object.

4. Select Add Object from the panel menu.

The Draw Layer appears in the timeline. You can alternatively drag a Draw Layer from Design view into the timeline (see Figure 24.18). Then, release the Draw Layer onto the desired animation channel and frame.

Caution

You will not be able to add a Draw Layer into frames of an animation channel already occupied by another object, and you will not be able to drop the same object into the frames of a different animation channel if it is already in those frames on another animation channel.

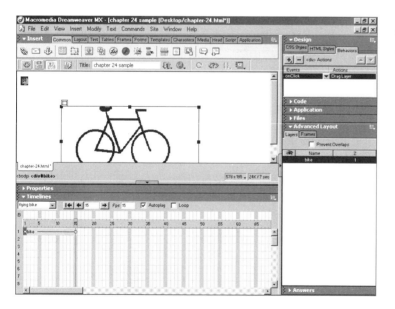

Figure 24.18
The Draw Layer being dragged onto the timeline.

You can modify Draw Layers within the timeline. These methods include

- **Delete**—Select a Draw Layer in the timeline, and then select Delete or Remove Object from the panel's pop-up menu.

- **Copy and Paste**—You can also copy, cut, or paste objects within the timeline using the panel's pop-up menu.

■ **Change**—Select a Draw Layer within the Timeline, and then select Change Object from the panel pop-up menu. Select a new Draw Layer to take this Draw Layer's place in the timeline.

All behaviors and motion associated with the previous Draw Layer will be transferred to the replacement Draw Layer.

Creating a Timeline Animation

Now that you have Draw Layers added to the timeline, you can begin to animate them, adding energy and interactivity to your design.

To determine how long an animation will last, divide the total number of frames by the number of frames per second being displayed.

Adding Motion

To precisely add motion using the timeline, you must create a straight line defined by beginning and end points.

To set up your animation's beginning and end points, follow these steps:

1. Click the end point keyframe marker of the animation bar and drag it to the right as far as you want the animation to last. You can change this later (making the animation longer or shorter as desired), but it is best to allow yourself plenty of space in the animation bar to work with.

➪ *To learn more about keyframes and animation, please see Chapter 24, "Draw Layers and Animation," p. 445.*

2. Add a keyframe to the timeline at the point you want the motion to begin and another keyframe for where you want the motion to end. To add keyframes in the timeline, place the playhead over the frame you want the keyframe in, select the animation bar or bars you want to add keyframes to at that point, and then select Add Keyframe from the panel pop-up menu. The frame becomes a keyframe indicated by a white circle. You can also, of course, use existing keyframes in the timeline rather than inserting new ones.

3. With the playhead on the end point keyframe for the animation, reposition the Draw Layer you want animated using one of these methods:

   ● In Design view, select the Draw Layer to be animated and change its top or left position using the Property inspector.

   ● In Design view, click and drag the Draw Layer to the desired position. You could also use the arrow keys to move the Draw Layer 1 pixel or hold down the Shift key to move 10 pixels at a time.

4. Repeat steps 2 and 3 as many times as desired to create curved motion.

5. After you have finished, click and hold the Next Frame button in the timeline to play the animation. At any time, you can adjust the position of the Draw Layer by clicking a keyframe and then use the methods previously mentioned to adjust it (see Figure 24.19).

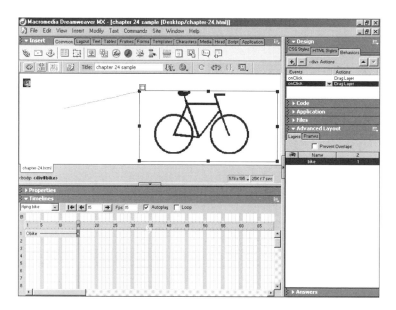

Figure 24.19
The Draw Layer with the bike has been moved across the screen. Notice that its animation path is indicated by a gray line.

After the timeline has been set up, if you did not check the Autoplay option in the Timeline panel, you will need to add a behavior to start the animation (see the section "Starting and Stopping the Animation," later in this chapter).

⇨*Unable to make changes to a Draw Layer? Find out why in "Draw Layers Versus Objects" in the "Troubleshooting" section later in this chapter.*

Tracing a Draw Layer's Path

Although you can precisely control the movement of a Draw Layer using the methods previously mentioned, an easier way to plot a complex movement for a Draw Layer is to have Dreamweaver trace its path as you move the Draw Layer around in the Design view.

To trace a path, follow these steps:

1. In Design view or the Timeline panel, select the Draw Layer to which you want to add a motion path.

2. In the Timeline panel pop-up menu, select Record Path of Layer.

3. Click and drag the Draw Layer around in Design view. As you drag, Dreamweaver adds keyframes to the timeline, recording the path you are following. After you are finished, release the mouse button.

The path will be plotted as the Draw Layer is moved around (see Figure 24.20).

Figure 24.20
Each dot represents a keyframe in the timeline for the plotted path.

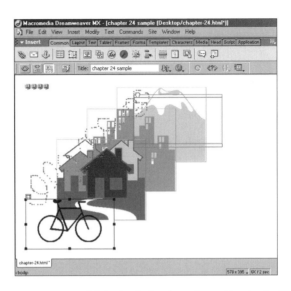

After the timeline has been set up, if you didn't check the Autoplay option in the Timeline panel, you will need to add a behavior to start the animation.

Changing Visibility, Size, and Stacking in the Timeline

In addition to changing a Draw Layer's position, you can also use keyframes to control other important attributes. Place the playhead on a keyframe or insert a keyframe at the spot you need (Command-click) [Ctrl+click] a frame), and then select a Draw Layer in the Timeline panel or Design view. Then, select the desired visibility state, Draw Layer size (width and height), clip, and Z-index in the Property inspector.

Adding Behaviors to a Timeline

Animated objects can have particular behaviors associated with specific frames in the timeline. This is a little different from adding behaviors to an object on the page because it does not use a JavaScript event. Instead, Dreamweaver adds a frame-specific event to trigger the action for the behavior when a particular frame in the timeline is run.

To add a behavior to a timeline, follow these steps:

1. In the Timeline panel, select the frame to which you want to add a behavior.

2. Select Add Behavior from the Timeline pop-up menu, and you will be alerted to immediately add a behavior.

3. In the Behaviors panel (Shift+F3), select the Add Behaviors drop-down list and add any desired behavior you require—adding JavaScript or checking for a browser. Follow the instructions for that behavior.

The action associated with the behavior is triggered whenever this frame is encountered in the timeline (see Figure 24.21).

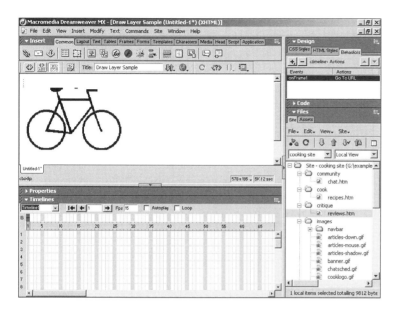

Figure 24.21
When a behavior exists for a frame, the Behavior channel has a light blue rectangle with a line through it in that frame. You can see this by opening your copy of Dreamweaver MX.

Are you finding that the behaviors are grayed out when you try to add one to your timeline? Check out "Activating the Behaviors Menu" in the "Troubleshooting" section of this chapter.

Starting and Stopping the Animation

After an animation has been created in the timeline, you can have it automatically play when the Web page loads either by checking the Autoplay option in the Timeline panel or by adding a behavior to the page to start and stop the timeline playing.

The start and stop options available include

- **Go to Timeline Frame**—This behavior enables you to move the animation forward or backward to a particular frame in an animation and then loop between the behavior and that frame as many times as you want.

- **Start Timeline**—Assign this behavior to a link or an image to turn it into an on button for a particular animation.

- **Stop Timeline**—Assign this behavior to a link or an image to stop a currently running animation. You should not assign a Start Timeline and Stop Timeline behavior to the same image or link using the same event because the last one will always be used. For example, if you assign onClick to start the animation and then use onClick again (with the same object) to stop the animation, the animation will not run.

> Timeline behaviors can be triggered within the timeline itself (see the section "Adding Behaviors to a Timeline," previously in this chapter).

You can associate multiple timeline behaviors from a single link or image, but each will have to be set up separately.

TROUBLESHOOTING

Draw Layers Versus Objects

I am having problems when trying to make changes to a Draw layer. What could be going on?

When clicking a Draw layer to select it, be sure you have clicked the Draw layer itself and not selected an object within it; otherwise, you will not be able to make changes. If you have selected the layer, the Draw Layer icon will be highlighted in the upper-left corner of the Design view and a selection box will appear above the Draw layer on the left side.

Activating the Behaviors Menu

I'm trying to add a behavior to the timeline, but all my options are grayed out. What's the problem?

You likely have an object selected somewhere in the timeline, markup, or Design view. Deselect your element and try again; the menu options should all be available now.

PEER TO PEER: NETSCAPE LAYERS VERSUS DREAMWEAVER DRAW LAYERS

If you've worked with DHTML before, you have probably heard of or used the `layer` element. This was a special element Netscape added to its version 4 browsers that was in many ways similar to Draw Layers—but they are *not* the same thing.

Netscape layers use one of two special elements instead of the `div` or `span` elements. The elements are

- `layer`—An independently positioned layer much like a Draw Layer that has been positioned

- `ilayer`—An inline layer that can be controlled and positioned, but is positioned with the rest of the content on the page

Although Dreamweaver allows you to define Draw Layers as Netscape layers using either of these elements, be aware that these are proprietary elements to Netscape—and then only in 4.x versions of the browser.

These elements *do not work* in any version of Internet Explorer or Netscape 6. IE never adopted the `layer` elements, and in a very interesting turn of events, Netscape chose to leave support for these elements out of its generation 6.0 browsers. Why? Because in an effort to support Web standards as defined by the W3C, Netscape chose to leave its own proprietary elements out of the new browser and focus instead on better compliance via nonproprietary elements, improved CSS, and an improved DOM.

Using the `div` and `span` elements in Dreamweaver Draw Layers is a recommended practice and will work in all modern browsers—Internet Explorer 4.0 and higher, some Netscape versions 4, Netscape versions 6.0 and higher, as well as browser such as Opera and OmniWeb.

24

VI

ADDING MULTIMEDIA

IN THIS PART

WORKING WITH PLUG-INS AND JAVA APPLETS

IN THIS CHAPTER

PLUG-INS

Although client-side scripting is a versatile way of extending Web pages beyond the capabilities of standard HTML/XHTML, browser plug-ins, ActiveX controls, and Java applets take client-side functionality a step further, enabling you to add multimedia and dynamic interaction features to your site. Some examples of this include navigation items, interactive menus, and slide shows. This chapter shows you how to add them to your pages.

Plug-ins have been an indispensable part of the Web experience for years now. *Plug-ins* are small programs that extend the capabilities of the browser beyond what could be accomplished otherwise. Like most programs, plug-ins work only on the platform for which they are designed. This means users must download a plug-in specific to their platforms (Windows, Mac, UNIX, and others) to view the specialty content the plug-in facilitates.

When you use a plug-in on a Web page, you are not actually embedding the plug-in itself into the document. Instead, you're simply inserting a reference to a content file with a specific multipurpose Internet mail extension (MIME) type. The browser then uses the MIME type to determine which plug-in to use to play the content. Unfortunately, this means that only one plug-in can be installed to play back a particular MIME type. For example, the multimedia player wars between Apple, Microsoft, and Real Networks, among others, have all produced plug-ins that can play back many of the same file formats, so you can never know for sure which player a particular user has installed.

25 | Checking for Plug-ins

If you're writing a page that supports plug-in content, you'll need a means to detect whether a user's browser has the plug-in installed or even has a browser capable of running it (see Table 25.1). An easy way to detect plug-ins is with the use of a Dreamweaver behavior. Both the Check Browser and Check Plugin behaviors can be attached to a link or a body tag to provide an alternative page to use if the plug-in can't be supported.

⇨ *To learn about behaviors, see Chapter 22, "Working with JavaScript and Behaviors," p. 415.*

⇨ *Is the Check Plugin behavior not working? Find out the reason why and what to do about it in "Checking for a Plug-in" in the "Troubleshooting" section of this chapter.*

Will My User Have the Right Plug-in?

When you use Dreamweaver to insert a plug-in, you are really just inserting the content. The browser determines the appropriate plug-in to use to play the content. If a plug-in to play the content isn't available, the user must download and install it to view your content. You can use the Check Plugin behavior to do this, or at least give the user information about any plug-ins required to view your content. One solution is to create a link to its download site using the icon of the plug-in.

Table 25.1 Common Plug-ins

Name	Use	URL
Apple QuickTime	The Apple QuickTime plug-in plays a variety of multimedia content formats, including QuickTime audio, video, and VR panoramas.	`http://www.apple.com/quicktime/download/`
Adobe Acrobat Reader	Adobe Acrobat is a popular format for transmitting documents over the Web.	`http://www.adobe.com/products/acrobat/readstep2.html`
Macromedia Flash and Shockwave	The most popular format for creating vector and image-based animations on the Web.	`http://www.macromedia.com/software/flashplayer/`
Macromedia Shockwave	An advanced multimedia format used for graphics, audio and video, and even games.	`http://www.macromedia.com/software/shockwaveplayer/`
RealOne Player	The latest version of Real Network's player plug-in for many multimedia formats, including Real Audio, Real Video, and MP3.	`http://www.real.com/realone/index.html`
Windows Media Player	Plays popular audio and video formats, including MP3, AVI, Windows Media Audio (WMA), and Active Streaming Format (ASF).	`http://www.microsoft.com/Windows/windowsmedia/download/plugin.asp`

25

Embedding a Plug-in

To embed plug-in content into a page, do one of the following:

- Place the cursor where you want the plug-in content to be inserted in the document. Click the Plugin button in the Media tab of the Insert bar (see Figure 25.1).

- Drag the Plugin icon to the location on the page that you want to embed the content.

- Place the cursor where you want to insert the control, and select Insert, Media, Plugin from the menu.

A plug-in placeholder is inserted into your document.

Figure 25.1
The Media category is used to insert all supported plug-in types.

Setting Plug-in Properties

Click the plug-in's placeholder in Design view to open the Plugin Property inspector (see Figure 25.2).

Figure 25.2
The Plugin Property inspector allows you to preview the plug-in in Design view.

The following plug-in options are available:

- **Plugin Name**—The Name property sets the name of the plug-in, which identifies the tag for scripting.

- **Width and Height**—The W and H properties enable you to change the displayed dimensions of the plug-in. The default units used are pixels, but you also can specify the size in alternative units: pc (picas), pt (points), in (inches), mm (millimeters), cm (centimeters), or % for a percentage of the page's dimensions.

- **Src**—The Src property specifies the data file to play with the plug-in. This contains the filename you chose in the Select Netscape Plug-in File dialog box in the previous step.

> The align, vspace, and hspace attributes are not available for use in transitional document types. If you are using HTML or XHTML strict documents or XHTML 1.1, these presentational issues should be placed into a style sheet.

- **Plg Url**—The Plg Url property specifies the URL of the site where the user can download the plug-in. If an appropriate plug-in to play the data file is not installed, the browser attempts to download it from this location.

- **Align**—The Align property sets how the applet should be aligned on the page. The various alignment options are the same as those for images and other elements and are covered in those chapters specific to those elements.

- **V and H Space**—You can use the V Space and H Space properties to set the amount of blank space bordering the plug-in. These values must be in pixels.

- **Border**—The Border property is used to specify the width of a border to put around the plug-in.

Setting Plug-in Parameters

The Parameters button on the Plugin Property inspector activates the Parameters dialog box (see Figure 25.3). The Parameters dialog box lets you enter any custom parameters that the control might need. These parameters will be specified by the documentation or sample HTML code that comes with the plug-in developer's documentation.

Parameters are special attributes of the plug-in's embed tag.

> **Caution**
> The use of embed is problematic in terms of standards because it doesn't exist in any recommended version of HTML or XHTML. Some very advanced workarounds are available, such as writing your own DTD (beyond the scope of this book), but alternatives do exist. See the "Troubleshooting" section at the end of this chapter for alternative options for embedding plug-ins.

To enter a parameter, do the following:

1. Click the Plus (+) button.

2. Enter the name of the parameter in the Parameter column.

3. Enter a value in the Value column.

You also can remove parameters, using the Minus (–) button, or rearrange parameters by clicking one and moving it up or down in the order using the arrow buttons.

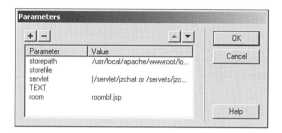

Figure 25.3
The Parameters dialog box is used to enter custom parameters for any type of plug-in, control, or applet.

ACTIVEX CONTROLS

ActiveX controls were developed by Microsoft using its Component Object Model (COM) for the Windows platform. ActiveX controls perform much of the same functions as plug-ins, but they are limited to Internet Explorer 3.0 or higher on the Windows platform. Netscape cannot run ActiveX controls without the aid of a third-party add-on.

25

Given the limitations of ActiveX controls, you might wonder why you would want to use them at all. The truth is that it makes sense to provide the ActiveX version of a plug-in when possible. Often, an ActiveX control provides more flexibility than its plug-in counterpart. Also, you can write your page in such a way that the ActiveX control is used on the Windows platform and the Netscape plug-in on others transparently, thereby providing the best possible experience to your site visitors no matter which browser they are using.

To find recent ActiveX controls, check out C:Net's Download.Com section for components, at http://download.com.com/ 2001-2206-0.html.

For more information on developing ActiveX, see the Microsoft Developer Network's section on ActiveX Controls, at http:// msdn.microsoft.com/ workshop/components/ activex/intro.asp?frame= true.

ActiveX controls are developed using languages such as Visual Basic, C++, or even Java, but you don't need to know any of these programming languages to use ready-made ActiveX controls on your pages.

Adding an ActiveX Control

To add an ActiveX control to a page, do one of the following:

- Place the cursor where you want the control to be inserted in the document. Click the ActiveX button in the Media tab of the Insert bar.

- Drag the ActiveX icon from the Insert bar to the location on the page that you want to embed the control.

■ Place the cursor where you want to insert the control, and select Insert, Media, ActiveX from the menu.

An ActiveX control placeholder is inserted into your document.

> **ActiveX controls are added to a** page using the `object` element. The `object` element is current and active in all versions of HTML and XHTML.

Setting ActiveX Control Properties

Click the ActiveX control's placeholder in Design view to open the ActiveX Property inspector (see Figure 25.4).

Figure 25.4
The ActiveX Property inspector is used to set the object tag's attributes.

Table 25.2 describes Dreamweaver options regarding ActiveX controls.

Table 25.2   ActiveX Controls

Option	Description of Action
ActiveX Name	The `name` attribute sets the name of the control, mainly for use in scripting.
Width and Height	The W and H properties enable you to change the displayed dimensions of the control. The default units used are pixels, but you also can specify the size in alternative units: pc (picas), pt (points), in (inches), mm (millimeters), cm (centimeters), or % for a percentage of the parent's dimensions.
ClassID	The `ClassID` property is unique to ActiveX controls. It specifies a 32-character unique identifier called a globally unique identifier (GUID) that is specific to the control. All ActiveX controls are identified using their unique Class IDs. The Class ID to use is provided with the documentation accompanying the control or is shown in sample HTML code that uses the control.
Embed	The `embed` element is used to specify an alternative Netscape-style plug-in to use for browsers that don't support ActiveX. The use of this property is discussed in the next section.
Align	The `align` attribute sets how the control will be aligned on the page. Values include `baseline`, `top`, `middle`, `bottom`, `textop`, `absmiddle`, `absbottom`, `left`, and `right`.
V and H Space	You can use the V Space and H Space properties to set the amount of blank space bordering the control. These values must be in pixels.
Base	The Base property sets the `codebase` attribute for the object. This gives the browser a URL from which an ActiveX control can be downloaded if it isn't already installed on the user's system.
Alt Img	The Alt Img specifies an image to display for browsers that don't support the `object` tag.
ID	The ID attribute sets a unique identifier for the object.
Data	Data is used to specify the data file the control should open. This is typically used for ActiveX controls that play a media file.

Setting ActiveX Control Parameters

The Parameters button on the ActiveX Property inspector activates the Parameters dialog box, which lets you enter any custom parameters the control might need. If a control that you download requires any special parameters, it should come with documentation that explains them.

Unlike plug-in parameters, which use attributes, ActiveX control parameters are added using `param` tags. To enter a parameter, click the Plus (+) button. Enter the name of the parameter in the Parameter column and a value in the Value column. You also can remove parameters by using the minus (–) button or rearrange them by clicking one and moving it up or down in the order using the arrow buttons.

Using ActiveX Controls and Plug-ins at the Same Time

The Embed option of the ActiveX Property inspector is used to insert a plug-in into the control's `object` tag code. This enables Netscape and other browsers that ignore the `object` tag to see just the plug-in, while Internet Explorer knows to ignore any plug-ins inside the `object` tag. This gives you a simple way to support both plug-ins and ActiveX controls without having to use a client (or server-side) script or a custom page for each browser.

The following code listing shows an example of an `embed` tag nested inside an `object` tag:

```
<!-- Object Tag for ActiveX
<object id="NSPlay1" width=320 height=240
  classid="clsid:2179C5D3-EBFF-11CF-B6FD-00AA00B4E220"
  <param name="FileName" value="netshow_sample.asx">
  <param name="ControlType" value="1">
  <!-- Embed tag for plug-in
  <embed type="applicaton/asx" width=320 height=240
    src="netshow_sample.asx" ControlType=1>
  </embed>
</object>
```

JAVA APPLETS

Java applets, like plug-ins, enable you to extend the capabilities of a page beyond what can be accomplished with DHTML and client-side scripting.

Java is a programming language developed and promoted by Sun Microsystems. It was developed with the idea that it would be a language that could be used to power smart appliances, such as TV set-top boxes. That idea might have been a little ahead of its time, but Java really came into its own with the advent of the World Wide Web. Java's "write once-run anywhere" philosophy and relatively small code size made it a natural fit for browser-embedded applications that could conceivably run on any hardware and operating system

Even though both have been around for years, there is still a misconception that JavaScript, the popular scripting language, is somehow related to Java. The truth is that they are entirely different languages, with different purposes. The only thing JavaScript has in common with Java is some syntax similarities and a name designed to piggy-back on the Java hype at the time.

25

platform. Java applications designed to be run on the client use a subset of the Java language and are known as *applets*.

Java applets consist of class files that can be downloaded individually or in an archive (known as a Java Archive, or JAR, file). These class files consist of compiled Java code (called Java *bytecode*) that is interpreted and run by a virtual machine. The virtual machine is the only component that must be written specifically for a particular host platform. After the user has it installed, along with the base Java classes, any Java applet should run.

Embedding Java Applets

Dreamweaver's extensive support for plug-ins extends to Java applets as well. Follow these steps to insert a Java applet:

1. Do one of the following:

   - Place the cursor where you want the applet to be inserted in the document. Click the Applet button in the Media tab of the Insert bar. Naturally, it's the button that looks like a cup of coffee.

   - Drag the Applet icon to the location on the page that you want the applet.

   - Place the cursor where you want to insert the applet, and select Insert, Media, Applet from the menu.

> The `applet` element has been deprecated in HTML 4.0 in favor of `object`. If you want to use the `applet` element instead of `object`, you'll need to use a transitional HTML or XHTML document type.

2. The Select File dialog box opens. Enter or browse to the class, JAR, or Zip file containing your Java applet. Be sure to set the file URL relative to the document and not the site root.

3. Click OK.

An `applet` tag (which again looks like a cup of coffee in Design view) is inserted in your document.

Setting Applet Properties

Click the applet representation to open the applet Property inspector (see Figure 25.5).

Figure 25.5
The Java applet Property inspector is used to set all applet attributes.

The following options are now available within the Property inspector:

- **Applet Name**—The Applet Name property is used to enter a unique name for the applet. This name can be used for controlling some applets from scripting.

- **Width and Height**—The W and H properties enable you to change the displayed dimensions of the applet. The default units used are pixels, but you also can specify the size in alternative units: pc (picas), pt (points), in (inches), mm (milli-meters), cm (centimeters), or % for a percentage of the page's dimensions.

- **Code**—The Code attribute specifies the filename of the file containing the applet's Java code. This is the file-name that was chosen in the Select File dialog box.

- **Base**—The Base property specifies the path to the folder containing the applet. This path is relative to the site root, so it can remain blank if the Java applet file is located in the same folder as the document.

- **Align**—The Align property sets how the applet should be aligned on the page.

- **Alt**—The Alt property can be used to specify alternative content to display in the event that the client browser doesn't support Java applets or has disabled them. You can specify either text to be displayed or an image filename. If you enter text, it will be inserted in the applet tag as the "alt" attribute. If you choose an image, Dreamweaver inserts an `img` tag, as shown in this example:

Properties for applets that are archived in a `.jar` or `.zip` file cannot be set solely using the Property inspector. If you used the Select File dialog box to choose the file, you must activate Code view to edit the tag by hand. Manually rename the code attribute to `archive`. Then, create a new code attribute that points to the main class in the archive. This class should be mentioned in any documentation or sample HTML files provided with the applet.

```
<applet code="recipes.jar" width="400" height="200" align="middle">
   <img src="images/cooklogo.gif" width="400" height="200" align="middle">
</applet>
```

Because browsers ignore tags they don't understand, any browser that doesn't recognize the applet tag displays the image instead.

- **V and H Space**—You can use the V Space and H Space properties to set the amount of blank space bordering the applet. These values must be in pixels.

How can you best accommodate those browsers that do not support Java applets? Find out how in "Applet Alternatives" in the "Troubleshooting" section later in this chapter.

Setting Applet Parameters

The Parameters button on the Applet Property inspector activates the Parameters dialog box. The Parameters dialog box lets you enter any custom parameters that the applet you are embedding might have. If a Java applet that you download requires any special parameters, it should come with documentation that explains them. The Java parameters dialog box adds `param` tags to the applet in the same way that it does for ActiveX controls. See the section "Setting Plug-in Parameters," earlier this chapter, for more information.

25

TROUBLESHOOTING

Checking for a Plug-in

I'm having trouble detecting plug-ins with IE. What's the problem?

The Check Plugin behavior is not always effective in Internet Explorer, which is, as you know, the most popular browser. Even though its usefulness is minimized by this limitation, the behavior still has value if you set the Always Go to First URL if Detection Is Not Possible option. This setting sends the browser on its way to download the plug-in if it can't detect whether it's necessary. It's better to take the chance on sending your user to re-download a plug-in he already has than to risk losing a visitor.

Applet Alternatives

I want to use an applet on my page, but I know it won't be accessible. How can I provide an alternative for those who can't access it?

You might choose to degrade gracefully to show the best alternative for all browsers. Choose an image to display in browsers that don't support Java applets, and select text for those that don't show images. Do this by specifying an image filename for the `alt` content in the Property inspector and then entering text for the `alt` attribute of the generated `img` tag (using Code view).

PEER TO PEER: ACCESSIBILITY FOR PLUG-INS AND JAVA APPLETS

There are several ways to ensure that objects are properly dealt with in terms of accessibility.

Here are some things to do to work toward creating an accessible document with plug-ins, applets, and objects:

- If you are using the `object` element to define objects on a page, you can provide text descriptions that will be helpful to everyone, including the disabled, as follows:

  `<object> Text description goes here . . . </object>`

- When using the `applet` element, use the `alt` attribute to describe the applet's purpose.

- Put descriptive cues within the text so people can understand the relationship between the object and the page in a very clear way. This is especially important if you are using objects for navigation.

26

INSERTING AUDIO AND VIDEO

IN THIS CHAPTER

AUDIO AND VIDEO FOR THE WEB

One sure way to add excitement to a Web page is to add audio or video to it. However, excitement isn't *always* what your site visitors want. What's more, almost all audio and video requires either browser support or a plug-in, so not everyone is going to be ready to play. As a result, an important step when using audio and video with Web pages is to be sure the use of either is appropriate to your audience.

Appropriate uses for audio would include

- Audio on a musician's Web site

- Audio on an entertainment Web site such as one promoting a film

- Audio to assist with educational or tutorial information

- Audio for pronunciation, such as on a language site or dictionary site

- Audio on a personal home page, such as a welcome or a recording of baby's first words

Similarly, good uses for video would include

- Trailers for film or video promotion

- Music videos on music-related sites

- Video showing close-ups of mechanical parts on an industrial Web site

- Video showing the inside of homes, hotel rooms, conference rooms, and other internal venues for rent or sale

- Personal videos of family and friends for a home page

Naturally, you will think of or encounter other applications for audio and video, but these ideas will help contextualize good and appropriate uses for audio and video. Inapproriate and bad uses for audio or video include any use where the content of the media is not appropriate for the audience visiting the site and any use where bandwidth and user control is limited.

After you've decided to use audio or video on your Web site, you'll first want to get familiar with supported file types and their advantages and disadvantages and learn a little about how to create and edit audio files. Then, using Dreamweaver tools, you'll add the audio or video selections to your site.

Audio and Video File Types

With the growing access worldwide to broadband, the use of audio and video on Web sites has become more realistic. Technological advances in compression and streaming (the capability to send the audio or video data in a constant stream from the server to the client) have also increased the desirability of audio and video, where appropriate, on Web sites.

The type of audio and video file type you choose will depend largely on what you're trying to accomplish and which tools are at hand. Table 26.1 shows common audio and video file formats used on the Web.

Table 26.1   Common Audio and Video Formats for the Web

File Type	Extension	Use	Pros and Cons
Audio Interchange File Format (AIFF)	.aif	Common format for Mac OS	No real compression. Large file sizes result.
Musical Instrument Digital Interface	.midi, .mid	Control interface for replay of sounds	No digital audio information, so small file size but is limited to synthesized sounds.
MPEG-1, Layer III	.mp3, .mpeg	Audio and video for Web	Near CD-quality sound with excellent compression. In very widespread use. It can also be streamed with appropriate server technology.
RealAudio	.ra, .ram, .rpm	Audio and video for the Web	Very high quality with small file size.
Apple QuickTime	.qt, .mov	Audio and video for the Web	Excellent quality. Very popular format for both Mac and Windows. QuickTime 4.0 has streaming options available.
Rich Music Format	.rmf	Combined digital and MIDI audio for the Web	Very tiny file sizes. Useful in adding sound effects to Web pages.
Shockwave Audio, Shockwave Flash	.swa, .swf	Audio and multimedia for the Web	Shockwave audio is high-quality and is based on MPEG compression. Flash has built-in sound capabilities with support for streaming.
RIFF WAVE	.wav	Common audio file type for Windows; developed by Microsoft and IBM	Even when compressed, WAV files can be fairly large.
Windows Media Audio	.wma	Streamed audio for the Web	High quality. Relies on Windows technology.

To play audio and video files, you and your site visitors must have plug-in software. Some of the primary and important plug-ins you'll want to have (and encourage your site visitors to get) include the following:

- **Apple QuickTime, `http://quicktime.apple.com/`**—Apple QuickTime Plug-in allows your audience to view your QuickTime video clips as well as many other audio and video formats.

- **Microsoft Media Player, `http://www.microsoft.com/windows/mediaplayer/`**—The new and improved Microsoft Media Player is available as a free download. This is one-stop shopping for most audio and video formats you will encounter, including RealVideo/RealAudio 4.0, MPEG 1, MPEG 2, WAV, AVI, MIDI, MOV, VOD, AU, MP3, and QuickTime files. The Media Player can run as a standalone or can be viewed within Internet Explorer and Netscape.

- **Beatnik Player, `http://www.beatnik.com/`**—Supports Beatnik RMF files. There's also a terrific amount of developer information, tools, and community support.

- **RealOne Player by Real, `http://www.real.com/products/player/`**—RealOne Player supports all three Real data types: RealAudio, RealVideo, and RealFlash. It also supports AVI, WAV, MIDI, MPEG, and others. Real is the leader in delivering audio and video over the Web.

When you're deciding on the best format for your audio and video files, you should consider the likelihood that your users will already have the software they need to see your work. Too often, users will not take the time to download a plug-in. You can provide a download for the required plug-in, which you'll learn to do later.

Producing Audio and Video

The first step to adding audio and video to your Web site is to create the source files or gather prerecorded source files. It's important to remember that good media content on the Web is the result of good media sampling. If you create a sound clip by taking your tape recorder to a concert and recording your favorite song from the 20th row, you will have quite a different quality clip from one produced in a studio.

You need a good microphone and good sound editing software if you're recording your own sound sample. For a good video sample, you need a high-quality capture device and encoding software.

26

▷ *Not sure what you have or what you need to do great editing? Check out "Learning More About Web Audio and Video" in the "Troubleshooting" section at the end of this chapter.*

About Audio

Most recording devices create analog recordings. To digitize an analog audio source, the signal must be processed through an analog-to-digital (A/D) converter. Most computers now come equipped with sound cards that have A/D converters. If your computer has a sound input jack, it already has an A/D converter. If your computer has only a sound output jack or an internal speaker, you probably only have digital-to-analog conversion capabilities. Even if you are recording audio from a digital source, such as a digital audio tape (DAT) or compact disc (CD), some kind of A/D conversion is usually involved because most computers do not come with digital audio inputs yet. Because of the quality available in more recent sound cards, if you do not have a sound card with these capabilities, it's time to upgrade the sound card.

An A/D converter uses a "sample and hold" circuit that records the voltage levels of the input signal at a fixed interval. This interval, or *rate*, at which the signal is sampled is determined by the A/D converter's *sampling rate*. The sampling rate also determines the highest frequency that can be recorded or played back. It is important that the recording be played back at the same sampling rate at which it was recorded.

After you create your sound file, you need to edit it with a good sound-editing application. Many shareware packages are available that will do the trick for simple projects. It wouldn't hurt to first try some shareware options before deciding to invest in professional software.

The following programs will help get you started with audio editing:

- **Cool Edit**—A digital sound editor for Windows. With this company, you have a variety of software choices, from a reasonably priced package, Cool Edit 2000, to a more sophisticated tool, Cool Edit Pro (`http://www.syntrillium.com/`). Figure 26.1 shows Cool Edit 2000.

- **SoundEdit Pro**—Offers good audio editing for a very reasonable price. You can download the demo, which is very user friendly, from `http://www.rmbsoft.com/` (see Figure 26.2).

- **Sound Forge**—This professional sound editing software for Windows is made by Sonic Foundry and includes an extensive set of audio processes, tools, and effects for manipulating audio. Sound Forge offers full support for the latest streaming technology, including Microsoft Windows NT Server NetShow Services and RealNetworks' RealAudio/RealVideo. Sonic Foundry also has numerous other sound and multimedia editing software to take a look at (`http://www.sonicfoundry.com/`).

If you decide you need more serious functionality (and you are willing to pay *serious* money for it), you should get a professional package such as Pro Tools by Digidesign (`http://www.digidesign.com/`). A good in-between application, both in terms of price and features, is SoundEdit 16 by Macromedia (`http://www.macromedia.com/`), which is only available for the Mac.

26

About Video

When considering the possibility of adding video to your Web site, you must look at a hardware investment as well as a software purchase. It was already mentioned that you must have a very high-quality audio source file before you add it to your Web page. That point is even more important when it comes to producing video content. There are two steps in the process of creating video when you will sacrifice quality if you do not have good tools.

When you encode video, you capture it to your hard drive. The faster the computer, the faster the video because frames are lost if your computer can't keep up with the video capture. To produce professional-quality video, you need a very fast machine and a high-quality video capture card.

You also will sacrifice quality if, during the compression process, you do not choose the best video bit rate, bit rate quality, and frame speed to meet your needs. Fortunately, much of the software available for editing video will assist you with managing these concerns.

Figure 26.1
Using Cool Edit 2000 to compress an audio file.

Figure 26.2
SoundEdit Pro is a low-cost tool that can get you editing audio quickly and easily.

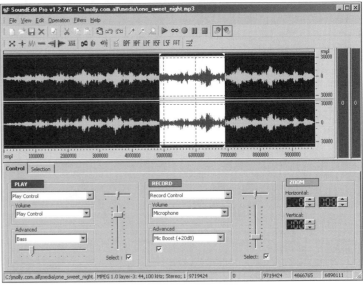

Selecting a video format and tools to manage video depends on a variety of factors, including platform availability, which tools you like to use for editing, and personal preference. MPEG and QuickTime tend to be popular choices over AVIs. MPEG is very widely supported platform-wise, and QuickTime tools and plug-ins are popular (see Figure 26.3). AVI tends to be Microsoft-centric, and although it runs inline in the IE browser, support does vary with other browsers.

Figure 26.3
Apple's QuickTime format is extremely powerful and popular. Apple also provides significant tools and support for QuickTime developers.

More About Streaming Media

Streaming media was brought to the forefront of the Web by Real, who remains the leader in streaming technologies and tools to this day. However, many companies, including Apple, Macromedia, and Microsoft, are adding streaming capabilities to their file formats and server technologies.

Most streaming media requires access to a special server, although that's not always the case. Streaming audio and video files can be easily created with tools from those companies interested in their use.

For more information on Apple QuickTime tools, see `http://quicktime.apple.com/`.

A tremendous wealth of information, support, and utilities can be found at Real Networks' site, `http://www.realnetworks.com/`.

Information on Windows Media Technology is available at `http://www.microsoft.com/windows/windowsmedia/`.

26

USING DREAMWEAVER TO ADD SOUND FILES TO A PAGE

After you have your sound files, you can choose either to link to them so a user can download the file or to embed them so they will play in the browser or spawn the required plug-in and play upon receipt of the file.

Linking to a Sound File

Linking to a sound file is as easy as linking to any other file type. Linking gives your site visitor the option to save the file or play the file. Because giving site visitors choices is a large part of Web site usability, this is a good option when you are unsure of your audience's preferences and capabilities.

To link to a sound file, follow these steps:

1. Place the text (or image or other media) you want to be linked to the sound file.

2. In Design view, select the text or media by highlighting it.

3. In the Property inspector, click the folder icon and find the audio file. Click to select it.

4. Click OK. Your file is now linked.

Typically, when a site visitor activates a link of this type, the file begins to download and play in the associated player (see Figure 26.4). Alternatively, visitors can save the file to their hard drives to play at a later time.

Figure 26.4
Downloading a sound file from a link created with Dreamweaver.

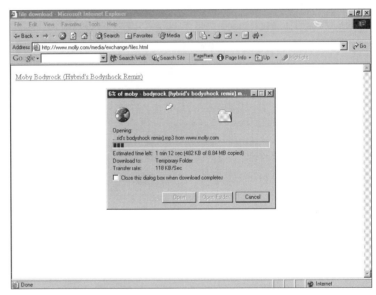

Embedding Sound

If you want your sound files to play inline and be generally more integrated into your page, you should embed them. A variety of attributes is available in Dreamweaver when you embed a sound file, as follows:

- **Plugin**—Enter a value here for name and id, which is necessary if you want to add behaviors or scripting to the sound file and player.

- **W**—Width is best controlled by pixels, but you can use a percentage to describe how much space within the browser frame you want the embedded file to take up.

- **H**—Height determines the height of the embedded sound file's plug-in player.

- **Src**—Location of the file.

- **Plg URL**—You can set a URL that takes users who don't have the correct plug-in to a plug-ins page to download it.

- **Align**—Allows you to align the player on the page.

- **Vspace**—Allows you to assign vertical spacing to the player.

- **Hspace**—Allows you to assign horizontal spacing around the player.

- **Border**—Allows you to set a border if you want one. A value of 0 ensures that no border will be present.

Caution

Using align, vspace, hspace, and border attributes is fine for transitional documents, but these attributes are not permitted in strict ones. Using CSS wherever possible to control layout is now the preferred method when modifying attributes of this nature.

To embed a sound file on a page, follow these steps:

1. Open the document to which you want to add the sound file in Design view.

2. Place your cursor in the location where you want to add the file. On the Insert bar, click the Media tab. Then, click the plug-in icon (see Figure 26.5). Alternatively, you can select Insert, Media, Plugin from the main menu. The Select dialog box appears.

3. Find the file you want to embed, and select it. Click (Open) [OK]. In Design view, you'll now see an icon that represents your file (see Figure 26.6).

4. The media file is now embedded. To manage any of the previously mentioned attributes, either select the plug-in icon in Design view or click within the embedded sound file in Code view. The Property inspector will activate.

Plug-In icon

Figure 26.5
The plug-in icon can be found on the Insert bar. Click the Media tab to access the icon.

Make any modifications you want using the Property inspector. When you're finished, save your file and test it by clicking Play from within the Property inspector.

➥ *Want to have your music play as the page loads or as the mouse pointer passes over a certain image? You can do so in certain browsers. Find out how, and which one, in "Controlling Music on Your Page" in the "Troubleshooting" section at the end of this chapter.*

Figure 26.6
After a file is embedded, the plug-in icon represents that file when you're viewing the page in Design view.

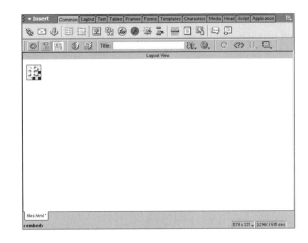

INSERTING VIDEO

Adding video to your page works exactly the same way that adding audio does. You can link to a video file, or you can embed the file. Which method you use depends on your audience and the type of site you're creating. Even though linking to video gives the user more options, embedding video can make the experience of the page more cohesive.

Linking to a Video File

To link to a video file, follow these steps:

1. Place the text (or image or other media) you want to be linked to the video file.

2. In Design view, select the text or media by highlighting it.

3. In the Property inspector, click the folder icon and find the video file. Click to select it.

4. Click OK. Your video file is now linked.

Your site visitor can now click the link to download and play it in a plug-in, or she can choose to save the file to disk for later viewing.

Embedding Video

As with audio, embedding is easily managed by following these steps:

1. Create a new document, or open one where you want to add a video file.

2. In Design view, place your cursor in the location where you want to add the file. On the Insert bar, click the Media tab. Then, click the plug-in icon—it's the same icon you'll see when inserting audio. Alternatively, you can select Insert, Media, Plugin from the main menu. The Select dialog box appears.

3. Find the video file you want to embed, and select it. Click OK. In Design view, you'll now see the icon that represents your video file.

Click the plug-in icon in Design view, or click within the embedded sound file in Code view. The Property inspector will activate.

Additional Attributes for Embedding Audio and Video

Additional attributes are available for embedding audio and video. They include

- `autoplay="true/false"`—Answer with `true`, and your movie starts when the page is first accessed. Answer with `false`, and the user must click the Play button on the console for the movie to play.

- `controller="true/false"`—This adds user controls to the movie. If you set this to `true`, you must find out how many pixels your controller needs for the display and then add that amount to the height of your movie. Otherwise, the movie and the controller are forced into the space required for the movie.

- `loop="true/false/palindrome"`—If you want the movie to play repeatedly, set this to `true`. If you want to play it once and stop, set it to `false`. `palindrome` plays from beginning to end and backwards in a continuous loop.

To add these attributes, bring up the Tag Inspector (select Window, Tag Inspector). In the top field, find the `embed` tag and highlight it. All the attributes that you are currently using and that you might like to use are found there. Simply click in the value section found next to the attribute name and fill in the value of these attributes manually. Dreamweaver automatically updates them to the code.

TROUBLESHOOTING

26

Learning More About Web Audio and Video

I'm having a difficult time getting more details about using Web audio and video. Where can I go for more information?

Learning the details of recording and managing audio and video for the Web can be a time-consuming process. A lot of online resources are available. Check the Web sites mentioned in this chapter, and be sure to stop by the very comprehensive About.Com section on home recording, at `http://homerecording.about.com/index.htm`. It's filled with excellent tutorials and references.

Controlling Music on Your Page

I would like my music to load immediately with the page or be attached to another event after the page has loaded. Can I do this, and if so, how?

You can do so by tapping into the power of Dreamweaver behaviors. But, you can do so only in IE browsers. Netscape and Mozilla do not support this particular behavior.

To add a sound for immediate loading, do the following:

1. Open the Design panel and click the Behaviors tab.

2. Click the Plus sign and select Play Sound from the drop-down menu.

3. The Play Sound dialog box appears. Use the folder icon to browse your computer for the sound file. Highlight it, and then click OK.

4. The sound file will be embedded into the document, along with some JavaScript.

The default event is onLoad, but you can change this by selecting the sound object and then high-lighting OnLoad in the Behaviors panel. A drop-down menu appears, and you can then select from one of the many play sound options.

PEER TO PEER: MAKING PAGES CONTAINING AUDIO AND VIDEO VALID AND ACCESSIBLE

Here's the bad news: Using the embed tag is actually forbidden in HTML and XHTML, period. It's simply not allowed if you want your documents to be valid. Instead, the object tag is supposed to be used, but support for this element is limited to newer browsers, especially Internet Explorer.

So, how do you make a document using the embed element valid? The truth is, unless you're willing to write your own Document Type Definition in Modular XHTML (which will be beyond the scope of almost all readers of this book), the answer is that you can't. So, either insert all audio using the object tag or make the choice to have an invalid document.

The other concern with audio and video is accessibility. People who are blind, visually impaired, deaf, or hearing impaired will miss out on aspects of audio and video content. The rule of thumb here is to ensure that you *do not rely* on audio and video to express your main point. Also, add descriptive text near the audio or video that provides context and adds detailed information about what you are displaying or playing for your visitors, no matter their physical abilities.

26

WORKING WITH FLASH
AND SHOCKWAVE

UNDERSTANDING FLASH AND SHOCKWAVE

Flash and Shockwave are two very rich media technologies Macromedia has brought to the Web with significant success. Despite the need for plug-ins on the part of the site visitor, both Flash- and Shockwave-generated media have contributed to some of the Web's richest design features.

As you read earlier in Chapter 8, "Adding Some Flash," Macromedia Flash is a vector-based tool for multimedia on the Web. In that chapter, you learned to use Dreamweaver MX's tools for adding Flash buttons and text. Here you'll be working with Macromedia Flash MX and taking a look at the interface of Macromedia Director Shockwave Studio. Even if you don't have these programs, you can either find them on the CD-ROM that came with this book or download demos of them from the Macromedia Web site.

The fact that Flash is vector-based is an appealing feature because of its capability to manage text and animation yet retain relatively small file sizes. Director Shockwave is also a vector-based multimedia tool, with specially detailed features for development of high-quality CD-ROM and kiosk media, as well as for the Web.

> Direct links to all Macromedia product demos can be found at http://www.macromedia.com/software/.

Both Flash and Shockwave share common features born of their vector-based environment, such as

- Potential for very high-quality color

- Excellent management of type

- Rich animation options

- Powerful audio delivery

- Potential for multiple Web delivery methods, including streaming and downloadable media

- Relatively small file sizes and capability for authors to make choices regarding quality and compression as necessary

The history of multimedia animation on the Web is an intriguing one, particularly because it started surprisingly early in the Web's life. Macromedia Director had been in use for some time for the development of CD-ROM and other multimedia, but until a plug-in was developed, no Director files could be played directly from the Web.

What's more, the expense and learning curve of Director were both prohibitive for most Web enthusiasts at the time. In fact, Director's interface remains quite complicated (see Figure 27.1).

The plug-in for Shockwave came out in 1995, and Macromedia began to add improvements to future versions of Director so as to better assist authors in porting their multimedia designs to the Web.

Shockwave caused quite a shake-up at the time because no one had really ever seen anything quite like it in the Web environment, which really had graphic support only for two short years prior to the introduction of the Shockwave plug-in. But, overcoming the need for the plug-in limited the distribution of Shockwave.

27

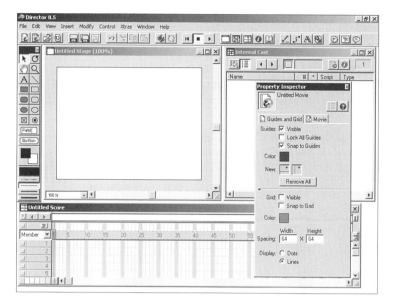

Figure 27.1
Shockwave Director Studio has a complicated interface with many floating palettes.

Around the same time, software engineer Jonathan Gay was working on developing a vector-based animation tool with excellent compression that looked very attractive for use on the Web. What's more, the interface was more streamlined and lightweight than Director, making it both more affordable and easier to use.

This product was released in mid-1996 as FutureSplash. FutureSplash inspired interest in a number of major Web sites, including the Microsoft Network (MSN) and the official *Simpsons* Web site. Also among those paying attention to this technology was Macromedia, who ultimately bought FutureWave Software, the parent company to FutureSplash. At the end of 1996, FutureSplash was re-presented to the public as Macromedia Flash, and the rest is truly history.

An interesting history of Flash written by its inventor, Jonathan Gay, is available at http://untoldhistory.weblogs.com/stories/storyReader$4.

Macromedia now reports that 96% of total Web users have a Flash player installed. The Shockwave player is much less widespread. It's therefore easy to contextualize the difference in their use by thinking that Flash is an excellent choice for many Web applications, whereas Shockwave is used in more specialized instances.

At this point, both Flash and Shockwave are completely scriptable. Flash uses ActionScript to extend its individual capabilities in the computing environment, and Shockwave uses a language known as Lingo.

27

DESIGNING ANIMATIONS

From Felix the Cat, El Kabong, Popeye, and Olive Oyl to the Flintstones, many a childhood has been enriched by these wonderfully drawn and animated characters.

Animation is an expression both useful and joyous. It can be used to entertain, promote (notice that most Web ads are animated), and draw attention to specific information on a page. Animations can be subtle, or they can be outrageous and detailed.

No matter their content, animations are created using design tools. The goal is to change the way a composition looks, and that change occurs in a specified period of time. The change can be movement, color, size, texture, or visual style. Animations can also have audio and interactivity, such as links and rollovers, connected to them.

Before creating animations, an understanding of animation concepts is essential. Three of the most basic but very important things to be aware of in creating vector-based animations are

- **Objects**—In the context of an animation, an object is something that can have any animation feature applied to it. Text and shapes are perfect examples of objects.

- **Duration**—This refers to the total amount of time the animation runs.

- **Keyframes**—Perhaps one of the most critical tools in the animator's toolbox, a *keyframe* is a single point in time (placed by you at an interval or numerous intervals within the duration of the animation) at which something changes to the object in question.

The goal of the exercises in this chapter is to get you to demo the capabilities of Flash and Director. Chances are some readers are already well-versed in Flash, but others won't have had the opportunity to try their hand at Flash animation, or any animation at all. These concepts will get you off to a great start.

Creating an Animation in Macromedia Flash MX

Here's a simple step-by-step bouncing ball exercise to give those readers a taste. Those folks more experienced with Flash can jump ahead to the next section, where you'll learn about other ways to create Flash animations.

First, you'll draw the ball. To do so, follow these steps:

1. Open Flash MX, and select File, New.

2. Select a color.

3. Select the Oval Tool by clicking it in the Tools window.

4. To retain aspect ratio, Shift-click and then use your mouse to draw a round ball (see Figure 27.2).

5. Save your file as bouncing-ball.fla.

The next step is to bounce the ball along the timeline. To do so, follow these steps:

1. In the Timeline, click frame 5; then select Insert, Keyframe (see Figure 27.3).

2. With the Arrow Tool, move the ball to its next position. This position will be the first "up" part of the bounce.

3. Click frame 10 in the Timeline, and select Insert Keyframe. Now drag the ball back down to the baseline.

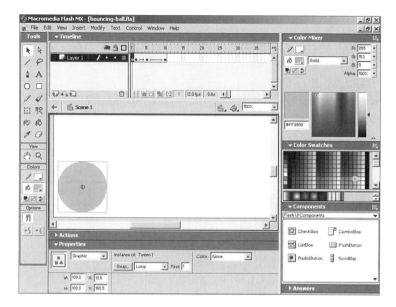

Figure 27.2
Drawing the ball in Macromedia Flash MX. The interface is leaner, meaner, and cleaner than Director and is consistent with all the MX studio products.

Flash Timeline Playhead

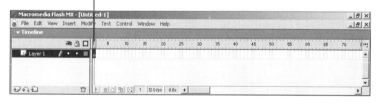

Figure 27.3
The playhead in Flash MX allows you to move through the Timeline frame by frame or all at once. Simply grab and drag.

4. Click frame 15 and create another keyframe by selecting Insert, Keyframe.

5. Move the ball up and slightly off the stage, so it appears as if the ball is leaving the visible area.

Save the updates to your file. The next step is to add *tweening*. This is the process of smoothing out the in-between frames of your animation.

Flash is particularly impressive in its capability to do this, saving you lots of time and effort. Without tweening, you would have to create every single frame in between the keyframes to smooth out the ball's movements. To tween the animation, click each keyframe; select the ball; and then select Insert, Create Motion Tween.

When you are finished with your animation, you should save the changes. To preview your animation, select Control, Play.

27

You now need to export your file in SWF format for inclusion in a Web page. This is necessary because the Flash player plays only SWF files, so it has to be in that format for your site visitor to view the file.

To do so, follow these steps:

1. Select File, Export Movie.

2. Save your movie with an appropriate filename.

3. The Export Flash Player dialog box appears (see Figure 27.4). You can use this dialog box to refine settings. For the purposes of this exercise, leave everything at default and click OK.

Figure 27.4
The Export Flash Player dialog box provides display, frame rate, and audio quality options.

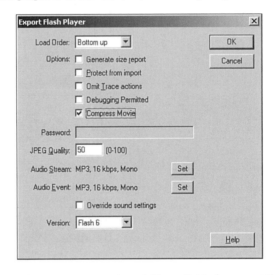

Flash now generates the movie as a compressed .swf file, suitable for use on the Web.

Creating a Flash Animation with Adobe LiveMotion

Another popular means of creating Flash animation is by using Adobe LiveMotion 2.0. This tool is easy to use—in fact, the user interface is appealing to those already familiar with Adobe products (see Figure 27.5). Adobe LiveMotion exports to a variety of file formats, including the .swf format, which is played by the Flash player.

To create a star animation using Adobe LiveMotion, do the following:

1. Set the frame rate of the animation by selecting Edit, Composition Settings. In the Composition Settings dialog box, select your frame rate from the drop-down menu. I selected 12, which is the default frame rate.

2. In a new canvas, draw a star-shaped object or select one from the Library. I chose a star and colored it red.

3. Size and position the star to your tastes. Select the 3D palette. Select the Ripple effect from the drop-down menu and set the options as follows: Depth, 1; Softness, 1; Lighting, 100; Rotation, 360; Edge, Straight; and Light, Dark Only.

4. Select the Type tool and set the word New in yellow in the center of the star.

5. With the text object selected, open the Object Layer palette and create a new layer. Fill this layer with white. Set the width to 1 and the softness to 10 using the Layer palette.

6. Save the file in LiveMotion format.

7. Open the Timeline/Composition Window and tile the windows so that you can easily move between both the editor and the composition.

8. Select the star. Click the triangle twist-down next to the star's Layer 1 track.

9. Drag the composition duration bar to a suitable duration point. I set mine to 6 seconds (6s in the Timeline).

10. Place the Current Time Marker (CTM, akin to the playhead in Macromedia Flash) at 00 and click the Stopwatch next to the Effect Angle track in Layer 1. In the 3D palette, set the rotation to 360.

11. Drag the CTM three segments to the right. Make a keyframe and, in the 3D palette, set the rotation to 90.

12. Move three more segments to the right, create a keyframe, and set the rotation to 360.

13. Set another keyframe three segments to the right and make the rotation 90.

14. Set the final keyframe at the end of the composition duration and make the rotation angle 360.

Save the updates to the file and preview the resulting effects by either clicking the Play button in the Timeline/Composition Window or switching to Preview mode (see Figure 27.6).

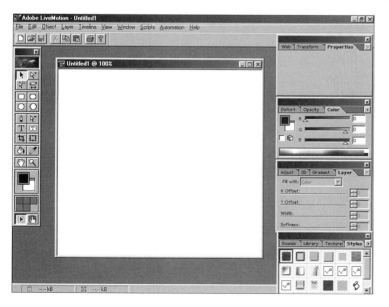

Figure 27.5
The Adobe LiveMotion 2.0 interface is familiar and comfortable for many designers.

27

Figure 27.6
Preview the star animation in
Adobe LiveMotion.

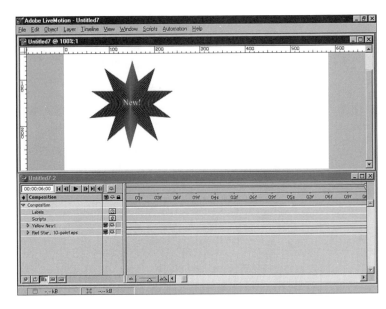

Just as with Macromedia Flash MX, you'll need to export the file to a .swf format so it can be viewed in the Flash player. To export an animation or multimedia presentation as an .swf file, complete the following steps:

1. Bring up the Export palette by selecting File, Export Settings (see Figure 27.7).

Figure 27.7
Using the Export palette to generate a .swf file suitable for playing
in the Flash player.

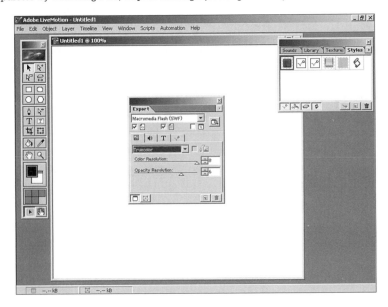

2. Select Flash as your export option.

3. Set the frame rate by clicking the Frame Rate tab in the Export Settings palette. The higher the frame rate, the slower the speed of the overall presentation or animation.

4. If you're using audio, you might want to modify the audio rate. You can do this in the Audio tab. The lower the number, the lower the quality of the audio.

5. If you'd like to embed fonts in your composition, do so by clicking the Embed Fonts tab and choosing the fonts you'd like to have embedded along with the composition.

For more information about Adobe LiveMotion, see http://www.adobe.com/products/livemotion/main.html. Also, the lead author of this book wrote *Teach Yourself Adobe LiveMotion 2.0*, available from Sams Publishing.

6. If the Export HTML Page check box isn't checked, check it now.

7. Select File, Export.

8. Name and save your file. Depending on the size of your animation or presentation, you might wait a few moments while the various components are created and saved.

Exploring Other Flash Animation Programs

Several other alternative software programs offer .swf export, too. Some of these programs are quite easy to use; others are aspects of more familiar graphical tools. All these products offer demos, and the URLS are provided here for you to give them a try:

- **Sothink Glanda 2001a**—This is a lightweight, template-based tool that will especially appeal to newcomers to Flash looking for fun buttons and easy-to-use applications. For Windows, see http://www.sothink.com/webtools/glanda/sample/index.htm (see Figure 27.8).

- **Coffee Cup Firestarter**—Also a fast, lightweight program with preset effects. For Windows, see http://www.coffeecup.com/firestarter/main.html.

- **Mix FX**—Offers text effects, background effects, and buttons for .swf export. For Windows, see http://www.mix-fx.com/.

- **e-Picture Pro**—This is a professional-level animation tool with 3D effects and .swf export. Definitely worth a look. For Windows and Macintosh, see http://www.beatware.com/products/epicture_pro.htm.

- **Corel Rave**—This product is part of the Corel Graphics Suite. "Rave" stands for "Real Animated Vector Effects." A professional-quality tool, it's available for Windows and Macintosh at http://www.corel.com/.

27

Figure 27.8
You can use Glanda to create a
Flash button with sound effects.

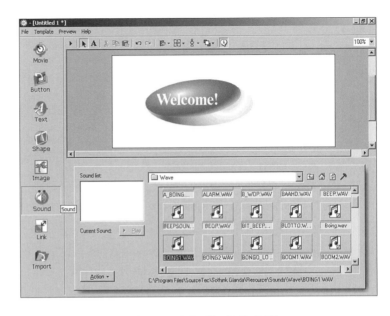

ADDING THE FLASH MOVIE TO A WEB PAGE

After you have a Flash movie source file, .swf, you can easily add it to a Web page using
Dreamweaver. You can do so three ways:

- Use the Media tab on the Insert bar, and click the Insert Flash icon.

- Drag the Flash icon to the point in the document where you want the Flash movie to appear.

- Select Insert, Media, Flash.

Whichever method you select will cause the Select File dialog box to appear (see Figure 27.9).
Search your hard drive for the correct file, and click OK. The Flash placeholder will appear (see
Figure 27.10).

Dreamweaver MX inserts both the object and embed tags for Flash to work properly in multiple
browser types. Listing 27.1 shows the Dreamweaver markup.

27

Listing 27.1 Combining object and embed

```
<object classid="clsid:D27CDB6E-AE6D-11cf-96B8-444553540000"
codebase="http://download.macromedia.com/pub/shockwave/cabs/flash/
swflash.cab#version=6,0,29,0"width="550" height="300">
    <param name="movie" value="export.swf" />
    <param name="quality" value="high" />
<embed src="export.swf" quality="high" pluginspage="http://www.macromedia.com/
go/getflashplayer" type="application/x-shockwave-flash"
width="550" height="300">
</embed>
</object>
```

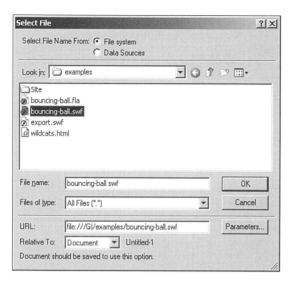

Figure 27.9
To select a Flash movie, you use the Select File dialog box to find and select the movie.

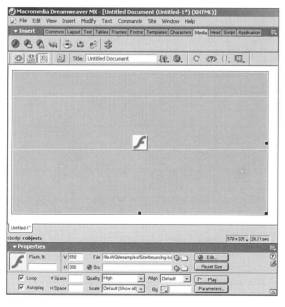

Figure 27.10
When you insert a Flash movie, Dreamweaver MX creates an active placeholder for it.

A problem with this markup is that the embed element and its attributes are not supported in HTML or XHTML. Ideally, you should be using only the object element, which is in the specifications for the long haul. If you are concerned about Netscape versions 4.0 and earlier, and any other early browser lacking support for the object element, then you can use this workaround, but be aware that you won't have a valid document.

For more information on working with object, see Chapter 25, "Working with Plug-ins and Java Applets," p. 475.

After the movie has been added, you can make adjustments to its attributes by selecting the Flash placeholder and changing any of the properties in the Property inspector.

For a complete list of properties for Flash and Shockwave, see "Flash Object Properties," p. 143.

You can preview your work in the Document window by following these steps:

1. Select the Flash placeholder for the file you want to preview by clicking it once.

2. In the Properties inspector, find the Play button and click it. The movie will now play.

3. If you want to stop the movie, click Stop at any time.

Of course, you should now save your file. You can browse it externally in any browser with Flash support. Figure 27.11 shows a page with the Flash movie that was created earlier active in a browser.

Figure 27.11
Play the Flash movie within the context of a Web page.

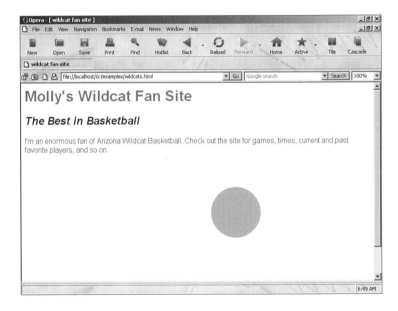

Does working with Flash seem like something you'd like to do, but you're having difficulty getting started? See "Planning Flash Applications" in the "Troubleshooting" section at the end of this chapter.

IMPORTANT FEATURES IN SHOCKWAVE

As mentioned earlier, the Director interface is more complex than Flash, and creating presentations in it can be a highly specialized activity. This is not to say that Flash doesn't have incredibly rich feature sets by this point in its history, but with the fact that Director is used for so many other industrial-strength multimedia, it only makes sense that it's a more complicated program.

Although you won't be stepping through an exercise here because it's really beyond the scope of this book, you should download the Director Shockwave Studio (or check the CD-ROM), install it, and look around (see Figure 27.12). Compare it to the Flash MX interface, and I know you'll find some interesting parallels. For example, both programs refer to the editing area as the "stage," and both programs use a timeline (although it's called *timeline* in Flash and *score* in Director) for animation.

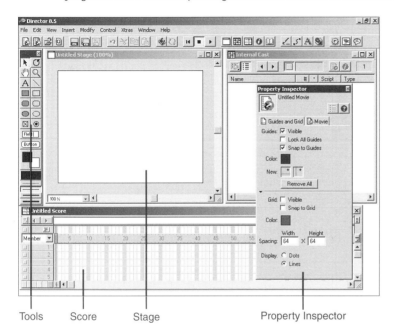

Tools   Score   Stage   Property Inspector

Figure 27.12
Examine this view of the Director interface in detail and compare it with the Flash MX interface in Figure 27.13.

But, you'll, also see that the interface improvements in the MX studio line have helped to organize tools, palettes, and inspectors more effectively (see Figure 27.13).

With all this detail, why would Shockwave be of use to Web designers? Well, some of the features that make Director Shockwave appealing in certain cases for Web designers include

- **Total control of presentation**—Flash has to limit the types of media and images it can use in order to properly compress for Web delivery. Shockwave, on the other hand, allows you create, import, and export a wide range of formats.

- **3D design**— Director Shockwave allows you not only to create 3D designs, but also to do so in a real-time rendering environment.

- **Greater interactivity**—With the Director Shockwave Multiuser server, you can create very sophisticated, real-time, Web-based games and chat rooms. The server can run live on any computer connected to the Internet (see Figure 27.14).

If you're interested in learning more about Director, check out *Special Edition Using Director 8.5*.

Want to explore Shockwave applications? Check out Shockwave. com, http://www.shockwave. com, for a firsthand look at Shockwave features for the Web.

27

Timeline

Figure 27.13
Comparing the Flash MX interface to Shockwave Studio, version 8.5.

Tools —

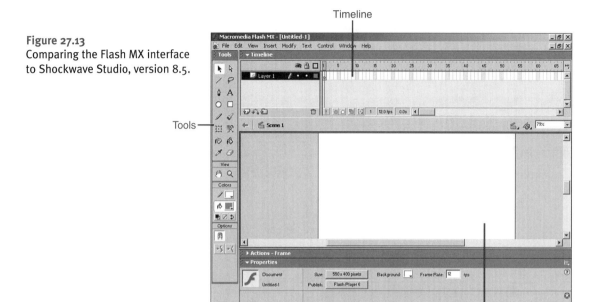

Property Inspector   Stage

Figure 27.14
The Director Shockwave Multiuser server running live on a Windows XP system with a high-speed Internet connection.

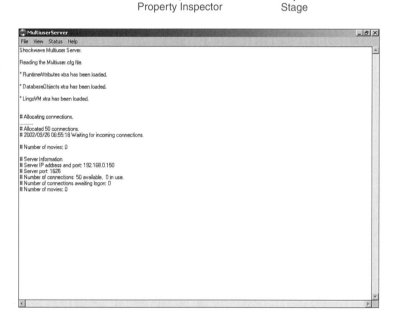

Figure 27.15 shows a Shockwave game being delivered live.

Figure 27.15
The game Dynomite is available at www.shockwave.com to play live online and is also downloadable as a standalone game. This flexibility in delivery exemplifies one of Shockwave's best features.

ADDING SHOCKWAVE TO A PAGE

As with Flash, a Shockwave movie is easily added to your page. If you have a Shockwave movie and want to add it to your page, here's how:

1. Place your cursor at the point on a page where you want your Shockwave content to appear.

2. Select Insert, Media, Shockwave; the Select File dialog box appears.

3. Find the file (it will have a `.dcr` extension) and click OK.

4. The Shockwave placeholder appears where you've inserted it on the page (see Figure 27.16).

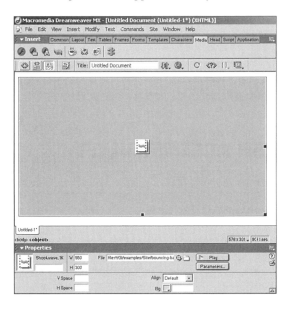

Figure 27.16
When you add a Shockwave movie to a page, Dreamweaver MX inserts a placeholder. To preview the movie, select it and then click Play in the Property inspector.

27

You can now make any additional modifications to your page. When you're ready, view your Shockwave movie in a browser to see how it looks.

⇨ *Shockwave files crashing your browser? Find out more in "System Crash," in the "Troubleshooting" section of this chapter.*

TROUBLESHOOTING

Planning Flash Applications

I'm trying to get started with Flash but am not sure how to plan for a complex animation. What's the best way?

Getting started in a new medium is never without its pitfalls. One critical point is to be sure you plan your animation! For more information on creating an excellent foundation for your Flash development, see `http://www.macromedia.com/desdev/mx/flash/extreme/`.

System Crash

Every time I try to load a Shockwave file in my browser, my system crashes. What's going on?

There are a number of reasons this could be happening. Some common problems include conflicts with your system, incompatible versions of software, and lack of available memory. Shockwave can be intensive to run! The best thing to do is be sure you have *the most recent* Shockwave player. If you do, try uninstalling it and then reinstalling it.

If the problem isn't solved, you can always try online help. For Windows, see `http://www.macromedia.com/support/director/ts/documents/tn3902.html`. Macintosh users should see `http://www.macromedia.com/support/director/ts/documents/tn3901.html`. Both of these pages provide a list of error reports and troubleshooting concerns.

PEER TO PEER: FLASH ACCESSIBILITY

Flash, with 96% saturation, is an extremely attractive media to use on the Web. However, one of the biggest concerns with Flash in the current Web design and development environment is that it has some serious problems with accessibility.

Macromedia is aware of this problem and is working to make significant advances in this area. Some of the primary ways that Macromedia is addressing the concern are as follows:

- **Provide accessibility features in Flash players**—Flash Player 6 is the first player in its class to make Flash content readable by screen reading hardware and software for the blind.

- **Provide accessibility features in the Flash MX development environment**—Flash MX provides an accessibility panel that enables developers to add descriptive text to any element in a Flash movie. So, the ball from our earlier example could be described using text, which would then be available to screen readers, making the Flash content more accessible than ever before (see Figure 27.17).

Visit the Macromedia Accessibility Resource Center to learn more about techniques for creating accessible rich media: http://www.macromedia.com/macromedia/accessibility/.

- **Provide education to designers and developers using Macromedia products concerning accessibility**—Via the Macromedia Accessibility Resource Center, designers and developers have access to articles, tutorials, examples, and tools that will help them create accessible sites at large, including those that contain rich media content from Flash or Shockwave.

Figure 27.17
Using the Flash MX Accessibility panel to add a name and description for the Flash content on a page.

VII

MANAGING YOUR SITE

IN THIS PART

VALIDATION, CROSS-BROWSER COMPATIBILITY, AND ACCESSIBILITY TESTING

IN THIS CHAPTER

MOVING TOWARD A PROFESSIONAL STANDARD

Throughout this book you've read "Peer to Peer" sections advocating standards and best practices. In this chapter, some of the most important contemporary practices are discussed at greater length.

As mentioned many times, Macromedia has been paying close attention to these contemporary practices and incorporating them over time into its products. Macromedia Dreamweaver MX is especially impressive in this regard, with plenty of tools to assist you in achieving that professional standard—far more so than with other, similar products for the Web.

Of course, the Web has been in such a state of rapid change and evolution that it's a challenge for anyone to keep up, much less software developers. As a result, some of the tools Macromedia has introduced into the MX line, although extraordinarily helpful, are also limited or not quite up to the ideal. Fortunately, there are workarounds for these problems, and future upgrades to the product line will have refined some of these tools rather impressively.

What Are Web Standards, Really?

To provide a little more context into why this book has such a focus on helping you use Dreamweaver MX in accordance with Web standards, one must get some context into what Web standards really are and just why they can be so helpful to you.

The term *Web standard* is ultimately a confusing one because it's not just inaccurate, but it also suggests conformity. We use the term *Web standard* to refer to what is actually a series of specifications and recommendations created by the World Wide Web Consortium (W3C). The W3C is not an authoritative standards body per se; its primary functions are to research, develop, and publish information on technologies and activities related to the Web.

Following a W3C specification—what is conventionally and broadly referred to as a *Web standard*—does not mean conformity in terms of design. In fact, it's probably the opposite. Innovation in design, especially on such a rapidly changing platform as the Web, requires a period of stability prior to and after the fact to come about. It's a pattern that history bears out. Building the next level of the Web's infrastructure as cleanly as possible provides the matrix for new levels of innovation to be achieved. Web professionals are sensing this, which is why many people and software developers such as Macromedia are starting to get interested in standards. They realize it's a cool—and necessary—issue.

The Bottom Line: Time and Money

Standards definitely can save time. Early case studies suggest that compliance probably saves money for everyone in the Web site development chain—from site owner to developer to ISP. Those are the immediate advantages. Longer term, working with standards addresses many technical, creative, and even social concerns as follows:

- **Technical advantages**—Technically, Web sites will be more easily maintained and also readily available for many platforms beyond the Web.

- **Creative advantages**—Creatively, you can apply style sheets that will easily make a site look good on a computer screen, on a PDA screen, and even in print.

- **Social advantages**—Socially, we remove barriers to access by cleaning up our hacked markup and paying attention to accessibility concerns.

Web standards in the big view are about the long-term benefits to business and technology. Learning Web standards on a professional level is a commitment that takes effort now and requires years of study to maintain and grow. That's the truth of it. Yet, if you are a professional interested in learning professional practices and using quality tools, it becomes very helpful to you to have at least an]awareness of how to achieve the long-term professional goal.

When to Switch?

The question of when to switch to standards practices can't effectively be addressed without looking at education and training for Web professionals. Being a Web designer or Web developer is no longer novel. We have complex jobs to do, and standards are a means of doing those jobs with maturity and excellence. When your team has a good overall understanding of and long-term commitment to standards, you can consider a switch.

Good times to look at introducing XHTML, layout with CSS, and validation of documents include

- **During a Web site redesign**—Much of the work being done by Web design firms and Web designers individually is redesigning of sites. This is an excellent time to introduce best practices and standards.

> If the cost to make all legacy documents compliant is prohibitive, begin to move forward from this point using standards. If, at some point, you can address the legacy concerns, do so.

- **Upon creation of a new Web site**—If you're about to create a new Web site, following the guidelines in this book in general, and this chapter specifically, will help ease you into Web standards.

Other means for assisting with the creation of a professional standard include such items as

- **Creating company style guides**—Create a company style guide for markup and content such as logos, colors, and any other relevant guidelines. Add sections for specific clients where necessary.

- **Research tools**—Research and try development tools such as highly flexible and affordable content management systems. Look at validation utilities and site management tools for link checking, statistical analysis, and other things that will make your work more successful.

- **Study browsers**—This might be the toughest part because the platform and versioning differences are vast.

- **Seek community and education**—Other professionals can assist in profound ways with advice and ongoing guidance. Continue finding means of educating individuals on your team about technology updates and options, so they can bring this knowledge back into the fold. Training, certification, and new products are often introduced at Web-related conferences, which provide short but intense options for community networking and continuing education.

28

Of course, there are also general business practices that influence your work. Know the client; know the client's needs and goals; and of course, know the client's audience. This will guide you away from falling into the problems that arise from rushing into anything without good research.

For example, if you find that a client's audience uses 4.0 browsers, especially Netscape, you have to facilitate that—and you can do so very effectively while following specifications. It just takes an understanding of the standards, and that's where the education and community aspects of professional understanding come into play.

> **The World Organization of** Webmasters (WOW) provides high-end certification, community, and educational resources for all Web professionals. This growing professional association is a non-profit organization working to provide you with the resources you'll need throughout your career. For more information about WOW, see http://www.joinwow.org/.

VALIDATING DOCUMENTS

One of the first ways you can begin learning about Web standards is to validate your HTML or XHTML documents. There are several ways to do this: You can use Dreamweaver MX tools, or you can use alternative tools. In this section, you'll learn the advantages and disadvantages of each, so you can make the best decision necessary for your workflow.

Using Dreamweaver MX Validation Tools

Dreamweaver MX comes complete with several built-in validators. The validators provide helpful warnings and errors to assist you in ensuring your documents pass muster.

⇨ *Trying to validate but having problems? Find out why in "Validator Trouble" in the "Troubleshooting" section at the end of this chapter.*

If you'd like to validate an HTML or XHTML document using Dreamweaver MX, first set your preferences as follows:

1. Select Edit, Preferences from the main menu. The Preferences dialog box appears.

2. Highlight the Validator category. The dialog box interface changes to show the validation options (see Figure 28.1).

3. Uncheck any checked items, and then check the type of document you are validating, such as HTML 4.0.

4. Click OK.

⇨ *To learn more about preferences, see Appendix A, "Setting Preferences," p. 617.*

Now that your preferences are set, open the document, in this case an HTML 4.0 document, in Dreamweaver MX. Validation reports will appear in the Reports panel (see Figure 28.2).

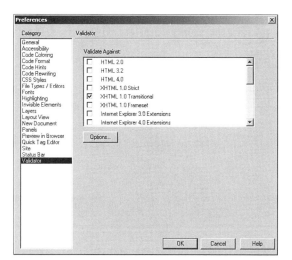

Figure 28.1
Before working with a validator, you need to set the preferences you want to use.

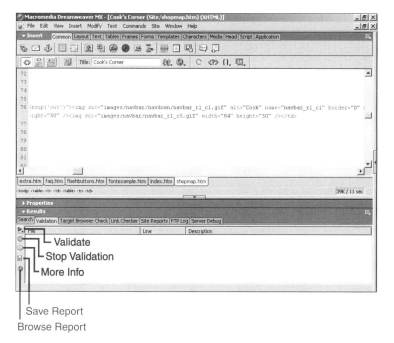

Figure 28.2
The Reports panel provides you with a look at the various validation reports.

After you have done that, follow these steps to continue the validation process:

1. Select File, Check Page, Validate Markup. Dreamweaver MX will run its validator.

2. The Results panel, if not already open, will open and display any warnings or errors (see Figure 28.3).

3. Examine the errors and make changes as you see fit.

28

Figure 28.3
The Results panel gives you the resulting errors and warnings of a validation report.

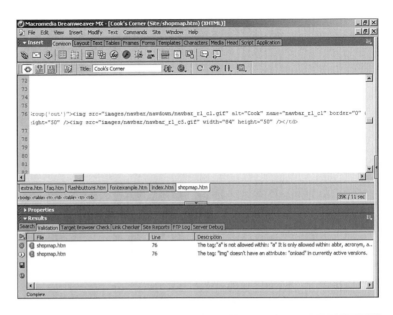

Validation using this method provides you with the following information:

- **File**—This is the name of the file being validated.

- **Line**—This feature helps you find the exact line where the associated problem that the error or warning is referring to resides. Double-click directly on any error or warning to go directly to the line where the problem is.

- **Description**—This area provides a description of the problem and ideas on how to fix it.

If your document passes with no errors, you can assume you have a valid document. Dreamweaver MX, however, doesn't explicitly say that your document is valid according to the DOCTYPE you've declared in your document.

It's important to remember that a warning is not an error in validation. A *warning* is just a suggestion for using an alternative means of doing something more in step with best practices. Warings do not affect the actual validity of a document. An *error* is a specific problem that must be addressed for the document to be considered valid.

Using the W3C HTML Validator

In this section, youlearn how to use the W3C validator to test your documents. First, consider testing an HTML document and then an XHTML document just to get the feel of the validator.

The W3C validator can validate a document online or by upload. To validate your document online, you first need to place it on a remote Web server. To validate your document by upload, just be sure you know the name and location of the document.

To validate a document, follow these steps:

1. Point your Web browser to `http://validator.w3.org/` (see Figure 28.4).

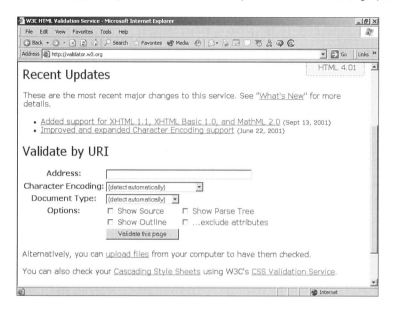

Figure 28.4
Use the W3C's validator is an alternative method.

2. If you are validating an online version, type the address of your document into the Validate by URI address field. If you are uploading your file, click the Upload Files link and add the file from your hard drive. Leave all the other options as they are.

3. Click the Validate This Page or Validate This Document button. The validator will now compare your document to the DTD you described in that document. After the validator is done processing, a report appears in a new browser page.

If any errors are reported, examine what they are, troubleshoot your document, make any necessary changes, and revalidate until your document passes the validation test.

Encoding Warnings at the W3C Validator

If you are uploading files, you will often generate a warning regarding proper encoding.

Encoding is ideally set on the server, so this error should not appear when you are validating from an online source—assuming your server is properly configured.

Another means of adding encoding is to place the proper encoding information into a meta tag. Any document using the XML prolog should not generate this warning on upload or online test because the prolog contains the encoding information.

Note that a warning of this nature does not interfere with your document's validity; it's simply a means of alerting you to a potential problem with the proper encoding and display of your document.

28

At this point it will serve you well to begin validating other documents you have worked on recently. Find a document you know might be problematic (has font tags, uses nested tables, uses proprietary browser tags—anything like that will do). Then, try validating the document with a range of DTDs.

➪ *To learn more about DTDs, see "Transitioning from HTML to XHTML," p. 240.*

Fixing Errors

If you are experiencing a high volume of errors, begin by correcting any obvious problems. Then, fix each error in order.

Many times, the existence of a single error can generate a long list of errors, and cleaning up that single error will remove the others, resulting in a valid, conforming document.

VALIDATING CSS DOCUMENTS

One thing that Macromedia Dreamweaver MX does not provide is a validation method for your CSS documents. But, validating CSS is as important as validating your HTML and XHTML if you want to have a compliant site.

The W3C provides an excellent CSS validation tool that works essentially in the same way that its HTML and XHTML validator does.

To validate a CSS document using this tool, follow these steps:

1. Point your browser to `http://jigsaw.w3.org/css-validator/` (see Figure 28.5).

Figure 28.5
Working with the W3C's CSS validator helps to ensure that your documents are all valid prior to uploading them.

2. As with the HTML and XHTML validator, you can validate in several ways, including by URL (if the document is online) and by upload.

3. Click the option you'd like. If you select by URL, you'll be asked for the location of the document. If you select to upload it, you'll be asked to browse for the document or type its path directly into the available text box.

4. Click the Submit This CSS File for Validation button.

The W3C's CSS validator will validate your CSS. As with HTML and XHTML, warnings can be generated; as long as no errors are generated, the CSS document is valid (see Figure 28.6). Warnings, again, can assist you in improving your document but do not influence the validity of the document.

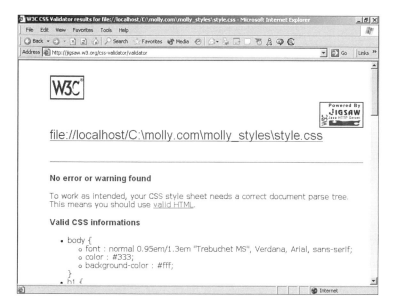

Figure 28.6
A valid CSS document produces no warnings or errors.

To learn more about CSS, see Chapter 16, "Using Cascading Style Sheets in Dreamweaver," p. 285.

CROSS-BROWSER COMPATIBILITY

Adhering to Web standards can help ensure that your sites are readable across browsers. It's important to remember that the W3C's guidelines are as much for Web browser manufacturers and software developers such as Macromedia to properly implement these features in their tools as they are for designers and developers.

The main problems faced by designers and developers over the past years have come from inconsistencies in these tools and in the browser support for the tools. But, the good news is that most of today's contemporary browsers contain good support for standards. These browsers include

28

- Microsoft IE 5.5 and later (Windows and Macintosh)

- Netscape 6.0 and later

- Mozilla 1.0 and later

- Opera

There are other browsers that do a good job adhering to standards, but they are in very limited use. The previously listed browsers also have some specific bugs or problems related to their standards compliance.

For example, even though the Opera browser has always been dedicated to creating excellent standards support for CSS, it currently lacks much support for the Document Object Model (DOM). This means that a great deal of scripting becomes disabled in that browser.

Another issue is that when migrating to Web standards, it often becomes necessary to consider the limitations of older or problematic browsers that site visitors might still be using. Style sheet layouts, for example, can use workarounds so that even if the layout is not maintained in a given browser, the content is still accessible and readable. But, if you have a situation in which you have a large user base of Netscape 4 users and are required to maintain the visual design, you will have to turn to transitional design techniques (using transitional DTDs in HTML or XHTML) and table-based layouts.

Unfortunately, there are no quick-fixes for the numerous cross-browser problems. However, most designers and developers are finding that if they can adhere to standards and develop for the previously mentioned browsers, their sites are not only more compatible across browsers, but also much closer to accessibility concerns because of the basic idea that, at their ideal, HTML 4/4.01 and XHTML 1.0 ask for the complete separation of presentation and document structure.

The bottom line is that all sites will have to be checked in multiple browsers. You can do this in Dreamweaver with ease. First, you must have multiple browsers installed. Then, you can check your work in a variety of browsers by selecting File, Preview in Browser and selecting the browser of your choice. To add a browser to the list, select File, Preview in Browser, Edit Browser List. This brings up the Preferences dialog box, and you can add browsers from there.

You can also use Dreamweaver MX to test for browser compatibility. To do so, follow these steps:

1. Save your file.

2. Select File, Check Page, Check Target Browsers.

3. Select a browser from the list.

4. Click Check.

To find a wide range of browsers and browser versions for testing purposes, check out http://browsers.evolt.org/.

The check will run and the results will appear in the Results Panel under the Target Browser Check tab.

It's also recommended that you have at least two testing computer platforms: Windows and Macintosh. This is because Macintosh versions of Web browsers are different in their capabilities from Windows versions.

28

VALIDATING FOR ACCESSIBILITY

As it does with markup, Dreamweaver MX provides a means to test and report accessibility problems. There are also several other public validators that you can use.

Before you attempt to validate for accessibility, you should examine your documents to see whether they adhere to the Web Accessibility Initiative (WAI) priority guidelines. The WAI of the W3C has an official document involving 14 guidelines that Web developers are encouraged to follow. Following these guidelines will help you carefully look at your documents and address concerns related to accessibility.

The 14 WAI guidelines are as follows:

1. **Provide equivalent alternatives to auditory and visual content**—If you're using sound or graphics, include text descriptions and employ HTML-based aids, such as the `alt` attribute in images, wherever possible.

2. **Don't rely on color alone**—Because many people cannot see color, have problems with color blindness, or are accessing the Web via noncolor devices, relying solely on color to convey information is problematic. To address this guideline, be sure to include explanations wherever color is being used to express important facts, and make sure that foreground and background colors have high enough contrast to be visible.

3. **Use markup and style sheets, and do so properly**—This guideline is an important one! It encourages the creation of well-formed documents in accordance with recommendations. What's becoming very evident is that the more separation you can get between presentation and document structure, the more accessible your pages will automatically become.

➪ *For more information on markup, see "Working with HTML and XHTML," p. 237. To learn about CSS, see "Designing with Style," p. 265, and "Using Cascading Style Sheets in Dreamweaver," p. 285.*

4. **Clarify natural language usage**—Any foreign pronunciations, acronyms, or abbreviations should be spelled out or accomodated using the `title` attribute in related elements.

5. **Create tables that transform gracefully**—Ideally, you're only using tables now for tabular data. Tables present specific problems, such as screen reader software reading across table cells, which can be very confusing. Some browsers support certain elements and attributes that can be used to make tables more accessible.

➪ *To work effectively with tables, see "Designing with Table-Based Layouts," p. 321.*

6. **Ensure that pages featuring new technologies transform gracefully**—All pages should be accessible no matter which technologies are being employed.

7. **Ensure user control of time-sensitive content changes**—Many users with disabilities are affected by things that move and blink. For example, a few members of my family have migraine headaches, and one sure trigger is fast-moving, blinking objects. Moreover, other people have mobility impairments and cannot keep up with any kind of moving object. Others with

28

learning disabilities might become confused. Anything that moves, blinks, or auto-updates should have controls that allow the user to stop, start, and pause the object to make the page more effective and usable.

8. **Ensure direct accessibility of embedded user interfaces**—If you're placing an embedded object within your page, such as an applet or Flash design, be sure that users have access to the interface of that embedded object.

9. **Design for device independence**—Individuals accessing the Web might be doing so using a number of devices, including keyboards, mice, voice commands, a head or mouth stick, and so on. General guidelines to manage this issue include using client-side imagemaps instead of server-side maps and providing tab order mechanisms in forms for easier navigation.

10. **Use interim solutions**—Older browsers and assistive devices do not often operate properly, yet many are in abundance in various government organizations, including those that provide services to disabled communities. So, if I wrote a document with a consecutive list of links (very common in navigation schemes), my screen reader might read the link as one uninterrupted link and attempt to resolve it, to no avail. Another problem is the pop-up window, which these days is often used in advertising.

11. **Use W3C technologies and guidelines**—The W3C provides recommendations for all browser and tools manufacturers as well as Web authors. When conformance is achieved, accessibility guidelines are that much more readily implemented.

12. **Provide context and orientation information**—The more complex a page or site, the more helpful it is to ensure that visitors know what they are doing at a given location and why.

13. **Provide clear navigation mechanisms**—Clear and consistent navigation not only is an imperative in accessibility, but is also an imperative in user interface design. Links should be clearly identified and organized, and graphical options should have appropriate alternatives available.

⇨ *For more information on creating navigation, see "User Interface Design Essentials," p. 314.*

14. **Ensure that documents are clear and simple**—The easier your content is to understand, the more you'll get your point across, no matter who the audience is.

> For additional tips when working with accessibility, see http://www.w3.org/WAI/References/QuickTips/.

Testing Accessibility with Macromedia Dreamweaver MX

Macromedia Dreamweaver MX provides several means of helping you to ensure that your documents are accessible. Even Macromedia points out that "no tool can automate" this process and acknowledges that its tools are there to assist you with achieving accessible sites.

You'll still need to know the WAI guidelines as recommended previously and study additional information if you are working on any sites that have legislative mandates requiring them to be accessible.

After you believe your document (or a section of a document) is ready to be tested, you can run an accessibility report using Dreamweaver MX tools.

If you'd like to browse your report results, click the Browse Report option. Your report will then be displayed in your default Web browser.

Running a Complete Report on a Document

To run an accessibility report on a document, follow these steps:

1. Open the document in Macromedia Dreamweaver MX.

2. Select File, Check Page, Check Accessibility (see Figure 28.7). The checker will run and provide a report.

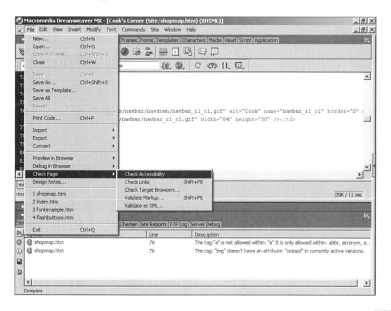

Figure 28.7
To check accessibility, select Check Accessibility from the File submenu.

3. Use the report to find and correct problems in the document.

As with the markup validation report, you will see the filename, line number where the error resides, and a helpful description of the problem with a suggestion for fixing it (see Figure 28.8).

You can run reports for an entire site. Simply select the site folder from the site panel and follow steps 2 and 3.

28

Figure 28.8
Dreamweaver MX provides a detailed accessibility report in the Results panel. Use this to help make changes to improve your page's accessibility features.

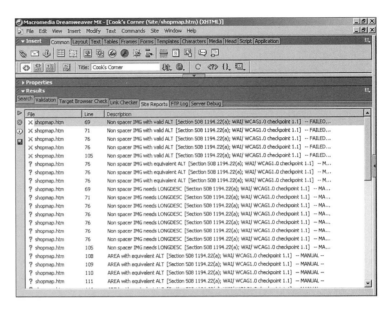

Running a Feature-Specific Accessibility Report

You can also run accessibility reports on specific content. To do so, follow these steps:

1. Open the document.

2. Select Site, Reports; the Reports dialog box appears (see Figure 28.9).

Figure 28.9
The Report Settings dialog box.

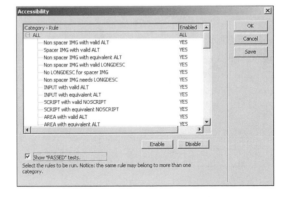

3. Click Report Settings, and the appropriate settings dialog box appears.

4. Specify which content you want the report reflect (see Figure 28.10).

5. Click Run.

A site report will be generated in the Results panel, and it will be specific to the options you selected.

You can save accessibility reports to document your workflow process as well as share with other co-workers. To save your report, click the Save icon in the Results panel.

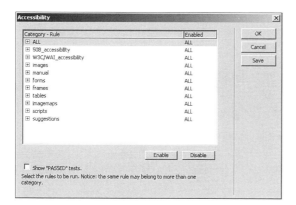

Figure 28.10
Setting detailed features for an accessibility report.

Following W3C Recommended Techniques for Accessibility Testing

If you'd like to do a step-by-step check, you can do so by following W3C WAI recommended testing techniques. As part of these techniques, you'll need to run the document through at least two recommended accessibility validators.

The Step-by-Step Process

To perform this kind of check, follow these steps:

1. Select a sampling of documents from the site you want to review. Include your home page in the test.

2. Using a graphical browser (or variety of browsers), examine the documents using the following guidelines:

   - Turn off all images and see whether the document is still logical.

   - Turn off any sound to ensure the document is understandable without it.

   - Change the font size, making it larger and smaller. Your content is ideally still readable.

   - Set the screen resolution to 640×480. If this forces a horizontal scroll, realize that this can cause difficulties for the mobility impaired.

   - Change your monitor's display to black and white (if you can) and see how the site looks.

   - Tab through links and form fields using the keyboard in place of the mouse. Can you get everywhere easily?

3. Test your documents with voice or text browsers. Perform these two checks:

   - Is the information you're hearing or seeing equivalent to what is experienced in a graphic browser? Does the information follow a logical order?

   - Validate your documents using at least two accessibility validators.

28

4. Summarize your testing results, making recommendations as to how any problems can be addressed and any follow-up steps to reach full conformance.

In situations where accessibility is a legislated concern, you will need to run these tests on your documents on a regular basis to ensure conformance.

Using the Bobby Validator

To check your site for accessibility using the Bobby validator—one of the most popular accessibility validation tools—you must either first have your page online (a free service) or purchase the standalone local version. The advantage of the standalone version is that you can run accessibility tests on entire sites.

To use the online validator, follow these steps:

1. Point your browser to `http://bobby.watchfire.com/`.

2. Enter the URL of the page you want validated.

3. Select a guideline. If you are testing to the most rigorous guidelines, click the Web Content Accessibility Guidelines option. If you are testing specifically for Section 508 guidelines, select that option.

4. Click Submit.

Bobby will now generate a report (see Figure 28.11). The report will generate warnings and errors and how to fix them, or it will approve your page.

Figure 28.11
Bobby returns a report showing this page to be Section 508 compliant.

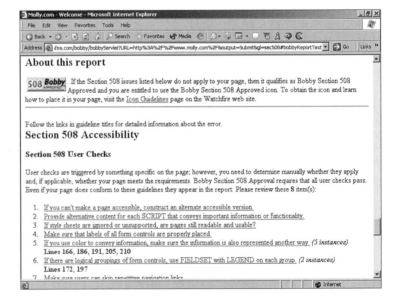

⇨ *Pages not validating properly in Bobby even though you've followed the accessibility guidelines? Find out what the problem is in "Accessibility Validation Problems" in the "Troubleshooting" section later in this chapter.*

Using the Page Valet Validator

Another online accessibility validator you can use is Page Valet. Page Valet can actually check for several validation concerns and provides very specific feedback in terms of your accessibility problems.

To use Page Valet, follow these steps:

1. Point your Web browser to `http://valet.webthing.com/page/`.

2. Scroll down to the Validate Your Document section, and enter the URL you want checked.

3. In the Accessibility Checks option, select the level and type of accessibility report you want. For most readers of this book, WCAG Level 1 or US Section 508 will be the most commonly used reports.

4. In Report Preparation, select Server-Side XSLT.

5. In Report Format, select Document View/HTML from the drop-down menu.

6. For Parse Mode, leave it at the Web mode default.

7. Click Validate.

> For a listing of other validation tools, please see `http://www.w3.org/WAI/ER/existingtools.html`.

Page Valet will run a check and provide you with an annotated report (see Figure 28.12). You can then work with the report's recommendations and make changes as you see fit.

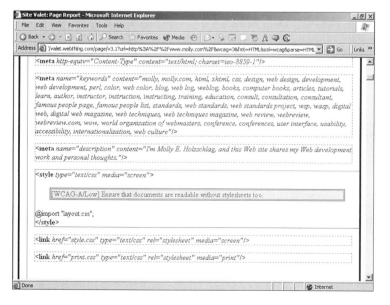

Figure 28.12
Page Valet provides a great interface, complete with annotations to assist you in adhering to accessibility concerns.

28

TROUBLESHOOTING

Validator Trouble

I tried to run my page through the validator, but it won't work. What's wrong?

For documents to be validated, they must contain the proper DOCTYPE declaration. Check your document to see whether the proper DOCTYPE is declared.

▷ *For examples of DOCTYPE declarations, see "Features of XHTML," p. 243.*

Accessibility Validation Problems

The Bobby accessibility validator is claiming my page isn't valid, but I looked through the errors and I've addressed each one according to the accessibility guidelines. What's wrong?

Working with accessibility validators sometimes means your page won't validate even if it is in fact valid. The reason for this is that certain checks must be performed by you. For example, if a text alternative is required for a media object, the validator might not find that alternative and will generate a warning. Manually check the error or warning, and if you've adhered to the guidelines recommended earlier in this chapter, your site is likely to be valid according to accessibility guidelines.

PEER TO PEER: USING MACROMEDIA EXTENSIONS AND PRODUCTS FOR ACCESSIBILITY TESTING

Macromedia has recently joined forces with accessibility experts to create a product called LIFT. This product can be downloaded from `http://www.usablenet.com/lift_dw/lift_dw.html`, and it will run complete reports on your sites and assist you with making appropriate changes.

Some extensions are available for assisting you with ensuring that you are including important accessibility features in your documents. Be sure to check the Macromedia Exchange site's accessibility section for a range of utilities to assist you with the accessibility validation process.

▷ *For more information on using Macromedia Exchange and extensions, see "About Macromedia Exchange," p. 556.*

28

WORKING WITH OTHERS

IN THIS CHAPTER

SETTING UP A REMOTE SITE

Working as part of a design team presents additional challenges and obstacles. If you've ever collaborated on a design project, you know that the most common concern is maintaining control over files when multiple developers are working on the same pages. Communication is another critical factor so the project proceeds smoothly.

If you've followed this book in a linear fashion, you undoubtedly have read about using templates and working in such a way as to streamline activities. Here, you learn to work with others to perform some tasks you've already learned to do on your own, such as setting up and working with a remote site, but with extended information on how to do so in groups.

As discussed in previous chapters, the most common method of uploading to the remote server is File Transfer Protocol (FTP). This method works just as well in a collaborative environment as it does on an individual basis. Dreamweaver offers additional tools—Check In/Out—to ensure that files aren't being uploaded or downloaded by multiple developers at the same time. If you're working with a team, however, there are other possible methods of communication with the remote server that might better suit your purposes.

WHAT IS VERSION CONTROL?

Let's say you and a team of five other developers are working on a site. You make changes to a file and save it. At the same time, however, another member of the team is editing the same file. When your co-worker saves his copy of the file onto the server, your changes disappear into the ether because the file is overwritten.

Version control prevents these aggravating mishaps. When one member of the team opens a file, it's locked to prevent others from editing the same file.

Dreamweaver uses a minimal form of version control when Check In/Check Out are enabled. The remote server shows that a file is currently checked out and lists the name of the team member who currently has access to the file. Other developers can still access the file, but only in a read-only state.

Larger development houses often use more sophisticated version control systems such as Visual SourceSafe and WebDAV. Not only do version control systems such as Visual SourceSafe and WebDAV protect against overwritten files, but they also keep a historical record for each file in the project. This enables you to revert to previous versions of a document.

Microsoft Visual SourceSafe

Microsoft Visual SourceSafe is a Windows-based version control system. To use SourceSafe as your method of interacting with the remote server, follow these steps:

1. Open the Site Definition dialog box for your site:

   - If you're in the initial creation stage of your site, this is done using Site, New Site.

   - If you've already defined the local folder information for the site, use the Site, Edit Sites command to open the Edit Sites dialog box, click the site name, and then click Edit.

2. Select the Remote Info category.

3. In the Access drop-down menu, select SourceSafe Database.

4. Click the Settings button to open the Open SourceSafe Database dialog box (see Figure 29.1).

5. In the Database Path field, enter the location of the SourceSafe database.

You can get the database path and project name from your product manager if your development team is using this form of version control.

29

6. In the Project field, enter the name of the project, as it's referenced by the SourceSafe database.

7. Enter your username and password to access the project.

8. Click OK.

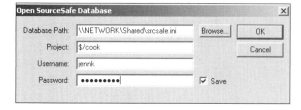

Figure 29.1
The SourceSafe Database settings give Dreamweaver access to the project database.

WebDAV

Web-Based Distributed Authoring and Versioning (WebDAV) is another version control system. It's currently less popular than VSS, but because it is an open standard, it has a growing audience. To set WebDAV as your method of access to the remote server, use the Site Definition dialog box (steps 1 and 2 in the previous procedure) to set the Access field to WebDAV. Click Settings to open the WebDAV Connection dialog box (see Figure 29.2). Enter the URL of the WebDAV server and your username and password to access it.

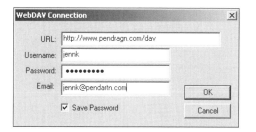

Figure 29.2
The WebDAV Connection settings enable Dreamweaver to communicate with the Web-based version control server.

Version Control Limitations in Dreamweaver

Version control software is useful, but it has its limitations. If you're using VSS or WebDAV with Dreamweaver, the Synchronize and Select Newer Files options are unavailable because Dreamweaver can't obtain an accurate timestamp from the remote server. Also, depending on how your collaborative environment is configured, it's still possible to overwrite an updated file with one

29

that's outdated if your local folder isn't current. If your development shop uses version control software, your product manager should be able to provide information about how to use and access the database.

CHECKING FILES IN AND OUT

Even if your development team isn't using version control software, Dreamweaver has tools to keep your project running smoothly. When you set up the Remote Info in the Site Definition dialog box, there are options at the bottom of this box to enable Check In/Out. Check In is similar to the Put or upload command, whereas Check Out is similar to the Get or download command.

The advantage of using these tools instead of the default Get and Put commands is that Check In/Out tracks which files are currently in use by other members of the team. If a file is in use, the Remote Site list of the Site window/panel shows that the file is checked out, designated by a check mark in the file list (see Figure 29.3).

The Check In/Out options are useful for individual developers who work on multiple machines and platforms. If you forget to upload changes to the remote server, the file will appear as checked out when you try to retrieve it on another machine, thus enabling you to avoid having multiple copies of the same file, each with different revisions.

Figure 29.3
The Site window displays files that are checked out by yourself or others on the team when Check In/Out is enabled.

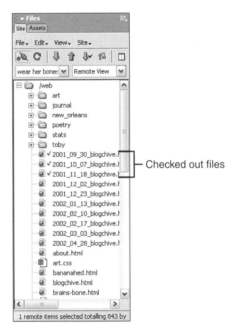

Checked out files

If you're using FTP in a team environment, it's important that every member of the team uses Dreamweaver's built-in FTP tools. If some developers are using a third-party FTP application while others are using Dreamweaver's FTP tools, the Check In/Out features will be rendered ineffective. Dreamweaver will have no way of knowing the files were downloaded by the other application.

To enable Check In/Out, select the Enable File Check In and Check Out box in the Remote Info category of the Site Definition dialog box. Upon selecting this option, additional selections will appear in the dialog box (see Figure 29.4).

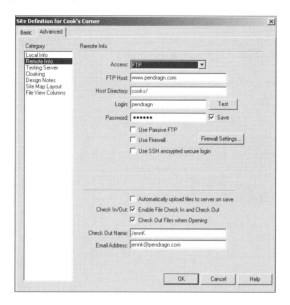

Figure 29.4
When the Enable File Check In and Check Out option is selected, other options become available, as well.

If you've been using the Site panel for long, you're probably used to double-clicking to open a document. Select the Check Out Files when Opening option to automatically check out files when you double-click.

This option works only if you're opening files by double-clicking or using the context menu within the Site panel or window. It doesn't work with the File, Open menu option.

To make the Check In/Out feature most effective, Dreamweaver needs to be capable of tracking who has checked out the files. This allows other members of the team to communicate directly with the person who's currently working on a file that might be needed by someone else, eliminating broadcast email messages to the entire group. To enable this feature, fill in the Check Out Name field with a unique username. If you also enter an email address in the appropriate field, team members will be able to click the email address in the Remote Site list to open an email addressed to the appropriate developer.

After the Check In/Out options have been selected, their use is identical to the Get and Put commands. The same Get/Check Out and Put/Check In buttons are used to upload and download files.

➪ *If you're having trouble with certain transfers, read "Checking the Transfer Log" in the "Troubleshooting" section later in this chapter.*

29

Cloaking Files and Folders

Often when you're making changes to the content of pages, the images and other elements of the site remain the same. When you've completed revisions and are ready to synchronize the local folder with the remote server, it's a waste of time to re-upload the image folder or other folders if no changes have taken place to the contents of those folders. Cloaking allows you to specify that certain folders are exempt from site-wide operations.

➡️ *Trying to cloak HTML pages and can't? Find out the problem in "Cloaking" in the "Troubleshooting" section later in this chapter.*

The Cloaking category of the Site Definition dialog box enables or disables cloaking for the site. Once enabled, you can also set an entire file type to be cloaked, regardless of the directory in which it's located on the site. To cloak a folder, activate cloaking using Site, Cloaking in the Site panel.

SYNCHRONIZING SITES

As files are checked in and out by various developers, your local folders can quickly become outdated. To bring the local and remote sites back into sync, use the Synchronize tool:

1. Select Site, Synchronize.

2. In the Synchronize dialog box, choose to synchronize only selected local files or the entire site (see Figure 29.5).

3. Choose whether to replace only the files on the remote server with their updated local counterparts, to replace only the files in the local folders with their more recent remote counterparts, or to synchronize in both directions as needed.

4. Decide whether to delete files that don't have a counterpart on the other server.

5. Click Preview to begin the synchronization process.

6. In the preview dialog box, verify which files should be uploaded, downloaded, or deleted (see Figure 29.6). All files are selected by default for action. If you want to leave a particular file as is, deselect it.

7. Click OK to complete the synchronization.

Figure 29.5
The Synchronize dialog box determines the direction of the synchronization process.

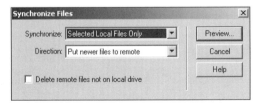

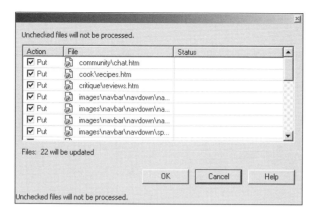

Figure 29.6
Confirm the actions to be taken by the Synchronize tool.

TROUBLESHOOTING

Cloaking

Why can't I cloak an individual file?

Cloaking can be done on folders or specified file types, not on individual files. Thus, you can cloak the entire images folder or all files ending in .jpg, but not an individual file named chef.htm.

Checking the Transfer Log

I'm having transfer problems. How can I figure out what's going on?

Whether you're getting/putting or checking in/out, Dreamweaver logs every FTP transaction between the local and remote sites. This log can help you track down transfer problems. To display the FTP log, select View, Site FTP Log from the Site panel or window. On the Mac, the Site FTP Log is under the Site menu. The log lists any error messages received.

The Site FTP Log appears in the Results panel group. This panel also allows you to enter commands directly to the FTP server.

PEER TO PEER: BUILDING THE WEB OF TRUST

Collaboration can be seen through the lenses of technology and work. But, it can also be seen as a part of the ideology of the Web.

One of the primary goals of the W3C is to build a "Web of Trust." What this means is that the collaborative nature of the medium should never be compromised because it is a fundamental aspect of innovation.

29

The W3C sums up its position on collaboration in this way:

"The Web is a collaborative medium, not read-only like a magazine. In fact, the first Web browser was also an editor, though most people today think of browsing as primarily viewing, not interacting. To promote a more collaborative environment, we must build a 'Web of Trust' that offers confidentiality, instills confidence, and makes it possible for people to take responsibility for (or be accountable for) what they publish on the Web. These goals drive much of W3C's work around XML signatures, annotation mechanisms, group authoring, versioning, etc."

To learn more about the specific vision of the W3C in seven quick and easy points, check out `http://www.w3.org/Consortium/Points/`.

LEARNING ABOUT YOUR SITE

30

PUTTING THE SITE REPORT TO WORK

Your site is, of course, a lot more than just a bunch of content and images in an eye-catching wrapper. It's code, links, knowledge of your audience, and marketing. The more you know about every aspect of your site, the more tactically you can manage it.

Site analysis begins with the markup itself. More than just a matter of wanting to write the best markup possible, HTML complications can have a tremendous impact on the usability of your site.

Consider the implications. If a site is laden with empty or redundant tags, the pages will take longer to load and might produce unexpected results in some browsers. If the pages don't have informative titles, visitors could become disoriented. Page titles also affect search engine rankings, which potentially makes this a return on investment issue, as well. If the images on the site don't have descriptive alt text, and if the site as a whole doesn't pass accessibility tests, potential visitors are lost.

The Site Report feature brings all these code issues together. To run the Site Report, follow these steps:

1. Select Site, Reports from either the Document window or Site panel menu.

2. The Reports dialog box contains a list of report categories (see Figure 30.1). Select the scope of the Report—the current document, the entire local folder, or specific files/folders.

3. Select the reports you require (see Table 30.1).

4. If the selected report(s) require additional settings, use the Report Settings button. This button must be clicked in conjunction with each selected report that requires additional information.

5. Click Run to initiate the report process.

Figure 30.1
The Report dialog box contains options for both workflow and HTML-related analysis.

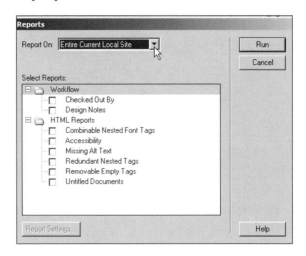

Table 30.1   Site Report Options

Report Name	Purpose	Report Settings
Checked Out By	Lists all documents checked out by a specified user	Specify the user name. If no user name is entered into the Report Settings, the report will list all files checked out by each user.
Design Notes	Lists all Design Notes attached to the site (or selected documents)	Enter search constraints to find Design Notes related to a particular user, revision, or file type.
Combinable Nested Font Tags	Generates a list of font tags that are defining the same block of text that can be combined	
Accessibility	Checks the site's compliance with Section 508 of the 1998 Rehabilitation Act for Accessibility	Each of the accessibility rules can be enabled or disabled for the report.
Missing Alt Text	Lists images that have not been assigned an alt text attribute to make the content accessible	
Redundant Nested Tags	Reports on instances where a tag (and attributes) are nested within the exact same tag	
Removable Empty Tags	Lists extraneous tags that contain no content	
Untitled Documents	Generates a list of all pages in the site that are untitled, either because they retain the default page title or because the <title> tag is missing	

There's a lack of commonality to the reports. Indeed, you might prefer to run separate reports for workflow, accessibility (including missing page titles and alt text for images), and tag issues.

Chapter 9, "Publishing Your Site," explains the use of the Clean UP HTML/XHTML command. This tool is useful for correcting some of the common coding problems, but it doesn't replace the need for the Reports tool because it addresses only a limited range of issues and can be used only one page at a time. It can and should certainly be used in conjunction with the Site Report tool, however, to clean up the mistakes identified in the Report.

➥ *For more information on cleaning up your HTML code, see "Cleaning Up Your HTML," p. 154.*

For accessibility and other issues not addressed by the Clean Up HTML/XHTML command, the Site Report itself can be used to track down problems directly on the page (see Figure 30.2). The Site Report can be sorted by filename, line number, or problem description.

The Accessibility report is also available for the current page by selecting File, Check Page, Check Accessibility.

When you run the tag-related reports, Dreamweaver validates the site and reports other problems in a pop-up warning box.

Figure 30.2
The report results appear in the Site Report panel of the Results panel group.

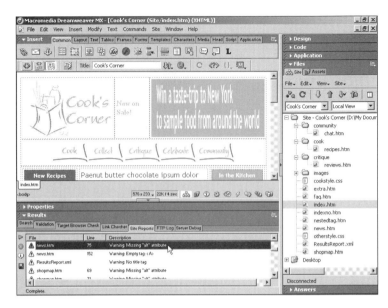

If you've run the report site-wide, the fastest method for fixing problems is to sort by filename. As you scroll through the report results, right-click an entry you want to address and select Open File. The file will be opened in the Document window in the split Design/Code view. If you don't already have line numbers enabled in Code view, turn them on when editing from the Site Report. The line number for each problem is listed in the report, making them easy to find in the document.

Particularly if you're running an Accessibility report for the first time, you might find some of the issues raised by the report to be confusing. To learn more about these issues, right-click an entry and select More Info from the context menu. This additional information appears in the Reference panel of the Code panel group (see Figure 30.3).

⇨ *Having trouble seeing the whole site? Check out "Site Report Visibility" in the "Troubleshooting" section later in this chapter.*

After you've made revisions to your site based on the report results, you should run the Site Report again. Your changes might have raised other issues. At the very least, you'll be reassured that the site is error-free.

Whenever making changes to your site—whether it be changes made by the Site Report, link validation tools, or any other type of maintenance—don't forget to put/check in the files on the remote server when you're done. Note that putting a file doesn't change its status, but checking a file in does ensure that the file's status is updated.

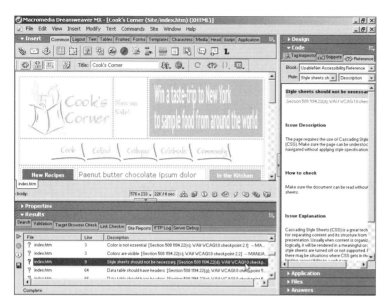

Figure 30.3
Additional information relating to the issues raised in the Site Report is available in the Reference panel.

MAINTAINING LINK INTEGRITY

Another essential site analysis chore is keeping diligent watch over the links within the site. As you already know, the Web changes so quickly that external links you create today can be outdated by tomorrow. Most Web design experts state that you should check external links at least once a month—although few developers heed this advice (including some of those very same experts).

For the record, broken external links are one of the major annoyances that will keep visitors from returning to your site. This is particularly true if you have a list of links to related sites, where a dozen or more links might be broken or outdated at any given time. If you don't plan to maintain the list, you should consider eliminating it from your site.

Internal linking, although not as common a problem due to Dreamweaver's capability to update links as pages are moved within the site's folder structure, is still fraught with some dangers. As you revise the site, it's not uncommon for pages to be *orphaned*—still available on the server but not linked from any other page of the site. Internal links can also break down if you edit a page in an external HTML editor or rename a page without electing to update the links to or from that page. Links to images are the most common type of internal link breakage because images are often deleted or renamed outside Dreamweaver.

Checking Links in a Site

The Check Links feature makes short work of these assorted link problems. Similar to the Site Report feature, the Check Links tool compiles a report of all broken links and orphaned files.

There are three types of Link reports, and each is accessed from a different menu:

- From the Site panel, select Site, Check Links Sitewide to check links throughout the entire site.

- From the main menu, select File, Check Page, Check Links to validate links within the current document.

- Select specific files and folders in the Site panel; then select Check Links, Selected Files/Folders from the context menu to check links only in those files and folders.

No matter the scope of the link checking, the report appears in the Link Checker panel of the Results panel group (see Figure 30.4). The report can be filtered to list only broken links, external links, or orphaned files by using the Show drop-down menu in the Link Checker panel. As with the Site Report, the link report results can be saved to an XML file or used directly to help you locate and repair the problems.

> *Want to validate external links? Find out what to do in "Validating External Links" in the "Troubleshooting" section later in this chapter.*

Figure 30.4
The Link Checker report is similar to the Site Report in appearance and functionality.

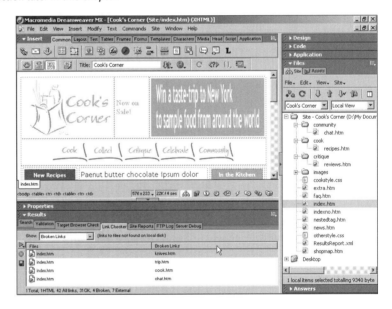

Repairing Links

To repair links using the Link Checker report, follow these steps:

1. Run the Check Links tool for the current page, selected pages/folders, or site-wide.

2. In the Broken Links column of the Link Checker report, select a broken link (see Figure 30.5).

3. Enter the correct path and filename or use the Browse icon to navigate to the correct file.

4. Press Enter or click another link to save the change.

5. If prompted to apply the same change to other broken links to this file, click Yes to automatically make the updates or click No to change only the specific reference in question (see Figure 30.6). If you click Cancel, your change will be undone.

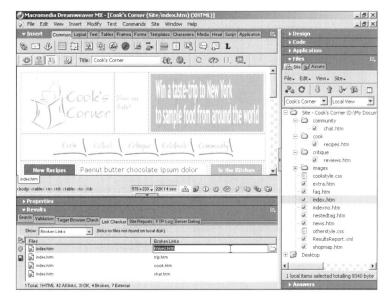

Figure 30.5
A Browse icon appears next to a broken link when it's selected for repair. Use this button to navigate to the correct location of the file.

30

Figure 30.6
If there are other broken links to the same file, Dreamweaver will ask whether those should also be updated.

As you repair each link, it disappears from the report. If you filter the report to show only each type of link at a time, you can work methodically through the list of broken links and orphaned pages without being distracted by external links. When the broken link and orphaned pages reports are empty, all the internal links have been validated. Because there's no way to validate external links in Dreamweaver, those links will always appear in an external link report.

You can also repair links directly in the document. Simply double-click the File column of a broken link, and the document will open in the Document window with the specific link selected (see Figure 30.7). The link can then be modified in the Property inspector. Although this process is more time-consuming, it's useful when you want to see the link in context or make additional changes to the link (such as modifying the source text).

Changing Links Throughout a Site

Even if a link isn't broken, it might need to be updated to refer to a different destination file. If you change email addresses, for example, you'll want to change all the mailto links in the site to point to the new address. In the case of the Cook's Corner site, the Now On Sale item might change from knives (`knives.html`) to cheese graters (`graters.htm`), even though the source text (Now On Sale) remains constant.

Figure 30.7
Double-clicking a broken link entry in the Link Checker report opens the document with the broken link highlighted in both the Document window and the Property inspector.

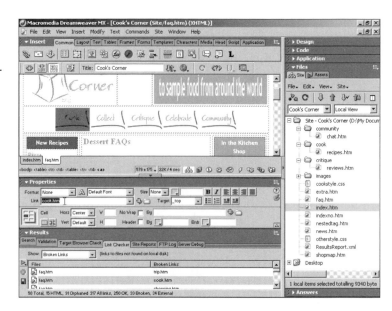

To change a link site-wide, do the following:

1. Select Site, Change Link Sitewide from the Site panel menu.

2. In the Change Link Sitewide dialog box, enter the current link destination in the Change All Links to field (see Figure 30.8). Use the Browse icon if you're unsure of the path.

Figure 30.8
Changing links site-wide saves time and ensures that you don't miss any stragglers.

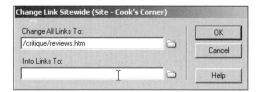

3. Enter the new link destination in the Into Links to field.

4. Click OK.

TROUBLESHOOTING

Site Report Visibility

I'm trying to use the Site Report features, but the display is limited. How can I get to the complete report?

One of the limitations of the Site Report is the size of the panel on the screen. Unless you manually adjust the panels to take up more than the default screen real estate, some of the report explanations are truncated. Use the More Info option to read the complete text of the problem in the Reference panel.

Validating External Links

I need to validate links to other sites. Can Dreamweaver help me do that?

Dreamweaver does not validate external links. The Check Links report will, however, provide you with a list of external links. You can then use this report to go down the list and manually check the integrity of each external link.

PEER TO PEER: TRACKING USAGE STATISTICS

Even after the site is complete and live, the site analysis doesn't end. Particularly if your site has an expectation of commercial success, you'll want to know whether it's living up to its return on investment. To do this, your site analysis changes emphasis from the development of the site to its usage, and it is critical that you track this information if you want to truly serve your visitors and achieve best practices.

Dreamweaver, however, doesn't offer any tools for tracking usage statistics. The Macromedia Exchange contains some extensions to enable counters, but these are commercial products that charge a fee to enable them on your site.

Many Web hosting services offer tools to allow their clients to track usage on their sites (see Figure 30.9). Also, several free and commercial services are available to track these statistics. They generally require a certain amount of manual labor to insert the necessary code into your site, but they'll provide you with all the information you need about your site's usage and the demographics of your visitors.

To learn more about statistics, check first with your Web service provider or systems administrator to see whether there are preexisting methods on your servers to do this. If not, you might want to look into a free service, such as `http://www.freestats.com/`, to accomplish this.

Figure 30.9
The molly.com Web site uses a statistics package known as Webalizer. It offers extensive visual demographic and other statistical information. Webalizer can be found at `http://www.mrunix.net/webalizer/`.

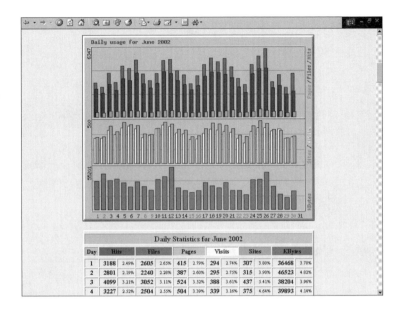

30

EXPANDING DREAMWEAVER AND USING THIRD-PARTY SOFTWARE

IN THIS PART

31

DOWNLOADING AND INSTALLING EXTENSIONS, BEHAVIORS, AND PLUG-INS

IN THIS CHAPTER

EXTENDING MACROMEDIA DREAMWEAVER

An impressive part of Macromedia's strategy for its products and how people use them is to allow its programs to be *extensible*.

This means that programmers, especially those with JavaScript, XML, and C++ programming, can create extensions and share or sell them. Typically, extensions are created by Dreamweaver users, developers, and designers who have a desire to automate a particular task that they might use regularly. Such tasks are usually expansions on existing features in Dreamweaver MX, although sometimes they are advanced features. Extensions provide all kinds of features that can help you with workflow, design concerns, and development issues.

Some of the most popular extensions include such things as the following:

- Table formatting and design presets

- Specialty scripting

- Accessibility features

Because Dreamweaver has been a very popular tool for some time, many extensions are available that you can find, download, and install. Once installed, extensions are integrated into Dreamweaver as part of the program—permanently extending the power of the program according to your needs.

ABOUT MACROMEDIA EXCHANGE

Macromedia Exchange is the Macromedia-run Web site where most extensions are submitted and are available for free (see Figure 31.1). Not all extensions that exist are free, but the ones available from the Exchange site are. Some of the more complex extensions, or those created by developers specifically for sale, can be found on individual Web sites.

Figure 31.1
The Macromedia Exchange Web site is a rich environment for designers and developers to share and create extensions.

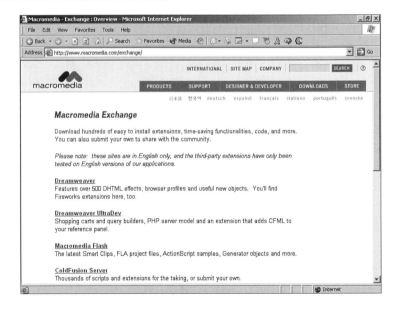

The Exchange Web site exists to

- Provide a repository of free extensions to Macromedia products, including Dreamweaver MX

- Provide community and support via discussion groups

- Enable users of extensions to rate and review individual extensions

- Provide information for designers and developers interested in writing their own extensions to Macromedia products

To access the Exchange site, point your browser to http://exchange.macromedia.com/. To go directly to the Dreamweaver Exchange, use this URL: http://exchange.macromedia.com/dreamweaver/.

On the Exchange Web site, you can also find support and extensions for other Macromedia products, including past versions of Dreamweaver, Dreamweaver UltraDev, Flash, ColdFusion, JRun, HomeSite, and Spectra.

MANAGING EXTENSIONS

31

If you'd like to add extensions to Macromedia Dreamweaver MX, you first need to register at the site. After that, you should download and install the Extension Manager, a program Macromedia provides for free to help you quickly add and install extensions.

Then, look through the variety of extension resources available to you, and download and install those of interest to you.

Registering for Macromedia Exchange

Before you can download, submit, or create reviews for any of Exchange's extensions, you need to register for the Exchange. Registration is a fairly simple process that provides you with several excellent resources, including

- Regular news updates via email regarding Macromedia resources and products

- Product tracking

- Full access to all Exchange services

To register for Macromedia Exchange, follow these steps:

1. Log on to the Macromedia Membership Center at http://www.macromedia.com/membership/ (see Figure 31.2).

2. You'll get to a page containing a form that asks you for your title, name, email address, and password. Fill in the fields.

3. Click continue and provide any information the registration process requests.

Figure 31.2
Membership to Macromedia is a great value because you'll get email updates, quick access to support, and rich online community.

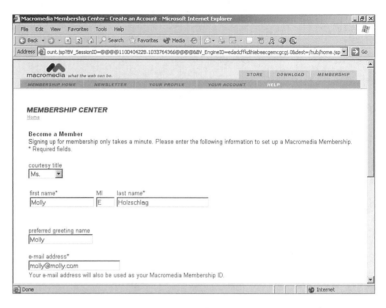

Membership is free and instant. After you go through this process, you can log in to the Exchange as well as use other convenient features on the Macromedia Web site, such as purchase tracking, which keeps a list of things you've bought from Macromedia and enables you to easily get updates, upgrades, or re-download software should you ever need to reinstall.

Having problems logging on even though you're a Macromedia member? See "Login Problems" in the "Troubleshooting" section later in this chapter for more information.

Downloading and Installing the Extension Manager

As mentioned, the Extension Manager assists you in quickly and easily adding extensions to your Macromedia products. Before you can download any extensions, you need to download the Extension Manager and install it on your local machine.

To download the Extension Manager, follow these steps:

1. Point your browser to `http://exchange.macromedia.com/`. After you are a registered user, you will be welcomed by the Exchange and provided with a page that helps you access both the Exchange and the program version you require.

2. Click the link and version appropriate for your system (Macintosh or Windows).

3. Direct your browser to download and open the application.

4. Follow the installation wizard's steps.

> The Extension Manager is available in a variety of languages, including French, German, Italian, Japanese, Korean, Portuguese, Simplified Chinese, Spanish and Swedish.

When you're done, the Extension Manager opens a browser window connecting you to a Welcome page, complete with help, links to Macromedia Exchange, and instructions on how to use the program.

To launch the Exchange from Dreamweaver MX, follow these steps:

1. Open Macromedia Dreamweaver.

2. Select Help, Manage Extensions. The Macromedia Extension Manager dialog box appears (see Figure 31.3).

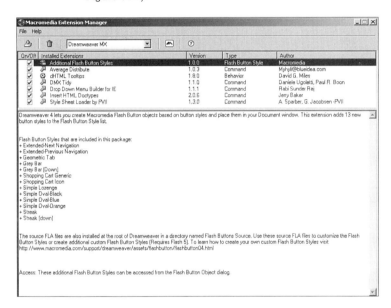

Figure 31.3
Here you see the Macromedia Extension Manager with a number of extensions installed.

31

3. In the dialog box, you'll see a list of any extensions you might have downloaded in the past. If no extensions are listed, it's because you've not yet used any version of the Extension Manager.

The Extension Manager dialog box provides the following options:

- **On/Off**—This option, found in the main window, allows you to check or uncheck a given extension to ensure that it is either activated or deactivated. You can download as many extensions as you like and enable or disable them using this option according to your needs.

- **Installed Extension**—This feature in the Extension Manager dialog box lists by name all the extensions you've downloaded.

- **Version**—In the Version section of the Extension Manager, you can find the numeric version release of the extension you're using. This is particularly helpful when determining whether an upgrade to a given extension you might have had for some time is necessary. Many extensions are upgraded on a regular basis, so it's always good to check with the Exchange if you want to find updates to the extensions with which you work.

- **Type**—This field describes the means by which the extension is accessed. In most cases with readers of this book, the means will be "command." This means the option is available to you from the Command menu in the Dreamweaver MX interface.

- **Author**—Because the Exchange is an open-distribution system, authors are acknowledged in this field. Some authors include their email addresses so you can email them if you have any concerns or problems using their extensions.

> To see a description of the extension in question, highlight it in the Extension Manager dialog box; a description will appear in the lower box, along with information on how to access the extension.

Even though extensions are provided on the Exchange site for free, sometimes you'll need specific support information regarding the feature. You can first try the newsgroups (described in the "Getting Help with Extensions" section later in this chapter), or you can email the author of the extension directly if she has made her contact information available.

Extensions At-a-Glance

Several extensions are available for Macromedia Dreamweaver. They are organized into categories so you can easily find those extensions most suited to your needs.

Table 31.1 describes the categories and the kinds of extensions you'll find in each category.

Table 31.1 Macromedia Extension Categories

Extension Category	Purpose
Accessibility	In this category are a range of extensions that can help you with accessibility concerns such as setting titles and a Check Page for Accessibility feature.
App Servers	This area is for those looking for information when working with applications.
Browsers	Tools to help you—and your site visitors—when working with browsers, such as browser upgrade notices.
DHTML/Layers	Look here for anything related to animation and working with Draw Layers.
Extension Development	This section provides tools for those Dreamweaver MX users who want to create their own extensions.
Fireworks	This section provides useful tools for Dreamweaver MX users who are also using Fireworks in an integrated setting.
Flash Media	This section provides additional Flash button styles, specialty menus, and panels to assist Dreamweaver MX users when working with Flash Media.
Learning	This section provides a variety of tools that will help you learn Dreamweaver more efficiently and create learning applications for your site visitors.
Navigation	Use these extensions to create pop-up windows, breadcrumb navigation, and specialty links.
Productivity	Increase your productivity by adding buttons to Dreamweaver that will help you quickly access frequently used features.

Table 31.1 Continued

Extension Category	Purpose
Rich Media	This area provides extensions to help you create interactive media and place it in your Web page.
Scripting	This section is for specialty scripts that can assist you with JavaScript and other scripting needs.
Security	Check this area for securing frames, disabling right-click, and other actions you'd like to have greater control over.
Style/Format	This section provides many cool tools to enhance your CSS and formatting options.
Tables	When working with tables, check out these extensions, which include colorizing tables and additional table designs.
Text	This section provides special characters, case control, math symbols—it's all in here.
eCommerce	Means of improving commerce aspects of a site can be found here, such as ads, shopping carts, and searches.

31

Getting Help with Extensions

The Macromedia Web site provides terrific support to all designers and developers using Dreamweaver MX, as well as those using and creating extensions. Support is delivered via Macromedia newsgroups (Web-based and standard newsgroups) and the Web site in general.

To access general support, follow these steps:

1. Point your browser to `http://www.macromedia.com/desdev/community/`.

2. Click the Dreamweaver link. The Designer and Developer Community Resources page loads (see Figure 31.4).

3. Use the list on the page to find items specific to your concerns.

To access Dreamweaver online forums, where you'll find the Dreamweaver Exchange Extensions forum, follow these steps:

1. Point your browser to `http://webforums.macromedia.com/dreamweaver/`.

You will notice two approval types. A *Basic* approval means that the extension has been looked at by the Dreamweaver team and found to be both useful and correct to install. If there's a Macromedia logo under the approval column, the extension is recommended by Macromedia.

To use a Macromedia standard newsgroup, you need to have a default email client configured. Once it is, you can find a range of support sites and newsgroups.

Figure 31.4
The Macromedia Designer and Developer center can assist you in finding support and information for a wide range of issues, including those involving extensions.

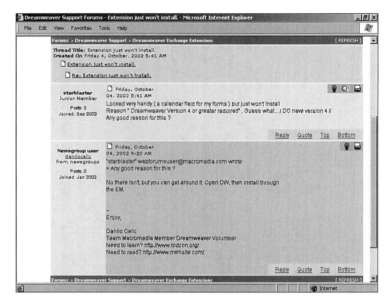

2. Click the Dreamweaver Exchange Extensions link.

3. You can browse through the topics on the forum's home page, use the search feature, read entries, or add entries as you require (see Figure 31.5).

Figure 31.5
Browsing through the Exchange Extensions forum.

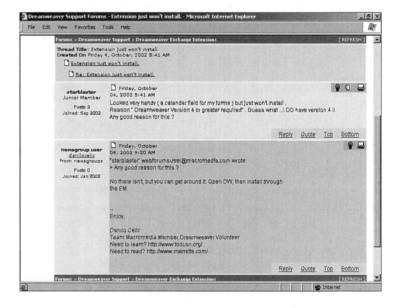

Support using these methods is typically swift and most frequently provided by peers rather than Macromedia.

ADDING AN EXTENSION

After you have your membership, have downloaded and installed the Macromedia Extension Manager, and are oriented to the site, download and install your first extension.

Although you can add any extension you like, the Additional Flash Button Styles Extension will serve as an example here.

To download and install the extension, follow these steps:

1. Browse to the Exchange site.

2. In the Browse Extensions drop-down menu, select the Flash Media option. The Flash Media page loads.

It is considered good Netiquette to search for topics before posting a concern. It's very possible that if you are having a problem with an extension, someone else had a problem, too. What's more, always follow appropriate, responsible posting behavior.

31

3. Search the list for the Additional Flash Button Style extension. When you've found the extension, click the link to it.

4. The Additional Flash Button Style Extension page loads (see Figure 31.6). Here you'll find information on the extension, a description of features, information about the author, the extensions rating, and of course clickable links for the extension download (divided into Macintosh and Windows).

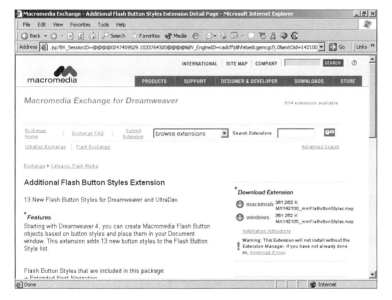

Figure 31.6
The Additional Flash Button Style extension's home page.

5. Click the download link you require for your operating system. Follow the prompts to download and run the installation.

6. After the application is finished downloading and installing, it will be available in the Extension Manager.

If you'd like to disable an extension, uncheck its check box in the Extension Manager.

7. Confirm that the extension has been downloaded and is showing up in the Extension Manager. Then, close Dreamweaver MX and restart.

Your new Flash Button styles are now available for use. Figure 31.7 shows a sample of a Flash button.

⇨ *To install Flash buttons, see Chapter 8, "Adding Some Flash," p. 141.*

Figure 31.7
Extended Flash button styles provide you with more options when adding Flash buttons.

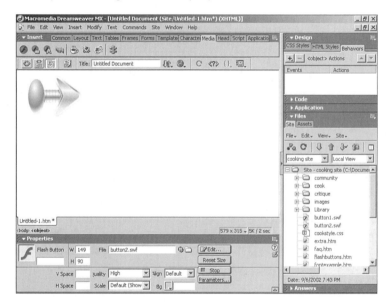

DOWNLOADING A BEHAVIOR

Downloading a behavior is exactly like downloading any other extension. In this example, you'll learn how to download a behavior from within Dreamweaver MX itself.

To do so, follow these steps.

1. Open the Behaviors panel. From the Actions (+) menu, select Get More Behaviors (see Figure 31.8).

2. Your default Web browser will open, and the Macromedia Exchange Web site will be available.

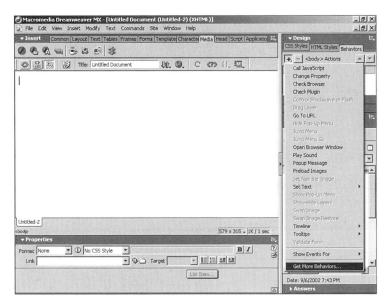

Figure 31.8
Using the Get More Behaviors option from within the Behaviors panel.

31

3. Select DHTML/Layers from the Browse Extensions drop-down menu.

4. Click the link to the behavior you want to add.

5. The behavior's page appears; click the appropriate download button for your platform.

6. Download and install the behavior. In some cases, as with the Flash button exercise described earlier, you will need to restart Dreamweaver MX for the behavior to be available.

To use a behavior extension, follow these steps:

1. Open the Design panel if it's not already available.

2. Click the Behaviors tab.

3. Click the (+) and select your newly installed behavior.

To learn more about behaviors, see "Using Behaviors," p. 426.

Many extensions are really mini-applications in and of themselves (see Figure 31.9). If you invoke a given command or behavior, either that extension will automatically execute or its related dialog box will appear so you can customize and control the extension's features.

Figure 31.9
The Drop-Down menu builder for IE is a perfect example of a mini-application extension. This extension lets you build DHTML drop-down menus for Internet Explorer.

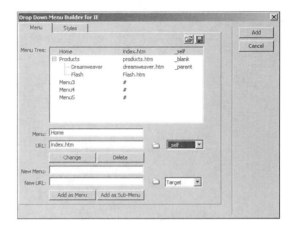

INSTALLING THIRD-PARTY PLUG-INS

Just as a site visitor must have a plug-in installed to display certain features such as Flash movies, so must you. To use plug-ins for displaying movies and any other type of specialty media, the plug-in *must* be in residence on your computer.

Every time you start Dreamweaver, it performs a quick search to find out which plug-ins are available locally, looking in your browser folders for the information.

However, if you want to directly install a plug-in for use in Dreamweaver, you can do so by following these steps:

1. Download the plug-in from the plug-in's home Web site. An example would be downloading the SVG plug-in from the Adobe.

2. When prompted to save the plug-in to a particular location, select Browse and find the `Dreamweaver MX/Configuration/Plug-ins` folder.

3. When the download is complete, you might need to double-click the executable file for the plug-in to finish the installation process.

The plug-in is now directly installed into Dreamweaver MX.

➡️ *Have you downloaded a plug-in and can play the associated media in Dreamweaver MX but not your browser? Find out why in "Plug-in Availability" in the "Troubleshooting" section.*

TROUBLESHOOTING

Login Problems

I'm a member of the Exchange, but I'm having problems logging in. What's going on?

The problem could be caused by several things. First, it's possible that you have incorrectly typed your UID or password into the dialog box. Try again. If this doesn't work, go to the Membership page, `http://www.macromedia.com/membership/`, and use the tools to retrieve a lost or forgotten password.

At regular intervals Macromedia does perform updates and upgrades to its site. When it does, you will get a page that tells you what's going on and that you'll need to return at a later time.

Plug-in Availability

My plug-in not working outside of Dreamweaver. Why?

If you install a plug-in directly into Dreamweaver rather than to your browser, it might not be available in your Web browsers. You'll need to reinstall the plug-in to its recommended browser location for it to be available in your Web browser.

PEER TO PEER: MACROMEDIA EXTENSIONS FOR MARKUP COMPLIANCE

Macromedia Exchange extension authors have written several important extensions related to proper markup. They include

- **DMX Tidy**—This is an extension version of Dave Raggett's famous HTML Tidy program, used to tidy up problems in HTML and XHTML, and even convert HTML to XHTML.

- **Entity Converter**—This extension converts characters into entities, and vice versa.

- **DOCTYPE Inserter**—Insert the appropriate DOCTYPE declarations into your documents.

31

WORKING WITH WEB GRAPHICS

MACROMEDIA AND WEB GRAPHICS

One of the biggest areas of in-depth study and growth is in Web graphic technology. New graphic formats have emerged, and more new ones are coming down the pike. Macromedia has played a significant role in improving its products with the Web in mind.

Dreamweaver MX has a companion program called Fireworks MX. It's an excellent graphic production program and is especially attractive to those individuals who want to tap into the tools the MX studio products share.

Knowing how to create professional graphics for the Web is important for any serious developer, and for the hobbyist, learning Web graphics skills will most surely assist your pages in being popular and worthy of regular visits.

IMPORTANT GRAPHIC FILE FORMATS

Understanding the available file formats used in Web graphic design is essential. One of the most daunting aspects of constructing a new Web site from scratch is the need for high-quality, well-designed graphics. The designer's responsibility isn't just limited to creating visual appeal: This is the Web, not clay or canvas, and working in a digital medium brings with it uniquely digital responsibilities.

Web graphic design is rife with myths about what Web graphics are and how they are created. On one hand, the core ideas are incredibly simple; on the other hand, many who try their hands at graphics just can't seem to get the process right. To get better results—and get them more quickly— software that is easy to use and integrates well with other development tools can really help.

File optimization—the act of working with files to achieve both quality appearance and acceptable download times—begins with an understanding of the file formats that are available. To gain a good foundation in terms of Web graphic production as well as transition to learning the tools, I'll begin by describing file formats available on the Web and which options are available to you in those formats. Then, after you've gained a strong understanding of file formats, we move on to the tools that will help you work with the format and optimization concepts you've learned.

Graphic Interchange Format

Graphic Interchange Format (GIF) has been the longest supported graphic file type on the Web, and it is extremely useful for a number of graphic file applications.

The GIF file format uses a type of compression known as *lossless*. GIF compression works by figuring out how much of the image uses the same color information. At that point, the compression algorithm saves those sections by using a numeric pattern.

GIF compression is limited to a total of 256 colors so that a numeric pattern must, in turn, be very specific. This is one of the main reasons it's so important to understand more about color theory and restrictions on the Web.

So, if you have 15 shades of blue in your graphic, that translates to 15 individual patterns. When more than 256 patterns appear in an image to compress, the algorithm has to decide what to leave out. It does this by limiting those blues to just a few or even just 1 total blue color.

Because of this process, your neon blue might end up a sky blue, and so forth. This is where experience and a skilled hand comes into play—knowing when and how to deal with color and file types enables you to gain control over colors in your graphics.

There are several important guidelines to determine whether you should select the GIF compression method for a specific graphic:

- **Line-drawn images**—Any graphic made up of mostly lines, such as a cartoon, is a good choice for GIF compression.

- **Images with few, flat colors**—With only a few colors and no light sources or gradations in that color, there's not going to be a lot of competition for those 256 colors in the compression.

The image in Figure 32.1 shows a line-drawn image. This image is an excellent choice for GIF compression. The logo in Figure 32.2 uses black, white, and gray—and all the colors are flat, with no light sources or gradations. This image is also perfect for GIF compression.

Figure 32.1
A line-drawn image is a perfect choice for GIF format.

Figure 32.2
This logo, using only black, white, and gray, is also a good choice for the GIF format.

Joint Photographic Experts Group

Frustrated with the limitations of GIFs, a group of photographic experts went to work on compression methods that would allow high-quality compression while retaining millions of colors. The results are what we know today as a Joint Photographic Experts Group file (JPEG).

The algorithm that makes up the JPEG compression is even more complicated than GIF. JPEGs use a *lossy* compression method. The algorithm focuses on removing data that is felt to be unimportant, instead of first mapping out areas of information that should be saved.

The appropriate file extension, or suffix, for JPEG files is .jpg. There's a lot of confusion around this issue because of the JPEG name. Always follow standard file-naming conventions and use the .jpg suffix for all JPEG images.

The JPEG method does this by dividing the image data into rectangular sections before applying the algorithm. On the one hand, this method gives you a lot of control in terms of how much information you're going to toss away; however, at high compression ratios, you can end up with a blocky, blotchy, blurry result. Working with JPEGs, just as with GIFs, requires a bit of skill and a fine hand to achieve the best results.

> **Blocky sections in an image are** known as *artifacts*. Artifacts occur when you've over-compressed an image. You'll look at this a bit later in this chapter when you step through the optimization process.

Because the JPEG format is specifically designed to manage files with a lot of color, certain types of images best lend themselves to JPEG compression. The following list is a helpful guide to use when determining whether JPEG is the best format for your image:

- Images with a lot of colors, such as color photographs

- Graphics using gradient fills (see Figure 32.3)

- Graphics using light sources

- Photographs with a lot of gradation, such as skies, sunsets, and oceans (see Figure 32.4)

Figure 32.3
Gradient fills are appropriate for the JPEG format. The reason has to do with JPEGs' capability to compress files without reducing the number of colors.

Figure 32.4
Sunset pictures, particularly when in full color, contain a lot of gradation and normally are processed by using the JPEG format.

Portable Network Graphics

The Portable Network Graphics (PNG) graphics format was defined during 1995–1996 to overcome copyright issues surrounding the GIF format at the time. However, aside from the goal of creating a public domain image format, the developers also attempted to improve on the standard set by GIF. This has resulted in a number of enhanced features:

- Indexed color, grayscale, and truecolor image support

- 1–16 bit depth

- Alpha channel for transparency

- Better interlacing, resulting in faster display of a usable image

One of the main ways in which PNG outperforms GIF is the capability to store images that include an alpha channel. This enables proper antialiasing and eliminates the jagged edges around fonts and images, and PNG's superiority is also one of the reasons Macromedia chose it to be the default image type when working in Fireworks.

Unfortunately, popular Web browser support for PNG has not yet been fully achieved. Although the current versions of the major Web browsers and graphic image software have added support for this new format, PNG support is incompletely implemented in some browsers, most specifically Microsoft IE. As a result of such a major browser not having sufficient PNG support, the GIF and JPEG formats are still far more common.

> To keep up with the status of PNG and Web browsers, please see `http://www.libpng.org/pub/png/pngstatus.html#browsers`.
>
> For related information on the PNG format, visit the World Wide Web Consortium's specification for PNG at `http://www.w3.org/TR/REC-png-multi.html`.

32

DESIGNING IMAGES WITH FIREWORKS

A Web site typically uses graphics to design, identify, and navigate.

Some of the images you'll have to consider for your pages include background images, headers, navigation buttons, bars and rules, and spot art.

Background images load into the background of the page. Sometimes referred to as *wallpaper*, background images set the tone of a page. Headers give an individual page its identity by incorporating the site's logo. Headers can also include the parent site's identity, too, as in "Molly's Site: What's New." One click of a navigation button and you're on your way to another page in a site. Bars and rules are used to separate text or elements on a page, and graphic bars and rules can customize a site's look. *Spot art* is the term used to describe clip art or photography that accentuates the textual content on a page. Other images include animations, imagemaps, and banner ads.

In these types of images are a variety of techniques you'll want to employ to ensure a professional-quality site.

Creating Background Images

Backgrounds come in a few varieties:

- **Wallpaper patterns**—These are small squares that tile to create a smooth, seamless texture that looks like well-installed wallpaper (no bumps, seams, or bungles!).

- **Margin tiles**—Also referred to as *strips* because they are wide and short, margin tiles can be functional or decorative in nature.

- **Watermark style**—This is one large background graphic, usually square, that adds an image, logographic material, or color to the background of a page.

One important issue to remember is that with HTML presentation, all backgrounds must be seen as tiles. They might not look like a tile, but they act like a tile whenever the resolution of a screen changes. Wallpaper patterns, which are squares, tile into the browser one-by-one until the available space is filled.

Tiling always occurs with HTML alone. Cascading Style Sheets (CSS) allows for more control over your background graphic's behavior, including the ability to fix the background and prevent its tiling.

To learn more about backgrounds and CSS, see "Setting the Background," p. 291.

Designing Wallpaper Patterns

Wallpaper patterns were the first wave of background graphics. You've probably seen lots of them, in all kinds of styles. They're problematic for a number of reasons, including the fact that if they're too dark or busy, they interfere with readability. They're also demanding on the designer—it takes a bit of skill if you're making them completely by hand.

However, if you design them properly, they can create an extremely attractive look for your site.

The following are some general guidelines to use when creating tiles:

- Individual tiles should be at least 50 pixels×50 pixels.

- Work hard to ensure that tiles appear seamless.

- Avoid allowing a small tile with a single image to repeat over and over. Imagine one egg in a single square, tiled repeatedly into the browser.

- Always ensure that you do *not* interlace background graphics.

In this exercise you can create a simple background tile. I'm going to use Fireworks MX, but you can follow along with almost any imaging program:

1. Open the program and create a new file by selecting File, New.

2. The New Document dialog box opens (see Figure 32.5). Enter the width and height of your image. In this example, you'll see an image that is 50×50. You can also add the resolution, which should be set to 72, and select the background color of the canvas.

3. Select any one of the drawing tools. You can choose to use a brush, create geometric shapes—whatever you'd like to try. The example shown in Figure 32.6 was done with a brush, set in the Fireworks Property inspector to the airbrush option.

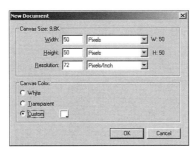

Figure 32.5
The New Document dialog box in Fireworks enables you to set the size, resolution, and color for the new image before you create it.

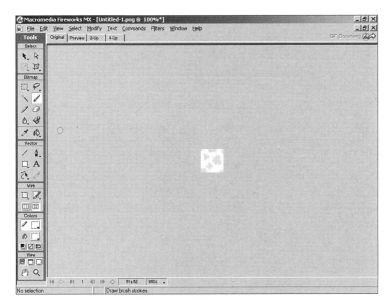

Figure 32.6
Drawing using Fireworks tools to create a wallpaper pattern.

32

4. From the Property inspector, select a color.

5. In the center of the tile, paint your design. This simple example uses brush strokes to emulate a flower, which will ultimately create a floral pattern.

6. Select File, Export Preview. The Export preview will give you a variety of options to optimize your image before saving it (see Figure 32.7). You can try looking at a variety of setting combinations for GIF, JPG, and PNG graphics.

7. After you've found the setting that has the highest quality yet lowest file size and download time, click Export to save your now-optimized file.

Now you can load the image as a background graphic in an HTML document. Figure 32.8 shows my flowery results!

Figure 32.7
Fireworks MX's Export Preview is an amazingly powerful dialog box in which you can choose a variety of settings and achieve the best graphic quality for your pages.

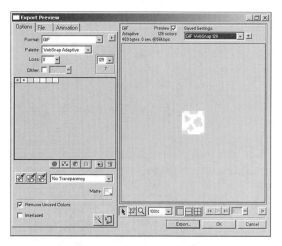

Figure 32.8
The single flower square becomes flowered, seamless wallpaper.

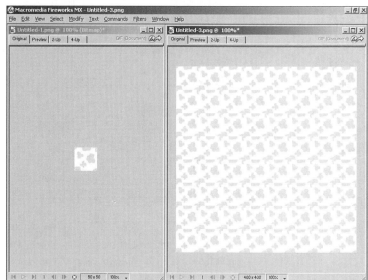

Margin Tiles

Margin tiles are quite prevalent on the Web. Essentially, two types of margin tiles exist:

- **Functional**—This is a background margin tile that uses the margin space for navigation or other graphic and text information. Because it will be a significant part of your color and design scheme, functional margin design means making sure text, links, and other functional items can be seen and integrated into the margin's space and design (see Figure 32.9).

- **Decorative**—Decorative margins serve to enhance a design aesthetically. They have no function other than to provide visual interest to a page. They are essentially the same as a functional margin in terms of design.

Graphic Optimization and Contemporary Tools

One of the most useful aspects of contemporary software for image creation and manipulation has been the addition of optimization tools. In the early days of Web graphic design, optimization usually had to be done by hand, which was time-consuming and generally less effective.

By using Fireworks' Export Preview dialog box, you can make the best decisions regarding your graphic compression by simultaneously changing the file type and compression settings for that file type while viewing the image live. This saves time as well as gives you the best output.

These valuable compression technologies are available in other software as well. Adobe Photoshop has a similar feature called Save for Web. Users of JASC's popular Paint Shop Pro will find excellent tools there as well. With such efficient tools on the market, there really is no excuse for not having the best optimization of graphics possible.

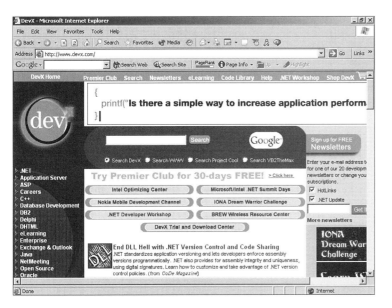

Figure 32.9
This site uses a functional margin background by using it to present the navigation for the site.

32

For effective margin tile design, follow these tips:

- **Create long tiles, anticipating various screen resolutions**—You'll want your background margin tiles to be *at least* 1,280 pixels wide. You might even consider making them 1,600 pixels wide, but it's up to you and your awareness of your audience. Choose longer tiles if many of them are using very high-resolution monitors. Height will range from around 50 pixels to 250 pixels or so, depending on your design.

- **Design using few colors, but be sure to add interest by employing shadow, shape, or texture**—Flat margin tiles are very common on the Web. Although they're not unattractive, challenge yourself a bit and create something with a bit more verve.

■ **Because you have to anticipate a wide range of screen resolutions, design your image to size**—Test your image at a variety of resolutions to ensure that it is pleasing and functional at as many resolutions as possible.

Functional

Here, you'll create a functional right-margin image with color and texture:

1. Open Fireworks and select File, New.

2. In the New Document dialog box, set the width of your image (this example uses 1,024) and the height (set here for 50). Select your background color.

3. Select the Marquee tool by clicking it from the left side of the tools palette (see Figure 32.10).

Figure 32.10
Selecting the Marquee tool from the Bitmap tools section in the Fireworks tools palette.

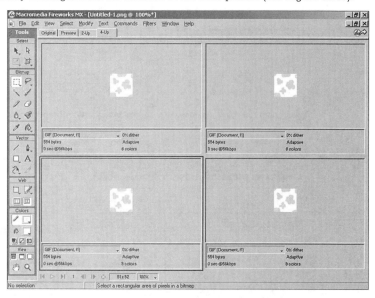

4. Draw a rectangular shape at the far left end of your tile.

5. Select a color from the Property inspector. You can use any of the options there to modify the color with texture, other colors, and gradients.

6. Using the Paint Brush tool, fill your selected area with the color or texture you've defined.

7. Select File, Export Preview. Make your settings choices for the best optimization possibility, and then click OK.

8. Select File, Export and save your file.

Figure 32.11 shows the results of my tile.

Bottom margins can get lost because they won't be immediately seen on longer pages. Use bottom margins for full pages or when you want to control the look of the page at its utmost bottom, even if it's not in view until the site visitor scrolls down.

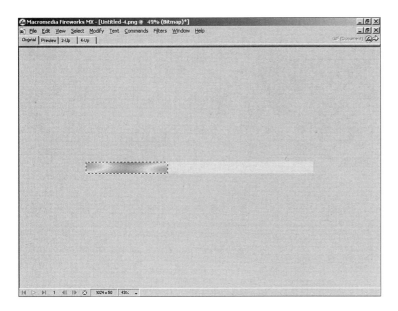

Figure 32.11
The dimensions of this margin background tile are 1280×50, and the file size is 1.81K, saved as a JPG to retain the gradient.

To create a decorative margin graphic, simply use the left, right, or top margin of your graphic and add a visual design. Unlike the textured margin background you just created, whose left section can be used as a navigation field, a decorative margin tile is there for aesthetic purposes only.

Watermark Style

Watermarks are especially difficult to use when relying on HTML presentation because of the tiling issue. The idea with watermarks is to keep them simple, with few, flat colors, and to keep file sizes low.

Here, you'll create a watermark starting with a large tile:

1. In Fireworks, create a New Document by selecting File, New.

2. Set the size of your file to 1,280×1,200 pixels.

3. Draw your design onto the page.

4. Select File, Export Preview and save your file.

In Figure 32.12 you'll see a watermark in use.

To ensure good contrast, keep background tiles very light or very dark and the body text the opposite. So, if you have a very light background, black text will help readability because it contrasts well with the background. Similarly, if you have a very dark green background design, a light color such as cream will provide you with good contrast.

32

Figure 32.12
The Oil of Olay Web site uses some interesting watermark backgrounds, as shown here.

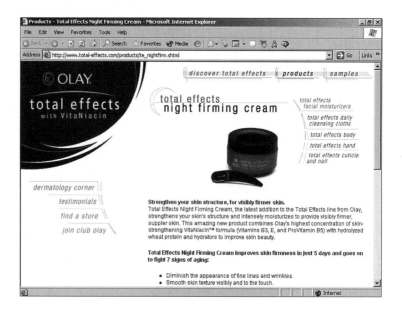

Header Graphics

32

Headers are used to identify a site and a page in a site. One type of header is the *splash* header. This typically fills a larger piece of real estate on the opening page only. It identifies the site with the company logo or brand and sets the visual tone for the rest of the site.

A *page* header is smaller but still boldly visible along the top and left, middle, or right of an internal page. In this example, you'll create a graphic page header:

1. In Fireworks, select File, New.

2. Set up the graphic to be 400×50 pixels.

3. Fill the image with a color suitable for transparency.

4. From the Window menu, make sure Layers is selected.

5. Create a new layer using the New Layer icon (see Figure 32.13).

6. On this layer, set your type using the Type tool.

7. When you're satisfied with the look of your graphic, select File, Export Preview.

8. Work with the Export Preview options until you're happy with the file type, size, and look. Click Export to save the file.

> Although undeniably helpful in certain designs, the advances made with CSS can help you leave most headers styled to the fonts and colors you require using CSS instead of graphics.

Figure 32.14 shows the header being designed in Fireworks. After you're finished, you can add the graphic to your Web page to see the results.

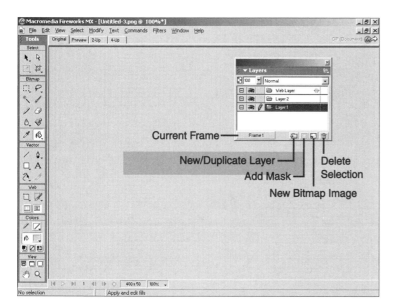

Figure 32.13
Using the Layers window to add a layer.

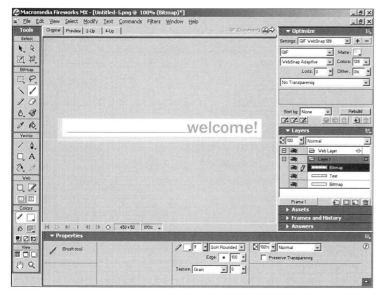

Figure 32.14
An internal page header can help keep a visitor oriented in a site, as well as add visual interest to the page.

32

To learn how to use your images on a Web page, see Chapter 4, "Adding Images," p. 63.

Bars and Rules

At times, an effective, decorative bar or rule can be used to demarcate visual sections of a document.

If you're going to create your own bar, here are some helpful guidelines:

- Don't stretch the bar from margin to margin. Instead, make a bar that is either centered with some whitespace to either side or aligned to the right or left. Cutting off the margins separates space dramatically and could cause disruption in the cohesiveness of both the design and the experience of the content.

- Use a treatment such as a drop shadow, curved or angled lines, something that's hand drawn, or broken lines—anything to give the rule a fresh look.

Graphic bars and rules can really make a site look uniform and well designed, but you should also consider using style to achieve the same goal.

⇨ *Thought your designing was going well until you tested your page in a browser and found that your graphics were busier than you'd like them to be? See "Effects" in the "Troubleshooting" section for some tips on how to make your graphics work well together without overdoing it.*

Working with Spot Art

Spot art serves to enhance and accentuate text. It can be clip art or photographs.

To make spot art stand out from the norm, it's sometimes fun to add edges, shadows, or other effects. However, you do have to be careful with the use of effects because of the additional weight they can add to a page. Effects should be planned so that they are consistent and blend well with the overall design.

Hand-drawn art, cartoons, and clip art can add variety and personality to your sites, too. Whichever you choose, you should be consistent and creative—not conflicting and cliche—throughout a site. It always surprises sophisticated site visitors to find that people have created a slick graphic only to mix it with a piece of overused, worn clip art!

Another concern is dimension. Spot art is akin to italic or bold on a page—it's about emphasis, not dominance. You want your spot art to blend well into the overall scheme of your design. Pay close attention not only to the dimension in relation to the screen size, but also from one photo to another.

Creating Buttons

Navigational buttons can be made up of text, images, or a combination of both. You can go simple by using a static navigation button as a link. To do so, create buttons using the techniques you've already employed in this chapter to create a graphic.

Or, you might prefer to create visually active buttons, which can be achieved using JavaScript. The really exciting news is that, if you are using Fireworks to create your graphics, you don't have to be a programmer to create visually active buttons of this nature—Fireworks MX has a Button Editor that will help do it all for you.

Try to select images that are going to be lightweight (small in file size) because you always want to keep your individual file weight down. Using lighter images for each state will make a difference in file weight when you combine all the images into the final format.

Table 32.1 defines the four states available when creating dynamic buttons in Fireworks MX.

Table 32.1 JavaScript States in Fireworks MX

State	Action
up	The default state of the button.
down	The way the button will appear when the mouse is pressed on it.
over	The appearance of the button as the pointer is moved over it.
over while down	This feature is a button state that changes in the down state when the mouse is moved. This can be helpful when showing a site visitor that the button is selected.

To create a JavaScript button using the Button Editor, you'll first need to prepare graphics that correspond to each state you'd like to use (you don't have to use every state).

For a simple two-state button with an up state and over state, first create the button as it should appear normally; then modify the button for the over state. This modification could be a change in color or text, text color, or the design of the button itself. Avoid using buttons that are different sizes.

After you have your two buttons, follow these steps:

1. In Fireworks MX, select Edit, Insert, New Button. The Button Editor opens (see Figure 32.15).

Figure 32.15
The Button Editor allows you to make multiple-state, dynamic buttons using JavaScript.

32

2. You'll see each state available in the editor on a tab across the top of the window. As you click the tab for that state, a new canvas is available. Be sure the Up tab is selected. Now you can import the up state graphic by following one of these options:

   • Drag and drop a graphic from another open document window into the up state of the Button Editor.

   • Draw the button right onto the Button Editor's canvas.

   • Click the Import a Button selection in the Button dialog box.

3. After you have your up button, click the Over tab.

4. Use one of the techniques outlined in step 2 to create the graphic used for the over state.

5. Click Done.

Now, the button with the JavaScript added to it will show up with a special icon showing that the button has scripting added to it. You can (Shift-click) [right-click] the center circle of the icon to bring up a submenu of various behavior-related parameters that you can set depending on your needs.

To make a button using any additional states, simply repeat the previous steps for each button state you'd like to include. If you want to export the image for use in Dreamweaver, simply click the Quick Export icon in the upper-right corner of the Document window (see Figure 32.16). If you select Dreamweaver, Export, HTML, Fireworks generates an HTML document including the JavaScript, which you can then copy and paste into Dreamweaver as needed.

Quick Export

Figure 32.16
Select the Quick Export icon to export your buttons for use in Dreamweaver.

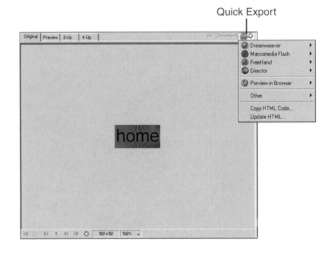

To learn more about rollovers, see "Creating a Rollover," p. 432.

Designing Imagemaps

Imagemaps enable a designer to take a single image and break it down into multiple sections of varying shapes. Each of those sections then can be linked to a different Web page.

Although this sounds convenient, and although imagemaps have certainly been a significant part of Web design for some time, the reality is that they are becoming less prevalent on professional sites. This likely has to do with several things, including the fact that more sophisticated and attractive technologies such as JavaScript are available, accessibility concerns when working with imagemaps, or that the fact mapping is too fixed for today's regularly updated Web sites.

Despite these issues, the technology and tools related to mapping have remained current, and you will certainly want to add an understanding of imagemapping to your repertoire of graphic skills.

The first step in creating an imagemap is to find a good map to use. Typically, useful imagemaps are those that make visual sense. Very often, these are literal maps! So, if you have a site in which camping information is different for areas around Flagstaff, Phoenix, and Tucson, Arizona, you might like to create a map with those three cities denoted. Then, each of those cities will be made "hot"—in other words, they are linked to different pages but all from the same graphic.

After you have the image you'd like to use, open it in Fireworks MX and follow these steps to add the hot spots:

1. From the Web section of the Tools panel, shown in Figure 32.14, select a tool to create the type of hot spot you'd like to use, as follows:

   - The Rectangle Hotspot tool creates square or rectangular hot spots.

   - The Circle Hotspot tool allows you to draw circular hot spots.

   - Odd-shaped hot spots can be drawn with the Polygon Hotspot tool.

2. Find the location on your image where you'd like to draw your hot spot. For circular and rectangular spots, simply click and drag to create the shape. For polygonal shapes, click at various points on the image until you have the shape you like.

3. Using the Property inspector, insert the various attributes you'd like for each of the hot spots you create. This includes the Link location, alternative text, and any link targets you might have.

As with buttons created with the Button Editor, you can use the Quick Export feature to export HTML for pasting into Dreamweaver MX. The final results of the imagemap in action can be seen in Figure 32.17.

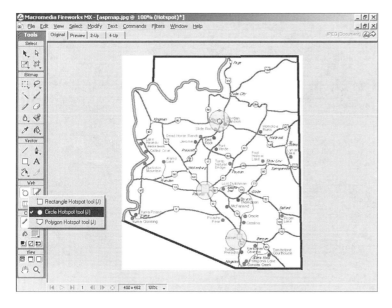

Figure 32.17
An imagemap with hot spots can be quickly created in Fireworks MX.

32

Having trouble with links in your imagemap not working properly? See "Links Won' t Work" in the "Troubleshooting" section at the end of this chapter for some timely tips on how to fix this problem.

Designing Advertising Banners

Ad banners are all over the Web. Their efficacy is greatly debated, and in fact there is no hard evidence that they work in any way other than to act similarly to billboards. Site visitors might see them, but click through rates are typically very low.

Ad banners still remain prevalent despite the fact that they are proving to be both a weak advertising platform and an annoyance to site visitors and designers—both of whom are more interested in the content of a given Web site than its ads.

For more information on design-ing ad banners, see *Designing Winning Ad Banners*, by Charlie Morris, at http://www.wdvl. com/Internet/Commerce/ BannerAds/.

If you're working as a professional Web designer, you will be called on to create banner ads. A variety of techniques are used in banner advertising, including animation, bright colors, and *rich media* (the use of Flash and scripting to achieve unusual advertisements).

Typically, advertising groups require specific, standardized sizes and guidelines for banner creation. A very familiar, common banner size is 468×60 pixels, with a recommended file size of 8KB or less (see Figure 32.18). You do have to check with the methods employed by the group you decide to work with, however, because their guidelines will differ.

468×60 banner

Figure 32.18
The ubiquitous 468×60 ad banner.

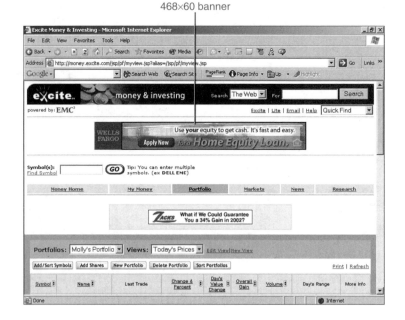

The following are some general specifications to keep in mind when creating banners:

- Save the file as a GIF or JPG.

- Use bright colors because this enhances appearance on the page.

- Animated GIFs are considered very effective. Looping is often acceptable with ad banners, but be sure to check with your ad banner partner for more specific guidelines.

TROUBLESHOOTING

Effects

I wanted to add some panache to to my page, so I grabbed up all the cool effects and filters I could find and got to work. The designing is going great, but the results are a bit busy—what happened?

Effects must be planned and appropriate to the design. Consistency is a big factor, too. You definitely do not want to do something just because you can.

In fact, effects have been overused. Even though they sometimes are exactly what is needed, still think carefully before using any effects. And, when you do use them, use them consistently.

Links Won't Work

I created an imagemap, but one of my areas isn't linking properly. What could be the problem?

Check your URLs first. You might have mistyped or incorrectly coded a link. If everything is fine with the addressing, you'll need to look more closely at the coordinates to be sure they are working properly.

PEER TO PEER: WEB GRAPHIC DESIGN BEST PRACTICES

There's no denying that graphics can bring a lot of life to a Web site. Still, one of the greatest challenges to the professional Web designer is to use graphics intelligently. Here are a few tips:

- If you can use a better method to achieve your goal, such as using a header styled with CSS instead of a graphic, do so.

- Rely on browser-based color, using style or HTML presentation, to make your pages more vibrant without having to add too many graphics.

32

- If possible, avoid the convention of slicing graphics. It's a time-consuming, difficult thing to do and demands complicated table designs to support.

- Don't rely on a graphic to convey the message. This is a checkpoint in accessibility guidelines—you've got to provide some type of context for the image.

- Always use descriptive alternative text in any image that is a visual image. This helps address the accessibility concern, as well as providing more context for all site users.

Finally, don't be afraid to start trying to create graphics that are compelling and unusual visually. Just because the focus is on minimizing graphic use in general doesn't mean the graphics we do design should be boring!

32

33

CONTENT MANAGEMENT USING
MACROMEDIA CONTRIBUTE

ABOUT MACROMEDIA CONTRIBUTE

Macromedia Contribute is a lightweight, live program that enables almost anyone to create and edit documents on existing Web sites. Contribute can be used along with features in Dreamweaver MX to help you—and co-workers who might not otherwise have extensive design or development experience—complete a range of tasks, including

- Maintenance and updates

- Adding new pages using a blank page, a Contribute "starter" page, or a template created in Dreamweaver MX

- Publishing documents created in other applications, including Microsoft Word and Microsoft Excel

- Adding or removing text, graphics, and other media on your existing sites

- Sharing site connections in a team environement

Macromedia Contribute can be used by anyone creating sites in Dreamweaver MX, production team members, and anyone responsible for updating content to existing Web sites. Contribute provides the designer and developer quick and easy access to pages so as to allow for general updates to content, including text, images, and media. Team members not otherwise tasked with design or development can also use Contribute for these updates.

Business users and content editors will especially enjoy Contribute because it enables them to rapidly update pages without having to use Dreamweaver MX itself, much less know how to work with complex code and layout structures. For these users, Contribute is especially attractive because its easy-to-use interface is very similar to a word processing program.

Consider the marketing manager who wants to update text to reflect a recent promotion, an online magazine section editor who wants to add a new article, or even a company's CFO who'd like to publish an Excel spreadsheet to the corporate intranet. Most of these people aren't designers, developers, or Web authors. Their job is to get the content published to the Macromedia Dreamweaver MX designed site without having to deal with the more complex features of Dreamweaver, which are far out of the scope for what these individuals need to achieve.

As the site designer, developer, or project manager, you can empower both yourself and anyone working on the site that you design by using Contribute for those situations or individuals in which the objective is to get the content online within the context of the site's design.

Contribute operates while connected to the Internet. You can work offline on certain tasks, but most tasks are best carried out in the live connection environment. In this chapter, you'll learn how Contribute is a convenient, related program to Macromedia Dreamweaver MX.

Getting Connected

Readers of this book might find themselves using Contribute for fast tasks or acting as administrators and providing Contribute for other members in their organizations to easily add and update pages. No matter the way Contribute is being used, it has to be properly configured to work.

The first step is to install Contribute. In large team instances, Contribute might already be installed on your computer. After it is, the first step is to get Contribute connected to the site, or sites, with which you'll be integrating it.

To set up Contribute, you must have either Network access or FTP access to any site you want to be editable:

- **Network access**—Network access is used when the Web server is running on the same local network as your computer. Go to Network Neighborhood and find the computer where your Web site resides.

- **FTP**—File Transfer Protocol is used when you are using a remote server to host a site.

In a networking situation, you might need to talk to your network administrator and have her help you with the setup. In the case of FTP, you can set this up on your own, but you'll need your FTP address, FTP login, and FTP password. After you have the connection information, you can set up Contribute using the Connection Wizard (see Figure 33.1).

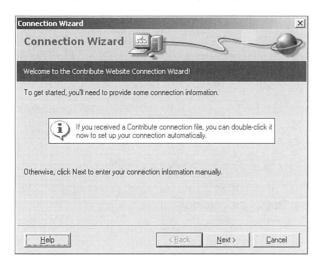

Figure 33.1
Use the Connection Wizard to set up your Contribute sites.

33

To get set up using the Web Connection Wizard, follow these steps:

1. Open Contribute and select Edit, My Connections.

2. Click New in the My Connections dialog box (see Figure 33.2).

3. Click Next. The User Information dialog box appears. Enter or edit any information found in that dialog box.

4. Click Next. In the Web Site Address dialog box, enter the address of the Web site. Once again, click Next. The Connection Information dialog box appears.

5. Select from FTP or Local/Network, depending on your personal needs. Complete the remaining data with your information.

Figure 33.2
The My Connections dialog box allows you to manage your connections and sites efficiently.

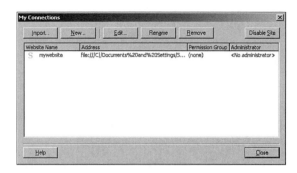

6. Click Next. The Summary panel now appears, allowing you to confirm the information.

7. Click Finish.

You are now able to edit the site using Contribute.

Importing a Contribute Site

Your administrator might send you email with a site setup file attached or provide you with a URL to download the file from your network. Connection setup files can be identified by a `.stc` filename extension. In this case, you need to double-click the file to import the connection to your site.

In some cases, your systems adminstrator will send you a site setup file for Contribute via email. This fil has an `.stc` extension.

To import a site from an attached `.stc` email file, follow these steps:

1. Find the setup file in your email application or on your computer after you've downloaded it. Double-click the setup file.

2. Contribute will launch and display the Import Site dialog box.

3. Enter your name; email address; and the file's password, which will be provided to you (usually in a separate email).

After you're done, click OK; the site will now be imported into Contribute. It is then available for you to modify immediately. On the other hand, you can close Contribute at any time and when you reopen it, the site (or sites) you've imported will be ready for you to use.

ABOUT THE CONTRIBUTE INTERFACE

Interestingly, Contribute works as a Web browser and page editor. The following two modes are available in Contribute:

- **Browse mode**—In this mode, Contribute acts as a Web browser, allowing you to open online Web pages, follow links, and even set bookmarks.

- **Edit mode**—You can browse to an existing page, switch into Edit mode, and begin making edits to the page.

Contribute is, as mentioned, very lightweight and extremely easy to use interface-wise. It contains a title bar, menu bar, toolbar, page navigation panel (which lists links and indicates published pages), Quick Help section, and document window. Figure 33.3 shows the Contribute workspace.

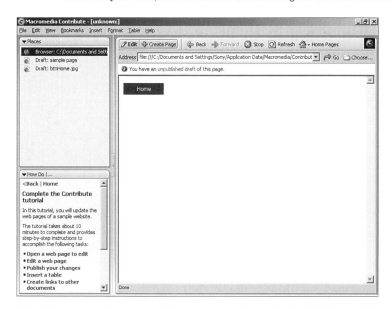

Figure 33.3
Viewing the Contribute work-space.

Working Offline

You can also use Contribute to work offline. This means you can make your changes and updates and transfer them to the site live at a later time. If you want to work in Offline mode, select File, Work Offline. To switch back, selece File, Work Online.

33

Using Browse Mode

When you use Contribute as a Web browser, you can browse to any Web page. Contribute picks up the preferences from those you have set in Microsoft Internet Explorer. Any changes to preferences regarding the Contribute Browse mode must be made through your IE preferences.

If you want to browse to a Web page using Contribute, simply follow these steps:

1. Type the URL into the address field found in the toolbar.

2. Click Go. If you are properly connected to the Internet, the page will load in the Contribute document window.

3. You can use the navigation buttons to move back and forth from pages you've visited.

You can switch to Edit mode via the Browse mode, but you can edit only Web sites that have been imported into Contribute and for which you have permissions to edit. If you do not have permissions—which are set by the network systems administrator—or the site is unaffiliated with your work, you will not be able to edit the site.

In the browse toolbar is a Create Connection button. If you want to add a site to the Contribute browser, you can click Create Connection while browsing button to add the site. Then, you can use the Choose button as a quick way to access the site.

Exploring Edit Mode

The editing toolbar options are available to help you achieve numerous editing options. You can

- Modify font sizes.
- Change colors.
- Edit style.
- Manage paragraphs.
- Add links.
- Add images.
- Add tables.

➩ *Is the Edit Page button disabled? Find out why in "Disabled Edit Button" in the "Troubleshooting" section at the end of this chapter.*

To edit a page in Contribute, follow these steps:

1. Enter the Web address in the browser toolbar. Alternatively, you can click the Home Page button and then select the site to navigate to the page you want to edit.

2. Click the Edit Page button to switch from Browse mode to Edit mode (see Figure 33.4).

Figure 33.4
Working in Contribute's Edit mode enables you to make changes to a Web page.

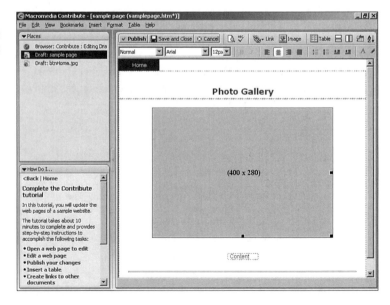

3. Make your editorial changes. When you're ready to publish the page, click Publish on the edit toolbar.

Contribute will publish your changes to the Web server. More details will be provided about this process as the chapter progresses.

CREATING A NEW PAGE USING CONTRIBUTE

You can create new pages in Contribute using two different methods. The first is to use the Insert Link method, and the second is to use the Add a Page button.

Using Insert Link

This method enables you to create a link from an existing page and create the new page for the link. To create a page using the Insert Link method, follow these steps:

1. Browse to the page you want to link to your new page.

2. Click Edit, and place the insertion point onto the page where you want the link to be.

3. Select Insert, Link. The Insert Link dialog box appears.

4. Enter the link text.

5. Click the Create a New Page button. The dialog box changes so you can make selections regarding the type of page you want to make. Make your selection.

6. Click the Examples tab, and then select a sample page design for your new page.

7. Enter a page title and click OK.

The link appears in the referring page, and the new page shows up in My Drafts. The page is automatically saved to the same location as the file that is linking to it. You can now add content to that page as is, use a template created in Dreamweaver MX for the design, and publish when ready.

Creating a New Page with the Add a Page Button

If you want to create a page within Contribute that is independent from a referring page, here's how:

1. Go to the folder where you want to create the new page.

2. Click the New Page button; the New Page dialog box appears.

3. Select the page type you want to create.

4. Click the Examples tab, and decide on your design.

5. Enter a page title, and click OK.

Even though you'll likely be doing most light editing chores using Contribute, if you want to use Macromedia Dreamweaver MX to modify pages, add templates, and perform validation and other tasks, you can do so easily. Simply open Dreamweaver MX and use the Site panel to view and edit the added documents.

33

The new page opens in Edit mode so you can begin working on it using Contribute right away.

IMPORTING WORD AND EXCEL DOCUMENTS INTO A PAGE

One of the most useful features of Contribute is that it enables you to quickly import Word and Excel content to your site. This is powerful because you don't have to re-create a table or content—Contribute does the work for you via a very simple, fast process.

To import a Word or an Excel document into a page, follow these steps:

1. Create a new page, or open an existing one.

2. Place your cursor on your Contribute page where you want the data to go.

3. Select Insert, and then select either Microsoft Word Document or Microsoft Excel Document.

Contribute will now add the content to your page.

Opening Word and Excel Files in Contribute

If you want to make editorial changes to Word or Excel files, you can do so using Contribute. The restrictions are that you must be running Windows 98 or later, have a copy of IE 5.0 or later, and have Microsoft Office 97 or later installed. Also, you need to have used IE to open Word or Excel documents before.

To open a Word or an Excel document in Contribute for the first time, follow these steps:

1. Using Contribute, browse to the page that contains a link to the file you want to open. Click the link; the File Download dialog box appears.

2. Uncheck the Always Ask Before Opening This Type of File check box.

3. Click Open.

The file opens in Contribute (see Figure 33.5).

Editing Word or Excel Documents Using Contribute

To make editorial changes to a Word or an Excel document in Contribute, follow these steps:

1. In Contribute, open the Word or Excel document you want to edit.

2. Click the Edit button.

3. Make your changes.

4. Select Finish Later, Cancel, or Publish, depending on your needs.

As soon as you open a file with Contribute, that file is locked. No one else can access it while you are editing it.

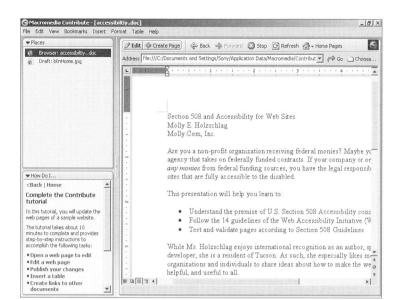

Figure 33.5
You can open a Word document in
Contribute.

EDITING PAGES IN CONTRIBUTE

In this section, you learn how to make modifications to pages in Contribute, including setting your page properties, undoing mistakes, saving draft pages, and exporting pages.

Setting Page Properties

The following page properties can be modified:

- **Page Title**—This specifies the page title as it appears in the title bar of a browser.

- **Page Margins**—You can set page margins using the left and top margins to determine the size of the page. If you want no margins, set these preferences to 0.

- **Background Color**—This sets the background color for the page.

- **Background Image**—This property enables you to add a background graphic to your page.

- **Text Color**—To set the color of your text, use this feature.

- **Document Encoding**—This sets the document encoding for your page.

- **Link Color**—This sets the default link color.

- **Active Link**—This sets the default link color as a link is clicked.

- **Visited Link**—This defines a default color for a visited link.

To set these properties using Contribute, follow these steps:

1. Browse to the page you want to edit, and click the Edit button.

2. Select Format, Page Properties. The Page Properties dialog box appears (see Figure 33.6).

Figure 33.6
You can use the Page Properties dialog box to set such properties as margins, background color and images, text color, and link colors.

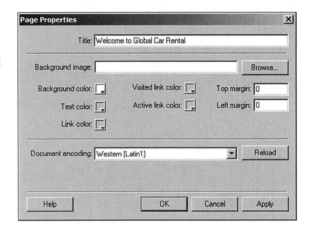

3. Set the various properties as needed.

4. Click Apply to see your changes, and then continue editing if necessary.

5. Click OK.

Your page now reflects the properties you've chosen.

Undoing Mistakes

We all make mistakes, so it's fortunate that software products such as Contribute let us undo them. It's too bad we can't have a similar feature for real life!

To undo a mistake you've made while editing in Contribute, simply select Edit, Undo. If you want to reinstate the edit, select Edit, Redo.

Both the Undo and Redo options will reflect your most recent edit.

Deleting Pages

To delete a page, you must first be connected to the site and you also must have permission to delete the page. Permissions, as mentioned earlier, are set by the network systems administrator. Permissions also are varied—for example, you might have permission to edit a given document but not to delete it. If you do not have permission to perform a certain task, either the buttons or menu options to perform that operation will be disabled.

To delete a page, follow

1. Browse to the pa

2. Select File, Del

3. Click Yes to d

Contribute now

Creating a Dra

As soon as   can see any drafts listed in the
Drafts sect   . The advantage of a draft is that
you can l   d return to editing it later. All
drafts st   page.

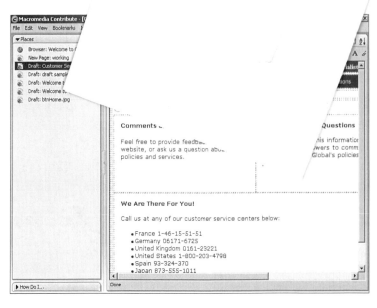

Figure 33.7
Viewing drafts in the Places section of the sidebar.

You can save your draft by selecting File, Save. If you decide to close a draft and return to it later,
you can do so by clicking the Web tab and browsing or editing as necessary. When you're ready to
return to the draft, you can click the draft, which is found in the Places sidebar.

Exporting a Page

To export a page from Contribute to HTML, Word, or Excel and save it on your computer, follow
these steps:

1. Open the page you want to export.

2. Select File, Export. The Export dialog box appears.

3. Decide where you want to save the fileand then name the file.

4. Click Save.

WORKING WITH TEXT

Contribute enables anyone to easily add and format text. Even though you might be using Dreamweaver MX to create your complex page designs, co-workers without the professional experience can easily make changes to those pages they are responsible for updating without having to deal with the complexity of Dreamweaver. Professional-level users of Dreamweaver MX can use Contribute to make quick changes while browsing through a site.

Adding Text to a Web Page

There are several ways to add text to a page. You can do any of the following:

- Type the text directly into the document you're editing.

- Copy and paste text from another application.

- Drag text from another application.

> **Caution**
>
> Contribute might carry formatting over from other applications, such as Word. You will have to reformat the text in this case to update styles to your page's design.

Formatting Text

You can change a variety of text features using Contribute. The following options are available on the edit toolbar when in Edit mode:

- **Text Style**—Select a preset text style from the drop-down menu. Options are Normal, SectionHead, TableDetail, TableHeading, and Headings 1–6.

- **Font**—Select a font from the drop-down menu.

- **Font Size**—Select a font size from the available drop-down list.

> See the following section, "Creating Lists," for more information on how to create specific types of lists.

- **Font Style**—Select a font style from either Bold or Italic.

- **Text Alignment**—Use the alignment buttons to align text to left, right, center, or justify.

- **Indent/Outdent**—Create visual tabs using the Indent and Outdent buttons.

- **Format Lists**—You can format lists, including bulleted lists, numbered lists, and definition lists.

- **Text Color**—You can change text color by selecting the text, clicking the Color button, and then selecting a color from the picker.

- **Highlight**—You can highlight text by selecting it, clicking the Highlight button, and then selecting a color from the Color picker.

To apply any of these options, simply select the text you want to modify and use the button or drop-down list for the option in question.

You can also make these, and other changes, through the Format menu on the main toolbar. For example, if you want to change text color using the main toolbar, you'd follow these steps:

1. Select the text you want to modify.

2. Select Format, Text Color. The Color dialog box appears.

3. Make your color choice and click OK.

Your color is updated. If you want to add strikethrough; style text as teletype (which simply will appear as monospaced text); or make text emphasis, or strong, follow these steps:

1. Highlight the text you want to modify to select it.

2. Select Format, Other (see Figure 33.8).

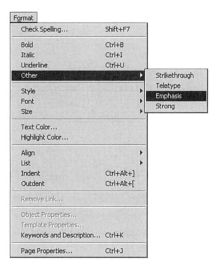

Figure 33.8
Selecting options from the Other submenu.

3. Select an option from the Other submenu.

Your special style is applied. You can also highlight text. To do so, select the text you want to highlight and then click the Highlight button in the editor.

CREATING LISTS

Lists are, of course, a very important means of organizing and presenting text on the Web. Contribute lets you create numbered lists, bulleted lists, definition lists, and sublists.

Creating Numbered Lists

Numbered lists are best used to organize numerical, ordered information. To create a numbered list, follow these steps:

1. In Edit mode, place your cursor where you want to add your first list item.

2. Click the Numbered List button on the toolbar, or select Format, List, Numbered List.

3. Type in the text for your first list item.

4. Press Enter and type in the next item. Contribute automatically adds the proper numbering.

You can turn off the automatic numbering by pressing Enter twice or pressing Enter once and then clicking the Numbered List button.

Creating a Bulleted List

Use bulleted lists to "chunkify" information that doesn't need to be in a specific order.

Creating a bulleted list is just like creating a numbered list. In Edit mode, place the cursor where you want to begin the list and then click the Bulleted List button on the toolbar. You can alternatively select Format, List, Bulleted List. Type in your item, press Enter, and continue adding text as you see fit.

You can create both numbered and bulleted lists from existing text by selecting that text and clicking the appropriate list button.

Adding a Definition List

Definition lists create a series of list items, each with an indented subitem.

A *definition list* is a series of items, each with an indented subitem. Definition lists are an excellent choice for longer lists that require details, such as lists of items and their descriptions.

To add a definition list, do the following:

1. Place your cursor on the page where you want to add your first item.

2. Select Format, List, Definition List.

3. Type in your list item, and press Enter.

4. Type in the indented definition text, and press Enter.

5. Type in your next list item, and press Enter.

6. Type in the definition text.

7. Continue adding items until you are finished.

To end the list, either press Enter twice or press Enter and then select Format, List, Definition List.

Creating Sublists

You can have nested lists in lists. You can also combine list types, such as having a bulleted list in a numbered list.

To create a sublist, follow these steps:

1. Place the cursor at the *end* of the line in an existing list where you want the sublist to go.

2. Press Enter.

3. Click the Indent button on the toolbar. You can also press the Tab key or select Format, Indent.

4. The new list appears on the new line, indented.

If you want to change the list type, click the appropriate list button on the toolbar. Click it again to return to the main list style.

Checking Spelling

Spell checking is always a good idea, especially when you're updating pages directly to the server, as you do in Contribute.

To check and correct your spelling, follow these steps:

1. Select Format, Check Spelling. Alternatively, you can click the Check Spelling button on the toolbar.

2. Contribute begins to run the spell checker. If, at some point, a misspelled word is found, the Check Spelling dialog box appears (see Figure 33.9).

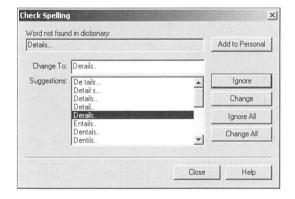

Figure 33.9
Performing spell checks on documents prior to publication is an excellent habit to get into.

33

3. Select one of the available options to fix the spelling problem.

4. Continue the check. After you are finished, either click Close in the Check Spelling dialog box or click OK in the Spell Checking Completed message box.

The spelling repair options include

- **Add to Personal**—This adds unrecognized words, such as industry terms or company names, to the main dictionary. The word will now become a permanent addition to the dictionary.

- **Ignore**—Using Ignore allows you to ignore the single instance of the unrecognized word.

- **Ignore All**—This option enables you to ignore all instances of a given word used in a document without adding the word to the dictionary.

- **Change**—This replaces the problem word with text that you type directly into the Change To text box. You can also choose a selection from the Suggestions list that appears.

- **Change All**—Use this option to change all instances of a word's spelling in your current document.

Make a habit of using spell checking prior to publishing a document. Your site visitors will appreciate reading properly spelled documents.

Using Search and Replace

As with Word and other editors, you can search for text as well as search for and then replace text.

To search for text, follow these steps:

1. Select Edit, Find. The Find and Replace dialog box appears.

2. In the Search For text box, type in the text you want to search for.

3. Click Find Next to find the first instance of the text you want.

You can continue clicking Find Next until you've found all instances of the text in your document. Click Close when you're finished.

To search and replace text, follow these steps:

1. Select Edit, Find. The Find and Replace dialog box appears.

2. In the Search For text box, type in the text you want to search for. You can limit your search by case by selecting the Match Case option.

3. In the Replace With text box, type in the text with which you want to replace the found text.

4. Click Find Next to find the first instance of the text you want. After you've found the text, you can either select Replace to replace the current instance of the text or select Replace All to replace all instances of the text.

5. When finished, click Close.

WORKING WITH IMAGES

Contribute allows you quick access to edit, add, and delete images from the pages in your site.

Adding an Image

To add an image to your page, first be sure your image is cropped, sized, optimized, and saved in a Web ready format.

➡️ *If you'd like to learn about file types and images for the Web, see Chapter 32, "Working with Web Graphics," p. 569.*

There are several ways to add an image. You can use the Insert menu, click the Image button, drag an image from an existing document, or copy and paste the image from one document into the document you're editing.

To add an image with the Insert menu or Image button, follow these steps:

1. In your page draft, place the cursor where you want the image to appear. Click the Image button on the toolbar, or select Insert, Image. The Select Image dialog box appears.

2. Use the dialog box to find the image you want.

3. Click Select.

The image is now inserted into your document.

To add an image by dragging it, follow these steps:

1. Reduce the size of Contribute so you can drag from the location of the image to the draft.

2. In your draft, place the cursor where you want to insert the image.

3. Select the image you want to insert in the source location, and then drag the image into Contribute.

The image now appears in your draft document.

To copy and paste an image, follow these steps:

1. Select an image from an application, such as a Web browser, Microsoft Word or Excel, the Contribute File Browser, or another file opened in Contribute.

2. In that application, select Edit, Copy.

3. Move to your Contribute draft, and place your cursor where you want the image to appear.

4. In Contribute, select Edit, Paste.

The image now appears in your draft.

CREATING A TABLE

Tables are easily created in Contribute. You can insert a custom table and modify it, or you can create a table and apply a preset style from Contribute.

33

Adding a Custom Table

To add a custom table to your page, follow these steps:

1. In Edit mode, place the cursor where you want to add the table.

2. Click the Insert Table button on the toolbar. Alternatively, you can select Insert, Table or use the Table menu by selecting Table, Insert, Table. No matter which option you select, the Insert Table dialog box now appears.

3. In the Insert Table dialog box, enter the number of rows and columns you want the table to have.

4. Work with the Table and Table Cell properties to modify your options.

5. When you're finished, click OK.

Your table is now added to the page. Available table options are as follows:

- **Table Alignment**—This option aligns the contents of the table to the left, right, or center.

- **Table Width**—Type in a numeric value for pixels or percent. Then, use the drop-down menu to set pixels or percentages.

- **Border Thickness**—This feature allows you to enter the table border in pixels.

- **Cell Padding**—Set the amount of space between the edge of the table cell and the cell's contents by adding a number in pixels here.

- **Cell Spacing**—Set the amount of space between each table cell by entering, in pixels, the numeric value you want.

To set table cell properties, click the Table Cell Properties tab in the Table Properties dialog box. The available options are

- **Horizonal Alignment**—Set the content cell alignment (default, left, right, or center) using the drop-down menu.

- **Vertical Alignment**—Set cell content alignment (default, top, middle, or bottom) using the drop-down menu.

- **Background Color**—Select a background color for your table cell using the Color picker.

- **Text Wrap**—For normal text wrapping, check the Wrap text check box. If you don't want text to wrap, uncheck the box.

After the table is inserted into your page, you can add content to it by typing in text and adding images. You can also modify it by adding rows and columns using the Insert Row and Insert Column buttons. Other options include inserting rows, columns, multiple rows and columns, or nested tables—use the main menu; select Table, Insert; and make your selection. To split a table cell, select Table, Split Cell.

Adding Preset Formatting

Macromedia Contribute enables you to make great-looking tables by using one of the available preset design formats. You can apply these only to data tables that are straightforward; complicated tables that contain merged cells and detailed formatting cannot accept these styles.

To add a preset design to a table, follow these steps:

1. Select the table, or place your cursor in a table cell.

2. Select Table, Format Table. The Format Table dialog box appears.

3. Using the dialog box, find a design scheme. Highlight the one you like, and click Apply to see it (see Figure 33.10).

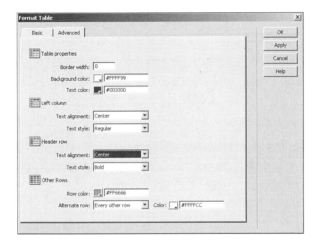

Figure 33.10
Design schemes are available in the Format Table dialog box.

4. You can make modifications to the table's properties by clicking the Advanced tab (see Figure 33.11). Here, you can set alignment, color, header row styles, and row coloring styles.

5. Click Apply to see your choices.

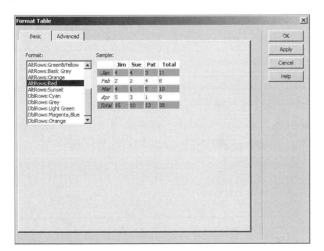

Figure 33.11
To customize a preset table design, use the Advanced tab features.

33

When you're happy with the table's formatting, click OK. The table now has the new format styles applied.

WORKING WITH LINKS

As with Dreamweaver, Macromedia Contribute enables you to create a variety of links, including text links, mail links, and linked images. You can also test your links from within Contribute.

Creating a Link

To create a link, follow these steps:

1. Browse to the page where you want the link to appear.

2. Click Edit to enter Edit mode.

3. Select the text or image you want to link.

4. Click the Link button on the toolbar, or select Insert, Link. The Insert Link dialog box appears.

5. Use the Insert Link dialog box (Figure 33.12) to determine which type of link and which type of document you want to link to. You have quite a few options, described in the following list.

Figure 33.12
The Insert Link dialog box enables you to create a variety of links.

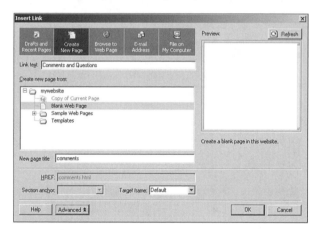

6. When you're finished with your selections, click OK.

The Insert Link dialog box offers a variety of options, including

- **Drafts and Recent Pages**—Click this option to bring up a list of drafts and recently edited or published pages. Find the document to which you want to link, and click OK.

- **Create New Page**—You can create a link and generate a new page by using this feature. Highlight the Blank Web Page option, and click OK.

- **Browse to Web Page**—To browse to a page and link to it, use this option.

- **E-mail Address**—This option allows you to create an email link. Add the email address into the E-mail Address text box, and click OK.

- **File on My Computer**—Link to an existing file on your computer using this option. Click the Browse button to find the file, or type the path into the file. Click OK when you're done.

Additional options are available in the Advanced section to perform such operations as targeting a frame.

Removing a Link

If you have a link you want to remove, you can do so by following these steps:

1. Open the page with the link.

2. Click Edit.

3. Highlight the link text, or select the link image.

4. Select Format, Remove Link.

Testing Links

As with spell checking, testing links is an excellent thing to do before publishing the page to the site. Contribute enables you to test links by previewing them in a browser and manually checking them.

To test your link, follow these steps:

1. Open the draft in Edit mode or browse to the page.

2. Select File, Preview in Browser. The draft opens in your default browser.

3. Click the link to make sure it works correctly.

When you're finished testing your links, you can publish your page.

For site-wide link checking, the tools in Macromedia Dreamweaver MX are much more sophisticated. However, this method is a quick and easy way of testing links on one or several pages at a time.

33

WORKING WITH FRAMES

Although you cannot create framed sites using Macromedia Contribute, you can edit frame content using Contribute. So long as permissions are properly set by your site administrator, you can access any frame page directly via the Contribute workspace—you don't have to browse to the individual frame page to edit it.

Editing Content in a Frame

To edit content in a frame, follow these steps:

1. Browse to the framed page.

2. Click Edit. The Choose a Page to Edit dialog box appears. In it, you'll find a list of page titles and URLs for the individual frame files.

3. Select the frame file you want to edit.

4. Click Edit; the page you selected appears in Contribute.

5. Make your changes as necessary.

Targeting Frames

As well as being able to edit frame content, you can manage link targets. So, if you have a navigation frame on the left and want information to open in the right frame, you can do so using Contribute.

Target options include

- **Default**—This option opens the linked page in the same frame.

- **Entire Window**—This replaces the entire frameset with the linked page.

- **New Window**—Use this option if you want the linked document to open in a completely new window.

Also, any named frames that exist within the site will appear so that you can target to them.

To apply a target, follow these steps:

1. Browse to a page with frames.

2. Click Edit.

3. Select the frame where you want to add the link to open a new page in another frame or window.

4. Click OK.

5. Place the cursor where you want the link text to appear. Type in the text and highlight it.

6. Select Insert, Link, or click the Link button in the toolbar. The Insert Link dialog box appears.

7. In the URL field, enter the location of the page to which you want to link. You can browse for the page by clicking the Browse button.

You can use the Link testing technique described earlier in the chapter to test the link.

8. Click the Advanced button. In the Target drop-down menu, select the name or type of frame target that you want to appear.

9. Click OK.

The link appears in the draft.

Publishing Frame Edits

As you are well aware, framesets are made up of individual frame pages. So, when you edit a frame page, you change only the information in that frame. As a result, you can easily publish your individual frame pages.

After you're done editing a frame page, follow these steps to publish the frame:

1. Click the Publish button. The full frameset, including your individual frame draft, appears in Contribute.

2. Click Preview, or you can select File, Preview in Browser. The page appears in the browser.

3. Check your work for spelling and link integrity.

You can now continue with the publishing process.

PUBLISHING YOUR DRAFTS

After you're done editing your draft pages, you might want to perform a number of checks and then publish it to the live Web site. Some of the options you'll consider before publishing include

- Preview in Browser

- Spell and Link Check

- Making the draft available for review, approval, and feedback

33

Previewing

As you've already seen in this chapter, you can preview your page in a browser. Unlike Dreamweaver MX, however, Contribute uses only your default browser and does not allow you to set numerous browsers for testing. This is somewhat of a disadvantage, particularly if your Web site uses style sheets or browser-specific proprietary markup. If your site does use these, you might consider testing your pages using Dreamweaver MX instead.

However, if you just want to take a quick look at the document changes and test links, you can do so by either selecting File, Preview in Browser or pressing the F12 key. The page then opens in the default browser.

Request for Review

Because Macromedia Contribute is mostly used in team environments, you might be required or prefer to request a review of the page from co-workers or anyone else, even if they aren't using Contribute or Dreamweaver.

The review process involves Contribute creating an email message in your default email software program with a temporary URL where the page will be made available for viewing. Contribute manages the temporary location, so you don't have to worry about that. The reviewer simply clicks the URL in his email client and is automatically brought to the temporary site.

After you send an email review request, the Contribute Edit mode changes status to alert you that the page has been sent to review. It also displays the date you sent the request. You can then continue working on other pages until the feedback comes back to you.

To request a review, follow these steps:

1. Open the page you want reviewed in Edit mode.

2. Select File, E-mail Review. Contribute will launch your email client with the message text and link in it (see Figure 33.13).

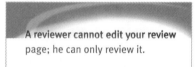

A reviewer cannot edit your review page; he can only review it.

Figure 33.13
Contribute launches a new email message via your default mail client, complete with a link to the temporary page.

3. Address the message.

4. Add any additional comments to the email.

5. Send the message.

If Contribute has trouble finding your email client, a dialog box will appear to assist you with configuring this feature.

Cancelling Drafts

If you are editing a published page and want to get rid of your entire draft, you can discard the draft and return to the original page.

To cancel changes to a draft of a previously published page, do the following:

1. In Edit mode, select File, Cancel Draft. An alert appears asking if you're certain you want to complete this action.

2. Click Yes.

The page is cancelled, and the original page is loaded into Contribute. If you want to cancel changes to a new page, select File, Delete Page. The page will be deleted.

Publishing the Page to the Site

After you've completed editing and reviewing your draft, performing spell and link checks, and viewing the page in your browser, you can publish the page to the site.

When you publish a page, Contribute makes the page live on your Web site and, if the page was previously published, Contribute replaces the existing page with the updated page.

To publish updates to an existing page, follow these steps:

1. Click the draft to open it, if it's not already opened.

2. Click the Publish button. If you have links to new pages in the draft, the Publish Linked New Files dialog box will appear.

3. In the dialog box, accept or change each filename, and then click Publish All.

Contribute will now publish the page, and any linked pages that you've selected, to the Web site. The page is then displayed by Contribute in Browse mode.

Rollback

Contribute provides a level of safety for its users by providing a Rollback feature. This feature enables you to undo a published page and revert to an earlier version of that page. Interestingly, you don't have to roll back to the most recent version—Contribute keeps a record of any published pages, so you can choose from any versions of a rollback file that you desire.

33

⇨ *Having trouble with images and media when rolling back pages? Find out why in "Problems with Assets" in the "Troubleshooting" section of this chapter.*

To roll back a page, follow these steps:

1. Open the published page in Browse mode.

2. Select File, Roll Back to Previous Version. The Roll Back dialog box appears.

3. Select a prior version of the page from the available list (see Figure 33.14).

4. If you like the page version you've selected, click Roll Back.

Contribute will publish the page and load the rolled back page in Browse mode.

Figure 33.14
Contribute's powerful rollback feature provides an additional level of safety by keeping track of your published pages and drafts.

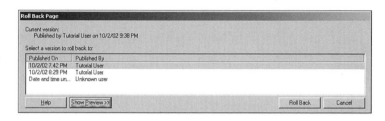

TROUBLESHOOTING

Disabled Edit Button

The Edit Page button is disabled. What's going on?

If the Edit Page button is disabled, another person is using Contribute or Dreamweaver to edit the page.

Problems with Assets

When rolling back a page, images and media are sometimes lost. What's the problem?

Contribute does not manage assets outside of the pages it creates. So some assets, such as images and other media that you've added or replaced (especially using other means than Contribute), will not necessarily be available in a given rollback file.

PEER TO PEER: MARKUP AND CONTRIBUTE

Because Contribute is meant for a variety of people who do not necessarily have Web design and development experience, the program has very little sophistication when it comes to markup. Text formatting uses font tags and the like. You can't edit style sheets, and although layer content is editable, the layers themselves are not.

As a result, it becomes imperative to have a style guide or other method with which to achieve conformance. The site designers and developers, if adhering to standards, can provide editors with guidelines as to which Contribute features to use and which to not use.

What's more, if compliance is a concern, either content editors should be given some guidelines on how to validate a page and make edits external to Contribute or the designers and developers working on the site should perform validation tasks.

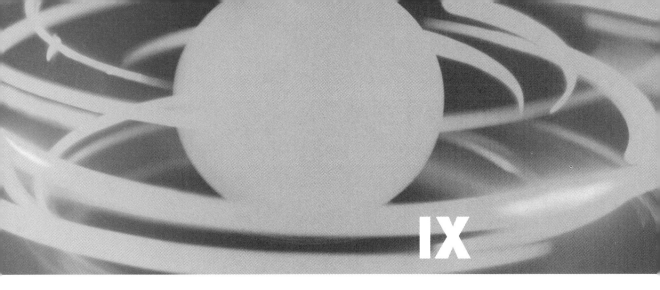

IX

APPENDIXES

IN THIS PART

SETTING PREFERENCES

IN THIS APPENDIX

CUSTOMIZING DREAMWEAVER MX

One of the most attractive things about Dreamweaver MX is the extent to which you can customize it. This appendix seeks to assist you in creating the best and most effective setup, which will both powerfully influence your productivity and increase your enjoyment of the process.

DEFINING THE WORKSPACE

The exciting news, at least for Windows users, is that the Macromedia Dreamweaver MX allows two workspace layouts:

- **One window integration**—This layout provides all the windows, menus, and panels in an integrated view.

- **Floating layout**—In this layout, panels are floating, similar to previous versions of Dreamweaver.

An additional view is available as a subset to the one-window integration layout, emulating the Homesite view and appealing to the more code-inclined users. Unfortunately, at this time, the Macintosh version offers only the floating layout.

Customizing the Workspace Layout

If you are using the Windows version of Dreamweaver MX, you can set up your workspace layout to the style of your choice. The first time you start the program, Dreamweaver MX provides a dialog box that lets you customize the layout.

The following options are available:

- **Dreamweaver MX Workspace**—This is the integrated workspace. In it, all windows, menus, and panels are integrated into a single window. Panel groups are docked on the right, with the Document window to the left. Most users will likely prefer this workspace, and it is used in the majority of screen shots throughout this book (see Figure A.1).

- **HomeSite/Coder-Style**—This view is the integrated workspace with special layout features. The panels are docked on the left, reminiscent of HomeSite and ColdFusion Studio. What's more, the Document window always shows Code view as its default. Anyone who has enjoyed working in HomeSite or ColdFusion will find this workspace sub-type very appealing (see Figure A.2).

- **Dreamweaver 4 Workspace**—In this case, the layout looks similar to the layout in Dreamweaver 4. Each document is contained in a separate window, which floats. Panel groups are docked together, but they are not docked to the application window itself. This look is best for those used to working with earlier Windows versions of Dreamweaver or those Macintosh users who find themselves using Windows to run Dreamweaver (see Figure A.3).

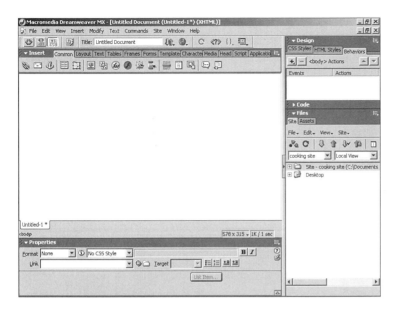

Figure A.1
The integrated workspace in Dreamweaver MX for Windows.

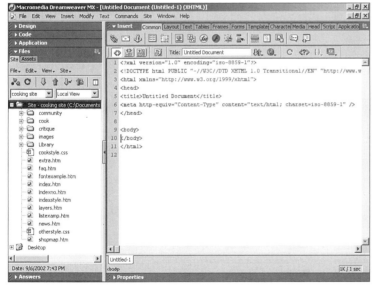

Figure A.2
The HomeSite/Code-Style view is a subset of the integrated workspace created to emulate HomeSite's simpler look.

Appendix A

Figure A.3
Floating panels and windows are used in the Dreamweaver 4 workspace.

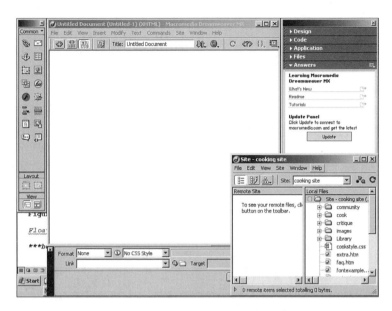

You can always change the workspace layout any time you like by following these steps:

1. Select Edit, Preferences from the main menu.

2. The Preferences dialog box appears (see Figure A.4).

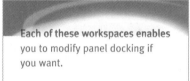

Each of these workspaces enables you to modify panel docking if you want.

Figure A.4
Using General preferences to set up or change the workspace.

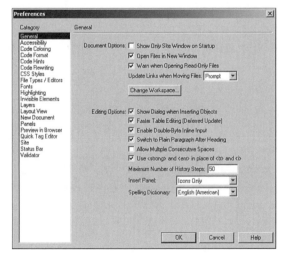

3. Highlight the Category, in this case, General. The dialog box changes to display the General preferences. Click the Change Workspace button.

4. The Workspace Setup wizard appears (see Figure A.5).

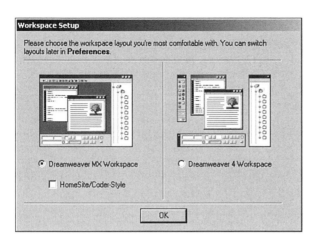

Figure A.5
Using the Workspace Setup wizard.

5. Check the radio box for the Workspace style you like. If you want to select HomeSite/Coder-Style, be sure to check the box. Click OK.

You'll be returned at this point to the Preferences dialog box. Click OK again, and your Windows workspace will modify.

SETTING UP GENERAL PREFERENCES

To control the overall appearance of Dreamweaver MX, you can work with these general preferences first. To access the Preferences panel, which provides you with a direct connection to most of Dreamweaver's customizable features, first select Edit, Preferences (or Dreamweaver, Preferences in Mac OS X). Then, highlight General in the Category column.

Table A.1 shows the options available in the General Preferences dialog box.

Table A.1 General Preferences

Preference	Purpose
Show Only Site Window on Startup	Check this option if you want Dreamweaver to open with only the Site window and panels available, *without* a new document available. This option is available only in floating layout.
Open Files in New Window	Use this option (Windows only) to open each file in a unique window.
Warn when Opening Read-Only Files	If a file is locked or checked out and you attempt to open it with this option checked, a dialog box appears to ask you whether you'd first like to unlock or uncheck the document.
Update Links when Moving Files	This option allows you to control the means in which you update links in a document when moving files. You have three options: Always (which always updates the links automatically), Never (which never updates the links), and Prompt (which provides a prompt each time you move a file).

Appendix A

Table A.1 Continued

Preference	Purpose
Change Workspace	This button enables you to change the workspace features described earlier in the chapter. This feature is for Windows only.
Show Dialog when Inserting Objects	This option enables you to choose whether a dialog box will open as you use the Insert bar and related menus to insert an object. Depending on the object, a different dialog box opens, allowing you to set preferences. If you uncheck this option, no dialog box appears and you will use the Property inspector to make adjustments to your inserted object.
Faster Table Editing (Deferred Update)	With this option, you can defer updates while working on tables until you click outside the table or update changes manually by pressing (Command-spacebar) [Ctrl+spacebar].
Enable Double-Byte Inline Input	This enables you to enter double-byte text into your document window when working in an environment and using double-byte characters such as those used in Japanese.
Switch to Plain Paragraph After Heading	When you press (Return) [Enter] after a heading in Design view, a new paragraph automatically is inserted. If this option is unchecked, pressing (Return) [Enter] causes a new heading with the same value as the one prior.
Allow Multiple Consecutive Spaces	This option automatically ensures that if you type two or more spaces while in Design view, a nonbreaking space is inserted. With this option disabled, any multiple spacing is ignored.
Use <strong> and <em> in Place of <b> and <i>	Check this to use the strong element for bold and the em element for italics. The W3C specification encourages the use of these options rather than b and i because strong and em are considered structural rather than presentational.
Maximum Number of History Steps	This enables you to determine the number of steps the History panel contains and displays. The default value of 50 is likely to be sufficient, but you can type in a number that best suits you.
Insert Panel (Insert Bar)	Set the Insert Bar icons using the drop-down menu. Your choices are to view the bar with icons and text, icons only, or text only.
Spelling Dictionary	Use the drop-down menu to select a dictionary appropriate to your language needs.

ACCESSIBILITY OPTIONS

The Accessibility section in the Preferences dialog box allows you to set the following accessibility options for various markup in a document:

- **Form Objects**—To add accessibility features to forms, check this option. Any time you insert a form, an accessibility dialog box specific to forms appears, enabling you to use the `label` element, `accesskey` attribute, and `tabindex` attributes for accessibility features.

- **Frames**—Adding accessibility to frames enables you to properly identify frames using the Frame Tag Accessibility Attributes dialog box (see Figure A.6).

- **Media**—This enables you to insert a title, an `accesskey` attribute, and a `tabindex` attribute to any media object (Flash, Shockwave, or Java applets).

- **Images**—Ensure your images are accessible by including alternative text and a long description.

- **Tables**—The Insert Tables with Accessibility Attributes option allows you to customize your tables for accessibility (see Figure A.7).

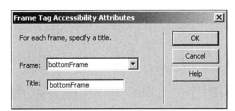

Figure A.6
The Frame Tag Accessibility Attributes dialog box.

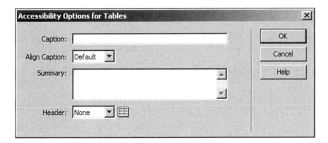

Figure A.7
This dialog box is more complex compared to the one shown in Figure A.6, due to the accessibility needs for tables.

Two additional options in the Accessibility preferences enable accessibility for you—the Dreamweaver user—rather than the audiences for whom you are creating the documents. These options include

- **Make Dreamweaver Use Large Fonts**—Allows you to use large fonts in the program.

- **Offscreen Rendering (disable when using screen readers)**—If you re using a screen reader to work with Dreamweaver, deselect this so rendering doesn't interfere with your screen reader.

To change any of these settings, simply select Edit, Preferences and check or uncheck the associated dialog box.

SETTING CODING PREFERENCES

The way you set your code preferences can help you be more efficient, find problems in your code more quickly, and organize your code in such a way that others can easily modify it, too.

Code Color

Coloring syntax is a feature in many types of editing environments. Dreamweaver MX enables you to customize your code color and style. Using specific colors to highlight tag types can be helpful in quickly identifying tags when working in Code view. For example, you can color all `table` tags green and style them as bold. This way, when working with complex table layouts, you can find and edit tags easily.

To manage the colors and text style in your code, follow these steps:

1. Select Edit, Preferences; the Preferences dialog box appears.

2. Highlight Code Coloring to bring up the Code Coloring options (see Figure A.8).

Figure A.8
Code coloring options in Dreamweaver MX provide you with effective means to manage code in Code view.

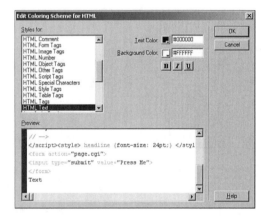

3. Highlight a document type. For most readers of this book, you'll want to set choices for HTML, CSS, Text, and JavaScript.

4. After you've chosen the document type, click the Edit Coloring Scheme button. This brings up the Edit Coloring Scheme dialog box, which will be slightly different for each document type option.

5. Select the items you want to colorize. You can set text color, background color, and font style (italics, bold, or underline).

6. The Preview pane will update the code color and style features to your tastes.

7. Click OK.

You'll now be returned to the Preferences dialog box set to Code Coloring. At this point, you can continue modifying code colors for additional document types.

Code Formatting

The way code is formatted can be a very personal issue. Some people like to indent tables, for example, whereas others do not. How you format your code might depend on a specific style for your company or a personal preference.

You can control a variety of code formatting features such as indentation, length of lines, and case of tags and attributes.

To set your formatting preferences, follow these steps:

1. From the main menu, select Edit, Preferences.

2. In the Preferences dialog box, highlight the Code Format category to bring up the Code Format options (see Figure A.9).

3. Adjust the various settings using the text boxes and drop-down menus available.

Caution

In XHTML, all tags and attribute names *must* be lowercase. Because you can never go wrong with lowercase when using HTML, it's recommended that you set case to lowercase unless you have a specific reason not to.

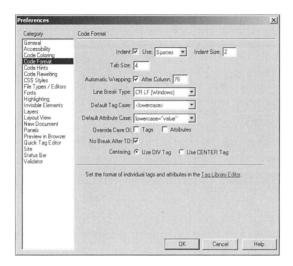

Figure A.9
Code Format options in Dreamweaver MX preferences.

The following options are available for formatting code in Dreamweaver MX:

- **Indent**—Check this box to use code indenting.

- **Use**—This provides a drop-down menu determining which indentation method to use: Spaces or Tabs.

- **Indent Size**—Use this text box to enter a number that manages the size of the indents. The size of the indent is based on the type of indent. So, if you've set the Use to Spaces and the Indent Size to 3, three spaces will be used rather than three tabs.

- **Tab Size**—This feature enables you to control how many spaces make up a tab. The default is set to 4.

- **Automatic Wrapping**—This feature enables you to set the point where text and code will wrap.

- **Line Break Type**—Depending on the type of remote server you're working with, you'll need to configure the proper type of line break. Windows, Mac, and Unix are all different. It's important to set the correct type of line break so that your source code appears using the formatting you've set up, breaking the lines in accordance with your settings. Also, you should set this depending on the type of external text editor you have. If you are working with Notepad, set the Windows option; for BBEdit, set the Macintosh option.

- **Default Tag Case and Default Attribute Case**—These options enable you to control the capitalization of tag and attribute names. Because HTML is not case sensitive, it has been common practice to mark up HTML in uppercase, mixed case, or lowercase, depending on the individual's tastes. However, as mentioned previously, XHTML is case sensitive, so be careful when using XHTML documents to ensure that all element and attribute names are lowercase.

- **Override Case Of**—This feature enables you to override past options with current settings for element and attribute case. When you open an uppercase or a mixed case document in HTML and you want to ensure that all the elements and attribute names are forced to lowercase, Dreamweaver MX converts to your specifications. Tags you type directly into Code view or the Quick Tag Editor also are converted to the case you've specified, as are any tags or attributes you insert.

- **No Break After TD**—Check this if you want all the output of table cell markup to appear on one line. This is especially important when working with image slices because breaks between cells containing slices will cause gaps.

- **Centering**—This option determines whether elements should be centered using the `center` element or the `div` element with a value of center, `<div align="center"> . . . </div>`. Both are available to you in Transitional specifications, but ideally, you should use Cascading Style Sheets (CSS) to accomplish centering.

When setting preferences, most of the options—with the exception of the Override Case Of option—do not affect older documents, even when you open them and begin editing. However, you can update these documents to your new settings. To do so, open the document in question and Select Commands, Apply Source Formatting. The new formatting will be applied.

Code Hints

Using Code Hints enables you to insert elements, attributes, and values as you enter code in Code view.

Available preferences for Code Hints are

> Even if Code Hints are disabled in Preferences, on the Windows platform you can invoke the hints by pressing Ctrl+spacebar.

- **Enable Auto Tag Completion**—This feature enables you to type in a portion of code and automatically completes the remaining code.

- **Enable Code Hints**—If you want to work with Code Hints while working with code in Code view, select this option. You can drag the Delay slider to set the time in seconds before you're provided a given hint.

- **Menus**—Use this feature to set which type of Code Hints you want displayed. So, if you want only hints related to HTML and markup, deselect those hint types that aren't appropriate.

To choose Code Hints preferences, follow these steps:

1. Select Edit, Preferences.

2. In the Preferences dialog box, highlight Code Hints. The dialog box changes to provide you with the Code Hints options.

3. Make your selections based on the options available.

Click OK to activate your new settings.

Code Rewrite

When you open a document in Dreamweaver MX, it can perform several rewrite options. The options are as follows:

- **Fix Invalidly Nested and Unclosed**—This option rewrites improperly nested (poorly formed) tags. So, if you have something in your markup that is improperly nested, such as `<strong><em>Hi!</strong></em>`, using this option will fix the problem, as well as insert quotations and any closing brackets if they aren't in the markup.

- **Rename Form Items**—When pasting code, this feature ensures that you don't have any duplicate names in your form objects.

- **Remove Extra Closing Tags**—This feature deletes any closing tag that has no corresponding opening tag.

- **Warn When Fixing or Removing Tags**—This option displays a list of the technically questionable or problematic markup that Dreamweaver tried to correct. You can find the location of the problem using line and column numbers, quickly find the problem that was corrected, and make sure your document is working the way you intended.

- **Never Rewrite Code:In Files with Extensions**—You can prevent Dreamweaver MX from rewriting any code with file extensions as determined. This is especially helpful if you are using any type of propietary code methods.

- **Encode Special Characters in URL Using %**—This feature ensures that URLs contain only those characters considered to be legal.

- **Encode <, >, &, and " in Attribute Values Using &**—This also ensures that any URL contains legal characters.

To modify preferences for code rewriting, follow these steps:

1. Select Edit, Preferences.

2. With the dialog box open, highlight the Code Rewriting option in the Category list.

3. Make your changes in the dialog box.

When you're finished, click OK to update your preferences.

Appendix A

CSS STYLE PREFERENCES

Setting these preferences controls how Dreamweaver generates CSS styles. CSS styles can be written using *grouping*, a short-hand form of style. Some people prefer using this, whereas others prefer long hand. Still others prefer a combination of the two.

The options available to you include the following:

- **Use Shorthand For**—Selecting this option enables you to set which CSS style properties Dreamweaver writes in shorthand. You can select from Font, Background, Margin and Padding, Border and Border Width, and List-Style.

- **When Editing CSS Styles**—Use the features here to determine whether your existing styles will be rewritten to your updated CSS preferences. Choose from

  - **If Original Used Shorthand**—Select this radio button if you want Dreamweaver MX to leave all styles as they currently are.

  - **According to Settings Above**—Selecting this option causes Dreamweaver to rewrite styles for the attributes defined in the Use Shorthand For section.

To edit CSS styles, simply bring up the Preferences dialog box, highlight CSS styles, and make your selections (see Figure A.10).

Figure A.10
You can use grouping (referred to in Dreamweaver MX as "short-hand") for a selection of properties.

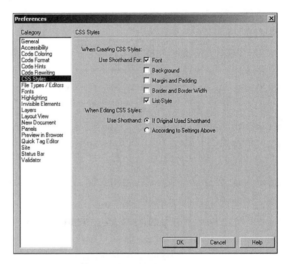

CONFIGURING EXTERNAL EDITORS

Although Dreamweaver MX's capabilities as a code editor are very rich, many people like to work with a variety of other editors, too. And, even though you might use Fireworks MX as part of the MX studio suite, some people commonly use other image editing programs, such as Adobe Photoshop. If you're working with media, such as audio, you can also customize the editors for that. Dreamweaver enables you to configure a range of external editors, providing you with extended options with which to do your work.

HTML/Code Editors

To configure an HTML/Code editor for use externally from Dreamweaver Code view, follow these steps:

1. Open the Preferences dialog box by selecting Edit, Preferences.

2. Highlight the File Type/Editors category (see Figure A.11).

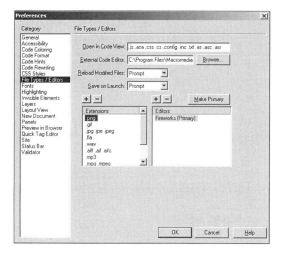

Figure A.11
You can set your favorite editors for working with various file types using the Preferences dialog box.

3. Click the Browse button and find the editor you want to associate with a given extension. Click OK.

4. Customize your options using the dialog box. When you're finished, click OK again to update your custom selections.

Your options are as follows:

- **Open in Code View**—In this section, add any of the extensions you want to have open in your external browser.

- **External Code Editor**—This option enables you to either input the path directly into the text box available or use the Browse button to find the program you want to use.

- **Reload Modified Files**—This enables you to specify which action Dreamweaver takes when it detects that external changes have been made. Your choices are Prompt, Always, and Never.

- **Save on Launch**—This option lets you choose whether Dreamweaver should save the current document you're working on *before* launching the editor. Your choices are Prompt, Always, and Never.

Macintosh users should be aware that if you want to use an editor other than BBEdit, which is already associated with code editing, you need to deselect the Enable BBEdit Integration option. If you want to use BBEdit as your primary HTML and code editor, leave this selected.

After your HTML/Code editor is selected, you launch it by simply selecting Edit, Edit with [name of external editor]. Figure A.12 shows the menu option with Homesite 5 as the chosen editor.

> **If you're unsure of which approach** to take with the Save on Launch option, select Prompt. This way, Dreamweaver MX will always ask you what you want to do each time you launch the external browser.

Figure A.12
After you've set up your HTML/Code editor, the Edit, Edit With menu option reflects your chosen editor.

Image Editors

If you want to set which file types a given image editor opens, select Edit, Preferences and highlight the File Types/Editors option—just as you did for HTML and code editors.

You can select image editors by file type, so if you want to work with PNG format in Fireworks MX and JPEG and GIF in Photoshop, you can do so.

With the Preferences dialog box open to the File Types/Editors, find the Extensions list and follow these steps:

1. In the Extensions list, select the file extension for which you are selecting the editor.

2. Find the Editors list. Click the Add (+) button. The Select External Editor dialog box appears.

3. Browse for the editor you want, and select it.

4. If you want this editor to be the primary editor for this file type, click the Make Primary button.

You can add more editors for a given file type by adding image editors for that type (see Figure A.13).

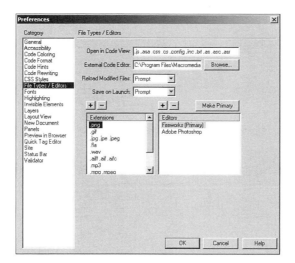

Figure A.13
You can have multiple image editors associated with a single file type, allowing you to determine which editor you want to use in a given instance.

CUSTOMIZING FONTS AND ENCODING

The Fonts portion of the Preferences dialog box (see Figure A.14) enables you to set numerous font properties and encodings including

- **Font Settings**—The font settings feature enables you to select the font types and encoding for a document. This is especially important when creating multilingual or other language sites. If you are working in Korean, for example, select Korean from the Font Settings list and then select the appropriate font features. Fonts must be installed on your computer in order to be available, so to use Korean text, you must have the proper Korean font.

- **Proportional Font**—A proportional font is used to display any type of normal text, such as is found in paragraphs and headers. You can use the default, or you can select another option for default. You can also choose a size, in points, for this font.

- **Fixed Font**—Typically used for preformatted text and code, a fixed font is also known as a *monospaced* font. In this type of font, each letter takes up the exact amount of space as another. You can choose from any fixed font installed on your system and size it to your tastes.

- **Code View**—This is the font that will appear in Code view and the Code inspector.

- **Tag Inspector**—Modify this selection for any text that appears in the Tag inspector.

With the exception of encoding for display purposes, the Fonts preferences relate only to the way *you* see these fonts, not the way you'll mark them up or style them for the browser.

Appendix A

Figure A.14
Setting global font preferences
using the Preferences dialog box.

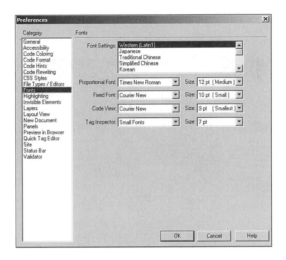

HIGHLIGHTING

These preferences are used to help you identify specific features with a specially colored highlight. You can change the defaults by selecting Edit, Preferences and then selecting the Highlighting options. The highlighting options you can choose from are

- Editable Regions

- Nested Editable

- Locked Regions

- Library Items

- Third-Party Tags

Outside of the scope of this book but pertinent to code-savvy readers are two options for Live Data: Untranslated and Translated. You can set a separate color to discern between the two.

INVISIBLE ELEMENTS

An *invisible* element is one that doesn't appear in the body of the browser. Examples include comments and scripting. Dreamweaver MX allows you to show a marker for these elements that doesn't otherwise display in Design view. To ensure that a given type of marker appears, follow these steps:

1. Select Edit, Preferences.

2. Highlight the Invisible Elements category.

3. In the Show section of the Invisible Elements list, check any element that you want to have display a marker.

To hide an element, uncheck it from the Highlight Preferences dialog box.

SETTING LAYERS PREFERENCES

To set preferences for layers, open the Preferences dialog box and highlight the Layers option in the Category list (see Figure A.15).

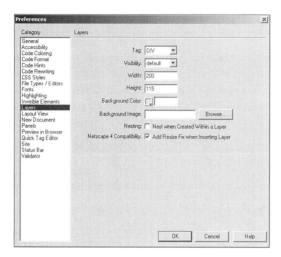

Figure A.15
Layer preferences enable you to customize the way in which your Draw layers are coded.

Your options include the following:

- **Tag**—Here, you can select div or span to indicate a CSS layer. Using the div element is the recommended method.

- **Visibility**—This provides default visibility for the layer. The options are default, inherit, visible, and hidden.

- **Width**—The default width of a layer is set to 200 pixels. You can change this to any measurement, in pixels, that you want.

- **Height**—The default height of a layer is set to 115. Simply type in a different number if you so choose.

- **Background Color**—To set a default background color for layers, use the color picker or type the color in the available text box.

- **Background Image**—You can set a default background image for layers. Type in the path or click the Browse button, and then find the image you want to use.

- **Nesting: Nest When Created Within a Layer**—This controls nesting in divisions. Select this option when you want to use layers within layers.

- **Netscape 4 Compatibility: Add Resize Fix When Inserting a Layer**—This inserts JavaScript code into the head portion of a document to fix a known problem with the way Netscape 4 deals with layers.

After you've set the preferences you want, click OK.

LAYOUT VIEW

To set preferences for Layout view, bring up the Layout view preferences in the Preferences dialog box (see Figure A.16). Your options include

- **Autoinsert Spacers**—This option automatically places spacers if the When Making Autostretch Tables is selected and never inserts them when the Never radio button is selected.

- **Spacer Image**—Sets a spacer image for your sites. First, select the site from the drop-down menu (only sites you've added to Dreamweaver MX will be available). Then, if you don't have a spacer image, you can create one by clicking the Create button and saving the file to the location of your choice. If you already have a spacer, you can click the Browse button and find the spacer image.

- **Cell Outline**—This allows you to modify the color of your table cell outlines in Layout view. Use the picker, or type in the color value.

- **Cell Highlight**—This changes the color as you move the pointer to point to a given cell.

- **Table Outline**—To change the outline of your layout tables, use the color picker or type in the color you desire.

- **Table Background**—To modify the background color of a Layout table where there are no layout cells, use the color picker or type in a color.

Figure A.16
Setting preferences for Layout view.

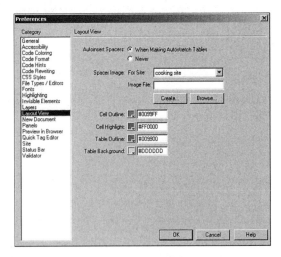

After you're happy with your choices, you can continue modifying preferences or click OK to update the preferences to Dreamweaver MX.

NEW DOCUMENT PREFERENCES

To set the features for a new document, you'll use these preferences. You can have a default document type, such as HTML, ASP, JSP, and so on. In most cases, you'll be leaving the default as HTML.

The options available for a New Document are

- **Default Document Type**—Select the default document from the drop-down menu.

- **Default Extension**—You can do this only by editing the document type XML file. There is an active link in the dialog box that you can click to perform this action (see Figure A.17).

- **Default Encoding**—To set a default document encoding, select one from the drop-down menu.

- **Show New Document Dialog on (Command-N) [Ctrl+N]**—This feature automatically creates a new document of the default document type when you use the keystroke command.

- **Make Document XHTML Compliant**—This feature ensures that your document will be structured as an XHTML document.

> **Caution**
> Be careful to not confuse Dreamweaver's use of the term *document type* with the formal definition of Document Type Definition used when referring to HTML and XHTML standards.

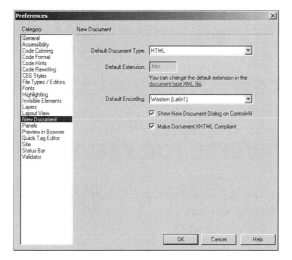

Figure A.17
To change the default extension from .htm means changing a .xml file that Dreamweaver MX uses to manage the extension. Click the link and follow the prompts to make the change.

SPECIFYING PANEL PREFERENCES

This preferences feature allows you to set the way panels and inspectors appear in the interface.

Options for panel preferences include

- **Always on Top**—This option lets you determine which of the many Dreamweaver MX panels always appear to the front of the Document window (see Figure A.18). Default settings provide panels and inspectors to be in front of the Document window. This feature doesn't apply in the integrated workspace because all panels in that workspace are docked.

- **Show Icons in Panels and Launcher**—This feature allows you to specify whether the Launcher bar appears. With this option on, the Launcher bar is added to the status bar area, with icons for each panel. You can then click these icons to open panels and inspectors (see Figure A.18).

- **Show in Launcher**—Here you can customize which icons appear in the Launcher bar (see Figure A.18).

Figure A.18
There are numerous panels in Dreamweaver MX. If you're using a floating layout view in Windows or Macintosh, you can determine which panels are on top.

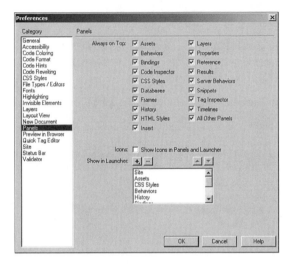

If you want to add or remove an icon to or from the Launcher bar, use the Add (+) or Remove (-) button. You can also change the order in which the icons appear by selecting an item and using the up or down arrows to move it in the list.

CONFIGURING BROWSERS FOR PREVIEW

Dreamweaver MX enables you to preview your documents in as many browser types as you like, making testing your pages across browsers and platforms very easy.

To add a browser to the list, follow these steps:

1. Open the Preferences dialog box, and highlight the Preview in Browser category.

2. In the dialog box, click the Add (+) button next to Browsers. The Add Browser dialog box appears (see Figure A.19).

3. Fill in the browser name, fill in the path to the application (use the Browse button if necessary to find the application), and set whether you want the given browser to be a primary or secondary browser.

4. Click OK. The browser is now added to the list (see Figure A.20).

> If you want to edit existing settings, simply click the Edit button on the Preview in Browser dialog box and make changes as required.

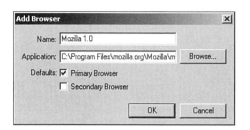

Figure A.19
The Add Browser dialog box.

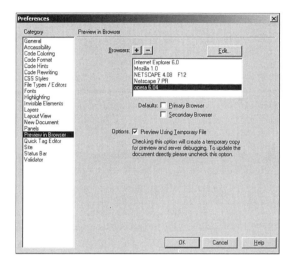

Figure A.20
View a customized browser list in the Add Browser dialog box.

To remove a browser, simply select the browser in the browser preferences and click the Remove (-) button. The browser is now removed from the list.

QUICK TAG PREFERENCES

You can change the Quick Tag preferences as follows:

- **Apply Changes Immediately While Editing**—This feature allows immediate updates to the document while you're using the Quick Tag editor. If this option is turned off, changes are updated only upon pressing (Return) [Enter].

- **Enable Tag Hints**—This feature provides you with tag information. If you don't want tag hints, turn off the feature by deselecting the check box.

- **Delay**—Use the sliding bar to make the tag hints box come up more quickly or more slowly.

SETTING SITE PANEL PREFERENCES

The site panel is where many people who use Dreamweaver find themselves working. You can check files in, check them out, upload them to your server, and perform numerous other functions.

Site panel options include

- **Always Show**—This option enables you to set whether the remote or local site is shown and in which panel each appears.

- **Dependent Files**—This enables you to set a prompt when transferring files that are dependent to a main HTML file (graphics, external style sheets, and external scripts). You can set it so the prompt appears on Get/Check Out and Put Check/In.

- **FTP Connection**—Use this to determine when to terminate the connection. Simply check the box and then add an amount of time, in minutes, to define when the connection should disconnect. The default is 30 minutes, which is usually plenty of time. In fact, most servers will likely disconnect sooner if they are receiving no incoming queries from you.

- **FTP Time Out**—This selection enables you to set how long Dreamweaver MX attempts to query the server for a connection. The default is 60 seconds, but you can change this to whatever you like. After the amount of time has passed, Dreamweaver will alert you with a warning.

- **FTP Transfer options**—This option lets you determine how Dreamweaver behaves if there is no user response during a file transfer.

- **Firewall Host**—Here, you'll select the address of the proxy server so you can connect to remote servers when behind security firewalls. For those individuals not behind a firewall, leaving this space blank is recommended.

- **Firewall Port**—Use this option to denote the port through which you will connect to the remote server. The default port for FTP is 21, but if you have a different port specified, you'll need to enter it here.

- **Put Options: Save Files Before Putting**—If this feature is activated, files are automatically saved before being uploaded to the server.

- **Edit Sites**—This button launches the Edit Sites dialog box. Here you can edit any existing site or add a new one.

SETTING STATUS BAR OPTIONS

There are two options for the status bar. The first is Window Size, which allows you to customize which window sizes you can display on the bar. These sizes are used to test your pages at different resolutions. The other option is the default speed necessary to calculate download time. You can change the default by selecting the speed you want from the drop-down menu (see Figure A.21).

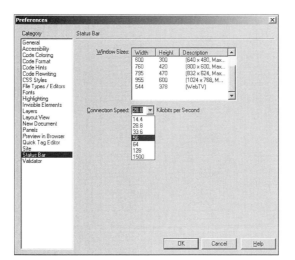

Figure A.21
Set options for the status bar, including Window Sizes and Connection Speed.

CONFIGURING VALIDATOR PREFERENCES

Validating documents is, of course, an important aspect of working with Web standards. This feature is helpful for you when working with standards, as well as correcting proprietary tags and attributes.

To set your validator options, follow these steps:

1. Select Edit, Preferences and then highlight the Validator category.

2. Check as many options in the Validate Against box as you require.

3. Click OK.

Your preferences for the validator are now set.

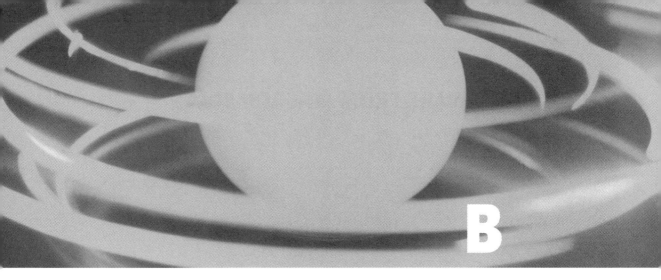

WHAT'S ON THE CD-ROM?

DEMO SOFTWARE FROM MACROMEDIA

- Dreamweaver MX

- Fireworks MX

- Flash MX

- Freehand

- Homesite

- Director

- ColdFusion

- Cool Edit Pro

HELPFUL CODE FROM THE AUTHORS

- Standards-based templates

USEFUL UTILITIES AND DEMOS

- HTML Tidy

- BBEdit for Macintosh

- LIFT

Appendix B

INDEX

How can we make this index more useful? Email us at indexes@quepublishing.com

How can we make this index more useful? Email us at indexes@quepublishing.com

Insert bar
  buttons, *179-181*
  tabs, *180-181*
menus, customizing
  (Macromedia Exchange),
  195
panels
  Advanced Layout, 189
  Answers, 193
  Application, 189
  Code, 186-188
  Design, 185
  Files, 185-186
  *groups, arranging,
    183-184*
  groups, closing, 184
  groups, docking, 184
  groups, grippers, 183
  groups, sizing, 184
  History, 193
  overview, 182
  Results, 191-192
  Timelines, 190
Property inspector
  context selection, 182
  docking/undocking, 182
  icons, 182
  *toggling between
    CSS/HTML views, 286*
workspace layouts, 170-173

**Internet Explorer, borderless
frame support, 363-364**

intra-page links, 87-88

intrinsic events
  scripts, 416
  W3C specifications, 430

**invisible elements, coding
options, 632**

italic fonts, 55

J - K

jaggies, 143

Java
  language development, 481
  versus JavaScript, 417, 481

Java applets. *See* **applets
(Java)**

**Java Server Pages (JSP), 98,
115-116**

JavaScript, 416-417
  behavior
    Control Shockwave, 427
    Jump Menu, 427
  behaviors, 419, 426
    adding to layers, 380-382
    attaching, 428-429
    behaviors panel, 428
    Call JavaScript, 427
    *Change Property,
      380-381, 427*
    Check Browser, 427
    Check Plugin, 427
    deleting, 429
    Drag Layer, 427
    editing, 429
    Go To URL, 427
    Hide Pop-up Menu, 427
    Jump Menu Go, 427
    *Open Browser Window,
      427*
    Play Sound, 427
    Pop-up Message, 427
    Preload Images, 427
    Set Nav Bar Image, 427
    Set Text, 427
    Set Text to Layer, 381
    Show Pop-up Menu, 427
    *Show-Hide Layers, 382,
      427*
    Swap Image, 427
    Swap Image Restore, 427
    Timeline, 427
    Validate Form, 427
  browser support, 417
  code, standalone capability,
    419
  DHTML animation, 462-468
  dynamic button states,
    582-584
  ECMAScript standardization
    efforts, 430
  editing, 423
  event handlers, 417-419
    OnAbort, 418
    OnBlur, 418
    OnChange, 418
    OnClick, 418
    OnDblClick, 418
    OnError, 418
    OnFocus, 418
    OnKeyDown, 418
    onKeyPress, 418
    onKeyUp, 418
    onLoad, 418
    onMouseDown, 418
    onMouseMove, 418
    onMouseOut, 418
    onMouseOver, 418
    onMouseUp, 418
    onResize, 418
    OnUnload, 418
  external files, 421
    *adding to Web pages,
      423*
    *setting up in Web pages,
      421-422*
  functions, 419
  noscript element, 421
  script containers, adding,
    420-421
  script element, 420
  Scripts category (Assets
    panel), 203
  snippets, 419, 424
    creating, 424-425
    deleting, 425
    editing, 425
    *inserting in Web pages,
      424*
  versus Java, 417, 481
  Web pages, adding, 420-421

**Joint Photographic Experts
Group.** *See* **JPEG**

**JPEG (Joint Photographic
Experts Group), 65**
  artifacts, 571
  background images, 33
  file extension, 571
  image suitability, 572
  lossy compression, 571
  uses, 65
  versus GIF compression,
    571

**JSP (Java Server Pages),
115-116**

Jump Menu behavior, 427

Jump Menu Go behavior, 427

How can we make this index more useful? Email us at indexes@quepublishing.com

X - Y - Z